CW00429643

BLOODY APRIL...
BLACK SEPTEMBER

BLOODY APRIL...
BLACK SEPTEMBER

Norman L R Franks
Russell Guest & Frank W Bailey

GRUB STREET · LONDON

Published by
Grub Street
The Basement
10 Chivalry Road
London SW11 1HT

Copyright © 1995 Grub Street, London
Text copyright © 1995 Norman Franks, Russell Guest and Frank Bailey

A catalogue record for this book is available from the British Library

ISBN 1 898697 08 6

All rights reserved. No part of this publication may be reproduced, stored in
a retrieval system, or transmitted in any form or by any means, electronic,
mechanical, photocopying, or otherwise, without the prior permission of the
copyright owner.

Typeset by Pearl Graphics, Hemel Hempstead
Printed and bound by Biddles Ltd, Guildford and King's Lynn

Contents

Acknowledgements

The authors wish to thank and acknowledge the help given by a number of friends and colleagues, together with advice, support and photographs. They are: Neal O'Connor, George Williams, Peter Kilduff, Ed Ferko, Richard Duiven, August Blume, Stewart Taylor, Stuart Leslie and D MacGuinness. Also to the Keeper and staff at the Public Records Office at Kew, Surrey, the Bureau Central d'Incorporation et D'Archives, de l'Armee de L'Air, the Service Historique de l'Armee de L'Air (SHAA) and the US National Archives.

We should also like to remember the late Russell Manning, O A Sater, Dennis Connell, Paul Chamberlain and Dr. Gustav Bock, all of whom were always generous in sharing information and helping their fellow historians.

Introduction

Military aviation in World War One was new. Only six years before the war began in August 1914, the Frenchman Louis Blériot became the first man to fly the English Channel, and only two years before the conflict did the Army grudgingly acknowledge the aeroplane by creating the Royal Flying Corps in May 1912. For its part, the Royal Navy had its own air-arm from the same date, the Naval Wing which in turn became the Royal Naval Air Service in July 1914.

In less than two years of armed conflict, the war had ground to the stalemate of the Western Front trench systems that stretched from the North Sea coast near Nieuport to the Swiss frontier. The generals that commanded the various armies in France had grown up with the ideals of open land warfare wherein cavalry not only made the occasional dramatic charge with lance and sabre gleaming, but as tradition had shown, were the eyes of those generals in finding out what the enemy were doing on 'the other side of the hill'. The trenches, with their barbed-wire entanglements, not to mention the quagmires of 'no-man's-land', made cavalry scouting patrols impossible. Almost overnight the generals turned to the aeroplane to be their eyes, for in flight they could not only see the other side of the hill, but photograph it as well.

Thus reconnaissance and aerial photography changed the whole nature of military flying in that both sides suddenly needed the means of both stopping the enemy from carrying out its reconnaissance sorties and ensuring its own aeroplanes were able to operate over the lines. Thus the struggle for air supremacy began.

This is not a book covering the study of wartime aviation development. Suffice it to say that over the period of 1915-16, both sides tried many means to achieve their aims in the air, and each side began producing fighting aeroplanes equipped with machine-guns to try to shoot down enemy two-seaters and oppose the single-seaters that were endeavouring to do the same thing to their own side's two-seaters.

Initially, the Germans assigned two or three fighters to each of its reconnaissance units, known as Feld-flieger Abteilung (FFA, later shortened to FA, Flieger Abteilung), to fly both protection sorties and hunting sorties against the British and French. The British and French, meantime, formed complete fighting units which they used in much the same way, although the Royal Flying Corps consciously adopted an offensive attitude under its overall commander, Major General Hugh Trenchard.

The Germans, for their part, with slightly fewer aeroplanes than the combined numbers of the British, French and Belgian air forces, were content to take on a more defensive posture, letting the enemy come to them so that they were generally able to dictate the terms of battle. Though this doctrine, in time, was proved wrong, by late 1916 that was the 'status quo' within which they had to operate.

The period known as the Fokker Scourge—the Germans using the nimble Fokker mono-planes with a forward-firing machine-gun(s), which covered the approximate period August 1915 to June 1916—created many of the early fighter aces among the German Fokker Eindekker pilots. Immelmann, Wintgens, Parschau, Berthold, von Mulzer, Frankl and Boelcke took their place in aviation history during this period, but the most well known was Boelcke. This was not just due to his successes in early air combat, but also to his foresight and help in creating the fighting squadrons of the German Air Service, the Jagdstaffeln, known individually in the abbreviated form of Jasta.

The German Jasta units were created in the autumn of 1916. The first seven were formed by the beginning of October and over the next few months more were established, so that by the early spring of 1917, 37 Jastas were in existence. Their birth coincided with the arrival of new single-seat biplane fighters, the Albatros DII and Halberstadt DII Scouts, each having machine-guns that fired through the propeller. These greatly outclassed the existing British and French fighters such as the DH2 and FE8 pusher-types and could give a good account of themselves against the FE2b two-seat pusher, and the single-seat Nieuport Scouts, Sopwith Pups and two-seater Sopwith 1½ Strutters.

As spring arrived on the Western Front in that fateful year of 1917, two things happened which together brought the air war to a head during April. Firstly, the German Jastas had begun to hone themselves into an aggressive fighting force during the winter months, when generally the chances of proving themselves and their aeroplanes against the Allied air forces were limited due to the weather. With the arrival of spring and better weather came at last the opportunity they'd been waiting for. Secondly, the Allied commanders had plans for a huge offensive as soon as the weather improved. The plan was to mount the offensive along a 100-mile section of the Western Front between Arras in the north and the Aisne River in the south. If it succeeded, British troops would attack at Arras while the French armies would make an assault from the southern end of the line. This, of course, was nothing new: such assaults had happened before, such as the disastrous Somme offensive in July 1916, but Allied commanders were nothing if not optimistic of success as each subsequent offensive came onto the drawing board. In hindsight, their perseverance and constant belief in success as each new battle was planned was something to behold.

Field Marshal Sir Douglas Haig would command the British, General Robert Nivelle, hero of Verdun, the French. Tasked with providing the necessary air support, Trenchard was well aware of the shortcomings of his aircraft, especially now that the Germans had reorganised their fighter force and had received superior aircraft. He had requested and been promised new types but nothing much had yet arrived in France. Some new types were on the way, such as a two-seater Bristol Fighter, and a new single-seater called the SE5, but the former had only just arrived (one squadron) and had yet to fly their first operational patrols, while the SE5 (again just one squadron) would not arrive until the second week of April and not be operational for another two. Meanwhile, Trenchard would have to start the battle with old DH2s, the FE2 squadrons, French Nieuports and the handful of Sopwith Pup squadrons. He did have the added support of some RNAS squadrons which had Sopwith Pups and Sopwith Triplanes, while the French had a lively little fighter, the Spad VII, some of which had been given to the British, but only two squadrons had them. The French were naturally more keen to get rid of their Nieuports than their new Spads.

The German Jastas became more aggressive during the first weeks of 1917 and it was obvious to Trenchard that with their new aircraft and therefore their new-found prowess, retaining air superiority over the coming offensive would be difficult. It made it even more essential that his airmen fly even more aggressively in an attempt to overwhelm the Germans, who were still, in the final analysis, inferior in numbers. However, aggression was one thing, the ability to be aggressive another.

Haig was kept well aware of the situation, and to his credit he wrote several times to the War Cabinet urging them to hurry along the new types promised, but these could not be produced overnight so Trenchard and his force would have to do the best with what they had.

Even before the April offensive, the Germans had the latest version of their Albatros Scout —the DIII—begin to make its appearance over the front. Boelcke, of course, had died in a collision on 28 October 1916, but his name lived on in several of his pupils, not the least of whom was a young cavalry officer, Baron Manfred von Richthofen. In January 1917 he was given command of Jasta 11, which would soon become the highest scoring of all the Jastas. By the end of March, von Richthofen would have a personal score of 31 victories, only nine short of the number his mentor Boelcke had achieved.

So, on the eve of battle, Trenchard knew that having survived the Fokker Scourge of the previous year, the tide of supremacy would soon turn against his airmen once more—and at a most critical time. At first he thought of conserving his forces, but the amount of information needed to plan the offensive made it necessary for photo and visual reconnaissance missions to be flown in number, which in turn increased the aerial activity over the front. Overall monthly personnel casualties since October 1916 had been in double figures, with 75 in October the highest. Now, in March 1917, the figure shot up to 143 airmen dead or missing. The number of sorties also increased, to 14,500, the highest recorded in any month so far.

The Arras offensive would see the British forces take the brunt of the fighting. For its part the RFC had 25 squadrons along this section of the front, with around 365 serviceable aeroplanes, of which about a third were fighter types. Other units covered the more northern sectors, opposite Lille and Ypres. Across the lines, the German 6 Armee covering the area Lille in the north to Cambrai in the south had 195 aircraft, of which half were fighters. But numbers were not totally relevant when one considered the quality of the German fighter force: in many respects the relationship between German fighters, Allied fighters and Corps aircraft would be akin to sharks among minnows in the coming battle.

Part One of this book will record in detail the air Battle of Arras and the air fighting which developed through that fateful month of April 1917—which would later be called Bloody April.

Part Two of the book skips 16 months of WWI, to September 1918—Black September. Much had happened during those intervening months and a brief résumé of what had occurred in the air war will be covered. By September 1918, several major things had happened in France. Germany had tried in vain to smash the Allied lines in March and April 1918, the Americans had finally arrived in force, and the August assault upon the Amiens front by the British had started the break-up of German might. In September came the St Mihiel offensive by the French and Americans, followed quickly by another in the Meuse-Argonne sectors.

When September ended, the First World War had just six weeks more to run, yet in that devastating month, the German Air Service and the Marine Jagdstaffeln up on the North Sea coast had inflicted upon the British, French and American air forces the largest ever number of losses and casualties the war was to see in one month. It certainly left the numbers of April 1917 way behind.

In this section of the book we shall see how things had developed over the preceding year and a quarter, how the aircraft, tactics and doctrines had changed, how air fighting had developed, and how the newest of the Allied air forces—the US Air Service—had fared in its great test of air strength over the battlefields of the Western Front.

The St Mihiel offensive lasted from 12 to 15 September, following a huge build-up of men and machines after the recent Aisne-Marne campaign. Colonel Billy Mitchell, the US air commander, had some 1,500 French and American aircraft available, Mitchell having persuaded the French to commit most of their available units in this sector to his battle plan. Opposite them were the crack Jasta formation of JGII (plus JGI late in the month), the Germans no longer fighting in just Jasta strength but in large group formations under experienced air leaders.

Then came the build-up for the final assault against the Meuse-Argonne front which commenced on 26 September. Meantime, on the British front the Royal Air Force (following the merger of the RFC and RNAS on 1 April 1918) gave full support to the Second Battle of Arras, beginning 3 September, and the assault on the Hindenburg Line on the 12th which coincided with the St Mihiel attack, to be followed by the assaults on Flanders Ridge and Ypres (28 September), then the St Quentin Canal (29th).

The casualties on both sides were appalling, but for the Allies they were almost catastrophic, although, of course, by that stage they could absorb the losses, whereas the Germans could not.

As in our recent WWI aces books, we have attempted to be accurate in both recording the air actions and making the analysis of losses and claims. Reference to all the surviving RFC/ RAF loss records has produced much information, but due to the period of time and so on, one cannot vouch for total accuracy or completeness. Some records we know are no longer available and have been lost, even over recent years.

Claims by both sides are as accurate as can be achieved, but the reader must realise the difference between claims and verified losses on either side. It doesn't take too much intelligence to realise there was over-claiming on both sides of the lines, mostly in good faith, and an awful lot of things can come between a claim and a confirmed victory. Many of course are in no doubt, while others might be queried by the reader due to some other previous publication saying something quite different.

In this particular respect, we have tried our utmost to study closely the relationship between a claim and a victory, taking into account time, location, and close scrutiny of maps, something which some people in the far or even more recent past seem to have taken little interest in. Even so, we are fallible, but generally we have good reasons for saying what we do but would welcome constructive comment should we have failed in one or two instances, for the sake of future reference if nothing else.

Generally speaking, the German claims are very good, one reason being that with the majority of the air fighting taking place over their own territory, aircraft or wreckage fell where it could be seen and recorded. The RFC/RAF on the other hand had generally to go on eye-witness verifications of what they saw—or thought they saw—and usually had no wreckage to inspect. The French, and later the Americans too, had a different system, being far more stringent in verification of claims, but this could still lead to a claim having no apparent corresponding loss. In the final analysis, we can only say what was claimed at the time, given credit for, and show what losses are known.

It has been difficult to verify all the German claims. Even so-called official sources note no losses whereas there is not the slightest doubt losses occurred—even aircraft having come down on the Allied side, that had to be a loss. However, we have had access to all the German personnel casualties—at least fatalities—so we can be fairly certain they are all correct. With aeroplanes it might be different. We do not know for certain if when an aircraft came down and, say, was destroyed by fire, but the pilot or crew scrambled clear unharmed, whether a pure aircraft loss was recorded, as opposed to an aircraft and crew. There is strong evidence to suspect that in some records, if there were no personnel losses, even if an aircraft was destroyed or subsequently written-off, that no loss record occurs. Therefore, in the German loss column at the end of each day, we have had to produce a figure from what we know, and this has no verification from any official source, but is given for information and comparison.

With Allied claims in these daily lists, we show the 'out of control' victories by the British, but as the French and American airmen had no comparable type of combat claim, there will be no figure for them under that heading.

Throughout the daily reporting we have tried to work chronologically but sometimes we do not know for certain the timing of a combat or a loss so these, while mentioned, will appear generally in the daily loss notes.

We have made little reference to losses due to non-combat sorties, or where an aircraft may have crashed returning from a sortie, but where the accident was not attributable to combat damage. Anyone reading through the daily aircraft loss reports will see just how many aircraft were lost, certainly by the British, through flying accidents and pilot error. To have included all those would have made the book unwieldy, so only crashes where combat damage was involved have been noted.

Where personnel casualties have been recorded, but the aircraft was not lost, even though damaged (which includes aircraft recovered from forced landings behind the front lines), a '*' will appear far right of the daily casualty entry to denote the aircraft was not a loss. Also, in the case of two-seater crews, the first named will always be the pilot; where only one crewman is recorded a (P) or (O) appears to denote pilot or observer.

In the narrative, during the periods where Allied and German times differed by one hour, reference to this will be emphasised by an (A) or (G) next to an Allied or German time, although generally the time attributable to an Allied or German action/report will, of course, be the time relevant to the side involved.

Royal Flying Corps Order of Battle 1 April 1917

Brigade	Wing	Sqdn	A/C	Base	Corps
GHQ	9th	35	AWFK8	Savy	Cavalry
Savy		27	Martinsyde G100	Fienvillers	
		55	DH4	,,	
		57	FE2d	,,	
		70	Sop 1½ Strutters	,,	
		19	Spad VII	Vert Galand	
		66	Sop Pups	,,	

I	1st	2	BE2	Hesdigneul	I
Château		5	BE2	La Gorgue (a)	XIII
du		10	BE2	Chocques	XI
Reveillon		16	BE2	Bruay	I Canadian
	10th	25	FE2b	Lozinghem	
		40	FE8	Treizennes (b)	
		43	Sop 1½ Strutters	„	
		8N	Sop Triplanes	Lozinghem (c)	
II	2nd	53	BE2	Bailleul	IX
Cassel		6	BE2	Abeele	X
		42	BE2	Bailleul	
		46	Nieuport XII	Droglandt (d)	VIII
		21	RE8	„	II Australian
	11th	1	Nieuport XVII	Bailleul	
		20	FE2d	Boisdinghem (e)	
		41	FE8	Abeele	
		45	Sop 1½ Strutters	St Marie Cappel	
III	12th	8	BE2	Soncamps	VII
Château		59	RE8	Bellevue	XVIII
de		12	BE2	Avesnes	VI
Sains		13	BE2	Savy	XVII
	13th	11	FE2b	Le Hameau	
		29	Nieuport XVII	„	
		48	BF2a	Bellevue	
		60	Nieuport XVII	Le Hameau	
		6N	Nieuport XVII	Bellevue (f)	
		100	FE2b	Le Hameau	
IV	3rd	7	BE2	Nesle	IV
Miséry		9	BE2	Morlancourt	XIV
		34	RE8	Foucaucourt	III
		52	BE2	Meaulte	XV
	14th	22	FE2d	Chipilly	
		24	DH2	„ (g)	
		54	Sopwith Pups	„ (h)	
		1N	Sop Triplanes	„ (i)	
V	15th	4	BE2	Warloy	I Australian
Albert		3	Morane Parasol	Lavieville	I Australian
		15	BE2	Lealvillers	V
	22nd	18	FE2b	Bertangles	
		23	FE2b/Spad VII	Baizieux	
		3N	Sopwith Pups	Marieux	
		32	DH2	Lealvillers	

Notes:
(a) 5 Squadron moved to Savy 7 April; (b) 40 Squadron moved to Auchel 25 April, then to Bruay 29 April; (c) Two flights of 8 Naval moved to Flez 26 April; (d) One flight 46 Squadron moved to Boisdinghem 16 April; followed by the main body on 25 April; (e) 20 Squadron moved to St Marie Cappel 16 April; (f) 6 Naval Squadron moved to Chipilly 11 April; (g) 24 Squadron moved to Flez 18 April; (h) 54 Squadron moved to Flez 18 April; (i) 1 Naval Squadron moved to Bellevue 11 April.

Wing Headquarters Locations

9th at Fienvillers
1st at Chocques
2nd at Eecke
10th at Lozinghem, moved to Château de Reveillon, Chocques 18 April
11th at Bailleul
12th at Avesnes, moved to Agnes-les-Duisans 24 April
13th at Le Hameau
3rd at Bouvincourt
14th at Chipilly, moved to Guizancourt 29 April
15th at Arqueves
22nd at Toutencourt

German Jastas attached to each Armee, April 1917

1 Armee—Jastas 2, 17, 29, 36
2 Armee—Jastas 2, 5, 20, 26
3 Armee—Jastas 9, 21, 29, 31
4 Armee—Jastas 8, 18
5 Armee—Jastas 7, 10, 13
6 Armee—Jastas 3, 4, 6, 11, 12, 27, 28, 30, 33
7 Armee—Jastas 1, 13, 14, 15, 17, 19, 22, 32
Abt 'A'—Jastas 24, 37
Abt 'B'—Jastas 16, 26, 35
Abt 'C'—Jastas 23, 34

German Jasta Bases, April 1917

Unit	Base	Armee	Location
Jasta 1	Vivaise	7	10 km NW Laon
Jasta 2	Pronville	1 and 2	15 km W Cambrai
Jasta 3	Guesnain	6	5 km SE Douai
Jasta 4	Douai	6	
Jasta 5	Boistrancourt	2	10 km SE Cambrai
Jasta 6	Aulnoy	6	2 km S Valenciennes
Jasta 7	Procher	5	
Jasta 8	Rumbeke	4	2 km S Roulers
Jasta 9	Leffincourt	3	50 km NE Reims
Jasta 10	Jametz	5	30 km SE Stenay
	—then Aincrevillers		14 km SE Stenay
Jasta 11	Douai-Brayelles	6	
	—then Roucourt		5 km SE Douai
Jasta 12	Epinoy	6	8 km NW Cambrai
Jasta 13	Reneuil Ferme	5 and 7	
Jasta 14	Boncourt	7	15 km ENE Laon
	—then Marchais		8 km E Laon
Jasta 15	La Selve	7	48 km N Reims
Jasta 16	Eisenheim	Abt 'B'	
	—then Habsheim		5 km SE Mulhouse
Jasta 17	St Quentin le Petit	7 and 1	
Jasta 18	Halluin	4	1 km SE Menin
Jasta 19	Thour	7	30 km N Reims
Jasta 20	Guise	2	30 km NE St Quentin
Jasta 21		3	
Jasta 22	Laon	7	
Jasta 23	Mars-la-Tour	Abt 'C'	15 km W Metz
Jasta 24	Morchingen	Abt 'A' and 1	
	—then Annelles		
Jasta 26	Habsheim	Abt 'B'	5 km SE Mulhouse
	—then Guisc-Ost	2	25 km ENE St Quentin
	—then Bohain-Nord		20 km NE St Quentin
Jasta 27	Ghistelles	6	15 km S Ostende
Jasta 28	Wasquehal	6	1 km SW Roubaix
Jasta 29	Juniville	3 and 1	15 km W Leffincourt
Jasta 30	Phalempin	6	10 km S Lille
Jasta 31	Mars-sous-Bourcq	3	10 km E Leffincourt
Jasta 32	Chéry-les-Pouilly	7	10 km N Laon
Jasta 33	Villers-au-Tertre	6	10 km SE Douai
Jasta 34	Mars-la-Tour	Abt 'C'	15 km W Metz
Jasta 35	Habsheim	Abt 'B'	5 km SE Mulhouse
	—then Colmar-Nord		
Jasta 36	Le Châtelet	1	
Jasta 37	Montinghen-Metz	Abt 'A'	

PART ONE

Bloody April

by Norman Franks
with Russell Guest and Frank Bailey

Sunday, 1 April 1917

British Front

There was not the slightest portent of things to come as the new day's grey light cast out the previous night's shadows across the shattered landscape of the Western Front on this first day of April 1917. There was no spring dawn, only scudding cloud that would bring rain on and off all day.

Deep in their trenches, the fighting soldiers of both sides tried to keep warm in their underground bunkers. Others began to move about, brewing the inevitable billy of tea, while making sure yesterday's left-over bread had not been 'got at' by the rats during the night. Outside, the luckless men who had been on guard duty in the chill of pre-dawn stood on the parapet woodwork. Occasionally they would peep out through a sand-bagged spy hole, or into those extended see-over parapet eyeglasses at the enemy lines.

What they saw was the familiar barbed wire entanglements in front of their trenchworks, the lifeless churned-up mud and earth of no-man's-land, then the German wire, with some parapet sandbags or pieces of timber beyond it. There was little growing other than perhaps the odd clump of grass, or a new weed. Trees and bushes had long since gone, smashed and shattered in countless bombardments. There might be the odd stubborn tree stump, but little else.

For the men in the trenches—on both sides—the day would be much like any other. Those on guard duty would turn out for their period of time-on, then time-off. The others would stay under cover, attending to household or personal chores. Perhaps a bit of urgent repair to their underground living quarters, replacing worn or broken duck-boards in the trenches, darning socks, washing a shirt or some item of underwear; fetching food and water from the rear, cleaning one's rifle, while all the time trying to think of anything other than their present soul-destroying lifestyle.

One could just about get used to trench-life. Nothing had ever prepared the men who fought World War One for such an existence, but like most things, once it was understood to be inevitable, then it could be endured—by most of them. Occasionally a sniper, British, French or German, might fire at a fleeting target. Minds would then be concentrated for a few minutes on the possible implications, but when it remained silent, things would return to normal. Occasionally something would disturb the tranquillity and a machine-gun might rattle out. Men would rush to the gun-slits, fire off a few rounds in panic, followed by other machine-guns. Suddenly it would stop, and after a few minutes, peace reigned once more.

There was no constant, daily fighting. Generally speaking unless some Field Commander decided that today was the day to launch yet another offensive to try and break the deadlock that was the Western Front, all would remain quiet. All quiet on the Western Front; it was often so. As the soldiers noted, it was only those intrepid aviators who 'went over the top' every day—and good luck to 'em. Leave us in peace and we'll be more than happy.

Yet on this day there was little flying either; the weather saw to that. But between the rain showers, the ever aggressive doctrine of the Royal Flying Corps saw to it that aeroplanes were sent up to make sure the Germans knew the war was still on. The artillery flyers went up to the front in order to guide shell-fire onto any enemy gun positions noted the previous day, or even during the current day, by over-zealous officers at the front who, as far as their men were concerned, couldn't leave well enough alone. It usually started with a 'tit-for-tat' episode. Someone would spot a likely target and after a wireless call, a gun battery would be ordered to lob a few shells at it. This would bring a response from the other side. Positions of guns would be noted and radioed back to Headquarters, who would then send up aircraft, or tethered kite balloons, both to range for the guns and to record the fall of shot. This might then escalate as each side sent up fighting aircraft to try to drive off the artillery flyers. Sometimes it all ended with everyone going home, sometimes all hell was let loose. War is sometimes like that. It just takes someone to stir up trouble.

Even so, on quiet days too, it was essential to keep an eye on the enemy. If either side seemed exceptionally quiet it could mean they were up to something. Planning an attack, bringing up troops and equipment, ammunition and guns. Each side needed to keep watch on the other, especially in the rear areas. Any unusual movements would in all probability mean something was afoot, then the other side would begin to move up troops to counter the threat, transferring men and equipment from another part of the front. And so it went on.

There were two ways of keeping an eye on the opposition – by aircraft being flown over the rear areas, or by observers being hoisted aloft in a basket beneath a static-line balloon. The balloon lines were some way back from the immediate front, so as not to be in danger of light ground fire, and the observers in the dangling baskets could observe their section of the front through powerful binoculars. They could see both movement and flashes or smoke from gun batteries. It followed, therefore, that the balloons too would be attacked, to be either destroyed if possible, or at least forced down. It took a while to haul them down and then get them back up, so forcing them down was a good second-best. Forcing the observer to jump out of his basket with the aid of a rudimentary parachute at least stopped him working—and he might even break a leg!

Time on the Western Front at this period was the same for both the Allied and German forces. It would not change until 16 April, when the German time would be advanced by one hour.

At this particular juncture on the British front, much of the area to the south-east of Arras was rather more fluid than usual, as German troops were gradually withdrawing to their Hindenburg Line positions. As British troops eased forward, there was some brisk fighting for the shattered remains of a few villages before they were forced to halt in front of the mighty German defence line.

On the British front the balloons were up early and so were the artillery flyers. Such were the conditions that the balloon of No. 10 Kite Balloon Section (10th Section, 2nd Company, 1st Wing), supporting the Canadians, was struck by lightning and destroyed. One of the Section's ground personnel, Private A Simpson, was also struck, and killed instantly.

Meanwhile, others were reporting German gun batteries, so RFC aircraft were up ranging the guns along the fronts of the 1st, 3rd and 4th Armies. A few German fighter pilots were called to take off and see if they could disrupt proceedings.

Jasta 2 (now called Jasta Boelcke in memory of the dead air hero) based at Pronville, 16 km due west of Cambrai, sent up a patrol, led by Leutnant Otto Bernert, who would command this Staffel in June. Taking advantage of the cloud, Bernert and his wingman nipped across the front line, and attacked the balloon of the 4th KB Section (4th Section, 13th Company, 5th Wing) at Villers-au-Flos at 1045, Bernert sending it down in flames; the two observers, Second Lieutenants Cochrane and Hadley, parachuted down. It was Bernert's 11th victory and the British had suffered their first air loss of April to the German fighter pilots.

While all this had been happening, a two-seat BE2c of No.15 Squadron RFC was engaged on artillery work in approximately the same area. Captain A M Wynne and his observer, Lieutenant A S Mackenzie, of 15 Squadron, based at Lealvillers, 12 km north-west of Albert, had taken off at 0925 that morning, so at way past 1130 they were just about to head for home after ranging for guns of V Corps, when they were spotted by a German pilot, again from Jasta Boelcke. Unfortunately for the two British airmen it was another expert fighter ace, seated in the cockpit of his Albatros DII, and he had twice as many victories as Bernert. Leutnant Werner Voss had spotted them and kept above some cloud so as to approach unobserved. Between Ecoust and St Leger, he swooped down through the cloud, diving down on the BE which was at 800 feet. Wynne saw the danger and headed west, Mackenzie opening fire with his Lewis gun. He fired two drums with no apparent effect, as Wynne headed down. At 100 feet, Mackenzie was hit in the heart and died instantly. Wynne immediately prepared to put down but was then hit in the leg by another burst from Voss. The BE scraped over the front line trenches, watched by soldiers who always knew no good would come of flying, and crunched into the ground near St Leger. Wynne was thrown out which was just as well, as Voss then dived on the wrecked BE and fired into it before flying back across the lines.

It was 1145 and the 19-year-old Voss (he would be 20 on 13 April) secured his 23rd victory following confirmation from front line German troops that his adversary had been successfully brought down and the machine then destroyed by shell-fire. This would not be the first time that a flyer of either side had shot up a downed adversary. The war had long since left the realms of chivalry often associated with WWI war in the air, something that was more often than not a dream of the 1930s pulp fiction writers of war flying adventures.

Within minutes of this victory, the British artillery two-seaters were getting their own back. Near Arras was a BE2c of 12 Squadron, flown by Second Lieutenants Douglas Gordon and H E Baker. Jasta 3 from Guesnain, just to the south-east of Douai, flew a patrol to the front led by its Staffelführer, Leutnant Alfred Mohr, an ace with six victories. He too was flying an Albatros DII—2016/16—and dived on the two-seater, but the alert gunner hammered the on-coming scout, hitting the German's fuel tank. Immediately it burst into flames and engulfed the machine, which fell into the British lines at 1150. Mohr died in the inferno, the wreckage of his aeroplane being given the number G.18 by the British, who numbered all (most) enemy aircraft that fell in their territory, whether intact or a smouldering mass. Jasta 3 was taken over by Oberleutnant Hermann Kohze from Kampfgeschwader 4 (a bombing unit) the next day.

The second British aircraft lost on this quiet day occurred in the early afternoon. In an attempt to provide protection for the artillery aircraft over the front, 11 Squadron at Le Hameau, 16 km west of Arras, had sent up a patrol of their two-seat pusher FE2b fighters at 1420. The weather was pretty bad at this time and one machine failed to make it home, last seen to the west of Boyelle. The Squadron thought the crew, Corporal A Wilson and 2AM F Hadlow, may have been brought down in a storm, but the Germans claimed an FE shot down by ground fire, credit going to the gunners of Flakzug 145 and Mflak 14. Both airmen were taken prisoner, having come down north-west of Pont de Couriers.

French Front
There was little real activity along the French front on this Sunday, with no casualties recorded either. There was only one combat noted with Sergent Goux of N.67 claiming a German two-seater sent down over the enemy lines. There is no corresponding loss, although an observer with a Bavarian artillery observation unit, Flieger Abteilung (A) 288b ('b' denotes a Bavarian unit), Leutnant Werner, was severely wounded, which may have been the result of an attack by Goux's Nieuport Scout.

	A/C	KB		DES	OOC	KB
British losses	2	1	British claims	1	—	—
French losses	—	—	French claims	1	—	
German claims	2	1	German losses	1	—	

German losses in aircraft have sometimes appeared difficult to reconcile. In the German Nachrichtenblatt for 1 April there are no losses recorded but clearly Jasta 3 had a most definite loss, and although FA(A)288 had a man wounded, it could be that the aeroplane itself was not lost.

British Casualties				
Aircraft type	No.	Squadron	Crew	
BE2c	2561	15 Sqdn	Capt A M Wynne	WIA
			Lt A S Mackenzie	KIA
FE2b	4954	11 Sqdn	Cpl A Wilson	POW
			2AM F Hadlow	POW
Balloon		4-13-5	2/Lt Cochrane	Safe
			2/Lt Hadley	Safe

Monday, 2 April 1917
British Front
Almost all the action occurred during the morning during a day of wind, rain and low cloud. Nevertheless, reconnaissance aircraft were sent out and no fewer than 32 ground targets were given the benefit of shell-fire by artillery with aeroplane observations and direction. Not unnaturally the German fighter pilots were up too, interfering with the RFC's daily incursions over the front.

Among the first off from the British side were five FE2b machines of 22 Squadron airborne from Chipilly, situated on the northern bank of the Somme River, 10 km due south of Albert, at 0635. 22 shared this airfield with 24 Squadron's DH2s, 54 Squadron with Sopwith Pups and 1 Naval Squadron, which had Sopwith Triplanes.

Two of the FEs carried cameras in order to take photos of German dispositions opposite the British 4th Army front, while the other three would act as escort. The formation headed north-east, crossed the lines to the north of Peronne then flew in the direction of Gouzeaucourt, by which time one photo FE had returned home with engine trouble. Meantime Jasta 5 at Boistrancourt, 10 km to the south-east of Cambrai, took off and headed for the front, having been told of approaching British aircraft. Very often the German pilots would not take off until front line observers reported Allied aircraft approaching or crossing the lines. This saved time patrolling up and down behind the front and stopped the problem of having to return to refuel just as enemy aircraft were finally spotted.

Jasta 5 found the FEs, which had now overflown Gouzeaucourt (south-west of Cambrai), between Beaucamp and Gouzeaucourt Wood, just before 0830 and attacked. The FE crews, now joined by some DH2s of 24 Squadron, later reported a force of 18 Albatros Scouts in two groups and in the fight which followed, the remaining photo machine was hit, began to burn, then fell in flames. The victor was Offizierstellvertreter Edmund Nathanael, who would return home having secured his 5th victory. Seeing the FE start to burn, Captain C R Cox and Second Lieutenant L C Welford (4855) tried to drive off the Albatros, but Cox was himself heavily engaged. Welford fired 60 rounds into another Albatros over the FE's left wing-tip, seeing it catch fire and go down out of control. He then saw a DH2 finish it off, the German crashing to the ground.

The five DH5s of 24 Squadron, which had taken off from Chipilly at 0730 to fly a line patrol, had seen the enemy aircraft attacking the four FEs over Havrincourt Wood and had come to engage. Lieutenant Kelvin Crawford (in 5925) fired three-quarters of a drum of Lewis ammunition at one Albatros, which caught fire, fell away and was reported as crashed near Gouzeaucourt. Lieutenant Sydney Cockerall (A2581) engaged another Albatros at close range, then during a circling manoeuvre got inside the German, fired, and sent it down out of control to crash. Another German fighter was driven down by Second Lieutenants Percy W Chambers and F O'Sullivan of 22 Squadron (A5959) and seen to land north-east of Gouzeaucourt.

In the event, there were no apparent fighter losses on the German side—certainly Jasta 5 suffered none. The Albatros Scouts did break off the action, leaving the three surviving FEs to fly home, but the crew of the one lost were both dead. The pilot had been Second Lieutenant Patrick Alfred Russell, aged 27 from Northumberland, who had seen action at Gallipoli with a Yeomanry Regiment, and his observer, a Canadian, Lieutenant H Loveland, attached to the RFC from the 78th Canadian Infantry Battalion.

Such claims became a feature of the fighting during the First War and it is difficult to reconcile the reports of the Allied airmen with the apparent lack of corresponding German losses. Crawford's burning victim was also confirmed by 22 Squadron, so why there appears to be no loss is a mystery, unless the German pilot(s) survived and only their aircraft were lost and not reported as such in the records. Over-claiming in respect of assumed out of control victories is understandable, but why so many German aircraft were seen burning and crashing, with virtually no losses admitted to is strange.

Even before this combat had taken place, the RFC had had its first loss of the day, losing an aircraft which had taken off some 45 minutes after 22 flew out. 60 Squadron based at Le Hameau (which it shared with 11 and 29 Squadrons), sent out aircraft at 0715 to fly an Offensive Patrol between Arras and Gommecourt. They spotted aircraft over the lines and headed towards Queant running into Jasta 2. In the ensuing fight, Second Lieutenant C S Hall (A6766) sent an Albatros spinning down over Fontaine Notre Dame, but 60 Squadron lost Second Lieutenant Vaughan F Williams, who fell in flames following an attack by Otto Bernert at 0830. Again there is no German loss recorded.

Meantime, the Sopwith Pups of 54 Squadron, who flew a five-man patrol which began at 0720, ran into seven enemy aircraft, five two-seaters and two single-seaters. They broke up the formation, Lieutenant Oliver Sutton (A637) claiming one shot down while Lieutenant W V

Strugnell, in A639, (a pre-war air mechanic who had learned to fly in 1912 as an NCO) attacked another two-seater from close range, seeing the observer slump down hit, but then his engine began to fail forcing him to break off and head back. He just made it, crash-landing at Aizecourt-le-Haut. There are no recorded losses on the German side.

Strugnell was not yet out of the woods. Getting his engine going again he attempted a take-off only to hit a post with his propeller, which shattered. The area was covered with shell-holes and he was unable to avoid a crash. The Pup was severely damaged. Men from the Squadron came to the site and dismantled the machine, but that night, before they could move off, the parts were further damaged in a severe gale.

Another photo operation was mounted by 13 Squadron from Savy, 15 km to the west of Lens, the BE2d taking off at 0745. Forty-five minutes later, the pilot, Lieutenant Pat Powell, was turning for home and diving, having seen some Albatros DIIIs coming for him. Despite fire from his gunner, Air Mechanic Percy Bonner, the BE was hit from the fire of the leading Albatros and, out of control, the two-seater ploughed into a house near Farbus, north-east of Arras. The Albatros pilot had just scored his 32nd victory and his first of the month. By the end of April his score would have risen to 52; his name was Manfred von Richthofen, leader of Jasta 11. Both 'Tommies' were killed.

Their aircraft having failed to return, 13 Squadron sent off another BE at 0950, crewed by Lieutenant C F Jex and AM J H Bolton. They fared a little better than their earlier comrades in that they survived an attack by four enemy scouts, but in evading, they were driven into cloud, lost their way and finally put down at No.2 Squadron's base at Hesdigneul, south-west of Bethune—where they crashed. It would seem that the four enemy fighters were from Jasta 11, for Karl Allmenröder certainly claimed shooting down a BE at 0930, near Angres, south-west of Lens.

However, so that the reader can begin to understand how difficult it is sometimes to try and sort out who was shooting down whom, the problems with this particular combat are worth noting.

On the one hand we have a definite claim by Allmenröder that he brought down a BE at 0930, in the location mentioned above. However, the reader will have noted that Jex and Bolton were said to have taken off at 0950. As British and German times were the same at this period, we seem to have a time problem, unless they took off at 0850 and the records are in error! Or perhaps the German made his claim at 1030, which would fit the combat details. Added to this, Angres is right on the front line, so did Allmenröder believe his victim fell just inside German lines, in no-man's-land or on the British side? There is also a note that the number of the BE credited to Allmenröder was 7061; Jex was flying 2510, although 7061 is a BE number. There are no other losses reported on this day—certainly not a 7061—and as we know, the BE was not lost in combat but crashed on landing at Hesdigneul. (Reference to the crash occurring at 23 Squadron's 'drome is wrong—23 were at Baizieux, 60 km south of the action.)

At 0800, FE2ds of 57 Squadron took off from Fienvillers, 8 km south-west of Doullens, and no less than 50 km due west of the front lines, to fly a line patrol between Lens-Arras-Bapaume. At 0945 they were engaged by Jasta 11 just north of Douai, Richthofen's squadron being based at Douai-Brayelles. The six FEs were east of Arras when Jasta 11 came down on them, the pushers then flying south-west. However, it could be that the FEs had split up or did split, as Jasta 11 engaged part of the patrol to the north of Douai while the others headed south-west and ran into Jasta 2. The gunners put up a spirited return fire which hit two of the attacking Jasta 2 Albatri: Leutnant Erich König, a six-victory ace, had his machine set ablaze, crashing at Wancourt, while Leutnant Hans Wortmann (two victories) crashed at Vitry-en-Artois. If the locations are correct, Wortmann would have gone down first, south-west of Douai, and König later and further south-west. However, König was reported down at 0945 and Wortmann five minutes later. If Wortmann did go down first he would more likely have crashed at Vis-(not Vitry-)en-Artois which is just east of Wancourt.

However, what is not in question is that Jasta 2 lost two pilots. What is not certain is who got them. Lieutenant E E Pope and Lieutenant A W Naismith (A1959) reported engaging the enemy machines but Naismith's gun jammed after one round. What is not known is if either of the 57 Squadron crews that were lost were successful before they fell, for 57 Squadron didn't get off scot-free. Two FEs were hit by Jasta 11 pilots, Leutnant Constantin Krefft (the Jasta's Technical Officer) and Vizefeldwebel Sebastian Festner shooting down one each. One fell at Oignies, 12 km north-west of Douai, the other south-east of Auby. The surviving four FEs began landing back at their base between 1020 and 1050. As they were doing so, 43 Squadron at Treizennes, south of Aire, were sending out six Sopwith 1½ Strutters led by Captain D C Rutter, to fly yet another photo op. Once over the lines they were in the territory of Jasta 11 and waiting for them were von Richthofen, his brother Lothar and Werner Voss.

Manfred von Richthofen, as leader, attacked first, managing to cut out one Strutter to the east of Vimy. The British pilot tried desperately to get into some nearby cloud but Richthofen's fire hit the fuel tank. With petrol spraying out and with the immediate danger of fire, Second Lieutenant A P Warren quickly put his machine down near Givenchy. Even so, his gunner, Sergeant Renel Dunn, who had been hit in the abdomen during the air attack, and undoubtedly knowing his wound was fatal, kept up a spirited return fire from his rear cockpit after the machine stopped, which hit von Richthofen's circling Albatros, he being just five metres up. Von Richthofen immediately dived on the grounded machine and shot it up. Whether he hit Dunn again is not known for certain—he certainly reported killing one of the occupants, but Dunn would have died anyway, and was certainly dead when Richthofen's claim was verified. Peter Warren, a 19-year-old from Oxfordshire, was taken prisoner.

While this was going on, the others of 43 were still being engaged, Second Lieutenant C E Berigny and 2AM E Bowen claiming an Albatros Scout which they said fell in flames east of Vimy, but there is no recorded loss on the German side, and certainly not by Jasta 11.

Here the authors would like to point out again that while German personnel casualties are pretty accurate there is some doubt about aircraft losses, so it may well be that while there is no reported aircrew killed, the aircraft may well have been lost and the occupants escaped from a crash-landing. What does become apparent is the number of German aircraft seen burning and/or crashed which had no corresponding aircrew losses, which means either the pilot/crew survived, or the British pilot/crew were in fact seeing an Allied plane going down and believed it was a German.

Other German casualties that did occur this day were up on the northern part of the front, Leutnant Karl Haan of Flieger Abteilung 19 (FA19) being killed by anti-aircraft fire over Langmarck. The British flak position was around Pilkem, just to the west, which reported the two-seater falling in flames but only one crew member is reported dead. Further south, an Albatros CVII (2217/16) of FA48 was hit by flak during a sortie over the British lines and had to make a forced landing where the crew, Offizierstellvertreter F Meixner and Oberleutnant W Puckert, were taken prisoner. The two-seater—Albatros CVII 2217/16—which was virtually intact, was given the RFC number of G.19.

Two BE2d aircraft from 2 Squadron were directing artillery west of Angres at 1030. Second Lieutenant E M Paul and Lieutenant L M Elworthy (5879) were attacked by two Halberstadt Scouts over Noeux-les-Mines, but the BE pilot rapidly dived away, as the two Germans then went for the other BE, flown by Second Lieutenants W J Stonier and H C W Strickland (6746). Again after a brief skirmish the two-seater crew escaped. BE crews were not always this lucky. Stonier, in fact, would not survive April 1917.

The German fighter pilots may not have been able to claim victories in this instant, but they had at least driven off the artillery flyers and stopped them from doing their work with the guns.

French Front

Again there is little to report from the French sectors apart from an observer in a Caudron being wounded by ground fire during a photo reconnaissance sortie for VII Armée. The French ground gunners did, however, bring down an Albatros DIII of Jasta 35 (2107/16), the pilot, Vizefeldwebel Rudolf Nebel making a forced landing near Grossen Belchen where he became a prisoner. But he was not a prisoner for long. On 5 May 1917 he managed to escape and got back to Germany via Switzerland.

A Nieuport Scout pilot was lost during the day, when he force-landed inside the German lines for unknown reasons.

	A/C	KB			DES	OOC	KB
British losses	8	—	British claims		5†	2	—
French losses	—	—	French claims		1		—
German claims	7	—	German losses		4‡		—

† Three of the British claims were to AA fire.
‡ Again the Nachrichtenblatt records no losses, when four are not in dispute; two fighter pilots killed, one captured and a two-seater crew captured. In addition one two-seater crew man was killed.

British Casualties

Aircraft type	No.	Squadron	Crew	
FE2b	6953	22 Sqdn	2/Lt P A Russell	KIA
			Lt H Loveland	KIA
Nieuport XXIII	A6763	60 Sqdn	2/Lt V F Williams	KIA
Sopwith Pup	A639	54 Sqdn	Capt W V Strugnell	Safe
BE2d	5841	13 Sqdn	Lt P J G Powell	KIA
			1AM P Bonner	KIA
FE2d	A1944	57 Sqdn	Lt H P Sworder	KIA
			2/Lt A H Margoliouth	KIA
FE2d	A5151	57 Sqdn	Capt H Tomlinson MC	DOW
			Lt N C Denison	WIA/POW
BE2e	2510	13 Sqdn	2/Lt C F Jex	Safe
			2AM J A Bolton	Safe
Sop 1½ Strutter	A2401	43 Sqdn	2/Lt A P Warren	POW
			Sgt R Dunn	KIA

French Casualties

Caudron G4		C.54	Lt Simonnet (O)	WIA
Nieuport XVII	2243	N.23	Adj Bertal	MIA

Tuesday, 3 April 1917

British Front

If all the action on 2 April had occurred during the morning, then all the action of the 3rd was in the afternoon, due of course to the continuing bad weather. Heavy rain had set in during the afternoon of the 2nd, storms and low clouds lasting till noon on this Tuesday. So strong had been the winds that 29 Squadron had had two of its Nieuport Scouts overturn while taking off in gales but both pilots had been unhurt.

Activity on the ground centred around the British 7th Division's attack on Ecoust and the 4 and 5th Australian Divisions capture of Noreuil, the last positions before the Hindenburg Line itself. The cost was over 600 casualties to the Australians and 400 to the British—in what was described at the time as a 'minor skirmish'.

As soon as the weather improved, RFC machines were brought out of hangars and prepared for flight. Among the first off were FE2s of 11 Squadron to fly a recce mission, away at 1300. A808 did not get back, being reported shot down by AA fire, crashing over the enemy's side of the lines. Both crewmen were killed and anti-aircraft batteries Flakzug 28, 185 and 47 were credited with an FE shot down after scoring a direct hit on the pusher two-seater, south of Feuchy.

At 1355 hours 40 Squadron sent out seven Nieuports to escort a photo machine of 43 Squadron, both units based at Treizennes. Led by Captain Robert Gregory, some enemy aircraft were spotted east of Arras but they were out of range. However, Lieutenant E L 'Lobo' Benbow chased one which quickly disappeared while Lieutenant K Mackenzie engaged three near Arras but without result. The Germans were a patrol of Jasta 30, Leutnant Gustav Nernst claiming one of the Nieuports at 1440 over Esquerchin, east of Arras. He had picked off Second Lieutenant S A Sharpe RFA/RFC who crash-landed to be taken prisoner. It was Nernst's second victory.

More FEs were out mid-afternoon. To the south of the front 23 Squadron sent out a photo aircraft from Baizieux, while a patrol of 25 Squadron took off from Lozinghem, west of Bethune, on a photo op to Mericourt-Gavrelle at 1530. Just as they were getting airborne, the 23 Squadron machine was being engaged and brought down near Essarts. The 25 Squadron machines now flew into Jasta 11's territory and south of Lens ran into Richthofen's fighters. The Baron brought down one, Karl Emil Schäfer another, at 1615 and 1620 respectively. Sebastian Festner may have attacked another but his claim was not upheld.

Just minutes earlier five DH2s of 32 Squadron took off from Lealvillers, led by Captain William G Curphey MC. Over the front they were engaged by enemy fighters, losing one at 1630—Lieutenant E L Heyworth—and in the subsequent fight, had another shot up. Lieutenant L W Barney struggled back to the lines, chased by an Albatros, and he eventually force-landed at 1700 hours inside British lines. So, who brought down these DH2s, and the 23 Squadron FE?

Edmund Nathanael of Jasta 5 claimed a 'Gitterrumpf' [lattice tail] north of Boursies. in front of the German lines, at 1635, while Vizefeldwebel Emil Eisenhuth of Jasta 3 claimed an FE at Hendecourt in British lines, 5 km due north of Lagnicourt, at 1655, Leutnant Adolf Schulte of Jasta 12 an FE due east of St Leger at 1710, also in British lines, and Sebastian Festner of Jasta 11, a DH2 unconfirmed at 1720 near Hendecourt.

Obviously Nathanael got Heyworth, Boursies being just to the east of Lagnicourt where the fight took place. Festner, who was either still in the air or had landed and taken off again, and Eisenhuth, probably went after Barney, so again his claim was not confirmed, but given to Eisenhuth. The 23 Squadron FE, piloted by Sergeant J A Cunniffe, had his gunner, 2AM J T Mackie, wounded, but got his machine down at Essarts, 20 km inside British lines, and well east of St Leger. Schulte said his FE went down north-east of St Leger, so in all probability he claimed this one, but there was no RFC loss, just a wounded gunner. Cunniffe had ten days to reflect on his narrow escape, before he would have a closer one!

While all this was going on, 15 Squadron at Lealvillers sent out another photo machine at 1625, which was shot down at 1730 near Croisselles by Hauptmann Paul von Osterroht, commander of Jasta 12. The Germans reported the BE down at Bullecourt, but both locations are right on the front line within a kilometre or so.

That really accounts for all the British losses, but there is one German claim outstanding, that of Unteroffizier Ludwig Weber of Jasta 3, who claimed a BE2e north-east of Brebières at 1450. There is no corresponding RFC loss for a BE, and Brebières is some 14 kilometres inside the German lines, just south-west of Douai.

The British only made one combat claim during the day, at 1435 hours. Sopwith 1½ Strutters of 43 Squadron were out and were attacked by some Albatros Scouts near Izel. Lieutenant Harold H Balfour and his gunner, Second Lieutenant A Roberts, claimed one which they reported falling in flames, but there is no reported loss of a German fighter pilot on the 3rd.

Also late in the day, Second Lieutenants G M Hopkins and 1AM Friend, 22 Squadron, who had taken off at 1620 in A5486 to fly a patrol over the 4th Army front, were forced to land near St Quentin after an attack by an enemy aircraft above the Hindenburg Line. They had been at the rear of the formation and had been hit from long range, the fuel tank being holed. They lost their engine and came down in the vicinity of Moislans, spending the night in a dug-out with front line troops. Next morning, a party of men arrived and dismantled the FE and they all returned to their base.

The day ended with an attack upon the British balloon lines between 1910 and 1955. Once again it was Otto Bernert of Jasta 2 causing the mayhem, claiming one balloon burned at Ervillers at 1910 and a second north of Bapaume twelve minutes later, both some 10 kilometres inside British lines. The Germans did claim another just before 2000 hours but only two were lost on this evening, 13 and 18 KB Sections each losing their 'gasbag', although the observers jumped to safety.

French Front

Escadrille Spa.67 had a Spad VII pilot, Caporal Bernard, wounded during the day but the exact circumstances are unclear. However, a two-seater crew of FA40, Leutnant Schumacher and Unteroffizier Scheinig, were engaged by what they said was a French Nieuport south of St Quentin and claimed they shot it down. Caporal Bernard force-landed near Noyon, south-west of this location but inside French lines, so perhaps it was him. The French made no claims.

	A/C	KB			DES	OOC	KB
British losses	6	2	British claims		1	—	—
French losses	—	—	French claims		—	—	—
German claims	10	3	German losses		—	—	—

British Casualties

Aircraft type	No.	Squadron	Crew		
FE2b	A808	11 Sqdn	Lt E T C Brandon	KIA	
			2/Lt G Masters	KIA	
Nieuport XVII	A6674	40 Sqdn	2/Lt S A Sharpe	POW	
FE2d	A6371	25 Sqdn	Lt L Dodson MC	POW	
			2/Lt H S Richards	DOW	
FE2d	A6382	25 Sqdn	2/Lt D P MacDonald	POW	
			2/Lt J I M O'Bierne	KIA	
FE2b	4897	23 Sqdn	Sgt J A Cunniffe	Safe	*
			2AM J T Mackie	WIA	
DH2	A2536	32 Sqdn	Lt E L Heyworth	WIA/POW	
DH2	A5012	32 Sqdn	Lt L W Barney	Safe	*
BE2c	7236	15 Sqdn	2/Lt J H Sayer	KIA	
			2/Lt V C Morris	KIA	
FE2b	A5486	22 Sqdn	2/Lt G M Hopkins	Safe	*
			1AM Friend	Safe	

French Casualties

Spad VII		N.67†*	Cpl Bernard	WIA	*

† While some French fighter escadrilles were flying Spads, unit designations were not changed from N. to Spa. until the unit became fully equipped with Spads later in 1917.

Wednesday, 4 April 1917

British Front

The bad weather continued with low cloud and rain—32 Squadron even reported a snow storm —which curtailed operations and only Jasta 4 at Douai saw any action. Leutnant Hans Klein gained his first of an eventual 22 victories by attacking a 12 Squadron BE2c which he shot down south of Arras at 0840, the two-seater crashing inside British lines. At 0905, Leutnant Hans Malchow brought down an 11 Squadron FE2b (his first and only victory), although the pilot of the 'Fee' managed to get over the lines before he force-landed, but German ground observers confirmed its apparent loss. 12 Squadron also had an observer wounded but his aircraft returned.

Nieuports of 40 Squadron took off for a line patrol at 0910, three aircraft patrolling the Lens-Bailleul line. Lieutenant E L Benbow had his petrol tank holed by ground fire which forced him to land at 2 Squadron's airfield at Hesdigneul at 1000.

Artillery aircraft successfully ranged guns onto several targets during the morning, before bad weather stopped virtually all flying.

There was an interesting incident up on the coast. Aircraft from the RNAS Dunkirk Seaplane base raided the sheds at Zeebrugge during the evening. Flight Sub Lieutenant Ernest John Cuckney dropped a 520lb bomb and two 65 pounders from 2,800 ft at 2008 but he evidently knocked off his engine switch as the throttle would not answer when he tried to open it. He glided down, followed by a searchlight beam, and landed on the water a quarter of a mile from the Mole. He was on the sea for about eight minutes before tracing the cause of his trouble. By this time a large tug with a searchlight was fast approaching and came within hailing distance. He then got his engine going and took off in the nick of time. Cuckney went on to make several more raids during April.

French Front
Nothing to report.

	A/C	KB			DES	OOC	KB
British losses	2	—	British claims		—	—	—
French losses	—	—	French claims		—	—	—
German claims	2	—	German losses		—	—	—

British Casualties

Aircraft type	No.	Squadron	Crew			
BE2c	2563	12 Sqdn	2/Lt K C Horner	DOW		
			2/Lt A Emmerson	DOW		
FE2b	A832	11 Sqdn	Lt W Baillie	Safe		
			AM E Wood	Safe		
BE2c		12 Sqdn	Cpl A V Scholes (O)	WIA		*

Thursday, 5 April 1917

British Front

The weather was misty and cloudy, but it had improved enough to bring forth aircraft from both sides to do battle as the build-up towards the Arras offensive got into its stride. Every headquarters needed photos of all sorts of things, so the observation squadrons were ordered up. With a retreat to new lines and the impending offensive against those new enemy positions —and the only maps came from photos—photo ops needed to be flown. And it was this day which can be said to have started Bloody April.

It was also the day which saw the first operational sorties flown by the new Bristol Fighters, the BF2a machines of 48 Squadron. Great things were expected of this aircraft, and one of its flight commanders was none other than Captain W L Robinson VC (also known as Leefe Robinson) who had won his Victoria Cross for bringing down the German Schutte Lanz airship SL11 over north London on the night of 2/3 September 1916. The other two flight commanders on 48 Squadron were veteran DH2 pilots from 24 Squadron's epic battles over the Somme the previous summer—Captains Alan Wilkinson, an ace, and A T Cull. The deputy leaders of each flight were also veterans.

Designed as a two-seat fighter the BF2a went into action with entirely the wrong tactical concept. Instead of taking on enemy fighters with the pilot's front gun, leaving the observer/ gunner in the rear to ward off any attacking aircraft from behind, it had been decided, by Robinson, that if attacked, the Bristols would merely close up and let the combined fire from the rear-gunners force away the would-be attackers. Later, as the BF2b, and using more aggressive tactics, it was to become one of the most dangerous opponents for German aviators, but that was some months in the future.

However, on this April morning six Bristols of 48 Squadron, led by Robinson, took off from Bellevue at around 1000 for an Offensive Patrol to Douai. Their base was over 40 km from the front at Arras, and by the time they had gained height, crossed the lines and were well east of Douai, it was nearing 1100. Having been reported by the German ground observers, a telephone call to Jasta 11's base at Brayelles had von Richthofen's pilot taking off within minutes, led by the Baron himself.

Spotting the Albatros Scouts, the Bristol pilots closed up while the gunners waited for the range to decrease. Down came the five men of Jasta 11, Spandau machine-guns blazing. First one then another Bristol was hit, dropping out of formation. Von Richthofen singled out one which he engaged, finally forcing it down near Lewarde, south-east of Douai. Having despatched Second Lieutenants Leckler and George, Richthofen chased after the other four, Festner already having knocked down Robinson's machine. He caught up with them over Douai and brought down Adams and Stewart near Cuincy, just west of Douai. Leutnant Georg Simon claimed the fourth, downed north of Monchecourt. The other two scraped over the lines, full of holes. The Bristol pilots, in all, claimed two of their attackers shot down but Jasta 11 were unharmed. Despite this disaster, the other two Flights set out in turn, according to orders, and claimed victories on each mission without loss.

Jasta 12 were also in the air to the south of Cambrai, engaged with FE2b pushers, but although Leutnants Röth and Otto Splitgerber were each credited with one brought down over

Gouzeaucourt and Honnecourt at 1105 and 1110, both locations well inside German territory, it is difficult to know where the FEs came from. Two FEs were indeed lost this day, but one fell to Leutnant Schlenker of Jasta 3 south-west of Moeuvres at midday (and the correct number A805 is recorded by the Germans) which is 12-14 km north of Jasta 12's claims and nearly an hour later. Schlenker's FE was a machine from 23 Squadron on a photo op to Inchy and was correctly reported as lost between Inchy and Pronville.

The other FE lost was a machine from 18 Squadron, on a photo op of the 5th Army front. But it did not take off until 1105 and although attacked by enemy aircraft, the mortally wounded pilot brought it down on the British side near Bapaume. The only other pusher-types in action were a DH2 single-seater of 32 Squadron, shot up and damaged by three enemy fighters at an unknown time, and a 20 Squadron FE which force-landed at Abeele in the late morning, but that was way up on the Ypres part of the front. That was claimed by Leutnant Ernst Weissner of Jasta 18 at 1145.

No.43 Squadron sent out a seven-man special recce mission at 1015 led by Major A S W Dore, from which Lieutenant F M Kitto and 2AM A W Cant had to return with engine trouble, Kitto crash-landing on Maison Bouche airfield just short of midday (A974). Seven or eight enemy fighters were spotted, which followed the formation from 1130 to 1150, finally making an attack near La Bassée. It was Jasta 30 that engaged the Strutters, Leutnant Nernst gaining his second victory of the month by bringing down one of them near Rouvroy at 1205. Lieutenants C R O'Brien and J L Dickson (A971) claimed one out of control, but Jasta 30 had no losses.

DH2s of 24 Squadron had mixed fortunes on a late morning OP, finding a two-seater doing artillery work, escorted by two, possibly three Albatros scouts. A combat began between the five British fighters and the four German aircraft. Captain Kent was leading the DHs, attacking one enemy machine but another got on his tail and had to break off. The two-seater was seen on the tail of a DH and going down in a spinning nose-dive, which was Second Lieutenant J K Ross, brought down east of Honnecourt by Leutnant Wolluhn and Unteroffizier Mackeprang of FA(A)210. Lieutenant H W Woollett claimed to have downed this two-seater, but again there does not appear to be a loss, certainly not in personnel. Woollett reported the observer stopped firing after his attack and saw the machine crash one and a quarter miles east of Honnecourt.

FEs of 20 Squadron were in a fight over Belgium just before midday, having sent out two northern OPs at 0950 and 1047. On the first, Captain Mahony-Jones and Captain R M Knowles (in A1961) followed an Albatros Scout down to 700 feet in company with A29, Second Lieutenant Pike and AM Sayers. They were then attacked by nine fighters, Jones and Knowles claiming one down over Courtrai and later another over Houthulst after a running fight.

Meantime, the other three aircraft attacked two German planes over St Eloi at 10,000 feet. As already mentioned one FE (flown by 2/Lt J Lawson/Sgt Clayton—A1942) was badly shot up and landed at Abeele airfield. A second FE, equally shot up (2/Lt Hugh G White/Pvt T Allum—A6385) flopped down on Abeele, but they had just shot down an Albatros Scout and were feeling pleased with themselves.

The opposing Germans were pilots of Jasta 18; Leutnant Weissner claimed an FE which was not credited, but the unit lost Leutnant Josef Flink, flying a DIII 1942/16. He was badly wounded in the hand by fire from Private Allum over Neuve Eglise, landed and was taken prisoner. His machine was given the number G.20.

Two Martinsyde G100s of 27 Squadron were brought down by ground fire further south on the French front around midday during a bomb raid on Hirson. Second Lieutenant W T B Tasker came down near Origny, due to engine failure, where he burnt his machine before being captured, Second Lieutenant M Johnstone crashing 12 miles east of Compiègne but inside French lines. Flakzug 407 and Flakbatts 4 and 64 claimed Tasker, while the other Martinsyde was seen to land at La Bouteille. Ground fire also accounted for two BEs of 13 Squadron on photo ops. Second Lieutenant G E Brookes and 2AM J H Bolton fell over Duissans on the British side, while Lieutenants O G F Ball and H Howell-Evans were unlucky enough to be hit by friendly fire and came down over St Catherine.

The Nieuports of 60 Squadron made a balloon attack just after midday, going for a 'drachen' near Cambrai. Lieutenant E J D Townsend, a Canadian from Vancouver, failed to return, later being reported severely wounded and a prisoner, to unknown ground fire.

The afternoon was fairly quiet, but it picked up in a last flurry in the early evening. A 29 Squadron Nieuport XXIII, part of an OP flown at 1810, was shot down. Vizefeldwebel Karl Menckhoff of Jasta 3 claimed a Nieuport just west of Athies which is in the right area. Lieutenant N A Birks was wounded and taken prisoner and he later reported that he was visited by his victor, who was of 'sergeant-major' rank—Vizefeldwebel.

The final loss of the day was from 6 Naval Squadron. Its pilots claimed one Albatros Scout in flames and two out of control by Flight Lieutenant E W Norton and Flight Sub Lieutenant A L Thorne, although Norton had to make a forced landing at Bouquemaison at 1700 hours. One of their Nieuport XVIIs was brought down between Arras and Cambrai at 1845, Flight Sub Lieutenant R K Slater being taken prisoner, by Leutnant Eberhard Voss of Jasta 20, who claimed his victim near Omissy. 6 Naval had another Nieuport shot up, Flight Sub Lieutenant M R Kingsford being injured when he crash-landed.

Twenty-nine enemy aircraft were claimed by the RFC and RNAS during this day, but again there is a lack of any evidence on the German side of losses. The Nachrichtenblatt finally acknowledged one loss which must be presumed to be that of Flink of Jasta 18. Other than a pilot of FA6 being killed in a landing accident at Courtrai, the only other personnel losses were Leutnant Karl Hummel killed at Ghent, Unteroffizier Albin Nietzold killed at St Marie and Gefreiter Simon Metzger killed at Mont d'Origny, units unknown, and they may not have been combat casualties.

While pilots of 18, 24, 25, 1 and 8 Naval Squadrons all made claims between 1200 and 1245, all eight were out of control victories over Albatros or Halberstadt Scouts. A patrol of 54 Squadron also claimed a balloon destroyed at Gouy. As the pilots flew back at low level, Captain Pixley fired at a horse and rider, seeing both fall, while Captain F N Hudson opened up on 100 soldiers unloading boxes from open trucks outside a railway station. Some were seen to fall as the rest scattered in all directions.

During the evening flurry, 60 Squadron claimed an Albatros destroyed and two out of control in the Riencourt area, 29 Squadron claimed three Albatros Scouts out of control between Douai and Vitry-en-Artois, while a 12 Squadron crew claimed an Albatros DII as destroyed.

French Front

Little to report, other than a Caudron GIV lost over Sillery, south-east of Reims, shot down by Leutnant Albert Dossenbach, Staffelführer of Jasta 36. It was the Jasta's first confirmed kill. Three single-seaters were in combat, one pilot being wounded near Lure, while Lieutenant de Mortemart of N.23 was forced to land after a fight near Verdun, but was unharmed. The Frenchman may have been Caporal Alfred Guyot of N.81. He received the Medaille Militaire on this day, following a fight with five hostile scouts, during which he was badly wounded. He force-landed in the front lines but had the strength to vacate his aircraft and regain French lines.

Leutnant Hans Auer of Jasta 26 claimed a Nieuport at Sennheim at 1806 which came down inside German lines, but it is not certain who the pilot was, although Caporal Herubel of Spa.78 was brought down at Jonchere.

	A/C	KB		DES	OOC	KB
British losses	15	—	British claims	7†	22	1
French losses	3	—	French claims	—		—
German claims	18‡	—	German losses	1		?

† Including one captured. ‡ Including two by ground fire.

British Casualties

Aircraft type	No.	Squadron	Crew	
BF2a	A3337	48 Sqdn	Capt W L Robinson VC	POW
			2/Lt E D Warburton	POW
BF2a	A3320	48 Sqdn	Lt H A Cooper	POW/WIA
			2/Lt A Boldison	POW/WIA

BF2b	A3343	48 Sqdn	Lt A T Adams	POW/WIA
			Lt D J Stewart	POW/WIA
BF2a	A3340	48 Sqdn	2/Lt A N Leckler	POW/WIA
			2/Lt H D K George	POW/DOW
Sop 1½ Strutter	A1073	43 Sqdn	2/Lt C P Thornton	POW
			2/Lt H D Blackburn	KIA
DH2	A2592	24 Sqdn	2/Lt J K Ross	POW/DOW
FE2b	A805	23 Sqdn	Lt L Elsley	KIA
			2/Lt F Higginbottom	DOW
FE2b	4967	18 Sqdn	Lt H A R Boustead	DOW
			2/Lt C MacKintosh	KIA
Martinsyde G100	A1578	27 Sqdn	2/Lt M Johnstone	Safe
Martinsyde G100	7485	27 Sqdn	2/Lt W T B Tasker	POW
BE2d	5787	13 Sqdn	2/Lt G E Brookes	WIA
			2AM J H Bolton	KIA
BE2d	2520	13 Sqdn	2/Lt O G F Ball	KIA
			Lt H Howell-Evans	KIA
Nieuport XVII	A6693	60 Sqdn	Lt E J D Townsend	POW/WIA
Nieuport XVII	N3202	6N Sqdn	FSL R K Slater	POW
Nieuport XVII	N3187	6N Sqdn	FC E W Norton	Safe *
Nieuport DVII	N3191	6N Sqdn	FSL M R Kingsford	Inj *
Nieuport XXIII	A6791	29 Sqdn	Lt N A Birks	POW/WIA

French Casualties

Caudron GIV	C.39	Lt d'Hericourt	KIA
		Sgt Mathieu	KIA
Nieuport Scout	N.23	Lt de Mortemart	Safe *
Spad VII	N.81	Cpl A Guyot	WIA
Spad VII	N.78	Cpl Herubel	MIA

Friday, 6 April 1917

British Front

Today was Good Friday. Parties to celebrate were reported in many locations despite the obvious build-up—or even because of it. Generally these sorts of things were for civilians in Britain, not for the men facing death and destruction in holes in the ground but whenever possible a chance of normality was taken. It could be their last.

The men knew too something was in the wind. There was to be an offensive soon. All the signs were there: troops moving up, supplies being brought forward, commanders going off to briefings and sergeant-majors checking that kit and rifles were in order. Some of the senior officers knew more than they were telling; the foot soldier who would have to go over the top would be the last to know. It was not that they could not be trusted, but both sides often tried to snatch a prisoner during a trench raid when things looked as if they were about to happen, in the hope of information.

RFC Headquarters were still tasked with bringing in useful aerial photographs of the enemy's positions, while hostile batteries needed to be sighted and shelled. Over the two days 5-6 April, some 1,700 aerial photographs were taken while bombing aircraft raided German aerodromes on 17 occasions. The weather both helped a little and hindered, for the morning was fine, rain and cloud not putting a dampener on things until the afternoon. Therefore most of the aerial activity was confined to the morning—a particularly busy morning, and for many flyers their last.

The first loss of the day came at 0800, a 1 Naval Squadron Sopwith Triplane going down amid bursting AA fire south-west of Moeuvres. The OP, led by Flight Lieutenant T F N Gerrard, had left Chipilly at 0630. Flight Sub Lieutenant N D M Hewitt's machine is presumed to have been hit and was seen circling Doignies and failed to get to the lines before he was forced down and taken prisoner. He was claimed by Flakbatterie 505 at Lagnicourt, two kilometres from Doignies.

In some accounts, N D M Hewitt is supposed to have been shot down by Karl Schäfer of Jasta 11, but Schäfer (a) did not score until 1020, (b) his victim fell at Givenchy some 32 kilometres to the north-east of Doignies and (c) it was a BE2 not a Triplane. Another classic case of someone not looking at a map or taking account of the hour.

In any event, this was the first Sopwith Triplane to fall to the enemy although it had been around in limited numbers for some weeks. Indeed, the prototype, N500, was being used at the front the previous July with 1 Naval Squadron. The design so impressed the Germans that Anthony Fokker, the Dutch designer building aircraft for the Germans (his services having earlier been rejected by the British and French) produced one of the most well-known fighters of WW1 later that summer, the Fokker Dr1 Triplane.

At Le Hameau the FE2b pushers of 11 Squadron were up early, sending out a reconnaissance sortie to the Arras area at 0735. FE2s of 25 Squadron flew a protection patrol, taking off at 0743, and were involved in the same fight as 11 Squadron. Over the front a fighter was encountered which attacked FE 7025 flown by Second Lieutenants D P Walter and C Brown, slightly wounding the pilot, forcing him to crash in a forced landing near Gavrelle at 0900.

The Germans were alive to all the sudden activity of the last 24 hours and on the alert. They sent off Jasta 4 from Douai led by Wilhelm Frankl, who had already claimed his first victim of the day. Frankl had shot down a night-flying FE2b at 0230 during a night raid by 100 Squadron. His victim had fallen at Quiery le Motte, his 15th kill of the war.

Victories over night raiders were rare in WW1, this one being the first by a German fighter aircraft. The difficulties in finding a hostile aircraft in a black sky when radio and radar aids were still in the far distant future were immense. Even an experienced flyer such as Frankl would find it hard, but he had done it this night, and must have been on a 'high', for today he would add a further three day victories to his tally. He already had the Pour le Mérite, awarded when his score had reached eight in August 1916.

Now, just on 0850, he saw the FEs east of Arras and led the attack. The two-seaters closed up but already Frankl was firing at one, hitting not only the engine but also the gunner. Crippled, the FE went down, its pilot making a crash-landing at Feuchy. Frankl was already firing at another which also went down, glided over the front line to crunch into the ground by the Arras-St Pol road, its crew scrambling safely from the wreckage. A third FE, shot up by either Frankl or one of his men, also headed down as it flew back over the trenches to make a forced landing at 0900, its pilot wounded. The Jasta, and Frankl, were credited with two victories.

Other FEs were in trouble just to the south of this action, 57 Squadron having sent out six from Fienvillers at 0700, led by Captain A C Wright to fly an OP between Somain, west of Valenciennes, and Beauvois, south-east of Cambrai. One FE left this formation at 0820 with engine trouble, leaving five to continue. At 0800 the FE crews spotted ten two-seaters south of Douai and attacked. Wright came in behind one of them, but the German observer put bullets into his FE and he was hit in the knee, just as the two-seater began to dive after being hit by the FE's bullets. Several single-seaters now joined in. Oberleutnant Adolf von Tutschek of Jasta Boelcke made an attack on them ten minutes later and claimed one brought down near Anneux, just to the south-west of Cambrai, while the others tried to fight their way out of trouble.

Tutschek was not immediately credited with this kill and it was only when Leutnant Werner Voss confirmed that von Tutschek's fire had done the initial damage that the latter was given credit. Adding to the confusion is that the FE in question was numbered A22 (Schreiber and Lewis), whereas somehow, von Tutschek's victim was recorded as A6. The confusion clears when one knows that A6 was the letter and number of an 'A' Flight machine from 57 Squadron, and nothing to do with the aircraft's serial number. (Even this leaves a slight question for the details of Captain Wright's fight do tally with Tutschek's combat, although perhaps there were two FEs seen going down with dead engines and being engaged by other fighters.)

Within minutes other Jasta 12 pilots were attacking the FEs again, one going down to the Staffelführer, von Osterroht, another to Leutnant Otto Splitgerber. Meantime Jasta 5 pilots had joined the fray, Edmund Nathanael claiming one at Douchy, south-west of Valenciennes, and Heinrich Gontermann another at Neuville just two kilometres further south-west. Parts of the aircraft numbers of these latter two claims were A6... for Nathanael and 1959 for Gontermann. Gontermann was later photographed in 'A4', which was A1959, so A6388 was that which Nathanael brought down.

Wright's FE was hit in the radiator, and it was not long before the FE's engine quit, the wounded Wright starting a long glide to the lines four miles away. As Wright was going down with a dead engine, two pilots of Jasta 12 spotted him and attacked. The FE crew steepened their dive, bullets being heard hitting the useless engine behind them. Finally, at low level and still gliding, Wright and Private Sibley came under small arms fire from German soldiers, Wright being hit again, this time in the thigh, but he scraped over the trenches, force-landing 50 yards in front of some Australian outposts.

For once the Germans didn't get off without injury, for Splitgerber's fighter was hit over Thiaut and he was wounded but got back. But by far the most serious loss occurred when two pilots of Jasta 5 collided north of Noyelles. Both men fell to their death: Vizefeldwebel Paul Hoppe and the Staffelführer, Oberleutnant Hans Berr, holder of the Pour le Mérite with ten victories.

If any of the FE gunners thought they'd caused the collision, none were in a position to put in a claim as none of 57 Squadron got back except for the earlier abort, and only Captain Wright and his observer lived to fight another day, having crashed just inside British lines after their fight with von Osterroht. This would not be the only occasion during April where complete, or almost complete, formations would be annihilated by the Jasta pilots.

It would seem that German anti-aircraft guns also fired on these FEs, three being claimed over the Anneux and Lagnicourt areas but these were all the same as the fighter pilots shot down. No doubt Wright's was one such joint claim.

Even as 57 Squadron's patrol was being annihilated, four Martinsydes of 27 Squadron were being engaged up on the northern part of the front during a bombing raid on Ath in Belgium, 80 km behind the front line. Once more it was Jasta 30 that made the interception, Leutnant Joachim von Bertrab shooting down two of the G100s over Ath at 0815, and south of Leuze at 0830, both British pilots being killed.

Captain A J M Clarke, who led the raid, made out a combat report on his return, which gives a vivid description of the German tactics:

> 'Over Ath at 5,000 ft, machine-guns were heard and on looking behind pilot saw one Martinsyde going down with one Halberstadt on its tail. This machine was last seen out of control in a spin close to the ground. The HA [hostile aircraft] then hovered above the formation while height was lost to 2,300 ft to drop the bombs. Formation then rendezvoused very quickly after bombing but hostile machines—at least three and probably more—kept up above in the sun, firing bursts at intervals.
>
> 'Eventually one dived on to the formation. Pilot engaged with the rear gun. The HA shot down the rear machine of the formation which went down in flames, and then, being fired on, kept up above the formation, firing occasional shots. The hostile formation kept up above and did not attack at close range and finally left the two remaining Martinsydes at Tournai.'

It seems that all the FE units were over the front that morning, 22 Squadron operating on the southern end of the British front, escorted by the Pups of 54 Squadron. At 0730, Captain F N Hudson of 54 attacked and shot down a two-seater over Le Catelet, confirmed by three men of 22 Squadron. Half an hour later, the Pups were engaged by some fighters above St Quentin, one attacking Lieutenant S G Rome MC. Lieutenant Oliver Stewart (A6156) fired at the Albatros at close range and it went down out of control, confirmed by Captain Hudson and Lieutenant Rome to have crashed.

Then the BE2s began flying photo ops over the front, giving the Jasta pilots more target practice. First away was a machine of 8 Squadron but at 0930 it was being shot down by German fighters, credit going to Frankl of Jasta 4 whose victim fell north of Boiry at 0955. The next one was a 15 Squadron BE, driven down into British territory where it was destroyed by German shelling.

Second Lieutenants A H Vinson and E L Gwilt had been engaged by six enemy Scouts over Bullecourt while taking photographs. During the combat both pilot and observer opened fire on their attackers, driving off five of the Germans but one continued the action. Vinson dived headlong earthwards, going over the vertical at which time both Lewis guns fell overboard. As the Albatros pumped bullets into the BE, three bullets grazed Vinson's face, while two more slashed through Gwilt's glove. Others pierced the petrol tank but thankfully did not ignite the fuel. The fight and pursuit lasted half an hour, until Vinson managed to scrape over the lines and put down near Lagnicourt. The Albatros had followed the BE down, firing all the time. As the two men leaped from the BE and took cover in a shell hole the German pilot came down and strafed the BE. The Albatros was finally driven off by ground fire, but then enemy artillery opened up; before the machine was hit by the falling 8″ shells, Vinson ran to it and retrieved the photographic plates and camera, which later produced good pictures of Bullecourt and the Hindenburg Line.

The German pilot was Werner Voss of Jasta 2, who returned to Pronville having secured his 24th victory. Voss almost got his 25th too, for he was also in combat with a 54 Squadron Pup (A6165?), flown by future ace Second Lieutenant R M Foster. Hit by the German pilot, Foster got across the lines and force-landed near Lagnicourt without injury to himself.

No.2 Squadron had two BEs up, one on a photo op to Lieven, the other doing artillery work with the 52nd Siege Battery. The first, with Captain V J Whittaker in the pilot's seat, was shot down by a fighter over Lieven at 1015 and fell in flames, probably by Karl Schäfer of Jasta 11. The other BE was chased away by enemy fighters.

The fourth BE loss of the morning came from 16 Squadron doing artillery observation east of Neuville St Vaast. They were attacked by a fighter, their machine falling in flames near Thelus at 1030, again brought down by Karl Schäfer, whose two BE claims were made over Givenchy at 1020, and south-west of Vimy at 1037.

The air was full of aeroplanes at this time, or perhaps it is more correct to say full of falling aeroplanes. 45 Squadron had sent out a formation of Strutters at 0910 to do a recce over Lille, which were attacked by Jasta 30. The attack so upset the British formation that two of the two-seaters collided, then a third was knocked down by machine-gun fire. Hans Bethge received credit for one Strutter (7806), von Bertrab the two that had collided (A1093 and A2381), which made four victories for von Bertrab on this day.

The RE8s of 59 Squadron headed for Vitry-en-Artois at 0935 on a recce sortie, only to be intercepted by pilots of Jastas 2, 3 and 11. Kurt Wolff of Jasta 11 shot one down over Bois Bernard at 1015, Jasta 3's Karl Menckhoff sending a second down over Fampoux at the same time. Finally, Bernert of Jasta Boelcke brought down a third RE over Roux on the Scarpe River.

By this time, to the north, more FEs were out, 20 Squadron mounting a bomb raid with ten aircraft, against Ledeghem between Ypres and Courtrai. Jasta 8 intercepted them and a running fight ensued between 1000 and 1020. The Fees claimed four shot down, two destroyed and two out of control, one over Ledeghem and three south of Roulers, one being seen to crash in a field when hit by Second Lieutenant E O Perry and Private Allum (A6370). The other claims were all made by the crew of Second Lieutenants E J Smart and H N Hampson (A3). Jasta 8 had no fatalities.

Leutnant Walter Göttsch shot down A6358 north of Polygon Wood, while AM Sayers, a gunner flying in A29, was wounded. FE A3 was also hit and force-landed on the right side of the lines, while A5147 was badly shot up but the pilot got down safely on Bailleul airfield.

The second Sopwith Triplane loss of the day came shortly after noon, 1 Naval flying an OP at 0956. Late in the patrol, they ran into Jasta 12 near Henin-Lietard, Hauptmann Paul von Osterroht claiming Flight Sub Lieutenant L M B Weil shot down, who crashed near Malakow station. While it was the second Triplane lost, it was the first brought down by a German pilot as well as the second kill of the day for the commander of Jasta 12.

British airmen were heavily engaged on this Good Friday, and although there was still a good deal of over-claiming, at least some Germans did come down. Again the number of aircraft actually lost is difficult to find but apart from the three fighter pilots already mentioned, Jasta 3 had Unteroffizier Ludwig Weber wounded in an Albatros DII (510/16), brought down near Biache on the Scarpe, possibly one of the two Albatros Scouts claimed out of control by 48 Squadron to the north-east of Arras.

The FEs of 25 Squadron also claimed two fighters shot down mid-morning, during a photo op over Farbus Wood and an assault by 14 Halberstadt and Albatros Scouts. Second Lieutenants A Roulstone and E G Green (A813) claimed an Albatros DIII in flames over Givenchy at 1030 just after it had shot down a BE in flames. Shortly afterwards Second Lieutenant B King and Corporal L Emsden claimed a Halberstadt DII destroyed east of Vimy. An FE was shot up; Second Lieutenant R G Malcolm and Lieutenant D E Holmes (4997) had to force-land by No.9 KBS at Bray.

Vizefeldwebel Reinhold Wurzmann of Jasta 20 was seen to fall in flames near Maray (or Marcy, east of St Quentin), probably the DIII claimed destroyed by Captain C M Clement and his gunner Second Lieutenant L G Davies, in a 22 Squadron FE at 0800 by St Quentin. This Squadron was on a photo-recce job south-east of Gouy when seven enemy fighters attacked and in the fight, one was sent down to land near Lesdins while a second spun away out of control. Another German casualty this day was Flieger Josef Eicholz, unit unknown, killed at Fampoux.

Two-seaters were also in evidence, 23 Squadron claiming one as early as 0730, the victor being Captain Ken McCallum, a Canadian (Spad A6709). Captain F N Hudson sent another down out of control near Le Catelet a few minutes later, while 24 Squadron claimed one out of control near Havrincourt Wood. The Germans had two-seaters come down at Lecluse (FA233, Vizefeldwebel Siegfried Thiele and Leutnant Karl Seyberth both killed) and another near Queant (FA(A)263, Unteroffizier Rudolf Temler and Leutnant Julius Schmidt both killed). FA221 also had a machine shot up and forced to land, flown by Feldwebel Hans Donhauser and Leutnant W Wolter. Donhauser later became a fighter pilot, ending the war with 19 victories. FA(A)243 also lost a crew at Colmar, on the southern French front, near the Swiss border, although this is not believed to be a combat loss.

Curiously, 18 Squadron's FEs also claimed two Albatros Scouts, one being noted as captured at Ecoust St Mein, but there is no record of it and certainly no G-number was issued on this day, nor is it mentioned in the RFC War Diary. A 12 Squadron BE was attacked by a fighter and was reported falling in flames.

The balloon at Sallaumines, just east of Lens was ordered to be attacked and it was claimed as destroyed at 1000 by Lieutenant H C Todd of 40 Squadron (A6677) near Neuvireuil, who hit it with three Le Prieur rockets from ten yards; the observer took to his parachute. However, Second Lieutenant H S Pell was brought down by ground fire (MFlak 60) and killed during this foray. His replacement in C Flight that evening was Lieutenant Edward 'Mick' Mannock!

The Naval pilots of 1, 3 and 6 Naval Squadron were engaged during the morning claiming a number of victories but it is difficult to reconcile them with reported losses, certainly with regard to German pilot casualties.

French Front

French fighter pilots were ranged against hostile balloons in an attempt to blind the Germans' view of the build-up for the coming offensive. Adjutant Gustave Douchy of Escadrille N.38 claimed two during the day, one at Hauvine, and a second at Montchalons at 1800 hours. Sous Lieutenant Emile Regnier of N.112 flamed one at Epoye. The other two were shot down by Brigadier Pierre Leroy de Boiseaumarie of N.78 at Ardeuil and Lieutenant Mistarlet of N.31 at Lavannes.

The Jasta pilots were alive to the sudden increase in activity and shot down a number of French aeroplanes. Caudrons were brought down by Oberleutnant Rudolf Berthold of Jasta 14, Vizefeldwebel Georg Strasser of Jasta 17 and Leutnant Walter Böning of Jasta 19. Four Caudrons were in fact lost during the day, with the observer of a fifth wounded. Farmans were also claimed by Leutnant Dieter Collin of Jasta 22 near Terny-Sorny and Leutnant Kreuzner of Jasta 13 (Collin's not being confirmed), the French losing at least one, with another hit by ground fire, its pilot being wounded. A Sopwith two-seater was also lost, the machine making a forced landing north of Laon. Berthold's victim was numbered 1559, which corresponds to a Caudron R4 lost by Escadrille F.35 near Malvel.

Two Spads were also claimed, one by Leutnant Bongartz of Jasta 36 and one (a delayed confirmation) by Leutnant Baldamus of Jasta 9, although no Spads are recorded as lost in surviving records. A Nieuport and another Caudron were claimed by two-seater crews from FA228 and FA212.

Leutnant Josef Jacobs of Jasta 22 shot down a French balloon of 21 Cié at Blanzy-Vailly at 1930 for his fourth victory of an eventual 48. Jasta 22 had taken off at 1905 because French fighters had burned a balloon right over their own airfield at Laon, and they wanted revenge. Jacobs found his balloon amid rain clouds, attacked and watched it erupt in flames as he flew off while the observer parachuted down.

	A/C	KB		DES	OOC	KB
British losses	24	—	British claims	13	15	1
French losses	6	1	French claims	—		5
German claims	40†	1	German losses	6‡		2

† Includes six by ground fire. ‡ Nachrichtenblatt admits five.

British Casualties

Aircraft type	No.	Squadron	Crew		
FE2b	7714	100 Sqdn	2/Lt A R M Rickards	POW	
			2AM E W Barnes	POW	
FE2b	A811	11 Sqdn	Sgt F H Evans	POW	
			2AM E Woods	KIA	
FE2b	A5000	11 Sqdn	2/Lt D S Kennedy	Safe	
			2AM J F Carr	Safe	
FE2b	7025	25 Sqdn	2/Lt D P Walter	WIA	*
			2/Lt C Brown	Safe	
Sop Triplane	N5457	1N Sqdn	FSL N D M Hewitt	POW	
BE2c	2879	8 Sqdn	Lt G J Hatch	KIA	
			Cpl E Langridge	KIA	
BE2c	A3157	15 Sqdn	2/Lt A H Vinson	Safe	
			2/Lt E L Gwilt	Safe	
Martinsyde G100	7465	27 Sqdn	2/Lt J R S Proud	POW/DOW	
Martinsyde G100	7478	27 Sqdn	Lt J H B Wedderspoon	KIA	
FE2d	A1959	57 Sqdn	Lt T F Burrill	POW	
			Pvt F Smith	POW/WIA	
FE2d	A22	57 Sqdn	Lt T B Schreiber	POW	
			2/Lt M Lewis	POW	
FE2d	A21	57 Sqdn	Lt D C Birch	POW	
			Lt J K Bousfield MC	POW	
FE2d	A6388	57 Sqdn	2/Lt H D Hamilton	POW/WIA	
			Pvt E Snelling	POW/WIA	
FE2d	A1952	57 Sqdn	Capt A C Wright	WIA	
			Pvt R Sibley	Safe	
FE2d	A6358	20 Sqdn	2/Lt R Smith	KIA	
			Lt R Hume	KIA	
Sop 1½ Strutter	A1093	45 Sqdn	Lt J A Marshall	KIA	
			2/Lt F G Truscott MC	KIA	
Sop 1½ Strutter	A2381	45 Sqdn	2/Lt C StG Campbell	KIA	
			Capt D W Edwards MC	KIA	
Sop 1½ Strutter	7806	45 Sqdn	2/Lt J E Blake	KIA	
			Capt W S Brayshay	KIA	
RE8	A3206	59 Sqdn	Lt C F Bailey	KIA	
			2AM V M Barrie	MIA	
RE8	A3421	59 Sqdn	2/Lt A C Pepper	POW	
			Lt W L Day	KIA	
RE8	A112	59 Sqdn	2/Lt R W M Davies	KIA	
			2/Lt J C D Wordsworth	KIA	
BE2d	5834	2 Sqdn	Capt V J Whittaker	KIA	
			2/Lt A R Brown	KIA	
BE2c	6823	16 Sqdn	Lt O R Knight	KIA	
			2/Lt U H Seguin	KIA	
Nieuport XVII	A6667	40 Sqdn	2/Lt H S Pell	KIA	

| BE2c | | 7 Sqdn | 2AM C G Mitchinson (O) | KIA (shellfire) | * |

French Casualties

Caudron R4		R.210	Sgt Gauron	WIA	
			S/Lt Cazier (O)	KIA	
			Pvt Brasseur (AG)	KIA	
Caudron G4		C.227	Sgt Lafaille	WIA	
			S/Lt Vrolyck	KIA	
Caudron G4		C.224	—Sommier	KIA	
			—Jouvenot	KIA	
Sopwith two-seater		N.62	MdL Clerisse (O)	MIA	
Caudron G4		C.220	Lt Berquet (O)	WIA	*
Farman 60		F.208	Capt Grimault	WIA	
			S/Lt Feltin	WIA	
Caudron G4	1559	F.35	S/Lt Desbordes	MIA	
			Lt Borgoltz (O)	MIA	
			Sol Lebleu (AG)	MIA	
Farman 61		F.211	Sgt Valence (P)	WIA	*

Saturday, 7 April 1917

British Front

After the blood-letting of the previous day, the 7th was quieter, despite the nearness of the offensive, but due no doubt to the low cloud and rain which persisted throughout much of the day.

Reconnaissance aircraft still went out, one machine of 16 Squadron making a valuable recce from 500 feet, facilitated by an effective shrapnel barrage by Canadian artillery. German batteries were still subjected to artillery fire with observations from Corps aeroplanes, 57 targets being dealt with.

Offensive Patrols were flown between the showers, 1 Squadron losing a Nieuport on the 0842 special mission to attack a balloon, with Lieutenant Robert J Bevington brought down by marauding fighters of Jasta 8, Hauptmann Hans von Hünerbein gaining his one and only victory. The Nieuport went down over Becelaere, east of Ypres. Von Hünerbein would take command of Jasta 5 before April was out, only to be killed the following month.

Air combat was very much restricted until clearer weather came to the Western Front in the late afternoon, the next losses not occurring until 1745 hours. 60 Squadron's Nieuports flew an OP at 1640 and were engaged by von Richthofen's Jasta 11 at 1745 north of Mercatel, right over the front. In fact the fight drifted over the British side, but near enough to the trenches for the German ground observers to confirm three Nieuports had gone down, as indeed they had. Two of the British pilots died, the third being wounded. Despite recording that the formation had been attacked by a superior force, von Richthofen only had three of his men with him, and he, Schäfer and Wolff secured the kills. One Albatros had been seen to fall too, credited to the two dead pilots, but Jasta 11 had no losses.

The British unit lost Second Lieutenants Hall and Smart, with D Norman Robertson wounded and forced down. Lieutenant J M Elliott's Nieuport—A6771—was badly shot up too, while Lieutenant H E Hervey MC—B1517—got a bullet in the engine but got back. Several of the Nieuport's guns had become frozen before the fight, which did not help while trying to defend themselves against the German pilots.

Shortly before this action, another pilot of 60, Lieutenant W A Bishop, had attacked the German balloon lines and claimed a balloon destroyed at Vis-en-Artois, as well as an Albatros DIII out of control.

Half an hour after 60 Squadron had been mauled, FE2s of 20 Squadron, flying a bomb raid south of Ploegsteert Wood, right on the lines in the northern part of the front (15 km south of Ypres) were attacked by German fighters. On this day, 20 Squadron had been assigned to bomb the aerodrome at Mouvaux, just north of Lille. They had bombed it that morning, having one aircraft crash on the way back through engine trouble, although its crew were safe and on the right side of the lines.

West of Arras, the British lost a balloon at 1645 hrs, to Leutnant Hans Klein of Jasta 4. In the basket of FM32, 9th KB Coy, was the unit CO, Captain G S Samson. He and Second Lieutenant W G Dreshfield were at 3,200 feet, 300 feet below the cloud layer. Samson heard machine-gun fire and turned to see a German fighter 200 feet away, diving straight at them. He immediately ordered Dreshfield to jump, and out he went. As soon as he was clear, Samson went over the side too. By the time his parachute opened, the enemy fighter had gone back into the cloud, but flame was now coming from the stern of the balloon, so Klein had got his first balloon and his second confirmed victory. He would claim 22 by the end of November 1917, but a wound the following February put him out of the flying war.

Interestingly, the War Diary notes that the enemy aeroplanes looked so much like a Nieuport Scout that a nearby aeroplane did not think to interfere until the attack proved the machine to be hostile, by which time Klein was on his way back home.

At 1712 eight FEs went back, bombed the base again then headed for home. After recrossing the lines, Captain George Mahony-Jones looked back and saw one of his crews being engaged by nine German fighters and he immediately turned to assist. The pilot of the other FE was then wounded and force-landed just inside British lines, but by now Mahony-Jones and his gunner, Second Lieutenant W B Moyes, a former 6th Royal Scots officer, were fighting for their lives in the midst of the enemy fighters. At first they seemed to succeed in driving off some of the fighters but finally a burst set their machine on fire and the FE fell in flames, both men being killed. Shortly afterwards, 20 Squadron received a letter from the Headquarters of the 34th Battalion, AIF:

To the Commandant, RFC Bailleul, 8 April 1917.

'The CO 34th Battn AIF has asked me to express a deep sense of admiration which was inspired by the gallant flying of an airman, apparently belonging to a squadron under your command. About 6 pm on the evening of the 7th instant, two of our planes were engaged with nine of the enemy's. One plane was damaged and the other, although retreat looked possible, turned and fought. Several of the enemy's planes scattered but unfortunately our plane was hit and immediately burst into flames.

The scene was witnessed by the men of the Battalion from the trenches and the conspired bravery was much spoken of by them and the gallantry is sure to foster a spirit of emulation for our men to strive hard on their parts, to act in the same heroic and self-sacrificing manner as this gallant airman. The true bravery of your fine Corps was thus strikingly brought home to our men.'

Adj, 34th Battn.

Mahony-Jones was brought down by Vizefeldwebel Max Müller of Jasta 28, his 6th victory, but the first for the Jasta, seen to fall in flames into the British lines. The other FE, with its pilot wounded, crash-landed south of Ploegsteert, with a dead gunner, claimed by Leutnant Walter von Bülow-Bothkamp of Jasta 18, his 10th victory.

More Nieuport patrols were out at this time, 29 Squadron meeting German fighters and losing two pilots, one falling to Leutnant Bernert of Jasta 2, south of Roeux, the other to Vizefeldwebel Linus Patermann of Jasta 4, north west of Biache.

Two hours later, at 1910, Wilhelm Frankl, CO of Jasta 4, would bring down yet another Nieuport, and yet another from 60 Squadron. This was Captain M B Knowles, from Ashford, Middlesex, who came down south of Fampaux where he was captured. It was Frankl's last victory.

Jasta 11 scored one final victory on this day, a Bristol Fighter of 48 Squadron. A patrol of 48 had flown out at 1802 to fly an OP north-east of Arras. In a brief skirmish with Jasta 11, Sebastian Festner had attacked what he identified as a two-seater Sopwith, which went down over the British lines to crash north-west of Maroeuil. The Bristol in fact force-landed at Saulty, with a dead gunner.

Lieutenant H C Todd of 40 Squadron claimed a balloon destroyed on this evening (his second in two days), while pilots of 8 Naval were in a fight with German fighters, claiming one destroyed and one out of control. 20 Squadron also reported a scrap, and also claimed one Albatros destroyed with another out of control.

Up on the coast, 5 Naval Squadron had bombed a destroyer alongside the Mole at Zeebrugge in the early hours, Flight Lieutenant I N C Clarke (Australian) dropping 12 LePecq bombs from 11,000 ft.

French Front

On the Chalons front one enemy aircraft was forced to land near Hourges, where it caught fire on the ground. Whether this had anything to do with Vizefeldwebel Ludwig Müller, of FA46, who was killed near St Mihiel, is uncertain. More likely it was the Rumpler CI (2605/16) of Schutzstaffel 7 flown by Gefreiter Schoop and Leutnant Hupe that was lost at this time.

	A/C	KB			DES	OOC	KB
British losses	8	1		British claims	3	3	2
French losses	—	—		French claims	1		—
German claims	10	1		German losses	1		?

British Casualties

Aircraft type	No.	Squadron	Crew		
Nieuport Scout	A6605	1 Sqdn	Lt R J Bevington	POW	
Nieuport XXIII	A6766	60 Sqdn	2/Lt C S Hall	KIA	
Nieuport XVII	A6645	60 Sqdn	2/Lt G O Smart	KIA	
Nieuport XVII	A311	60 Sqdn	2/Lt D N Robertson	WIA	*
Nieuport XVII	A6671	60 Sqdn	Lt J M Elliott	Safe	*
Nieuport XVII	A6692	29 Sqdn	Capt A Jennings	KIA	
Nieuport XVII	A6775	29 Sqdn	2/Lt J H Muir	KIA	
FE2d	A1961	20 Sqdn	Capt G J Mahony-Jones	KIA	
			2/Lt W B Moyes	KIA	
FE2d	A6400	20 Sqdn	2/Lt J Lawson	WIA	
			2/Lt H N Hampson	DOW	
Nieuport XVII	A6773	60 Sqdn	Capt M B Knowles	POW	
BF2a	A3317	48 Sqdn	2/Lt J W Warren	Safe	*
			2/Lt G C Burnard	KIA	
BE2c		15 Sqdn	2AM A O Dilley (O)	WIA	*

French Casualties

Spad VII	224	N.31	Lt Mistarlet	MIA
Spad VII		N.48	Lt Lorillard	MIA
Spad VII		N.48	S/Lt de Larminat	MIA

Sunday, 8 April 1917

British Front

Easter Sunday; a fine day but cloudy. In preparation for the offensive, British ground troops pushed forward in the vicinity of the Bapaume-Cambrai road on a front of 3,000 yards north of Louverval.

While people in Britain and France were celebrating communion services, 60 Squadron were taking off for an 0835 Offensive Patrol, among whom was Major J A Milot, a Canadian from Quebec, who despite his rank was a relatively inexperienced pilot and former infantry officer. After a few days with 13 Squadron, he had joined 60 on 15 March. East of Vimy they spotted German fighters ahead and within moments were in a dog-fight. It was Jasta 11 again, and Festner turned in behind one Nieuport and opened fire, sending Major Joseph Milot down on fire. In the scrap, Second Lieutenant Hamilton Hervey had his gun jam, so he pulled off to one side and headed for the lines. Later he wrote from a prison camp:

'In the first fight we had, my gun jammed and by the time I had got it going again I had lost the other machines. I waited about for a bit and then, as more of them had turned up, started for home. I had already got over our lines when I saw four enemy machines scrapping with some others and so went back to join in. On the way, when I had got some distance over and rather low, I think something or other to do with my engine was hit by a bit of "archie"; anyway, several shots burst very close to my machine and then my engine started to run very badly and finally stopped altogether. I turned back at once but could not reach our lines and landed about two miles behind the German front line. I broke the petrol glass as soon as I landed and let all the petrol out of my tank but some soldiers came up and got me away from the machine before I could set light to it.'

Hervey had most probably been hit by fire from KFlak 43, who claimed a Nieuport Scout east of Arras. But these were not the first losses of the day. Night victories might have been rare, but the German Air Service claimed its second of the month at 0440. FEs of 100 Squadron had flown a bomb raid against Douai airfield, home of Jasta 4, soon after midnight and Jasta 4's Hans Klein had taken off to try an interception. He was lucky and brought down 7669 south-east of the town.

Artillery observation and reconnaissance missions were flown throughout the day, with Offensive Patrols flown by British scouts to ward off hostile attacks. For the most part this worked, for it was not until late morning that another British machine was lost.

Sopwiths of 43 Squadron were flying a line patrol when Manfred von Richthofen and two of his Staffel attacked the three 1½ Strutters over Farbus, bringing down A2406 with a wounded pilot and a dead gunner at 1130.

Noon saw FE2s of 57 Squadron taking off for an OP with six aircraft, and these got into a fight near Arras with an equal number of enemy fighters. Three of the FEs were shot about but all got back over the lines before having to put down. Thus no German pilots made any claim, but one pilot and two gunners had been wounded and one FE lost. The third crew, Lieutenant Erlebach and Trotter, who force-landed near Arras, later flew back with their aircraft after temporary repairs, three days later.

Jasta 4 took off after lunch when more enemy machines were reported heading for Etaing. These were RE8s of 59 Squadron, out on a photo op. Like some other two-seater observation units, 59 tended to escort its own photo machine with its own aircraft, rather than hope that fighter patrols would be in the area to protect them against the nimble Albatros Scouts. This was fine in theory but in practice, a slow two-seater was no real help to an equally slow two-seater. This Squadron had already found this out on 6 April, and were about to learn the lesson again.

Jasta 4 swept down on them, one RE8 almost immediately falling away while the others were harried as they sped for the lines. A second RE8 was shot up, both crewmen being wounded while the gunner in a third was also hit. There seems little doubt that Wilhelm Frankl shot down the one which failed to get back, but as we shall see, he did not have the opportunity to claim this victory.

Frankl's RE8 went down at 1330, but he still had fuel enough to continue to patrol behind the front. At 2 o'clock, 48 Squadron were taking off to fly an OP between Arras, Lens and Vitry and they were intercepted by Frankl's Jasta 4 pilots as soon as they crossed the lines. In the brief fight which followed, 48's gunners claimed two Albatros Scouts as shot down, one by Captain D M Tidmarsh/Second Lieutenant C B Holland, the other by the combined fire from three other crews, both over Remy-Eterpigny. Frankl's Albatros, 2158/16, fell between Vitry and Sailly, breaking up as it did so. Continuing with their patrol, 48 Squadron were later intercepted by Jasta 2. Otto Bernert quickly despatched one near Remy at 1510, at the same time claiming an RE8. The Bristol was A3330, of that there is no question, but the RE8 is a bit of a mystery. The Bristol was timed at 1510, the RE8 five minutes later. There are no known RE8s lost at this time, only the 59 Squadron machines being in combat and that was at 1330, one hour and twenty minutes earlier. It is possible that once the other RE8s were driven off they may have returned and at least one had run into Bernert—48 Squadron may even have seen the two-seater and tried to give it some protection. The Bristol went down south of Eterpigny, where the Bristols would have been, but the 'RE8' five minutes later is reported as being brought down north of Bailleul-Sir-Berthoult, just west of Gavrelle, about 12 km to the north-west (not to be confused with the more famous Bailleul, 56 km to the north-west).

While this was going on, de Havilland 4 bombers of 55 Squadron were raiding a château at Hardenpont, up near Mons. This Squadron was based at Fienvillers, south-west of Doullens, and was the first DH4 Squadron to operate in France, having come out from England in March. Their first operation was flown on 3 April. Today it would suffer its first losses.

The château housed the Headquarters of Crown Prince Rupprecht's Army Group although the raid did not cause him any personal problems. On the return journey, Jasta 11 were waiting for the bombers, and met them north of Cambrai at 1425. In the fight which ensued, two 'Fours' were brought down, one by Schäfer (A2140), the other by Wolff (A2141), one at Epinoy, one at Blecourt, while a third (A2160) was hit by flak, coming down south-west of Amiens. This was probably the 'grosskampf aircraft' claimed by Flakzug 17, seen to go down over Amigny.

On the northern, Ypres sector, a 46 Squadron Nieuport XII two-seater ran into trouble on a photo op, coming up against three Albatros Scouts of Jasta 18. The two-seater was hit by Leutnant Walter von Bülow-Bothkamp, wounding both of the crew, but the pilot struggled over the lines to crash to the east of Ypres. From there the aeroplane was in full view of the Germans who promptly shelled it.

Manfred von Richthofen gained another victory for himself and his Jasta 11 by shooting down a 16 Squadron BE2g west of Vimy at 1640, both British airmen being killed. It was the Baron's 39th kill. The day ended in a flurry of late afternoon activity, six aircraft of 25 Squadron flying a bomb raid on Pont-a-Vendin, led by Captain C H C Woolven (A782), losing an FE2b to flak—claimed by several flak units north of La Bassée at 1900. Ten minutes later, Leutnant Georg Schlenker of Jasta 3, picked off a Nieuport of 29 Squadron flying an evening OP, the Scout coming down north-east of Croisselles, for the German's 7th victory.

An untimed German victory was one by Offizierstellvertreter Walter Göttsch of Jasta 8 who shot down a Belgian BE2c from the 6me Escadrille, east of Dixmude. They were on a recce to Bruges and came down south of Couckelaere. Another was a balloon claimed by Heinrich Gontermann of Jasta 5, west of St Quentin.

The RFC had been in amongst the balloons during the morning, 1 Squadron's Nieuports flaming two. One was at Quesnoy at 0830 by Lieutenant E S T Cole (A6668), the second by Captain C J Quintin-Brand at Moorslede around 1130. Also during the morning, 60 Squadron had been in some air fights, Major A J L Scott and Lieutenant W A Bishop claiming an Albatros two-seater destroyed near Douai at 0930, Bishop also claiming two Albatros Scouts out of control. In the afternoon 66 Squadron's Pups claimed three more out of control, and 3 Naval Squadron two more north-east of Pronville. 22 Squadron's FEs, led by the six-foot-four-inch Canadian, Lieutenant Carlton M Clement, had been helped out by the Pups. They had been on an OP between Mont-d'Origny, Fonsomme and Homblières, east of St Quentin.

Just on 1700 they had been approached by two Albatros Scouts. As the two Germans attacked, the FEs' return fire appeared to hit one Albatros whose pilot promptly went down and landed on the airfield at Mont d'Origny, while the Sopwiths drove off the other. The FEs then spotted four two-seaters (they recorded them as Halberstadt types) which were between them and St Quentin. The Fees attacked, firing at close range. The leading two-seater went down vertically, losing part of a wing before hitting the ground near Regny. A second two-seater was driven down and seen to land heavily in a field just north of Marcy.

No.29 Squadron claimed one destroyed south-east of Arras, in the fight in which Second Lieutenant Owen was lost.

Other than Frankl, the only German pilot listed as a casualty this day on the British front was Leutnant Alfred Trager of Jasta 8, who was wounded by an exploding bullet, plus Flieger Helmut Naudszus, killed at St Quentin, possibly in one of 22 Squadron's victories. The Nachrichtenblatt noted three aircraft lost in all. Sebastian Festner force-landed his Albatros DII (223/16) due to a wing cracking, and may have been one of the enemy scouts claimed by 60 Squadron.

Second Lieutenant Walter B Wood, who had just reached France and 29 Squadron, but who would win the MC and bar in 1917 and gain several victories, wrote home on this day:

'It does make me wild to see articles in the papers running down our Flying Corps on account of the casualties. If you only knew the work we do compared to the Hun, you would realise how ridiculous it all is. Very rarely do we see a Hun machine over our lines, and, regularly, our patrols go, perhaps three times a day, 15 or 20 miles over their lines and wait over their aerodromes for the Huns going up. We have them beaten.'

However, the casualties were real and the truth is that neither the British nor the French were inflicting anywhere near the hurt on the Germans they thought they were.

French Front

On the Chalons front Caudrons were active against front line targets, both G4s and R4 escort gunships. The R4 was the French answer to the problem of escorting their bombing/reconnaissance aircraft by having a more powerfully armed machine of the same general type, rather than relying on Spad or Nieuport Scout single-seat escorts. Two Caudron crews claimed German aircraft shot down, one north of Berry-au-Bac, and a second at 1615 over Aguilcourt.

On the Chauny sector, Lieutenant de Laage de Meux, flight commander of N.124—the famous Lafayette Escadrille, manned mostly by American volunteers—shot down a single-seater north of St Quentin at 1330, which force-landed inside French territory. The pilot, Leutnant Roland Nauck of Jasta 6, was flying Albatros DIII 2234/16, actually coming down at Villevecque, but either died in his aircraft or very soon afterwards. His aircraft was given the RFC number G.21. De Laage also claimed a two-seater north of Moy—possibly a FA61 aircraft—receiving the Legion d'Honneur for this day's work. A Vizefeldwebel Josef Schreiner was killed at Amifontaine/Prouvais this day, unit unknown.

However, French losses were quite severe. On the Chauny front no fewer than ten Caudrons were either brought down in combat, or flew home with wounded crewmen plus one Farman shot up. Escadrille C.46 were involved in a fight with four enemy fighters, losing one aircraft, probably to Oberleutnant Erich Hahn, leader of Jasta 19 based at Le Thour, 30 km north of Reims, who claimed a Caudron down north of Loivre. Another Caudron was claimed by a two-seater crew of FA23, at Effigny.

	A/C	KB			DES	OOC	KB
British losses	14	1		British claims	4	11	2
French losses	1	—		French claims	4		—
German claims	18†	1		German losses	3		?

† Includes one Belgian aircraft.

British Casualties

Aircraft type	No.	Squadron	Crew		
FE2b	7669	100 Sqdn	2/Lt L Butler	POW	
			2AM R Robb	POW	
Nieuport XXIII	A6764	60 Sqdn	Maj J A Milot	KIA	
Nieuport XXIII	A3111	60 Sqdn	2/Lt H E Hervey MC	POW	
RE8	A4178	59 Sqdn	Lt K B Cooksey	KIA	
			2AM A H Jones	KIA	
RE8	A4185	59 Sqdn	Lt E L Hyde	WIA	*
			Lt R M Grant	WIA	
RE8	A3418	59 Sqdn	Lt Leake	Safe	*
			2/Lt P L Hogan	WIA	
Sop 1½ Strutter	A2406	43 Sqdn	2/Lt J S Heagerty	WIA/POW	
			Lt L H Cantle	KIA	
DH4	A2140	55 Sqdn	Lt R A Logan	POW	
			Lt F R Henry	POW	
DH4	A2141	55 Sqdn	Lt B Evans	KIA	
			2/Lt B W White	KIA	
DH4	A2160	55 Sqdn	Lt A J Hamer	KIA	
			2/Lt J A Myburgh	DOW	
FE2b	A1955	57 Sqdn	Lt A D Pryor	WIA	
			AM C Goffe	WIA	
FE2b	A1957	57 Sqdn	Lt T Grosvenor	Safe	*
			2/Lt W W Glen	WIA	
BF2a	A3330	48 Sqdn	2/Lt O W Berry	KIA	
			2/Lt F B Goodison	DOW	

BE2g	A2815	16 Sqdn	2/Lt K I MacKenzie	KIA	
			2/Lt G Everingham	KIA	
Nieuport XII	A156	46 Sqdn	2/Lt J E de Watteville	WIA	
			Lt R A Manby	WIA	
Nieuport XXIII	A6765	29 Sqdn	2/Lt T J Owen	KIA	
FE2b	A813	25 Sqdn	2/Lt E V A Bell	WIA/POW	
			Lt A H K McCallum	WIA/POW	
DH2		24 Sqdn	2/Lt E Kent	DOW	*
BE2c		4 Sqdn	2/Lt A C Finlayson	DOW	*

French Casualties

Caudron R4		C.46	MdL Theron (G)	KIA	
Caudron R4		C.46	S/Lt Wilmes (O)	KIA	
			Adj de Cuyper (G)	WIA	
Caudron G4		C.219	Adj de Saint Pierre (P)	WIA	*
Caudron R4		R.209	Sol Pichot (G)	DOW	*
Caudron R4		R.209	Cpl Picquot (G)	WIA	*
Caudron R4		R.209	Lt Charpiot	WIA	*
Caudron R4		R.209	Lt Conby (O)	WIA	*
Caudron G4		C.212	S/Lt Villemy (O)	KIA	*
Caudron G4		C.212	Cpl Debrie (P)	WIA	*
Caudron G4		C.30	Sgt Munier (P)	WIA	*
Farman 40		F.201	Lt Martin (O)	WIA	*

Belgian Casualties

| BE2c | | 6me Esc | Adj A Glibert | KIA | |
| | | | Lt J Callant | KIA | |

Monday, 9 April 1917

British Front

At around midnight the shelling began. It was always so before a battle. It was a prerequisite that artillery fire would pound the enemy trenches and wire to demoralise, if not kill, maim and bury, the opposing soldiers and cut the barbed-wire entanglements so that the troops who would storm the enemy's positions at dawn would have a reasonable chance of getting across 'no-man's-land' and into the German trenches before they were mown down by machine-gun and rifle fire. Sometimes it worked, often it didn't. The Germans replied in kind but with less ferocity.

Soldiers on both sides easily read the signs and kept themselves deep inside their bunkers, hoping a direct hit would not cave in their otherwise fairly strong shelters. Both knew that they would have to sit and bear it as the rain of steel and explosives fell on them. It was no easier for the old hands as it was for the new. What was a shock for the new was anxiety for the old. The shelling went on all night. It gave some small comfort to the men who would be 'going over the top' on the morrow, and discomfort to the recipients—so the attackers hoped.

Dawn, when it came, was cold, with low clouds and a strong wind that persisted most of the day. But as light filtered across the barren but smoke-filled landscape, the men in the Allied trenches stood ready, each with his own thoughts and fears. Had the wire been cut? Had the enemy been pounded and destroyed? Would today be a walk-over? Could they at last break through to open countryside? Would they all be dead five minutes from zero hour!?

The order to fix bayonets was given. This was it. Dawn. A last dawn? Officers moved among their troops, occasionally checking a watch, looking up at the grey sky. The last minutes ticked by and still the shells whistled and screeched overhead and into the German trench systems. Was this really Easter Monday; peace on earth, good will to all men? 0530 hours; whistles blew. It was time.

Scrambling up ladders, or steps made in the side of the trench-works, the khaki-clad soldiers, encouraged by their officers and cursed by their NCOs, went 'over the top'. Ahead lay the shattered dead ground between them and their enemy. Smoke blew across this pulverized moon-like landscape, the noise of explosions got nearer but would soon stop, then move on as the artillery gunners upped the range. Where was the wire? When would the first rattle of machine-gun fire come to their ears, quickly followed by scything metal and death? Breathing became difficult; feet and legs felt like lead. There were some snow flurries. God be with us all.

The front stretched from Lens to St Quentin. South of Arras and west of Cambrai British troops stormed Hermies and Boursies. West of St Quentin, Fresnoy-le-Petit was captured. North of Arras the prize of Vimy Ridge was under assault by the Canadians.

Despite the wind and snow showers, the BE crews were out soon after 0600 to support this Battle of Arras. Their job was to make contact with forward elements of the soldiers, to see how far they had progressed, then report back. Contact Patrols they were called. Make contact and report.

Unlike the dreadful carnage of the Somme the previous July, the soldiers of the British 1st and 3rd Armies reached their initial objectives, had got through the wire and into the shattered German trenches. From behind the British lines the balloons went up despite the strong wind, eager eyes also seeking information through the smoke via powerful binoculars.

A 16 Squadron BE2 skimmed over the battle front, seeking signs of both friend and enemy. Machine-gun fire greeted them, so the enemy was not totally knocked out. Bullets zipped through the wood and fabric of the BE, finding flesh. With both men wounded, the pilot headed back and they were lucky to survive. Another BE, this time from 13 Squadron, was also met by guns and shell fire, but this only found wood and fabric. The pilot crash-landed inside British lines, both men safe. A machine from the 1st Brigade located a German gun battery moving to the rear and the pilot dived, firing with his machine-gun. The guns were abandoned, temporarily.

Triplanes of 1 Naval Squadron flew an early OP to Cambrai at 0640, one machine flown by Flight Commander C A Eyre (N5478) having to return with a dud engine, crash-landing at Dancourt.

As the morning progressed targets observed behind the enemy front were engaged by shell fire, the fall of shot being registered and corrected by both aeroplane and balloon observers by radio, while fighter patrols were flown behind the battle front to protect the artillery machines and balloon lines from attack. It succeeded pretty well, but the weather helped too. Despite the fact that this was the opening day of the new offensive, enemy air opposition was almost nil.

By 0815, the advance was starting to falter. German artillery had begun to pound the front lines despite the work of the artillery flyers. A 12 Squadron BE came back with a wounded observer. However, by noon it could be reported that Highland troops had reached Roclincourt; Canadian troops, after a struggle, took Les Tillenes. As the day progressed St Martin-sur-Cojeul and the chapel at Feuchy village were captured. Further Contact Patrols spotted British troops in St Laurent Blagny and Athies, then Fampoux and Point du Jour, mostly to the north of the Scarpe River. To the south of the river, the German resistance was stronger. Another 13 Squadron BE (5875) with Lieutenant D H Ball and Captain W W Boyd was hit by machine-gun fire from the ground, forcing them to make a landing near Arras, but they were safe.

When weather permitted, some fighters attempted to shoot up German troops and positions, much to the delight and satisfaction of the Allied soldiers. A Spad from 19 Squadron (A263) was hit in turn by ground fire, Lieutenant F L Harding safely getting down on Lille-Villers airfield.

The Bristol Fighters of 48 Squadron got into a scrap with some Albatros two-seaters late morning claiming two destroyed and another out of control. FA202 had Unteroffizier Eugon Reuter killed and Leutnant Schröder wounded over Vitry on the 6 Armee front and were probably the victims of 48 Squadron. There was also a Offizierstellvertreter Franz Hermann and Gefreiter Oskar Weller killed on this day, unit unknown. Pilots of Naval 6 and Naval 8 were also involved in air fights in the Cambrai-Arras-Noyelles area around noon, claiming three fighters out of control. Upon returning from this action, the 6 Naval pilots were caught in a storm and two of its Nieuports crashed, having Flight Sub Lieutenant A L Thorne killed and Flight Sub Lieutenant J deC Paynter (a future ace) injured.

There was less reported action during the afternoon and it was not until evening that fresh fighting occurred in the air. At 1835, a 2 Squadron BE2d (6253), crewed by Captain F Fernihough and Second Lieutenant R Hamilton MC, was attacked while on an artillery patrol at 5,000 feet. Their aggressor flew an all-black Albatros with a white cross on the rudder but Hamilton's fire appeared to hit the German, who turned away and went east, losing height.

48 Squadron again got into a fight and claimed two DIIIs out of control at around 1800, although Lieutenant Jack Letts had his gunner mortally wounded and 25 Squadron got an out of control near Lieven at 1905. Captain A M Wilkinson of 48 Squadron shared in all five of 48's claims, and in his subsequent DSO citation it records his help in gaining these four victories on this day.

It fell to Jasta 11's Karl Schäfer to make the German Air Service's only confirmed kill of the day. Over the front he spotted a 4 Squadron BE2d and, with four other Jasta pilots, dived to the attack. It was 1900 hours, and the BE went down to crash at Aix Noulette, seven kilometres west of Lens, but inside British lines. Lieutenants J H Brink and R E Heath had taken off at 1850 to recce the Queant area. They came under AA fire which in turn attracted Schäfer and his men who dived to the attack. Heath saw the five Halberstadts coming down and began to fire the rear gun which jammed after a few rounds. As he began to clear it he was hit in the foot.

Getting his gun going again, he fired back once more but then Johannas Brink received a bullet in the back and slumped forward, the BE beginning a spiral downwards. Heath attempted to take control but Brink signalled that he could land it, and did so, but the BE turned over and Heath was thrown out. Heath, despite his wound and being winded, dragged his pilot from the wreck and laid him on the ground.

Two of the German fighters then came down to strafe them. Heath grabbed a Lewis gun from his cockpit and called to a nearby soldier—an Australian private—hoisted the gun onto the man's shoulder and began firing at the two Halberstadts, driving them off. Brink died of his wound two days later, but it is not recorded if the Australian soldier was temporarily deafened by the Lewis gun being fired next to his ear!

By the end of the day's fighting, the British front had moved east by some 6,000 yards along a 15,000 yard stretch, the most important victory being the capture by the Canadians of Vimy Ridge. In this predominantly flat landscape, any high ground was an important and strategic feature. It had been in German hands since October 1914, but now the Allied forces could look down on the Douai plain from its 200-feet heights, while it also became the defensive flank for the British 3rd Army along the Scarpe.

French Front

With everything concentrated up on the British front, and Nivelle still planning his part of the overall strategy, there was little activity in the south. There were no losses and no claims. The Germans, however, lost a two-seater crew of FA(A)276 at Manningen, near Metz, probably an accident at Manningen Bar aerodrome. Leutnants Rudolf Müller and Max Trautmann were killed.

	A/C	KB		DES	OOC	KB
British losses	3	—	RFC claims	3	6	—
French losses	—	—	French claims	—		—
German claims	1	—	German losses	—		—

British Casualties

Aircraft type	No.	Squadron	Crew			
BE2g	6818	16 Sqdn	2/Lt E B Smythe	WIA		
			2/Lt S Cooper	WIA		
BE2e	2878	13 Sqdn	Lt J H Norton	Safe		
			Capt T L Tibbs	Safe		
BE2d	5742	4 Sqdn	Lt J H Brink	DOW		
			Lt R E Heath	WIA		
BE2c		12 Sqdn	2/Lt O D Norwood (O)	WIA		*
BF2a	A3315	48 Sqdn	Lt J H T Letts	Unhurt		*
			Lt H G Collins	DOW		

Tuesday, 10 April 1917

British Front

On the Arras front British troops reached the outskirts of Monchy-le-Preux while further south the British line advanced to the north of Louverval. In spite of the land battle raging along these sectors, continued strong winds and snow kept aeroplanes of both sides on the ground through much of the day. Certainly the Germans made no fighter claims and the RFC only made one out of control claim at 1900 hours that evening, by two 48 Squadron crews over Remy.

Two BE2 pilots were wounded during the day by ground fire while on either Contact Patrol or artillery observation work, and an AWFK8—'Big Ack'—of 35 Squadron had to force-land at Monchy-le-Preux at 1600 after being hit by flak, and was written off.

Major W S Douglas (later Sir W Sholto Douglas) and his observer 2AM A W Cant in a 43 Squadron Strutter (A7804) had their petrol tank shot through by AA fire and force-landed north-west of Arras at 1710. In the above-mentioned fight of 48 Squadron, one Bristol Fighter (A3334) was damaged by the fire from an Albatros Scout, Captain A T Cull and his gunner Corporal Edwards making a forced landing near Queant, fortunately on the right side of the lines.

French Front

Just one Nieuport Scout was lost, piloted by Brigadier Chautard of N.31, and he came down inside German lines, due to becoming lost in bad weather, and is presumed to have been taken prisoner. An observer in a Salmson two-seater was wounded by ground fire. There were no claims.

	A/C	KB			DES	OOC	KB
RFC losses	1	—		RFC claims	—	1	—
French losses	1	—		French claims	—	—	—
German claims	—	—		German losses	—	—	—

British Casualties

Aircraft type	No.	Squadron	Crew		
AWFK8	A2683	35 Sqdn	2/Lt H S Lees-Smith	Safe	
			2/Lt H L Storrs	Safe	
BE2c	2829	12 Sqdn	Lt J H Cooper	WIA	*
			2/Lt W A Winter	Safe	
BE2e	2839	8 Sqdn	2/Lt P B Pattison	WIA	*
			2/Lt E M Harwood	Safe	

French Casualties

Nieuport XVII	1930	N.31	Brig Chautard	POW	
Salmson-Moineau	F.41		—Lefrancois (O)	WIA	*

Wednesday, 11 April 1917

British Front

A very slight improvement in the weather during the morning brought renewed activity in the air-war, but more high wind, low clouds and snow storms restricted afternoon sorties. On the ground, Monchy was taken and La Bergère. The 4th Australian Division attacked—without any artillery support—and broke into the Hindenburg Line, but were thrown back with enormous losses. The 4th Brigade lost 2,339 out of 3,000 men, with 1,000 captured, the single biggest prisoner loss of Australians in the war. This 'experiment' was a totally useless blunder by General Gough. As will be seen, in September 1918, an under strength Australian Division would smash right through.

No.4 Squadron sent out machines to bomb targets at Cambrai at 0708, while 40 minutes later, 23 Squadron were sending out Spads to provide some form of escort. 23 had only recently become a single-seat unit, having previously flown FE2s, with the arrival of Spad VIIs from the French.

Most of the early German combats over the front came on or after 0845, but between 0800 and 0820, 48 Squadron were in combat with some Albatros Scouts over Fampoux, claiming one destroyed and two out of control. They then continued with their patrol, eager for more action. They were to get it in an hour's time.

Just on 0845, Jasta 12 intercepted the 4 Squadron BEs that were turning for home. The BEs had sacrificed a gunner/observer for extra bomb weight, so only carried pilots. Leutnant Georg Röth came down on Second Lieutenant F Matthews, hitting his BE and sending him down to crash-land north of Abancourt, just a few kilometres east of the Jasta's base at Epinoy. It was Röth's first confirmed victory which would, like all pilots, bring him the coveted Ehrenbecher—the silver Victory Cup (see photo).

The running fight continued, the BEs being harried slightly to the north-west, so when Lieutenant F L Kitchen went down to Leutnant Adolf Schulte, ten minutes after Matthews, at 0855, he fell near Tilloy right on the line. Another pilot, Second Lieutenant A F T Ord was wounded but brought his BE back to base.

Meantime, Jasta 2 had become airborne and spotted the Spads, Leutnant Hermann Frommherz shooting down one at Cuvillers, north-east of Cambrai at 0900, for his first victory— the BEs having long gone. Sopwith Pup pilots from 3 Naval Squadron were also in the air over Cambrai at this period, Flight Commander Lloyd Breadner claiming an Albatros in flames and another crashed, while Flight Lieutenant Joe Fall claimed three out of control, Flight Sub Lieutenant P G McNeil a fourth. Neither Jasta 2 or 12 suffered any personnel losses, but 3 Naval did. Towards the end of the scrap, Joe Fall's Pup (N6158) was hit, he lost his engine and had to land in German territory west of Neuvireuil, being legitimately claimed by Leutnant Adolf Schulte, his second victory of the morning, and his 7th overall. However, Fall managed to get his engine going again, and before anyone arrived to take him prisoner, he took off and flew home, his machine riddled with bullet holes! Flight Sub Lieutenant S Bennett's Pup (N5199) was also shot up but he got it home, but it was so badly damaged it was later scrapped.

Also in the air was Jasta 11, led by Manfred von Richthofen. At just on 0900, Sebastian Festner spotted a BE (5848), attacked and shot it down into the British lines near Monchy with a wounded pilot. Within minutes the Jasta pilots saw more aircraft, this time the patrol formation of 48's Bristol Fighters. Jasta 11 dived upon them, inflicting a second defeat on the new two-seater and taking another flight commander, Captain Tidmarsh, leaving Alan Wilkinson as the only one left. Lothar von Richthofen, Kurt Wolff and Schäfer each blasted one from the sky, the machines falling around Fresnes.

No sooner had this victory been achieved than the Baron himself spotted another BE on artillery work. Going down on it in company with Wolff, von Richthofen shot it down into the British lines at 0925, by Willerval—another 13 Squadron machine. That made five kills for the Jasta and they were not finished yet, but first they flew back to Douai to refuel and rearm.

Almost an hour later, Jasta 4 were on patrol, Hans Klein seeing more BEs working over the front. He singled out yet another 13 Squadron machine (5851) and shot it down at Biache, on the Scarpe, well inside German lines. Forty minutes later, at 1100, he was after another BE, which he put into the ground at Feuchy, inside the British lines. This was probably the 12 Squadron machine (7242) which was on a contact patrol, and which was wrecked when forced down by a German fighter—having made contact of the wrong sort!

The Germans had not finished with the poor Corps machines yet. Jasta 11 were back on the hunt at midday, Lothar von Richthofen spotting a British 'Tommy' just after 1230. Attacking it he watched it fall into the British lines north of Fampaux, noting it as a Sopwith. However, no Sopwiths appear to have been brought down this day, so it was either an RE8 of 59 Squadron, on a lone Line Patrol having taken off at 1215, or one of two 8 Squadron BEs lost at this time. The two 8 Squadron aeroplanes had taken off after midday, one being claimed by Schäfer who went down on a BE at 1250, shooting it down east of Arras.

The pilot of one of these BEs got his damaged machine down at Neuville, inside British lines, where it turned over, but both men scrambled clear. The other crew were seen to be attacked by four German fighters whilst on a shoot south-east of Arras and shot down, apparently on the right side of the front line. Their BE was wrecked and both men wounded.

The only other loss at this time was a 52 Squadron BE2e which had begun a front line patrol at 1205. However, this was lost on the German side of the lines, so could not have been either Schäfer's or Lothar's victim.

While Jasta 11 was causing all this mayhem around Arras, Otto Bernert was doing his best to curb the British Corps aircraft further south, nearer Bapaume. At 1230 he is reported to have downed a Morane north-west of Lagnicourt. This was a 3 Squadron machine, operating out of Lavieville, to the west of Albert, who lost a Parasol at exactly 1230 between Vaux and Morchies while on artillery observation. It fell into British lines, both crewmen being killed. Then Bernert went after a 23 Squadron Spad (A6696), although it has been reported in the past as an FE2. However, 23 Squadron having recently been a FE unit, some past historian may have noted the 23 Squadron loss, assumed it to have been an FE and thus recorded the incorrect type. The Spad, piloted by Lieutenant F C Troup, had taken off at 1140 and force-landed at Hendecourt-Ecoust area, in the British lines, Troup reporting that he had been shot down by a DIII that had just shot down a Parasol.

This ended the day's air fighting of any note, as the weather worsened. During the day the artillery flyers had directed shell fire onto several targets, helping to knock out gun positions and troop concentrations all along the front. Captain Bird of 16 Squadron, observing for the 5th Canadian Siege Battery, had seen four pits of a five-gun battery completely destroyed. Aircraft, especially those of 43 and 25 Squadrons, had again attacked ground troops with machine-gun fire, an activity that was very much on the increase.

French Front

The main emphasis of action was still in the northern sectors, but along the French front more activity took place than had been the case the previous day. On the Chalons front Lieutenant Armand Pinsard of N.78 brought down an Albatros Scout south-east of St Souplet, which had been flown by Vizefeldwebel Karl Möwe of Jasta 29, who was dead when ground troops got to the scene—the Jastas' first pilot loss.

A Farman of F215 was brought down north of Berry-au-Bac by Leutnant Albert Dossenbach of Jasta 36, while the observer of another Farman was wounded by ground fire while a Caudron of R.214 force-landed at Harmonville with a wounded crew.

On the Chauny front, Adjutant Jeronnez of N.26 also claimed a victory over Cerny-le-Laonnois, for his third kill. This was probably Leutnant Heinrich Karbe of Jasta 22 on a balloon hunt around noon. He was engaged by three Spads and was hit a grazing shot above the right eye, but it was enough to knock him unconscious. His next recollection is of being on the ground and running, luckily on the right side of the lines.

Escadrille N.73 were in a fight with Jasta 14, near Berry-au-Bac, losing two Spad VIIs, with one pilot missing and one wounded. This was at 1145, the victors being Rudolf Berthold, his 11th, and Offizierstellvertreter Hüttner, his second. N.62 had one of their Nieuport two-seaters forced down inside their own lines, although it is not certain if the crew were casualties. Another Caudron returned with a wounded observer after being hit by ground fire.

Leutnant Gebhardt Salzwedel of Jasta 24 got his first victory by downing a Nieuport Scout at Xures, in the French lines way down on the Nancy sector, which was Maréchal-des-Logis Preher of N.68, who failed to return.

	A/C	KB		DES	OOC	KB
British losses	15†	—	RFC claims	3	6	—
French losses	4	—	French claims	2		—
German claims	19	—	German losses	1‡		

† Including one finally written off on 27 April. ‡ Nachrichtenblatt admits to one aeroplane loss.

British Casualties

Aircraft type	No.	Squadron	Crew		
BE2c	2769	4 Sqdn	2/Lt F Matthews	POW/WIA	
BE2d	5849	4 Sqdn	Lt F L Kitchin	KIA	
BE2		4 Sqdn	2/Lt A F T Ord	WIA	*
Spad VII	A6690	23 Sqdn	2/Lt S Roche	POW	
Pup	N5199	3N Sqdn	FSL S Bennett	Safe	SOC

BE2d	5848	13 Sqdn	2/Lt E R Gunner	WIA	
			Lt C Curtis	WIA	
BF2a	A3323	48 Sqdn	2/Lt G N Brockhurst	POW/WIA	
			2/Lt C B Boughton	POW	
BF2a	A3338	48 Sqdn	Capt D M Tidmarsh	POW	
			2/Lt C B Holland	POW	
BF2a	A3318	48 Sqdn	2/Lt R E Adeney	KIA	
			2/Lt L G Lovell	KIA	
BE2e	2501	13 Sqdn	Lt E C E Derwin	WIA	
			2AM H Pierson	WIA	
BE2d	5851	13 Sqdn	2/Lt E T Dunford	POW/DOW	
			Cpl G Steward	KIA	
BE2e	7242	12 Sqdn	2/Lt G H Jacobs	WIA	
			2/Lt P L Goudie	WIA	
Morane Parasol	A6722	3 Sqdn	Lt M A A Lillis	KIA	
			2AM A Fyffe	KIA	
Spad	A6696	23 Sqdn	Lt F C Troup	Safe	*
FE2b		18 Sqdn	2/Lt J R Smith	WIA	*
RE8	A4190	59 Sqdn	Lt G T Morris	KIA	
			Lt G M Souter	KIA	
BE2c	2838	52 Sqdn	Capt A F Baker	KIA	
			2/Lt A J Etches	KIA	
BE2c	2813	8 Sqdn	2/Lt F J E Stafford	WIA	*
			Lt G E Gibbons	Safe	
BE2e	5811	8 Sqdn	Sgt V J Bell	WIA	
			2/Lt H Q Campbell	WIA	

French Casualties

Nieuport XVII	1955	N.68	MdL Preher	MIA	
Farman 61		F.71	Lt Grabes (O)	WIA	*
Farman 61		F.215	Sgt Perseyger	KIA	
			Asp Nardon	KIA	
Caudron R4		R.214	Sgt Bodin	WIA	
			S/Lt Grignon (O)	WIA	
			Sol Dermirgian	WIA	
Spad VII		N.73	Sgt Paris	WIA	
Spad VII		N.73	Adj Barioz	MIA	
Caudron G4		C.42	Lt Clerc (O)	WIA	*
Nieuport XII		N.62	Cpl Mougeot	?	
			Lt Lemaignen	?	

Thursday, 12 April 1917

British Front

A clear morning, followed by cloud and snow storms for the rest of the day, reflected the reduced activity in the air. Ground fighting secured the capture of Wancourt, Heninel, Gauche Wood, Gouzeaucourt Village and its woods.

What combat there was only took place in the morning, beginning with a photo and escort job by FEs of 18 Squadron over the 5th Army front, taking off just before to just after 0900. The FEs were intercepted by aircraft of Jasta 12 near Eterpigny at 1035, Sopwith Pups of 3 Naval Squadron also joining in.

Hauptmann von Osterroht engaged one of the Pups near Bourlon Wood, as the formation headed north-west for the lines. Acting Flight Commander R G Mack, flying a Pup named 'Black Tulip' and with the letter 'M' on its side, was hit and Mack wounded. He came down at Marquin on the Arras-Cambrai road where he was taken prisoner.

Meanwhile, Vizefeldwebel Arthur Schörisch attacked and brought down FE 4984, which force-landed at Eterpigny, but Leutnant Adolf Schulte, in Albatros DIII 1996/16, collided with FE 4995, and all three men fell to their deaths between Roumaucourt and Barelle at 1040. This would have been Schulte's 9th victory.

The other Pups dog-fought the Albatros Scouts above Jasta 2's base at Pronville, claiming three down out of control, but Schulte was the only reported casualty. 18 Squadron's gunners also claimed two Scouts out of control over Cagnicourt, one possibly being Schulte, although his Albatros, seen falling with wings smashed, was the one credited—in his absence—to Mack.

A 34 Squadron RE8, crewed by Captain F L J Shirley and Lieutenant L T Smith, took off on a photo sortie at 1000, and were engaged by Kurt Schneider of Jasta 5, in his all-black Albatros DIII. Shirley was wounded, being hit in the pit of his stomach and force-landed in British lines at Ascension Farm, near Herbercourt. Smith got Shirley clear before their machine was destroyed by German shelling. That ended the main activities, although 48 Squadron crews also reported shooting down an Albatros DIII out of control during the morning.

French Front

There was considerably more action along the French sectors despite the snow storms. A Nieuport two-seater was brought down south of Nauroy at 1100, by Unteroffizier Eduard Horn of Jasta 21, his first and only victory. This machine was from N.38, engaged on a photo mission. In the evening three fighters were shot down inside German lines; one, a Spad VII of N.112 was brought down by Leutnant Helmut Baldamus of Jasta 9 for his 17th victory, Adjutant-Chef Chemet being taken prisoner. The Frenchman came down near Attigny north of Pont Faverger, north-east of Reims, at 1900 hours.

Perhaps it should be pointed out again that while some French fighter squadrons were operating with Spads, their main equipment was still the Nieuport. Squadron designations of, say, N.38, would not become Spa.38 until later in the year once the whole unit had re-equipped with Spads.

Some of the other French losses came down through unknown causes, but the Germans knew the causes. Two pilots got themselves lost. One from N.26 landed on the wrong side of the lines. Another, from N.112, equally lost, actually landed on Leffincourt airfield, the home of Jasta 9.

In combat, a Salmson-Moineau of SM.106 brought down at Orainville was the victim of Oberleutnant Erich Hahn, Staffelführer of Jasta 19, despite Hahn's claim for a Caudron. A Caudron from R.214 that was brought down, fell to Flakzug 54 at Le Beau Château.

In turn, French pilots claimed two German aircraft, an Albatros Scout south of Epoye by Lieutenant Armand Pinsard of N.78, his 7th victory, and an aircraft by Maréchal-des-Logis Marcel Nogues of N.12 over the Bois de Cheval, for his second of an eventual 13 victories.

The Germans did lose personnel from Flieger Abteilungen on this day: Gefreiter Arno Rebentisch and Leutnant Ernst Beltzig of FA(A)272 were killed at Alincourt, and Flieger Max Vogl of FA46 was also killed. Gefreiter Richard Streubel was thought to be another casualty on the French front, unit unknown.

	A/C	KB		DES	OOC	KB
British losses	4	—	British claims	1	6	—
French losses	6	—	French claims	2		—
German claims	8†	—	German losses	1		—

† Including one to flak; plus two forced to land inside their lines.

British Casualties

Aircraft type	No.	Squadron	Crew	
FE2b	4984	18 Sqdn	Lt O D Maxted	POW
			Lt A Todd MC	DOW
FE2b	4995	18 Sqdn	Lt O T Walton	KIA
			2AM J C Walker	KIA
Sopwith Pup	N6172	3N Sqdn	FC R G Mack	POW/WIA
RE8	A104	34 Sqdn	Capt F L J Shirley	WIA
			Lt L T Smith	Safe

French Casualties

Nieuport XVII	2779	N.112	Cpl Carre	POW
Nieuport XII		N.38	MdL Richard	MIA
			Lt Hallier	MIA
Spad VII	184	N.26	MdL de Tascher	POW

Spad VII	2507	N.112	Adj-Chef Chemet	POW	
Salmson-Moineau		SM.106	Lt de Montfort	MIA	
			Sol Portolieu (O)	MIA	
			Brig Robillard (G)	MIA	
Caudron G4		R.214	Brig Brunet	MIA	
			S/Lt Hembrat (O)	MIA	
			Sgt Levy (G)	MIA	
Caudron G4		C.222	Lt Guimberteau (O)	WIA	*

Friday, 13 April 1917

British Front

Fine weather brought out the aviators on this Friday the Thirteenth which was to prove unlucky for a good number of young British airmen. The ground fighting still raged around Vimy and near the Drocourt-Queant switch line, so the various Army HQs still called for Contact Patrols and photographs.

British infantry took Givenchy-en-Gohelle, Angres and Wancourt tower, while Fayet to the north-west of St Quentin was also taken. Since the offensive had started, 13,000 German prisoners had been taken as well as 166 pieces of artillery.

Six FEs of 57 Squadron lifted off from Fienvillers at 0700 to fly an OP, led by Captain Jones, but Jones and Lieutenant Cullen had to return home with engine troubles, the latter having to make an emergency landing west of Arras, so that left four.

Just over an hour later, RE8s of 59 Squadron, assigned the task of bringing back photos of the rear areas around Etaing, also took off. It was only a week since 59 had taken a drubbing at the hands of Jasta 11, and now they were flying into von Richthofen's area again. They once more provided their own escort—RE8s escorting RE8s. There were fighter patrols in the general area of the front, but direct escort operations had not yet become a normal occurrence.

Of course, there were some valid reasons why direct escort had its problems. One has to remember that there was no radio communication between aircraft in WWı, so it was difficult to make a rendezvous, and other than hand signals and wing-waggling, no means of making contact with other aircraft when in sight of one another. Different speeds made it necessary for the single-seater pilots to throttle down and therefore become more vulnerable to sudden attacks. Official thinking, by commanders who had never flown a fighter aircraft, preferred their fighters to patrol the area of activity and intercept enemy fighters—and any hostile two-seaters they found—leaving the British two-seater machines to get on with their work unmolested. All very fine, but it didn't work. The sky is a big place and what is more, the Germans were well aware of the tactic and the more experienced would choose the most favourable moment to pick out a British two-seater.

Generally at this time, German fighters patrolled only in Jasta strength, usually no more than five or six aeroplanes. 59 Squadron may have thought that with a sortie of six aircraft they were more or less equal to any hostile patrol they might encounter. Undoubtedly 59 Squadron were trying to overcome a difficult problem but this wasn't the answer as they were about to find out yet again.

Nieuport two-seaters of 46 Squadron were operating, flying as escort to artillery machines over Polygon Wood, taking off at 0800. The Nieuports were attacked by two German scouts from the rear. Lieutenant K W Macdonald in one machine heard his gunner begin to fire but then the gun jammed after three-quarters of a drum. Whilst trying to clear it, the observer, Second Lieutenant C P Long, was hit in the neck and collapsed. Seeing he was seriously wounded, Macdonald dived straight for the lines and landed at Abeele airfield, but Long had bled to death.

The FEs of 57 Squadron were not too far to the north as the big hands on clocks and watches ticked towards 0900, but then the pushers were engaged by Jasta 5 just east of Gavrelle, between there and Vitry-en-Artois. They were suddenly busy having taken on a hostile patrol, and it let Jasta 11 have an open sky to engage 59 who were then alone.

Heinrich Gontermann, more remembered for his attacks on Allied balloons, and Kurt

Schneider, both of Jasta 5, each shot down an FE2, claimed—as most pusher-types were—as a Vickers. Gontermann shot down A5150, Schneider A1950. In fact Schneider claimed two FEs, but the other two returned home safely. One of his victories was reported as having gone down on the British side, so either one had flown back very low which deceived ground observers into thinking it had crashed, or perhaps someone had seen Cullen going down earlier and it had been confused with Schneider's claim.

Meantime, six pilots of Jasta 11, led by the Baron himself, with at least one fighter from Jasta 4, fell upon the six RE8s minutes before 0900. The two Scotsmen aboard the photo machine—A3203—headed for the lines while the other five tried to protect it. There was no contest. First to go down was A3199 to Festner, the RE8 falling north of Dury at 0854. Lothar von Richthofen knocked out two within seconds at 0855, A4191 hitting the ground north of Biache, A3126 at Pelves. Then the photo machine fell to Hans Klein of Jasta 4, and A3225 to Kurt Wolff, both at 0856. Klein's kill fell south-west of Biache, Wolff's north of Vitry. Oddly enough, the Baron's victim was the last to fall, at 0858, A3190 falling in flames between Vitry and Brebières.

As if in deference to the men who had just died, there was more than two hours of respite in the air on the Arras front. Jasta 11 went back to Douai victorious to refuel and rearm their Albatros fighters. The 'sharks' had tasted blood and the day might not yet be over.

At 1125, 11 Squadron sent out FEs for an OP, into Jasta 11's area. The signal came for the pilots to get back into the air and they needed no second bidding. With Manfred von Richthofen leading, they found 11 Squadron east of the lines, west of Douai. Wolff went in as the FEs headed west, pursued one and, after a chase across the lines north of La Bassée, the pusher (A827) force-landed near Bailleul at 1235. This was credited to the German as his 11th victory. This, of course, was Bailleul-Sir-Berthoult, just north-east of Arras. (This should not be confused with Bailleul town, which lies south of Poperinghe and Ypres, way up on the more northern part of the front. Germans working on the Arras front generally recorded this southern town plain Bailleul, which has led to much confusion over the years with the more famous northern location.)

Von Richthofen, in company with Leutnant Georg Simon, chased another south-west, his fire wounding both men in the two-seater which went down and crash-landed inside British lines between Feuchy and Monchy at 1245.

Once more Jasta 11 went home victorious, and why not. As the morning ended, Jasta 11 had been credited with seven kills thus far, with 39 British aircraft brought down so far in April, and the day was far from over, let alone the month.

The Bristols of 48 Squadron operated a Line Patrol at 1450 to the east of Arras and had a scrap with some Albatros Scouts, Captain A M Wilkinson and his gunner claiming one destroyed, Lieutenant J W Warren and his back-seater another out of control. However, the Squadron lost one machine which was hit by ground fire, claimed by Flakzug units near Courcelles.

Again there was a lull in the air fighting, and it wasn't until 1630 that Spandau machine-guns were again stitching a line of bullets into a RFC machine. No. 29 Squadron flew a Defensive Patrol at five minutes to four, only to be engaged by Jasta 11, Kurt Wolff gaining another kill by forcing Second Lieutenant B Scott-Foxwell to land inside British lines south of Monchy. The British flyer scooted for cover as artillery shells began to rain down, blasting the Nieuport into scrap.

Two hours later Jasta 11 were once more east of the lines. More FEs were out as well as the Martinsydes of 27 Squadron which were to bomb Henin-Lietard. 11 Squadron's 'Fees' were on another OP and so were six machines of 22 Squadron, and as 22 were to report: '... enemy aircraft very active.' The FEs were engaged by Jasta 11 and Jasta 3, but it is not clear who was engaged with whom. No.22 Squadron had an engagement with four enemy aircraft near Itancourt, which is five kilometres south-east of St Quentin, reporting one crashed by Second Lieutenant J V Aspinall and Lieutenant M K Parlee (4983) at 1830. No.11 Squadron had their fight much further north. Karl Schäfer of Jasta 11 claimed his victim down in British lines south-west of Monchy at 1830, which is more than 50 km north-west of Itancourt, and in any event they only had an FE shot up and a crewman wounded, although it is possible it force-landed and was recorded as a kill.

No.11 Squadron also had one of their machines shot up, the pilot being forced to crash-land in British lines. Leutnant Karl Bauer of Jasta 3 was credited with a FE2b on the British side of the lines at 1915 south of La Bassée, well north of Lens. It would be Bauer's only victory and he would die in combat a month later.

If one tries to determine what other Jasta 3 and 11 pilots were doing at around this time, one finds that Wolff was shooting down the 27 Squadron Martinsyde at 1852 near Rouvroy, south-east of Lens, while Leutnant Karl Stobel of Jasta 3 was gaining his one and only victory, over a BE2, south-west of Oppy, inside British lines. The only BE lost this day was a 5 Squadron machine on a Line Recce over Oppy, which came down inside its own lines, so this one is beyond doubt.

This 5 Squadron machine was attacked by two fighters, described as Halberstadts, and had its elevator controls shot away. Being unable to level out, the pilot made a rapid landing into what he later reported to be the enemy's lines, but most probably it was right in the middle of the battle area. The crew of Second Lieutenants N C Buckton and G L Barritt clambered out of their wrecked machine and decided to take the Lewis gun and make for a nearby sunken road. As they were doing so, a patrol of German soldiers appeared—they counted eight—so they opened up with the Lewis and the soldiers retreated. A few minutes later an advanced Canadian patrol came up and the two airmen were able to give them valuable information as to the whereabouts of the enemy. They also saw an FE2b brought down in flames near Farbus by the 'same hostile aircraft' almost immediately after they had come down. The two men also found a wrecked RE8, No. A112, with a dead pilot and observer. The only identity found was that the pilot was a former Northumberland Fusilier and the observer had been in a light infantry regiment.

What is interesting is that one must assume that the FE was brought down by Jasta 3 as well, and as fire is mentioned, must presumably be the 11 Squadron machine; thus it seems more likely that it was Bauer's victim. The RE8 wreck—A112—was one of the 59 Squadron machines brought down not on this day, but the previous Good Friday, the crew being Second Lieutenants Davies and Wordsworth, Robert Davies having indeed been in the 16th Northumberland Fusiliers and Joe Wordsworth having served with the 8th Durham Light Infantry.

Second Lieutenant Buckton in fact had quite an eventful Friday the 13th. Quite apart from being shot down into 'no-man's-land' and rescued by Canadian soldiers, he had flown two test flights that morning. After lunch he had flown with Lieutenant Steele on a recce sortie, attacking a party of 30 enemy troops, and then another group they had found near Bailleul—who had not unnaturally scattered in all directions. All flights had been in the machine now lying wrecked—7156.

An interesting note in 5 Squadron's records states that aircraft wanting to cross the lines should fire off a red Verey Light to attract the attention of patrolling fighters. However, it also notes that one of its machines had in fact fired red flares twice at a couple of FEs which had ignored them—twice! So much for help and co-operation, and one supposes that if there are no obvious friendly aircraft about, the two-seater crew must continue on alone!

At Douai Jasta 11 were congratulating Schäfer on what appeared to be his 17th victory, when once more the call to become airborne came. Nine 25 Squadron FE2s had taken off at 1840 on a bomb raid against Henin-Lietard. Taking the air, the Jasta pilots were too late to stop the attack, and the air battle began while the FEs were still dropping their bombs. The clash came over Henin at 1930, the FE crews claiming no fewer than four Albatros DIIIs destroyed as the running fight ensued. Klein of Jasta 4 also showed up again so the two units were obviously flying together, attacking the FEs at the front of the stream that were now heading for home.

The first FE to go down went under the guns of Klein, A6372 falling near Vimy, having almost made it. Sebastian Festner shot down A784 near Harnes at 1915, while Manfred von Richthofen got 4997 at 1935 over Henin itself, the pusher falling into a house at Noyelles Godault. Klein's victim was Captain L L Richardson, an Australian who had achieved seven victories with his gunners since mid-1916 and was about to receive the MC. He and his observer were both killed.

The RFC had two other losses during the day, but they appear not to have been claimed by any German pilots. At 1815 a Morane Parasol of 3 Squadron on a photo op crashed near the front lines at Queant after being attacked by three fighters, both RFC men being wounded. And a Nieuport XII two-seater from 46 Squadron was also brought down inside British lines, the dead observer being buried at Lijssenthoek, having been killed in combat with a German aircraft. This machine had almost got back to its base at Droglandt and was 16 kilometres from the front line, thus was not seen to go down and land by German front line observers.

Claims by German anti-aircraft units amounted to three, including a BE and an FE at Willerval, Brebières and Quiery-la-Motte—the latter being a type unknown. Willerval is just north of Oppy and this may be the same 5 Squadron machine claimed by Jasta 3.

During the day the RFC pilots had made several claims in addition to those already mentioned. 66 Squadron drove down a two-seater and a scout on an early morning patrol, while Lieutenant G S Buck of 19 Squadron, claimed a DIII out of control over Brebières. At 1130, Lieutenant H E O Ellis of 40 Squadron claimed a C-type Albatros as destroyed over Courrières. He put just 20 rounds into it but must have hit the pilot, for the two-seater cart-wheeled, turned over, went down in a spin and crashed.

Two German airmen are reported casualties. Unteroffizier Binder of Schusta 24, severely wounded on the 6 Armee front, and a Jasta 37 pilot wounded on the French front (see below). The Nachrichtenblatt records no aircraft lost and one Unteroffizier pilot wounded.

In the evening, Jasta 5 made an attack on the balloon lines west and south of St Quentin and claimed two destroyed, although it seems only one British balloon, that of the 34th Section of 4 Wing, was actually lost, the observers making a safe parachute descent. Nathanael and Gontermann were the claimants, their attacks timed at 1935 and 1940, Gontermann's being the French balloon of 55 Cié.

During the ground battle, troops of the 4th Canadian Division entered a recently abandoned German dugout, finding two wounded RFC officers, Second Lieutenants Smythe and Cooper of 16 Squadron, who had been missing since the 9th. They had been brought down by machine-gun fire during one of the first Contact Patrols upon the opening of the Arras Battle.

Although non-combat casualties are not being specifically covered in this work, the RNAS did lose one of its squadron commanders on this day, Squadron Commander J J Petrie DSC, CO of 6 Naval, killed in a flying accident. He was flying Nieuport XVII N3206.

French Front

Combat on the French sectors was confined to just three claimed successes. A Farman crew from F.41 claimed a victory over Mont Sapigneul on the Chalons front, while Adjutant Bertrand of N.57 claimed another near Guignicourt. In fact the pilot of the Farman was Louis Gros, later to become an ace flying with Spa.154. Adjutant Raoul Lufbery, the ace of the Lafayette Escadrille—N.124—claimed a two-seater north-west of St Quentin for his 8th victory.

The French lost a Spad VII at 1400 hours in combat with Jasta 36 near Sapigneul. The German, Leutnant Albert Dossenbach, holder of the Pour le Mérite, downed Sous Lieutenant Marcel Nogues of Spa.12, who was captured. Nogues had two victories at this time, but he was to escape his captors five weeks later and return to active duty, and by the war's end he had increased his score to 13.

A Salmson two-seater of F.72 on the Chalons front was downed near Chalons-sur-Vesles by Leutnant Heinrich Bongartz of Jasta 36 at 1700, the second victory for this future ace, who would eventually gain 33 successes. In the heat of combat, Bongartz had claimed a Caudron. In other actions, a Letord, a Sopwith and a Farman had returned with dead or wounded aircrew, mostly following combats with enemy fighters.

Balloons were attacked, Gontermann of Jasta 5 as already mentioned shooting down one of 55 Cié, while Jastas 34 and 37 made assaults against the 'drachens'. Oberleutnant Eduard Dostler of Jasta 34 made a claim at Genicourt but this was not confirmed, while Unteroffizier Simon Ruckser of Jasta 37, based at Montingen, by Metz, flamed one but was severely wounded by ground fire. It also happened to be Jasta 37's first success and first casualty.

At 1955, Leutnant Josef Jacobs of Jasta 22 spotted a Farman over the French side of the lines, flying in and out of cloud. Despite French AA fire, Jacobs attacked and watched as the

Farman went down 'end-over-end' over Barisis, 20 kilometres west of Laon. Confirmation came from German gunners that the Farman had gone down although it may not have crashed.

	A/C	KB			DES	OOC	KB
British losses	18	1	British claims		5	3	—
French losses	2	2?	French claims		3		—
German claims	27	3	German losses		?†		

† No losses recorded in the Nachrichtenblatt, just one NCO pilot wounded.

British Casualties

Aircraft type	No.	Squadron	Crew			
FE2d	A5150	57 Sqdn	Capt L S Platt	KIA		
			2/Lt T Margerison	KIA		
FE2d	A1950	57 Sqdn	2/Lt G W Gillespie	KIA		
			Pvt R Sibley	MIA		
RE8	A3225	59 Sqdn	Lt A H Tanfield	KIA		
			Lt A Ormerod	KIA		
RE8	A3190	59 Sqdn	Capt J Stuart	KIA		
			Lt M H Wood	KIA		
RE8	A4191	59 Sqdn	Lt H G Mc Horne	KIA		
			Lt W J Chalk	KIA		
RE8	A3199	59 Sqdn	Lt A Watson	POW		
			Lt E R Law	POW		
RE8	A3216	59 Sqdn	Capt G B Hodgson	KIA		
			Lt C H Morris	KIA		
RE8	A3203	59 Sqdn	Lt P B Boyd	KIA		
			2/Lt P O Ray	KIA		
Nieuport XII	A258	46 Sqdn	Lt K W Macdonald	Safe		*
			2/Lt C P Long	KIA		
FE2b	A827	11 Sqdn	Lt C E Robertson	Safe		*
			2/Lt H D Duncan	Safe		
FE2b	A831	11 Sqdn	Sgt J A Cunniffe	WIA		
			2AM W J Batten	WIA		
FE2b		22 Sqdn	Lt E A Thomas	WIA		*
BF2a	A3322	48 Sqdn	2/Lt H D Davies	POW		
			2/Lt R S Worsley	POW		
Nieuport XXIII	A6768	29 Sqdn	2/Lt B Scott-Foxwell	Safe		
BE2f	7156	5 Sqdn	2/Lt N C Buckton	Safe		
			2/Lt G L Barritt	Safe		
Martinsyde G100	A1564	27 Sqdn	2/Lt M Topham	KIA		
FE2b	4997	25 Sqdn	2/Lt A H Bates	KIA		
			Sgt W A Barnes	KIA		
FE2b	A784	25 Sqdn	Sgt J Dempsey	POW		
			2/Lt W H Green	WIA/POW		
FE2b	A6372	25 Sqdn	Capt L L Richardson	KIA		
			2/Lt D C Wollen	KIA		
Morane Parasol	A6760	3 Sqdn	Lt L F Beynon	WIA		
			Lt A C Lutyens MC	WIA		
FE2b	A819	11 Sqdn	Lt E T Curling	WIA		
			2/Lt J Rothwell	Safe		

French Casualties

Aircraft type	No.	Squadron	Crew			
Salmson-Moineau		F.72	S/Lt Fequand	KIA		
			Lt Locquin (O)	KIA		
			Sol Hutreau (AG)	KIA		
Spad VII	1057	N.12	MdL M J M Nogues	POW		
Letord L J		R.210	Ens de la Tullaye (O)	WIA		*
			Sgt Lentrain (AG)	KIA		
Sopwith 2		F.2	S/Lt Pauli-Krauss	Safe		*
			S/Lt Clave	WIA		
Farman 40		F.41	MdL Gros	Safe		*
			S/Lt de Dreux	WIA		

Saturday, 14 April 1917

British Front

With Vimy Ridge firmly in Allied hands and the line dented if not smashed, Field Marshal Haig now awaited General Nivelle's promised attack along the French front to the south. Not that Haig trusted the Frenchman to carry out what he had promised. Nobody knew more than Haig that to effect a breakthrough was almost impossible. Not totally impossible, or no General would even try, but Haig had his doubts that Nivelle would do it now.

Nevertheless, for five days the British forces had taken the battle to the enemy, hoping to take any pressure off the French sectors before the French launched their attack. Haig, having halted his attacks on Vimy and at the Scarpe now awaited Nivelle's mighty thrust, but it was delayed. Pressure along the 25-mile British front would need to be maintained—but for how long? Meantime, this Saturday saw Lieven and Lens taken as well as Gricourt to the south.

German troops were coming up from the rear, which is why the railhead at Henin-Lietard had been attacked the previous day. At 0420, 10 Squadron sent out some 'pilot-only' BE2s for a late night raid on Henin. They made their attack but machine-gun fire brought down one aeroplane and its pilot was put into a prison camp.

With the dawn came the Corps machines, and up went the fighters to fly their Offensive Patrols. The morning looked fine enough but the forecast was for a more cloudy afternoon. Pups of 54 Squadron flew a dawn patrol and had one pilot wounded in a fight, but the pilot got back so there was no victory for the German pilot. However, Leutnant Schöll of Jasta 30 did claim a Sopwith over Douai at 0810. In fact he claimed a two-seater Sopwith, but in all probability it was a Pup of 54 Squadron. A Pup pilot, Lieutenant M B Cole, encountered a two-seater over Gonnelieu at 0810 (in A6168) and claimed it out of control, reporting the observer hit by his fire and seen hanging over the side of the rear cockpit.

No.29 Squadron sent out machines to escort the two-seaters at 0840, and got tangled up with Jasta 4 south-east of Fresnoy and lost Second Lieutenant E J Pascoe to Oberleutnant Kurt von Döring at 0934, his first of an eventual 11 victories.

At the same moment, Hermann Frommherz of Jasta 2 was savouring his second victory, a 9 Squadron BE2c which he had just forced down at Ribecourt, south-east of Cambrai. He would end the war with 32 kills and we will meet him again in September 1918.

The Corps machines hopeful of some protection over the Arras battle area found, nevertheless, that the Albatros Scouts were getting to them. An 11 Squadron FE on a photo mission was attacked by an Albatros and its gunner was killed. The pilot scooted back over the lines, heading down, still being chased by the German who finally had to let him go, but not before he saw him hedge-hopping low over the ground. Vizefeldwebel Menckhoff's claim for the FE was not upheld. He hadn't seen it crash, only reported it close to the ground near Ecoust St Mein, but the FE pilot got his shot-up pusher down at his base of Le Hameau at 1010. As men watched the shot-up FE land, the chaps of 60 Squadron, which shared the airfield with 11 and 29 Squadron, were anxiously awaiting the return of their 0830 OP to Douai.

Douai! One might have guessed; Richthofen country! The patrol, with a mixture of Nieuport XVIIs and XXIIIs ran into Jasta 11 at 0915 and in just eight minutes four were shot down. Captain Alan Binnie MC, leader, was hit in the upper left arm as he reached for his wing-mounted Lewis gun, shattering the bone. The Australian, from New South Wales, saw his blood spurting all over his instruments, then passed out and came to amid wreckage and German soldiers. He'd been hit by Lothar von Richthofen's fire. Cock, a New Zealander, went down under Wolff's, while Festner hit and mortally wounded Chapman from south London. The other Londoner fell to the Baron over Bois Bernard and he too was taken prisoner. Alan Binnie later had his left arm amputated at the shoulder and was repatriated in January 1918 but flew again despite his disability. (He died in an accident during WW2.) So Le Hameau had had five of its Nieuports lost (four from 60 and one from 29) and had an FE return shot about and with a dead gunner on board.

The Nieuports had been engaging a German two-seater recce plane when Jasta 11 intervened, and one wonders if this had been the FA(A) 224 aircraft flown by Vizefeldwebel Karl Meckes and Leutnant Paul Otto, engaged on reconnoitring railway movements, spotting numerous rail-cars at Grenay Station, six kilometres north-west of Lens. They were attacked by three British fighters and hit in the propeller, wings and observer's seat, Otto being slightly wounded. Meckes received the Württemburg Golden Military Merit Medal on 2 August as a result of this day's action.

Another BE went down to Jasta 5's Gontermann over Metz-en-Couture during a front-line photo job, and although it came down inside British lines both RFC men—from 52 Squadron—were killed.

An RE8 of 34 Squadron failed to return from a photo op, having taken off at 0920 from its base at Foucaucourt. No German pilot seems to have claimed it (although reference has been made to Schäfer of Jasta 11, but the time is wrong). Perhaps it was the aircraft claimed by Flakzug 50.

In the late afternoon, Captain L C Coates with Second Lieutenant J C Cotton, of 5 Squadron, were engaged on a Line Recce and artillery patrol, and at 1830 were west of Willerval. Here they were attacked by half a dozen German fighters, and a running fight ensued. Returning fire, Cotton thought he'd sent one fighter down—confirmed later by Canadian troops on Vimy Ridge as going down out of control—and despite being wounded in seven places, he still continued to fire back until his gun finally jammed with a broken cartridge guide spring. Coates was also wounded but kept the BE under control and, despite having his aileron controls shot away, landed the BE without further injury to either himself or his observer.

Schäfer and Jasta 11 were in action at 1700 to 1730, Schäfer attacking a lone 25 Squadron FE2b (4877) during a patrol between Lens and Arras, that went down in flames near Lieven at 1705 inside British lines just west of Lens. Schäfer then chased after a BE2 of 2 Squadron, on artillery duty over the Bois de l'Hirondelle, seen to be shot down by two enemy fighters at 1720.

Wolff shot up another BE of 2 Squadron (2525), but its crew, Second Lieutenant W P M Brettell and Lieutenant C E Leggett, escaped despite having to make a forced landing inside British lines, thanks to another BE crew.

Brettell and Leggett had also been on an artillery patrol near the Cité St Theodore at 3,500 feet. At 1910, over Lens, they were attacked by two German fighters, Brettell diving away rapidly. One German—Wolff—followed them down, the observer firing back at him, with several rounds appearing to hit Wolff's machine. Another 2 Squadron BE flying nearby, with Captain H Fowler and Lieutenant F E Brown (2521), an experienced couple who had had several encounters with German fighters and survived (Fowler had already had a fight with Jasta 11 during the afternoon), saw the action and came to assist their comrades. They attacked Wolff, drawing him away from Brettell, only to have Wolff turn on them, but Brown fired another drum of Lewis ammunition at him and saw the fighter spiral down towards Maroc, before flying off, helped on its way by gunfire from Maroc and Grenay. Brettell's BE had been hit in several places, and eight bullets had pierced the petrol tank.

An hour later Jasta 11 were on the prowl again, this time finding Spads of 19 Squadron on an OP along the line Bailleul-Vitry-Sains-Bullecourt. Lothar von Richthofen claimed one in British lines south of Vimy, Wolff another west of Bailleul. However, 19 only lost one machine and its pilot, Lieutenant E W Capper, although it had Lieutenant J W Baker wounded. Edward Capper very nearly shot down Wolff before the German got on his tail and brought him down.

French Front

Most of the air combat took place around noon. Two Caudrons were claimed by Jasta 14 at Craonelle and Juvigny, north of Soissons, while Rudolf Berthold claimed a Spad two-seater over the Bois de Marais. However, this latter victory was more probably a Sopwith two-seater of N.15 that came down near Pontavert, west of Berry-au-Bac, after a combat with three enemy fighters. Josef Veltjens was also credited with a Spad at this same time, his first victory. The Jasta lost Leutnant Otto Weigel who was killed at 1215 over Craonelle, probably by the crew of a C.46 Caudron whose 'ace' crew (Capt Didier Lecour Grandmaison, Adj Marie Vitalis and MdL Achille Rousseau) claimed a German fighter south of Craonne at 1210.

The French made several claims on the 14th. On the Belfort sector, Maréchal-des-Logis de Belleville of N.49 brought down a fighter in flames at Elsbach. The German pilot was Leutnant Fritz Grunsweig of Jasta 16, who was engaged in a balloon attack when shot down. N.93 claimed three enemy planes and a balloon, Adjutants Gustave Daladier and Vieljeux claiming the aircraft, Adjutant Hamel the balloon. For Daladier, who claimed a two-seater, it was his first of an eventual 12 victories, and he received the Medaille Militaire for this combat.

During a mission on the Nancy sector, Adjutant Grelat and Lieutenant Cavinet of GB4 claimed an aircraft over Brisbach, the Germans also losing Unteroffizier Hermann Jopp of Jasta 37 on this front, brought down by the 71st Balloon Section near Mont Toulon, when Jopp attacked it.

Also on the Soissons front, Sous Lieutenant Languedoc of N.12 claimed an enemy plane over the Bois de Noyelles at 0600 hours. Capitaine Georges Guynemer of N.3 claimed an Albatros in flames by La Neuville at 1030 (the Frenchman's 36th victory), while Lieutenant Thiriez of N.15 got one over Corbeny.

On the Chalons front Lieutenant Armand Pinsard of N.78 shot down a two-seater north of Somme-Py—his 8th victory—while a Farman and a Caudron crew each claimed one EA shot down during the day.

The Germans had several losses: Vizefeldwebel Ludwig Demmel and Unteroffizier Simon Stebel of Schutzstaffel 26 were both killed near Neubriesach; Leutnant August Schlorf and Oberleutnant Erich Schwidder of FA(A)251 were brought down near Wibeah Ferme, Pauvres, north-east of Reims; Leutnant Otto Druck and Unteroffizier Erich Hartmann of FA(A)243 were shot down near Diebolshausen, Alsace; and Leutnant Friedrich Bierling of FA(A)253, was killed just west of Anicy le Château. Another two-seater observer, Leutnant Theodor Aichele of FA14 was killed at Rusach in Alsace. KG4 also lost Leutnant Kurt Matthias, who was brought down with his pilot—Ruger—at Clermont les Fermes. The losses from SS26 and FA(A)251 were probably caused by N.93.

By far the most serious loss to the Germans this day was that of Helmut Baldamus of Jasta 9 shortly before midday. The unit was in combat with Nieuport Scouts of N.37 near St Marie-a-Py, Baldamus colliding with Caporal Simon, both German and Frenchman falling to their deaths. The Germans gave credit to Baldamus for the Nieuport, his 18th and final victory.

Another victory this day went to Eduard Dostler of Jasta 34, south-west of St Mihiel, while Flakzug 79, 171 and 413 claimed another Spad south-east of Moyenmoutier. For once, the Germans seemed to have claimed more aircraft than actually lost.

However, on the French front, the British 3 Naval Wing mounted a raid upon Freiburg, Germany, just across the Rhine south of Strasbourg. It was planned as the Wing's last bomb raid before reorganisation and supposedly as a reprisal for the recent sinking of hospital ships. The bombing force comprised Sopwith two-seaters and they were intercepted by Jasta 35, who shot down two of the Strutters, Vizefeldwebel Gustav Schindler claiming N5171 down at Schlettstadt, and Vizefeldwebel Rudolf Rath N5117 down at Scherweiler. A third Sopwith (9667) was brought down by ground fire. In one of the downed aircraft was Wing Commander C E H Rathborne, and although he was taken prisoner, he was later to escape. In the 1930s he would command the RAF in the Mediterranean as an Air Commodore CB DSO & bar. Harold 'Gus' Edwards, one of the other pilots brought down, would become an Air Marshal in the RCAF in WW2. One of the victorious observers, the Australian Bert Hinkler, would gain immortality as a pioneer aviator in the 1920s, flying from Britain to Australia.

The Navy flyers claimed three Albatros Scouts shot down during the raid and Jasta 35 did indeed have three pilots brought down. Leutnant Gerhard Anders was wounded, and so was Leutnant Margraf. The third was the Staffelführer, Oberleutnant Herbert Theurich, flying a DIII 2097/16, who was mortally wounded.

The Germans also claimed two French balloons, one to Leutnant Fritz Pütter of Jasta 9, 48 Cié east of Suippes and another to Leutnant Hans Adam of Jasta 24, a balloon of 57 Cié west of St Mihiel.

	A/C	KB		DES	OOC	KB
British losses	15	—	British claims	4	9	—
French losses	3	2	French claims	12		1

| German claims | 27† | 2 | German losses | 9 | 1‡ |

† Seven to flak and ground fire. ‡ The Nachrichtenblatt notes nine aircraft lost (four in combat, four missing, one by flak) with two pilots and three observers killed, four pilots and one observer wounded, plus one balloon lost.

British Casualties

Aircraft type	No.	Squadron	Crew		
BE2f	2567	10 Sqdn	2/Lt C W D Holmes	POW	
Sopwith Pup	A661	54 Sqdn	Lt R N Smith	WIA	*
FE2b	7702	11 Sqdn	2/Lt A W Gardner	Unhurt	*
			Cpl W Hodgson	KIA	
Nieuport XXIII	A6794	29 Sqdn	2/Lt E J Pascoe	KIA	
RE8	A78	34 Sqdn	Lt H R Davies	POW	
			Lt J R Samuel	POW	
BE2c	7241	52 Sqdn	2/Lt C T L Donaldson	KIA	
			2/Lt S R Carter	KIA	
BE2c	2562	9 Sqdn	Lt W Harle	POW/WIA	
			2/Lt W B E Cramb	KIA	
Nieuport XXIII	A6772	60 Sqdn	Capt A Binnie MC	POW/WIA	
Nieuport XVII	B1511	60 Sqdn	2/Lt J H Cock	KIA	
Nieuport XVII	B1523	60 Sqdn	2/Lt L C Chapman	DOW	
Nieuport XVII	A6796	60 Sqdn	Lt W O Russell	POW	
Spad VII	A6746	19 Sqdn	Lt E W Capper	KIA	
Spad VII		19 Sqdn	Lt J W Baker	WIA	*
FE2b	4877	25 Sqdn	Lt H E Davies	WIA	
			2/Lt N W Morrison	KIA	
BE2g	6814	5 Sqdn	Capt L C Coates	WIA	*
			2/Lt J C Cotton	WIA	
BE2c	2527	2 Sqdn	Capt G B Lockhart	KIA	
			Lt A P Wilson	KIA	
Sop 1½ Strutter	N5117	3N Wing	WC C E H Rathborne	POW	
			GL/AM1 V Turner	KIA	
Sop 1½ Strutter	N5171	3N Wing	FSL H Edwards	POW	
			GL/AAM1 J L Coghlan	KIA	
Sop 1½ Strutter	9667	3N Wing	Lt G R S Fleming	DOW	
			GL/AM1 A G Lockyer	KIA	
BE2c		42 Sqdn	Lt G C Walker (O)	WIA	*
BE2c		13 Sqdn	2AM W S Boon (O)	WIA	*

French Casualties

Nieuport XVII	2539	N.37	Cpl Simon	KIA
Sopwith 2		N.15	S/Lt de Maison Rouge	DOW
			S/Lt Revi	WIA
Caudron G4		C.225	Lt Floret	Unhurt
			S/Lt Piquet	Unhurt

Sunday, 15 April 1917

British Front

Low cloud and rain which persisted throughout the day precluded any air combat at all on the northern sectors, although Corps aircraft did operate a few recce sorties and a few guns were ranged; otherwise all was quiet. On the ground the Germans made a counter-attack at Lagnicourt, south-east of Arras, opposite Cambrai, breaking into the Australian lines, but were then thrown back from almost all their initial gains during the day. The Australians suffered 1,010 casualties; the Germans 2,313.

Effective co-operation between the RFC and the artillery helped blunt the attack, and there was no interference from Germany's airmen evident. The guns fired over 43,000 shells!

As at this date, RFC HQ listed the following aircraft states:

9th Wing	19 Sqdn	16 Spads
	27 Sqdn	18 G100s
	55 Sqdn	18 DH4s
	56 Sqdn	13 SE5s
		1 Nieuport Scout

57 Sqdn	17 FE2ds	
66 Sqdn	19 Sopwith Pups	
70 Sqdn	19 Sop 1½ Strutters	
SD Flt	5 BE12/2cs	
I Brigade	69 BE2s	(2,5,10 and 16 Sqdns)
	11 FE2bs	(25 Sqdn)
	3 FE2ds	„
	17 Nieuports	(40 Sqdn)
	15 Sop 1½ Strutters	(43 Sqdn)
	17 Sopwith Triplanes	(8N Sqdn)
II Brigade	24 BE2s	(6 and 53 Sqdns)
	44 RE8s	(21 and 42 Sqdns)
	17 Nieuport XIIs	(46 Sqdn)
	18 Nieuport Scouts	(1 Sqdn)
	17 FE2ds	(20 Sqdn)
	18 FE8s	(41 Sqdn)
	16 Sop 1½ Strutters	(45 Sqdn)
III Brigade	70 BE2s	(8, 12 and 13 Sqdns)
	18 RE8s	(59 Sqdn)
	18 AWFK8s	(35 Sqdn)
	26 FE2bs	(11 and 100 Sqdns)
	36 Nieuport Scouts	(29 and 60 Sqdns)
	11 BF2as	(48 Sqdn)
	18 Sopwith Triplanes	(1N Sqdn)
IV Brigade	56 BE2s	(7, 9 and 52 Sqdns)
	16 RE8s	(34 Sqdn)
	17 FE2bs	(22 Sqdn)
	18 DH2s	(24 Sqdn)
	18 Sopwith Pups	(54 Sqdn)
	13 Nieuports	(6N Sqdn)
V Brigade	17 Morane Parasols	(3 Sqdn)
	35 BEs	(4 and 15 Sqdns)
	18 Spads	(19 and 23 Sqdns)
	18 DH2s	(32 Sqdn)
	17 FE2bs	(23 Sqdn)
	17 Nieuports/Pups	(3N Sqdn)

In the general Order of Battle there had been only a few subtle changes since the start of the month, although one or two squadrons had changed equipment and bases. One squadron (No.42) had now been equipped with RE8s, so with the other two units, there were now 78 on the front. But still the main Corps machine was the various BE2s—numbering 259—taking the brunt of the artillery and contact patrol work.

Fighters—that is Pups, Triplanes, Spads and Nieuports—only totalled 143. The DH2s and FE8s were hardly being used, the units which had them awaiting new equipment. The single unit of Bristol Fighters was now down to just 11 machines, and the main long distance fighting was being handled by the FE2 squadrons which had 90 aircraft on strength (the other FEs were used by 100 Squadron for night bombing). Long distance recce missions were in the main being flown by the three RFC 1½ Strutter units. The new AWFK8 would soon prove itself as a front line recce and contact patrol machine that also took to bombing, ground attack and artillery work.

The one glimmer of hope in Trenchard's arsenal was the arrival of the first of the promised 'new types' from England—the single-seat SE5. No.56 Squadron had arrived from England on 7 April, although its pilots were still working-up at their base at Vert Galand, north of Amiens, on the Amiens-Doullens road. Its 13 machines were the forerunners of several thousand of the type—mainly the improved SE5a—to be built and see action over France for the remainder of the war and which, with the Sopwith Camel that began to arrive later in the year, would bear the brunt of the fighter air war. But for April 1917, 56 would be the only SE5 squadron in front line service.

The reason why 56 had a single Nieuport on charge was due to its senior flight commander, the famous and well-known Captain Albert Ball DSO MC, who had scored over

30 victories (of the period) during 1916 while still only 20 years old. In deference to his ability with and liking of the Nieuport, he was allowed to have a personal one for his own use—B1522—a type XVII. Ball made two lone flights across the lines on the 14th although 56 itself would not make its first war patrols until the 18th.

French Front

Still Nivelle was not ready to start his offensive. At 1040, Lieutenant Albert Deullin of Spa.73 claimed a German aircraft shot down over Festieux—the only positive encounter of the day. The only German loss admitted to was a two-seater of FA(A)242, lost to ground fire. A pilot, Unteroffizier Franz Kassel of FA2, was killed, while Leutnant Paul Dörr of FA45 was wounded, and died on 17 April.

However, the German fighter pilots were more successful. In a fight with N.15, Leutnant Dossenbach of Jasta 36, having already forced a Nieuport Scout of N.83 down into French lines at Betheny near Reims with a wounded pilot, shot down Adjutant Epitalon at St Fergeux. Two more N.15 pilots fell, one over Thugny to Vizefeldwebel Hans Mitkeit, also of Jasta 36, and Lieutenant Bergeron to Unteroffizier Max Zachmann of Jasta 21, falling near Sery at 1030. Leutnant Werner Albert, Staffelführer of Jasta 31 downed another Spad of N.3—the Storks Group—over Nauroy, north of Reims.

A Spad of N.102 which fell near Prouvais was the 4th victory of Vizefeldwebel Julius Bückler, a future leading ace who would end the war with 35 victories and the Pour le Mérite.

Two Nieuports failed to get back, Dossenbach's and a machine of N.519 on the Nancy front. The only claim for a second Nieuport was that made by Leutnant Dotzel of Jasta 19, his one and only victory, which fell into the French lines at La Neuvillette.

The crew of Schusta 10 claimed a Farman over Oulcher Wald, although there are no Farmans listed as lost, but a Salmson-Moineau of F.71 was hit and its pilot wounded, although this is believed to have been caused by AA fire.

	A/C	KB			DES	OOC	KB
British losses	—	—	British claims		—	—	—
French losses	6	—	French claims		1		—
German claims	8	—	German losses		1		—

British Casualties
Nil

French Casualties

Aircraft type	No.	Squadron	Crew		
Nieuport XXIII	2539	N.519	Adj Sirieys	MIA	
Nieuport XXIII		N.83	S/Lt Senechal	WIA	*
Spad VII	1059	N.15	Lt Bergeron	POW	
Spad VII	1234	N.15	Adj Epitalon	POW	
Spad VII	373	N.15	Sgt Buisson	POW	
Spad VII	117	N.3	Sgt Papeil	MIA	
Spad VII	1056	N.102	Cpl Quaissaron	MIA	
Salmson-Moineau		F.71	MdL Wang (P)	WIA	*

Monday, 16 April 1917

THE READER MUST NOTE that on this day the times changed on the Western Front. From now until 9 April 1918 German time was one hour ahead of Allied time, and any historians or enthusiasts trying to match events should remember to take account of the time difference.

British Front

There seemed little let-up in the poor weather, rain and low clouds persisting all day although there were a few bright intervals. Despite this there was more activity along the Arras front, with contact patrols, artillery observation and recce missions all being flown. This naturally brought up the German fighters with the consequential casualties. Men died in those few bright intervals.

A Line Patrol and recce sortie was flown by 43 Squadron, starting out at 0630, to La Bassée and Bailleul. They encountered a two-seater of Schutzstaffel 4 over Douai, Leutnant Figulla and Unteroffizier Steudel making a fight of it at 0810 which resulted in the Strutter falling with a dead gunner and a wounded pilot. Further south, FEs of 18 Squadron were flying a photo op and escort sortie and had a fight with German single-seaters. One of the observers was Lieutenant O J Partington, formally of the Queen's Royal West Sussex Regiment. He recorded in his log-book:

'16.4.17. FE 4898 pilot [2/Lt E W A] Hunt. 6.55—9.10 am.
    11,000 ft, visibility poor owing to clouds; archies good. Formation attacked by six HA, one shot down. Combat north-east of Cagnicourt. Followed HA down to 4,000 ft when he disappeared into clouds; we then went home. Steam tractor seen moving NW on road Cambrai-Arras.'

The Squadron, in fact, claimed two Albatros DIIIs out of control over Cagnicourt.

Whether 60 Squadron had got over its defeat of two days earlier cannot be known, but the pilots must have had it on their minds this day when they took off at 0805 to fly a patrol to the Vitry area. Jasta 11 rose to meet them. At 0930 (1030 German time) the two formations met. In a running fight between Biache and Roeux, Lothar von Richthofen, Wolff and Festner each shot down one Nieuport. In fact four Nieuports went down, three of the British pilots being killed while the fourth died at Douai the next day. Lieutenant Pidcock drove down two enemy aircraft but made no substantial claim. Nobody seems to have claimed or been credited with the fourth Nieuport.

The next action came during an artillery observation sortie by a BE2d of 7 Squadron. It attracted anti-aircraft fire in the early afternoon, and was hit and shot down near Savy, accounted for by KFlak 93, falling just inside British lines with a wounded crew. A Morane from 3 Squadron also returned from a sortie with a wounded observer, probably the 'BE' claimed by KFlak 63 north-west of St Quentin. A pilot of 9 Squadron was also wounded during the day.

The final loss came in mid-afternoon: another artillery crew, this one ranging for guns on 17 Corps' front. Manfred von Richthofen, having missed out on the morning show, was out hunting, spotting the BE two-seater belonging to 13 Squadron north of Gavrelle. He attacked unseen, his fire causing the BE to smoke as it fell. The wounded pilot just managed to scrape over the lines, landed and turned over. The machine was smashed up and then shelled, so the Baron had his 45th victory, and Jasta 11 its 56th of the month.

At 1650 German time, Heinrich Gontermann attacked the British balloon lines at Manancourt, north of Peronne. He flamed a balloon of the 6th Company (6-15-4), and then went for one of the 29th Company. Ground observers saw and reported the Albatros flying round and round the balloon as it was pulled down, firing at it from well below 2,000 feet but it did not catch fire. Gontermann must have believed he'd damaged it sufficiently to claim a kill, although it may be significant that while the first balloon was his 10th official victory, he had been credited with six more kills before the second balloon was made official, to become his 17th victory. However, it seems that his second balloon was a 14th Company one (14-14-4), lost this day.

French Front

General Nivelle finally launched his attack, named the Second Battle of the Aisne. Aerial activity, therefore, was great along the Aisne sector with casualties high.

Fighter squadrons flew in support of their bombing and recce machines, three German aircraft being claimed as shot down, one each by N.12 (S/Lt Henri Languedoc) at 0600 east of Cauroy, and N73 (Brig Rigault) at 1025 over Cormicy, and the third by N.26 (Brig Thomassin) west of Juvincourt. In addition, balloons were claimed as destroyed by N.73 (also Brig Rigault) at Bruyères at 1510 and another by N.67 (Cpl Cordelier) at Gros Usage. Another aircraft was claimed by gunners of F.72 and C.222 during a bomb raid north of Hermonville.

On the French front the Germans lost Leutnant Hans-Olaf Esser of Jasta 15, killed near Winterberge; the two-seater Abteilungen lost Leutnant Karl Helbig (O) of FA278 on the Aisne sector; Leutnant Hans-Jurgen Kalmus (O) of FA208 over Liesse; and Leutnant Walter Utermann (O) of FA(A)248 over Juvincourt (possibly Thomassin's victim). The crew of Unteroffizier Walter Koppen and Leutnant Heinrich Wecke of FA(A)248 fell over Villers Franqueux. Another single-seat pilot shot down was Vizefeldwebel Rieger of Jasta 17. His controls were damaged and in crash-landing he was severely injured.

The French, however, paid a heavy price. A Caudron G4 was attacked by five enemy fighters and crashed north of Sapigneul—probably the victim of Emil Thuy of Jasta 21 who downed a Caudron near Berry-au-Bac at 1505. Four fighters were lost, three Nieuports and a Spad. Three Nieuports were claimed by Leutnant H Wendel of Jasta 15 over Prouvais, Vizefeldwebel Buckler of Jasta 17 over Berry-au-Bac, and Unteroffizier Janning and Gefreiter Reimers of Schusta 5, north-west of Reims. The Spad was claimed by another two-seater crew, Gefreiter May and Unteroffizier Wiehle of Schusta 3, over Corbeny.

The fourth Nieuport was brought down by AA fire and flown by an American volunteer with the Lafayette Escadrille, Caporal Edmund Genet of N.124. Raoul Lufbery was leading a patrol between St Quentin and La Fere when they came under AA fire, shells bursting close to Genet's machine. The American turned for home, presumably wounded or his aircraft damaged, but then went into a spin, the wings of the Nieuport coming off, and it finally ploughed into the ground near Ham.

Another Caudron failed to return—from C.47, probably the one attacked by Leutnants Rose and Parlow of Jasta 22, east of Cernay. Several other two-seaters were hit by ground fire and a number of airmen were brought back wounded.

French balloons were once more a target, Josef Jacobs of Jasta 22 claiming one during the afternoon despite interference from several Caudrons. Jasta 22 had in fact taken a leaf from the RFC's book on this day, Jacobs and Vizefeldwebel Graf Biessel strafing French trenches and forward observation posts.

	A/C	KB		DES	OOC	KB
British losses	7	2	British claims	—	2	—
French losses	6	—	French claims	4		2
German claims	16†	3	German losses	6		2‡

† Three by flak. ‡ The Nachrichtenblatt states four of the losses were Schusta aircraft of the 7 Armee; five pilots/observers killed or wounded, one observer missing. Two balloons lost with their observers killed.

British Casualties

Aircraft type	No.	Squadron	Crew		
Sop 1½ Strutter	A7804	43 Sqdn	2/Lt J G Frew	POW/WIA	
			1AM F Russell	KIA	
Nieuport XVII	B1501	60 Sqdn	2/Lt D N Robertson	KIA	
Nieuport XVII	B1509	60 Sqdn	Lt J Mc Elliott	KIA	
Nieuport XVII	B1507	60 Sqdn	Lt T Langwill	DOW	
Nieuport XXIII	A6769	60 Sqdn	2/Lt R E Kimbell	KIA	
BE2d	5869	7 Sqdn	2/Lt W Green	WIA	
			2/Lt C E Wilson	KIA	
BE2e	3156	13 Sqdn	2/Lt A Pascoe	WIA	
			2/Lt F S Andrews	DOW	
BE2c	7163	9 Sqdn	2/Lt W R Baldwin (P)	WIA	*
Morane Parasol		3 Sqdn	1AM H Copstake (O)	WIA	*

French Casualties

Aircraft type	No.	Squadron	Crew		
Caudron G4		C.228	Sgt Pissavi	KIA	
			S/Lt Bekkers	KIA	
Farman 40		F.41	Lt Clavier (O)	KIA	*
Nieuport XXIII	2827	N.75	Lt Moreau	MIA	
Nieuport XVII		N.124	Cpl E C C Genet	KIA	
Nieuport XXIII		N.65	Cpl Cavinet-Lagrange	MIA	
Spad VII		Spa.48	S/Lt P de Larminat	MIA	
Caudron G4		C.47	S/Lt Houmens	MIA	

Nieuport XXIV	N.83	Brig Thomassin	WIA	*
Nieuport XXIII	N.83	MdL Dagonnet	WIA	*
Farman 40	F.226	S/Lt Desmyttere (O)	WIA	*
Farman 40	F.8	Lt Leloup (O)	WIA	*
Salmson-Moineau	SM.106	Lt Crosnier (O)	WIA	*
Caudron G4	C.47	Lt Caudillot (O)	WIA	*
Caudron G4	C.39	Lt Petit (O)	WIA	*
Caudron G4	C.104	Asp Humbert (O)	WIA	*
Farman 40	F.206	S/Lt Cote (O)	WIA	*
Sopwith 2	F.16	Lt Goisbaualt (O)	WIA	*
Farman 40	F.201	Lt Touard-Riolle (O)	WIA	*

Tuesday, 17 April 1917

British Front

With rain almost non-stop throughout the day there was very little aerial activity over the front. A few Corps aircraft registered for some artillery fire and some recce work was achieved but that was all. Lieutenant F Wessel, a Danish volunteer with 15 Squadron, successfully ranged guns of the 152nd Siege Battery on some new wire, five direct hits being achieved. During the night of 17/18th, FE2 of 100 Squadron flew bombing raids to a transport park at Cantin and some MT columns near Brebières. There were no losses.

French Front

A similar story here, with just one casualty, a Farman pilot being wounded by AA fire.

On the ground the French ground assault was already starting to falter. The attack against Laffaux which began the previous day, despite strong artillery support and barrage of the previous ten days, was not going well. It appears that the French commanders had not taken fully into account the natural obstacles their troops would encounter. The French V and VI Armees trying to go forward in the Chemin des Dames area—the buttress of the Campagne front—faced prepared defenders holding higher ground. These inflicted crippling casualties on the French troops. In just over a month this would lead to many desertions followed by the famous French army mutinies.

		French Casualties		
Aircraft type	No.	Squadron	Crew	
Farman 42		F.54	Adj Gealagas (P)	WIA

Wednesday, 18 April 1917

British Front

Low clouds and rain prevented all work. One German two-seater of FA17 was shot down by infantry fire. On the ground, however, the British moved on Epehy and captured Villers-Guislan.

French Front

Despite the casualties, the French troops managed to drive into German positions to take Chavonne and Chivy, advancing as far as Braye-en-Laonnais, reporting several thousands of prisoners and 75 guns. There were no claims in the air but a Spad VII of N.78 was lost, claimed by MFlak 54 near Donnrein. At 0800 Leutnant Joens of Jasta 31 reported downing a Voisin at Auberive for his first victory.

	A/C	KB		DES	OOC	KB
British losses	—	—	British claims	—	—	—
French losses	1	—	French claims	—		—
German claims	2†	—	German losses	1‡		—

† One to flak. ‡ Infantry fire.

		French Casualties		
Aircraft type	No.	Squadron	Crew	
Spad VII		N.78	S/Lt de Pasquier	MIA

Thursday, 19 April 1917

British Front

The wet weather continued all day, and practically no work was possible. A balloon of the 14th Section was attacked by a German aircraft and damaged but there was no claim made. The only casualty of the day was the balloon company commander of the 17th Company, Major A C B Geddes MC, killed by shell-fire.

French Front

Some slight activity resulted in five combat claims, although only two are recorded in any detail: an LVG two-seater was brought down by Sous Lieutenant Paul Tarascon of N.62 east of Trucy for his 10th victory, and Sous Lieutenant René Dorme of N.3 scored his 19th kill by downing a single-seater north-east of Brimont at 1450.

The Germans admitted one aircraft lost in combat and one officer wounded by ground fire, but at least two men were killed. Schutzstaffel 28 lost an aircraft in combat with a Caudron (possibly one of the three French claims where no details have been found), Gefreiter Hermann Brauer landing unhurt, but his observer, Unteroffizier Friedrich Schneider, was hit in the head and killed, the machine being forced down at Warmoville, near Prosnes. Brauer survived until his own death over Zonnebeke in July. Leutnant Paul Herrmann of Jasta 31 was killed in action in combat with a Spad over Bois Malvel—probably the victim of René Dorme. The French ace claimed his 19th official victory north-east of Brimont at 1450.

Escadrille N.38 lost a Morane Parasol, and N.69 had a pilot wounded. The Morane was brought down at Prosnes, south-east of Reims, by Leutnant Willi Daugs of Jasta 36 for his first victory. Other claims by the Jasta pilots comprised a Spad by Leutnant Werner Marwitz of Jasta 9 south-west of Auberive at 1100; Leutnant Adolf Frey of the same unit downed a Farman south of Moranvillers; and Leutnant Richard Wenzl of Jasta 31 also claimed a Spad in the same area, all three locations being within the French lines.

	A/C	KB		DES	OOC	KB
British losses	—	—	British claims	1	—	—
French losses	1	—	French claims	5		—
German claims	4	—	German losses	1		—

French Casualties					
Aircraft type	No.	Squadron	Crew		
Spad VII		N.69	Lt Conneau	WIA	*
Morane Parasol		N.38	Capt Fevre	KIA	
			Lt de Broglie-Revel	KIA	

Friday, 20 April 1917

British Front

British troops took Gonnelieu. After three days of wet weather the rain eased but left a pall of mist and low cloud over the battle front, making the work of the RFC very difficult. But the aeroplanes were out in small packages, 15 Squadron operating a BE over the 5th Corps area on artillery observation duties until attacked by five aircraft of Jasta 12. The BE had flown out at 0620 and was intercepted at 0735, Jasta 12's Vizefeldwebel Arthur Schörisch claiming his victim at 0940(G) near Ecoust St Mein, inside the British lines. The pilot was the same Danish volunteer, Lieutenant Wessel, who had ranged so successfully three days earlier.

Another BE, from 8 Squadron, took off at 0745, and was attacked by a German aircraft, damaged and forced to land, probably by the crew of Leutnant Peters and Vizefeldwebel Schopf of FA235 who forced down an aircraft near Vimy, although they claimed it was a 'Vickers'.

In the afternoon Sopwith 1½ Strutters of 43 Squadron flew a line patrol over the Loos Salient and seeing troops, descended to 200 feet to fire at small parties on the Gavrelle-Fresnes road. Second Lieutenant the Hon. S H D'Arcy and Lieutenant A E Pickering dispersed several of these as well as troops in some trenches, but Second Lieutenants Crisp and Newenham were not so fortunate and were brought down by ground fire from Flakzug 46. Newenham had only joined the Squadron on 8 April.

AA fire also accounted for the other loss of the day, a 16 Squadron BE2f which started as patrol at 1610 between Avion and Willerval and was shot down by Flakbatterie 503 between Fresnoy and Oppy.

Lieutenant W A Bishop of 60 Squadron claimed an Aviatik two-seater in flames over Biache-St-Vaast at 1458. The Germans only record an observer killed near Peronne, 40 km to the south of Bishop's claim.

French Front

French troops occupied Sancy on the Vregny plateau, while areas near Moron-Villiers in the Champagne region were taken. In air actions no claims were made in the south. Two Farmans were attacked, one being brought down by Leutnant Schurz of Jasta 13 at Landricourt. The Germans had a Jasta 10 pilot wounded, Vizefeldwebel Viktor Hebben, but the cause is uncertain.

	A/C	KB		DES	OOC	KB
British losses	3	—	British claims	1	—	—
French losses	1	—	French claims	—	—	—
German claims	6†	—	German losses	—	—	—
† Three by flak.						

British Casualties

Aircraft type	No.	Squadron	Crew		
BE2c	A2868	15 Sqdn	Lt F F Wessel	WIA	
			2/Lt S E Toomer	Unhurt	
BE2e	A2823	8 Sqdn	Lt J D McCall	Unhurt	*
			2/Lt F J Martin	Unhurt	
Sop 1½ Strutter	A1098	43 Sqdn	2/Lt A E Crisp	POW/WIA	
			2/Lt G A Newenham	POW/WIA	
BE2f	2553	16 Sqdn	Sgt J Dangerfield	POW	
			2AM E D Harvey	POW	

French Casualties

Farman 42	F.1	Adj Bondaire	KIA	
		Lt Blanchi	DOW	
Farman 60	F.44	Lt le Barbu (O)	WIA	*

Saturday, 21 April 1917

British Front

Low cloud and mist prevailed most of the day, not clearing until 1700 hours. Some recce and artillery observation work was carried out on the Arras front and 9 Squadron scored a particular success. Captain Lowcock and Lieutenant Macartney spotted a motor convoy moving along a road and sent out a Zone Call to the guns. Artillery fire destroyed the road ahead of the trucks and lorries then blasted them to destruction.

In the land fighting, British troops gained ground along the northern banks of the Scarpe River, east of Fampoux.

Evidence of the mist and cloud came as a 32 Squadron DH2 crashed into trees in the early afternoon at the unit's forward landing ground, killing the pilot. Captain Billinge had led a sortie to the enemy balloon lines between Bapaume and Cambrai but three enemy fighters were seen patrolling above them so they came back.

Of the many artillery squadrons operating, it was to prove a rough day for 16 Squadron's BEs. At 1345, Second Lieutenants Bishop and Milligan took off to operate over Vimy and they were brought down by AA fire inside British lines where their machine was wrecked—probably the BE claimed by KFlak 105 north of Vimy. Shortly after 1500 the Squadron sent out aircraft to fly a photo op over Vimy and were met by Jasta 11. Kurt Wolff despatched a BE, which went down in flames between Vimy and Maricourt. In some records, Lothar von Richthofen also shot down a BE, and a second 16 Squadron machine was brought down at about this time, although other records only note him with one kill on the 21st (see next paragraph) and another unconfirmed.

Just as this fight was going on, a six-man flight of 29 Squadron, led by Captain E F Elderton was taking off on an OP of the front now that the Corps aircraft were out. They too fell victim to Jasta 11 as soon as they reached the lines. Coming down on the Nieuports from the broken cloud, three went down under the guns of Lothar, Wolff and Schäfer. It brought Jasta 11's victories for the month so far to a devastating 60—for no loss! (Other than Festner's forced landing on the 16th.) Or was it no loss. Karl Schäfer in fact crash-landed near the front line after another combat—chasing a BE2 at low level—having then been hit by ground fire, but he got back to Douai that night, so at least one of the Jasta's Albatros Scouts may have been lost or certainly badly damaged.

Further south, at 1730, between Queant and Cagnicourt, the Pups of 3 Naval had a fight with some Albatros DIIIs, claiming three out of control and one destroyed. J J Malone (N6208) also claimed a two-seater Albatros out of control at 1740, five miles north of Queant.

An aircraft the Germans did not apparently claim was a 25 Squadron FE2 on a photo op in the late afternoon. The crew of Captain J L Leitch and Lieutenant G M A Hobart-Hampden were engaged by enemy aircraft and badly shot up but the pilot got them back over the lines where they later crashed at 1845, but the flyers themselves were safe. However, the crew did claim an Albatros shot down, while the other crew claimed one driven down which was then finished off by a RNAS pilot. Pilots of 8 Naval Squadron who were patrolling nearby came to the two pushers' assistance and were quickly in the fight. Flight Sub Lieutenant R A Little and Flight Lieutenant A R Arnold each claimed Scouts brought down, Rex Arnold's coming down inside British lines. It was given the RFC number G.22.

It was a fine effort by Rex Arnold, for his gun had jammed soon after attacking the first Albatros but he continued to harass the other Germans, trying to frighten them off. After a few moments of this, he looked down but could not see the FE although he did see a German aircraft falling towards the ground with two of its planes floating down slowly after it.

Bob Little, meantime, had engaged three Albatros Scouts claiming one out of control, but then the FE stalled and Little almost flew into it, the fighting being so close. His gun shoot then broke and he had to break off but saw the FE gliding west and went down towards it. He followed it until it hit the ground near Bouvigny Wood. Little then landed beside the FE to see if he could be of help but both crew members were all right. Little would make a similar landing on the 24th but with an embarrassing ending.

It was Jasta 30 pilots who were in the fight with 25 and 8 Naval and they lost Leutnant Gustav Nernst who fell into the British lines near Arras. He had attacked the FE flown by Lieutenant R G Malcolm and Second Lieutenant J B Weir (A8373), was hit by their fire, then finished off by Rex Arnold, in Triplane N5458. Flying Albatros DIII 2147/16, Leutnant Oskar Seitz, who had been with the Jasta just five days, was brought down by Bob Little (N5449, after presumably crippling Leitch's FE) but got away with a crash landing. However, there is some suggestion that Nernst and Seitz in fact collided first.

Among two-seater losses this day, Unteroffizier Brosius and Leutnant Koehler of Schusta 11 were brought down on the Arras front, while Flieger Julius Oettinger of FA275 died of wounds. Lieutenant R H Stocken of 23 Squadron, flying a Spad (A6697), claimed a two-seater out of control over Souchy-Lestrée, north-west of Cambrai at 1810. This and Malone's C-type at 1740 were the only German two-seaters claimed this date.

French Front

On the ground Nivelle's offensive was becoming bogged down while the casualties amongst his troops became nothing less than appalling. The battle area was littered with dead and wounded, lives thrown away for a few yards of dirt. Sadly a feature of the war on the Western Front.

For once, on a day seeing some air action, the French recorded no combat losses but did achieve some victories. Sous Lieutenant Henri Languedoc of N.12 gained his 7th victory by bringing down an enemy aircraft over Somme-Suippes, but the day went to Armand Pinsard of Spa.78.

His first victory of the day was over Leutnant Wichard of Jasta 24, flying Albatros DIII 2096/16, who came down between Nauroy and Moronvillers where he was taken prisoner. His machine became well known due to a number of photographs of it appearing in several magazines and books, with the large-lettered name VERA painted on the fuselage. It was later sent to America where it was photographed even more.

Pinsard's second victory came that evening. This time he shot down Leutnant Gunther von der Heyde of Jasta 9, whose comrades last saw him in action with three Spads over Nauroy at 2000 hours.

	A/C	KB			DES	OOC	KB
British losses	7	—	British claims		5	7	—
French losses	—	—	French claims		3		—
German claims	6†	—	German losses		4‡		—

† Includes two by flak. ‡ The Nachrichtenblatt notes one two-seater and three scouts missing.

British Casualties

Aircraft type	No.	Squadron	Crew	
BE2g	A2888	16 Sqdn	2/Lt Bishop	Unhurt
			2/Lt C N Milligan	WIA
BE2g	A2766	16 Sqdn	Capt E J D Routh	WIA
			2/Lt MacKenzie	Unhurt
BE2g	A2915	16 Sqdn	2/Lt J P C Mitchell	KIA
			Lt G R Rogers	MIA
Nieuport XXIII	A6797	29 Sqdn	2/Lt F Sadler	KIA
Nieuport XVII	A6755	29 Sqdn	2/Lt C V deB Rogers	KIA
Nieuport XXIII	B1568	29 Sqdn	2/Lt A B Morgan	DOW
FE2d	A6383	25 Sqdn	Capt J L Leitch	Unhurt
			Lt G M A Hobart-Hampden	Unhurt

French Casualties
Nil

Sunday, 22 April 1917

British Front

Today the aviators of both sides awoke to fine but cloudy weather. With the ground fighting still going on around Havrincourt Wood and Trescault village, as well as south-east of Loos, although on a reduced scale, Haig was anxiously waiting on the break-out from Nivelle's offensive. Still trying to exert pressure on the British sectors, the flyers needed to be up for artillery shoots and contact patrols.

Three Triplanes of 1 Naval were out early: Flight Commander R S Dallas, with Flight Sub Lieutenants T G Culling and Carr, taking off at 0430. Carr became separated but the other two found and engaged 14 enemy aircraft—unsupported—making 20 individual attacks and claiming three Scouts shot down, two destroyed and one out of control.

The RFC's 1 Squadron was also out early, nine Nieuports taking off at 0555 to patrol Lille-Seclin-Carvin-La Bassée, led by Captain E D Atkinson. Two aircraft returned home with engine troubles, escorted by a third. This third man was Second Lieutenant E S T Cole and having seen them safely across the lines he headed back, spotting a balloon up over Wervicq. He attacked and shot it down in flames at 0640. The rest of the patrol were engaged by eight fighters, Atkinson and Lieutenant S M Wright claiming two down out of control at 0705(A) but one British pilot failed to make it back. They had fought Jasta 28, Leutnant August Hanko bringing the Nieuport down over Wavrin for his first victory. Lieutenant Walter Wood was taken prisoner.

Nieuports of 60 Squadron were also after balloons, Lieutenants H G Ross and G L Lloyd each burning one north of Drury and Boiry Notre Dame at just after 0700, Lieutenant W E

Molesworth claiming a third smoking. At 0730 Lieutenant A R Penny flamed another at Vis-en-Artois.

Spads of 19 Squadron, led by Lieutenant W E Reed, took off at 0608 to patrol Bailleul-Vitry-Sains-Bullecourt on the north, along with Lieutenants Applin and Hamilton. Applin became separated so when a German two-seater was located, it was just Reed and Hamilton who attacked. Hamilton's gun jammed, forcing him to break off. Reed continued the attack (in B1563) and claimed the Albatros C-type as brought down at Quiery, as well as driving down two others over Courcelles before his gun too jammed. On the way home he was hit by ground fire and slightly wounded.

In this scrap there were also a couple of Naval Triplanes involved but it is uncertain who other than Dallas and Culling were around, although Flight Sub Lieutenant A R Knight popped up from somewhere and claimed an Albatros out of control east of Oppy at 0730, but only Reed claimed a two-seater at this time. It seems apparent that the two-seater was from FA(A)211, flown by Leutnant Martin Mobius (who was wounded) and his observer Leutnant Goldhammer. They came down at 0830(G), so the time is approximately right, although they reported being brought down by two Sopwiths. They may have mis-identified the Spads, and one might assume they would have said Triplanes rather than Sopwiths if Triplanes had been involved. Mobius had only joined FA(A)211 on 10 April but the wound to his leg was not serious and he got their burning machine down without further injury. He was a recipient of the Knight's Cross of the Military St Henry Order in June but was later killed as a fighter pilot with Jasta 7.

The Germans made a determined effort to blind the British with Jasta 5 attacking their balloon lines during the morning. Heinrich Gontermann claimed one at Arras at 0935(G), while Kurt Schneider flamed two, one at Epehy, the other at Essigny-le-Grand, at 1130 and 1145. These latter two were 28 km apart, so he certainly worked hard for his kills.

The British lost balloons of No.3 and 14 Sections. Gontermann got the 3rd Section's (a second claim was disallowed), Schneider getting the 14th, then a French balloon of 55 Cié. (In the afternoon, Nathanael of Jasta 5 attacked and was credited with another balloon at Bus—perhaps Section 13.) At No.16 Section at Ficheaux, Arras, Captain E A Twidale (Canadian) was killed due to his parachute failing to deploy when he jumped during an attack—probably Gontermann's second effort. Major R L Farley, No.10 Balloon Company commander, and 2/Lt C W Berry of the 28th Section were also wounded.

With one exception (see later) this ended the morning action (apart from a single Albatros Scout claimed out of control by Bishop of 60 Squadron east of Vimy at 1120) and it was not until the early afternoon that aircraft clashed once more. 11 Squadron flew a photo operation and ran into the exuberant Jasta 11 at 1610.

Manfred von Richthofen led his staffel down onto the pushers, shooting one down at Lagnicourt, just inside the British lines, Kurt Wolff getting his to fall at Hendecourt. A third FE was badly shot about and caught fire in the air, the pilot finding most of his controls shot away. His observer fell mortally wounded, slumping over the side of his front cockpit. Lieutenant C A Parker grabbed onto him as he brought the FE down for a forced landing, then got him out of the burning aeroplane, carrying him to cover despite falling shell fire. Unfortunately the man succumbed to his wounds. Four other FEs returned with wounded observers, one making a forced landing, another a crash-landing. However, despite the losses, Jasta 11 were only credited with two kills, even though Parker's FE must have been seen to land on fire as well as being subsequently shelled.

Meantime, Spads of 23 Squadron were escorting more FEs, this time those of 18 Squadron. At 1900 they came under attack from Jasta 12 and 5 between Marcoing and Havrincourt Wood. Two of the Spads were quickly shot down, one by von Osterroht the Jasta 12 Staffelführer, the other by Nathanael of Jasta 5, whose victim fell at Ribecourt. Vizefeldwebel Reinhold Jorke was credited with another Spad seen to go down over the British lines but although the British pilot was wounded he got down safely. Leutnant Röth also received credit for an aeroplane shot down over Marcoing, but it is unclear who or what this might have been, as all the known British losses have been accounted for. One of 18 Squadron's FEs was hit by ground fire, its pilot wounded.

Jasta 11's Kurt Wolff ended the day's scoring by downing a 3 Squadron Morane at 2005(G), also near Havrincourt. Karl Schäfer was also credited with a BE at 2020(G) west of Monchy in the British lines. There is no corresponding British loss; the only BE coming down during the day was a 13 Squadron machine which had taken off that morning at 0644. It came down just north of Fampoux. If there has been a mistake with the time, and the claim was at 0820 (0720 Allied time), then time and approximate location might fit. Suggestions that this was another of the downed FEs do not stand up as regards time, being more than an hour after the FE action of the afternoon.

French Front

Three hostile aircraft were brought down on the Soissons front by French fighter pilots, two at least being two-seaters. Lieutenant Albert Deullin gained his 14th victory with a kill at 1750 west of Craonne, then N.3's Sous Lieutenant René Dorme and Capitaine Alfred Auger scored their 20th and 4th victories respectively with two-seaters at 1835 and 1910, over Beaurieux and Lierval.

Lierval is 4 km from Chevrigny where FA212 lost the crew of Unteroffizier Gustav Richter and Leutnant Erich Bersu. Another crew, Flieger Albert Karzmarek and Unteroffizier Karl Schulz, came down at Oulcherswald and Oulchers is just to the west of Craonne. All four men died.

Losses amounted to just one Caudron G4 of C.42, claimed by Leutnant Gerlt of Jasta 19 and his first and only victory, over St Etienne.

	A/C	KB		DES	OOC	KB
British losses	7	2	British claims	2	15	5
French losses	1	1	French claims	3		—
German claims	10	4	German losses	3		1†

† According to the Nachrichtenblatt, which also records one pilot and two observers wounded.

British Casualties

Aircraft type	No.	Squadron	Crew		
Nieuport XVII	A313	1 Sqdn	Lt A W Wood	POW/WIA	
BE2e	7089	13 Sqdn	2/Lt H S Robertson	Safe	*
			Lt G J Farmer	Safe	
FE2b	A5501	11 Sqdn	Sgt T K Hollis	DOW	
			Lt B J Tolhurst	KIA	
FE2b	A5500	11 Sqdn	2/Lt J J Paine	Injured	
			2/Lt J Rothwell	Injured	
FE2b	A820	11 Sqdn	Lt C A Parker	Safe	
			Lt J E B Hesketh	DOW	
FE2b	A810	11 Sqdn	Capt E R Manning	Safe	*
			Cpl R Tollerfield	WIA	
FE2b	7020	11 Sqdn	Lt W F Fletcher	WIA	*
			Lt W Franklin	WIA	
FE2b		11 Sqdn	2AM J F Carr (O)	WIA	*
FE2b		11 Sqdn	2/Lt P A de Escofet (O)	WIA	*
Spad VII	A6695	23 Sqdn	2/Lt K R Furniss	POW/DOW	
Spad VII	A6682	23 Sqdn	2/Lt F C Craig	POW	
Spad VII		23 Sqdn	Capt K C McCallum	WIA	*
FE2b		18 Sqdn	Capt H L H Owen (P)	WIA	*
Morane Parasol	A6727	3 Sqdn	2/Lt F L Carter	KIA	
			Cpl A E Morgan	MIA	
BE2c		13 Sqdn	2/Lt L A Davis	WIA	*
			2/Lt G G Fairbairn	WIA	
Nieuport Scout		29 Sqdn	2/Lt W P T Watts	WIA	*
Spad VII	B1563	19 Sqdn	Lt W E Reed	WIA	*

French Casualties

Caudron G4		C.42	MdL Le Clerc	MIA	
			Lt Mercier	MIA	

Monday, 23 April 1917

British Front

Today was St George's Day, and with it came fine weather—and death. With the French offensive crumbling Haig launched a new offensive, with the main attack commencing at 0445 along the nine-mile front from Croisilles to Gavrelle covering both sides of the Scarpe River. At the same moment another, smaller attack went towards the south-west of Lens. The British 3rd Army pushed forward to Pelves, Cherisy and Fontaine. All met heavy opposition.

The Army, as usual, were soon calling for information as to where their troops were in the battle area, HQ RFC sending out aircraft to make contact. Not only visual contact, for the soldiers were supposed to signal the aeroplanes with flares, but in the heat of battle, it was not always possible or perhaps advisable to start lighting flares so that some aviator could spot them, so it was difficult. Other aircraft went out to shoot up ground targets, especially troops who might be either holding up the advance, massing for a counter-attack, or reinforcements moving up to the line.

Some early air-fights took place between 0630 and 0800(A), the pilots of 1 and 3 Naval mainly involved. 3 Naval claimed one Albatros Scout destroyed and four out of control between Croisilles and Havrincourt, while further north Dallas and Culling each claimed a DFW two-seater out of control west of Douai.

Captain Albert Ball of 56 Squadron opened the Squadron's account by shooting down an Albatros two-seater over Abancourt at 0645, in his personal Nieuport. He chased another two-seater but its gunner put several bullets through the Nieuport's wings, so Ball broke off.

A BE of 13 Squadron was the RFC's first casualty, flying a contact patrol over the 17th Corps area. It was hit by ground fire 500 yards north of Fampoux and while the pilot got it down safely it was soon wrecked by gunfire. RE8s were also out attacking ground troops, taking a leaf from the Schutzstaffeln book. Sopwith 1½ Strutters and Martinsyde G100s were also sent into the fight, while DH4s took bombs to the rear areas. The bombers were given an escort of Pups from 66 Squadron while Spads would patrol the area too.

Captain C M Clement of 22 Squadron led a six-machine OP and photo sortie, seeing numerous enemy fighters between Cambrai and St Quentin. Over Le Verguier at 0710 they were attacked by six scouts, FE 7681 at the rear of the formation spiralling down in flames. However, the pilot got it down inside British lines where it overturned, although he and his observer were badly burned and the FE destroyed. A 15 Squadron BE was also hit by ground fire near the Hindenburg Line, and returned with a wounded observer.

Offensive Patrols were meant to saturate the battle area, but the sky is a big place and the Germans were expert at dodging the fighters and picking off the two-seaters. AWFK8s—Big Acks—of 35 Squadron entered the arena sending out aircraft at 0900. Two hours later they ran into Jasta 12. It is not clear what happened in this fight. 35 Squadron lost one aircraft which came down at Wancourt on the British side, and Arthur Schörisch claimed one down at this location at 1200(G). Another Big Ack returned home with a wounded gunner. However, Jasta 12 claimed and was credited with four 'Sopwiths' (the AWFK8 being a newish type to the front), which seems rather excessive. Possibly 66 Squadron's Pups may have been involved, although they did not lose anyone.

At 0925 16 Squadron sent out aircraft on a photo op, which were met by the two von Richthofen brothers just after midday German time, 1105 Allied time. Two BEs went down, both falling inside British lines but close enough for them to be reported by German ground observers. Manfred's score rose to 47, Lothar's to ten. Lothar's victims were Second Lieutenants Crow and Turner. In making for the lines, Crow was hit in the head and chest and died instantly, Turner being fortunate to survive the subsequent crash although he was wounded.

One spectacular event of the morning was an encounter by Flight Sub Lieutenant L S Breadner, a Canadian, with a huge Gotha GIV (610/16) bomber over Vron at 1030(A). The machine, of Kaghol III/16, came over in daylight—the first many had ever seen. Lloyd Breadner was on his way to the airfield from his billet when he heard anti-aircraft fire and looking up saw the large twin-engined aeroplane right overhead at around 10,000 feet. Rushing to his Pup he took off, chased the bomber and from directly behind it, fired 190 rounds at both engines. Crippled, the bomber came down near Vron inside British lines where it became G.23.

Its crew, Leutnants K Schweren, O Wirsch and Offizierstellvertreter A Hecher were taken prisoner. It was the first Gotha brought down by a British fighter aircraft.[1]

The RFC pilots put in more claims late morning, Captain Ball reporting a DIII in flames at 1145 over Cambrai, 40 Squadron claiming a Halberstadt Scout out of control over Lens.

Artillery flyers were in trouble after lunch, 12 Squadron losing a machine in flames but with no German claim. Then at 1530(A) 55 Squadron with the Martinsydes of 27 Squadron flew a bomb raid on Boue and a factory at Lechelle, escorted by four Nieuports of 29 Squadron. After bombing, they returned via St Quentin and 12 miles south of Boue they were engaged by a reported seven Albatros Scouts from the north-west (Jastas 12 and 26). A big fight developed during which several British planes were shot up, with men wounded, but all staggered back across the lines, denying the German pilots any definite successes. Second Lieutenant A D Taylor, observer to Second Lieutenant I V Pyott DSO, opened fire at one attacker from 300 yards and it dived steeply. Ian Pyott (he had won his DSO in 1916 for shooting down Zeppelin L36 over England) saw a red enemy fighter go down out of control, but then Taylor was hit in the arm by a fighter which dived underneath and then across them.

Second Lieutenant F L Oliver in another 'Four' had his gun jam after two shots and he was then hit in the foot, while another bullet smashed his Lewis gun. 1AM W Bond fired two bursts at a fighter on his tail and it went down in a spinning nose dive. However, the Four's engine was damaged and they began to lose height but they crossed the lines to crash-land at Buire. A7408 crash-landed at Ervillers and was wrecked, its pilot dead and gunner wounded.

Despite the lack of sure kills, Unteroffizier Jorke and Vizefeldwebel Grigo of Jasta 12 were credited with DH4s brought down. Lt M H Coote in a G100 was engaged by Offizierstellvertreter Rudolf Weckbrodt (although he claimed a DH4) south-west of Itancourt. Coote was wounded in the leg but he got back.

Two of the four Nieuports were brought down, both making forced landings at Rochincourt at 1645 where they came under German artillery fire and were destroyed. Only one pilot had been wounded and all came down inside British lines.

The FE2s of 22 Squadron were out again this afternoon, and were once again engaged by Jasta 5 over the same locality as they had been that morning—Bellenglise. And it was Kurt Schneider who did the damage. He engaged a DH2 escort, of 24 Squadron, and in trying to evade the Albatros, the luckless pilot collided with one of the Fees, all three men falling to their deaths. Schneider was credited with two more kills, bringing his score to ten.

Another FE2b claimed at this time was a machine of 18 Squadron on a bomb raid which was engaged over Barelle by Leutnant Hermann Göring of Jasta 26. The FE pilot was wounded and came down north-east of Arras, on the British side. The FE gunners claimed four Albatros Scouts out of control. The Pups of 3 Naval were also involved in this fight as were Jastas 12 and 33. The Naval pilots claimed several enemy fighters shot down and among those who did fall was Jasta 12's leader, Paul von Osterroht, who came down west of Cambrai at 1800 hours. A Jasta 33 pilot was also brought down, Unteroffizier Nauczak being severely wounded over Queant.

Heinrich Gontermann of Jasta 5 brought down an RE8 of 34 Squadron south-east of Arras at 1925(G), making the final claim of the day. No.29 Squadron flew a ground attack sortie in the late afternoon, led by Major Hugh Champion de Crespigny, Captain E F Elderton being wounded by small arms fire, but he got home.

The afternoon fighting had seen several more claims by RFC units, Lieutenant Bishop reporting downing a two-seater and a scout in flames east of Vitry while Lieutenant J M Child of 19 Squadron claimed an Albatros two-seater crashed north-west of Douai. No.48 Squadron had also seen action, claimed one destroyed and four out of control over Vimy, and had one gunner wounded by ground fire. Another victory was scored by the CO of 19 Squadron, Major H D Harvey-Kelly DSO. He had attacked a DIII between Graincourt and Cambrai at 1910, firing 60-80 rounds into it from 50 yards. It went down vertically and crashed about a mile outside of Cambrai. The German pilot had apparently tried to flatten out but then hit the ground.

---

[1] The French ace Georges Guynemer claimed a Gotha on 8 February 1917.

German losses this day were Flieger Adam Föller and Unteroffizier Kaiser of Schusta 7 who had to make a crash-landing but were otherwise unhurt. (Foller was to be killed over Gavrelle on 1 May.) Kampfgeschwader Nr.4 suffered several casualties: Leutnants Werner Steuber, Fritz von Massow, H Steibel, Eberhard Stettner and Oberleutnant Heinrich Möller.

Balloons were again attacked by the Jasta pilots, Vizefeldwebel Leopold von Raffay of Jasta 34 shooting at one near Belrupt. Others were also attacked but no claims made. Balloon Sections 5 and 16 both reported attacks, their balloons considerably hit but not destroyed. However, the balloon sections did sustain casualties: Lieutenant H E Goody of No.16 Section and 2AM G W N Kidney of No.3 were both wounded.

French Front

On the Nancy sector, a Nieuport two-seater crew of N.23, Maréchal-des-Logis Morizot and Lieutenant Gouin, brought down an Albatros Scout over the Bois de Avocourt, flown by Vizefeldwebel Arno Schramm of Jasta 7, who was reported killed over Montfaucon. Along the Chalons front Sous Lieutenant Juguin brought down a hostile aircraft north-west of Itancourt while the crew of a Farman of F.7 claimed another. A two-seater was also claimed by Capitaine Jean Derode, CO of N.102, over Prosnes, his 3rd of an eventual seven victories, although his machine was damaged in the action and he had to force-land. Leutnant Friedrich Feldmann of FA(A)252 was wounded over Prosnes, dying on the 26th, and it is likely he was hit during this fight.

On the debit side an observer in N.23 was wounded, and during Lieutenant Juguin's fight, his aircraft was set on fire but he got down without injury. A Caudron of C.8 was damaged and a gunner wounded, while a Morane Parasol of N.124 was shot down, claimed by Leutnant Willi Schunke of Jasta 20 for his first—and only—victory, south-west of St Quentin.

The Lafayette Escadrille, apart from having Nieuport Scouts, also had several other assorted aeroplanes, but not for general use over the lines. On this day, Sergeant Ron Hoskier, an American from New Jersey, son of a New York banker—and whose parents were now based in Paris—took the Morane up with Soldat Jean Dressy in the observer's cockpit. Dressy was the orderly to Lieutenant de Laage (having been with the family for years), who loved to fly but was not a regular aviator, although he hoped to become an air force gunner.

Having been told the Moranes would soon be taken away when Spads would totally equip N.124, Hoskier had decided to make one last flight in the old machine and Dressy asked to go too. They were attacked by three Albatros Scouts of Jasta 20, and after a struggle, in which Hoskier was wounded, the Morane fell into the French communication trenches, both occupants being killed instantly.

	A/C	KB			DES	OOC	KB
British losses	14	—	British claims		13	27	—
French losses	2	—	French claims		5		—
German claims	17	1	German losses		2		—†

† The Nachrichtenblatt records one large aircraft lost due to flak(!), one scout, and eight pilots wounded.

British Casualties

Aircraft type	No.	Squadron	Crew		
BE2e	7089	13 Sqdn	2/Lt H S Robertson	Safe	
			Lt G J Farmer	Safe	
BE2e	2840	15 Sqdn	Lt Vachell	Safe	*
			2AM F A Blunden	WIA	
FE2b	7681	22 Sqdn	2/Lt J A Rossi	WIA	
			2/Lt P H West	WIA	
BE2f	A3168	16 Sqdn	2/Lt E A Welch	KIA	
			Sgt A G Tollervey	KIA	
BE2f	A2876	16 Sqdn	2/Lt C M Crow	KIA	
			2/Lt E T Turner	WIA	
AWFK8	A2709	35 Sqdn	2/Lt F H Reynell	KIA	
			Capt S Barne MC	KIA	
AWFK8		35 Sqdn	2/Lt N C Yonge (O)	WIA	*
BE2e	7182	12 Sqdn	Lt A Ralphs	KIA	
			Lt L W Mott	KIA	

DH4	A7410	55 Sqdn	Lt T Webb	Safe	
			1AM W Bond	Safe	
DH4	A7408	55 Sqdn	Capt A T Greg	KIA	
			1AM R W Robson	WIA	
DH4	A2147	55 Sqdn	Lt I V Pyott DSO	Safe	*
			2/Lt A D Taylor	WIA	
Nieuport XVII	B1520	29 Sqdn	Lt W P T Watts	WIA	
Nieuport XVII	B1516	29 Sqdn	2/Lt J D Atkinson	Safe	
Nieuport XVII	A6752	29 Sqdn	Capt E F Elderton	WIA	*
Martinsyde G100		27 Sqdn	Lt M H Coote	WIA	*
RE8	A88	34 Sqdn	2/Lt H O W Hill	KIA	
			Lt H P Illsley	KIA	
FE2b	6929	22 Sqdn	Lt E A Barltrop	KIA	
			2/Lt F O'Sullivan	KIA	
DH2	7909	24 Sqdn	2/Lt M A White	KIA	
FE2b	A823	18 Sqdn	2/Lt E L Zink	WIA	*
			2/Lt G B Bate	Safe	
BF2a		48 Sqdn	Lt L E Porter (O)	WIA	*

French Casualties					
Sopwith 2		N.23	Lt Gouin (O)	WIA	*
Nieuport Scout		N.84	Lt Juguin	Safe	
Caudron R4		F.8	Sol Le Guino (G)	WIA	*
Morane Parasol	1112	N.124	Sgt R W Hoskier	KIA	
			Sol J Dressy	KIA	

Tuesday, 24 April 1917

British Front

A return to fine spring weather again brought forth increased activity with the resulting casualties, but they were not as heavy as the previous day. On the ground the intense fighting by the British extended their grip in the south, along the banks of the St Quentin canal near Vendhuille. In the north, though several counter-attacks were mounted by the Germans at Gavrelle, these had been broken up by well-directed and concentrated shell-fire. Further gains to the north-east of Fampoux—at Greenland Hill—north of the Scarpe, and east of Monchy to the south of the Scarpe had also been achieved. Soon after first light, up to 3,000 German prisoners had been taken as the British blunted the attacks and counter-attacked themselves.

The first air loss of the day came at just after 0700(A), Oberleutnant Heinrich Lorenz, CO of Jasta 33, bringing down a Pup of 66 Squadron, part of an escort to a recce of Solesmes. The RFC pilot was last seen near Cambrai, Lorenz shooting him down near Bourlon, the first kill for the Jasta.

Six FE2s of 20 Squadron were across the lines by 0700 escorting a 45 Squadron Sopwith two-seater on a photo job, getting into a fight with an estimated 18 Albatros Scouts of Jastas 8 and 18 west of Ledeghem twenty minutes later. The crew of Lieutenant R E Johnson and Captain F R Cubbon claimed two of the V-Strutters shot down. In turn Jasta 8's Offizier-stellvertreter Walter Göttsch and Leutnant Werner Junck claimed their 9th and 1st victories respectively by downing two of 20 Squadron's FEs, while Leutnant Walter von Bülow-Bothkamp of Jasta 18 claimed a third pusher over Ypres, on the British side. Göttsch's victim too came down on the British side, thus Junck must have brought down A6385, the only one of 20's machines that didn't recross the lines.

FE No. A5144 caught fire during the fight but Lieutenant Robertson, although wounded, got his burning aeroplane down. A6403 was in the running fight for the lines, the crew of Lieutenant E O Perry and 2AM E H Sayers claiming an Albatros down in flames, but they too had their machine set on fire but came down inside British lines. Jasta 18 had Leutnant Fritz Kleindienst killed. His Albatros caught fire north of Comines and he jumped to his death. The Staffelführer, Rittmeister Karl von Grieffenhagen, had his machine badly hit and he crash-landed, losing a leg and part of his lower jaw.

Confusing the issue somewhat is the fact that Marine Feld-Jagdstaffel I was also operating opposite Ypres this morning and they too claimed two FEs shot down, one near Ypres and another over Becelaere, the latter inside German lines. They also lost the pilot who was believed to have got these two pushers, Vizeflugmeister Josef Wirtz, who fell over Polygon Wood, possibly after colliding with the second FE. As Wirtz died in the crash, we have no way of confirming if he indeed caused the two FEs to go down, or even collided with one. Although MFJ claimed two victories, it is more probable that the 'live' pilots of Jasta 8 and 18 received official credit.

Later a letter was passed to the Squadron from Major James Abbey, OC of the A/103 Battery, Royal Field Artillery, which read:

> 'I beg to report that an aeroplane, No.5144 [sic], belonging to your squadron, landed in flames on my battery position about 8 am this morning and was totally destroyed.
>
> 'The machine burst into flames at a great height and was landed safely in our lines owing to the gallant conduct and great presence of mind of the two occupants, the pilot Lt Robertson and observer Capt Knowles.
>
> 'Though both these officers were wounded, the pilot rather seriously in two places, and both were burnt slightly, they managed to keep the flames under control until within 200 feet of the ground, Knowles then jumped clear just before the machine turned over and pulled Robertson from under the burning wreckage.
>
> 'Captain Knowles was full of praise at the manner in which Lt Robertson piloted him safely to the ground.'

Captain R M Knowles, an officer of the Norfolk Regiment attached to the RFC, had only recently received the Military Cross. By one of those strange quirks of fate, Knowles had shot down and wounded Göttsch on 3 February 1917; now Göttsch unknowingly had got his revenge.

The 1½ Strutters of 70 Squadron were up early, nine beginning a recce of Cambrai at 0535 hours, led by Captain Williams, escorted by some Pups. After some time they were engaged by six pilots of Jasta 2, and although the RFC men claimed two Halberstadt DIIs out of control the Jasta had no losses.

An Albatros attacked Sergeant Thomson's machine (A8213), his observer, 2AM Impey firing a drum at it. Hits were seen on the engine and it stalled and fell away. Impey changed the drum, then fired into its fuselage and saw it go down out of control. Lieutenant Gotch engaged another Albatros, his observer, Lieutenant Kiburz, scoring hits and it too went down, in a nose dive.

Otto Bernert, however, clawed one Strutter down, which fell in flames south of Vaucelles for his 20th victory. This was Lieutenant Halse and 2AM Bond. They were hit in the engine early in the fight and began to glide away, but they were then attacked again and shot down. Only the previous day had Bernert been notified of the award of the Pour le Mérite, and if this victory was in any way a celebration, then this day would see his celebrations extended.

Still with fuel and ammunition Bernert soon spotted other targets, three BE2e aircraft of 9 Squadron who had flown out on a bomb raid at 0540 without gunners so as to increase their bomb load. Bernert swooped down on them as they headed for home and between 0840 and 0845(G) shot down all three, one falling north of Joncourt, the second north of Levergies and the last south of Bellicourt, north of St Quentin. The mechanics at Morlancourt waited in vain for their three BEs to return. For some reason the Squadron thought they had been brought down by AA fire, so the fact that the three aircraft had virtually no defence probably wasn't considered.

Within five minutes Bernert had spotted another victim, a DH4 bomber of 55 Squadron, also out early to bomb La Briquett. Bernert attacked it and it went down inside British lines where the pilot crash-landed west of Bony at 0850(G) with a dead gunner and a wounded pilot.

Five victories in one day would have been a record, but five victories in one sortie, all scored between 0830 and 0850, was outstanding. No other German pilot had achieved that sort of success, nor had any Allied pilot in France come to that. The fact that he wore spectacles didn't preclude success in air combat either, and he had now achieved 24 victories. He would add three more to his score before being wounded. He was destined to die of influenza a month before WW1 ended.

Just on 0900(G), Heinrich Gontermann of Jasta 5 shot down a Triplane of 8 Naval Squadron near Bailleul, on the British side. One Naval pilot claimed an Albatros out of control.

During the morning, near Lens, German two-seater crews claimed two victories, a Sopwith to Unteroffizier Stegmann and Vizefeldwebel Merzel of Schusta 27 at 0750, and an unspecified type to Lieutenant Reigel and Vizefeldwebel Tötsch of FA211 at 0930(A). There were no RFC losses at these times that match up in this area.

Naval 8's was the last loss until after lunch, although the RFC made claims for hostile aircraft brought down. 1 Naval Squadron claimed one destroyed and two out of control fighters in the Sailly-Noyelles area at 0815/40(A) while 18 Squadron's FEs claimed three destroyed—one in flames—over Barelle at the same time. One of these was probably Offizierstellvertreter Rudolf Weckbrodt of Jasta 26. He was wounded during a fight with some FEs, but he was back with the Jasta by the end of the month. At 1110(A) the SE5s of 56 Squadron attacked and claimed a two-seater destroyed over Bellone, credit going to Captain C M Crowe and Lieutenants L M Barlow and M A Kay.

Flight Lieutenant C D Booker of 8 Naval Squadron saw a two-seater being 'archied' (fired at by AA guns) near his aerodrome (Auchel, also known as Lozinghem), so gained height, following it towards Arras. He lost it momentarily then spotted it amongst some further AA bursts, chased after it and then attacked under its tail. The observer still managed to fire into the Triplane (N5482) and scored some hits, but Booker's fire also struck home and the observer disappeared into his cockpit, obviously hit. The German pilot then put his nose down and headed towards Douai, trailing a thin line of smoke but under control. Booker did not make a claim.

It is not certain who was in the two-seater, but Vizefeldwebel Richard Schleichardt of FA(A)224 made two flights over Allied lines this day, and on the second was forced down by a British fighter inside his own lines.

Two German two-seaters were brought down in the front lines around noon. The first, an Albatros C-type, came down at Grenier Wood, south-west of Armentières, after a combat with Second Lieutenant T F Hazell of 1 Squadron. Tom Hazell was on a Line Patrol at midday flying at 14,000 feet when he spotted two two-seaters 4,000 feet below. He dived on one, firing 30 rounds from 20 yards under its tail. Volumes of smoke came out of the bottom of the fuselage, and as it went down, it burst into flames, falling into the German front line trenches. The crew of Unteroffizier Otto Haberland and Leutnant Heinrich Klofe of FA227 were both killed.

Twenty-five kilometres to the south two Nieuport pilots of 40 Squadron, Lieutenants I P R Napier and J G Brewis, engaged what they described as an Aviatik west of Lens. Flight Sub Lieutenant R A Little of 8 Naval then joined in flying a Triplane (N5469). The Australian Bob Little had been on his airfield at Auchel around noon, had received a message that a German aircraft was approaching, and was sent off to engage it. So for the second time this morning, 8 Naval had engaged enemy aircraft near their base. He spotted the two Nieuports and the two-seater right over Auchel as he gained height; the German turned north, Little following, firing whenever the opportunity arose. When he noticed the observer was not firing, he closed in, the two-seater starting to lose height; then it nose-dived and landed in a field inside British territory near Lens. It was a machine of FA18 and the crew of Leutnants Hans Huppert and Friedrich Neumüller were taken prisoner. Whether Little decided to capture his victims himself and attempted to land next to the downed machine, is uncertain. In his report he stated he could not get his engine going after the dive and had to land beside the two-seater. Whatever the reason, Little ran into a ditch and turned his Triplane over. Neumüller went to his aid and helped free him from the wreck! The German machine became G.24, recorded as a DFW CV.

At 1300 British time, Nieuports of 1 and 60 Squadrons went for a massed attack on the German balloon lines. Lieutenant A V Burbury of the former unit flamed one while Lieutenant W E Molesworth of 60 Squadron got another at Boiry Notre Dame.

Meanwhile, Second Lieutenant Reginald Burton Clark (Australian) of 60, while diving at a balloon, was attacked by four Albatros Scouts. He was hit in the upper part of his left leg and a subsequent shot hit him in the lower part of the same leg; his fuel tank was also holed. Despite his injuries, he tried to engage the enemy, firing off half a drum of Lewis at them but could not wait to see any effects. His Nieuport was hit again, his flying wires being cut and he quickly came down. The machine crunched into a shell-hole and caught fire on landing but Clark was pulled clear by Corporal Summers of the 1st Canadian Pioneer Battalion. There were signs that he may have to lose the leg, but he gave his report of the fight before allowing his wounds and burns to be attended to, but he died of his injuries on 1 May. There is no German claim for his Nieuport.

Mid-afternoon saw patrols and fights by 56 Squadron, who claimed two EA out of control; then at 1650, Flight Lieutenant H T Travers of 3 Naval made it three two-seaters captured for the day, by bringing down another DFW CV, this time of FA26. Travers, with Flight Sub Lieutenants F D Casey and J J Malone engaged the German between Morchies and Louverval. It came down near to the front line at Doignies with its pilot, Unteroffizier Max Haase, and his observer Leutnant Karl Keim both wounded, the latter fatally. No sooner had the DFW landed than German artillery opened up and the two-seater was soon reduced to matchwood and scrap iron, the wreckage designated G.25 by the RFC. In the absence of tangible evidence, it was recorded as an Aviatik. However, the DFW's number was 5927/16. Malone's Pup developed engine trouble during the combat (although it is possible his motor was hit by Keim) and he had to make a forced landing, and had to take shelter in the same shell-hole as his two victims until they could be rescued. Keim died ten minutes later, and Malone's Pup was also blown to pieces by shell fire.

The last RFC casualties of the day came in the late afternoon. A 10 Squadron BE2g on a special bombing mission was hit by ground fire but got back across the lines before being forced to crash-land. Then a 59 Squadron RE8, one of three flying a line patrol over Monchy le Preux, was hit by AA fire over Guemappe at 1845, wounding the observer, but the pilot brought him back safely. Flakbatterie 701 claimed a two-seater hit near Wancourt which was probably this machine.

Just on 1700, a six-man patrol of 60 Squadron—Fry, Horn, Young, Penny, Percival and Rutherford—were near Vis-en-Artois. They spotted four red-fuselaged Albatros Scouts, one with green wings, the others with red. One was going down on a BE at 1,500 feet. Three of the Nieuports dived to protect the two-seater, and joined by a Sopwith Triplane, they succeeded in driving off what was obviously Jasta 11. The Albatros pilots rapidly broke off and dived east.

At 1730, FE2s of 25 Squadron had a scrap with some Albatros Scouts over Billy Montigny, claiming one destroyed. Also during the day, 48 Squadron claimed three DIIIs destroyed around Arras, while Lieutenant R N Hall of 40 Squadron claimed a two-seater out of control east of Lens. This may have been a machine of FA(A)235 who lost Leutnants Richard Zeglien and Carl Timm who fell at Acheville, which is about three miles south-east of Lens.

French Front

French fighter pilots were busy this day, claiming at least five German two-seaters shot down— it was a bad day generally for German two-seaters—and two scouts, at least one being a DIII.

Adjutant Georges Madon of N.38 claimed an Albatros down at Cornilette which was not confirmed (of an eventual total of 65 such claims), and an Albatros C in flames for his 9th victory (of an eventual 41 confirmed). Capitaine Robert Massenet-Royer de Marancour, commander of Groupe de Combat 14 (GC14) and Caporal Lejeune of N.83 crashed a two-seater also at Courson, near Courcy le Château at 1640 while Adjutant Baudoin of N.80 shot down a two-seater in flames at 1700 hours over l'Ange Gardien. Adjutant Raoul Lufbery, the American star of the Lafayette Escadrille, shot down an Aviatik two-seater east of Cerisy on the Somme— where N.124 were now operating—at 1725 for his 9th victory.

A fighter was claimed by Maréchal-des-Logis Marcel Henriot of N.65 at 1720 over the Forêt de Pinon, with Sergent Edmund Pillon of N.82 claiming a DIII down at Dannemarie for his 3rd victory (he was promoted to Adjutant the next day and ended the war with eight official victories). Pillon's victim was probably Vizefeldwebel Rudolf Rath of Bavarian Jasta 35 flying 2020/16, who came down at Hagenbach and was killed at 0722(G). The other known scout pilot brought down was Vizefeldwebel Max Wackwitz of Jasta 24, who was compelled to land at Bignicourt, near the Jasta's aerodrome after a combat with a French fighter, but was otherwise unharmed. This may well have been Madon's unconfirmed victory.

French losses were just two, both Nieuport XXIIIs, Sergeant Boiteux-Levret of N.81 and Caporal Menard of N.85. Two Nieuports were claimed, one by Vizefeldwebel Albert Haussmann of Jasta 23 over Beaurieux at 1605(G) for his 2nd victory, the other by Leutnant Ernst Udet of Jasta 15 for his 5th, shot down over Chavignon at 1930. A Spad was claimed by Offizierstellvertreter Felsman of Jasta 24, east of Prunay at 1012 in the morning but records do not identify the French unit. Similarly, a Caudron two-seater was claimed by Oberleutnant Eduard Dostler of Jasta 34 over Ablonville as his 6th victory.

German two-seaters lost over the French front were: Vizefeldwebel Otto Hartung and Leutnant Friedrich Krowolitski of FA252 killed at Nauroy by Madon; Leutnants Werner Hecht and Hugo Schneider of FA(A)222 killed over Courcy le Château by Baudoin of N.80; Leutnants Karl Jaeger and Walter Rudatis of FA253, killed in the Laon-Allemant area, by de Marancour and Lejeune of N.83. In addition Leutnant Karl Schmidt, observer in FA(A)251, was killed over Clermont, and Flieger Josef Reuber of FA250 was killed at Sissone, crashing on take-off, although his observer survived. AA fire wounded Leutnant Blum of FA46 south of St Mihiel.

A German pilot not claimed was Oberleutnant Rudolf Berthold, leader of Jasta 14, wounded during a combat with a Caudron, although not serious enough for him to leave his command.

	A/C	KB			DES	OOC	KB
British losses	12	—		British claims	16	10	3
French losses	2	—		French claims	7		—
German claims	22†	—		German losses	15‡		?

† Four by flak. ‡ The Nachrichtenblatt states 11 aircraft lost, including two behind enemy lines, three missing and one collided with enemy aircraft. In addition one officer was killed and three wounded.

British Casualties

Aircraft type	No.	Squadron	Crew		
Sopwith 1½ Strutter	A1002	70 Sqdn	2/Lt C II Halse	KIA	
			2AM W Bond	MIA	
BE2e	7195	9 Sqdn	Lt G E Hicks	POW	
BE2e	A2937	9 Sqdn	2/Lt F A Matthews	KIA	
BE2e	A2941	9 Sqdn	Lt C L Graves	KIA	
DH4	A2149	55 Sqdn	Lt A M N de Lavison	WIA	
			2AM K Oliver	KIA	
FE2d	A5144	20 Sqdn	Lt N L Robertson	WIA	
			Capt R M Knowles MC	WIA	
FE2d	A6385	20 Sqdn	2/Lt A R Johnson	KIA	
			Lt H R Nicholson	KIA	
FE2d	A6403	20 Sqdn	Lt E O Perry	Safe	
			2AM E H Sayers	Safe	
Sopwith Pup	A6175	66 Sqdn	2/Lt R S Capon	POW/WIA	
Triplane	N5467	8N Sqdn	FSL E B J Walter	KIA	
Nieuport XXIII	A6777	60 Sqdn	2/Lt R B Clark	DOW	
BE2g	A2843	10 Sqdn	2/Lt A W Watson	Safe	
RE8	A3213	59 Sqdn	Sgt Smith	Safe	*
			Lt R S Stone	WIA	
Pup	N6208	3N Sqdn	FSL J J Malone	Safe	

French Casualties

Nieuport XXIII	2937	N.81	Sgt Boiteux-Levret	MIA
Nieuport XXIII		N.85	Cpl Menard	WIA
Spad ?				
Caudron ?				

Wednesday, 25 April 1917

British Front

Low clouds again curtailed the intensity of air fighting, although the artillery flyers were able to operate often. This helped the movement of troops on the ground, the British line advancing slightly south of the Scarpe. It was announced that since the 23rd, over 3,000 German prisoners had been taken.

A successful Zone Call was made by a crew of 15 Squadron, Second Lieutenants W G Barker and Goodfellow, after spotting an estimated 1,000 enemy troops in trenches. They then directed the shell-fire onto the trenches and followed this by directing gunfire on other troops and two gun batteries. Canadian Billy Barker later became one of the leading Allied air aces and won the Victoria Cross in October 1918.

Today was Jasta 11's day, but the first victim was a 59 Squadron RE8 that had taken off at 0515 to fly a recce-line patrol south-east of Arras. It failed to return, but as no German pilot made a claim for a British machine at this early hour, it must be assumed to have been brought down by AA fire. KFlak 63 claimed a BE on this date, brought down near Omissy which they may have mistaken for the RE. Both crewmen were captured, the pilot being the same Sergeant Smith who had brought back a wounded observer the previous evening.

The first air fight came at 1030(G) over Guemappe, Karl Allmenröder of Jasta 11 shooting down a BE right over the lines. A 12 Squadron BE2e is the only machine to fit the claim although the exact time it was lost has not been discovered, but the crew were both killed.

Jasta 11 also spotted six FE2bs shortly after this encounter, which were 25 Squadron aircraft escorting line-patrol aircraft between Lens and Arras, led by Captain A de Selincourt. Emil Schäfer went down behind A837 and shot it down between Willerval and Bailleul but inside British lines. A5505 was also hit by a Jasta pilot but it got back over the lines only to crash attempting a forced landing later, but the crew were unhurt.

By this time, however, Jasta 11 had become aware that one of its pilots was missing. Sebastian Festner had been part of the early patrol and near Oppy had spotted the 1½ Strutters of 43 Squadron. He attacked, but the rear gunner of A8232, crewed by Lieutenant C R O'Brien and Second Lieutenant J L Dickson, had hit the red Albatros (2251/16) at 0815(A) — 0915 German time—and Festner fell to his death. He had scored 12 victories, ten during Bloody April. He was also the only German aircraft claimed by the RFC on this morning, although British AA fire also claimed the Albatros over Gavrelle. The Albatros fell just inside British lines and was noted as G.26, but as it was under shell fire from the German artillery it was not salvaged. 43 Squadron had a gunner wounded in this fight but the pilot brought the Strutter home.

Not until the evening did further air action occur, Schäfer again being involved. 48 Squadron's Bristol Fighters were on a Combined Offensive Patrol east of Arras, and AA observers reported seeing a machine go down during a combat with enemy fighters. Schäfer's claim for a Bristol down by the railway station at Roeux was confirmed. Lieutenant W T Price and his observer Lieutenant M A Benjamin claimed an Albatros destroyed at 1900 but Jasta 11 had no other losses.

Another BE was the last casualty, 10 Squadron having sent out a machine at 1725 for artillery observation work against the Cité St Pierre. At 1945(A) it was attacked by Albatros Scouts and shot up. The pilot, Lieutenant R V Kann, was flying fairly low to avoid the clouds when he and his observer, Second Lieutenant C Bousfield, saw five or six hostile aircraft approaching. The largest, painted red, opened fire and hit Kann in the back. Bousfield opened fire and his bullets seemed to enter the red machine's fuselage. Meantime, Kann had begun to spiral down, finally landing in a shell hole near to Cité St Pierre. So close was it to the line that it could not be salvaged. Nobody seems to have put in a claim for it.

French Front

Nothing of note to report.

	A/C	KB			DES	OOC	KB
British losses	6	—	British claims		2	—	—
French losses	—	—	French claims		—	—	—

| German claims | 4† | — | German losses | 1 | — |

† One to flak.

British Casualties

Aircraft type	No.	Squadron	Crew		
RE8	A3213	59 Sqdn	Sgt F C Smith	POW	
			Lt E J Dilnutt	POW	
Sop 1½ Strutter	A7799	43 Sqdn	2/Lt C L Veitch	Safe	*
			2/Lt E S W Langton	WIA	
BE2e	7191	12 Sqdn	Lt T Thomson	KIA	
			Lt A M Turnbull	KIA	
FE2b	A837	25 Sqdn	2/Lt C V Darnell	KIA	
			2AM G Pawley	KIA	
FE2b	A5505	25 Sqdn	2/Lt M A Hancock	Safe	
			Lt V Smith	Safe	
BF2a	A3352	48 Sqdn	2/Lt W J Clifford	KIA	
			2/Lt H L Tomkies	KIA	
BE2g	A2899	10 Sqdn	Lt R V Kann	WIA	
			2/Lt C Bousfield	Safe	
Nieuport XVII	A6790	1 Sqdn	2/Lt A V Collins	Injured†	
Nieuport XVII	A6624	1 Sqdn	2/Lt L J Mars	Injured†	

† Collision in bad weather on return from an OP; both men suffered severe concussion.

French Casualties
Nil

Thursday, 26 April 1917

British Front

The cloudy weather persisted until the evening, therefore most of the air action took place either after lunch or during the evening. On the ground the Germans made an attempt at retaking Gavrelle but they were heavily repulsed. An assault by British troops on some quarries on the eastern outskirts of Hargicourt was successful.

Ten FEs of 20 Squadron flew to Rumbeke aerodrome—home of Jasta 8—each carrying two 112-pound bombs. Take-off was at 0600 and they were engaged by about eight Albatros Scouts, the gunners claiming two shot down out of control. One FE was hit, its observer being mortally wounded in the chest but the pilot regained the lines near Watou.

Ground fire hit a Nieuport XVII of 60 Squadron at 1010, while on an OP, compelling Second Lieutenant N P Henderson to make a forced landing in a lake, during which he sustained a cut under one eye. The machine was unable to be salvaged and was therefore written off.

At midday, 1 Squadron mounted a balloon attack, Lieutenant Arthur V Burbury MC shooting down one in flames, and he was last seen heading his Nieuport down towards another but he failed to get back. He was hit by gunfire from KFlak 2 east of Wytschaete, coming down near Houthem to be taken prisoner.

Captain D C Rutter/Second Lieutenant B J Venn leading a squad of 43 Squadron was patrolling the line over Oppy at 1530, when he spotted four red Albatros Scouts coming from Douai—Jasta 11! They proceeded to attack a BE2c working over Oppy but Rutter led his patrol down and drove them off. The hostile scouts turned south and attacked another BE2c over the Scarpe River. Rutter followed as quickly as he could but they easily outpaced his Strutter. Seeing the danger, Rutter opened fire from 1,000 yards but he was too far away and before he could do anything further, the BE was going down in flames and the Albatri heading back towards Douai. That was Kurt Wolff at work.

Kurt Wolff brought his score to 21 with this kill at 1635(G), bringing down a BE of 5 Squadron working with the 57th Siege Battery near Gavrelle, despite the attempt by 43 to help. Thus Rutter and company had saved one Corps crew at the expense of a second. Such was fate—or luck.

Two hours later Karl Allmenröder and Lothar von Richthofen went down on two 16

Squadron BEs also engaged on artillery observation over Vimy. One fell in flames on the German side of the Ridge, the other crash-landing west of Vimy, its pilot wounded.

Jasta 30 claimed its first victory since 6 April: Leutnant Paul Erbguth, a former Schlasta pilot, shot down yet another BE, this one from 10 Squadron flying a photo sortie. It went down at 1725(A) between Hulloch and Wingles to crash at Haisnes right on the front line.

The FEs of 22 Squadron flew two sorties in the late afternoon, the first at 1615 being a photo op to Flesquières and the Bois de Vaucelles with six aircraft. They came under heavy AA fire, one FE being hit and wounding its pilot in the chin, but he got back. The second sortie, at 1735, went to bomb Bohain Station. One pusher developed engine trouble and turned back, dumping its bombs into front line trenches north-west of St Quentin.

The rest met Jasta 5 north of St Quentin and lost two of their number to Offizierstell-vertreter Sturm for his first (and only) victory and Leutnant Rudolph Nebel for his first (of two) victory. Sturm got Hopkins and Stewart in A825, Nebel claiming Captain H R Hawkins, an Australian, and his gunner, Second Lieutenant McEntee. The Fees came down at Brancourt le Grand and Joncourt at 0800 and 0805(G) hours.

Jasta 5 claimed two balloons downed during the day, Gontermann one at Arras at 1150, Leutnant Kurt Schneider one at Seraucourt at 1600. In all there were three balloons claimed, the other by Vizefeldwebel Julius Buckler of Jasta 17 by de Genicourt Wood. Buckler's victim was French, 35 Cié. Gontermann's balloon was the 1st Brigade's 8th KB Section, which was destroyed after three determined attacks by the German, the last from below 500 feet.

There were numerous combats during the afternoon and evening, all except two against Albatros Scouts. The two were C-types engaged by FE8s of 41 Squadron near Hooge around midday, both being claimed as destroyed. Once more there were more claims for destroyed enemy aircraft than lost by the Germans, plus the usual crop of 'out of controls'.

The FEs of 25 Squadron were operating in the Lens-Arras area, claiming one of each category at 1720(A) near Drocourt, north-east of Arras. One FE had to make a forced landing near Lens after a fight with a German Scout but both crewmen were unhurt. In the same fight, Booker of 8 Naval Squadron claimed a DIII in flames, as did Flight Sub Lieutenant E D Crundell.

Naval Triplanes nearly added to the British losses during this late afternoon period by attacking Spads of 19 Squadron. No. 19 had started an OP at 1740, saw the activity over Douai and went to investigate. Just north-east of Arras Lt J M Child (B1537) was attacked by five Triplanes which put shots through his tailplane, fuselage and both wings. Child put his Spad into a spin with engine full-on and managed to force-land at Bellevue at 1900. Lieutenant Holmes (B1588) also received the attention of two Triplanes but managed to evade and get away. It is hoped that these were not the two Albatros Scouts 8 Naval claimed!

Further south another group of FEs were flying north of Cambrai shortly after 1900. Captain Albert Ball of 56 Squadron was flying in the same area, spotting the FEs approaching and also saw a number of Albatros Scouts climbing up from the direction of Cambrai itself. Biding his time until the Scouts came up to his height—13,000 feet—he then attacked and claimed one went down and crashed.

He was then heavily engaged by five other Scouts and after a brief skirmish he headed away south-east but was chased by the Germans. One outpaced the others and when it was almost in range, Ball turned quickly and fired into it, the Albatros catching fire and falling in flames. Ball had then to fight his way back, which he managed successfully, finally landing at Vert Galand at 2030, with his SE5 badly shot about. It is believed that it was Jasta 3 that engaged Ball and they lost Vizefeldwebel Emil Eisenhuth in a DIII, 2207/16, who fell in flames near Hayencourt, north-west of Cambrai and was killed.

At 1920 hours, Lieutenant H E O Ellis of 40 Squadron, on an OP to Salome, made an attack on a balloon over the town but was attacked by four Albatros Scouts. Ellis manoeuvred into a favourable position and fired from 25 yards into one of them. This machine turned over on its starboard wing and crashed east of Salome, a second Albatros being seen to land close beside it.

Up over the coast, off Ostende, 7 Naval Squadron lost a Handley Page 0100, shot down by German seaplanes while four HPs were attempting to bomb a destroyer outside the port.

Credit went to Vizeflugmeister Müller of Seeflug 2, flying a Rumpler 6B1 (No.1037), the HP falling into the sea three miles north-west of Nieuport. The British pilot drowned but two others were rescued by the Germans. The fourth was rescued by a French FBA flying boat, one of two which attempted to get to the men, one being shot down by flak and then towed into Ostende by one of the German destroyers originally under attack. On board, so the Germans then discovered, were the other two Naval survivors. The HPs were from the Manston Squadron, but were operating from Coudekerque aerodrome under 5 Naval Wing.

French Front

There was more activity over the French sectors, with a total of at least seven German aircraft claimed as being shot down. N.48 brought down an Albatros C-type at Ville-aux-Bois at 0615(A), credited to three of the Escadrille's pilots, Lieutenant Armand de Turenne, Caporal Rene Montrion and Caporal Conan. La Ville-aux-Bois is just to the east of Cerny where a machine of FA(A)255 had observer Leutnant Traugott Milbrandt killed.

That evening N.48 made it two for the day as Sergent Bajac and Caporal Jacques Roques downed a hostile machine at Loivre at 1740. The Lafayette Escadrille claimed two. Sergeant Charles Johnson got another two-seater Albatros east of St Quentin at 1800, while Lieutenant William Thaw and Sergeant Willis Haviland sent a second down over Juvincourt, half-way between Laon and Reims, at 1830.

The other three victories were claimed by N.79 at Itancourt, and N.93 north of Res d'Ailette, while R.46 gunners shot down one over Fort Brimont. One German loss was the Staffelführer of Jasta 15—Oberleutnant Max Reinhold – who went down near Lierval at 1930(G) after a fight with three Spads.

In addition to the German losses above, Observer Leutnant Sigismund Steinfeld of FA(A)271 died over Ripont and Leutnant Franz Blum of FA46 was killed at Chambley.

Three French losses are recorded. Capitaine Doumer of Spa.76 failed to return from a patrol having taken off at 1600 hours heading towards Fresnes, shot down by Oberleutnant Hahn of Jasta 19 north of Brimont; Caporal Egret of N.78 was downed by Leutnant Albert of Jasta 31 over Nauroy; and a Caudron G4 of C.56, hit by ground fire south of Fort Brimont. The latter machine got back, but Lieutenant Burville, the pilot, had been wounded; it was claimed by Flakzug 87, 102 and 180 and KFlak 53.

	A/C	KB		DES	OOC	KB	
British losses	10	3?	British claims	10	15	—	
French losses	2	—	French claims	7		—	
German claims	11†	3	German losses	2‡		1	

† Two by flak. ‡ The Nachrichtenblatt states two scouts lost in combat, one balloon, two two-seaters FTL inside German lines and one officer killed by flak. This does not include the seaplane claimed at Zeebrugge.

British Casualties

Aircraft type	No.	Squadron	Crew		
FE2b	A6393	20 Sqdn	Lt F D Stevens	Safe	*
			Sgt A Clayton	KIA	
Nieuport XVII	B1549	60 Sqdn	2/Lt N P Henderson	WIA	
Nieuport Scout	A6671	1 Sqdn	Lt A V Burbury MC	POW	
BE2g	2806	5 Sqdn	Lt H B T Hope	KIA	
			2/Lt L E Allan	KIA	
BE2g	A2859	16 Sqdn	Lt W K Mercer	WIA	
			Pvt Lea	Safe	
BE2e	A2826	16 Sqdn	2/Lt W S Spence	KIA	
			2/Lt W A Campbell	POW	
FE2b	A796	22 Sqdn	Lt L W Beal	WIA	*
			2/Lt G Bell	Safe	
BE2e	5870	10 Sqdn	Lt H F Roux	WIA/POW	
			2/Lt H J Price	WIA/POW	
FE2b	A825	22 Sqdn	2/Lt G M Hopkins	POW	
			Lt J D M Stewart	POW	
FE2b	4883	22 Sqdn	Capt H R Hawkins	POW	
			2/Lt G O McEntee	POW	

BE2		9 Sqdn	Capt R J Lowcock (P)	WIA	*
BE2		2 Sqdn	2AM T Aspinall (O)	WIA
Sopwith Baby	8171	SDF	F/Cdr W L Welch	Safe
Handley Page 0/100	3115	7N Sqdn	FSL R S S Hood	Drowned
			LM R H Watson	POW/Died
			AM2 F C Kirby	WIA
			ACM W C Danzey	POW/Died

French Casualties

Spad VII	1447	N.76	Capt R Doumer	KIA
Spad VII		N.78	Cpl Egret	MIA
Caudron G4		C.56	Lt Burville (P)	WIA	*

Friday, 27 April 1917

British Front

There was no improvement in the weather, low clouds prevailing all day. With very little activity in the air, there were a number of 'shoots'—59 targets being dealt with by artillery with aircraft observation, plus 26 by balloon observers. Crews of 8 and 13 Squadrons were particularly successful against German batteries.

A BE2c of 2 Squadron was brought down by AA fire while flying an artillery observation sortie for the 219th and 150th Siege Batteries at 1115 hours, following a successful shoot on German trenches. It was claimed by Flakzug 145, and as the machine fell one of the crew fell out near the Cité St Pierre. This must have been the pilot as the observer was later reported burnt to death. The whole episode was witnessed by another 2 Squadron crew, Captain W A Skeate and Second Lieutenant R V Waters while working with the 224th Siege Battery.

The only other combat losses of the day came in the evening. FE2bs of 11 Squadron flew a Line Patrol, taking off at 1720, only to run into pilots of Jasta 11. Gunners claimed two Scouts destroyed south-west of Vitry, one in flames and another out of control. Lothar von Richthofen brought 4850 down at Fresnes where the crew were taken prisoner, while Kurt Wolff forced 7698 down to make a crash-landing south of Gavrelle, inside British lines. The victories were timed by the Germans at 2015 and 2020. Jasta 11 had no recorded losses.

Five minutes later Karl Allmenröder claimed a BE2f, in British lines, west of Fampoux. The only possible victim was a 12 Squadron BE, that reported a fight with a German scout who wounded the observer, but the two-seater was not a loss.

Two balloons were claimed by RFC pilots, Lieutenant Bishop of 60 Squadron attacking one at 0655 near Vitry-en-Artois, seen to go down smoking heavily, while Lieutenant H E O Ellis of 40 Squadron destroyed one at Salome at 1000 hours. 48 Squadron Bristols also claimed a two-seater destroyed, seeing it crash in the Scarpe River, near Vitry.

Two other losses of note were a 43 Squadron 1½ Strutter flown by Captain H H Balfour and Second Lieutenant E H Jones. Flying along the crest of Vimy Ridge they were hit in the engine by ground machine-gun fire, which promptly stopped. Balfour quickly turned for the lines, made it—just—then ploughed into the ground, catapulting him and his observer into the mud in front of the wreck. Despite a few moments of unconsciousness, both men were only slightly injured and rescued by Canadian troops. Balfour had been recently discussing whether a crew should strap themselves in firmly when about to crash-land, the majority of his Squadron comrades thinking it was better not to do so. He disagreed, but in this final moment he changed his mind and undid his seat belt. When he scrambled back to his shattered Strutter, he saw that the engine had been smashed back into the cockpit where his legs would have been had he remained strapped in!

The other loss was a Nieuport XVII of 60 Squadron. Second Lieutenant F Stedman took off from No.2 ASD at Candas, to deliver a new machine to the Squadron at Le Hameau. Instead of flying directly there, he obviously decided to take a look at the front (unless he became completely lost), for he ended up behind the German lines as a prisoner of war.

French Front

The French claimed just three German aircraft during the day. One was a two-seater of FA14 crewed by Leutnants Herbert Zimmermann and Ernst Naumann. They were brought down at Gerardner and were either killed or died of wounds in a French hospital. A scout was claimed by the crew of a Farman of F.71, which was probably Leutnant Friedrich Vonschott of Jasta 14 who came down near Montchalone with wounds so severe he died on 14 May. Two other fighter pilots were casualties, Leutnant Eissfeldt of Jasta 10, severely wounded in combat and Leutnant Rudolf Hepp of Jasta 24. Hepp's machine, Albatros DIII 1731/16, was badly damaged and he crashed at Leffincourt, but without injury. It is possible he was shot up by Alfred Auger of N.3 who forced a hostile machine to land north of Betheniville.

A Farman 42 of Escadrille F.19 was attacked by an Albatros and forced to land inside French lines with 49 bullet holes in it, the observer having been wounded. There is no German claim for this action, although KFlak 93 did claim a Caudron shot down over Essigny-le-Grand.

Jasta 36 pilots made attacks on the French balloon lines, claiming three destroyed, Leutnant Albert Dossenbach claiming one—which was not confirmed—Leutnant Heinrich Bongartz two, one at Berry-au-Bac the other south-east of Thillois.

	A/C	KB		DES	OOC	KB
British losses	4	—	British claims	3	2	2
French losses	—	?	French claims	4	—	—
German claims	6†	2	German losses	1‡	—	—

† Three by flak. ‡ The Nachrichtenblatt records one aircraft missing, one officer and one NCO killed with four officers wounded.

British Casualties

Aircraft type	No.	Squadron	Crew		
BE2c	2713	2 Sqdn	2/Lt W J Stonier	KIA	
			2/Lt F R Croker	KIA	
Nieuport XVII	B1570	60 Sqdn	2/Lt F Stedman	POW	
Sop 1½ Strutter		43 Sqdn	Capt H H Balfour	Injured	
			2/Lt E H Jones	Injured	
FE2b	4850	11 Sqdn	2/Lt J A Cairnes	POW	
			1AM E G Perry	POW	
FE2b	7698	11 Sqdn	2/Lt P R Robinson	WIA	*?
			2AM H Tilley	WIA	
BE2		12 Sqdn	2AM T C Coe (O)	WIA	*

French Casualties

Farman 42		F.19	Sgt Bouchon	Unhurt	*
			Lt Fabre	WIA	

Saturday, 28 April 1917

British Front

Low cloud once more prevailed over the shattered Western Front. On the ground the British attacked on a front of several miles to the north of the Scarpe; fighting became severe. Canadian troops captured Arleux-en-Gohelle, three miles east of Vimy Ridge, and progress was made north-east of Gavrelle as well as the western slopes of Greenland Hill. South of the Scarpe ground was gained north of Monchy-le-Preux.

In the air it was to be the Germans' day with virtually no losses despite a few claims by RFC. It began soon after dawn with a 13 Squadron BE2e on a Contact Patrol over 17 Corps' area being brought down by ground fire from the trenches, so they knew they had made 'contact'! The machine was later salvaged.

A second 13 Squadron BE took on the job of artillery spotting an hour later, but this time it was a red Albatros Scout that ended the Squadron's task. Manfred von Richthofen shot down the BE into the south-east corner of the wood east of Pelves at 0930(G). The BEs were persistent, and at 1120, Kurt Wolff sent a machine of 16 Squadron down south of Oppy for his 23rd victory.

It wasn't going to be a good day for 16 Squadron either. Another dawn patrol machine had already been brought down by ground fire at o600, being forced down with its fuel tank shot through, only to crash into a front line shell-hole with a wounded observer. At 1005 two Canadians, Major E O McMurty and Lieutenant H D Mason, had taken off to patrol over Thelus. They were nearing the end of a long sortie when ground observers saw their BE come down—the apparent victim of Allied shell-fire. McMurty, from Montreal, having served in France with the Canadian Infantry since 1915, had only joined the RFC in January, became a pilot and had returned to duty in France on 18 April—ten days earlier.

Sopwith 1½ Strutters of 43 Squadron had left their base at 1050 to fly a Line Patrol between Lens and Neuvireuil and one failed to get home. The only Sopwith claimed this day was by Offizierstellvertreter Edmund Nathanael of Jasta 5. The Sopwith two-seater went down at La Vacquerie at 1315(G) for his 12th victory. Flak did claim one Sopwith on the British front, south of Tournai, but it is doubtful that a 43 Squadron machine from this sortie would have been so far over, so what it was is a mystery; but then again, Nathanael's victim was some distance from the patrol line but had obviously seen the Jasta 5 machines and the Strutters had had a go.

Not long after Major McMurty was killed by 'friendly fire', a BE2c of 2 Squadron was also hit by Allied shells while working with the 219th and 150th Siege Batteries, but this time the crew managed to get their damaged machine home. 5 Squadron's BEs also suffered. Second Lieutenant A E Clark was attacked by a German fighter soon after lunch and he was wounded in the leg but got back. At 1745(G) another 5 Squadron BE received the attention of Kurt Wolff, while on a photo op to Gavrelle.

Second Lieutenants Buckton and O'Sullivan had been trying for some time to get across to take photos that were of some importance but had been thwarted three times. Determined to carry out his assignment, Buckton made a fourth attempt. Seeing two Nieuport Scouts nearby, Buckton fired off two red lights and the two British fighters took up an escort position, but as they headed for the line again, six Halberstadt Scouts appeared, so Buckton circled, hoping they would fly off. This seemed to let the Nieuports off the hook as they flew away, leaving the BE unprotected once more.

Buckton saw the Halberstadts head away and quickly crossed the trenches to complete his task. They had exposed just one plate when the Jasta 11 pilots came back, Wolff swooping down from the low cloud. O'Sullivan began firing in defence but the BE was driven down, riddled with bullets from the German's fire. At least twenty holes were punched in the petrol tank, Buckton quickly switching off the engine to prevent fire.

O'Sullivan's fire kept at least two of the Halberstadts at bay, but Wolff's fire had taken effect, Buckton being forced to crash-land into the British lines west of Gavrelle. The BE broke in two, Buckton and O'Sullivan being obliged to get beneath the wreckage as one of the Halberstadts—perhaps Wolff himself—came down to strafe them, the German trenches being just 140 yards away. British soldiers began firing white lights at the German who then broke away and headed east.

Another BE brought down was a 52 Squadron machine at 1410(A). Second Lieutenants W D Thom and B H Armstrong were patrolling near the front, 2,000 yards north-east of Villers Plouich. Attacked by a German fighter, Thom began to spiral down, his observer's gun then jamming. The fighter followed them down, Thom force-landing south of Villers Plouich just inside British lines, the German being driven off by ground fire.

Flakbatterie 709 claimed an FE2b shot down over Villers Plouich, south-west of Cambrai but for once there were no pusher casualties on the 28th. Leutnant Julius Schmidt of Jasta 3 claimed a balloon south of Mareouil, behind Arras at 1815 hours, presumably the one lost by the 6th KBS.

What claiming the RFC did was limited to a two-seater shot down over Salome at 1000 by Lieutenant Ellis of 40 Squadron, another over Oppy at 1225 by Flight Sub Lieutenant Bob Little of 8 Naval Squadron. Later, Captain Albert Ball crashed an Albatros two-seater over Fontaine, west of Cambrai, at around 1630 while Flight Commander Ray Collishaw of 10 Naval claimed an Albatros Scout destroyed over Ostende at 2000. However, there are no German losses recorded despite all three claimants being very experienced air fighters. Collishaw, of course, may have claimed a Marine Albatros, but loss records are not available.

The Ball fight was witnessed by others of 56 Squadron, for the Flight had attacked three of the C-type machines and seen one go down and land, then saw another fall to pieces and crash. After chasing another two-seater, Ball's SE5 (A4850) was hit by AA fire which left his port elevator controls connected by a single thread and the fuselage badly damaged, but he brought it home to a safe landing.

The main feature of the fighter aircraft this day was in ground strafing, notably by aircraft of 56, 32 and 23 Squadrons, while three 56 Squadron SE5s led by Captain C M Crowe patrolled defiantly over one of the German airfields at Douai at 3,500 feet but were not challenged.

French Front

There are no records of any losses or claims on the 28th, despite the fact that Jasta 26 engaged French Sopwith two-seaters, claiming two and receiving credit for one destroyed. Vizefeldwebel Langer claimed an 'enemy aircraft' south of St Quentin at 1830(G), thinking this might have been a 1½ Strutter. He didn't receive confirmation of his claim as it went down on the Allied side.

Leutnant Hermann Göring also claimed a French Sopwith two-seater at approximately the same time, noted as being from Escadrille Sop.27, this and Langer's unconfirmed claim both being from this unit.

Leutnant Jakob Wolff of Jasta 17 also received confirmation of a claim over a Caudron at Brimont and KFlak 41 also reported shooting down a French Sopwith two-seater near Reims.

	A/C	KB			DES	OOC	KB
British losses	6	1		British claims	4	—	—
French losses	—	—		French claims	—		—
German claims	9†	1		German losses	—		—
† Three by flak.							

British Casualties

Aircraft type	No.	Squadron	Crew			
BE2e	A1843	13 Sqdn	2/Lt J H Jones	Safe		
			2/Lt G Hall	Safe		
BE2e	A2896	16 Sqdn	Capt Bird	Safe		*
			2/Lt A G Perryman	WIA		
BE2e	7221	13 Sqdn	Lt R W Follit	DOW		
			Lt F J Kirkham	WIA/POW		
BE2e	A2745	16 Sqdn	2/Lt J V Wischer	WIA/POW		
			2/Lt A A Baerlein	POW		
BE2e	A2944	16 Sqdn	Maj E O McMurtry	KIA		
			Lt H D Mason	KIA		
Sopwith 1½ Strutter	A993	43 Sqdn	2/Lt C M Reece	POW		
			2AM A Moult	WIA/POW		
BE2e	7165	52 Sqdn	2/Lt W D Thom	Safe		*
			2/Lt M H Armstrong	Safe		
BE2f	2551	5 Sqdn	2/Lt A E Clark	WIA		*
			AM Morley	Safe		
BE2c	2543	2 Sqdn	2/Lt F W Crawford	Safe		*
			Lt F B Scullard	Safe		
BE2g	2557	5 Sqdn	2/Lt N C Buckton	Safe		
			2/Lt G R O'Sullivan	Safe		

French Casualties
None recorded

Sunday, 29 April 1917

British Front

Fine weather at last, but with it came the blood-letting of the final two days of April. Ground fighting continued on a large scale with British troops capturing trench systems to the south of Oppy along a mile-long front. First figures of captured German soldiers came to 976 over the two days 28/29th.

Contact patrols were again flown, trying to locate front line troops and positions so that the Generals could plan. Among the first of these was a 12 Squadron BE2e brought down by machine-gun fire soon after its 0610 take-off time. The crew were both wounded, the machine wrecked.

Nieuports of 40 Squadron patrolled from 0645; Lieutenant J A G Brewis and Second Lieutenant W A Bond came under intense ground fire which hit Brewis' machine which crashed, killing its pilot. Flak 61 and 68 claimed him, north of Hendecourt.

Two hours later—1015—57 Squadron's FEs were flying a Line Patrol between Lieven and Noreuil. They saw two SE5s fighting five or six enemy fighters over Dury and joined in. Captain N G McNaughton and Second Lieutenant H G Downing (A6365) attacked an Albatros; the German pilot, as he dived, was seen to fall from it before the machine hit the ground. The FEs were engaged in turn by the Albatros Scouts from Jasta 12. Unteroffizier Friedrich Gille came down on A6355 and as the rest of the FEs fought their way west—claiming one Albatros destroyed and two out of control—they saw their companions turning on to the tail of one Albatros near Noyelles, but that was the last they saw of them. The dog-fight drifted south, but finally Gille got the upper hand and sent the FE down north of Barelle at 1055(G) where the crew got down but were taken prisoner. Gille had his first victory of an eventual six. Jasta 12 itself did not record any losses in personnel.

It was a good day for German flak gunners too, with so many low flying RFC machines over the front, either on contact work or low strafing sorties. 29 Squadron's Nieuports came in for some rough handling during a late morning OP where they obviously dropped down to try some strafing mayhem on the ground but came under fire from MFlak 63 south of Dury. Two of the nimble Nieuports were hit and brought down, putting two more young pilots in a prison camp.

The Naval boys were much in evidence in the last hour before noon, 1 and 3 Naval claiming three hostile aircraft destroyed, one in flames, plus six out of control, including a C-type. Shortly before midday, Lieutenant Bishop of 60 Squadron claimed a Halberstadt DII in flames east of Epinoy. Once again there is a lack of recorded losses by the Germans. However, the two-seater, although only claimed as 'out of control', may well have been the FA2 machine that came down near Barelle, north-west of Cambrai, in which Leutnants Bruno Kittel and Hermann Waldschmidt died. Flight Sub Lieutenants C B Ridley and H V Rowley claimed the two-seater near Villers- les-Cagnicourt, which is just to the west of Barelle.

The 3 Naval's Pups had been escorting FEs, led by Flight Lieutenant H G Travers with five machines, and Flight Lieutenant Lloyd Breadner with another five. They had picked up the pushers south of Cambrai and saw them safely back from their recce job, keeping position between the sun and the FEs at 14,000 feet. They attacked three enemy machines over Villers Outreaux but they quickly dived away east. It was in the subsequent fight with eight scouts that Flight Sub Lieutenant S L Bennett was lost while Breadner's men fought them. Travers then returned having seen the FEs safely across the lines.

Obviously Jasta 5 was one of the units involved in the fighting, for Leutnant Kurt Schneider claimed a Pup over Elincourt, inside German lines, Bennett going down near this location. 3 Naval claimed three scouts out of control, but needless to say the Germans were again spinning down out of trouble.

The most serious loss to the Royal Flying Corps this day was the CO of 19 Squadron, Major H D Harvey-Kelly DSO. As is well known, Harvey-Kelly was the first RFC pilot to land in France after war had been declared, as a pilot with 2 Squadron on 13 August 1914. He had been commissioned into the Royal Irish Rifles in 1900 and had transferred to the RFC in 1913. He had received the DSO in February 1915 and took command of 19 Squadron in January 1916.

In the late morning of this day, Harvey-Kelly led a three-man patrol between Lens, Fontaine and Noreuil in their Spad VIIs—Jasta 11 country. Shortly after they took off, General Hugh Trenchard and his right-hand man, Major Maurice Baring, arrived at Vert Galant where 19 (66 and 56 Squadrons too) were based. They had come to see Harvey-Kelly and have lunch, only to learn that he had just flown off but would be back in an hour or so. They had lunch but were destined never to see Harvey-Kelly again.

The three Spads were spotted by von Richthofen, flying with several of his Jasta, and attacked them near Lecluse, south of Douai just after midday German time. Von Richthofen shot his man down into the swamps—Second Lieutenant Richard Applin's Spad falling in pieces—while brother Lothar brought down Lieutenant W N Hamilton near Izel after a chase north-west. It fell to Wolff to bring down Harvey-Kelly, shot down over Sailly-en-Ostrevent. This brought the Baron's score to 49. Would he reach 50 before the end of April?

Back at Vert Galant, with lunch over and no sign of the three pilots, Trenchard took his leave saying, 'Tell Harvey-Kelly I was very sorry to miss him.' Baring was to record that the tone of Trenchard's voice made it clear that he never expected the message to be delivered and neither did Baring.

FE2bs of 18 Squadron took off at 1420 to escort a photo machine to the 5th Army area and clashed with Jasta 11 over the front lines. They just had time to refuel, rearm and have some quick refreshment before they were off once more. Manfred von Richthofen and Kurt Wolff each despatched one FE, the Baron's falling inside German lines, south-west of Inchy, Wolff's in British front line trenches with a dead gunner. Another 18 Squadron pilot was wounded in the fight but he brought his machine back to base. It also brought von Richthofen's score of kills to 50 and Wolff's to 26—and the day was far from over.

The FE crews later reported being attacked by three Albatros Scouts (in fact there were five), the gunners claiming one Scout shot down in flames and another out of control. The 'surviving' Albatros shot up Second Lieutenants Dinsmore and Bate's FE, but Dinsmore succeeded in recrossing the lines, followed closely by Wolff, who watched it force-land south of Pronville. As Wolff headed back, troops from the Border Regiment helped Dinsmore get the wounded Bate from the machine but he died soon afterwards.

The British troops confirmed the action and saw one of the enemy machines wrecked on the ground and the other falling. As Jasta 11 had no casualties in this action, one wonders what they saw. Probably they were seeing the other FE go down—it fell in flames and the crew fell or jumped out—and von Richthofen reducing height as he followed it down.

One of the FEs to escape the main fight was that flown by Second Lieutenant G A Critchley (A851) whose observer, Lieutenant Oliver Partington, noted in his log book:

'Duty: Photography. Ht. 10,000 ft. Five photos taken, large camera. Six HA attacked the formation E of Cagnicourt, no combat owing to pilot diving and losing touch with the rest of formation. AA normal, visibility fair.'

Partington sounded a bit miffed, but if he had known it was von Richthofen and his pilots, he may have thought Critchley's move a good one.

More FEs, this time 20 Squadron's, headed for the northern part of the front, taking off between 1545 and 1600 hours, carrying bombs to raid Bisseghem Dump, just outside Courtrai. Jasta 18 rose from Halluin and met the pushers west of Courtrai, Leutnants Paul Strähle and Ernst Weissner each bringing down one. 20 Squadron reported being attacked by 20 Albatros Scouts, and in the fight that ensued claimed two shot down in flames, a third crashed and another out of control, while losing two FEs. Another FE, its fuel tank holed, force-landed at 42 Squadron's base, but was otherwise unharmed.

A third FE was crewed by the veterans Second Lieutenant E O Perry and 2AM T E Allum, both wounded north-west of Sanctury Wood—by AA fire, so they said—although Leutnant Gustav Nolte also claimed an FE shot down into British lines at Hooge. Perry got A29 down safely but the machine was burnt out. Jasta 18 suffered no losses.

Meantime, Jasta 11 had again landed and refuelled. No sooner had they done so than reports of more aircraft over the front sent the Richthofen brothers to their machines. Two 12 Squadron BE2s were working with artillery over the front, having taken off at 1645 and 1648 respectively. The brothers attacked them at 1925(G)—1825 British time—Manfred's victim falling without its wings near Roeux on the Scarpe, near the front line trenches, Lothar's crashing north-west of Monchy-le-Preux, again right by the front lines.

Lieutenants J H Westlake and C J Pile, in the BE attacked by Lothar von Richthofen, also had wing problems. The lower wing was shot away and the upper was damaged.

Westlake got it down under some sort of control but it collapsed as soon as he touched down. Cyril Pile suffered injuries including a broken thigh, but died while being carried to the aid station of the 9th Battalion of the Essex Regiment.

There were several other skirmishes throughout the day, mainly against the artillery observation squadrons, several machines returning with wounded pilots or observers, as well as one wounded 55 Squadron bomber pilot. The final flurry of aerial activity embraced a large dog-fight between Spads, Nieuports and Triplanes near Henin-Lietard and which netted for Manfred von Richthofen his 52nd victory, and his fourth for the day.

For many years the results of this battle have been wrongly assessed merely because von Richthofen did not mention the actual type of aircraft that he shot down. In his combat report he certainly mentions all three of the above types and early historians looked for an obvious victim and came up with Captain F L Barwell of 40 Squadron (Nieuports) who was lost during this evening. However, Barwell took off at 1820 and Richthofen's timing of his combat at 1940 German time seemed to fit, although it would have been 1840 British time; ie. 20 minutes after Barwell left Lozinghem.

Richthofen had only just shot down his 12 Squadron BE a short time before when he became embroiled in this final action of the day. If the earlier historians were to be believed, Barwell, in his final 20 minutes, had to fly the 25 km to the lines while gaining height, then have a 'long' air fight. An infantry report of the fight between the red Albatros and the British machine said that it lasted almost half an hour! So much for the 20 minutes Barlow had from take-off to falling. In any event, Richthofen stated his victim fell after 'a short time' so we can discount the half an hour fight as being with Richthofen.

Richthofen's 52nd victim was Canadian Flight Sub Lieutenant A E Cuzner of 8 Naval in a Triplane—the same type as recorded in the Nachrichtenblatt as Richthofen's victim. Richthofen and Jasta 11 were in action mainly with the Triplanes of 1 and 8 Naval, one ace (Little) and two future aces being in evidence: R P Minifie and Victor Rowley of 1 Naval, Bob Little of 8 Naval. So it was these men who were in action with Richthofen and Jasta 11. In fact it was Little who saw a red Albatros bring down a BE over Monchy (Lothar von Richthofen) and dived on it. Only heavy AA fire deflected Little from closing in, which allowed the younger Richthofen to escape. Little and Minifie then got into a fight with an Albatros which ended with a German fighter crashing on Douai aerodrome. Minifie was then worked over by several enemy fighters, which put several holes through his Triplane and one through the left longeron. On his way back, Richard Minifie shot up some troops on a road for good measure. His shared victory was his second of the day and his second of an eventual 21 victories.

But what of Barwell? Who shot him down at the end of the half-hour combat? There were two claims for aircraft at around this time: Edmund Nathanael of Jasta 5 and Hermann Göring of Jasta 26. However, Jasta 26 was operating too far to the south, east of St Quentin, so that discounts Barwell. 6 Naval did have a scrap at 1855(A) over Guise, near St Quentin, claiming one EA in flames and two out of control, Göring shooting down Flight Sub Lieutenant A H V Fletcher north-east of St Quentin at 1945(G). Flight Sub Lieutenant R R Winter in a Nieuport XVIIbis (N3199) was badly shot up but got back. Perhaps the late confirmation of Oberleutnant Bruno Loerzer, Jasta 26's commander, at 1930 near Bellenglise which was eventually credited as his 5th victory

According to Jasta 5 records, Nathanael shot down a Triplane at 2100(G) over Beaumont, inside German lines. In the Nachrichtenblatt Nathanael's victory is recorded as a Rumpf Eins —single-seat with fuselage! (As opposed to a pusher type without the usual fuselage body, ie: gitter-rumpf.) Nathanael's claim is timed at 2100 (ie: 2000 British time) which is a better fit for Barwell, who would have been in the air for an hour and 40 minutes by then.

1 Naval Squadron had put up three Triplanes at 1700(A) and 45 minutes later, over Beaumont, they had an indecisive fight with two hostile scouts. Soon afterwards, when east of Lens, Flight Sub Lieutenant A P Heyward engaged another enemy machine which dived vertically, but then Heyward was attacked by three more scouts and was wounded in the arm but got back and landed south of Bethune.

Another 1 Naval Squadron patrol set out at 1805 with five Triplanes. Near Gavrelle, Flight

Sub Lieutenant H V Rowley attacked a red 'Nieuport' and fired 50 rounds at 50 yards, the hostile scout going down out of control for his first victory of an eventual nine, but he was then engaged by three more scouts. His engine was hit so he made straight for the lines and made an emergency landing in a field south of Bethune, but his machine turned over when landing on soft ground. As far as time is concerned, Nathanael's 'Triplane' claim seems to fit Rowley better than Heyward, despite the German saying his victim came down inside German lines, which Rowley did not—nor did Heyward. To add to all this confusion, another 1 Naval Triplane came down in the area south of Bethune. Flight Sub Lieutenant H D M Wallace developed engine trouble and was forced to land, but thinking he was in enemy territory, set fire to his machine which burnt out before he knew he was on the right side of the lines. So, if Nathanael's Rumpf Eins was not a Triplane, but a Nieuport, then Barwell had to have been brought down by him.

The crew of a BE2g, flying a recce sortie between Bailleul-Sir-Berthoult and Gavrelle, just north-east of Arras, had a lucky escape. Lieutenant A E Illingworth and Second Lieutenant F Tymms (6277) were at 5,000 feet when they spotted six German fighters almost directly overhead; two were coloured red, so one can assume they were Jasta 11 aircraft. It was 1815 as Arthur Illingworth saw the leader commence a dive. Illingworth side-slipped and endeavoured to manoeuvre his BE out of the attacker's line of fire. The other fighters came down too and each made at least two attacks on the two-seater as it headed west, twisting and turning as it went. As they reached Mont St Eloi (which is within sight of Vimy Ridge) the fighters gave up the chase, but none had come too close for fear of the observer's rear gun, although Tymms had had no opportunity to fire, hoping in vain that one of the hostile machines would come in close.

An Albatros two-seater was claimed out of control near Pont Rouge on the River Lys just north of Armentières, by Captain E D Atkinson of 1 Squadron, at 1740. Atkinson (A6678) saw the two-seater approaching the lines opposite Ploegsteert Wood at 16,000 feet. The British pilot climbed between Ploegsteert and Armentières, then attacked as the two-seater turned and headed for Lille, its observer firing back at the Nieuport. Over Pont Rouge he got in 25 rounds from 30 yards which caused smoke to stream from the engine. The observer appeared to have been hit but then the machine went down in a vertical dive, in fact going over beyond the vertical. Atkinson then saw three Albatros Scouts below in his line of dive, so he pulled out and headed back. Apart from the two-seater 1 Naval claimed, this is the only other C-type accounted for this day. The Germans did incur some two-seater casualties but it is difficult to tie up victories with victims.

Oberleutnant Georg Kraft, observer with FA4 was killed over Marsoenel, Arras; Vizefeldwebel Rener of FA(A)48 was wounded over Carvin, north-east of Lens; his observer, Leutnant Alois Stegmann, was killed.

French Front

Four hostile aircraft were claimed by French fighter pilots, one two-seater Albatros being claimed at 1343(A) at Fleuricourt by Sous Lieutenant 'Pere' Dorme of N.3. It was Dorme's 21st victory. A scout fell north-east of Nauroy at 1500, shot down by Lieutenant Beraud-Villars of N.102. This was probably flown by the Staffelführer of Jasta 29, Leutnant Ludwig Dornheim, who was killed over Biene-Nauroy.

Sous Lieutenant Baudoin of N.80 shot down a two-seater at Moulins, the crew being captured, while Sous Lieutenant Lebeau of N.12 claimed his fourth victory by downing a machine over Orainville at 1745 hours.

Losses for the Germans on this front were Leutnant Peckman of Jasta 15, wounded; observer Leutnant Erich Bamm of FA(A)201, killed over Marchais, near Liesse; Flieger Ernst Deutchman of Schutzstaffel 22, killed over Bray-en-Laonnois.

On the debit side a Caudron G4 of C.9 was attacked by two enemy machines on the Nancy front, wounding the pilot, Caporal Luizet. On the Soissons sector, Maréchal-des-Logis Ravet, piloting a Morane Parasol of C.122, was also wounded along with his gunner, Soldat Cassonnet, Ravet being forced to make an emergency landing near Ferme d'Alger.

Sergent Leroy of N.12 was wounded and his Spad VII damaged, while a Letord of C.46

failed to return from a mission. This was probably the 'Caudron' claimed by Leutnant Walter Böning of Jasta 19 for his 3rd victory which fell at Brimont. Two other Caudrons were claimed during the day, one by Gefreiter Reichardt and Leutnant Zupan of FA7 near Marcoing at 1150, while Leutnant Heinrich Geigl of Jasta 34 claimed one south of Pont-à-Mousson at 1415(G), which was inside French lines. This may have been the Caudron of C.222 that returned with a wounded observer.

A Voisin of VB.114 also failed to get home. This machine suffered from engine trouble which forced the pilot to put down north of Pouvres where he and his observer were taken into captivity.

Leutnant Richard Ernert of Jasta 34 claimed a balloon at Fort Genicourt which was that of 87 Cié.

	A/C	KB		DES	OOC	KB
British losses	20	—	British claims	11	21	—
French losses	2	—	French claims	4		?
German claims	23†	1	German losses	4‡		1

† Four to flak. ‡ The Nachrichtenblatt records two aircraft in German lines, two missing, one balloon lost; three airmen killed in action plus three wounded.

British Casualties

Aircraft type	No.	Squadron	Crew		
BE2e	6768	12 Sqdn	Lt N H Mackrow	WIA	
			Lt J M Musson	WIA	
Nieuport XVII	A6739	40 Sqdn	Lt J W Brewis	KIA	
FE2d	A6355	57 Sqdn	2/Lt F A W Handley	POW	
			2/Lt E Percival	POW	
Nieuport XXIII	B1579	29 Sqdn	Lt H B M Milling	POW	
Nieuport XXIII	A6684	29 Sqdn	Sgt G Humble	POW	
Sopwith Pup	A6160	6N Sqdn	FSL S L Bennett	KIA	
Spad VII	A6681	19 Sqdn	Maj H D Harvey-Kelly	KIA	
Spad VII	A6753	19 Sqdn	Lt W N Hamilton	POW	
Spad VII	B1573	19 Sqdn	2/Lt R Applin	KIA	
Nieuport XVII	N3192	6N Sqdn	FSL A H V Fletcher	POW/WIA	
FE2b	4898	18 Sqdn	Sgt G Stead	KIA	
			Cpl A Beebee	KIA	
FE2b	A5483	18 Sqdn	2/Lt G H Dinsmore	Safe	
			2/Lt G B Bate	KIA	
FE2b		18 Sqdn	2/Lt R C Doughty (P)	WIA	*
FE2d	A29	20 Sqdn	2/Lt E O Perry	WIA	
			2AM T E Allum	WIA	
FE2b	A19	20 Sqdn	Sgt S Attwater	POW	
			2/Lt J E Davies	POW	
FE2b	A6391	20 Sqdn	2/Lt V L A Burns	POW	
			2/Lt D L Houghton	POW	
BE2e	7092	12 Sqdn	Lt J H Westlake	WIA	
			Lt C J Pile	DOW	
BE2e	2738	12 Sqdn	Lt D E Davies	KIA	
			Lt G H Rathbone	KIA	
Sop Triplane	N5484	1N Sqdn	FSL A P Heyward	WIA	*
Sop Triplane	N5441	1N Sqdn	FSL H M D Wallace	Safe	
Sop Triplane	N5463	8N Sqdn	FSL A E Cuzner	KIA	
Nieuport XVII	A6745	40 Sqdn	Capt F L Barwell	KIA	
BE2c		9 Sqdn	2/Lt H J Grogarty (P)	WIA	
BE2c		7 Sqdn	2/Lt J H Haywood (P)	WIA	
DH4		55 Sqdn	Lt C G Sturt (P)	WIA	

French Casualties

Caudron G4		C.9	Cpl Luizet (P)	WIA	*
Morane Parasol		C.122	MdL Ravet	WIA	*
			Sol Cassonnet	WIA	
Spad VII		N.12	Sgt Leroy	WIA	*
Letord	90	C.46	Lt Campion	MIA	
			MdL Lamy	MIA	
			Cpl Bousque	MIA	

Voisin	1746	VB.114	Adj Durand	POW	
			Lt Lalaune	POW	
Caudron G4		C.222	S/Lt de Bussy (O)	WIA	*

Monday, 30 April 1917

British Front

Weather-wise it was another fine day for this last day of April. While British troops continued to fight along their front, the French made an attack in the Champagne region, taking several German trenches at Mont Carnillet to the south of Beine. Also significant was the announcement that General Henri Philippe Pétain had been appointed as Chief of the French General Staff, replacing General Nivelle, thus becoming the new Commander in Chief.

For the RFC this last day of April was to be another period of losses to the German Jasta pilots and ground gunners. This day also heralded a new phase in German air policy. For the first time four German Jastas were grouped together into one fighting formation. The four units were Jastas 3, 4, 11 and 33, all based in the Douai area.

While it would be difficult for the four units actually to fly together in formation, simply because up to 20-25 aircraft in one group was almost unheard of, it was almost impossible for a single man even to attempt to control such numbers in the air. In reality, however, the units continued to fight individually, but sometimes in two Jasta strength. The main reason for the grouping was so that a large body of fighting aeroplanes could be moved as a mass unit to various parts of the battle front, wherever they were needed most. This grouping became more official in June 1917 upon the formation of Jagdesgeschwader Nr.I (Jastas 4, 6, 10 and 11) under the leadership of Manfred von Richthofen.

Due to the constant moving of the group from sector to sector, plus the highly imaginative colouring schemes being painted on their scouts by individual German fighter pilots, it was little wonder that the group soon became known as the Circus. Late on 30 April, however, von Richthofen left the front for some well-earned leave, his brother Lothar taking temporary command of the Jasta.

Dawn on this Monday saw the BEs rising from their aerodromes to start the day's work of contact patrols and artillery registration sorties. Always ready for the rich pickings, just like anglers on a river bank at first light, the German fighter pilots too headed for the front lines, their keen eyes ready to pick out the early 'fish'.

Sopwith 1½ Strutters of 45 Squadron provided escort for a photo sortie first thing, on the northern part of the front. Vizefeldwebel Max Müller saw the British machines flying near Armentières and attacked one of the escorts. The one he singled out, flown by Second Lieutenant W A Wright with his gunner 2AM B G Perrott, put up a good fight, but Perrott was hit and dropped out of sight into his cockpit. Bill Wright, a future ace on both Strutters and later Camels, got his machine back across the lines and put down at Lillers, where the machine was written-off, only to find his rear man dead.

Second Lieutenants N A Lawrence and C R Y Stout of 16 Squadron (Stout was about to receive the MC) took off from Bruay at 0540 to fly a contact patrol 3,000 yards east of Vimy Ridge. They were almost at the end of their patrol time when the sharp stutter of machine-guns heralded a diving Albatros. Lothar von Richthofen watched as his victim nosed over and went down in flames to crash; victory number 16.

A 9 Squadron BE on patrol was attacked and shot down at Le Pave by Leutnant Friedrich Kempf of Jasta 2, having also left its base at 0540. Meantime, 57 Squadron flew a line patrol between Lieven and Noreuil, led by Captain Harker, and ran into a grinder in the shape of Jastas 11, 12 and 33 (not the new group formation!) near Douai.

Lothar von Richthofen was still in the air following his downing of the 16 Squadron BE forty minutes earlier. Seeing the FEs he attacked and brought down one at Izel. Adolf von Tutschek, leader of Jasta 12, clawed down a second FE at the same location and time—0755(G). The fight must have broken up for these two FEs were the only ones lost, but some of the surviving FEs obviously continued with their mission, for more than half an hour later, Leutnant Geiseler from Jasta 33 attacked an FE and chased it over the lines near Oppy, but he did not have his victory confirmed. The FE finally made a forced landing near Roclincourt and although the machine was wrecked, the crew were unhurt. They were Lieutenants C S Morice and F Leathley, who had claimed one Albatros out of control. They then flew west, followed by four or five fighters, having their radiator hit. They continued to evade the worst of the enemy's fire as they also lost height, then had to run the gauntlet of ground fire as they flashed over the trenches at 500 feet. Finally the FE's engine seized and they force-landed at Roclincourt, 3,000 yards inside British territory.

Amidst all this, the Squadron CO, Major L A Pattinson, with Lieutenant Angus Mearns, had taken off to do an engine test. They saw the fight going on over the lines and despite the engine overheating flew to help out, claiming one Albatros down out of control and another driven down with a dead engine, but by this time the main casualties had occurred.

This wasn't the end of 57 Squadron's misery, for another patrol took off at 0900 and also ran into hostile aircraft, Lieutenant J H Ryan being mortally wounded and his gunner, Second Lieutenant B Soutton, also hit. Ryan got his machine down inside British lines at Miraumont at 1020 but died soon afterwards.

Near Armentières at 0855(A), Captain C J Quintin-Brand of 1 Squadron closed in on two two-seaters he'd seen going west over Wytschaete five minutes earlier. He finally engaged one south of Neuve Eglise, firing from 100 yards. He hit the observer, who was seen to drop down into his cockpit. Now free to close right in, he did so, shooting the two-seater down into Allied lines at Houplines. This was an Albatros C of FA204 flown by Vizefeldwebel Max Baatz and Leutnant Alexander Schleiper. Both men were killed and the machine was numbered G.27 by the British.

Later this morning, 16 Squadron had sent out another BE to photograph sections east of Vimy but this had the bad luck to run into a machine of FA(A)233 crewed by Vizefeldwebel Brokmann and Leutnant Pedell who shot the British machine down over Fresnoy at 1010(G). This was just inside British lines; the BE was wrecked but both men scrambled clear relatively unharmed.

More FEs ran into trouble on this sunny morning, 18 Squadron flying escort to their own photo machines. They were attacked by fighters and fought a defensive battle back to the lines, one with a dead gunner and a wounded pilot, while a second had to make a crash-landing but the crew were unhurt. There were no German claims as they had no firm idea how much damage had been inflicted. Once again Oliver Partington was observer to G A Critchley and noted in his log-book:

> 'Photography: FE A851. 0810-1030. Ht. 11,000 ft—two photos taken, large camera. AA normal, visibility fair. Formation attacked by about 20 HA Scouts over Baralle. One HA came direct for our tail, fired ½ drum from back gun into him; he swerved past on left and I fired another half drum from front gun. HA then dived with engine trailing cloud of smoke. Fired three-quarters of a drum from front gun at another HA flying E about 1,500 ft below; he nose-dived, apparently out of control.'

The new SE5s of 56 Squadron flew an OP between Vitry and Villiers on this morning, taking off at 0805. They were engaged by some Albatros Scouts of Jasta 5 and Lieutenant M A Kay was shot down east of Fresnoy by Edmund Nathanael. Lieutenant J O Leach was then reported to have attacked the victorious German pilot having seen him shoot down Maurice Kay. The Albatros caught fire and crashed, but as far as is known, Nathanael was not shot down nor did Jasta 5 lose any pilots in this action. In fact Nathanael would claim one more victory (his 15th) before being killed in May 1917.

There were more combats taking place along the front during mid-morning operations. An OP by 1 Naval, led by Dallas, provided escort for 48 Squadron's Bristols. An estimated 20 enemy fighters tried persistently to engage the two-seaters south of Douai for more than 20 minutes but only succeeded in wounding one observer. Dallas claimed a two-seater Rumpler crashed near Hayencourt (see later). As the two-seaters headed home, the Triplanes went to help some FEs and managed to drive the Albatros pilots away, Dallas sending one down out of control.

Another 9 Squadron BE was in the air at 1000, flying a photo op east of Vimy—the generals were determined to get their pictures—but the German fighter pilots were equally determined to stop it. Hans Klein of Jasta 4 went down on this BE at noon German time, sending it crashing at Ribecourt, the first kill by Jasta 4 since the 14th.

The Spads of 19 Squadron took off at 1130 to fly an OP between Lens, Le Forest, Fontaine and Noreuil, led by Captain D A L Davidson MC. This was the Squadron's third OP of the day. On the second Davidson and Lieutenant J M Child had a fight with three EA near Vitry but had to return with gun jams. Taking off again they found a two-seater of Schutzstaffel 19 over the front, but in the attack, Davidson's Spad was hit badly and disintegrated—blown to pieces was one description—and fell to earth. The German crewmen were Vizefeldwebels Voigt and Woldt, their victim falling over Sallaumines on the outskirts of Lens at 1320(G).

Further north, Nieuports of 1 Squadron escorted FE2s on a bomb raid late morning, and as the formation turned west after dropping their bombs, a number of German fighters engaged them between Gulleghem and Ypres. The Nieuports were led by Captain C J Quintin-Brand, who had brought down a two-seater a couple of hours earlier, and in the fight, a couple of Germans were sent down out of control, while the FEs drove down another.

After lunch it was the turn of 15 Squadron to have problems during an artillery shoot in their Corps area. A crew took off at 1330 and did some good work for two hours, almost at the end of their duty, but the BE was a tempting target and finally it was hit by fire from KFlak 61 and Flakzug 28. Lieutenant Paris couldn't make the trenches and he and his observer were taken prisoner after a forced landing east of Cherisy.

Yet another BE was brought down in mid-afternoon, 13 Squadron having put up a machine to take photos over the 17th Corps front at 1508. Kurt Wolff of Jasta 11 was watching and waiting west of Vitry, swooping down with Spandaus blazing at 1735(G). His fire knocked out the observer and wounded the pilot, but he got his machine over the lines and force-landed west of Fresnes. 13 Squadron had another observer wounded during the day and so too did 12 Squadron; in fact it had two observers wounded in air fights.

Nieuports of 29 Squadron were on escort duty over the front at this time and were engaged by Jasta 3. Second Lieutenant R H Upson was in a brand new machine when fire from Karl Menckhoff smashed his engine and forced him to put down at Cantin at 1850(G) after one hour's flying time. As the Nieuport only had a total of one hour 45 minutes recorded, it must have just run up about 45 minutes of flight testing and delivery time prior to this sortie, and its career was now at an end. Menckhoff had his 3rd victory of an eventual 39.

One other Nieuport, but one which was not confirmed, had been attacked by Leutnant Karl Deilmann of Jasta 6 near Roupy. It came down near Monchy le Preux, after a fight with Albatros Scouts. This had been flown by Major A J L 'Jack' Scott, CO of 60 Squadron, but he was safe and unharmed.

The final loss of April was a Naval Pup of 3 Naval Squadron. The Naval boys were providing escort to FEs of 18 Squadron west of Cambrai, the Pups having taken off at 1615. Flight Sub Lieutenant J J Malone was on his second sortie of the day, having flown escort to 4 Squadron BEs bombing railway yards at Cambrai that morning. The Pups got tangled up with Albatros Scouts from Jasta 12, and despite his experience—John Malone had achieved ten victories in air combat since the beginning of March and won the DSO – he was bested in this action by the embryo pilot Leutnant Paul Billik, who shot him down over Remaucourt at 1810(G). It was Billik's first confirmed victory—the first of an eventual 31. He had been with Jasta 12 just over a month.

On the RFC side, once again a number of German aircraft had been claimed shot down; in fact seven destroyed and 23 out of control. Among the destroyed had been a Rumpler two-seater by Roderick Dallas of 1 Naval Squadron over Haynecourt at 0835 and another C-type by Captain J O Andrews of 66 Squadron between Brebières and Vitry at 0845. Of two machines that came down inside British lines this Monday, one became G.28 in the RFC numbering system, noted as a DFW CV, brought down by ground fire, its crew taken prisoner, the other recorded as an Albatros C, and numbered G.27, which was Quintin-Brand's victim.

Another German artillery unit—FA(A)233—recorded the loss of observer Leutnant August Rodenbeck on the 30th, killed near Oppy, which was right on the British front line. Yet another

—FA(A)238—recorded the death of Oberleutnant Hermann Benckiser at Roucourt. A third two-seater crew from the 2 Armee area, FA(A)259, Vizefeldwebel Max Reichle and Leutnant Erich Hampe were reported missing. These two men force-landed at Hendicourt with a damaged machine and are obviously the crew of G.28 reported captured.

Another crew who came off second best were Leutnants Tüxen and Wissemann of FA250, who were both slightly wounded. Kurt Wissemann would later become a fighter pilot and fly with Jasta 3 the following month and be credited with bringing down the French ace Georges Guynemer in September.

It is also noted that Lieutenant W A Bishop of 60 Squadron claimed a two-seater crashed south-east of Lens at 1115 and another forced to land south of Lens shortly afterwards, both inside German lines.

The only recorded casualty of a German fighter pilot was Leutnant Friedrich Mallinckrodt of Jasta 20, a six-victory ace, severely wounded while operating over the southern sectors of the British front, possibly the victim of Captain W J C K Cockran-Patrick of 23 Squadron, who claimed an Albatros in flames at 1640, west of Cambrai.

The Belgian pilot, Andre de Meulemeester of 1ere Escadrille, claimed a C-type this day, over Lecke—just inside German lines—flying a Nieuport. It was his first victory of an eventual 11.

French Front

A claim was made by a French fighter pilot, Lieutenant Bailly of N.81 when he shot down a two-seater in flames at Moranvillers, for his first victory. This is believed to have been a machine from KG2 that fell over Reims, Leutnants Karl Beckmann and Ernst Poetsch being killed. Adjutant Lucien Jailler of N.15 gained his 8th victory near Laon at 0940, type not recorded.

One of the iron men of French fighter aviation, Lieutenant Jacques Leps of Spa.81, took on two Albatros Scouts—and lost. Shot up, he crashed his Spad VII on Mont Cornillet, after just making it back across the lines. Leps would score 12 victories by the end of the war.

Two more fighters were brought down. A Nieuport Scout of N.38, flown by Caporal Leroy, failed to return, being forced down in a combat with Leutnant Otto von Breiten-Landenberg of Jasta 9 at 1100 hours, near St Hilaire le Petit. Sergent Baudson of N.15 was wounded flying a Spad VII in the Soissons sector. Jasta 9 claimed three Spads: Leutnant Friedrich von Hartmann south-west of Nauroy at 0925(G) and Leutnant Hermann Pfeiffer at 1030 at Moranvillers, and finally Leutnant Adolf Frey at 1115, again over Moranvillers. One of them was probably Leps.

Frey, however, was then shot down in flames near Nauroy while attacking a Caudron R4, and Leutnant Werner Marwitz was also killed over Nauroy, although there are no records to indicate how Marwitz met his end.

Jasta 19 attacked the French balloon lines in force, claiming three destroyed at Guyencourt and two near Reims. Oberleutnant Erich Hahn claimed two, Vizefeldwebel Arthur Rahn two and Leutnant Walter Böning one. Leutnant Matthaei of Jasta 21 claimed a sixth balloon at 1440, over Montbre-Trois. The French lost balloons Cié 19, 59, 62 and 91.

	A/C	KB		DES	OOC	KB
British losses	15	—	British claims	8‡	23	—
French losses	2	?	French claims	1		—
German claims	19†	6	German losses	8*		—

† Three by flak. ‡ Plus one more if indeed ground fire brought down G.28. * The Nachrichtenblatt records six aircraft lost in combat plus two more missing, with two officers killed and four wounded.

British Casualties

Aircraft type	No.	Squadron	Crew	
BE2g	A2942	16 Sqdn	2/Lt N A Lawrence	KIA
			2/Lt G R Y Stout	KIA
BE2g	A2949	9 Sqdn	2/Lt D McTavish	POW
			Capt A S Allen MC	KIA
Sop 1½ Strutter	A1080	45 Sqdn	2/Lt W A Wright	Safe

			2AM B G Perrott	KIA	
FE2d	A6402	57 Sqdn	Lt P T Bowers	POW	
			2/Lt S T Wills	POW	
FE2d	A6352	57 Sqdn	2/Lt E D Jennings	POW	
			2/Lt J R Lingard	POW	
FE2d	A1966	57 Sqdn	Lt C S Morice	Safe	
			Lt F Leathey	Safe	
FE2d	A6380	57 Sqdn	Lt J H Ryan	DOW	*
			2/Lt B Soutten	WIA	
FE2b	A5143	20 Sqdn	Lt D Y Hoy	Safe	
			Sgt E H Sayers	Safe	
BE2g	A251	16 Sqdn	2/Lt Stewart	Safe	
			2/Lt Boyle	Safe	
SE5	A4866	56 Sqdn	Lt M A Kay	KIA	
FE2b	6998	18 Sqdn	Sgt T Whiteman	WIA	*
			2AM J H Wynn	DOW	
BE2e	A2916	9 Sqdn	2/Lt R P C Freemantle	KIA	
			2/Lt P Sherman	KIA	
Spad VII	B1562	19 Sqdn	Capt D A L Davidson	KIA	
BE2e	7060	15 Sqdn	Lt D K Paris MC	POW	
			2/Lt A E Fereman	POW	
BE2e	A2910	13 Sqdn	2/Lt W K Trollope	WIA	
			2/Lt A Bonner	KIA	
Nieuport XVII	B1601	29 Sqdn	2/Lt R H Upson	POW	
Sopwith Pup	N6175	3N Sqdn	FSL J J Malone DSO	KIA	
BE2c		12 Sqdn	2AM J J Cameron (O)	WIA	*
BE2c		12 Sqdn	2AM D W Imber (O)	WIA	*
BE2c		13 Sqdn	1AM L Baines (O)	WIA	*
BF2a		48 Sqdn	Cpl R Edwards (O)	KIA	*

French Casualties

Nieuport XVII	N.38	Cpl Leroy	MIA	
Spad VII	N.15	Sgt Baudson	WIA	*
Spad VII	Spa.81	Lt A L J Leps	Safe	

APPENDIX I
RFC Victory Claims for April 1917

1 April 1917

Time	Pilot/Crew	Sqdn	Vic No	E/A	Location	How
1050	2/Lt D Gordon &	12	1	Albatros DIII	Arras	DF
	S/Lt H E Baker	12	1			

2 April 1917

Time	Pilot/Crew	Sqdn	Vic No	E/A	Location	How
0745	S/Lt C S Hall	60	1	Albatros DIII	Fontaine Notre Dame	OOC
0800	Lt O M Sutton	54	1	2-seater	Peronne	OOC
0850	Lt S Cockerall	24	5	Albatros DII	Gouzeaucourt	D
0855	Lt K Crawford	24	4			
	Capt C R Cox &	24	2	Albatros DII	Gouzeaucourt	DF
	Lt L C Welsford	24	1			
0945	S/Lt E E Pope &	57	1	Albatros DIII	SE Arras	DF
	Lt A W Naismith	57	1			
0945	2/Lt E E Pope &	57	2	Albatros DIII	SE Arras	DF
	Lt A W Naismith	57	2			
1105	2/Lt C E Berigny	43	1	Albatros DIII	E Vimy	DF
	2/AM E Bowen	43	1			
	1st Army AA			Albatros DII	Lens	POW
	2nd Army AA			2-seater	Pilkem	DF
	5th Army AA			2-seater		POW

3 April 1917

Time	Pilot/Crew	Sqdn	Vic No	E/A	Location	How
1435	Capt H H Balfour &	43	2	Albatros DIII	Izel	DF
	2/Lt A Roberts	43	2			

5 April 1917

Time	Pilot/Crew	Sqdn	Vic No	E/A	Location	How
1000	Lt P Pike &	48	1	Albatros DII	Douai	OOC
	2/Lt H D Griffith	48	1			
1015	Capt W Leefe-Robinson &		2	Albatros DII	Douai	OOC
	2/Lt E D Warburton	48	2			
1100	Lt H W Woollett	24	1	2 seater	E Honnecourt	D
1135	Capt G J Mahony-Jones &		1	Albatros DII	Courtrai	OOC
	Capt R M Knowles	20	2			
1140	Capt Mahony-Jones &	20	2	Albatros DII	Courtrai	OOC
	Capt R M Knowles	20	3			
1145	S/Lt H G White &	20	1	Albatros DIII	Neuve Eglise	POW
	Pvt T Allum	20	1			
1145	Lt C R O'Brien &	43	2	Albatros DII	E La Bassée	OOC
	Lt J L Dickson	43	1			
1200	Sgt J Dempsey &	25	1	Albatros DII	Vimy Ridge	OOC
	Sgt C H Nunn	25	1			
1200	F/C R S Dallas	1N	8	Albatros DIII	E St Quentin	OOC
1200	2/Lt V H Huston &	18	2	Albatros DII	Inchy	OOC
	Lt G N Blennerhasset	18	2			
1200	2/Lt V H Huston &	18	3	Albatros DII	Inchy	OOC
	Lt G Blennerhasset	18	3			
1200	Capt R H Hood &	18	1	Albatros DII	Inchy	OOC
	2/Lt J R Smith	18	4			
1200	Capt A M Wilkinson	48	11	Albatros DII	Douai	OOC
	Lt L G Allen	48	1			
1245	FSL R J D Compston	8N	2	Halberstadt DII	SE La Bassée	OOC
1345	2/Lt F H Kolligs &	22	1			
	2/Lt J O Stewart	22	1	Albatros DII	Honnecourt	OOC
	2/Lt G M Hopkins &	22	1			
	2/Lt G O McEntee	22	1			
1645	Lt G A H Pidcock &	60	1	Albatros DIII	Reincourt	D
	Lt T Langwill	60	1			
1645	Lt C S Hall	60	2	Albatros DIII	Reincourt	OOC
1645	Lt D M Elliott	60	1	Albatros DIII	Reincourt	OOC

1700	F/C A W Norton	6N	4	Albatros DIII	W Douai	D
1700	F/C A W Norton	6N	5	Albatros DIII	W Douai	OOC
1700	FSL A L Thorne	6N	1	Albatros DIII	Douai	OOC
1700	FSL R R Thornely	6N	1	Albatros DIII	W Douai	OOC
1835	2/Lt E J Pascoe	29	1	Albatros DIII	Vitry-en-Artois	OOC
1835	Lt C V Rogers	29	1	Albatros DIII	Vitry-en-Artois	OOC
1900	2/Lt Scott-Foxwell	29	1	Albatros DIII	Douai	OOC
	Capt Pixley,	54	2⎫			
	Lt M D G Scott,	54	2⎪	Balloon	Gouy	DF
	Capt R N Hudson &	54	3⎬			
	2/Lt R M Charley	54	1⎭			
	S/Lt H S Pell	40	1	Albatros DII	S Bailleul	D
	Lt Lavarack &	12	1⎫	Albatros DII		D
	Lt Baker-Jones	12	1⎭			
	Patrol	48	—	Albatros DIII	Douai	D

6 April 1917

0730	Capt F N Hudson	54	4	2-seater	Le Catelet	OOC
0730	Capt K McCallum	23	1	2-seater		D
0800	Lt D Stewart	54	1	Albatros DIII	St Quentin	D
0800	Capt C M Clement &	22	3⎫			
	2/Lt L G Davies	22	1⎪			
	Lt Gladstone &	22	1⎪			
	Lt Friend	22	1⎬	Albatros DIII	St Quentin	D
	Lt J V Aspinall &	22	3⎪			
	2/Lt M K Parlee	22	2⎪			
	Lt J F A Day &	22	3⎪			
	2/Lt J K Campbell	22	2⎭			
0855	2/Lt D P Walter &	25	1⎫	Albatros DIII	SW Arras	OOC
	2/Lt H C Brown	25	1⎭			
1000	2/Lt H C Todd	40	2	Balloon	Neuvireuil	DF
1000	2/Lt Parkinson &	18	2⎫			
	2/Lt Power	18	1⎪	Albatros DII	Beaumetz-Beugny	D
	2/Lt Reid &	18	1⎬			
	Lt G N Blennerhasset	18	1⎭			
1000	Capt R H Hood	18	2⎫	Albatros DII	Ecoust St Main	POW
	2/Lt J R Smith	18	5⎭			
1010	2/Lt F D Ferry &	20	1⎫	Albatros DIII	Ledeghem	D
	Pte T Allum	20	2⎭			
1015	2/Lt E J Smart &	20	1⎫	Albatros DIII	Roulers	D
	2/Lt Hampson	20	1⎭			
1020	2/Lt E J Smart &	20	2⎫	Albatros DIII	S Roulers	OOC
	2/Lt Hampson	20	2⎭			
1020	2/Lt E J Smart &	20	3⎫	Albatros DIII	S Roulers	OOC
	2/Lt Hampson	20	3⎭			
1020	F/L L S Breadner	3N	1	Halberstadt DII	Bourlon Woods	D
1020	FSL J S T Fall	3N	1	Halberstadt DII	Bourlon Woods	D
1020	FSL A W Carter	3N	1	Halberstadt DII	Bourlon Woods	OOC
1020	FSL F C Armstrong	3N	1	Halberstadt DII	Bourlon Woods	OOC
1030	2/Lt G H Cock &	45	1⎫	Albatros DII	Lille	D
	2/Lt Murison	45	1⎭			
1030	2/Lt P T Newling &	45	1⎫	Albatros DII	Templeuve	OOC
	2/AM B G Perrot	45	1⎭			
1030	2/Lt A Roulstone &	25	1⎫	Albatros DIII	E Givenchy	DF
	2/Lt E G Green	25	2⎭			
1045	2/Lt B King &	25	1⎫	Halberstadt DII	E Vimy	D
	Cpl L Emsden	25	4⎭			
1135	Lt C R Kerry &	24	1⎫	2-seater	Havrincourt Wood	OOC
	2/Lt T C Arnot	24	1⎭			
1145	F/C B C Clayton	1N	1	Albatros DIII	NE St Quentin	OOC
1150	FSL T G Culling	1N	1	2-seater	Se St Quentin	OOC
	Lt G O Smart	60	1	Albatros DIII	Arras	OOC
	Lt F Holliday &	48	1⎫	Albatros DII	NE Arras	OOC
	Capt A H Wall	48	1⎭			
	2/Lt W T Price &	48	1⎫	Albatros DII	NE Arras	OOC
	2/Lt M A Benjamin	48	1⎭			

	Capt A J Clarke,	27	1	⎫			OOC
	2/Lt E W Kirby &	27	1	⎬	Halberstadt DII		
	Lt W Wedderspoon	27	1	⎭			
	Capt A J Clarke,	27	2	⎫			OOC
	2/Lt E W Kirby &	27	2	⎬	Halberstadt DII		
	Lt W Wedderspoon	27	2	⎭			

7 April 1917

1700	Lt W A Bishop	60	3		Albatros DIII	Arras	OOC
1710	Lt W A Bishop	60	4		Balloon	Vis-en-Artois	DF
1745	2/Lt C S Hall &	60	3	⎱	Albatros DIII	Mercatel	D
	2/Lt G O Smart	60	2	⎰			
1748	Lt H C Todd	40	3		Balloon	Sallaumines	DF
1830	Lt N C Robertson &	20	1	⎱	Albatros DIII	Tourcoing	D
	2/Lt L G Fauvel	20	1	⎰			
1830	2/Lt S N Pike &	20	1	⎱	Albatros DIII	Tourcoing	OOC
	2/AM E H Sayers	20	1	⎰			
1930	FSL R A Little	8N	7		Albatros DIII	SE Lens	D
	FSL C D Booker	8N	1		Albatros DIII	Lens	OOC

8 April 1917

0820	2/Lt E S T Cole	1	2		Balloon	Quesnoy	DF
0930	Lt W A Bishop	60	5		Albatros DIII	NE Arras	OOC
0930	Maj A J L Scott &	60	2	⎱	2-seater	Fouquières	D
	Lt W A Bishop	60	6	⎰			
1010	Lt W A Bishop	60	7		Albatros DIII	Vitry-en-Artois	OOC
1130	2/Lt F M Kitto &	43	3	⎱	Albatros DIII	NE Vimy	OOC
	AM A Cant	43	1	⎰			
1130	Capt C Q Brand	1	5		Balloon	Moorslede	DF
1400	2/Lt G Brockhurst &	48	1	⎫			
	2/Lt C B Boughton	48	1	⎪			
	2/Lt R E Adeny &	48	1	⎪			
	2/Lt L G Lovell	48	1	⎬	Albatros DIII	Remy-Eterpigny	OOC
	2/Lt A G Riley &	48	1	⎪			
	2/Lt L G Hall	48	1	⎭			
1400	Capt D M Tidmarsh &	48	4	⎱	Albatros DIII	Remy-Eterpigny	OOC
	2/Lt C B Holland	48	1	⎰			
1445	F/C R S Dallas	1N	9		2 seater	E Cambrai	OOC
1500	FSL F D Casey	3N	2		Albatros DIII	NE Pronville	OOC
1500	Capt G W Roberts	66	1		Halberstadt DII		OOC
to	Lt C C Montgomery	66	1		Halberstadt DII		OOC
1735	2/Lt A J Lucas	66	1		Halberstadt DII		OOC
1510	F/Lt H G Travers	3N	3		Albatros DIII	NE Pronville	OOC
1700	Lt C M Clement &	22	4	⎫			
	2/Lt L G Davies	22	2	⎪			
	Lt L W Beale &	22	1	⎪			
	Lt G G Bell	22	1	⎪			
	Lt J F A Day &	22	3	⎪			
	2/Lt Taylor	22	1	⎬	Albatros DIII	Beugny	D
	Lt J V Aspinall &	22	4	⎪			
	Lt M K Parles	22	3	⎪			
	Lt C M Furlonger &	22	1	⎪			
	Lt C W Lane	22	1	⎪			
	2/Lt J Campbell &	22	3	⎪			
	2/Lt H Spearpoint	22	1	⎭			
1910	2/Lt A Sutherland	29	2		Albatros DIII	SE Arras	D
	Capt R W Oxspring	54	1		2-seater		D

9 April 1917

1145	FSL R A Little	8N	8		Halberstadt DII	Noyelles-Lens	OOC
1145	FSL F C Norton &	6N	6	⎱	Albatros DIII	Cambrai	OOC
	FSL A R Thorne	6N	1	⎰			
1200	F/C E W Norton	6N	7		Albatros DIII	Cambrai	OOC
am	Capt A Wilkinson &	48	12	⎱	2 seater	Lens	D
	2/Lt H B Griffiths	48	3	⎰			
am	Capt A Wilkinson &	48	13	⎱	2 seater	Lens	OOC
	2/Lt H B Griffiths	48	4	⎰			

am	2/Lt W T Price &	48	2 ⎫			
	2/Lt M A Benjamin	48	2 ⎭	2-seater	E Arras	D
1800	Capt A Wilkinson &	48	14 ⎫			
	Lt L W Allen	48	1 ⎪			
	Lt J H T Letts &	48	1 ⎪	Albatros DIII	E Arras	D
	Lt H G Collins	48	1 ⎭			
1800	Capt A Wilkinson &	48	15 ⎫			
	Lt L W Allen	48	2 ⎪			
	Lt J H T Letts &	48	2 ⎪	Albatros DIII	E Arras	OOC
	Lt H G Collins	48	2 ⎭			
1905	Lt T H Southon &	25	1 ⎫			
	2/Lt H Freeman-Smith	25	1 ⎭	Albatros DIII	Lievin	OOC

10 April 1917

1900	Capt D Tidmarsh &	48	5 ⎫			
	2/Lt C B Holland	48	2 ⎪			
	2/Lt G Brockhurst &	48	2 ⎪	Albatros DIII	Remy	OOC
	2/Lt C B Boughton	48	2 ⎭			

11 April 1917

0800	Capt D Tidmarsh &	48	6 ⎫			
	2/Lt C B Holland	48	3 ⎪			
	2/Lt R E Adeney &	48	2 ⎪			
	2/Lt L G Lovell	48	2 ⎪	Albatros DIII	Fampoux	D
	2/Lt G Brockhurst &	48	3 ⎪			
	2/Lt C B Boughton	48	3 ⎪			
	2/Lt A G Riley &	48	2 ⎪			
	2/Lt L G Hall	48	2 ⎭			
0800	Capt D Tidmarsh &	48	7 ⎫			
	2/Lt C B Holland	48	4 ⎪			
	2/Lt R E Adeney &	48	3 ⎪			
	2/Lt L G Lovell	48	3 ⎪	Albatros DIII	Fampoux	OOC
	2/Lt G Brockhurst &	48	4 ⎪			
	2/Lt C B Boughton	48	4 ⎪			
	2/Lt A G Riley &	48	3 ⎪			
	2/Lt L G Hall	48	3 ⎭			
0820	2/Lt A G Riley &	48	4 ⎫			
	2/Lt L G Hall	48	4 ⎭	Albatros DIII	Fampoux	OOC
0845	F/C L Breadner	3N	3	Albatros C	Cambrai	DF
0855	F/C L Breadner	3N	4	Albatros DII	Cambrai	D
0900	FSL J S T Fall	3N	1	Albatros DII	Cambrai	OOC
0900	FSL P G McNeil	3N	1	Albatros DII	Cambrai	OOC
0905	FSL J S T Fall	3N	2	Albatros DII	Cambrai	OOC
0905	FSL J S T Fall	3N	3	Albatros DII	Cambrai	OOC

12 April 1917

1030	F/C R G Mack	3N	2	Albatros DII	Pronville	D
1030	FSL A T Whealy	3N	1	Albatros DII	Pronville	OOC
1030	FSL E Pierce &	3N	1 ⎫	Albatros DII	Pronville	OOC
	FSL F C Armstrong	3N	1 ⎭			
1030	FSL E Pierce	3N	2	Albatros DII	Pronville	OOC
1040	2/Lt E L Zink &	18	3 ⎫	Albatros DII	Cagnicourt	OOC
	Pte N G Jones	18	1 ⎭			
1040	2/Lt E W P Hunt &	18	1 ⎫	Albatros DII	Cagnicourt	OOC
	2/Lt K Fearside-Speed	18	1 ⎭			
	Capt A M Wilkinson &	48	16 ⎫			
	Lt L W Allen	48	4 ⎪	Albatros DIII		OOC
	2/Lt W O Winkler &	48	1 ⎪			
	2/Lt E S Moore	48	1 ⎭			

13 April 1917

0840	Lt G S Buck	19	1	Albatros DIII	Brebières	OOC
1130	Lt H E O Ellis	40	1	Albatros C	Courrières	D
am	Capt R Oxspring	66	—	Albatros C	Douai	DD
am	Lt J T Collier	66	—	Albatros DIII	Douai	DD
1620	2/Lt Scott-Foxwell	29	2	Albatros DII	Monchy-le-Preux	OOC

1830	2/Lt J Aspinall &	22	5	Albatros DIII	Itancourt	D
	Lt M K Parlee	22	4			
1930	Capt J L Leith &	25	2	Albatros DIII	Sallaumines	D
	Lt Hobart-Hampden	25	2			
1930	2/Lt R G Malcolm &	25	3	Albatros DIII	Henin-Lietard	D
	Cpl L Emsden	25	1			
pm	Capt A M Wilkinson &	48	17	Albatros DIII	Vitry-en-Artois	D
	Lt L W Allan	48	5			
	Lt J W Warren &	48	1			
	2/Lt H B Griffith	48	4			
pm	Capt A M Wilkinson &	48	18	Albatros DIII	Vitry-en-Artois	OOC
	Lt L W Allan	48	6			
	Lt J W Warren &	48	2			
	2/Lt H B Griffith	48	5			

14 April 1917

0810	2/Lt M B Cole	54	1	2-seater	Gonnelieu	OOC
0815	Capt W V Strugnell	54	4	2-seater	Buissy-Inchy	OOC
0820	F/C T F N Gerrard	1N	1	Albatros DII	Epinoy	OOC
0905	FSL E D Crundell	8N	1	2-seater	Henin-Lietard	OOC
0910	FSL E D Crundell	8N	2	2-seater	E Douai	D
0910	F/L C D Booker	8N	2	2-seater	Henin-Lietard	OOC
0950	Lt Jones-Williams	29	1	Albatros DII	Neuvireuil-Vitry	OOC
1200	Lt W E Reed	19	1	2-seater	Douai	OOC
1720	Lt D de Burgh &	40	1	Albatros DII	Mericourt	D
	Lt I P R Napier	40	1			
1930	Sgt W Burkenshaw &	25	1	Albatros DIII	Lens	OOC
	Capt A Binnie	60	3			
	Sgt J H Brown	25	3	Albatros DII	Henin-Lietard	D
	2/Lt R G Malcolm &	25	4			
	2/Lt J B Weir	25	2			
	2/Lt R C Savery &	11	2	Albatros DIII		OOC
	2/AM Toilerfield	11	2			
	2/Lt W R Exley &	11	1	Albatros DII		OOC
	Capt J A Le Royert	11	1			
	Capt L C Coates &	5	1	Albatros DIII	Willerval	D
	2/Lt J C Cotton	5	1			

16 April 1917

0830	2/Lt S J Young &	18	1	Albatros DIII	Cagnicourt	OOC
	2/Lt G N Blennerhasset	18	5			
0830	2/Lt E W A Hunt &	18	2	Albatros DIII	Cagnicourt	OOC
	2/Lt O J Partington	18	2			

21 April 1917

1730	FSL F D Casey &	3N	2	Albatros DIII	Heudecourt	D
	FSL H S Broad	3N	1			
1730	F/Lt H G Travers	3N	4	Albatros DII	Cagnicourt	OOC
1740	FSL J J Malone	3N	3	Albatros C	N Queant	OOC
1810	Lt H R Stocken	23	1	2-seater	Sauchy-Lestrées	OOC
1840	2/Lt R L Keller	23	1	Albatros DIII	Cagnicourt	OOC
1840	FSL F D Casey	3N	3	Albatros DIII	Cagnicourt	OOC
1850	F/C A R Arnold &	8N	2	Albatros DIII	Thelus	POW
	Lt R G Malcolm	25	5			
	2/Lt J B Weir	25	3			
1855	FSL R A Little	8N	9	Albatros DIII	NE Oppy	D
1855	Capt J L Leith &	25	8	Albatros DIII	Oppy-Rouvroy	OOC
	Lt Hobart-Hampden	25	3			

22 April 1917

0705	2/Lt H G Ross	60	1	Balloon	N Dury	DF
0705	2/Lt G L Lloyd	60	1	Balloon	NE Boiry	DF
0705	2/Lt E M Wright	1	1	Albatros DIII	Flers	OOC
0705	Capt E D Atkinson	1	2	Albatros DIII	Lille	OOC
0710	Capt E D Atkinson	1	3	Albatros DIII	Lille	OOC
0715	Lt W E Reed	19	2	Albatros C	S Quiery	DF

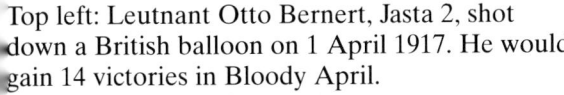

Top left: Leutnant Otto Bernert, Jasta 2, shot down a British balloon on 1 April 1917. He would gain 14 victories in Bloody April.

Top centre: Karl Allmenröder, Jasta 11, downed four British planes in April.

Top right: Emil Schäfer, yet another ace in Jasta 11, claimed 15 April kills.

Above left: Manfred and Lothar von Richthofen, Jasta 11, would between them shoot down 36 Allied aeroplanes in April.

Above right: Unteroffizier Ludwig Weber of Jasta 3, wounded on 6 April. He had taught Hermann Frommherz and Hermann Göring to fly.

Top left: Joachim von Bertrab, Jasta 30, scored four kills on 6 April.

Top centre: Heinrich Gontermann, Jasta 5, 12 victories in April, including seven balloons.

Top right: Hans Klein, Jasta 4, eight victories in April.

Above: All that remains of one of von Bertrab's victims of 6 April. Sopwith 1½ Strutter of 45 Squadron (A2381). 2/Lt C StG Campbell drowned after colliding with another Strutter.

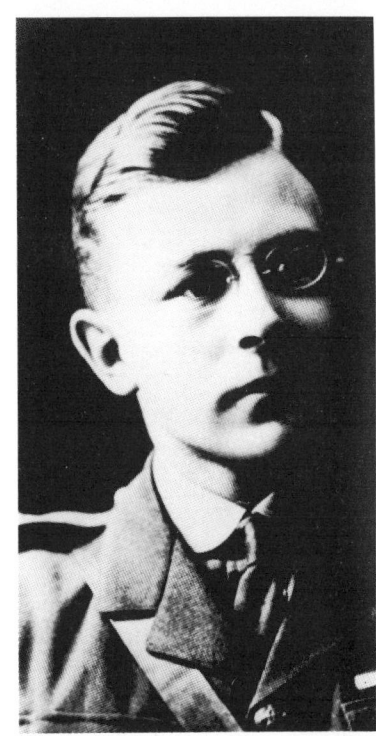

Top left: Leutnant Walter Göttsch of Jasta 8 scored three victories in April, including a Belgian BE2c on the 8th.

Top centre: Captain W L Robinson VC, 48 Squadron, prisoner of war, 5 April, brought down by Sebastian Festner, Jasta 11.

Top right: Lieutenant Francis G Truscott MC, 45 Squadron, killed 6 April.

Above left: Lieutenant John H B Wedderspoon, 27 Squadron, killed 6 April.

Above centre: Second Lieutenant Colin StG Campbell, 45 Squadron.

Above right: Captain William S Brayshay, 45 Squadron, killed 6 April.

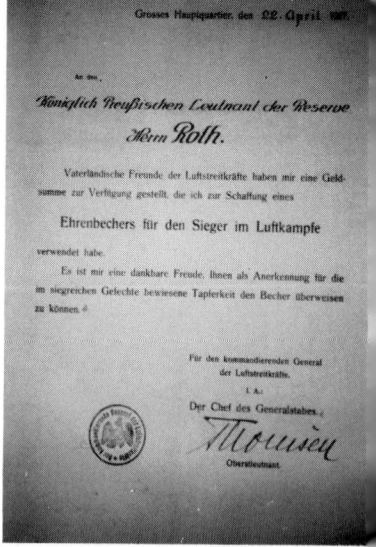

Top left: Second Lieutenant G C Burnand, observer, 48 Squadron, killed by Festner on 7 April.

Top right: Sebastian Festner, Jasta 11. He did not survive Bloody April, being killed in action on the 25th, while in combat with 43 Squadron.

Middle left: Lieutenant H G Collins, observer, 48 Squadron, died of wounds he received on 9 April after an attack by an Albatros Scout.

Bottom left: Lieutenant A J Hamer, 55 Squadron, killed in action 8 April; hit by flak on a bomb raid near Mons.

Bottom centre: Leutnant Georg Röth's Victory Cup (Ehrenbecher) denoting his first victory – a BE2c on 11 April 1917.

Bottom right: Röth's victory certificate which accompanied the Cup.

Top left: Rumpler C two-seater reconnaissance machine.

Top right: Leutnant Adolf Schulte, Jasta 12, killed in a collision with a British FE2b, 12 April.

Above left: German Kite Balloon about to be winched up, the observer's basket still on the ground.

Above right: Pilots of Jasta 2 (Boelcke) and 12, in April 1917; (l to r): Hpt von Seal, Oblt Adolf von Tutschek, Vfwbl Arthur Schörisch, Oblt Otto Bernert, Vfwbl Grigo, Ltn Hans Eggers, Vfwbl Robert Riessenger, Ltn Georg Röth.

Bottom left: A 15 Squadron BE2c, one of several brought down during April.

Bottom right: Squadron Commander J J Petrie DSC, CO of 6 Naval Squadron, killed in a flying accident on Friday 13 April.

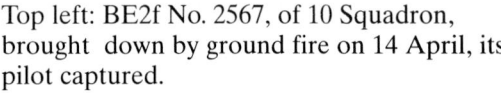

Top left: BE2f No. 2567, of 10 Squadron, brought down by ground fire on 14 April, its pilot captured.

Top right: RE8 No. A78, 34 Squadron, shot down on 14 April, crew prisoners.

Middle: No. 1 (Naval) Squadron flew Triplanes. This pilot group had a number of men who saw action in April; (l to r): S M Kinkead, J H Forman, H LeR Wallace, A G A Spence, Everett, H V Rowley, Luard, W S MacGrath, W F Crundell, W H Sneath, Burton, A R McAfee, S W Rosevear, R P Minifie, R S Dallas, C B Ridley, H R deWilde, White and Holden (EO).

Bottom left: Sopwith Pup; both RFC and RNAS Pups saw action during April.

Bottom right: Another Sopwith, the Triplane, also saw action during April, with the RNAS.

Top left: Albatros C two-seater, one of the main German recce machines.

Top right: Lieutenant Bernard J Tolhurst, observer with 11 Squadron; killed in action 22 April.

Middle left: BE2e, A3168, 16 Squadron, brought down by Manfred von Richthofen, 23 April.

Bottom left: The RE8 was meant as a replacement for the BE2 machines, but they were just as vulnerable to the Jasta pilots.

Bottom right: Captain H L H Owen, 18 Squadron, wounded by flak 22 April 1917.

Top left: AWFK8, No. A2709, 35 Squadron, brought down by Jasta 12, 23 April.

Top right: Lieutenant I V Pyott DSO, 55 Squadron, had his observer wounded during a bomb raid on 23 April, and was forced to land.

Middle left: Jack Malone, 3 Naval Squadron, in a Sopwith Pup.

Bottom left: A No. 5 Wing Sopwith 1½ Strutter, which came down in Holland, 23 April, with engine failure. FSL D H Nelles DSC, interned.

Bottom right: Lieutenant Tom Hazell of 1 Squadron, had his second victory on 24 April, going on to score 43 by the war's end.

Top left: Lieutenant Gabriel Coury VC, won his award while with the 3rd South Lancashire Regt in 1916. Flew as an observer with 13 Squadron in Bloody April.

Top right: Capitaine Armand de Turenne, N. 48, with the wreckage of an Albatros Scout he shot down on 26 April.

Middle left: Adjutant Gustave Douchy of N. 38, destroyed a balloon on 6 April.

Bottom right: Sopwith 1 ½ Strutter of 43 Squadron, brought down by Edmund Nathanael, Jasta 5, 29 April.

Bottom left: Lieutenant Jean Chaput of Spa. 57 scored his ninth and tenth kills in April.

Top left: Edmund Nathanael had a long fight with Barwell of 40 Squadron before bringing him down. He accounted for nine victories during April, but was himself killed on 11 May, with his score at 15.

Top right: By the end of April, Flight Lieutenant E W Norton DSC, 6 Naval Squadron, had nine victories, scored during the month - three on the 29th.

Above left: Captain F L Barwell, 40 Squadron, killed in action by Edmund Nathanael, Jasta 5, 29 April.

Above centre: Lieutenant N W Hamilton, 19 Squadron, the sole survivor after a fight with Jasta 11, 29 April 1917.

Above right: Jack Malone DSO, 3 Naval, killed in action in a fight with Paul Billik, Jasta 12, 30 April

Top left: Spad fighter of Spa. 103 of the Cigognes (Storks) Group.

Top right: Second Lieutenant J O Donaldson, 32 Squadron, PoW, 1 September.

Middle left: All that remains of a British Kite Balloon after a successful air attack, April 1917.

Bottom left: Sopwith Camel, 73 Squadron, shot down 1 September, probably by Oblt Robert Greim, Jasta 34b.

Bottom right: Two Americans serving with 73 Squadron taken prisoner on 1 and 2 September. Lt H V Fellows had been flying D1922 and Dan Sinclair D8114.

Top left: 1/Lieutenant Linn H Forster, 148th Aero, PoW, 2 September.

Top centre: 2/Lieutenant Johnson D Kenyon, 148th Aero, PoW, 2 September.

Top right: 2/Lieutenant Oscar Mandell, 148th Aero, PoW, 2 September.

Above left: 1/Lieutenant Jesse O Creech, 148th Aero

Above centre: Lieutenants Geo M Comey and Ralph B Bagby, shared in shooting down a German two-seater, 2 September; 1st Aero Salmson 2A2.

Above right: Second Lieutenant W H Rochford, 70 Squadron, PoW, 4 September.

Top: Lieutenant S D Lavelle, 3 Squadron, claimed a Fokker on 4 September. Note Squadron markings.

Middle right: French Bréguet XIV day bomber.

Above right: French Salmson 2A2 recce machine.

Middle left: Lieutenant J L Gower, 70 Squadron, PoW, 4 September.

Bottom left: US Bréguet XIV of the 96th Aero.

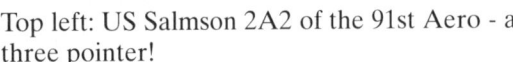

Top left: US Salmson 2A2 of the 91st Aero - a three pointer!

Top right: Lieutenant W K Swayze, 62 Squadron, PoW, 4 September.

Above left: Lieutenant C R Thompson, 84 Squadron, scored three balloon kills in September, to bring his score to seven.

Above right: Lt Simpson, Lieutenant Sydney W Highwood DFC, Captain A F W Beauchamp Proctor MC DFC (later VC DSO), and Lt J E Boudwin USAS. Highwood destroyed nine balloons and one aircraft during September, BP four balloons.

Right: SE5a machines of 84 Squadron.

Top left: Captain H A Patey DFC, 210 Squadron, brought down into captivity by Ltn Beckmann of Jasta 56, 5 September, having gained his own eleventh victory two days earlier.

Top right: 1/Lieutenant David Putnam, 139th Aero, with Captain Dudley Hill. Putnam was one of the great US fighter pilots, but died in combat with Georg von Hantelmann on 12 September.

Above left: Von Hantelmann also shot down Joe Wehner of the 27th Aero, on 18 September.

Above right: Georg von Hantelmann, Jasta 15, downed no fewer than 12 Allied planes during September, most being American, and amongst them were three aces, two American and one French.

Left: The amazing Frank Luke Jr, of the 27th Aero. He gained 18 combat victories in September, but was killed on the 29th. He later received the Medal of Honor.

Top left: German observation balloon. Luke destroyed 14 of these well defended and highly dangerous targets.

Top right: 1/Lieutenant Frank Hunter, 103rd Aero, received an Oak Leaf to his DSC for his actions on 13 September. In WW2 he commanded the US 8th Air Force Fighter Command.

Above left: Carl Spaatz flew with the 13th Aero to gain combat experience. He too rose to high rank with the USAAF in WW2.

Above centre: Ray Brooks of the 22nd Aero, gained four of his six victories during September, winning the DSC on the 14th.

Above right: 1/Lieutenant W W White Jr, 147th Aero, won the DSC for his action on 14 September, downing a balloon and a defending Fokker.

Right: Captain Jerry Vasconcells and Don Hudson, 27th Aero.

0720	2/Lt E S T Cole	1	5	Balloon	Wervicq	DF
0730	2/Lt A R Penny	60	1	Balloon	Vis-en-Artois	DF
0730	FSL A R Knight	8N	1	Albatros DIII	E Oppy	OOC
0745	2/Lt J T Collier	66	2	Albatros DIII	Vitry	OOC
1120	Lt W A Bishop	60	8	Albatros DIII	E Vimy	OOC
1121	Lt W A Bishop	60	9	Albatros DIII	E Vimy	OOC
1350	2/Lt W T Walter	40	1	2-seater	Henin-Lietard	D
1720	Lt W E Molesworth	60	1	Albatros DIII	Vitry	OOC
1720	FSL T G Culling	1N	2	Albatros DIII	Arleux	OOC
1722	F/C R S Dallas	1N	10	DFW C	Arleux	D
1725	F/C R S Dallas	1N	11	DFW C	Arleux	DF
1820	2/Lt R L Keller	23	2	Albatros DIII	E Cambrai	OOC
1830	Capt C K C Patrick	23	4	Albatros DIII	Fontaine Notre Dame	OOC
1900	Capt C K C Patrick	23	5	Albatros DIII	Flesquières	OOC
1910	FSL H S Kirby	3N	1	Albatros C	Cambrai	OOC
1915	FSL E Pierce	3N	3	Albatros DIII	Cambrai	OOC
	Capt A M Wilkinson &	48	19 ⎫	Albatros DIII	Vitry-en-Artois	OOC
	Lt L W Allan	48	7 ⎭			
	Capt E F Elderton	29	1	Balloon		DF
	2/Lt J S Leslie &	16	1 ⎫	EA		OOC
	Lt A R Sortwell	16	1 ⎭			
				Anti-Aircraft	Albatros DIII	D

23 April 1917

0630	FSL H F Beamish	3N	1	Albatros DIII	Croiselles	OOC
0630	FSL G B Anderson	3N	1	Albatros DIII	Croiselles	OOC
0630	FSL E Pierce	3N	3	Albatros DIII	Croiselles	OOC
0630	FSL J J Malone	3N	4	Albatros DIII	Croiselles	OOC
0645	Capt A Ball	56	32	2-seater	Abancourt	D
0710	Lt R H Upson	29	1	Albatros DIII	Biache-Sailly	D
0715	FSL J J Malone	3N	5	Albatros DIII	Croiselles	OOC
0745	FSL J J Malone	3N	6	Albatros DIII	Havrincourt	OOC
0800	F/C R S Dallas	1N	12	DFW C	W Douai	OOC
0800	FSL T G Culling	1N	3	DFW C	W Douai	OOC
1020	F/Lt L Breadner	3N	4	Gotha G	Vron	POW
1105	2/Lt N H England &	43	1 ⎫	Albatros DIII	SE Mericourt	D
	Lt L F Bettinson	43	1 ⎪			
	1/AM E Bowen &	43	2 ⎪			
	2/Lt C de Berigny	43	2 ⎭			
1140	Lt K MacKenzie &	40	1 ⎫	2-seater	Lens	OOC
	Lt H E O Ellis	40	2 ⎭			
1145	Capt A Ball	56	33	Albatros DIII	Selvigny	DF
1520	Lt J M Child	19	1	2-seater	NW Douai	OOC
1530	Lt W A Bishop	60	10	2-seater	Vitry-en-Tardenois	D
1559	Lt W A Bishop	60	11	Albatros DIII	E Vitry	D
1630	2/Lt A Sutherland	29	3	Albatros DIII	Vitry	OOC
1630	2/Lt A G Jones-Williams	29	3	Albatros DIII	Vitry	OOC
1630	2/Lt A G Jones-Williams	29	4	Albatros DIII	Vitry	OOC
1630	2/Lt J D Atkinson	29	1	Albatros DIII	Vitry	OOC
1640	2/Lt F A Handley &	57	1 ⎫	Albatros DIII	SE Arras	OOC
	2/Lt E Percival	57	1 ⎭			
1730	2/Lt H A Trayles &	18	1 ⎫	Albatros DIII	Baralle	OOC
	Cpl A Beebee	18	1 ⎭			
1730	2/Lt E L Zink &	18	4 ⎫	Albatros DIII	Baralle	OOC
	2/Lt G B Bate	18	1 ⎭			
1730	2/Lt Reid &	18	2 ⎫	Albatros DIII	Baralle	OOC
	2/Lt Fearnside-Speed	18	2 ⎭			
1730	Capt C E Bryant &	18	1 ⎫	Albatros DIII	Baralle	OOC
	2/Lt N Couve	18	1 ⎭			
1730	FSL A W Carter	3N	2	Albatros DIII	Epinoy	D
1730	FSL H S Kerby	3N	2	Albatros DIII	Le Pave	D
1730	FSL H S Kerby	3N	3	Albatros DIII	Le Pave	D
1730	F/Lt L Breadner	3N	5	Albatros DIII	Bourlon Wood	OOC
1730	FSL J S T Fall	3N	5	Albatros DIII	Bourlon Wood	OOC
1800	FSL F D Casey	3N	4	Albatros DIII	Saudemont	OOC
1800	FSL A W Carter	3N	3	Albatros DIII	Epinoy	OOC
1810	FSL A T Whealy	3N	2	Albatros DIII	N Cambrai-Arras Road	OOC

Time	Crew	Sqn	No.	Aircraft	Location	Result
1910	2/Lt F Williams	66	1	Albatros DIII	Lecluse	OOC
1932	Maj H D Harvey-Kelly	19	3	Albatros DIII	Cambrai	D
	Lt F Holliday &	48	2⎫	Albatros DIII	Vimy	D
	Capt A H Wall	48	2⎭			
	Lt F Holliday &	48	3			
	Capt A H Wall	48	3			
	Lt W O B Winkler &	48	2			
	2/Lt E S Moore	48	2⎫	Albatros DIII	Vimy	D
	Lt R B Hay &	48	1			
	?????	48	–			
	Lt W T Price &	48	3			
	Lt M A Benjamin	48	3⎭			
	Capt E R Manning &	11	1⎫	Albatros DIII		OOC
	Lt Duncan	11	1⎭			
	2/Lt I V Pyott &	55	2⎫	Albatros DIII	Bove	OOC
	2/AM W Bond	55	1⎭			

24 April 1917

Time	Crew	Sqn	No.	Aircraft	Location	Result
0640	Lt Gotch &	70	1⎫	Halberstadt DII	SE Cambrai	OOC
	2/Lt Kibbutz	70	1⎭			
0640	Sgt Thompson &	70	1⎫	Halberstadt DII	SE Cambrai	OOC
	2/AM Impey	70	1⎭			
0720	Lt R E Johnson &	20	1⎫	Albatros DIII	W Ledeghem	D
	Capt F R Cubbon	20	1⎭			
0720	Lt R E Johnson &	20	2⎫	Albatros DIII	W Ledeghem	D
	Capt F R Cubbon	20	2⎭			
0725	2/Lt R H Stocken	23	2	Albatros DIII	NW Cambrai	OOC
0755	Lt E O Perry &	20	2⎫	Albatros DIII	Becelaere	DF
	2/AM E H Sayers	20	2⎭			
0815	F/C R S Dallas	1N	13	Albatros DIII	SE Lens	OOC
0815	F/C T F N Gerrard	1N	2	Albatros DIII	Noyelles	D
0815	Sgt J Whiteman &	18	1⎫	Albatros DIII	Baralle	DF
	Lt Fearnside-Speed	18	4⎭			
0815	Collided	18		Albatros DIII	Baralle	D
0815	Collided	18		Albatros DIII	Baralle	D
0830	F/C T F N Gerrard	1N	3	Albatros DIII	Noyelles	OOC
0840	FSL G G Simpson	8N	2	Albatros DIII	Sailly	OOC
1010	F/Lt A M Shook	4N	1	Fokker D	Ghistelles	OOC
1110	Capt C M Crowe,	56	2⎫			
	Lt L M Barlow &	56	1⎬	2-seater	Bellone	D
	Lt M A Kay	56	1⎭			
1200	2/Lt T F Hazell	1	2	Albatros C	Bois Grenier	POW
1200	Lt I P R Napier,	40	2 ⎫			
	Lt J G Brewis &	40	1 ⎬	Aviatik C	Lens	POW
	FSL R A Little	8N	10⎭			
1300	Lt A V Burbury	1	1	Balloon		DF
1300	Lt R B Clark	60	1	Albatros DIII	S Tilloy	D
1305	Lt W E Molesworth	60	2	Balloon	Boiry-Notre Dame	DF
1515	Lt G C Maxwell &	56	1⎫	Albatros DIII	NE Cambrai	OOC
	2/Lt C R W Knight	56	1⎭			
1645	2/Lt K J Knaggs	56	1	Albatros DIII	Fresnoy	OOC
1650	F/Lt H T Travers,	3N	5⎫			
	FSL F D Casey &	3N	5⎬	DFW C	Morchies	POW
	FSL J J Malone	3N	7⎭			
1730	Lt A Roulstone &	25	2⎫	Albatros DIII	Billy-Montigny	D
	2/Lt E G Green	25	2⎭			
1900	Lt W T Price &	48	4⎫	Albatros DIII	E Arras	D
	Lt M A Benjamin	48	4⎭			
	Lt L M S Essell	29	1	Balloon		DF?
	Lt Le Gallais	29	1	Balloon		DF?
	Lt F P Holliday &	48	4⎫	2-seater	SE Arras	D
	Capt A H W Wall	48	4⎭			
	Lt F P Holliday &	48	5			
	Capt A H W Wall	48	5			
	2/Lt W O Winkler &	48	3⎫	Albatros DIII	Cagnicourt	D
	2/Lt E S Moore	48	3⎪			
	Lt R B Hay &	48	2⎪			
	????	48	–⎭			

	Lt R N Hall	40	1	2-seater	E Lens	OOC

25 April 1917

0815	Lt C R O'Brien &	43	3⎱	Albatros DIII	Oppy	D
	2/Lt J L Dickson	43	2⎰			

26 April 1917

1155	2/Lt E Bartlett	41	2	2-seater	Hooge	D
1200	Patrol	41		2-seater		D
1530	FSL A J Chadwick	4N	1	Albatros DIII	S Bruge	OOC
1615	FSL Collins	SDF	1	Seaplane	Zeebrugge	D
1720	Sgt J H R Green &	25	4⎱	Albatros DIII	Drocourt	OOC
	Lt H Freeman-Smith	25	2⎰			
1720	Lt C Dunlop &	25	3⎱	Albatros DIII	Izel-les-Esq	D
	Lt J L B Weir	25	4⎰			
1720	F/C C D Booker	8N	3	Albatros DIII	Drocourt	DF
1720	FSL E D Crundall	8N	3	Albatros DIII	Drocourt	D
1830	Capt K C McCallum	23	2	Albatros DIII	Cambrai	OOC
1830	Capt K C McCallum	23	3	Albatros DIII	Cambrai	OOC
1840	2/Lt R L Keller	23	3	Albatros DIII	Fontaine-Notre Dame	OOC
1840	2/Lt G C Stead	23	1	Albatros DIII	Fontaine-Notre Dame	OOC
1900	Lt D Y Hay &	20	1⎱	Albatros DIII	Moorslede	OOC
	2/AM T E Allum	20	3⎰			
1915	Lt H L Stachell &	20	1⎱	Albatros DIII	SW Roulers	D
	2/AM M Todd	20	1⎰			
1910	Capt F N Hudson	54	5	Albatros DIII	Premont	OOC
1910	2/Lt R M Charley	54	1	Albatros DIII	Premont	OOC
1910	Lt S G Rome	54	1	Albatros DIII	Premont	OOC
1915	FSL C J Moir	4N	1	Albatros DIII	Dixmuide	OOC
1915	FSL F D Casey	3N	6	Albatros DIII	Cambrai	OOC
1915	FSL J J Malone	3N	7	Albatros DIII	Cambrai	OOC
1920	Lt H E O Ellis	40	3	Albatros DIII	E Salome	D
	FSL R R Thornely	6N	1	Albatros DIII		OOC
	FSL G G Simpson	6N	3	Albatros DIII		OOC
1930	Capt A Ball	56	34	Albatros DIII	Hayencourt	D
1930	Capt A Ball	56	35	Albatros DIII	E Cambrai	DF

27 April 1917

0655	Lt W A Bishop	60	12	Balloon	Vitry-en-Artois	DF
1000	Lt H E O Ellis	40	4	Balloon	Salome	D
2000	2/Lt D S Kennedy &	11	1⎱	Albatros DIII	SW Vitry	DF
	Capt J A Le Royer	11	2⎰			
2000	2/Lt D S Kennedy &	11	2⎱	Albatros DIII	SW Vitry	D
	Capt J A Le Royer	11	3⎰			
	Lt W T Price &	48	5⎫			
	Lt M A Benjamin	48	5⎬	2-seater	Vitry	D
	Lt R B Hay &	48	3⎭			
	?????	48	—			
	Patrol	6		Albatros DIII		OOC

28 April 1917

1225	Lt R A Little	8N	11	2-seater	Oppy	D
1630	Capt A Ball	56	34	Albatros C	Fontaine	D
2000	FSL R Collishaw	10N	5	Albatros DII	Ostende	D

29 April 1917

1000	Capt H Meintjes	56	5	Albatros DIII	Hamel-Recourt	OOC
1020	2/Lt A Erlebach &	57	1⎱	Albatros DIII	Noyelles	OOC
	2/Lt C H Trottrt	57	1⎰			
1030	Capt McNaughton &	57	1⎱	Albatros DIII	Noyelles	OOC
	2/Lt H G Downing	57	1⎰			
1030	Lt J H Ryan &	57	1⎱	Albatros DIII	Noyelles	OOC
	2/Lt B Soutten	57	1⎰			
1100	FSL F D Casey	3N	7	Albatros DIII	Bantouzelle	DF
1100	FSL J S T Fall	3N	6	Albatros DIII	Bois de Gard	D
1110	F/C T F N Gerrard	1N	4	Albatros DIII	Epinoy	OOC

Time	Name	Sqn	No.	Aircraft	Location	Result
1110	FSL R P Minifie	1N	1	Albatros DIII	Epinoy	D
1115	F/Lt L Breadner	1N	6	Albatros DIII	SE Cambrai	OOC
1115	FSL A W Carter	1N	4	Albatros DIII	SE Cambrai	OOC
1115	FSL H S Broad	3N	2	Albatros DIII	SE Cambrai	OOC
1150	FSL C B Ridley &	1N	1 ⎫	2-seater	Cagnicourt	OOC
	FSL H V Rowley	1N	1 ⎭			
1155	Lt W A Bishop	60	13	Halberstadt DII	E Epinoy	DF
1315	F/C E W Norton &	6N	7 ⎫	Albatros DIII	E Honnecourt	OOC
	FSL A H V Fletcher	6N	1 ⎭			
1400	FSL E D Crundall	8N	4	Albatros DIII	Henin-Lietard	DF
1500	Capt C M Crowe	56	2	Albatros DII	Waziers	OOC
1500	Lt J O Leach	56	1	Albatros DII	Bugnicourt	OOC
1550	2/Lt G Dinsmore &	18	1 ⎫	Albatros DIII	Inchy-Proville	DF
	2/Lt G B Bate	18	3 ⎭			
1700	2/Lt F E Conder &	20	1 ⎫	Albatros DIII	Courtrai	OOC
	2/Lt H G Neville	20	1 ⎭			
1705	Capt F H Thayre &	20	2 ⎫	Albatros DIII	E Menin	DF
	Capt F R Cubbin	20	3 ⎭			
1710	Capt F H Thayre &	20	3 ⎫	Albatros DIII	E Zillebeke	DF
	Capt F R Cubbon	20	4 ⎭			
1725	2/Lt E J Smart &	20	4 ⎫	Albatros DIII	Courtrai-Ypres	D
	2/Lt T A M S Lewis	20	1 ⎭			
1740	Capt E D Atkinson	1	4	Albatros C	Pont Rouge	OOC
1800	FSL A P Heywood	1N	1	Albatros DII	E Lens	OOC
1830	2/Lt E S T Cole	1	5	Albatros DII	Ypres-Menin Road	OOC
1850	FSL R H Winter	6N	1	Albatros DIII	Guise	OOC
1855	F/C E W Norton	6N	8	Albatros DIII	Guise	DF
1855	F/C E W Norton	6N	9	Albatros DIII	Guise	OOC
1900	FSL F H M Maynard	1N	1	Albatros DIII	Fresnoy	OOC
1915	FSL R P Minifie &	1N	2 ⎫	Albatros DIII	Douai	D
	FSL R A Little	8N	12 ⎭			
1930	FSL H V Rowley	1N	2	Albatros DIII	Gavrelle	OOC
	Lt Knight &	6	1 ⎫	Albatros DIII		OOC
	F/Sgt Cardno	6	1 ⎭			

30 April 1917

Time	Name	Sqn	No.	Aircraft	Location	Result
0630	Lt G A Gyde	54	2	Albatros DIII	Walincourt	OOC
0645	FSL R J Compston	8N	2	Albatros C	E Douai	OOC
0700	FSL R J Compston	8N	3	Albatros C	W Douai	OOC
0700	FSL C D Booker	8N	4	Albatros DIII	W Douai	OOC
0710	FSL R A Little	8N	13	Albatros DIII	E Arras	OOC
0725	FSL R A Little	8N	14	Albatros DIII	E Arras	OOC
0835	F/C R S Dallas	1N	13	Rumpler C	Hayencourt	D
0845	Capt C M Crowe	56	3	Albatros DIII	E Douai	D
0845	Lt M A Kay &	56	1 ⎫	Albatros DIII	E Douai	OOC
	Lt J O Leach	56	2 ⎭			
0845	Capt J O Andrews	66	8	2-seater	Brebières-Vitry	D
0855	Capt C J Q Brand	1	6	Albatros C	Houplines	POW
0920	F/C R S Dallas	1N	14	Albatros DIII	Hayencourt	OOC
0930	2/Lt M M Kaizer &	18	1 ⎫	Albatros DIII	Baralle-Bourlon	D
	Sgt F Russell	18	2 ⎭			
0930	2/Lt S H Bell &	18	1 ⎫	Albatros DIII	Marquion	OOC
	Lt D W MacLeod	18	1 ⎭			
0930	2/Lt I C Barkley &	18	1 ⎫	Albatros DIII	Baralle	OOC
	2/AM L B Adcock	18	1 ⎭			
0930	2/Lt M M Kaizer &	18	2 ⎫	Albatros DIII	Baralle-Bourlon	OOC
	Sgt F Russell	18	3 ⎭			
0930	2/Lt S H Bell &	18	2 ⎫	Albatros DIII	Marquion-Bourlon	OOC
	Lt D W MacLeod	18	2 ⎭			
0930	2/Lt G Critchley &	18	1 ⎫	Albatros DIII	Baralle	OOC
	2/Lt O Partington	18	1 ⎭			
0945	2/Lt D Marshall &	57	1 ⎫	Albatros DIII	Buissy	OOC
	Lt J T Anglin	57	1 ⎭			
0945	Lt C S Morice &	57	1 ⎫	Albatros DIII	Buissy	OOC
	Lt F Leathley	57	1 ⎭			
1115	Capt W A Bishop	60	14	Albatros C	E Lens	D
1145	Lt E S T Cole	1	6	Albatros DIII	N Ypres	OOC

1150	FSL A R Knight	8N	1	Albatros DIII	E Lens	OOC
1245	FSL L F W Smith	4N	1	Albatros DIII	E Nieuport	OOC
1640	Capt C K C Patrick	23	7	Albatros DIII	Inchy-en-Artois	DF
1640	2/Lt S C O'Grady	23	1	Albatros DIII	Inchy-en-Artois	OOC
1730	FSL R Collishaw	10N	6	Albatros DIII	E Cortemarck	D
1900	FSL C J Moir	4N	2	Albatros DIII	S Nieuport	OOC
	2/Lt T Middleton &	48	1 ⎫			
	Lt C G Claye	48	1 ⎬	Albatros DIII		OOC
	Lt H Game &	48	1 ⎭			
	2/Lt C Malcomson	48	1	Albatros DIII		OOC

D = Destroyed   DF = Destroyed in flames   OOC = Out of Control   P = Probable victory   POW = Captured

APPENDIX II

French Victory Claims April 1917

1 April 1917

Time	Pilot/Crew	Unit	Vic No	E/A	Location	How
	Sgt L Goux	N67	1	2-seater		D

5 April 1917

| | S/Lt J Chaput | N57 | 9 | EA | | D |
| | S/Lt J Chaput | N57 | 10 | EA | | D |

6 April 1917

1805	Adj C Jeronnez	N26	2	Balloon	Montchalons	DF
	S/Lt V Regnier	N112	5	Balloon	Epoye	DF
	Adj G Douchy	N38	6	Balloon	Hauvine	DF
	Brig P Leroy	N78	1	Balloon	Ardeuil	DF
	S/Lt P Tarascon	N62	9	Albatros	Marechalpot	DF
	Lt J Mistarlet	N31	1	Balloon	Lavannes	D
	Cpl Montagne	N112	1	EA		

7 April 1917

| | S/Lt L Bucquet | N3 | 1 | EA | Forges | DF |
| | Lt A Lorillard | N48 | – | Balloon | | P |

8 April 1917

1330	Lt A de Laage	N124	–	EA	N St Quentin	FTL
1350	Lt A de Laage	N124	3	2-seater	N Moy	FTL
1530	Cpl Damanez (P)	R46	– ⎫			
	Cpl Rivière (G) &	R46	– ⎬	EA	Orgeval	P
	MdL Theron (G)	R46	– ⎭			
1615	Lt Bloch,	R46	1 ⎫			
	Sgt Joussen (G) &	R46	2 ⎬	EA	Aguilcourt	D
	Sgt Roye (G)	R46	1 ⎭			
	Brig Brunet (P),		1 ⎫			
	Sgt Levy (G) &		1 ⎬	EA	N Berry-au-Bac	D
	Sgt Gerard (G)		1 ⎭			

9 April 1917

| | S/Lt P Tarascon | N62 | 10 | LVG C | Pinon | D |

11 April 1917

| 1050 | Adj C Jeronnez | N26 | 3 | EA | Cerny-le-Laonnois | D |
| | Lt A Pinsard | N78 | 6 | Albatros D | SE St Souplet | D |

12 April 1917

| | Lt A Pinsard | N78 | 7 | Albatros D | S Epoye | D |

	MdL M Nogues	N12	2	EA	Bois de Cheval	D
	Adj L Jailler	N15	7	Scout	Rethel	FTL

13 April 1917

1730	Adj R Lufbery	N124	8	EA	NW St Quentin	D
	MdL L Gros (P) &	F41	1 ⎫	EA	Mont Sapigneul	D
	S/Lt de Dreux (O)	F41	1 ⎭			
	Adj A Bertrand	N57	2	EA	Guignicourt	D
	Adj Poli-Krauss (P) &		1 ⎫	EA		D
	S/Lt Clave (O)		1 ⎭			

14 April 1917

0600	S/Lt H Languedoc	N12	5	EA	Bois de Noyelle	D
1030	Cpl Benedictus (P),		1 ⎫			
	Soldat Bassière (G) &		1 ⎬	EA	Mont Sapigneul	D
	S/Lt Lullert (O)	R214	1 ⎭			
1030	Capt G Guynemer	N3	36	Albatros	Neuville	DF
1100	MdL de Belleville	N49	1	EA	Elbach	D
1215	Capt Lecour Grandmaison		5 ⎫			
	Adj Vitalis (G) &	C46	7 ⎬	EA	S Craonne	D
	MdL Rousseau (G)	C46	5 ⎭			
1315	S/Lt Mauduit (P),	F41	1 ⎫			
	Lt Tartet (O) &	F41	1 ⎬	EA	SW Conde	D
	Brig Kissel (G)	F41	1 ⎭			
	Adj G Daladier	N516	1	2-seater	Ste Marie-aux-Mines	D
	Mdl P Vieljeux	N516	1	2-seater	Bonhomme	D
	Adj J Hamel	N516	1	Balloon	Saulxures	DF
	Adj Grelat (P) &	GB4	3 ⎫	EA	Brisach	D
	Lt Cavinet (O)	GB4	3 ⎭			
	Lt A Pinsard	N78	8	EA	N Somme-Py	D
	Lt E Thiriez	N15	1	EA	Corbeny	DF
	71st Balloon Co			EA		DF
	Capt G Matton	N48	–	2-seater		P

15 April 1917

1040	Lt A Deullin	N73	13	EA	Festieux	DF
	S/Lt P de Larminat	N48	–	EA		P
	Lt A Deullin	N73	–	EA	Festieux	P

16 April 1917

0600	S/Lt H Languedoc	N12	6	EA	E Cauroy	D
1025	Brig R Rigault	N73	2	EA	Cormicy	DF
1030	Lt Balme (P) &	C222	1 ⎫	EA	Hermonville	D
	Lt Liort (O)	F72	1 ⎭			
1510	Brig R Rigault	N73	2	Balloon	Bruxières	DF
1520	Cpl A Cordonnier	N57	1	Balloon	S Bois de Grands Usages	DF
	Brig E Thomassin	N26	1	EA	Juvincourt	D
	Sgt G Triboulet	N57	–	EA		P

19 April 1917

1451	S/Lt R Dorme	N3	19	EA	W Orainville	D
	S/Lt Tarascon	N62	10	LVG C	E Trucy	D
	????			EA	W Moronvillers	D
	????			EA	SE Fresnes	D

21 April 1917

	Lt A Pinsard	N78	9	EA	Nauroy	D
	Lt A Pinsard	N78	10	EA	Nauroy-Moronvillers	D
	S/Lt H Languedoc	N12	7	EA	Somme-Suippes	POW
	Adj de Fourneaux	N78	1	EA	Somme-Suippes	D

22 April 1917

1710	Adj F Bergot	N73	–	EA	Aumenaucourt	P
1750	Lt A Deullin	N73	14	EA	W Craonne	D
1835	S/Lt R Dorme	N3	20	EA	Beaurieux	D
1910	Capt A Auger	N3	4	EA	Lierval	D
	Sgt P Pendaires	N69	–	EA		P

23 April 1917

1815	S/Lt Juguin	N84	1	Rumpler C	NW Itancourt	D
	MdL L Morizot (P) &	N23	1⎫	EA	Bois de Avocourt	D
	Lt J Gouin (O)	N23	2⎭			
	Sgt Reyzal (P),	F7	1⎫			
	Lt Climens (O) &	F7	1⎬	EA		D
	Brig Leclair (G)	F7	1⎭			
	Adj E Pillon	N82	3	LVG CV		D
	Capt J Derode	N102	3	2-seater	Prosnes	D
	????			EA	Epine de Chrevigny	D

24 April 1917

1640	Cpl R Lejeune &	N83	1⎫	2-seater	Courson	D
	Capt R de Marancour	GC14	3⎭			
1700	Adj R Baudoin	N80	2	2-seater	l'Ange Gardien	DF
1720	Mdl M Henriot	N65	1	Scout	Forêt de Pinon	D
1725	Adj R Lufbery	N124	9	2-seater	E Cerisy	D
1800	S/Lt F Battesti	N73	2	EA	Ste Croix	D
	Adj G Madon	N38	8	2-seater	Courson	D
	Adj G Madon	N38	9	Albatros	Cornilette	D
	Adj E Pillon	N82	4	Albatros D	Dannemarie	D
	????			EA	W Bois de l'Enclume	D
	MdL C Soulier	M26	–	EA		P
	Sgt G Triboulet	N57	–	EA		P

26 April 1917

0615	Lt A de Turenne,	N48	2⎫			
	Cpl R Montrion &	N48	1⎬	Albatros C	Ville-aux-Bois	D
	Cpl J Conan	N48	1⎭			
1000	S/Lt R Baudoin	N80	–	Scout	Reservoir-Trucy	P
1740	Sgt R Bajac &	N48	1⎫	EA	Loivre	D
	Cpl J Roques	N48	1⎭			
1800	Sgt C Johnson	N124	1	Albatros C	E St Quentin	D
1830	Lt W Thaw &	N124	2⎫	Albatros C	Juvincourt	D
	Sgt W Haviland	N124	1⎭			
	Lt G Luc Pupat	N79	1	EA	Itancourt-St Quentin	D
	Sgt Gendronneau,	R46	2⎫			
	Asp Breuil &	R46	1⎬	EA	N Ft Brimont	D
	Cpl Cadot	R46	1⎭			
	????			EA	Gratreuil	D

27 April 1917

	Sgt E Breton &	N501	1⎫			
	Sgt P Barthes	N501	1⎬	2-seater	N Reservoir d'Ailette	D
	Cpl Sigaud (P),	F71	1⎭			
	S/Lt Guye (O) &	F71	1⎫	EA		D
	Sol Lehemade (G)	F71	1⎭			
	????			EA	Gerardmer	D
	????			EA	S Beine	D
	Sgt J Naegely	N15	–	Albatros	Eppes-Coucy	FTL

29 April 1917

0545	S/Lt R Baudoin	N80	3	2-seater	Moulins	POW
1343	S/Lt R Dorme	N3	21	Albatros C	Fleuricourt	D
1745	S/Lt G Lebeau	N12	4	EA	Orainville	D
	Lt J Beraud-Villars	N102	2	EA	NE Nauroy	D
	????			EA	Aguilcourt	D

30 April 1917

0940	Lt L Jailler	N15	8	EA	Laon	D
	Lt R Bailly	N81	1	EA	N Moronvillers	DF
	Adj H Peronneau	N81	–	EA		P
	MdL Diesbach	N15	–	EA	Berry-au-Bac	P

D = Destroyed   DF = Destroyed in flames   POW = Prisoner of War   FTL = Forced to Land
P = Probably destroyed   (P) = Pilot   (O) = Observer   (G) = Gunner   (B) = Bombardier

APPENDIX III

German Victory Claims April 1917

1 April 1917

Time	Pilot/Crew	Sqdn	Vic No	E/A	Location
1045	Lt O Bernert	2	11	Balloon	Villers-au-Flers
1145	Lt W Voss	2	23	BE2c	E St Leger
	Flakzug 145 & MFlak 14			FE	Pont de Courriers

2 April 1917

Time	Pilot/Crew	Sqdn	Vic No	E/A	Location
0830	Lt O Bernert	2	10	Nieuport	Queant
0835	Oblt M v Richthofen	11	32	BE2d	Farbus
0930	Lt K Allmenröder	11	5	BE	Angres
1000	Vfw S Festner	11	3	FE2d	SE Auby
1000	Lt K Krefft	11	1	FE2d	Oignies
1120	Oblt M v Richthofen	11	33	Sop 1½	Givenchy
	OfStv E Nathanael	5	5	FE2b	NE Gouzeaucourt
			FTL	Nieuport	Poix Terron

3 April 1917

Time	Pilot/Crew	Sqdn	Vic No	E/A	Location
1450	Lt G Nernst	30	3	Nieuport	Esquerchin
1450	Uffz L Weber	3	1	BE2e	NE Brebières
1615	Obltn M v Richthofen	11	34	FE2d	Cité St Pierre
1620	Lt K Schäfer	11	9	FE2d	La Coulotte
1635	OfStv E Nathanael	5	9	DH2	N Bourssies
1655	Vfw E Eisenhuth	3	2	FE2b	Hendecourt
1717	Vfw S Festner	11	6	FE	Lens
1719	Lt A Schulte	12	6	FE	NE St Leger
1720	Vfw S Festner	11	7	FE	Hendecourt
1720	Hptm P v Osterroht	12	2	FE	N Bullecourt
1910	Lt O Bernert	B	12	Balloon	Ervillers
1922	Lt O Bernert	B	13	Balloon	N Bapaume
1955	????			Balloon	Athies-Thelus
	Lt Schumacher &	FA40	1⎫	Nieuport	S St Quentin
	Uffz Scheinig	FA40	1⎭		
	Flakzug 28, 47 & 185			FE	S Feuchy
	Lt A Schulte	12	—	DH2	

4 April 1917

Time	Pilot/Crew	Sqdn	Vic No	E/A	Location
0900	Lt H Klein	4	1	BE2e	SE Arras
0930	Lt H Malchow	4	1	FE	SW Arras

5 April 1917

Time	Pilot/Crew	Sqdn	Vic No	E/A	Location
1100	Vfw S Festner	11	5	Nieuport	SW Bailleul
1105	Lt F Röth	12	2	FE2b	Gouzeaucourt
1105	Lt A Schulte	12	—	FE2b	Lepave
1108	Obltn M v Richthofen	11	35	BF2a	Lewarde
1110	Lt O Splitgerber	12	2	FE2b	Honnecourt
1120	Lt G Simon	11	1	BF2a	N Monchecourt
1128	Obltn M v Richthofen	11	36	BF2a	Quincy
1200	Lt G Schlenker	3	6	FE2b	SW Moeuvres
1205	Lt G Nernst	30	2	Sopwith 2	W Rouvroy
1806	Lt H Auer	26	1	Nieuport/Spad	Sennheim
1830	Vfw S Festner	11	7	BF2a	Aniche
2230	Ground fire			FE	Bailleul
	Vfw K Menckhoff	3	2	Nieuport	W Athies
	Lt E Weissner	18	1	FE2d	S Ypern
	Lt E Voss	20	1	Nieuport	Omissy
	Lt A Dossenbach	36	10	Caudron	Sillery
	Lt Wolluhn &	FAA210	1⎫	EA	Ribecourt
	Uffz Mackeprang	FAA210	1⎭		

	Flakzug 407 &				
	Beh Flakbatt 4.64			Sopwith	Origny
	Forced to land			Martinsyde	La Bouteille

6 April 1917

0815	Lt J v Bertrab	30	1	Martinsyde	Ath
0815	Lt H Gontermann	5	6	FE2d	Neuville
0820	OfStv E Nathanael	5	7	FE2d	Douchy
0825	Lt O Splitgerber	12	3	FE2d	Thiaut
0830	Hptm P v Osterroht	12	5	FE2d	Lagnicourt
0830	Oblt A v Tutschek	B	9	FE2d	Anneux
0830	Lt J v Bertrab	30	2	Martinsyde	SE Leuze
0830	Lt A Schulte	12	—	FE2b	Anneux
0850	Lt W Frankl	4	16	FE2b	Fauchy
0850	Lt W Frankl	4	17	FE2b	Arras
0945	Lt W Voss	B	24	BE2e	S Lagnicourt
1000	Lt W Frankl	4	18	BE2e	NE Boiry
1010	MFlak 60			Nieuport	Neuvireuil
1015	Lt O Bernert	B	17	RE8	Roeux
1015	Vfw K Menckhoff	3	1	RE8	Fampoux
1015	Lt K Wolff	11	6	RE8	Bois Bernard
1018	????			EA	Loosbogen
1020	Lt K Schäfer	11	10	BE2d	Givenchy
1037	Lt K Schäfer	11	11	BE2c	SW Vimy
1048	Lt J v Bertrab	30	3	Sopwith 2	N Becq
1048	Oblt H Bethge	30	5	Sopwith 2	NE Templeuve
1050	Lt J v Bertrab	30	4	Sopwith 2	NE Pecq
1215	Hptm P v Osterroht	12	3	Triplane N	Henin-Lietard
1810	Lt H Baldamus	9	16	Spad	NW Fresnes
1930	Lt J Jacobs	22	2	Balloon	Blanzy-Vailly
	Lt W Frankl	4	19	FE2b	Quiery-la-Motte
	OfStv W Göttsch	8	7	FE2d	NE Polygonwald
	Lt Kreuzner	13	1	Caudron	S Vailly
	Oblt R Berthold	14	10	Caudron	Malval-Ferme
	Vfw G Strasser	17	1	Caudron	N Pontavert
	Lt W Böning	19	1	Caudron	S Berry-au-Bac
	Lt D Collin	22	—	Farman	Terny-Sorny
	Lt E Kreuzer	36	2	Caudron	Berry-au-Bac
	Lt H Bongartz	36	1	Spad	Vitry-les-Reims
	Lt Zywitz &	FA228	1 ⎫	Nieuport	Berry-au-Bac
	Lt Lexow	FA228	1 ⎭		
	Lt Hansen &	FA212	1 ⎫	Caudron	Berneuil
	Vfw Gonella	FA212	1 ⎭		
	KFlak 35			EA	Fayet-Gricourt
	KFlak 82			FE	Richtung-Holnon
	Flakbatt 505			FE	Lagnicourt
	Flak 709, Flak 507 or				
	a pilot			FE	Anneux
	Forced to land			Triplane	Mons
	Forced to land			Sopwith 2	N Laon
	MG fire from ground			FE	Quiery-le-Motte
	????			Caudron	Souain

7 April 1917

1700	Lt H Klein	4	2	Balloon	W Arras
1710	Vfw L Patermann	4	1	Nieuport	NW Biache
1710	Lt O Bernert	B	14	Nieuport	S Roeux
1745	Oblt M v Richthofen	11	37	Nieuport	NE Mercatel
1745	Lt K Wolff	11	7	Nieuport	NE Mercatel
1745	Lt K Schäfer	11	12	Nieuport	NE Mercatel
1815	Lt W v Bülow	18	10	FE2d	S Ploegsteertwald
1815	OfStv M Müller	28	6	FE2d	Ploegsteertwald
1910	Lt W Frankl	4	18	Nieuport	SE Fampoux
1910	Vfw S Festner	11	6	Sopwith/BF2b	NW Maroeuil
	Hptm H v Hunerbein	8	1	Nieuport	Becelaere
	MFlak 60			Nieuport	Fresnes

8 April 1917

0440	Lt H Klein	4	3	FE2b	SE Douai
0930	Vfw S Festner	11	7	Nieuport 23	E Vimy
1140	Rittm M v Richthofen	11	38	Sopwith 2	Farbus
1330	Lt W Frankl	4	20	EA	Arras
1430	Lt K Wolff	11	8	DH4	NE Blecourt
1440	Lt K Schäfer	11	13	DH4	Epinoy
1510	Lt O Bernert	B	18	BF2a	SE Eterpigny
1510	Lt O Bernert	B	19	RE8	N Bailleul
1640	Rittm M v Richthofen	11	39	BE2g	W Vimy
1900	KFlak 12, Flakzug 38, Flakzug 46, Flakzug 72, & MFlak 70			FE2b	N La Bassée
1910	Lt G Schlenker	3	7	Nieuport 23	NE Croiselles
	Lt H Gontermann	5	8	Balloon	W St Quentin
	OfStv W Göttsch	8	8	BE2d	E Dixmuide
	Lt W v Bülow	18	11	Nieuport	E Ypern
	Oblt E Hahn	19	2	Caudron	N Loivre
	Lt Weinschenk &	FA23	1⎫	Caudron	Effigny
	Lt Camphausen	FA23	1⎭		
	Vfw Finkendel &	FA225	1⎫	Nieuport	SW St Quentin
	Lt Weber	FA225	1⎭		
	Flakzug 17			Grosskampf	Amigny
	KFlak 43			Nieuport	E Arras

9 April 1917

1900	Lt K Schäfer	11	14	BE2d	Aix Noulette

10 April 1917

	Forced to land			Nieuport	Aleucourt

11 April 1917

0845	Lt G Röth	12	1	BE2c	NE Abancourt
0855	Lt A Schulte	12	7	BE2d	Tilloy
0900	Lt H Frommherz	B	1	Spad	Cuvillers
0900	Vfw S Festner	11	8	BE	N Monchy
0905	Lt A Schulte	12	8	Pup	W Neuvireuil
0910	Lt K Schäfer	11	15	BF2a	SW Fresnes
0910	Lt K Wolff	11	9	BF2a	N Fresnes
0915	Lt L v Richthofen	11	2	BF2a	N Fresnes
0925	Rittm M v Richthofen	11	40	BE2d	Willerval
1020	Lt H Klein	4	4	BE	Biache
1100	Lt H Klein	4	5	BE	Feuchy
1145	Oblt R Berthold	14	11	Spad	S Corbeny
1145	OfStv Huttner	14	2	Spad	Berry-au-Bac
1230	Lt O Bernert	B	15	Spad	Arras
1235	Lt L v Richthofen	11	3	BE2e	NE Fampoux
1240	Lt O Bernert	B	16	Morane	NW Lagnicourt
1250	Lt K Schäfer	11	16	BE2c	E Arras
	Lt G Salzwedel	24	1	Nieuport	Xures
	Lt A Dossenbach	36	11	Farman	Berry-au-Bac

12 April 1917

1035	Hptm P v Osterroht	12	4	Pup	NW Bourlon
1035	Vfw A Schorisch	12	2	FE2b	SE Eterpigny
1040	Lt A Schulte	12	9	FE2b	N Baralle
1100	Uffz E Horn	21	1	Sopwith 2	S Nauroy
1900	Lt H Baldamus	9	17	Spad	N Pont Faverger
	Lt K Schneider	5	2	BE2c	Herbecourt
	Oblt E Hahn	19	3	Caudron	Orainville
	Flakzug 54			Caudron R4	Le Beau Château
	Forced to land			Spad	Attigny
	Forced to land			Nieuport	Leffincourt

13 April 1917

0854	Vfw S Festner	11	9	RE8	N Dury

0855	Lt L v Richthofen	11	4	RE8	NE Biache
0856	Lt H Klein	4	6	RE8	SW Biache
0856	Lt K Wolff	11	10	RE8	N Vitry
0856	Rittm M v Richthofen	11	41	RE8	E Vitry
0900	Lt K Schneider	5	3	FE2d	S Gavrelle
0905	Lt H Gontermann	5	3	FE2d	S Gavrelle
1235	Lt K Wolff	11	11	FE2b	S Bailleul
1245	Rittm M v Richthofen	11	42	FE2b	W Monchy
1400	Lt A Dossenbach	36	12	Spad	Sapigneul
1520	Flak			EA	Quiery-la-Motte
1630	Lt K Wolff	11	12	Nieuport	S Monchy
1700	Lt H Bongartz	36	2	Caudron	Cormicy
1830	Lt K Schäfer	11	17	FE2b	SW Monchy
1830	Lt E Dostler	34	—	Balloon	Gernicourt
1852	Lt K Wolff	11	13	Martinsyde	Rouvroy
1910	Lt H Klein	4	7	FE2d	Vimy
1915	Lt E Bauer	3	1	FE2b	La Bassée
1930	Vfw S Festner	11	10	FE2b	E Harnes
1935	Rittm M v Richthofen	11	43	FE2b	Noyelle-Godault
1935	Lt J Jacobs	22	4	Farman	Barisis
1935	OfStv E Nathanael	5	8	Balloon	W St Quentin
1940	Lt H Gontermann	5	9	Balloon	S St Quentin
	Lt L v Richthofen	11	5	RE8	Pelves
	Uffz S Ruckser	37	1	Balloon	
	Lt Stobe	3	1	BE2g	SW Oppy
	Lt K Schneider	5	4	FE2d	Gavrelle
	Lt G Bassenge	5	—	Gitterrumpf	W St Quentin
	KFlak 12			BE	Willerval
	Flakzug 155			FE	Brebières
	KFlakbatt 101, KFlak 12, }				
	Flakzug 31, Flakzug 75, }			Bristol	Courcelles
	Flakzug 145 & Flakzug 188 }				

14 April 1917

0500	MG Ground fire			BE2f	Salome
0810	Lt H v Schöll	30	1	Sopwith 2	Douai
0915	Rittm M v Richthofen	11	44	Nieuport	S Bois Bernard
0920	Lt K Wolff	11	14	Nieuport	SE Drocourt
0920	Lt L v Richthofen	11	6	Nieuport	W Fouquières
0923	Vfw S Festner	11	11	Nieuport	Gavrelle
0930	Lt H Frommherz	B	2	BE2e	Ribecourt
0934	Vfw K Menckhoff	3	—	EA	Ecoust St Mein
0934	Oblt K v Döring	4	1	Nieuport	SE Fresnoy
1140	Lt F Putter	9	1	Balloon	E Suippes
1140	Lt H Baldamus	9	18	Nieuport	St Marie-à-Py
1200	Uffz H Kramer	14	1	Caudron	Juvigny
1200	Oblt R Berthold	14	12	Spad	Bois de Marais
1200	Lt J Veltjens	14	1	Spad	Craonne
1705	Lt K Schäfer	11	18	FE2b	SW Lievin
1720	Lt K Schäfer	11	19	BE	La Coulotte
1823	Lt L v Richthofen	11	7	Spad	SE Vimy
1829	Lt K Wolff	11	15	Spad	E Bailleul
	Lt H Adam	34	2	Balloon	W St Mihiel
	Lt H Gontermann	5	11	BE2e	Metz-en-Couture
	Vfw O Gerbig	14	2	Caudron	Craonelle
	Oblt E Dostler	34	5	Nieuport	SW St Mihiel
	Vfw G Schindler	35	1	Sopwith 2	Schlettstadt
	Vfw R Rath	35	1	Sopwith 2	Scherweiler
	Flakbatt 511			Nieuport	Crenay-les-Reims
	Flakzug 79			Nieuport	Rotbach-Rainhof
	Flakzug 21			Spad	Lauchensee
	Flakzug 50			EA	Monchy
	Flakbatt 507, 509 &				
	Flakzug 30			EA	Sains-les-Marquion
	Flakzug 79, 171 & 413			Spad	SE Moyenmoutier

15 April 1917

1030	Uffz M Zachmann	21	1	Spad	Sery
	Vfw J Buckler	17	4	Spad	Prouvais
	Lt Dotzel	19	1	Nieuport	La Neuvillette
	Lt W Albert	31	3	Spad	Nauroy
	Lt A Dossenbach	36	13	Nieuport	Betheny
	Lt A Dossenbach	36	14	Spad	St Ferguex
	Vfw H Mitkeit	36	2	Spad	Thugny
	Uffz Rath	SchSt 10	1 ⎫	Farman	Oulcher Wald
	Gefr Musch		1 ⎭		
	Forced to land			Nieuport	Barricourt
	Cause unknown			Nieuport	Prosnes
	Cause unknown			Spad	Nauroy
	Lt R Matthaei	21	—	Spad	Nauroy-Moronvillers

16 April 1917

1030	Lt L v Richthofen	11	8	Nieuport	E Roeux
1030	Lt K Wolff	11	16	Nieuport	NE Roeux
1030	Vfw S Festner	11	12	Nieuport	NE Biache
1030	Lt R Oertelt	19	FTL	Caudron	Laneuville
1040	Lt Glinkermann	15	FTL	Farman	Juvincourt
1130	Vfw G Strasser	17	3	Caudron	S Cormicy
1505	Lt E Thuy	21	2	Caudron	N Berry-au-Bac
1650	Lt H Gontermann	5	10	Balloon	Manancourt
1700	Lt H Gontermann	5	11	Balloon	Manancourt
1730	Rittm M v Richthofen	11	45	BE2e	NW Gavrelle
	Lt H Wendel	15	1	Nieuport	Prouvais
	Vfw J Buckler	17	5	Nieuport	Berry-au-Bac
	Lt J Jacobs	22	5	Balloon	Laffaux
	Gefr May &	SchSt 3	1 ⎫	Spad	Corbeny
	Uffz Wiehle	SchSt 3	1 ⎭		
	Vfw Jehle &	FA295	FTL ⎫	Farman	Juvincourt
	Lt Calliebe	FA295	FTL ⎭		
	Uffz Janning &	SchSt 5	1 ⎫	Nieuport	NW Reims
	Gefr Reimers	5	1 ⎭		
	Lt Rose &	FA22	2 ⎫	Caudron	E Cernay
	Lt Parlow	FA22	1 ⎭		
	Lt Figulla &	SchSt 4	1 ⎫	Sopwith	Douai
	Uffz Steudel	SchSt 4	1 ⎭		
	KFlak 63			BE	NW St Quentin
	KFlak 93			BE	SW St Quentin
	KFlak 47			Nieuport	Craonne

18 April 1917

0800	Lt H Joens	31	1	Voisin	Auberive
	MFlak 54			Spad	Donnrein

19 April 1917

1000	Lt W Marwitz	9	1	Spad	SW Auberive
1145	Lt A Frey	9	2	Farman	S Moronvillers
	Lt R Wenzl	31	1	Spad	S Moronvillers
	Lt W Daugs	36	1	Morane	Prosnes

20 April 1917

0745	Lt Peters &	FAA235	1 ⎫	Vickers	Vimy
	Vfw Schopf	FAA235	1 ⎭		
0940	Vfw A Schörisch	12	3	BE2e	Ecoust St Mein
	Lt Schuerz	13	1	Farman	Landricourt
	Flakzug 31, 188,				
	KFlak 105 & Flakbatt 503			BE2f	Fresnes-Oppy
	Flakzug 46			Sopwith	NE Beaucamp
	KFlak 1, 8, 96 & 112			Bristol	E Urvillers

21 April 1917

1728	Lt L v Richthofen	11	9	BE2g	SE Vimy

Time	Name	Unit	No.	Aircraft	Location
1730	Lt K Wolff	11	17	BE2g	N Willerval
1745	Lt K Wolff	11	18	Nieuport	E Fresnes
1745	Lt K Schäfer	11	20	Nieuport	Fresnes
	KFlak 105			BE2g	N Vimy
	Flakzug 103			BE	E Ypern

22 April 1917

Time	Name	Unit	No.	Aircraft	Location
0630	Uffz F Gille	12	—	BE	Croiselles
0810	Lt A Hanko	28	1	Nieuport	Wavrin
0935	Lt H Gontermann	5	23	Balloon	Arras
1130	Lt K Schneider	5	6	Balloon	Epehy
1145	Lt K Schneider	5	7	Balloon	Essigny-le-Grand
1430	OfStv E Nathanael	5	11	Balloon	Bus
1710	Lt K Wolff	11	19	FE2b	Hendecourt
1710	Rittm M v Richthofen	11	46	FE2b	Lagnicourt
2005	OfStv E Nathanael	5	12	Spad	Ribecourt
2005	Lt K Wolff	11	20	Morane	Havrincourt
2005	Hptm P v Osterroht	12	6	Spad	S Marcoing
2005	Lt F Röth	12	2	EA	Marcoing
2010	Vfw R Jorke	12	2	Spad	W Havrincourt
2020	Lt K Schäfer	11	21	BE2e	W Monchy
	Lt Gerlt	19	1	Caudron	St Etienne

23 April 1917

Time	Name	Unit	No.	Aircraft	Location
0815	Lt K Schneider	5	8	FE2b	Bellenglise
0830	Uffz F Gille	12	—	Sopwith	Javrincourt
0920	Lt Pedell &	FA 233	1 ⎫	EA	Gavrelle
	Vfw Brockmann	FA 233	1 ⎭		
1200	Vfw A Schorisch	12	4	Sopwith	Wancourt
1200	Hptm P v Osterroht	12	7	Sopwith	Fontaine
1205	Rittm M v Richthofen	11	47	BE2f	Mericourt
1205	Lt K Schock	12	1	Sopwith	Dainville
1205	Vfw Grigo	12	2	Sopwith	Neuville
1210	Lt L v Richthofen	11	10	BE2g	N Vimy
1400	Lt W Schunke	20	1	Morane	SW St Quentin
1700	Vfw Frantz	33	1	Sopwith 2	Boisleux
1715	Vfw L v Raffay	34	1	Balloon	Belrupt
1720	Lt H Göring	26	4	FE2b	NE Arras
1800	OfStv R Weckbrodt	26	2	DH4	SW Itancourt
1925	Lt H Gontermann	5	13	RE8	SE Arras
2000	Vfw Grigo	12	4	EA	St Martin
2000	Uffz R Jorke	12	5	EA	Neuville
	Lt K Schneider	5	9	FE2b	Bellenglise
	Lt K Schneider	5	10	DH2	Bellenglise
	Lt Rohr	22	2	Farman	Leuilly

24 April 1917

Time	Name	Unit	No.	Aircraft	Location
0805	Oblt H Lorenz	33	2	Pup	Bourlon
0830	Lt O Bernert	B	20	Sopwith 2	S Vaucelles
0840	Lt O Bernert	B	21	BE2e	N Joncourt
0842	Lt O Bernert	B	22	BE2e	N Levergies
0845	Lt O Bernert	B	23	BE2e	S Bellicourt
0850	Lt O Bernert	B	24	DH4	W Bony
0850	Lt K Krefft	11	—	EA	Arras
0850	Uffz Stegmann &	SchSt 27	1 ⎫	Sopwith	Lens
	Vfw Menzel	SchSt 27	1 ⎭		
0900	Lt H Gontermann	5	14	Triplane	Bailleul
1012	OfStv P Felsmann	FA 24	2	Spad	E Prunay
1030	Lt Reigel &	FAA 211	1 ⎫	Sopwith	Lens
	Vfw Tötsch	FAA 211	1 ⎭		
1605	Vfw A Haussmann	23	2	Nieuport	Beaurieux
1930	Lt E Udet	15	5	Nieuport	Chavignon
	OfStv W Göttsch	8	9	FE2d	E Ypern
	Lt W Junck	8	1	FE2d	Ypern
	Lt W Kypke	14	—	Spad	Berry-au-Bac
	Lt W v Bülow	18	11	FE2d	Ypern

	Oblt E Dostler	34	6	Caudron	Ablonville
	Vflgmt Wirtz	MFJI	2	FE2d	Polygon Wald
	KFlak 94 or pilot			BE	S Krylon Ferme
	Flakbatt 701			BE	Wancourt
	Flakbatt 512			FE	E Ypern
	Flakzug 120			BE	Seidelli
	Cause unknown			FE	NW Menin

25 April 1917

1030	Lt K Allmenröder	11	7	BE2e	Guemappe
1040	Lt K Schäfer	11	22	FE2b	N Bailleul
2030	Lt K Schäfer	11	23	BF2a	Bahnhof Roeux
	KFlak 63			BE	Richtung-Omissy
	Forced to land			BE	S Valenciennes

26 April 1917

0920	Vfw J Buckler	17	7	Balloon	Bois de Genicourt
1115	Lt H Gontermann	5	15	Balloon	Arras
1600	Lt Schneider	5	15	Balloon	Seraucourt
1635	Lt K Wolff	11	21	BE2g	E Gavrelle
1818	Lt P Erbguth	30	1	BE2e	SE Haisnes
1840	Lt L v Richthofen	11	11	BE2g	SE Vimy Ridge
1845	Lt K Allmenröder	11	8	BE2g	Vimy Ridge
2000	OfStv A Sturm	5	1	FE2b	Brandcourt
2005	Lt R Nebel	5	1	FE2b	Joncourt
	Oblt E Hahn	19	4	Spad	N Brimont
	Lt W Albert	31	4	Spad	Nauroy
	KFlak 2			Nieuport	Houthem
	Flakzug 87, 102, 180 &				
	KFlak 53			Caudron G4	S Ft Brimont
	Cause unknown			EA	Cambrai

27 April 1917

0900	KFlak 93			Caudron	Essigny-le-Grand
2015	Lt L v Richthofen	11	12	FE2b	Fresnes
2020	Lt K Wolff	11	22	FE2b	S Gavrell
2025	Lt K Allmenröder	11	9	BE2	W Fampoux
	Lt A Dossenbach	36	—	Balloon	
	Lt H Bongartz	36	3	Balloon	Berry-au-Bac
	Lt H Bongartz	37	7	Balloon	SE Thillois
	KFlak 12			BE	S Bois Bernard
	Flakzug 145			BE	E Loos

28 April 1917

0830	Lt J Wolff	17	2	Caudron	Brimont
0930	Rittm M v Richthofen	11	48	BE2e	SE Pelves
1120	Lt K Wolff	11	23	BE2g	Oppy
1515	OfStv E Nathanael	5	12	Pup	La Vacquerie
1710	Flakbatt 709			FE2b	Villers Plouich
1745	Lt K Wolff	11	24	BE2f	W Gavrelle
1815	Lt J Schmidt	3	2	Balloon	S Mareouil
1830	Lt H Göring	26	5	Nieuport 17	Harly
1830	Vfw Langer	26	—	EA	S St Quentin
	KFlak 41			Sopwith	Reims
	Beh Flakzug der EtInsp	6		Sopwith	S Tournai

29 April 1917

1055	Uffz F Gille	12	1	FE2d	Baralle
1130	Lt K Schneider	5	11	Pup	Elincourt
1150	Gefr Reichardt &	FA7	1 ⎱	Caudron	Marcoing
	Lt Zupan	FA7	1 ⎰		
1205	Rittm M v Richthofen	11	49	Spad	E Lecluse
1210	Lt K Wolff	11	25	Spad	Sailly
1215	Lt L v Richthofen	11	13	Spad	Izel
1415	Lt H Geigl	34	1	Caudron	S Pont-à-Mousson
1655	Rittm M v Richthofen	11	50	FE2b	SW Inchy

1700	Lt K Wolff	11	26	FE2b	S Pronville
1900	Lt G Nolte	18	1	FE2d	Hooge
1925	Rittm M v Richthofen	11	51	BE2e	S Roeux
1925	Lt L v Richthofen	11	14	BE2e	NE Monchy
1930	Oblt B Loerzer	26	—	EA	Bellenglise
1940	Rittm v Richthofen	11	52	Triplane	N Henin-Lietard
1945	Lt Kempf	8	1	BE2c	SW La Pave
1945	Lt H Göring	26	6	Nieuport 17	Remicourt
2045	Lt H Stutz	20	—	FE2b	Douai
2100	OfStv E Nathanael	5	14	Pup	Beaumont
	Lt P Strahle	18	4	FE2d	N Courtrai
	Lt E Weissner	18	1	FE2d	Courtrai
	Lt W Böning	19	3	Caudron R11	Brimont
	Lt R Ernert	34	1	Balloon	Genicourt
	Vfw T Himmer	34	1	Farman	Genicourt
	Flakzug 28, 40 &				
	KFlak 61 and 68			Nieuport	N Hendecourt
	MFlak 63			Nieuport	S Dury
	MFlak 63			Nieuport	S Dury
	Flakbatt 530			Nieuport	E Luneville
	Forced to land			Vickers	N Courtrai
	Forced to land			Voisin	N Pauvres

30 April 1917

0700	OfStv M Müller	28	7	Sopwith 2	E Armentières
0715	Lt L v Richthofen	11	15	BE2g	SE Vimy
0755	Lt L v Richthofen	11	16	FE2d	Izel
0755	Oblt A v Tutschek	12	4	FE2d	Izel
0820	Uffz F Gille	12	—	EA	Recourt
0845	Lt H Geiseler	33	—	FE2d	Oppy
0925	Lt v Hartmann	9	1	Spad	SW Nauroy
1005	OfStv E Nathanael	5	—	Pup	S Fresnes
1010	Vfw Brokmann &	FAA223	2⎱	BE	Fresnoy
	Lt Pedell	FAA233	2⎰		
1030	Lt H Pfeiffer	9	10	Spad	Moronvillers
1100	Lt v Breiten	9	1	Nieuport	St Hilaire-le-Petit
1115	Lt A Frey	9	3	Spad	Moronvillers
1200	Lt H Klein	4	8	BE2e	Ribecourt
1200	Vfw W Wagener	21	4	Sopwith 2	Prosnes
1320	Vfw A Franz	33	—	EA	Monchy
1320	Vfw Voigt &	SchSt19	1⎱	Spad	Sallaumines
	Vfw Woldt	SchSt19	1⎰		
1440	Lt R Matthaei	21	3	Balloon	Montbre
1735	Lt K Wolff	11	29	BE2e	W Fresnes
1810	Lt P Billik	12	1	Pup	Romaucourt
1850	Vfw K Menckhoff	3	3	Nieuport	Cantin
	Lt W Böning	19	2	Balloon	Guyencourt
	Oblt E Hahn	19	5	Balloon	Guyencourt
	Oblt E Hahn	19	6	Balloon	Guyencourt
	Vfw A Rahn	19	1	Balloon	Reims
	Vfw A Rahn	19	2	Balloon	Reims
	Lt K Deilmann	6	—	Sopwith	Roupy
	LtzS T Osterkamp	MFJ1	FTL	Nieuport	Oostkerke
	KFlak 93			BE	N Fayette
	KFlak 61 & Flakzug 28			BE	E Cherisy
	Flakzug 165			Farman	Rapes

APPENDIX IV
Known German Casualties April 1917

(NB. Although compiled from official sources neither this list nor that for September 1918 casualties can be taken as complete, but are given as an aid to the overall picture. Although we have tried to list the known operational casualties, there may well be a few non-operational losses included.)

1 April

Ltn Alfred Mohr	J3	Alb DIII 2012/16, KIA 1150 nr Arras, 6 Armee
Ltn Werner (O)	FAA 288b	Severely WIA, 6 Armee

2 April

Ltn Erich König	J2	KIA over Wancourt
Ltn Hans Wortmann	J2	KIA over Vitry-en-Artois
Vfw Rudolf Nebel	J35	Alb DIII 2107/16—POW, (Escaped 5 May)
Ltn Karl Haan	FA19	KIA over Langmarck, 4 Armee
Ltn Hahn ??		WIA
OffStv Fritz Meixner	FA48	POW, Bapaume
Oblt Friedrich Pückert	"	POW

3-4 April

Nil

5 April

Ltn Josef Flink	J18	WIA/POW; FTL Nr Neuve Eglise in Alb DIII 1942/16
Ltn Karl Hummel		Killed, Ghent
Gfr Simon Metzger		Killed, Mont d'Origny
Uffz Albin Nietzold		Killed, St Marie

6 April

Vfw Ludwig Weber	J3	Alb DII 510/16, WIA nr Biache
Vfw Paul Hoppe	J5	Collided with Berr, N Noyelles; Killed
Oblt Hans Berr	J5	Killed—see above
Ltn Otto Splitgerber	J12	WIA over Thialt, 0825
Flg Josef Eichholz		Killed, Fampoux
Vfw Reinhold Wurzmann	J20	KIA, down in flames N Noyelles
Vfw Siegfried Thiele (P)	FAA233	KIA, 6 Armee
Ltn Karl Seyberth (O)	"	KIA, Lecluse
Ltn Walter Dieckmann	FAA243	KIA, Colmar
Ltn Hans Müller	"	KIA, Colmar
Uffz Rudolf Temler	FAA263	KIA, Queant
Ltn Julius Schmitt	"	KIA, Queant
Vfw H C F Donhauser	FA221	F/L—shot up
W Walter	"	"

7 April

Gfr Schoop (P)	S7	MIA
Ltn Hupe (O)	FAA233	MIA, 6 Armee
Vfw Ludwig Müller	FA46	KIA, St Mihiel

8 April

Ltn Wilhelm Frankl	J4	KIA, Alb DIII 2158/16. 1415, N Vitry-en-Artois, 6 Armee
Ltn Roland Nauck	J6	KIA Villeveque, St Quentin, Alb DIII 2234/16 in Br lines
Flg Helmut Naudszus		Killed, St Quentin
Vfw Josef Schreiner		Killed, Amifontaine-Prouvais
Uffz Ferdinand Hinkemeyer		Killed, Cheret

9 April

Ltn Schroeder (O)	FA202	WIA, 6 Armee
Uffz Eugen Reuter (P)		KIA, Vitry
Ltn Rudolf Müller (P)	FAA276	Killed, Manningen by Metz
Ltn Max Trautmann (O)		Killed
OffStv Franz Hermann		Killed, Le Thone
Gfr Oskar Weller		Killed, Cheppy

10 April

Flg Adam Diewald		Killed, Ghent
Gfr Karl Steecher		Killed, Montmedy

11 April

Vfw Karl Möwe	J29	KIA, Juneville
		Ardennes, between Auberive & St Souplet
Ltn Heinrich Karbe	J22	slightly wounded

12 April

Ltn Adolf Schulte	J12	KIA in Alb DIII 1996/16
		N Barelle, Rumaucourt
Gfr Richard Streubel		Killed, Asfeld la Ville
Flg Max Vogl	FA46	Killed, Jarny
Flg Paul Weiss		Killed, Cohartville
Ltn Ernst Beltzig (O)	FAA272	KIA, Alincourt
Gfr Armo Rebentisch (P)	„	KIA, Alincourt

13 April

Uffz Binder	SS24	Severely WIA; 6 Armee
Uffz Simon Ruckser	J37	Severely WIA

14 April

Ltn Helmut Baldamus	J9	KIA over St Marie-à-Py
Vfw Paul Ruger (P)	KG4	KIA, Clermont les Ferme
Ltn Kurt Matthias (O)	KG4	KIA, Clermont les Ferme
Flg Johann Ploes		Killed, Manonvilliers
Ltn Heinrich Schönberg		Killed, Aisne-Champagne
Ltn Erich Schwidder (O)	FAA251	Killed, Pauvres (Wibeah Ferme)
Ltn August Schlarf (P)	„	Killed, Pauvres
Ltn Otto Weigel	J14	KIA, Craonelle
Ltn Fritz Grunzweig	J16	KIA after KB attack nr Ellbach, Obertraubach
Ltn Gerhard Anders	J35	WIA
Ltn Margraf	J35	WIA
Oblt Herbert Theurich	J35	KIA Alb DIII 2097/16 over Neubreisach
Uffz Hermann Jopp	J37	KIA by flak in KB attack nr Mont Toulin
Uffz Erich Hartmann (P)	FAA243	KIA, Elsass
Ltn Otto Druck (O)	„	KIA
Ltn Friedrich Bierling (O)	FAA253	KIA, W of Anicy le Château
Ltn Theodor Aichele (O)	FA14	Killed, Rusach, Alsace
Vfw L Demmel	SS2b	Killed, Neubriesach
Uffz Simon Stebel	SS2b	Killed, Neubriesach
Ltn Paul Otto	FAA224	WIA

15 April

Ltn Paul Dörr (O)	FAA45b	WIA by ground fire at Bouchain. DOW 17th. 6 Armee
Unnamed officer	FAA242	WIA

16 April

Ltn Hans-Olaf Esser	J15	KIA, Laon
Vfw Rieger	J17	MIA
Uffz Hans Precht		Killed, Aisne-Champagne
Ltn Hugo Sommer		Killed, Chivy
Ltn Hans Strathmeyer		Killed, Chivy
Uffz Walter Köppen (P)	FAA248	KIA, Villers Franqueux
Ltn Heinrich Wecke (O)	FAA248	KIA, Villers Franqueux
Ltn Walter Utermann (O)	FAA228	Killed, Juvincourt nr Verdun
Ltn Hans-Jorgen Kalmus (O)	FA208	Killed, Liesse

17 April

Flg Johann Schönhofer		Killed, Douai
Ltn Karl Helbig	FA278	KIA, Aisne-Champagne (or 16th?)

18 April

Vfw Bernard Schattat		Killed, Dailly Ferme
(one aircraft of FA17 lost to infantry fire)		

19 April

Ltn Paul Herrmann	J31	KIA over Bois Malvel
Uffz Friedrich Schneider (O)	SS28	KIA, Warmoville, Prosnes
		Gfr Hermann Brauer OK but he will be KIA 27 July

20 April

Vfw Viktor Hebben	J10	WIA

21 April

Ltn Günther v d Heyde	J9	KIA, over Nauroy
Ltn Gustav Nernst	J30	KIA in Alb DIII 2147/16, Arras
Ltn Oskar Seitz	J30	Brought down unhurt
Ltn R Wichard	J24	POW in 'VERA' 2096/16
Uffz Brosius	SS11	? 6 Armee
Ltn Koehler	„	?
Flg Julius Oettinger	FA275	DOW, Zeithain
Ltn Karl Schäfer	J11	Brought down by gnd fire—safe

22 April

Uffz Gustav Richter (P)	FA212	Killed, Chevrigny
Ltn Erich Bersu (O)	„	Killed, Chevrigny
Flgr Albert Karzmarek		Killed, Oulcherwald
Uffz Karl Schulz		Killed, Oulcherwald
Ltn Martin Möbius (P)	FAA211	WIA, Oppy
Ltn Goldhammer (O)	„	safe

23 April

Vfw Arno Schramm	J7	KIA over Montfaucon
Hpt Paul v Osterroht	J12	KIA 1800, nr Ecoust St Mein, Cambrai. 6 Armee
Uffz Nauczak	J33	Severely WIA over Queant
Ltn Eberhard Stettner		Killed, Monceau
Oblt Heinrich Möller (O)		Killed, Monceau
Ltn Werner Steuber (O)	KG4	Killed, Monceau
Uffz Fritz Bruno		Killed, Monceau
Ltn Fritz v Massow (P)		Killed, Monceau
Flgmstr Josef Wirtz	MFJ1	Killed, Becelaere. Collided with FE2d over Polygon Wood in Alb DIII 2281/16
Ltn Karl Schweren	⎫	
Ltn Otto Wirsch	⎬ KG3/15	All POWs; Gotha GIV G610/16, Montreuil, nr Vron
OffStv Alfred Hecher	⎭	
Uffz Kaiser	SS7	crash-landed
Flgr Adam Föller	„	„ „ (killed 1 May 1917)
Oblt Georg Schmidt (O)	FAA254	KIA, Seclainvillers, Somme

24 April

Oblt Rodolf Berthold	J14	WIA with a Caudron
Ltn Fritz Kleindienst	J18	Down in flames, N of Comines
Rittm Karl v Grieffenhagen	J18	Crashed after combat
Vfw Rudolf Rath	J35	Alb DIII 2020/16, KIA over Hagenbach, cr at Altkirch
Ltn Blumm	FA46	WIA by flak over S St Mihiel. Armee Det 'C'
Ltn Werner Hecht (P)	FAA222	Killed, Concy le Château
Ltn Hugo Schneider (O)	„	Killed, Concy le Château
Flg Josef Reuber		Killed, Sissone
Vfw Otto Hartung (P)	FA252	Killed, Nauroy
Ltn Friedrich Krowolitski (O)		Killed, Nauroy
Ltn Walter Rudatis (P)		Killed, Allemont, Laon
Ltn Karl Jaeger (O)	FAA253	Killed, Allemont, Laon

Ltn Karl Schmidt (O)	FAA251	Killed, Clemont
Ltn Hans Huppertz	FA18	POW, Bethune 6 Armee
Ltn Friedrich Neumüller	„	POW
Uffz Max Haase (P)	FA26	WIA/POW. DFW CV 5927/16: brought down at Havrincourt
Ltn Karl Keim (O)	„	DOW
Ltn Karl Timm (O)	FFA235	KIA Acheville
Ltn Richard Zeglin (P)	„	KIA, 6 Armee
Uffz Otto Haberland (P)	FAA227	KIA, over Armentières
Ltn Henrich Klofe (O)	„	KIA, nr Lille
Vfw Max Wackwitz	J24	F/landed damaged at Bignicourt
Vflgmt Josef Wirtz	MFJ1	KIA, Polygon Wood

25 April

Vfw Sebastian Festner	J11	KIA, Gavrelle, Alb DIII 2251/16
Flg Kurt Hebel		Killed, Lille
Ltn Werner Kachler (O)	KG5	KIA, Verdun

26 April

Vfw Emil Eisenhuth	J3	KIA, Alb DIII 2207/16, nr Hayencourt, NW Cambrai
Oblt Max Reinhold	J15	KIA, over Lierval, Laon
OfStv Rudolf Weckbrodt	J26	WIA
Ltn Traugott Milbrandt (O)	FAA255	Killed, Cerny
Ltn Franz Blumm (O)	FA46	Killed, Chambley (see 24 Apr)
Ltn Sigismund Steinfeld (O)	FAA271	Killed, Ripont
Ltn Friedrich Feldmann (O)	FAA252	KIA, Prosnes

27 April

Ltn Herbert Zimmermann (P)	FA14	POW/DOW; Bogeien, Gerardner
Ltn Ernst Naumann (O)		KIA, Gerardner
Ltn Eissfeldt	J10	Severely WIA
Ltn Friedrich Vonschott	J14	Severely WIA over Montchalons, DOW 14 May
Flg Alfred Huherman		Killed, Bergnicourt
Ltn Rudolf Hepp	J24	Damaged Alb DII 1736/16, and crashes in flames at Lefricourt

28 April

Nil

29 April

Ltn Peckmann	J15	WIA
Ltn Ludwig Dornheim	J29	KIA, over Beine
Vfw Rener (P)	FAA48	WIA
Ltn Alois Stegmann (O)	„	KIA, over Carvin
Flg Ernst Deutchmann	SS22	Killed, Braye-en-Laonnois
Ltn Bruno Kittel (P)	FAA45	KIA, Baralle, NW Cambrai
Ltn Herman Waldschmidt (O)		KIA
Ltn Erich Bamm (O)	FAA201	KIA, Marchais, Liesse
Oblt Georg Krafft (O)	FA4	KIA Marsoenel, Arras

30 April

Ltn Adolf Frey	J9	KIA in flames nr Nauroy
Ltn Friedrich Mallinckrodt	J20	Severely WIA. 2 Armee
Vfw Max Reichle (P)	FA259	POW, Heudicourt
Ltn Erich Hampe (O)	„	POW
Vfw Max Baatz (P)	FAA204	KIA, Houplines/Armentières
Ltn Alexander Schleiper (O)		POW/WIA; Albatros C captured
Ltn August Rodenback (O)	FAA233	KIA over Oppy. 6 Armee
Ltn Hermann Benckiser	FAA238	KIA over Rocourt. 6 Armee
Ltn Werner Marwitz	J9	KIA Nauroy
Ltn Ernst Poetsch (O)	KG2	KIA, Aussonce-Reims
Ltn Karl Beckmann (P)	„	KIA, Reims

Assessment and Introduction to Part Two

The main feature of Bloody April was the casualties inflicted on the Royal Flying Corps, and to a lesser extent on the French Air Service. Over the years numbers have been talked about or published, but at this distance it is difficult with any real certainty to be exact in this numbers game.

One established figure of RFC losses gives 316 British aviators killed or missing for this month and we would not argue with this. What we can show is that according to research into surviving loss records, operational casualties were some 245 aircraft destroyed as a direct result of air actions. Others of course were written off in crashes, many not in any way attributable to operations, even though they might be taking off or returning from an operational duty. In other words, the 245 aircraft were as a direct result of enemy action, both by German aircraft or German ground fire.

In the RFC's Summary of Work for April 1917, the list of casualties, claims and hours flown indicates the following: †

Date	Hrs flown	Missing	Enemy Casualties			
			Dest	OOC	DDD	KB ‡
1st	517	not recorded	not recorded			
2nd	517	„	„			
3rd	753	„	„			
4th	517	„	„			
5th	1,358	„	„			
6th	1,279	17	34			1
7th	605	not recorded	2			1
8th	1,735	10	22			2
9th	941	2	11			
10th	480	—		1		
11th	720	10	11			
12th	395	3	1	4		
13th	1,250	14	5	5		
14th	1,363	10	18			
15th	346	—	—			
16th	917	5	5			
17th	38	—	—			
18th	47	—	—			
19th	379	—	—			
20th	829	2	1			
21st	708	4	4	6		
22nd	1,663	5 (+ 5 KBs)	6	15		7
23rd	1,966	2	10	19		
24th	2,202	6	10	19	14	2
25th	1,047	3	4	1	2	
26th	1,017	6	3	1	2	1
27th	1,274	4	5	11	4	
28th	1,082	3	3	2		
29th	1,814	15	7	12	10	
30th	1,842	10	8	19	20	

† The RFC day, for official purposes, ran from 6 pm to 6 pm, which can confuse issues when something happens after 6 pm on, say, the 21st and appears to be recorded as the 22nd.
‡ As claimed by RFC pilots and aircrew. Detailed breakdown between those destroyed, out of control and driven down damaged not given until later in the month.

Remarkably this only shows a total of 131 aircraft missing and five balloons. Perhaps it only indicated truly 'missing' aircraft, and did not include those known to have been lost? The figures given for claims against the Germans speak for themselves.

Another interesting statistic in this Summary is the RFC strength. This is shown on 1 April as being 821 available aircraft, with 70 more unserviceable and 849 pilots available, 496 of which were actually flying (operational?). At the end of April, the figures showed 761 aircraft available, 148 being u/s. Pilot strength was 854, with 745 actually flying.

Figures, of course, can be manipulated to show almost anything that their author(s) wish to present, but here we are just showing the figures that seem to apply here from our researches. The loss of flying men—the often quoted 316—is not that far out from our research. Our breakdown is 211 killed, missing or died of wounds, plus 108 taken prisoner. That makes 319. To this figure must be added several who were killed or injured in crashes and accidents, although it is not clear if the original 316 figure included those killed in this way. In addition, around 116 pilots and observers were wounded, not taking into account those captured men who were also wounded. (As a comparison, the RFC lost 499 pilots and observers between 1 July—the opening of the Somme offensive—and 22 November 1916; ie: in four and a half months.)

As a matter of academic interest, the breakdown of the 245 aircraft by types known to be lost directly to enemy action shows the following:

BE2	75	Martinsyde G100	5
FE2	58	Sopwith Triplane	4
Nieuport Scouts	43	Morane Parasol	3
RE8	15	DH2	2
Sop 1½ Strutter	14	AWFK8	2
BF2a	9	SE5	1
Spad VII	8	Sopwith Baby	1
Sopwith Pup	7	Handley Page 0/100	1
DH4	6	Nieuport XII	1

Staying for a moment with the losses, the known French losses, which cannot be said to be 100% accurate, give figures of 55 aircraft lost, 63 airmen killed, missing or died of wounds, with at least 11 more prisoners and 55 wounded. The breakdown of aircraft types shows:

Spad VII	18	Morane Parasol	2
Nieuport Scout	12	Salmson-Moineau	2
Caudron G4	11	Voisin	1
Farman	4	Nieuport XII	2
Sop 1½ Strutters	2	Letord	1

As can readily be seen, the British Corps (observation) aircraft suffered severely, whether engaged on pure Corps work—contact patrols, reconnaissance or artillery patrols and registration missions —or bombing. These types (BE, RE8, Parasol, and 1½ Strutters) totalled 107, or just about one third of all losses. However, it is acknowledged that some FEs were also engaged on photo and recce work, as well as escort duties, while some Strutters were used on fighting patrols.

Pure fighting aeroplanes (Nieuport, Spad, Pup, Triplane, SE5) lost 65 of their number, but again, some of the FE2s would also come into this category and so, one supposes, did the new Bristol Fighters.

The overwhelming feature, however, has to be the Corps aircraft, sent out daily to gather photographs, help range guns, locate enemy artillery positions or to make contact with a fluid battle front. In poor aircraft they were shot to ribbons and anyone with less than reasonable front-line experience was easy prey to the Albatros and Halberstadt fighter pilots of the German Jastas.

This was nothing new, of course, and is emphasised by the Arras Battle, which just happened to come with the culmination of the spring weather, a spring offensive and a meeting head-on with the newly formed Jastas, whose pilots had been eagerly awaiting just this sort of confrontation since the previous autumn (fall).

An analysis of the Jasta pilots' claims is of interest. Some Jastas of course were very active and in the forefront of the battle areas, while others were not. But a full breakdown of individual unit claims for this month are:

Jasta	1	0	Jasta	13	6	Jasta	26	6
Jasta	2	21	Jasta	14	7	Jasta	27	0
Jasta	3	10	Jasta	15	2	Jasta	28	3
Jasta	4	16	Jasta	16	0	Jasta	29	0

Jasta	5	32	Jasta	17	6	Jasta	30	7
Jasta	6	0	Jasta	18	6	Jasta	31	4
Jasta	7	0	Jasta	19	12	Jasta	32	0
Jasta	8	5	Jasta	20	2	Jasta	33	1
Jasta	9	10	Jasta	21	5	Jasta	34	7
Jasta	10	0	Jasta	22	4	Jasta	35	2
Jasta	11	89	Jasta	23	1	Jasta	36	12
Jasta	12	23	Jasta	24	2	Jasta	37	1

(Jasta 25 is not shown for they were operating in Macedonia, not on the Western Front.)

Total claims were 298, which is not a bad average alongside the known losses of both British and French aircraft—299—although one has to remember a number of the Allied losses were to ground fire or anti-aircraft defences. German claims would also include balloons, which are not part of the 299 loss figure. (German pilots were credited with 34 balloons.)

The top four scoring Jastas—11, 5, 12 and 2—claimed 55% of these victories (165). Of the successful German aces in April, 14 scored five or more kills, the top being Kurt Wolff, and in total they accounted for 155 Allied aeroplanes and balloons. These 14 men claimed:

Kurt Wolff	Jasta 11—23	Sebastian Festner	Jasta 11—10
Manfred v Richthofen	Jasta 11—22	Edmund Nathanael	Jasta 5—9
Karl Schäfer	Jasta 11—21	Hans Klein	Jasta 4—9
Lothar v Richthofen	Jasta 11—15	Paul v Osterroht	Jasta 12—6
Otto Bernert	Jasta 2—15	Wilhelm Frankl	Jasta 4—6
Heinrich Gontermann	Jasta 5—11	Erich Hahn	Jasta 19—5
Kurt Schneider	Jasta 5—10	Karl Dossenbach	Jasta 36—5

Of these, nine had or would receive the Pour le Mérite, two were killed during April and only two would survive WW1—Klein and Lothar von Richthofen.

Just why were the German fighter pilots so successful? Mention was made earlier of experience. The policy of the day for the British Royal Flying Corps and Royal Naval Air Service—and a policy which remained virtually unchanged for the whole war—was that pilots and observers were thrust into front line squadrons as demands to replace casualties increased, often straight from flying schools. Total flying time, in most cases, could be counted in a few modest hours, perhaps 40 or 50 if they were lucky. Others may, of course, have had more, especially if they had been fortunate enough to be retained as instructors, or test pilots and so on, or even been lucky enough to get to the front at a quiet period, during which they might be able to gain extra flying hours without having to cope with the demands of an offensive. (Some Naval pilots were fortunate enough to go via No.12 Naval Squadron which was a training unit formed in this April at St Pol, where they could acclimatise to France and prepare for war flying.)

This was as true for Corps or bombing pilots, as it was for fighter pilots or scouts as they were called in WW1. The Germans, on the other hand, generally came to the Jastas after a period as a two-seater pilot, having spent some months, certainly several weeks, at the front in this capacity. Having shown a desire or an aptitude for single-seat fighter work, they could volunteer to be transferred to fighters, and after a brief period at one of the Jastaschules, be assigned to a fighter unit, if the school instructors approved. In this way, therefore, the new Jasta pilot was already something of a front-line veteran, and at the very least knew what it was all about and had acquired a degree of battle experience, as well as the 'feel' of air fighting. Having, therefore, flown two-seaters, and now faced with, in the main, two-seater opponents, he knew exactly what it was like to be engaged by a fighter and in consequence how to approach and attack two-seat opponents.

In contrast, his opposite number, flying a Nieuport, a Pup or such like, was just about competent enough to take off and land, and fly his aircraft straight and level. To be thrust into the maelstrom of a whirling air-battle was often something which the embryo scouting pilot did not survive.

The two-seater Corps pilots too were just as inexperienced, and very often their observers were former artillery men, who had either asked or been asked to transfer to flying because they knew about artillery firing and the fall of shot. But if they became too embroiled in watching the ground, that is when the German air fighters were upon them before they knew the danger was close.

The RFC was still lacking an adequate fighting aeroplane to counter the new Albatros Scouts or the Halberstadts. Experienced Nieuport or Pup pilots had a reasonable chance against them in a fight, and the new Sopwith Triplanes were a good match, but the FE8 and DH2 pusher-types were now on their way out, and while the FE2 crews could give a good account of themselves, they were beginning to take heavy punishment, as the April losses show. The Spad wasn't bad—with experience—but the Bristol Fighter had proved a disaster and only with new tactics and an aggressive attitude would it become a deadly opponent in the future.

What made the success achieved by the German fighter pilots even more remarkable, despite their superior equipment, was their comparatively few numbers. On the actual Arras battle front there were only six fighting Jastas, increased to only eight after 12 April.

The nominal strength of a Jasta was 12 aircraft and 14 pilots, although this figure was rarely if ever reached or even approached, owing to losses and the slow rate of production in Germany which delayed the replacement of lost or damaged machines.

The average Jasta aircraft strength on any one day was about seven fit to fly; thus at Arras, for the period 1 to 11 April, there were no more than 42 operational German fighters, increased to just 52 from 12 April. The mistake made by the British and French in estimating the German strength as higher than it was, was due mainly to the devotion by both the German air and ground personnel, the former willing to fly three or four times a day, the latter working round the clock to ensure every possible aircraft was serviceable and ready for combat.

Perhaps the fact that Allied formations often reported far more hostile aircraft in an air fight than could possibly be there, had something to do with being unwilling to accept that they could lose so many men and machines to a much smaller number of opponents. But this is purely an observation and may be unfair in fact. However, having studied some of Jasta 11's fights, whereas Richthofen would often report flying with just three or four of his men (his average aeroplane strength in the last week of April was only seven) his opponents' combat reports often stated the enemy strength as anything up to 20 to 30. Even if a second Jasta was in evidence, it would be rare for such numbers to be available.

The Germans had long since ended the practice of flying defensive patrols, being considered useless, and wasteful of resources. Generally speaking, the single-seater fighters would be sent into action only at such times when the Allied flyers seemed especially active. These Allied activities were watched and monitored by special air protection officers—Luftschutz Offizier—situated just behind the front, who had at their disposal observation and signalling equipment. Reports from these officers, via Air Unit Commanders at Corps HQ, gave the HQ staff a good picture of events from which they could decide or not to get fighters into the air, and in what opposing strength.

As the German fighter pilots' main task was to gain mastery over the front, a move was made to try and group some Jastas together. Jastas 3, 4, 11 and 33 were among the first, which later led to the formation of von Richthofen's Jagdesgeschwader Nr.1 in the early summer (Jastas 4, 6, 10 and 11).

However, during the Arras battle, no central command had overall control of the fighters, this being left to the Air Unit Commanders at Corps HQ. Their fighter zones generally coincided with the close reconnaissance areas of these Corps.

Turning to the question of claims made by British and French airmen, although to some degree we do not fully understand what losses the Germans incurred, it appears obvious that they did not sustain anything like the losses the two Allied sides were claiming. It would seem fair to assume that German official 'losses' were more associated with men than aircraft, but we are just not certain. But knowing what the fighter pilot losses were in relation to killed, taken prisoner and wounded, we can say that personnel casualties in the Jastas were not as high as

Allied claims would tend to indicate. Unfortunately two-seater losses are recorded even less accurately, or records have not survived.

However, by analysing the British and French claims and showing them next to known or admitted 'losses', we can see that at best the Allied flyers were overclaiming.

		Destroyed	OOC	KBs	
RFC claims for April		126	206	16	
French claims		70	—	8	
	Totals:	196	206	24	(not including AA or Corps two-seater claims)
Known German losses		76	N/A	7	(to air combat actions)

In a post-war study into claims and losses, the German Air Ministry provided figures to the British Air Ministry for the VIth Army zone. The ones relevant to this period indicate the following:

	Total Br Losses	In German Lines	Dead	German Personnel Miss	Wounded	Air-craft
31 March to 7 April 1917	37	32	2	1	3	2
8 April to 14 April 1917	47	31	2	2	2	3
15 April to 20 April 1917	17	12	1	—	1	—
21 April to 26 April 1917	37	11	7	7	1	11
27 April to 3 May 1917	40	26	12	6	6	10

The VIth Army boundaries on 9 April were Wervicq-Cassel-Boulogne in the north, Bullecourt-Ervillers-Acheux-Canaples-Conde-Folie in the south, and the coast to the mouth of the Somme in the west.

The Battle of Arras ended on 4 May, following a third Battle of the Scarpe two days earlier. All that had really been achieved was the important capture of Vimy Ridge, and the centre of activity soon shifted to the Flanders front further north, for the start of another scheme. This one was designed to free the Belgian coast by pushing the Germans back to the Scheldt River. It didn't work. On the French front, Nivelle's failure at Champagne effectively stopped all French offensive action for the rest of the year, the British having to take the brunt of the fighting on their northern and central sectors. There followed the Battle of Messines (7 to 14 June); Battle of Ypres (31 July to 10 November including the Battle of Passchendaele—12 October to 10 November); then the Battle of Cambrai (20 November to 3 December).

Meantime, the new SE5 fighter became established, 56 Squadron merely being the fore-runner of some 14 squadrons on the Western Front by 1918. The other new fighter was the Sopwith Camel, which arrived in France during June 1917. By 1918, 15 British squadrons would be operating this machine in France, plus two American squadrons attached to the RAF.

In the new year of 1918, there was the familiar lull of winter, but with the release of German troops from the Russian front following the Russian Revolution and the ending of the war in the East, the Germans mounted a huge offensive with the First Battle of the Somme (20 March to 5 April), which so nearly achieved a complete breakthrough for the Central Powers. Other battles followed: the Lys (9 to 29 April), the Aisne (27 May to 6 June); while in the south, the Germans reached the Marne on 31 May.

The failure of the Germans' March offensives sent a chill through the German High Command, for it knew only too well that finally, after almost a year since declaring war on Germany, American might was beginning to arrive in France. Once men and munitions from across the Atlantic became a flood, Germany knew her ability to wage war would begin to crumble. The Allies just had too many men from the Empire and from the Americas to call upon.

Fully aware of the strength of American industrial might and men, the Germans had formulated their 'Amerika Program' over the winter of 1917-18 which led to an increase in the size of their Air Force. The number of Jastas was increased from 40 to 80, but it did not mean an immediate doubling of opposition for the Allied airmen. Many of the newly created units took time to become established, generally they had inferior aircraft types to begin with, and mostly the personnel were inexperienced, although led by an acknowledged veteran or ace.

The two-seater Schutzstaffeln were renamed Schlactstaffeln and used for infantry support and ground attack, first used with some effect at Cambrai in late 1917. With the ending of the war in Russia, a number of experienced flyers were released for duty on the Western Front in the spring of 1918.

The French began the Fourth Battle of Champagne (15 to 18 July) and as this ended came the Second Battle of the Marne which lasted until 7 August. The British fought the Battle of Amiens (8 to 11 August), which really began to cut deep into German territory, and began a series of battles which broke the German Army apart. The British advance in Flanders (18 August), the Second Battle of the Somme (21 August) and the Second Battle of Arras (26 August), all hit home. These latter two came to an end on 3 September and now the stage was set for a mighty attack upon the German Hindenburg Line, while the French and Americans opened an assault at St Mihiel (12 September) to be followed by the Champagne and Argonne Battles on the 26th.

In broad terms the air war had changed little since April 1917. The RFC had become the Royal Air Force, with the amalgamation of the RFC and Royal Naval Air Service on 1 April 1918, but was still fighting an offensive war, taking the fight to the Germans. For their part, the German Air Service were content to let the British and French come to them, and continued to let the Allied airmen dash themselves against their Jastas.

This German tactic had evolved since late 1916, due at that time to numbers. The British and French were always numerically superior in men and aircraft and so the German fighter pilots took up a defensive war. In many ways they were happy to be able, more or less, to choose the moment of combat, or decline it if odds and conditions proved unfavourable. They could wait on their fighter airfields until their enemies were reported to be crossing the lines and still have time to gain height and be ready to attack. They could also break off any time and land, whereas the British and French had always to remember that they had to fly back over the lines to reach safety. With drying fuel tanks, running short of ammunition and often against a prevailing west to east wind, the Allied airmen often had a bitter struggle to get back to the safety of their own lines. Knowing this, other German Jasta pilots would be waiting for them to do just that, but with full petrol tanks and gun-belts.

By the summer of 1918, the SE5a and Camel, plus the two-seater Bristol Fighter, were the main fighter equipment for the British, plus four squadrons of Sopwith Dolphins, a machine that was every bit as good as the Camel but could operate at greater altitudes too. The French fighters were now mostly all Spad XIIIs, while the Americans had come through their initial period with the Nieuport 28s and were also flying Spad XIIIs.

The Germans still flew Albatros Scouts, but had progressed from the DII and DIIIs of April 1917 to the DV and DVa, although neither was a real match for the Allied fighter opposition. Nor was another type, similar in general appearance to the Albatros, the Pfalz DIII, which swelled the Jasta ranks in the summer of 1917. In a few weeks in early autumn of that year, the Germans had brought out the Fokker DrI Triplane, which produced a flurry of activity and success until a weakness in the upper wings—causing the death of several pilots —had caused the new type to be withdrawn and modified. In the spring of 1918 it reappeared, and for another brief period became a deadly opponent, notably in the hands of von Richthofen. But now, in the summer of 1918, the German Jasta pilots had perhaps their best ever fighter, the Fokker DVII biplane, a type with which both the novice and the expert fighter could meet any opposition on more than equal terms. And by this time, the Allied types were all beginning to look a bit long in the tooth, although far from being outdated.

Tactics and ideas had changed however. In mid-1917 the Germans had built on an earlier idea to group Jastas together, the first being Jastas 4, 6, 10 and 11. These became Jagdesgeschwader No.1 (JG1) under the command of the leading German ace, Manfred von Richthofen. The purpose of this permanent grouping was so that as a unit it could be moved to various parts of the battle front wherever it was needed, to oppose, for instance, an Allied offensive, which would naturally be supported in some strength by additional British or French squadrons.

With this mobility, and the increasingly colourful garb used by the German fighter pilots on their aircraft, these Jagdesgeschwader units soon became known as Flying Circuses. In total there were four Jagdesgeschwaderen, three Prussian—JG1, JG2 and JG3—and one Bavarian, JG4.

The reader will notice we said 'permanent grouping'; there were, in addition, several non-permanent groupings of Jastas, and these became known as a Jagdgruppe, eg: JGr1, JGr2 and so on. These were grouped together for specific duties and could be interchanged or even disbanded as was found necessary or expedient. Whether it was a JG or a JGr, a senior pilot would command such a unit, although not necessarily a leading ace. The German Air Service, like the Army and Navy, went on rank and ability, not just ability. Therefore one can find a number of Jasta or Jagdgruppes commanded by a pilot with few or even no air combat victories, leading other pilots with some quite sizeable scores. Even individual Jastas would not necessarily be commanded by a top-notch fighter pilot.

The Germans continued to employ a defensive stance, letting the Allied aircraft still come to them. In many ways this was still a good tactic, as it continued to give the German fighter pilots the choice of when to attack as well as the ability to break off combat and land if necessary, without being taken prisoner. The disadvantage, of course, was that German front line troops would constantly see more Allied aircraft over them, often, by this later stage of the war, strafing and bombing them from low level, with very little interference from their own Fokker and Albatros pilots.

It also allowed the Allied airmen to become adept at forcing their way through packs of German fighters to raid a target, and even though several attacking bombers might be brought down, the target was often either destroyed or severely hit, causing not only casualties but the destruction of stores, ammunition, etc. and disruption to road and rail traffic bringing much needed troops and/or supplies to the front.

Numbers were still in the Allies' favour, which is why the Germans continued in the overall defensive air war, but this also hindered the German two-seater recce and artillery observation crews from doing their work. Any reconnaissance of the Allied rear areas was always flown unescorted, the crews using cloud cover and height for their main protection.

Both sides used front line ground attack aircraft. The Allied airmen were generally fighting pilots—mostly Camels flyers—who would take on this duty in addition to air fighting, whereas the SE5 pilots tended to keep to air combat, but not strictly so. Dolphins and Bristol Fighters could also be used in the ground strafing role.

On the German side, they used two-seaters such as the Halberstadt CLII or III, and the Hannover CLIII, with extra armour, in units called Schutzstaffeleln. Some units also used the Junkers J1 armoured monoplanes.

In fact, ground attack and ground strafing had really begun during April 1917, and by the summer of that year was used with increasing regularity by the British in particular, especially in the Cambrai battle. By the spring of 1918 and certainly by the summer, the RAF had this tactic down to a fine art. It often cost them men and aircraft, but the effect on the German ground soldiers was marked.

By 1918 the British and French were also using aircraft in groups, although they were not so rigidly organised as the German Jagdesgeschwader formations. The French formed Groupes de Combat (GC), the British using Wings, although this title should not be confused in any way with the Wings of WW2. When used, the British formation tended to be made up of specialist aircraft, eg: Camels at a lower level, SE5s higher with Dolphins or Bristols above them. Bombing aircraft, such as the now well established DH4 and DH9s, or the Bréguet XIVs of the French, were now regularly escorted by fighters. It didn't always happen as planned, for this was still the era before air-to-air radio communications, so bombers and fighters making a rendezvous could lose each other/not find each other, and when the bombers 'pressed on' unescorted, they would find themselves under attack without any single-seater protection.

There was still no direct fighter protection for the Corps aircraft, their 'protection' still being in the form of fighter patrols in their area of activity. The poor old BEs had long gone, the main artillery machine being the RE8. This was still a 1917 machine but at least the crews were better trained now.

The French had begun to group their units together as early as 1916, although the French tended to fight a less aggressive air war than their British counterparts. These Groupes de Combat totalled sixteen by early 1918, and by February there were 21.

By 1918, larger groups of aircraft were needed by the French, to cover expanding ground operations, and under a central control. Therefore, they began reorganising a number of Groupes de Combat (GC) into Escadres de Combat, commanded by a Chef de Battaillon. Like the Germans, these units would be commanded by a senior officer, not necessarily a leading air ace. And just as JG1 had become known as the Richthofen Geschwader, so too did some of the Escadres de Combat become known by the name of their commander, eg: Escadre de Combat No.1 was known as Groupement Menard (being commanded by Victor Menard).

In turn, units, groupes and escadres could be built into an even larger establishment of both fighter and bomber units. In May 1918 the French created the 1er Division Aerienne, under the command of a general, which consisted of Groupement Menard, plus three other Groupes de Combat plus Escadre de Bombardement No.12 (which was itself made up of three Groupes de Bombardement), together with Escadre No.2 (Groupement Fequant), three GCs and another full Escadre de Bombardement.

Each GC would generally have some 72 Spads, while each GB would muster 45 Bréguet bombers. In addition there were also some Escadrilles de Protection, equipped with large Caudron R11 aircraft, used in effect like gun ships to ward off attacking fighters. Both the British and the French had night bombing units, and the RAF also had its Independent Air Force bombers, de Havilland 4s and 9s, and Handley Page 0/400 twin-engined three-seat bombers, used for attacking deep behind enemy lines, or even Germany itself.

For their part, by mid-1918, the American Air Service (USAS) were now operating in strength in support of their own and French ground troops. During August 1918 Colonel William (Billy) Mitchell was made commander of a recently organised (US) First Army Air Service and in co-operation with the ground commanders was preparing for an assault against the St Mihiel front. Therefore, as the British to the north were pressing the Hindenburg Line, the French and Americans would attack at St Mihiel, commencing 12 September.

For the drive on this front, Mitchell had convinced the French to fall in with his overall plan and had also managed to persuade them to put a large part of their air force at his disposal. As it turned out, by the time the attack began, Billy Mitchell had under his command, or co-operating with it, the largest number of units and aircraft to engage in a single offensive operation during WW1.

His own American forces consisted of 12 fighter (pursuit) squadrons, three day bombing squadrons, ten observation (reconnaissance) squadrons and one night reconnaissance squadron. To this force the French assigned their 1er Division Aerienne, which consisted of 42 fighter and day bombardment squadrons, two squadrons of French and three Italian night bombing squadrons and 12 squadrons of French observation aircraft. He also had four French fighter squadrons attached to his 1st Pursuit Group (which itself consisted of four pursuit squadrons), which would move to this part of the front on the eve of the battle. To this force he could also call upon the eight bomber squadrons of Sir Hugh Trenchard's Independent Air Force, and while these were not under Mitchell's direct orders, they undertook missions in support of his overall battle plan.

As the St Mihiel drive began, the number of aircraft Mitchell had under his orders was reputed to have been 701 fighters, 366 reconnaissance, 323 day bombers and 91 night bombers; a total of 1,481. Opposing this mighty force, the Germans had an estimated strength of some 213 aircraft—72 fighters, 24 bombers, 105 reconnaissance, six battle (ground attack) and six long distance photo machines. Some of the fighter units were in the midst of re-equipping from Albatros and Pfalz Scouts to the new Fokker DVII type.

The day after the drive began, the Germans reinforced their air units with the four Jastas of Jagdesgeschwader Nr.2, commanded by Oskar von Boenigk. Towards the end of the month, the 28th, JG1 arrived, under Hermann Goring, but by this date the St Mihiel offensive had ended, and the Meuse-Argonne battle had begun two days earlier.

Despite the numerical superiority of the combined American and French air forces, the German fighter pilots still managed to inflict tremendous losses on them. In fact, as will be seen in Part Two, September was to be the worst month for Allied air casualties during the whole of WW1—and this all happened just six weeks prior to the Armistice. Thus, despite a gradual decimation of the top aces of the German Air Service, those who survived, supported by the successful up and coming air fighters, were able to wreak havoc upon the generally less aggressive French and the keen but more inexperienced Americans. JG2, in fact, claimed more than 80 victories for just five casualties. In the final analysis, however, it was weight of numbers, lack of adequate pilot replacements and scarcity of fuel which tended to defeat the Germans.

On the British fronts, gone were the days of 1917. Generally speaking the new pilots arriving to fill gaps in the single and two-seater squadrons had more flying hours in their log books than those of a year or eighteen months before. They also had the benefit of a more structured and aggressive training, especially in mock air combat, at such places as the School of Air Fighting at Ayr in Scotland. The instructors too were far more experienced, thanks to the School of Special Flying at Gosport, Hampshire, which helped not only to train new pilots but to train instructors how to instruct. The improved techniques were followed by other training establishments.

By September 1918 there were hardly any men still flying combat in the RAF who had been in action in April 1917. Those that had survived were by this time either instructors, squadron commanders (many non-flying), working at various headquarters or back in England. The British had the luxury of a constant stream of eager young airmen only too willing to take their place on the Western Front, not merely from Britain but from Canada, Australia, New Zealand, South Africa and other lands of the Empire.

The Germans, on the other hand, did have some of their spring 1917 flyers still in action. Many had fallen, among whom were some of the great aces such as Manfred von Richthofen, Werner Voss, Kurt Wolff, Karl Allmenröder, Emil Schäfer and so on. But Hermann Göring was a Jagdesgeschwader commander, and so too was Bruno Loerzer; Hermann Frommherz was an active Jasta commander while Julius Buckler was about to command Jasta 22, having been with Jasta 17 since 1916. Robert Greim, commanding Jagdgruppe 9 had been flying since 1915, and so had Josef Jacobs, who now commanded Jasta 7 as he had done since August 1917. Reinhold Jorke had scored his second kill in April 1917 and in September 1918 was commanding Jasta 39. Emil Thuy also gained his second victory in April 1917, having then been Staffelführer of Jasta 28 since September of the same year. Ernst Udet, second only to von Richthofen in air victories, was still active, having downed his first adversary in March 1916, and now led Jasta 4. Josef Veltjens was another Bloody April veteran, and now commander of Jasta 15.

There were any number of others, either flying fighters in early 1917 or operating in two-seater units, who were still 'operational' in September 1918. Friedrich Altemeier had been scoring steadily with Jasta 24 since December 1916! Paul Baümer, Hermann Becker, Walter Blume, Franz Büchner, Carl Degelow, Alois Heldman, Rudolf Klimke, Otto Könnecke, Josef Mai, George Meyer, Karl Odebrett, Karl Ritscherle, Fritz Röth, Fritz Rumey, Emil Schäpe, Eduard von Schleich, Otto Schmidt and Paul Strähle, were just some of the aces of 1918 who had gained vast experience of air fighting and were still passing on their knowledge and skills to the latest recruits to their Jastas.

Among the French, there were some aces still flying over the front who had been active in the spring of 1917. René Fonck, the French ace of aces, was still scoring with Spa.103, having been with this unit for 16 months and recording victories since the summer of 1916. Bernard Barny de Romanet had been flying since 1915, and was now commanding Spa.167; François Battesti had gained his first victory in April 1917 with N.73 and was still operating with it. Maurice Boyau had been with N.77 in early 1917 and was still with it, his score now in the thirties. Jean Casale was another 1915 veteran, now flying Spads with Spa.38, while Gustav Deladier had gained his first kill in April 1917 flying Nieuports and was still with Spa.93.

Paul d'Argueff had been fighting the Germans over the Russian front in early 1917, and was now with Spa.124. Armand de Turenne gained his second victory in April 1917, and was now commander of Spa.12. Claude Haegelen would score heavily in September 1918, having been with the Storks since early 1917, and Henri de Slade, commander of Spa.159, had been flying since 1916. Georges Madon had scored 40 victories by the end of August 1918, his 9th having been achieved during April 1917, all with Spa.38. Gilbert Sardier commanded Spa.48, and he too had been active since 1916.

So here too was experience after a long apprenticeship, with knowledge being passed to the embryo fighter pilots. Admittedly the French fought a less aggressive war than the RFC/RNAS/RAF, and often they generally faced less aggressive German units, but over many battles and especially during the heavy and prolonged fighting at Verdun, the French pilots had done well.

The scene was thus set for this mighty, final clash which took place in the September 1918 skies of France. The outcome was heavy material and personnel losses for the Allied air forces, but already the die was cast; Germany would be forced to sue for peace six weeks after Black September came to an end. For the German Jasta pilots, it was their last fling.

American Order of Battle

1st US ARMY AIR SERVICE HEADQUARTERS
Colonel William Mitchell
(Ligny-en-Barrois)

AMERICAN AIR SERVICE UNITS WITH REINFORCEMENTS

1st Pursuit Group, USAS
Major Harold E Hartney
(Rembercourt)

27th Pursuit Sqn 1/Lt Alfred A Grant	94th Pursuit Sqn Capt Kenneth Marr
95th Pursuit Sqn Capt David McK Peterson	147th Pursuit Sqn 1/Lt James A Meissner

218th, 'C' Flt 648th Sqn

1st Pursuit Wing USAS
Major Bert M Atkinson
(Toul)

2nd Pursuit Group
Maj Davenport Johnson
(Toul)

13th Pursuit Sqn Capt Charles J Biddle	22nd Pursuit Sqn Capt Ray C Bridgman
49th Pursuit Sqn 1/Lt George F Fisher	139th Pursuit Sqn 1/Lt David E Putnam†

'A' Flt 255th Sqn

3rd Pursuit Group
Major William Thaw
(Vaucouleurs #1)

28th Pursuit Sqn 1/Lt C Maury Jones	93rd Pursuit Sqn Major W F M Huffer

---

† Acting CO in place of Major L C Angstrom who was ill, but who returned to duty on 13 September 1918.

103rd Pursuit Sqn
Capt Robert L Rockwell

213th Pursuit Sqn
1/Lt John A Hambleton

360th Sqn

Groupe de Combat 16
Capitaine Jules Menj
(Vaucouleurs #2)

Escadrille Spa.78
Capt Gustave Lagache

Escadrille Spa.112
Capt Pierre Merat

Escadrille Spa.150
Lt Albert Achard

Escadrille Spa.151
Lt Henri de Sevin

1st Day Bombardment Group
Major J L Dunsworth
(Amanty)

11th Bombardment Sqn (DH 4)
1/Lt Thornton D Hooper

20th Bombardment Sqn (DH 4)
1/Lt Cecil G Sellers

96th Bombardment Sqn (Bréguet 14.B2)
Capt James A Summersett, Jr

'A' Flight 648th Sqn

Corps Observation Wing, USAS
Major Lewis H Brereton
(Toul)

1st Corps Observation group, USAS
Major Melvin A Hall
(Saizerais)

1st Observation Sqn (Salmson 2A2)
1/Lt Arthur J Coyle
(Toul)

12th Observation Sqn (Salmson 2A2)
1/Lt Stephen H Noyes
(Toul)

50th Observation Sqn (DH 4)
1/Lt Daniel P Morse, Jr
(Toul)

'B' Flight 648th Sqn
(Toul)

Escadrille Br.208
Capt Proust
(Bicqueley)

Escadrille Br.214
Lt Pierre de la Chapelle
(Bicqueley)

Balloon Wing Company 'A'
1/Lt Allan P McFarland
(Saizerais)

1st Balloon Company
1/Lt Walter J Reed
(Domevre-en-Haye)

2nd Balloon Company
1/Lt Ira R Koenig
(Griscourt)

5th Balloon Company
1/Lt M R Smith
(Dieulouard)

42nd Balloon Company
1/Lt Ray W Thompson
(Ville-au-Val)

4th Corps Observation Group, USAS
Major Harry B Anderson
(Ourches)

8th Observation Sqn (DH 4)
1/Lt John G Winant

90th Observation Sqn (Salmson 2A2)
1/Lt William Gallop‡

---

‡ Acting CO in place of 1/Lt W G Schauffler, who was ill, and who returned to duty on 15 September 1918.

135th Observation Sqn (DH 4)
1/Lt Bradley J Saunders, Jr

'C' Flight 25th Sqn

Escadrille Br.218
Capt Petit

Balloon Wing Company 'C'
Capt Paul Patterson
(Toul)

3rd Balloon Company
Capt Birge M Clark
(Hamonville)

43rd Balloon Company
Capt O B Anderson
(Ansauville)

9th Balloon Company
1/Lt C M Felt
(Raulecourt)

69th Balloon Company
1/Lt James B Haight
(Neuf-de-Mandres)

5th Corps Air Service USAS
Lt Col Arthur R Christy
(Souilly)

5th Corps Observation Group
Major Martin F Scanlon

88th Observation Sqn (Salmson 2A2)
Capt Kenneth P Littauer

99th Observation Sqn (Salmson 2A2)
Capt James E Meredith

104th Observation Sqn (Salmson 2A2)
1/Lt Clearton H Reynolds

Escadrille Spa.42
Capt de Saint Seran

Balloon Wing Company 'B'
Major John H Jouett
(Benoite-Vaux)

6th Balloon Company
1/Lt S W Ovitt
(Villers-sur-Meuse)

8th Balloon Company
Capt M L Witherus
(Dieue-sur-Meuse)

7th Balloon Company
1/Lt Samuel T Moore
(Ft Genicourt)

12th Balloon Company
1/Lt Ashley C McKinley
(Sommedieue)

Army Observation Group, USAS
Major John N Reynolds
(Gondreville)

24th Observation Sqn (Salmson 2A2)
1/Lt Maury Hill

91st Observation Sqn (Salmson 2A2)
1/Lt Everett R Cook

'B' Flt 255th Sqn

Army Artillery Observation Group, USAS
Capitaine P A Block
(Ligny-en-Barrois)

Escadrille Br.206
Capt Tastevin
(Bicqueley)

Escadrille Br.234
Capt Emile Jansen
(Lay St Remy)

Escadrille Br.219
Capt Touchard
(Lay St Remy)

Escadrille Br.225
Capt Antoine Moraillon
(Belrain)

(All with Bréguet 14 A2)

10th USAS Balloon Co
1/Lt Dale Mabry

11th USAS Balloon Co
1/Lt Charles E Barber

16th USAS Balloon Co
1/Lt Oscar Roman

39th, 41st & 93rd French Balloon Companies

| 39th French Balloon Co
(Minorville-Domevre) | 41st French Balloon Co
(Jouy-sous-les-Cotes) | 93rd French Balloon Co
(Genicourt-sur-Meuse) |

FRENCH NIGHT BOMBARDMENT GROUP
Commandant Emile Villome
(Epiez)

| Escadrille CAP 115 (Caproni) | Escadrille CAP 130 (Caproni)
Capt Leon Hebard |

Italian Gruppo di Bombardement 18
(Capitano De Riso)

Italian Squadriglia 3, 14 & 15 (Caproni CA.3)
(Chermisey)

USAS 9th Night Recon Sqn (DH 4)
1/Lt Thomas A Box
(Amanty)

FRENCH 1st DIVISION AERIENNE
Colonel Albert Peting de Vaulgrenant
(Tannois)

1st Brigade d'Aviation
Chef de Bataillon Louis de Goys de Mezeyrac
(St Martin Sorcy)

Escadre de Combat No 1
Chef de Bataillon Victor Menard
(Ochey)

Groupe de Combat 15
Capitaine François Glaize
(Ochey)

| Spa.37
Lt Roger Poupon | Spa.81
Lt Jacques Leps |
| Spa.93
Capt Georges d'Geyer d'Orth | Spa.97
Lt Herve Conneau |

Groupe de Combat 18
Capitaine Andre Laurent
(Ochey)

| Spa.48
Lt Gilbert Sardier | Spa.94
Lt Benjamin Bozon-Verdurez |
| Spa.153
Capt Jean Gigodot | Spa.155
Capt Edmond George |

Groupe de Combat 19
Capitaine Albert Deullin
(Ochey)

| Spa.73
Lt Pierre Jaille | Spa.85
Lt Paul Dumas |
| Spa.95
Capt Marcel Hugues | Spa.96
Lt Pierre Fauquet-Lemaitre |

Escadre de Bombardement No 12
Chef d'Escadrons Joseph Vuillemin
(Chaudeney)

Groupe de Bombardement 5
Capitaine Petit
(Martigney)

Escadrille Br.117
S/Lt Charles Renard-Duverger

Escadrille Br.120
Lt Henri Lemaitre

Escadrille Br.127
Lt Blanchard
(All equipped with the Bréguet 14.B2)

Groupe de Bombardement 6
Capitaine Roux
(Tantonville)

Escadrille Br.11
Lt Lucien Bozon-Verduraz

Escadrille Br.66
Lt Jean Ardisson de Perdiguier

Escadrille Br.108
Lt Jean Luciani
(All equipped with the Bréguet 14.B2)

Groupe de Bombardement 9
Capitaine Guy de Lavergne
(Neufchâteau)

Escadrille Br.29
Lt Mongin

Escadrille Br.123
Lt Roger Delaitre

Escadrille Br.129 Lt Pierre Pascal
(All equipped with the Bréguet 14.B2)

Escadrilles de Protection

Escadrille C 239
Lieutenant Jean de Verchere

Escadrille C 240
Capitaine de Durat

(Both equipped with Caudron R 11)

2eme Brigade d'Aviation
Chef d'Escadrons Philippe Fequant
(Combles)

Escadre de Combat No 2
Chef d'Escadrons Edouard Duseigneur
(Combles)

Groupe de Combat 13
Capitaine Jean D'Harcourt
(Brabant-le-Roi)

Spa.15
Capt Fernand Chevillon

Spa.65
Capt Louis Sejourne

Spa.84
S/Lt Pierre Wertheim

Spa.88
Lt Arthur Coadou

Groupe de Combat 17
Capitaine Joseph de l'Hermitte
(Rancourt)

Spa.77
Capt Henri Decoin

Spa.89
Capt Guy Tourangin

Spa.91
Capt Robert Lafon

Spa.100
Capt Louis Koenig Belliard de Vaubicourt

Groupe de Combat 20
Capitaine Raymond Bailly
(Pargny)

Spa.69
Capt Paul Malavaille

Spa.99
Lt Rougevin-Baville

Spa.159
Lt Henri Hay de Slade

Spa.162
Capt Daniel Chambarière

Escadre de Bombardement No 13
Chef d'Escadrons Armand des Prez de la Morlais
(Villers-en-Lieu)

Groupe de Bombardement 3
Capitaine Hubert de Geffrier
(Combles)

Escadrille Br.107   Escadrille Br.126
Capt Hubert de Geffrier   Lt Louis Barjaud

Escadrille Br.128
Capt René le Forestier
(All equipped with Bréguet 14.B2)

Groupe de Bombardement 4
Capitaine Pierre Etournaud
(St Dizier)

Escadrille Br.131   Escadrille Br.132
Capt Albert Mezergues   Capt Jean Jennekeyn

Escadrille Br.134 Lt Pierre Rousselet
(All equipped with Bréguet 14.B2)

Escadrille de Protection
Capitaine Marcel Bloch
C 46 (Caudron R 11) St Dizier

Chief of Air Service 2nd Colonial Corps (French)
Commandant Pennes
(Rumont)

Sal. 28	C 47	Br.236	Sal. 277
Rumont	Rumont	Belrain	Rumont

20th French Balloon Co	52nd French Balloon Co	53rd French Balloon Co
(Thillombois)	(Boncourt)	(Vignot)

183rd Aero Squadron (Mobile Park No 1)

British Independent Air Force
Major General Hugh Trenchard
(Azelot)

Day Bombardment

No 55 Sqn	No 99 Sqn	No 104 Sqn	No 110 Sqn
Maj A Gray	Maj L A Pattinson	Maj J C Quinnell	Maj H R Nicholl
DH9/DH9a	DH9a	DH9/DH10	DH9/DH9a

Night Bombardment

No 97 Sqn	No 100 Sqn	No 115 Sqn
Maj V A Albrecht	Maj C G Burge	Maj W E Gardner
HP 0/400	HP 0/400	HP 0/400

No 215 Sqn	No 216 Sqn
Maj J F Jones	Maj W R Read
HP 0/400	HP 0/400

PART TWO

Black September

by Russell Guest
with Norman Franks and Frank Bailey

Sunday, 1 September 1918

British Front

This late summer opened with fair visibility but a high wind. The British Army was pushing forward along both sides of the Somme River, following up a series of attacks that had begun on 8 August 1918, with the Canadians and Australians breaking open the German front facing Amiens. On this day the Australians attacked the heavily defended Mont St Quentin, just north of Peronne and Peronne town itself. Peronne lay on the Somme, and crossing the river here would roll up the Germans to the north, forcing a retreat behind their prepared positions on the Hindenburg Line.

Further to the north, August had seen General Sir Julian Byng's 3rd Army attack on the 21st. They were now facing the infamous Drocourt-Queant switch-line of April 1917 fame. They would attack it on the morrow. Bapaume had fallen on the 29th and the northern flank of the 4th Army was also closing on the Hindenburg Line. The German Army was on the defensive and showing increasing signs of disintegration.

In the air, things were different. The RAF had suffered heavily in August, and now faced well equipped opposition in the shape of firmly established Jastas flying Fokker DVIIs. The RAF's day bombers needed escorting now as a matter of course, otherwise casualties were high. The four types of RAF fighters had seen long service, and indeed, only the Sopwith Dolphin was a 1918 aeroplane, and there were only four squadrons of them. The SE5a could hold its own with Fokker DVIIs but the main fighter, the Sopwith Camel, was rapidly becoming obsolete. This was evidenced in the last ten days of August, which witnessed the loss of five American-flown Camels in one fight on the 26th, while 43 Squadron lost another six the next day. The last main fighter-type was the Bristol F2b two-seat fighter, which had started life so ingloriously in April 1917, but which now had become a formidable foe. There were six squadrons of 'Brisfits' in France, used also extensively for long range reconnaissance sorties. The Germans were suffering their own difficulties, attrition was hard to replace, aviation fuel was in short supply, while their two-seater crews were now restricted in their operations by their lack of ability to avoid, out-fly or out-fight Allied fighters.

Aerial operations on the RAF's front as the month opened can be characterised in terms of the three main sectors of aerial activity: army co-operation, day bombing and fighter operations—including low bombing and strafing. (Night bombing was also becoming a regular feature, especially with the Independent Air Force's Handley Page bombers, under Hugh Trenchard.)

The prime initiation of aerial combat was when RAF patrols encountered patrols of German fighters that were prepared to engage. The German pilots still preferred to engage only when they had a distinct advantage, whereas the British and American pilots invariably attacked everything whatever the odds against them. As the Germans concentrated their resources on key sectors of the front, aerial activity was much more intense over the area of an offensive by the Army. In early September the active Jagdgeschwader on the British front was JGI and JGIII, both of which operated near Cambrai. Also still near Cambrai was Jasta 5, which was by far the most successful non-'Circus' staffel in September 1918. Consequently, most of the major encounters in September were over the Cambrai area, the Arras area, and later in the month in the north, around Ypres, following an Allied ground attack there.

Almost separately was something of a small private, but intense war between the mainly ex-RNAS squadrons (de Havilland bombers and Camel fighters) based around Dunkirk, and the German Marine Jastas, along the North Sea coast. The combatants also resorted to intensive night bombing, and the RAF also had a dedicated night fighter squadron in France to counter this threat—No.151, with Camels.

The morning of the 1st was fairly quiet, but Lieutenant W E G 'Pedro' Mann, in a Camel of 208 Squadron, claimed a German two-seater at 0750, in flames south of the Scarpe River for his 8th victory. Of its crew of Unteroffizier Gottfried Ebert and Vizefeldwebel Pilarz, of FA(A)294, only the latter survived, wounded. 40 Squadron's SE5s claimed another, Captain George Dixon achieving his 6th victory at 0815, south-east of Henin Lietard. The Germans only made one claim before midday: the commander of Bavarian Jasta 34b, Oberleutnant Robert Greim claiming a Camel at 1000 near St Pierre Vaast Wood, just south of Sailly-Saillisel—probably a 73 Squadron machine. The four or five other victories of the morning were balloons by Allied pilots:

0740	Lt Len Taplin	(7th victory)	4 AFC Sqdn	at Fromelles
0745	Lt Roy King	(14th victory)	4 AFC Sqdn	at Le Grand Riez
0830	Lt Fred Luff	(3rd victory)	74 Sqdn	at Menin
1025	Capt Ernest Hoy	(8th victory)	29 Sqdn	nr Armentières

and a Fokker DVII by Lieutenant J W Wright of 4 AFC, south-east of Bailleul at 0925—his first victory.

At 1100 hours, Captain Basil Catchpole MC DFC led out six Bristols of 'L' Flight—a long range recce unit—to photograph the Sensee Canal, north of Cambrai. They lost one of their number, probably to Unteroffizier Schaack of Jasta 28—his second victory. It seemed that the crew failed to spot the others turn for the lines and became separated—highly dangerous when enemy fighters were about. Later Catchpole returned alone to the area but with a large fighter escort and completed the photo sortie, producing a fine mosaic for 1st Army HQ. Further south over the Somme bridges at Brie, Lieutenant Russell McCrae of 46 Squadron claimed a Fokker out of control at 1125.

In the afternoon, at 1345, 57 Squadron lost a DH4 while bombing Cambrai and had another shot up by an estimated 20 attacking fighters. Their escort of 62 Squadron lost a Bristol and had another force-land. 57 Squadron crews claimed four Fokkers and 62, three more. Sergeant Mechanic J Grant, gunner to Lieutenant E M Coles of 57, saw a Fokker coming up beneath the 'Four' next to them, and shot it down.

The Fokkers were from Bruno Loerzer's JGIII, which consisted of Jastas 2, 26, 27 and 36. Loerzer claimed one Bristol for his 34th kill, Leutnant Ernst Bormann of Jasta 2 (Boelcke), another south of Lecluse for his 5th. The DH4 was brought down by Vizefeldwebel Skworz of Jasta 36 at Brunemont. Despite the RAF claims, there are no known German losses.

To the north, near Armentières, one of the many Americans serving with the RAF, Lieutenant Fred Gillet, in a Dolphin of 79 Squadron, shot down an LVG C at 1310, the 4th victory of the pilot who would be the most successful RAF pilot between the beginning of September and the end of the war. Another successful pilot, but on the German side, was Flieger Hans Nülle of Jasta 39. The Jasta intercepted Camels of 209 Squadron at 1650, Nülle gaining his first victory, Vizefeldwebel Gockel his third. More will be heard of Nülle during the month.

A Dolphin of 79 Squadron was lost to flak around Armentières at 1830 the pilot, Second Lieutenant D S Merton, chancing his luck. He had taken off at 1645 for a practice flight and strayed too close to the front lines. If he was looking for trouble he found it, ground fire bringing him down south of the town to become a prisoner. German flak fire had been very active during the day, three artillery observation aircraft having been hit, damaged, and forced to land.

More engagements between fighters occurred in the early evening, 29 Squadron having a scrap near Armentières at 1830, claiming two Fokkers, one to Captain Hoy for his second of the day, 7th overall. Another of the unit's aces, Lieutenant Arthur Eden Reed, a South African, claimed his 15th victory. Nos. 208 and 56 Squadrons each claimed a Fokker shortly before 1900. More fights went on near the Ypres Salient, Lieutenant Edwin Swale of 210 Squadron claimed a Fokker east of the city at 1830, then 88's Bristols got a Fokker in flames east of Becelaere at 1910. Despite these claims, no German aircraft were apparently lost, certainly no pilots.

On the German side, Leutnant Wilhelm Sommer of Jasta 39 achieved his first victory by burning the Tilloy balloon—SR59 of the 28th Balloon Company—at 2110. The observers, Lieutenants Kitcat and Freshney, both parachuted to safety. Flieger Abteilung (A) 208 lost Leutnants Hermann Aschoff and Friedrich Ohlf at Handecourt during the day, presumably to anti-aircraft fire, as no two-seaters were encountered anywhere near this area. Another two-seater crew, Vizefeldwebel Gunther and Leutnant Schwertfeger, of FA(A) 252, shot up a British tank which burst into flames, then directed artillery fire onto another which was also destroyed. This night, the RAF lost a night bomber, either to flak or to engine failure.

French Front

The French front line stretched from south of the Somme to the Swiss border. The Americans were arriving in force opposite the St Mihiel salient, south of Verdun and held the line to the north and south of Verdun. Although we shall record the activities of both air forces separately, both French and American forces were defending what was the French Front. Due to the vagaries of the French climate, there was rather more low cloud and rain over the French lines than further north today, thus air activity was rather slow.

Vizefeldwebel Karl Schlegel, a recent and rapidly rising 'Kanone' (the German term for what the French called an ace) from Jasta 45, made an intrusion over the French lines and scored his 19th victory by flaming the balloon of the French 29th Company, in the X Armée sector. The observer, Adjutant Proust, took to his parachute and landed safely. Balloon observers were the only Allied participants in the air war to have parachutes as escape routes. Unlike the Germans, who had registered successful jumps from aeroplanes in combat from June 1918, Allied aircrew never had the opportunity. This was a bureaucratic if not autocratic (even murderous) decision that was to cost the lives of countless British, French and American airmen in the last year of the war. One line of thought was that with a way out, the airmen would be more inclined to bale out if in a fix, whereas most probably the pilot would have been more aggressive, knowing that he had a line of escape if all else failed. It has also been said that as the Allies had so many airmen there was less inclination from on high to save a few! The Germans, with dwindling numbers, obviously had the opposite view.

On the Aisne River front, the 29-year-old, devoutly religious Sous Lieutenant Leon Bourjade combined with Sous Lieutenant Ernest Maunoury to burn the German Balloon at Pont Arcy at 1840. It was the 16th and 6th victories respectively of these two pilots of Spa.152. Over Flavy le Meldeux, Spa.150 claimed two aircraft, one credited to Sergent Charles Veil, an American serving with the French, the other shared between Lieutenant Henry Stickney, yet another American, and Sergent Bagarry, for their joint first victory. Vizefeldwebel Friedrich Poeschke of Jasta 53 claimed a Spad for his second victory, over Bretigny.

Thirty-seven aircraft of Escadre de Bombardement 14, comprising Groupes de Bombardement 8 and 10, carried out night raids against railway depots at Laon, Marie, Ham and other sites, dropping a total of 9,866 kilos of bombs and firing 700 rounds at barrack lights. One Voisin bomber was lost, probably to flak.

	A/C	KB			DES	OOC	KB
British losses	14	1		British claims	13	11	5
French losses	1	1		French claims	2		1
American losses	—	—		American claims	—		
IAF losses	—	—		IAF claims	—	—	—
German claims	12†	2		German losses	3		2

† Includes two to flak.

British Casualties

Aircraft type	No.	Squadron	Crew		
AWFK8	D5134	35 Sqdn	2/Lt H Phillips	Safe	
			2/Lt H G Griffiths	Safe	
RE8	E67	15 Sqdn	Capt C C Snow	Safe	
			2/Lt R C Capel-Cave	WIA	
DH4	F6096	57 Sqdn	2/Lt J C Dugdale	POW	
			2/Lt F B Robinson POW		
DH4	D8382	57 Sqdn	Sgt D E Edgeley	Safe	*
			Sgt N Sandison	WIA	
BF2b	E2521	L Flt	Lt G L Barritt	POW	
			2/Lt R H G Boys	POW	
BF2b	E2479	62 Sqdn	2/Lt L B Raymond	MIA	
			2/Lt D S Hamilton	MIA	
BF2b	E2494	62 Sqdn	Lt L W Hudson	Safe	
			2/Lt J Hall	WIA	
BF2b	C843	20 Sqdn	Lt F E Smith	Safe	
			Pbr E S Harvey	Safe	
SE5a	B7890	32 Sqdn	Lt E C Klingman	MIA	
SE5a	E5939	32 Sqdn	2/Lt J O Donaldson	POW	

Dolphin	E4433	79 Sqdn	2/Lt D A Martin	POW	
Camel	E4388	209 Sqdn	2/Lt H V Peeling	POW	
Camel	E4393	209 Sqdn	2/Lt R L Scharff	POW	
Camel	D1922	73 Sqdn	Lt H V Fellows	POW	
Camel	B7162	203 Sqdn	2/Lt T Nolan	Inj	
FE2b (night)	C9790	101 Sqdn	2/Lt M E Challis	POW	
			2/Lt R D Hughes	POW	
AWFK8		8 Sqdn	2/Lt T Brandon (P)	WIA	*
BF2b		L Flt	2/Lt M Wallace (O)	WIA	*
BF2b		48 Sqdn	2/Lt J N Kier (O)	WIA	*
RE8		53 Sqdn	2/Lt O C Burke (O)	WIA	*
SE5a		74 Sqdn	Lt T Adamson	WIA	*
DH4		57 Sqdn	Lt J Howard-Brown (O)	WIA	*
SE5a		32 Sqdn	Lt A E Sandys-Winsch	WIA	*
RE8		5 Sqdn	Lt E A Locke-Walters (P)	WIA	*
RE8		53 Sqdn	Lt S W Cowper-Coles (P)	WIA	*

French Casualties

Voisin	V106	Cpl Revolte	MIA	
		Soldat Robin	MIA	

Monday, 2 September 1918

British Front

At 0500 the Canadian Corps of the British 1st Army and the XVIII Corps of the 3rd Army attacked the Drocourt-Queant switch line, supported by tanks. V Corps attacked between Sailly-Saillisel and Le Transloy, IV Corps between Haplincourt and Beugny and VI Corps between Morchies and Lagnicourt. The Canadians broke right through and by mid-morning they had captured Cagnicourt. By the end of the day the British had reached a line along the Sensee River and the Canal du Nord. Along the Somme front, they were pressing up to the Hindenburg Line. On the British right, the French were also advancing, with the Germans losing all their gains from the March 1918 offensive.

In the air on this day, despite showery weather and an abundance of cloud, there were clear bright intervals with good visibility. Over the offensive, 5 and 52 Squadrons co-operated with the Canadians, 13 Squadron with XVII Corps and 8 Squadron with the Tank Corps. The Camels of 73 Squadron bombed and strafed enemy tank defences, while 40 and 22 Squadrons provided air cover directly over the advance.

The German policy of giving the elite Circus units the best equipment paid off, as the BMW-engined Fokker biplanes of JGIII had a significant impact on the air war. BMW Fokkers looked identical to the Mercedes-powered ones but they had 20—plus more horsepower, giving a significantly better performance. JGIII flew three main missions this day, claiming 26 victories out of the 35 or 37 claims made against the RAF. In all, the Germans claimed a massive 59 victories, details of 57 being presented here. It is assumed that the other two were by JGIII—as 24 are known—or by Jastas flying near JGIII and winning disputed claims. Certainly other Jastas claimed in the same area and time as JGIII. Another possibility is that two-seater crews made the claims.

The carnage began at 0630, as 201 Squadron attacked 12 Fokker DVIIs at 12,000 feet over Heudicourt. Captain Reg Brading, a 19-year-old Englishman, claimed his 9th victory by sending one down 'out of control' and 45 minutes later he got another. He attacked Fokkers operating under the cloud layer at 4,000 feet that were attacking Corps aircraft, shooting down his second victim over Lagnicourt. At the same time Lieutenant Ron Sykes, another 19-year-old, claimed a Fokker after his flight had been pounced on by 25 of these biplanes. This was confirmed at 1530 that afternoon, Brading seeing another wrecked Fokker near the crashed DVII he brought down, flying over to take a look at it. However, this could be deemed somewhat circumstantial.

The first major fight was at 0820, Jasta 36 clashing with the Camels of 3 Squadron, who lost Lieutenant Vic McElroy to Leutnant Quandt. However, the German then spoilt his performance somewhat by shooting up a Rumpler CIV of FA(A) 210 by mistake. Quandt would eventually lose a fight and be killed by a French fighter pilot, but not until June 1940—in World War Two!

From 0930 onwards, Jasta 27 of JGIII was in action, encountering two Bristols of 22 Squadron, one of which the Jasta commander promptly shot down. This was Hermann Frommherz's 17th victory. No. 22 claimed two Fokkers in return, one by the crew of Lieutenant Ian O Stead and Second Lieutenant W A Cowie, before they had to force-land—unharmed—in British lines, apparently not being claimed by the Germans. No. 22 also reported the presence of Camels and SE5s in this fight, and Pfalz DXIIs—which looked so similar to the more numerous DVIIs that few were actually reported that summer.

Then Jasta 26 claimed two SE5s at Villers at 1015/1020, one to Leutnant Otto Fruhner, his 19th, the other to Leutnant Herman Lange, his 5th. They were fighting 40 Squadron who lost just one aircraft; the other claim may have been a Camel. Jasta 26 went on to engage Camels, the whole Geschwader encountering a formation of Camels and two-seaters between 1100 and 1130, east of Cambrai. They made the following seven claims, making ten in all for the sortie:

Ltn F Noltenius	Jasta 27	Camel	Etaing	1100	5th victory
Ltn O Löffler	Jasta 2	Camel	S Pelves	—	5th victory
Ltn E Bormann	Jasta 2	Camel	Drury	—	6th victory
"	"	Camel	Souchy	—	7th victory
Ltn F Heinz	Jasta 2	Camel	Boiry	—	1st victory
Ltn O Fruhner	Jasta 26	SE5a	Barelle	1110	20th victory
Ltn F Noltenius	Jasta 27	DH4	Rumaucourt	1120	6th victory

Whilst this was going on, another of the Bloody April veterans, Vizefeldwebel Jörke of Jasta 39, claimed an RE8 of 5 Squadron over Ballieul-Sir-Berthoult at 1125—his 13th victory. For JGIII this was an example of accurate claiming, as 208 and 209 both lost two Camels, 73 and 201 one each. No. 56 Squadron lost an SE5a—probably to Fruhner—and Noltenius's claim was probably a 35 Squadron AWFK8—the Germans often confusing DH4s, AWFK8s and BF2bs.

Meanwhile, at 1005, Lieutenant M D Sinclair in a SE5a of 60 Squadron attacked an LVG C at the extremely low altitude of 30 feet, got underneath it(!) and opened fire from 100 yards, killing the observer moments before the C-type dove into the ground. Ten minutes later, Major F I Tanner, from 80 Squadron, claimed a DFW C, south of Cartigny, which spun in and burnt. At the same time, Lieutenant J Collier, also from 80 Squadron, claimed another just south of Mons-en-Chaussée—two rare victories for this Camel unit, dedicated to supporting British tanks.

Just after midday, JGIII and other Jastas were airborne again, this time making no fewer than 14 claims between 1220 and 1250 German time:

Vzfw C Mesch	Jasta 26	Camel	Haucourt	1240	7th victory
Oblt F Dahlmann	JGIII	Camel	Haucourt	1240	4th victory
Vzfw C Mesch	Jasta 26	Camel	Haucourt	1242	8th victory
Ltn Ehlers	Jasta 26	Camel	NE Barelle	1245	1st victory
Ltn H Lange	Jasta 26	Camel	NE Barelle	1245	6th victory
Hpt B Loerzer	JGIII	Camel	Dury	1245	35th victory
Vzfw A Lux	Jasta 27	RE8	Hamel	—	5th victory
Ltn Stoltenhoff	Jasta 27	RE8	—	—	2nd victory
Vzfw A Lux	Jasta 27	BF2b	Vis/Artois	—	6th victory
Ltn O Löffler	Jasta 2	Camel	Beugnatre	—	6th victory
Ltn E Bormann	Jasta 2	Camel	W Havrincourt	—	8th victory
Fw W Kahle	Jasta 27	Camel	Beugnatre	—	1st victory
Ltn O Löffler	Jasta 2	Camel	S Palleul	—	7th victory
Ltn M Demisch	Jasta 58	RE8	Vis/Artois	1220	5th victory

Either Martin Demisch (sometimes spelt Dehmisch) was flying with JGIII, or more likely he won a disputed claim with a JGIII pilot, giving JGIII 24 confirmed kills rather than the initial 26 claimed for the day—for no loss. After both their engagements, JGIII remained over the battlefield and engaged in some extensive ground strafing. The root cause of their success—

apart from superior aeroplanes—was the capacity of Bruno Loerzer to co-ordinate four Jastas into one large force, which simply swamped the flight-sized RAF patrols. Co-ordination between RAF units was hindered by their vertical separation which only seemed to work well when there were no clouds interfering with visual contact between each layer. The SE5a top cover often arrived too late, not having seen anything. Unfortunately, all too often no top cover was provided at all.

For example, the 148th Aero Squadron had been flying in two Flights, with 'A' Flight, led by First Lieutenant Field Kindley in front, passing under a large bank of cloud which was at 3,000 feet south of Rumaucourt, while First Lieutenant Elliott Springs and 'B' Flight were in the open behind and below. When Jasta 26 dropped out of low cloud right into the middle of B Flight, Kindley turned his Flight back into the fight, just as the other Jastas arrived. He claimed a Fokker but had 36 bullet holes punched into his Camel, ten of which had hit his guns a foot in front of his face!

The Camels were fighting a continuously reinforced formation of Fokkers, as Springs' combat report noted four Fokkers at 1145, four miles south-east of Haucourt on the Arras-Cambrai road, reinforced by three more, followed by a further seven from the south-east, and finally more to bring the total to 25. Elliott Springs also left an account of this fight, quoted in his biography *War Bird*, by Burke Davis:

'The Huns meant business and so did we. As soon as I would get on the tail of one, another would get me and as soon as I would shake him off there would be another... My lower left wing buckled. I went into a spin. I thought my machine was falling to pieces and reflected with pleasure that I had forgotten my pocketbook. I thought of Mac [1/Lt John Grider USAS, KIA 18 June 1918, and a close friend of Springs] and how glad he would be to see me. But my plane held together... and I got out of the spin in time to hop a Hun. I don't know how many Huns we got out of it. I'm the only one of my Flight who returned.'

First Lieutenant Jesse Creech had earlier fallen out of the patrol due to a broken con-rod, getting down unhurt, but the rest had been severely mauled. Kindley claimed a Fokker at 1150 south of Rumaucourt, which he saw turn over onto its back and spin in. Lieutenant Charles MacLean claimed another over Buissy after he had shot at it, the Fokker nose diving. Soon afterwards, MacLean flew back past Buissy and saw a wreck burning on the ground where the Fokker would have crashed. This would, without doubt, have been a burning Camel and is another indication of how the optimism of a fighter pilot results in exaggerated claims. Lieutenant Walter Cox claimed another destroyed.

The RAF lost at least three RE8s to fighters. No. 52 Squadron sent nine machines to bomb Vitry and the last vic of three were shot up and force-landed in Allied lines—shades of 59 Squadron in April 1917. At least this time the Camels of 148 had been covering them, but they were decimated by JGIII. In the fight too were the SEs of 64 Squadron and the BF2bs of 22 Squadron, who between them claimed a further five Fokkers, the former being engaged in ground strafing. One of the SE pilots, Sergeant A S Cowlishaw, was obviously on a balloon hunt when he joined combat, for his guns were primed with the highly sensitive Buckingham ammunition, designed for igniting balloons, but he drove down a Fokker over Marquion, smoking!

For the two American Camel Squadrons serving with the RAF, it was their second hiding in a week from JGIII. The other Squadron, the 17th Aero, were the main sufferers on 26 August. The reason was the same; caught low down and having to fight their way out against high odds. JGIII double-claimed on the Camels in this fight, as can be seen by two claims at the same time and/or location for most of the victims, i.e. ten claims, four losses if we ignore Creech, who it is believed dropped out before the fight began.

During this period the 'lesser' Jasta were also active and at 1220 Leutnant Wilhelm Sommer of Jasta 39 scored for the second day straight, shooting down an RE8 over Fampoux, in British lines, probably one of 52 Squadron's machines—and he wasn't finished for the day yet. Jasta 7's Leutnant Willi Nebgen claimed an AWFK8 at 1230 over Lomme, near Lille, for his 3rd victory while Vizefeldwebel Maack of Jasta 63 got his first, another Big Ack, at exactly the same time and place. However, 82 Squadron only lost one Ack-W!

During the day, Hauptmann Eduard von Schleich claimed an RE8 (his 31st kill) near Bapaume and in the late evening the Richthofen Circus (JG1) made its first claim in September. Oberleutnant Erich von Wedel, commander of Jasta 11, brought down another RE8 near Le Catelet at 1945 for his own 11th kill. Wilhelm Sommer got his second of the day by burning the 43 Company's balloon near Bapaume at 2100 hours.

This evening also saw a fight between Bristols of 48 Squadron and Jasta 20 over Gheluvelt at 2000. Leutnant Raven von Barnekow scored his 5th and Leutnant Bruno Hobein his 3rd, shooting down the two Brisfits which failed to return. No. 48's crews claimed four Fokkers, but Jasta 20 suffered no losses as far as is known. In fact the only known Fokker loss on the whole front was that flown by Vizefeldwebel Heinrich Gockel of Jasta 33. He baled out of his burning fighter, believed near Cambrai, while his young Staffelführer, Leutnant Karl von Schönebeck, scored his 7th victory.

During the day, the RAF organised a mass strafe of Linselles aerodrome. The SE5s of 29 and 74 Squadron bombed from 6,000 feet and then remained above while 41 Squadron and the Camels of 70 strafed from 100 to 50 feet. The aerodrome was reported as gutted, and none of the raiders were lost, a demonstration of air power that the RFC was incapable of 18 months earlier.

Another significant feature of the day was that just like Bloody April, the German fighters broke through and got to a large number of artillery observation and close support aircraft. However, unlike Bloody April, this was happening about once a month of late, and was not to happen significantly again during the war. The RAF fighters managed to keep the Jastas off the front most of the time, but more importantly, the far better trained RE8 and AWFK8 crews could now look after themselves, far better than the flyers of the previous spring.

French Front

The weather improved here and aerial combat picked up. In the V Armée sector, three Spad two-seaters of Spa.20 on a photo-recce mission were engaged in combat near Thil at 1030 by eight Fokkers. During the fight, Adjutant Dutrey and Sergent Latapie claimed a biplane at 1030 over La Neuvillette, 3 kilometres north-west of Reims, but were in turn attacked by Leutnant Gustav Dörr of Jasta 45. Latapie was wounded but Dutrey evaded the attack and they managed to return to base. Dörr then attacked the photo Spad and shot it down, the crew posted as missing. Dörr was credited with his 23rd and 24th victories. Leutnant Meixner of Jasta 45 also claimed a Spad at this time for his first victory. The third Spad of the trio, Sous Lieutenant Clavel and Lieutenant Puisieux, claimed a Fokker in the fight.

Twenty minutes later, Jasta 45's commander, Leutnant Konrad Brendle, attacked a balloon near Reims, but did not return. He was killed in action behind the French lines but received credit for his 8th victory through his colleagues for downing a balloon.

In the X Armée sector, during the course of a combat with five Fokker DVIIs, Maréchal-des-Logis Verges and Lieutenant Barat, of Spa.34, succeeded in downing one near Courcy-la-Ville. However, during the scrap Verges was killed, although Barat managed to fly their two-seater, which had been riddled with bullets, down safely into French territory. Also in this sector, near Reims, Caporal Fournier and Lieutenant de Boeuxis of Br.289, were shot down by three Fokkers; this time the pilot was wounded and the observer killed. Two-seaters were claimed by Leutnant Werner Preuss of Jasta 66—for his 13th victory—and Leutnant Herman Habich of Jasta 49, his second, the latter claiming near Chalons-Suippes at 1220, although the Jasta had Unteroffizier Hennies wounded.

Spad two-seaters were also claimed by Gefreiter Jakob of Jasta 17 at Savigny at 1000 hrs, and Leutnant Buddeberg of Jasta 50 over Braisne at the same time. Two more Bréguets were claimed in French lines near the Remser Wald, by Verdun by Jasta 68—Leutnant Rudolf Otto, Staffelführer, and Vizefeldwebel Huar.

Over the V Armée sector, another Bréguet, from Br.260 on a two-plane photo mission, was engaged by six Fokkers. Lieutenant Fournier was wounded, his observer being killed. Fournier managed to force-land in French lines. A Spad two-seater from an unknown unit was shot up as well, Caporal Maurel being wounded, his observer, Lieutenant de Boeuric, unhurt.

During the day Adjutant Lucas of Spa.97 claimed a balloon for his first victory. Another Spad escadrille that was climbing back from being heavily thrashed by the Germans during the early summer was Spa.159, under the expert guidance of their new CO, Lieutenant Henri Hay de Slade; they claimed two victories. De Slade got one between Terny and Sorny at 1045, Sergent Rozes the second, over Sorny itself. Both villages are due north of Soissons. De Slade was 25 years old and had been operational since December 1916 with Spa.86, before taking over Spa.159 in late July 1918.

Another French ace, Lieutenant Ferdinand Bonneton, 28, now flying with Spa.69, had already served in Russia, Romania and Italy. He shot down a balloon at Pontavert for his 7th victory, followed by a probable Fokker DVII over Beaurieux.

There were no end of combats over the front on this day, the Germans claiming nine Spad fighters:

Unt O Bieleit	Jasta 45	Baslieux	0820	1st victory
Ltn Fritz Höhn	Jasta 81	Courcy le Château	—	10th victory
Ltn A Brandenstein	Jasta 49	Suippes	1010	5th victory
Ltn Christians	Jasta 21	NW Fismes	1110	1st victory
”	”	E Fismes	1640	2nd victory
Ltn Hentzen	Jasta 9	W Terny Sorny	1733	2nd victory
Flgr F Wolff	Jasta 17	Savigny	1830	1st victory
Ltn H Brünig	Jasta 50	Fismes	1920	7th victory
Flgr Eyssler	Jasta 66	N Soissons	—	1st victory

The 22-year-old ace of Spa.88, Lieutenant Gabriel Thomas, had a fight with a German two-seater crew and was wounded for his pains. He would return in October and bring his wartime score to seven.

The French also attacked the German balloon lines during the day. At 0900 the 'drachen' of Ballonzug 22 was burnt by Lieutenant Henri Dencaussée of Spa.90 at Geline. Half an hour later Spa.90 struck again, Sous Lieutenant Marc Ambrogi, Adjutants Maurice Bizot and Jean Pezon shared the flaming of Ballonzug 36's gasbag at Juvelize, thereby gaining their 9th, 6th and 3rd victories respectively. During this team attack (normal for the French as it increased the chance of success while splitting the defensive fire) Bizot was hit by shrapnel from a defending gun but was able to fly home.

Spa.124 'Joan d'Arc' Escadrille, the French unit that replaced the earlier unit of the same number—the famed Lafayette Escadrille of American volunteers—claimed two balloons. The first went to Adjutant Bentejac and Sergent Grillot at Manre, the second to Lieutenant Berge and Sergent Caton at Bois de la Taille. Meantime, a patrol of Spa.163 burnt the German balloon at Bouconville.

In reply the Germans made determined efforts to go after French balloons. In the V Armée sector, the balloon of the 27th Company was destroyed at 1430 (A) by Leutnant Krayer of Jasta 45, Aspirant Simondi, the observer, parachuting to safety. The balloon of the 72nd Company was lost in the IV Armée sector, and again the observer—Sous Lieutenant Brutus—descended safely. The aircraft that flamed this balloon was shot down near Arcy St Restitute, and was probably Leutnant Gottfried Clausnitzer of the Saxon Jasta 72, who was shot down in flames after downing a balloon for his first victory. Two other balloons were attacked but not destroyed—probably those attacked by Brendle of Jasta 45 as mentioned above. The loss of Brendle—the experienced ace—and Clausnitzer makes it evident that the downing of a balloon was still no easy task, no matter how experienced the pilot.

A further two French balloons were lost in the II Armée sector by Jasta 67 pilots. Unteroffizier Baumgartner got the balloon of Sous Lieutenant Lamaud of the 81st Cié (Company), who made a safe jump, while Leutnant Quartier destroyed that of the 52nd Company, Sous Lieutenant Gravier parachuting down. Gravier was no doubt delighted to learn that his victor had been shot down by ground fire and captured, after having gained his second victory.

Three balloons were lost in the VII Armée sector in the late afternoon. Leutnant Josef Filbig of Jasta 80 got the 34th Company one at 1600, while the 89th Company lost theirs to

Leutnant Gustav Burck of Jasta 54 at 1615. Earlier, the Americans had lost the balloon of their 3rd Balloon Company, which was flamed at 1400 hours by Jasta 80's commander, Oberleutnant Gottlieb Rassberger—his first victory.

American Sector

Also operating near Reims was a squadron of the USAS. The 88th Observation Squadron was in the IV Armée sector and three of their Salmson 2A2s, engaged on photo work, were attacked by eight German fighters. The Americans claimed the German leader shot down but lost Lieutenants R W Hitchcock and F M Moore behind the lines near Dhuizy. Hitchcock had only recently been awarded the DSC for an action which had occurred on 11 August, after his observer had been killed and his body had jammed the controls. Despite this impediment, Hitchcock managed to bring the plane home, but this time he was not so lucky. Captain Richard Page and Lieutenant Pitt F Carl came down in French lines south of Reims.

Unfortunately, no time is known for this action and it may relate to Jasta 45 and the loss of Brendle, but more likely to three Spad two-seaters claimed by this unit near Magneux at around 1600. Leutnant Hans Rolfes claimed two—his 12th and 13th victories—the other credited to Leutnant Koennemann for his second. Another casualty mentioned as being related to this fight is the two-seater crew of Unteroffizier Josef Kraemer and Leutnant Eugen Weber of FA2, who came down in French lines. However, they were lost further north-west, near Nesle, probably falling to a patrol of GC14 that downed a DFW which had had the audacity to attack the 68th Company balloon.

The Spads of the 22nd Aero Squadron shot down a Rumpler C at 0942, near Armaucourt, the victor being Lieutenant Arthur Ray Brooks, the third of his six victories. Ray Brooks died on 17 July 1991, the last USAS—but not the last American ace—to die.

	A/C	KB		DES	OOC	KB
RAF losses	32	2	RAF claims	15	8	—
French losses	5	6	French claims	9		7
American losses	1	1	American claims	2		—
IAF losses	—	—	IAF claims	—	—	—
German claims	51	11	German losses	4		6

British Casualties

Aircraft type	No.	Squadron	Crew		
FE2b (night)	B1879	148 Sqdn	Lt E Alder	Safe	
			Lt A V Collins	Safe	
RE8	C2729	5 Sqdn	Lt L Coleman	KIA	
			2/Lt C E Gardner	KIA	
RE8	C2536	5 Sqdn	Lt C C Fraser	Safe	
			2/Lt A J Bishop	WIA	
RE8	C4590	5 Sqdn	Lt J Town	Safe	
			Lt A C Pollard	Safe	
RE8	E91	6 Sqdn	Lt Martin	Safe	
			Lt Churchward	Safe	
RE8	F5880	6 Sqdn	Lt Fenwick	Safe	*
			Lt Holmes	Safe	
RE8	C5072	6 Sqdn	Lt Pettit	Safe	
			Lt Clark	Safe	
RE8	F5978	13 Sqdn	2/Lt J S Stringer	POW	
			Lt R A Pope MC	POW	
RE8	F6015	52 Sqdn	2/Lt J G Garlake	Safe	*
			2/Lt L Sharp	WIA	
RE8	C2467	52 Sqdn	2/Lt R G Walton	WIA	*
			2/Lt G Bradbury	WIA	
RE8	D4899	52 Sqdn	2/Lt J B Elton	Safe	*
			2/Lt W E China	Safe	
RE8	D4903	53 Sqdn	2/Lt A J Macqueen	Safe	
			2/Lt D A Watson	Safe	
AWFK8	D5185	8 Sqdn	Capt G H Dykes	WIA	
			Lt Birkett	Safe	
AWFK8	B4161	8 Sqdn	2/Lt W L Chapman	Safe	
			2/Lt E E L Elliott	Safe	

AWFK8	F4268	8 Sqdn	Lt Spriggs	Safe	*
			Lt J A Cogan	WIA	
AWFK8	F7394	8 Sqdn	2/Lt C W Appleby	KIA	
			2/Lt R E Talbot	KIA	
AWFK8	F4263	10 Sqdn	2/Lt R A Coulthurst	WIA	
			2/Lt A R Macpherson	Safe	
AWFK8	B4174	35 Sqdn	2/Lt H Nottrass	WIA	*
			Lt F A Lawson	WIA	
AWFK8	D5174	82 Sqdn	2/Lt D Rose	POW	
			2/Lt J B Cockin	POW	
DH9	D3226	206 Sqdn	2/Lt H A Scrivener	POW/WIA	
			Sgt C H Davidson	KIA	
BF2b	E2516	22 Sqdn	Lt I O Stead	Safe	*
			2/Lt W A Cowie	WIA	
BF2b	D7990	22 Sqdn	Capt B L Dowling	KIA	
			Lt V StB Collins	KIA	
BF2b	E2453	48 Sqdn	2/Lt O O'Connor	POW	
			2/Lt J J Ambler	POW	
BF2b	E2455	48 Sqdn	2/Lt I M B McCulloch	POW	
			2/Lt L P Penny	KIA	
SE5a	D8445	40 Sqdn	2/Lt H W Clarke	MIA	
SE5a	C8706	56 Sqdn	Lt W M Strathearn	POW	
SE5a	C6468	74 Sqdn	Capt S Carlin	Safe	
Camel	C8344	3 Sqdn	Lt V H McElroy	KIA	
Camel	F6190	3 Sqdn	Lt G F Young	KIA	
Camel	F5968	54 Sqdn	Capt E J Salter	WIA	*
Camel	F2145	54 Sqdn	2/Lt W J Densham	Safe	*
Camel	D8114	73 Sqdn	2/Lt D B Sinclair	POW	
Camel	E1471	148th US	2/Lt J E Frobisher	DOW	
Camel	E1414	148th US	2/Lt O Mandel	POW	
Camel	D6700	148th US	2/Lt D Kenyon	POW	
Camel	E1412	148th US	Lt L H Forster	KIA	
Camel	E4399	201 Sqdn	2/Lt W A Hall	POW	
Camel	E1545	208 Sqdn	2/Lt C H Living	KIA	
Camel	D1873	208 Sqdn	Lt J W Marshall	POW/WIA	
Camel	F5970	209 Sqdn	Capt R C Grant	KIA	
Camel	E4381	209 Sqdn	Lt W M Wormold	KIA	
RE8		5 Sqdn	2/Lt G J Carr (O)	WIA	*
RE8		6 Sqdn	Lt E C Clegg (O)	WIA	*
RE8		7 Sqdn	2/Lt J McAslan (O)	WIA	*
RE8		13 Sqdn	Lt P J Travis (O)	WIA	*
AWFK8		8 Sqdn	Lt H A Mould (O)	WIA	*
DH4		18 Sqdn	Lt R S Aslin (O)	WIA	*
SE5a		41 Sqdn	1/Lt E H Barksdale	WIA	*

French Casualties

Bréguet XIV	Br.207		Capt de Ribes	KIA	
			Soldat Peret	Safe	
Bréguet XIV	Br.224		Capt Lamasse	KIA	
			2/Lt Jean-Marie	KIA	
Bréguet XIV	Br.260		Lt Fournier	WIA	*
			Soldat Guimbertau	KIA	
Bréguet XIV	Br.289		Sgt Proiss	MIA	
			Cpl Gamain	MIA	
Bréguet XIV	Br.289		Cpl Fournier	WIA	*
			Lt de Boeuxis	WIA	
Bréguet XIV	Br.104		Lt Hoppelt (O)	DOW	*
Spad XI	Spa.34		MdL Verges	KIA	*
			Lt Barat	Inj	
Spad XI	Spa.20		Sgt Deglise-Favre	MIA	
			Lt Brasseur	MIA	
Spad XI	Spa.20		Adj Dutrey	Safe	*
			Sgt Latapie	WIA	
Spad XIII	Spa.99		MdL Billiet	MIA	
Spad XIII	?		MdL Poitte	WIA	*
Spad XIII	Spa.88		Lt G Thomas	WIA	*
Spad XIII	?		S/Lt Bouisset	WIA	*

Spad XIII	Spa.38	Sgt Juge	WIA	*
Spad XIII	?	Cpl Perier	WIA	*
Spad XIII	Spa.90	Adj Bizot	WIA	*
Spad XI	?	Cpl Maurel	WIA	*
		Lt du Boueric	Safe	

American Casualties

Salmson 2A2	88 Sqdn	1/Lt R W Hitchcock	KIA	
		2/Lt F M Moore	KIA	
Salmson 2A2	88 Sqdn	Capt R Page	Safe	*
		1/Lt P F Carl Jr	Safe	

Tuesday, 3 September 1918

British Front

At 0630, Captain W A Southey led a patrol of 84 Squadron to start the day, during which the weather improved to being fine but cloudy. The SE5s trapped a Rumpler C-type over Manancourt to Nurlu Road and shot it down. Continuing their patrol, Southey burnt the balloon at Fins—his 12th victory—at 0645. The Germans lost another two-seater, this time a DFW, over Barelle at 0630, to a RE8 crew of 5 Squadron, Lieutenants H E Searson and T K Green, who spotted it flying along above the Canal du Nord.

On the ground this day, the two leading brigades of the 4th Canadian Division continued to advance, in order to secure the high ground overlooking the Canal du Nord, then pushing beyond it. Two-seater recce aircraft reported no sign of Germans west of the canal, while an 8 Squadron machine, on a tank contact patrol, was able to strafe German soldiers without seeing any enemy aircraft. With little opposition to their jobs, crews such as Canadian Lieutenants C F Galbraith and A T Sprangle of 5 Squadron were able to range artillery on guns and troops to good effect.

The Australians, as was their manner, were out hunting early and at 0705, Lieutenant Len Taplin of the Camel-equipped 4 AFC Squadron, burnt a balloon at La Plouich, thus achieving his 11th victory. Also out early were the Camels of 54 Squadron, who just five minutes earlier, but much further south, had claimed a Hannover CLIII at Moeuvres. No. 54 had been out low bombing but Lieutenant M G Burger spotted the two-seater and sent it down to crash.

The first fighter versus fighter battle occurred at 0710, 56 Squadron meeting Fokker DVIIs at 13,500 feet near Etaing and claiming four for the loss of Second Lieutenant Alfred Vickers, a new boy from Northampton, who had only arrived on 19 August with under 52 hours in his log book.

The Germans claimed no fewer than nine SE5s on this day, two over Abancourt and Aubenscheul (time unknown), and seven more in the afternoon, Jasta 36's Vizefeldwebels Wilhelm Skworz and Alfred Hübner made the untimed claims. However, Skworz failed to return, and was found the next day having crashed next to his victim at Sancourt, south of Abancourt. This is near to where Captain W R Irwin of 56 shot a Fokker in flames off Vickers' tail, which seems to tie these combats together.

There were more combats, and then 12 Squadron lost an RE8—most likely to ground fire, but possibly the one claimed by Leutnant Frommherz of Jasta 27 near Beugnatre between 1000-1100 for his 18th victory.

To the north of Ypres, the first serious fighting of the month occurred at 0910 as 70 Squadron ran into Fokkers south of Roulers and claimed four, three being out of control. At 0935, Lieutenant J A Glen flamed a balloon near Deulemont. At 0915, Leutnant W Schramm of Jasta 56 gained his 3rd kill by claiming a BF2b over Moorseele. None were in fact lost and the only fight recorded in this area was 70 Squadron's. No. 84 were out again, flaming a balloon south of Poeuilly at 0930.

The next main action was mid-morning, Captain John Doyle of 60 Squadron claiming another Fokker over Inchy at 1010. Once again the fight was with Jasta 36 and once more

Leutnant Quandt claimed, bringing down Lieutenant J F M Kerr, who force-landed at Cagnicourt at 1025.

The action swung back north of Ypres around 11 o'clock, 65 Squadron's Camels claiming four Fokkers over Engel. The pilot of a Fokker shot down at 1150 by Captain Fred Lord—his 6th—the young (supposedly 18-year-old) American ace of the notably 'Colonial' 79 Squadron, baled out of his burning fighter, but the parachute caught fire and the German fell to his death over Armentières.

Camels of 204 Squadron fought Fokkers at 1150, gaining three victories. The pilots had mixed experience: Ronald C Pattullo was a 22-year-old Canadian who'd been just three weeks with the Squadron. Lieutenant Bliss Edward Barnum was another Canadian, aged 21 but a veteran of nine months. The last claimant was Lieutenant Robert M Gordon, a Scot who would turn 19 on the last day of September, by which time he would have a DFC for his three months of active service. Gordon would live to the 1990s, serving his community as a Doctor, including WW2 in which he would win the DSO as a medic with the 51st Highland Division.

After midday the action intensified. Another two-seat Hannover was claimed at 1315, in flames east of Moeuvres, having received 200 rounds from Lieutenant A S Compton of 54 Squadron whilst it was flying at 1,500 feet. Five minutes later, Captain Gates of 201 claimed another two-seater he encountered at 3,500 feet. 500 rounds sent it diving into the ground.

The other American Dolphin pilot in 79 Squadron, Lieutenant Fred Gillet, reached his 5th victory at 1325, by burning the balloon at Armentières. One hour later another Fokker was claimed by 208's Captain 'Pedro' Mann at Marquion. This victory, his 9th, was made returning from patrol, spotting four Fokkers attacking the balloons along the Cambrai-Arras road. The 19-year-old Mann attacked one of them, firing from 100 to 50 yards, whereupon the Fokker spun away, engine on, out of control. This action matches Jasta 39's attack described in the next paragraph, and although this unit reported no loss, it is possible a Fokker got back over German lines without a pilot casualty. As will be seen, it certainly was not the victor over the two balloons lost by the RAF.

They were burnt at 1415 and 1417 by Gefreiter Hans Nülle. These, his 2nd and 3rd victories, were the 37-3-1 and 5-10-1 balloons positioned at Vis-en-Artois and Haucourt. The 10th Balloon Company balloon was numbered AR71, Lieutenant Henry and Corporal Banks both parachuting down after Nülle's attack. For the second day in a row, Nülle burnt the 5th Company balloon—AR74—with Lieutenant Lockwood and Acting Corporal Knights baling out.

No.57 Squadron were escorted on a bomb raid to Roisel, by 56 Squadron. Eight Fokkers engaged the SEs at 1520, one attacking Lieutenant E G Bowen, a Canadian, head-on. Bowen ducked, then stalled his machine upwards under the Fokker, firing 100 rounds from close range, seeing it spin down out of control.

Just after this, at 1525, Jastas 2 and 23 intercepted the DH9s of 98 Squadron, shooting down two. One crew fell near Cambrai, a second, with its observer dead, managed to scrape back over the lines to force-land near Cappy. Unteroffizier Michael Hutterer of Jasta 23 had thus achieved his 4th kill at Arleux, Jasta 2's Leutnant Otto Löffler his 8th at Epehy. Also at this time, Captain Southey of 84 Squadron made it three for the day and his 13th overall, by downing a balloon north of Fins.

Hauptmann Bruno Loerzer got into a fight with 32 Squadron, shooting down an SE5 near Douai at 1640 for his 36th victory, five minutes after Leutnant Otto Fruhner got his 21st—claimed as a Camel—at Sin le Noble. No. 32's Lieutenant H R Carson reported a Fokker shot down over Douai at 1645. Flieger Hermann Wirth of Jasta 32b was killed on this day over Douai, possibly in this fight.

This shows how difficult it can be to tie up claims and losses when even some of the more experienced fighter pilots did not identify their opponents accurately. At around 1700, Frommherz got his 19th victory by downing an RE8 at Beugny, and soon afterwards, two BF2bs were claimed by Leutnant Alfred Lindenberger of Jasta 2 Boelcke—his 9th kill—at Combles on the Allied side of the line, with the other claimed by the prolific Theo Quandt, his 14th. The one loss was probably, in fact, a DH4 of 18 Squadron, whose crew were killed west of Bourlon Wood.

At 1740, another pilot, Leutnant Friedrich Vollbracht of Jasta 5, who like Lindenberger would live to see fighter combat in WW2, gained his second victory by downing another BF2b. The vastly experienced pilots of Jasta 5 were in amongst 20 Squadron south of Peronne. Leutnant Josef Mai claimed one, his 24th, Leutnant Fritz Rumey shooting down his 30th. In fact only one Bristol was lost, although Captain H P Lale's machine was badly shot up and his observer killed, but he got back. 20 Squadron claimed three Fokkers and two Pfalz DXIIs.

Meantime, the undisputed 'ace' RE8 crew of the war, 12 Squadron's Lieutenants C R Pithey and H Rhodes (in F6097), who never hesitated to attack anything despite the type of machine they flew, shot down an LVG two-seater over Lagnicourt at 1715. Harvey Rhodes later became Lord Rhodes, although Croye Pithey was to die in 1919, but both men had won the DFC and bar for their unique achievements. Their ten victories included two balloons, three two-seaters and five fighters, and Rhodes made his own score 11 with another pilot. Not bad for the old 'Harry Tate'.

The Fokkers did not have it all their own way. No. 27 Squadron's DH9s, escorted by 1 Squadron, were south-west of Valenciennes at 1815, meeting a Fokker which appeared to be returning to its lines with engine trouble. Lieutenants E J Jacques and N P Wood dived on it, Wood firing three bursts to send the biplane into a flat spin before diving straight into some houses on the outskirts of Valenciennes.

At 1820, the diminutive American, Lieutenant Howard Kullberg, of 1 Squadron, serving in the RAF because the USAS said he was too small, attacked a Fokker as the formation returned over Cambrai. Kullberg engaged the biplane as several went for the DHs they were protecting, sending it down to crash near Avesnes-le-Sec.

There were numerous combats during this evening period. No. 210 Squadron fought several Fokkers after initially scrapping with a Fokker pilot they described as a 'star', although they eventually shot him down. Then 41 Squadron got mixed up with Jasta 29 at 1900, and although the Germans claimed three, only Second Lieutenant C E Turner crashed, wounded, at Arras. 41 claimed one in return.

Just as this action ended, Jasta 23's Unteroffizier Hutterer got his second of the day by downing Lieutenant F W Ferguson of 87 Squadron, the British squadron also claiming two Fokkers. Later that evening, Lieutenant Leslie Hollinghurst, also of 87 Squadron, (a future Air Chief Marshal) shot down a Hannover CLIII at Masnières.

Other British squadrons in action were DH4s of 18 Squadron at 1915, 29 Squadron at 1930 and 201 Squadron at the same time. Captain George Gates of the latter unit got an Albatros C-type east of Metz-en-Couture, watched by his patrol as it fell burning. Gates was the scourge of two-seaters in September, and his likely victims were Gefreiter Karl Noelpp and Leutnant Wilhelm Asmius of FA(A)248.

Up in the far north, a 205 Squadron DH4 on a recce along the Channel coast was shot up and forced to land with a dead observer, which was probably the 'Bréguet' claimed by Leutnant Brockhoff of MFJ 3 at Furnes at 1950. And the incomparable balloon buster, Belgium's Lieutenant Willy Coppens, shot down the Tenbrielen balloon for his 29th victory—his 27th balloon in 1918. More was to come from Coppens; nobody would get near his total of destroyed 'drachens'.

Over the day the German losses had been relatively light. Most RAF claims have to be discounted, as there is simply no evidence of any losses in the records of the Jastas they are known to have been fighting. Only two Jasta pilots appear as casualties: Vizefeldwebel Willy Skworz of Jasta 36 over Abancourt and Flieger Hermann Wirth killed over Douai.

French Front

The air war was quieter on this southern part of the front, due to bad weather. Most of the French losses of two killed, one missing and five wounded were to ground fire. However, Jastas 9, 17, 60 and 81 did claim five Spads between them. In addition, the Germans claimed five French and American balloons, but only details of four are known.

The balloon of the 76 Cié was working in the 5th Armée sector when it was flamed at 0905, the observer making a safe descent. The balloon of 44 Cié was also burnt in this sector, Adjutant J Branche also jumping to safety. One other French balloon was lost in the Aisne sector, the observer too surviving a jump. The three victors were Vizefeldwebel Willi Stör of Jasta 68, near Remy Wald; Unteroffizier Friedrich Engler of Jasta 62, who was severely wounded in the arm for his pains; and Leutnant Gustav Wember of Jasta 61, timed at 1600.

In the German 19 Armee sector, Gefreiter Erich Mix of Jasta 54 claimed the balloon of the American 1st Balloon Company, at 0940, near Tremblecourt as his second victory. His Fokker was hit at least 19 times by protective fire and was smoking badly on his return flight, forcing him to put down south-west of Preny. Mix would have to wait until WW2 to add two more victories to his final WW1 score in order to make 'ace' status. By 1941 his overall score was 13. On the French side, Adjutant Jean Pezon of Spa.90 burnt the Ballonzug 152 balloon at 1700, near Goin. Spa.98 claimed two enemy aircraft.

Further north, one of the great figures of French fighter aviation, Lieutenant Georges Madon, claimed another victory north of Fismes, his 41st and last confirmed kill. Because of the strict French confirmation system, he had upwards of 60 probable victories. Under the RAF method of scoring, Madon, like Capitaine René Fonck, would have over 100 victory claims by this time.

Pilots in Spa.91 and Spa.152 claimed aircraft this day, Spa.15 adding two balloons at Concevreaux and north of Fismes, while Spa.77 also added a balloon to their tally. A Bréguet XIV crew of Br.203 also reported downing a two-seater as well. The Germans lost a two-seater crew at Anizy-le-Château, and a pilot at Reims. In turn, the Germans claimed a number of French aircraft: Unteroffizier Mack of Jasta 60, a Spad: Leutnant Fritz Höhn and Vizefeldwebel Dietrich Averes of Jasta 81, two Spads near Soissons—one probably being flown by Caporal Dumont of Spa.91 who failed to return; Leutnant Walter Blume, CO of Jasta 9, brought his score to 20 (he would be the post-war designer of Arado aircraft); and Leutnant Herbert Rolle, also Jasta 9, downing two Spads at 1030 near Fismes. Of the two casualties of Spa.15 in this last attack, one had probably just flamed the balloon kill—Lieutenant Schneider—who was wounded, while Caporal Chambert was killed. Rittmeister von Bredelow, the CO of Jagdgruppe II, also claimed a Spad near Soissons, as did Vizefeldwebel Christian Donhauser of Jasta 17. Caporal Pradel of Spa.96 failed to return.

American Sector

During a bomb raid over Conflans, six Bréguets of the 96th Bombardment Squadron, which had departed at 1710(A) hours, was attacked by five Pfalz scouts with green and brown fuselages and yellow tails. The fight ran from Hannonville to Lebeuville, the whole flight being credited with a share in one which was shot down.

	A/C	KB			DES	OOC	KB
British losses	12	2		British claims	29	28	7
French losses	2	3		French claims	4		4
American losses	—	1		American claims	1		—
IAF losses	—			IAF claims	—		
German claims	33	6		German losses	5†		?

† At least; Schlasta 16 had a crew killed, supposedly in action, and the Germans had an airman killed at Valenciennes and another at Reims. There was also another pair (crew?) killed at Anizy-le-Château, but no unit shown.

British Casualties

Aircraft type	No.	Squadron	Crew		
RE8	F5885	5 Sqdn	Lt J Scholes	Safe	
			Lt R Boyle	Safe	
SE5a	E4064	56 Sqdn	2/Lt A Vickers	MIA	
RE8	B7888	12 Sqdn	Lt A W MacNamara	KIA	
			Lt H Johnson MC	KIA	
RE8	F5874	59 Sqdn	Capt G J Scott	WIA	*
			2/Lt J N Schofield	WIA	
SE5a	E6000	60 Sqdn	Lt J F M Kerr	Safe	*
RE8	C2377	53 Sqdn	Lt D C Dunlop	Safe	*
			Lt B E Scott	WIA	
DH9	D511	108 Sqdn	2/Lt A Preston	POW	
			Sgt H Stewart	POW	

DH4	F5839	18 Sqdn	Lt F M Macfarland	MIA	
			2/Lt A Peterson	KIA	
DH4	A7852	18 Sqdn	2/Lt H Cardwell	Safe	*
			2/Lt H O'Mort	Safe	
SE5a	D6935	32 Sqdn	2/Lt F C Pacey	MIA	
SE5a	C1124	32 Sqdn	Capt H L W Flynn	MIA	
DH9	D7202	98 Sqdn	2/Lt R T Ingram	KIA	
			2/Lt K J W Dennitts	MIA	
DH9	D2863	98 Sqdn	Lt Gowing	Safe	*
			2/Lt J G W Halliday	KIA	
DH4	D9235	25 Sqdn	Lt S Crossfield	Safe	*
			2/Lt C F Boyce	KIA	
SE5a	B8503	60 Sqdn	Lt C S Hall	Safe	
BF2b	B1344	20 Sqdn	2/Lt W F Washington	MIA	
			2/Lt K Penrose	MIA	
BF2b	E2181	20 Sqdn	Capt H P Lale	Safe	*
			2/Lt F J Ralph DFC	KIA	
Dolphin	C4163	87 Sqdn	Lt F W Ferguson	KIA	
SE5a	C9259	41 Sqdn	2/Lt C E Turner	WIA	
DH9		49 Sqdn	2/Lt A Dewhurst (O)	WIA	*
RE8		4 Sqdn	2/Lt P Ff Giles (P)	WIA	*
AWFK8		10 Sqdn	2/Lt W J Miles (O)	DOW	*
BF2b		48 Sqdn	2/Lt P A Clayson (O)	WIA	*

French Casualties

Salmson 2A2		Sal.?	Cpl van Troyen	WIA	*
			Adj Langlois	WIA	
Spad XIII		Spa.15	Brig Robert Hazemann	WIA	*
Spad XIII		Spa.96	Cpl Pradel	MIA	
Spad XIII		Spa.91	Cpl Dumont	KIA	
Spad XIII		Spa.15	Cpl Chambert	WIA	*
Spad XIII		Spa.15	Lt Schneider	WIA	*
?		?	S/Lt F Wachter (O)	WIA	*
Bréguet XIV	B2	Br.66	1/Lt D Schaeffer (O) USAS	WIA	*

Wednesday, 4 September 1918

British Front

The air action on this day began at 0555, with 4 Australian Flying Corps Squadron's Captain E J K McCloughry destroying a balloon at Erquinghem, near Armentières, for his 18th victory. Ten minutes later Lieutenant O B Ramsey got another over La Bassée—for his first. As it got lighter, the airmen could see that the day was bringing the best weather so far this September —fine but cloudy.

Further south, on the Cambrai front, the action started as eleven SE5a fighters from 60 Squadron, patrolling above the US 148th's Camels, attacked five Fokker biplanes, claiming three, between 0630 and 0635. Second Lieutenant M D Sinclair shot down one off the tail of Lieutenant McEntagart, the Fokker spinning in between Paillencourt and Bourlon. A second Fokker went down in flames to an American with 60, Lieutenant Oliver Johnson over Epinoy, following which five others got on his tail:

> '...shot me up and drove me to the ground. My engine had cut out and my prop was completely shot off. Ten Fokkers were between the lines and me and I had to dive steeply and land near Queant at 0700.'

A third Fokker went to a 19-year-old Scot from Edinburgh, Lieutenant George Metcalfe Duncan at Cambrai—his 6th victory. Duncan reported the initial five Fokkers, then five more —then another five! This was typical of the way the multiple layered Jasta formations fed into a fight. Duncan claimed the leader of the last five.

Leutnant Theo Quandt of the blue-tailed Jasta 36 claimed again, this time an SE5a over

Queant for his 15th victory, but the unit lost Leutnant Kurt Waldheim over Abancourt and Unteroffizier Reinhold Neumann, the latter being shot through the stomach, although he got back and landed at base. He died in hospital later that day. The Americans of the 148th located the fight over Marquion, west of Cambrai, claiming five Fokkers.

First Lieutenant Henry Clay, who claimed two, saw an SE5 being chased by ten DVIIs across the Canal du Nord, south of Sains les Marquion, which, he said, sported blue tails and black noses. Clay's first victim was witnessed by McEntagart of 60, then he shot another from the tail of Lieutenant Starkey's Camel. Clay had then to be rescued from the attentions of three Fokkers by Lieutenant Clayton Bissell, who also claimed two kills. His first dove into a wood near the Canal du Nord, then as he went into a vertical dive and climbing turn, he got on to the tail of a second Fokker, firing 300 rounds before it went down out of control.

Vizefeldwebel Alfred Hübner of Jasta 36 claimed another SE5 over Mercatel which was flown by Lieutenant H T McKinnie of 64 Squadron. This unit was seen entering the fight by Duncan. McKinnie was initially reported missing at about 0700 but was later found wounded inside British lines. Earlier on 64's patrol, at 0645 above Hernu, Lieutenants A M Stahl and T C Sifton collided, with only Sifton surviving a crash-landing—injured—in Allied lines.

Something truly unusual occurred at 0700. The very experienced and aggressive DH9 two-seat bomber crew of Captain R N G Atkinson and Second Lieutenant W T Ganter burnt a balloon over Frelinghien having spotted gas-bags up! Atkinson later reported:

'...three dives were made on one of these and 200 rounds fired into it. While aiming through the Aldis sight, the HKB started smoking at 500 feet, and on turning around to avoid collision, same was not visible and a shroud of smoke only was seen rising from the ground.'

Both 10 Squadron and 15 Corps ground observers saw it burn. At 0745, Captain Sidney 'Timbertoes' Carlin of 74 Squadron, so named because of a wooden leg, shot down another balloon north-west of Armentières for his 9th victory. (Carlin would serve in WW2, flying as a gunner on bombers before being killed on 9 May 1941.) Twenty minutes later, Lieutenant Fred Gordon of the same unit claimed another balloon south of Roulers.

To the south, meantime, the Australian Lieutenant Roy King brought down an LVG CV over Wattignies at 0710 for his 15th victory. Five minutes later, Captain A H 'Harry' Cobby scored his 29th and last victory, sending down a Fokker DVII out of control over the same locality.

Coming back from a bomb raid on Aubigny-au-Bac, 18 Squadron were intercepted by Fokkers, the bomber crews claiming two. One of the crews, Captain G W F Darvill and Lieutenant W Miller, both already with over five kills to their name, turned into the attack. Darvill then discovered his front gun had jammed, so he turned west with a Fokker following. Miller fired back at it, the DVII falling in flames at Cantin at 0750. Miller was then wounded, but continued to fire at another Fokker which they both saw crash at Aubigny. Their bomber (A7815) was shot about and they had to force-land inside the front line.

The initial interception was by Jasta 27, Leutnant Noltenius shooting up Darvill and getting as good in return, as will be seen. 18 Squadron lost A7853 to Leutnant Frommherz at Recourt—the German's 20th victory. Immediately after this, Jasta 27 and Jasta 26 became involved in a fight with 70 Squadron's Camels.

This occurred soon after 0800, a patrol, 12-strong, running into serious trouble in the form of JGIII. Of the twelve Camels—two entire flights—only four returned. Two Camel pilots claimed two victories over Escaillon (some 12 km due east of Douai) at 0815, one destroyed in flames, by the Canadian Lieutenant Ken Watson, and the other shared by Lieutenants D H S Gilbertson and J S Wilson. Gilbertson's victory was reported by Wilson on his return, as the former was among the missing. Both claims were for the ubiquitous Fokkers of JGIII, who in this combat inflicted the single biggest loss of fighters in one fight, suffered by the Allies in WW1. Wilson described the fight as beginning when Gilbertson and he:

'...dived on several EA. We engaged one machine and I fired about 120 rounds into it. The EA stalled and spun towards the ground well out of control. I also saw another Fokker diving vertically with clouds of smoke coming from the cockpit.'

This was confirmed by Captain Morgan, the only other returnee. Ken Watson reported:

'While on OP at 0815 over Escaillon, the patrol dived on 15 Fokker biplanes and a further 15 Fokkers dived on the patrol, coming out of clouds from 12,000 feet. I saw one EA on Lt Gower's tail. I engaged him at close range and shot him down in flames.'

JGIII claimed eleven Camels between the Sensee Canal and Douai, to the west of Escaillon, credited as follows:

0810	Ltn Ehlers	Jasta 26	Palleul	2nd victory
0810	Oblt F Dahlmann	JGIII	Palleul	5th victory
0812	Vzfw E Buder	Jasta 26	Cantin	11th victory
0812	Oblt F Dahlmann	JGIII	Palleul	6th victory
0815	Ltn O Fruhner	Jasta 26	Cantin West	23rd victory
0818	Vzfw F Classen	Jasta 26	Cantin	6th victory
0820	Hptm B Loerzer	JGIII	Monchecourt	37th victory
0820	Ltn O Fruhner	Jasta 26	S Douai	24th victory
0825	Vzfw E Buder	Jasta 26	Gouy	12th victory
0830	Ltn O Fruhner	Jasta 26	S Douai	25th victory
—	Vzfw A Lux	Jasta 27	Cantin	6th victory

Of the eight pilots lost, four were captured, including patrol leader Captain John Forman and Second Lieutenant Bill Rochford, younger brother of Captain L H 'Tich' Rochford, the star turn of 203 Squadron and one of its flight commanders. In Rochford's book (*I Chose the Sky*, Wm Kimber, 1977) he noted that 70 Squadron had been caught well over the lines by superior numbers. Certainly two of JGIII's three BMW Fokker DVII Jastas were involved and, significantly, 70's Camels were described as Clerget-powered machines, with 20 less horsepower than the Bentley-motored machines 203 were flying. Bill Rochford and Forman escaped from their captors and were at large for a few days, but were eventually picked up again. Leutnant Noltenius may have been directly involved, as evidenced by this extract from his diary:

'After a while a lively aerial battle with a strong Sopwith squadron commenced. I tried hard to get higher up in order to catch one of them, if possible, when he attempted to fly back to his lines. I was successful in this: I caught one and spiralled downward with him to 300 metres. Then a section of my top wing broke off—the part aft of the second main spar—and I had to give up. [In a fight with "Bristols"—most likely 18 Squadron's DHs—he had been well shot up, including a grazing hit along his flying helmet.] The Sopwith afterwards landed in a normal manner. In the course of the fight another Sopwith came to the assistance of the first one. I evaded him and continued to pursue the first opponent. This plane was later shot down by Lux. Fruhner also claimed this one. The decision had not yet been made, but it will no doubt be like this: Lux one, Fruhner the other one.'

Noltenius was not happy with the way some of what he saw as his victims were awarded to other pilots. The Germans, unlike the Allies, did not 'share' victories. They were also, on this occasion, credited with three more Camels than were lost. Jasta 57, led by Leutnant Paul Strähle, was also involved in this fight, observing JGIII shoot down two DH4s. They were then attacked by 23 (!) Camels and survived until JGIII attacked. Leutnant Johannes Jensen and Vizefeldwebel Hechler were severely shot about, and Gefreiter Tegtmeyer badly wounded by a shot in the stomach.

Oberleutnant Fritz Röth, the leader of Bavarian Jasta 16, claimed a DH9 over Neuf Berquin at 0830 for his 23rd victory. This was either a 4 Squadron RE8 that force-landed at 0815, or it may have been a Bristol from 88 Squadron, who were in a fight timed slightly later. This was at 0900, 88 becoming involved in a half-hour combat south-west of Lille with

Fokker DVIIs and Triplanes. Captain Edgar Johnston and his gunner, Lieutenant W J N Grant, claimed two of the former and one of the latter. Four more German machines were claimed, mostly out of control, although Johnston's veteran machine—C4867—which he'd flown since March, was damaged. The four Bristol crews were all 'ace' teams.

Soon after this, DH9s of 107 Squadron, out on a bombing raid to Valenciennes, were intercepted. The bombers, as was usual at this stage of the war, were escorted by Bristols—this time from 62 Squadron. The resulting fight lasted half an hour and drifted well to the south and east of Cambrai, where Jasta 58's aerodrome at Emerchicourt was situated. Leutnant Martin Demisch of this unit captured the Bristol of Lieutenant W K Swayze and his observer Second Lieutenant W E Hale at 1000. After the war, 'Pete' Swayze, who had achieved six victories, reported that he had suffered engine failure and was then forced down onto the German airfield. Swayze only survived the war by a few months, dying in 1920 in Toronto.

Meantime, Jasta 58 shot down two DH9s, one falling to Leutnant Spille at Helesmes, the other to Vizefeldwebel Jeep at d'Hivergies Ferme. One Fokker was seen in flames over La Sentinelle, being hit by Second Lieutenant F T Scott and Sergeant W J Palmer from 107 Squadron. Jasta 39 pilots saw the scrap and waded in, shooting down two more DHs; Unteroffizier Müller at Chelmes at 1010, and Unteroffizier Nülle at St Aubert five minutes later. 107 lost three aircraft, while Jasta 58's Vizefeldwebel Dünnhaupt was wounded.

Pilots of 2 AFC, 32 and 48 Squadrons were in action shortly before 1000, and just after the hour, Camels of 3 Squadron, operating in the Bapaume to Cambrai area, encountered Fokkers. Lieutenant David Hughes was driven back to the lines by three of them when two broke off. The other continued to fight, but Hughes, a Welshman, in F1972, managed to shoot it down. Flieger Otto Wagner of Jasta 79b fell into British lines and was captured. Hughes also had to come down, his Camel having been hit in the fuel tank, and written off.

Wagner was the fourth of five victories for Hughes, who was still only 19 years old. He had only been in the services since August 1917. As an interesting aside, Hughes trained between then and November, then served as an instructor at 37 TDS. Taught to fly fighters in April 1918, he became an instructor again until June at which time he joined 3 Squadron with a total of 270 flying hours—far above the average. He obviously had talent which he used to good effect.

Other 3 Squadron pilots were engaged and three more Fokkers were claimed, but they lost a 20-year-old Londoner, Second Lieutenant Ralph Tedbury, who had been with the unit since 10 August. He died of his injuries later this day. Aside from Jasta 79b, this combat involved Jastas 1 and 6. Vizefeldwebel Georg Staudacher, aged 20, shot down a Camel at 1010 in the Sailly-Cambrai area, while Leutnant Richard Wenzl got one south of Paillencourt. Lieutenant William Hubbard, an experienced ace of 23, claimed one of the Fokkers which had a yellow tail with black and white stripes on elevators and top wing. Hubbard had first attacked a biplane which was shooting down a Camel but had to turn in pursuit of the colourful machine described. On the edge of this action, 57 Squadron's bombers were returning from a raid on Marcoing, claiming one Fokker crashed and another out of control.

Bristol Fighters of 11 Squadron had a fight east of Cambrai at 1045, and at the same time Captain Tom Falcon Hazell gained his 38th and 39th victories by downing two balloons at Bernes and Gouzeaucourt. One of his flight, Lieutenant Ernest P Crossen, strafed the parachute of one of the observers. This may sound a bit unsporting, but this often happened, the view being that a downed balloon was one thing, a dead observer who would no longer be able to bring fire and destruction to Allied troops, a bonus. More likely it was spite too, as balloonists had parachutes and Allied pilots did not.

Near Arras, Leutnant Ernst Bormann of Jasta 2 gained his 9th victory by downing the SE5a flown by Lieutenant V H Harley of 64 Squadron. Ten minutes later, an American who would run up the highest score in 92 Squadron, Lieutenant Oren J Rose, claimed a Halberstadt C-type just west of Douai.

Shortly after midday, 4 AFC burnt two balloons south-east of La Bassée and south of Armentières. Later in the afternoon, 84 Squadron flamed the Douvieux balloon, shared by Second Lieutenants Stephen Highwood and C R Thompson. Steve Highwood was a 21-year-old from Morden, Kent. An exceptionally aggressive pilot, his claim was the first of nine balloons and an aeroplane during September. 'Ruggles' Thompson, whose 5th victory this was, was a 23-year-old South African.

One of the former RNAS veterans from April 1917, Captain Art Whealy DSC DFC of 203 Squadron, brought down, at 1615, a Fokker which had just set a balloon on fire near Trescault. The balloon, 11-9-13, had been shot down by Leutnant Erich Just of Jasta 11, his 6th victory, causing Lieutenants H Tallboy and J McGilchrist to parachute to safety. In fact Just survived the encounter and Whealy's victim was likely to have been Vizefeldwebel Hans Reimers of Jasta 6, who had achieved two victories, and who was shot down and mortally wounded by a Camel. He died the next day. This was the Canadian's 27th and last victory, and by the end of this momentous month, he was on his way back to Canada.

Another April 1917 veteran was in combat at 1815 near Auberchicourt south of Douai. Six Bristols out on a recce job were attacked by five Fokkers from cloud. Captain Alex Morrison, a 24-year-old from Middlesborough on his second tour with 11 Squadron, saw one coming and his observer, Sergeant R Allan, shot it down into a field near Hamel. The Squadron claimed another out of control south of Douai. (As a matter of interest, the post-war idea that small formations of two or three Bristols cruised about over the lines looking for Germans was a total myth by this stage of the war. Where opposition was expected, the recce squadrons like 11, sent out large patrols of one or two Flights.)

Another top German pilot gained a kill this day, Leutnant Arthur Laumann, Staffelführer of Jasta 10 being credited with his 28th and final kill of the war. No details are known, other than that the German daily communiqué specifically mentioned it. The most likely victim was Lieutenant E O Champagne, who force-landed mid-afternoon after being hit by a Fokker, following which his Camel burnt out.

During the day, the leading balloon buster of the war, Belgian Lieutenant Willy Coppens, burnt the Boverkerke balloon, to bring his score to 30.

French Front

As with the British front, the weather was good in the morning before clouding over in the afternoon. The French suffered seven combat casualties as well as losing four balloons.

Three of the balloons were shot down by the Germans on the 7 Armee sector. The first by Unteroffizier Heinrich Haase of Jasta 21 west of Sarcy at 0915 was that of a V Armée balloon of the 27 Cié, from which Sergent Euribert baled out. Another balloon was lost in this sector, that of 26 Cié, which burnt at 1104, Adjutant Boitard jumping safely. This was the 20th victory of Vizefeldwebel Karl Schlegel, who had been with Jasta 45 since May 1918. Obviously the loss of the unit's Staffelführer a few days before had not deterred Schlegel from his path to becoming the third most successful balloon buster on the German side. Coincidentally, Jasta 45 was also the third highest claimer against balloons and the highest scoring Jasta of the 'Amerika Program' Jastas formed from late 1917.

Interestingly, the German communiqué noted that at the location of Haase's and Schlegel's claims, an unsuccessful attack was made on a balloon, resulting in a Fokker landing in French territory, with 30 hits from three Spads. The unknown pilot then repaired the engine and flew home before being captured! Adjutant Armand Berthelot, a 24-year-old from the Finistère area of France, shared an EA with Sergents Faucade and Barat at 1130, and these events are believed to be connected. It was Berthelot's 8th victory, the others' first.

Leutnant Berling, another Jasta 45 pilot, claimed a balloon at 1830 and whilst Sergent Godefroy was injured jumping from the basket, his balloon did not catch fire. The 25 Cié's balloon was lost to Unteroffizier Baumgarten of Jasta 67, with both observers, Caporals Aboucaya and Guilbert, making safe landings.

Not to be outdone, the French too attacked balloons. Spa.152's leading balloon buster, Sous Lieutenant Leon Bourjade, aided by Sous Lieutenant Ernest Maunoury and Caporal Etienne Manson, combined to burn the Pont Arcy balloon (west of Soissons) at 0645.

Capitaine Jean de Luppe, the CO of Spa.83, attacked the German balloon lines near Filain, in company with Sous Lieutenant Devilder. They flamed one but de Luppe was brought down and captured near Celles-sur-Aisne, probably falling to Leutnant Arthur Korff of Jasta

60. It is often very difficult to tie up victim and victor with certainty, and this applies to the loss of a Bréguet of Br.19 in the IV Armée sector. It was hit by AA fire and came down in the front lines, its pilot wounded. However, Leutnant Werner Preuss of Jasta 66 gained his 14th victory by downing a French two-seater near Crécy-en-Mont, which may relate to this event, pilots and flak units often contesting claims.

Two other German aircraft were claimed by pilots of GC13 and GC17, covering the sector across from the 18 Armee. Adjutant Jacquot of Spa.100 claimed a fighter near Breuil-sur-Vesles at 1145, while Sous Lieutenant Marcel Coadou, aged 21, of Spa.15 and Adjutant Delzenne of Spa.88—both future aces—shared, with Adjutant Pinot of Spa.84, a scout in German lines. At midday, near Lavannes, Sous Lieutenant Robert Volmerange, who had joined Spa.38 on 1 June, claimed a C-type.

On the debit side, Jasta 17's Leutnant Seifert claimed a Spad near Souilly at 1130. Sergent René Touchard of Spa.68 was killed in action by either Offizierstellvertreter Gustav Dörr or Leutnant Hans Rolfes, both of the highly active Jasta 45. They claimed Spads north of Fismes at 1300, their 26th and 16th victories respectively. Maréchal-des-Logis Camille Chambrey of Spa.92 was shot down and captured, probably by Leutnant Werner Pechmann of Jasta 9, timed at 1715 near Soissons. At an unrecorded time, Vizefeldwebel Fritz Jacobsen of Jasta 73 downed an AR2 for his 8th victory.

The British Independent Air Force sent 55, 99 and 104 Squadrons to bomb Buhl and Morhange aerodromes, without loss.

American Sector

Concentrating now on the St Mihiel Salient, the Americans suffered six casualties, plus two balloons, against claims for three aircraft with two more probables.

First Lieutenants J Dickenson Este and Rob Roy S Converse of the 13th Pursuit Squadron were on patrol and engaged a Rumpler C above Nancy, which, they reported, had a green fuselage and white tail. They chased it from 1019 to 1027, last seeing it going down in a wide spiral over Pont-à-Mousson. This was not credited, nor was another two-seater—an Albatros—chased by the veteran commander of the 13th, Captain Charles Biddle, near Mamey at 1015. Biddle, who was 28, and a cool leader, had previously served with the French Spa.73 and then the US 103rd Pursuit, before becoming the CO of the 13th Aero 'Grim Reapers' in July 1918.

The 96th Bombardment Squadron, sent out eight aircraft to bomb the rail facilities at Dommary-Bareancourt at 1050. The formation was attacked by ten Pfalz scouts, some sporting red fuselages; one was seen to have black wings and another a white triangle pennant-shaped design on the fuselage, aft of the cockpit. One Pfalz, caught in the cross-fire from the Bréguets, was seen to crash near Laubeville. First Lieutenants Arthur Hadden Alexander and John Charles Earle McLannan were both wounded, Alexander in the small of the back, McLannan four times in the legs, but the pilot brought them back. For this action Alexander received the DSC. Two other observers were wounded, First Lieutenants Donald D Warner being hit in the hip, while Avrone N Hexter caught a bullet above the eyes. The bloodletting of the 'First Team'—as the American day bombers have since been called—was beginning.

Four Salmson 2A2s of the 91st Observation Squadron were operating over Rembercourt, but were spotted by four Fokkers. One of the two-seaters, crewed by 25-year-old First Lieutenants Frederick Vernon Foster and Raymond R Sebring, had taken off late and was trying to catch up the others. Leutnant Eugen Siemplekamp of Jasta 64w dived on them at 1105, shooting them down over Thiaucourt for his 4th victory. Foster survived as a prisoner and lived well into his nineties. Meantime, First Lieutenant Victor Strahm and Captain James E Wallis, shot down a Pfalz over Rembercourt, with another EA unconfirmed. These were the first victories by the 91st Aero. Strahm, from Nashville, Tennessee, would become a two-seater ace.

One of the balloons lost on the American sector was that of the 10th Balloon Company, which was flamed at 1230, with observers Lieutenants E R Likens and D G Boyd making safe descents. The other loss was a French balloon of the 43rd Cié, burnt near Ansauville five minutes earlier. Unteroffizier Bader of Jasta 64 got the American balloon—his 2nd victory—

but he was pounced on by Lieutenants Frank B Tyndell, Arthur Raymond Brooks and Clinton Jones of the 22nd Aero, who sent his Fokker down into German lines after wounding the man.

	A/C	KB			DES	OOC	KB
RAF losses	24	1		RAF claims	30	21	11
French losses	3	4		French claims	4		3
American losses	1	2		American claims	3		—
IAF losses	—			IAF claims	—	—	—
German claims	40†	6		German losses	5		9
† Four to flak.							

British Casualties

Aircraft type	No.	Squadron	Crew		
RE8	E111	4 Sqdn	Lt E L Barrington MC	Safe	*
			2/Lt W G Greenaway MC	Safe	
DH4	A7853	18 Sqdn	Lt W B Hogg	MIA	
			2/Lt A E Stock	MIA	
DH9	D3106	107 Sqdn	2/Lt J C Boyle	POW	
			2/Lt F C B Eaton	KIA	
DH9	F6172	107 Sqdn	Lt E R L Sproule	POW	
			2/Lt G T Coles	POW	
DH9	C6169	107 Sqdn	Lt B E Gammell	KIA	
			2/Lt F Player	KIA	
BF2b	D7945	62 Sqdn	Lt W K Swayze	POW	
			2/Lt W E Hall	POW	
BF2b	C4867	88 Sqdn	Capt E C Johnston MC	Safe	*
			2/Lt W J N Grant	Safe	
Camel	F1972	3 Sqdn	Lt D J Hughes	Safe	
Camel	C8333	3 Sqdn	2/Lt R N Tedbury	DOW	
Camel	B5434	46 Sqdn	2/Lt C H P Killick	POW	
Camel	B9269	70 Sqdn	Lt J L Gower	POW	
Camel	D9416	70 Sqdn	Lt J A Spilhaus	KIA	
Camel	D9458	70 Sqdn	2/Lt K H Wallace	KIA	
Camel	E1472	70 Sqdn	Lt D H S Gilbertson	KIA	
Camel	D3406	70 Sqdn	2/Lt W M Herriott	POW	
Camel	D9418	70 Sqdn	2/Lt S W Rochford	POW	
Camel	C8239	70 Sqdn	Capt J H Forman	POW	
Camel	D1930	70 Sqdn	Lt R McPhee	POW	
Camel	D9501	80 Sqdn	2/Lt E O Champagne	Safe	
SE5a	E5991	60 Sqdn	Lt O P Johnson	Safe	
SE5a	D6988	64 Sqdn	Lt T C Sifton	Inj	
SE5a	E1273	64 Sqdn	2/Lt A M Stahl	MIA	
SE5a	E4002	64 Sqdn	2/Lt H T McKinnie	WIA	
SE5a	E5979	64 Sqdn	Lt V H Harley	POW	
AWFK8		10 Sqdn	Lt A H E King (O)	WIA	*
DH4	A7815	18 Sqdn	Capt G W F Darvill	Safe	*
			Lt W N Miller (O)	WIA	
DH4		18 Sqdn	Sgt G A Cribbes	WIA	*
Dolphin		87 Sqdn	Lt V G Snyder	WIA	*
RE8		13 Sqdn	2/Lt H Dobing	WIA	*

French Casualties

Bréguet XIV	3.309	Br.9	Sgt Gauthier	WIA	*
			Sgt Mulot	Safe	
Bréguet XIV		?	S/Lt Malot	WIA	*
			S/Lt Chevrel	DOW	
Spad XIII		Spa.68	Sgt R Trouchard	KIA	
Spad XIII		Spa.92	MdL C Chaimbaz	MIA	
Spad XIII		Spa.83	Capt J de Luppe	POW	
?		Esc.104	Lt Hoppelt (O)	WIA	*
?		Esc.289	Sgt Tardieu (P)	WIA	*

American Casualties

Salmson 2A2	5225	91st	1/Lt F V Foster	POW	
			1/Lt R S Sebring	KIA	

Bréguet XIV B2	#18	96th	1/Lt A H Alexander	WIA	*
			2/Lt J C E McLannan	WIA	
Bréguet XIV B2		96th	2/Lt A N Hexter (O)	WIA	*
Bréguet XIV B2		96th	1/Lt D D Warner (O)	WIA	*

Thursday, 5 September 1918

British Front

The weather this day was described as warm and hazy. Activity built up slowly but by late evening the RAF had made 67 claims. 4 AFC started the ball rolling with another of their early morning marauding raids, during which Lieutenant A H Lockley burnt the Perenchies balloon at 0625. Half an hour later, east of Ploegsteert Wood, Lieutenant C L Childs of 70 Squadron flamed a Fokker DVII. On the German side, Leutnant Fritz Rumey of Jasta 5 shot down the SE5a of Second Lieutenant W A F Cowgill of 64 Squadron, north of Bouchain.

The next action was down at Cambrai at 0950. No. 84 Squadron burnt two balloons south of Poeuilly, credited to the Highwood/Thompson team, a repeat performance of the previous day.

At 1015, a further patrol by 64 Squadron met Fokkers—again Jasta 5. Although the SE pilots claimed four either destroyed or out of control, the Jasta only recorded Unteroffizier Schenk wounded. Soon afterwards, 60 Squadron lost an SE5a to ground fire, north of Hayencourt. Between 1030 and 1100, 80 and 74 Squadrons had tussles with Fokkers, claims being made, for one 74 Squadron loss.

The first large-scale encounter of the day happened at 1100 hours. No. 92 Squadron's SE5s ran into JGIII, flying in company with Jastas 37 and 46. The British unit lost three with another pilot forced to land:

1100	Ltn G Meyer	Jasta 37	E Havrincourt	16th victory
1110	Hpt B Loerzer	JGIII	Inchy/Brebières	38th victory
1110	Ltn Himmer	Jasta 37	NE Ribecourt	2nd victory

Both of the Jasta 37 claims were disputed by Leutnant Auf den Haar of Jasta 46 who failed to have either awarded. No. 92, in turn, claimed three Fokkers shot down: one by the CO, Major Arthur Coningham MC (a future Air Marshal); one to Lieutenant Evander Shapard; the third to a 1917 Spad veteran, Captain W E Reed, on his second tour. Jasta 37 lost Unteroffizier Otto Roesler killed over Flesquières. Lieutenant H B Good, one of the pilots lost by 92, was an ace; another a flight commander, the Australian Captain George Wells, who was captured. The pilot who was lucky to get back was Shapard, being forced to spin almost to the ground, then flying back at a height of 20 feet. On landing it was found that the main spars of all four wings had been shot through as well as both longerons, while a bullet had also lodged in one of the magnetos.

The usual advantage of SE5a units can't be seen from this fight. This was the worst loss suffered by the most junior SE unit in France—only operational since late July; and generally they had the capacity to take someone with them. SE5s could, unlike Camels, run from the huge formations which, the RAF communiqués noted, were cruising around all day. Mostly, the SEs also operated at height, which gave them the capacity to dive away from trouble, again unlike the recent Camel slaughters, which had all taken place at very low level. Camel pilots generally had to fight their way out of tight spots.

The bombers of 57 Squadron were on a raid at this time, near Marcoing, and also claimed Fokkers. Captain Andrew MacGregor, with Sergeant J Grant, claimed one over the town at 1125, other crews claiming two more. One victim was possibly Leutnant Heinrich Hagar of Jasta 32, wounded at 1200 (G). If not, he was likely to have been a victim of 92 Squadron. MacGregor ended his air force career as an Air Vice-Marshal with many decorations. The 20-year-old Scot had started as an infantry officer in the Argyll and Sutherland Highlanders in 1917 before flying training, joining 57 in March 1918. He would die the day before his 87th birthday. For Sergeant Grant, this victory was his 6th.

There were a number of isolated skirmishes from just before noon until the late afternoon, when an avalanche of fights occurred from 1700 hours onwards. One reason for this was that the RAF were slackening their rate of offensive operations, preserving strength for the major offensives. This was a vast change from the previous year. The pilots did not complain, glad of any respite, and this one was an actual request by RAF HQ in a memorandum dated 5 September, only to react if enemy activity increased. Fine words, but there was still a good deal of work to do supporting the ground battles.

One of the encounters involved an April 1917 veteran, Captain Edmund Zink, a former FE2b pilot and now flying an SE5 with 32 Squadron. He manoeuvred behind a two-seater and shot it down over Equancourt for his 5th victory. Another was a scrap between 48 Squadron's Bristols and Jasta 20, the second encounter this month. 48 lost a crew to Leutnant Bruno Hobein over Espières at 1250 although the Squadron did claim a Fokker in flames and another out of control. At 1315 the Germans reported that a single-seater landed near Ostricourt due to engine failure, which was a 73 Squadron Camel.

There was also action up on the North Sea coast. Camels of 65 Squadron claimed five Fokkers east of Ostende, the unit being led by another Bloody April pilot, Captain A G Jones-Williams MC. Their opposition was generally German Marine units, which had, on 2 September, been formed into the Marine Jagdgeschwader, comprising all five MFJ units under the command of Leutnant Gotthardt Sachsenburg.

Another unit who often tangled with the Marine pilots was 213 Squadron, formally the Dunkirk Seaplane Defence Flight of the RNAS. Their Camels claimed two Fokkers this afternoon just south of the German air base at Varsenaere. Second Lieutenant C E Francis was lost to MFJ 4's Vizeflugmaatrose Mayer at Stalhille at 1425. Flugmaatrose Karl Engelfried of MFJ 5 made his second kill by downing a DH9 of 218 Squadron west of Knocke, that had been bombing Bruges. Getting into trouble, Lieutenants J G Munro and T W Brodie staggered across into nearby neutral Holland. This was normal procedure for airmen that could not make it back down the coast. It was also usual for the Marine pilots to claim them. MFJ 5's records do not time this action, but 218 did claim a Pfalz DIII over Bruges at 1650.

In the early afternoon, down on the Bapaume front, the Germans launched an assault on British balloon lines, Vizefeldwebel Kautz of Jasta 46 burning one at Beugny at 1415. Ten minutes later Jasta 6 shot down two at Croisilles, 45-12-3 and 35-12-3, credited to Leutnants Richard Wenzl and Fritz Schliewen. The observers, Lieutenant C T L Smith from the 45th's and Second Lieutenant E F Caton and Sergeant Mechanic A W Woolgar from the other, all jumped safely.

Major Raymond Collishaw, CO of 203, attacked a Fokker that had been balloon strafing near Inchy-en-Artois at 1500 and shot it down into Allied lines where it burned. It was the Canadian's 56th victory—the highest of any pilot still operational in the RAF.

Between 1605 and 1610, 57 Squadron were once more intercepted on a bombing raid. In the area of Marcoing and Avesnes-le-Sec, Captain A MacGregor and Sergeant Grant claimed two destroyed in flames, from the second of which the pilot baled out but his parachute apparently failed. These claims brought Grant's score to eight. Another claim took one of the rare Sergeant Pilots to his 5th victory—Sergeant D E Edgley's observer, Sergeant J H Bowler, sending down a Fokker out of control.

Bristols of 22 Squadron and Camels of the 148th had fights during the afternoon, but on the Ypres front, near Roulers, 210 Squadron got into a scrap with Fokkers. One was claimed by an 18-year-old from Buckinghamshire, Lieutenant Ivan Sanderson for his 11th and final victory. Another was credited to Lieutenant Lowell Yerex, a 23-year-old American from Indiana —both timed at 1730. Upon their return, 210 posted Yerex and his flight commander, Captain Herbert Patey—a 6 Naval Squadron veteran of Bloody April, and an 11-victory ace—as missing. Patey would spend his 20th birthday (25 September) as a prisoner before dying during the influenza epidemic, in February 1919. Yerex was also captured, these pilots being shot down by Jasta 56's Leutnant Lutz Beckmann, the Staffelführer, for his 8th kill, at Winckel St Eloi, and Unteroffizier Ludwig Jeckert.

Captain Harry Cobby, the most successful Australian Flying Corps ace, had finished his tour on the previous day. On the 5th, his old Flight went out without him, and only the leader,

Lieutenant Norman Trescowthick, returned. No. 4 AFC were supposed to sweep the Douai area in conjunction with two other Flights, one of Bristols of 88 Squadron, and one of 2 AFC's SE5s.

Rendezvous was made over Serny aerodrome but they became separated in cloud, so that south-west of Douai only the Camels met two sudden formations of Fokkers, that sandwiched the patrol of five. Four pilots were shot down, only Lieutenant Len Taplin, an ace, surviving as a prisoner. They had been caught at 1800, well south of Brebières by Jastas 26 and 27 of JGIII. The Camels had been flying in the usual 'V' formation and were attacked from above and from two directions at once. Trescowthick gave the signal to avoid action and dived away, but the others were unable to do so and went down to the Fokker pilots:

1800	Ltn H Frommherz	Jasta 27	Marquion	21st victory
1800	Vzfw C Mesch	Jasta 26	Cuincy	9th victory
1805	Vzfw A Lux	Jasta 27	Baralle	7th victory
1805	Vzfw F Classen	Jasta 26	Henin Lietard	7th victory

Leutnant Noltenius briefly mentioned the fight in his diary:

'Almost no activity, when suddenly I saw a burst of flak on my port side over our territory. I did not notice the Englishmen until suddenly two Sopwiths passed by in front of me. I immediately pursued and hit one of them, for a mighty petrol vapour streamer began to issue from the machine, but I had to let him go as the other Sopwith prepared to attack me. Was unable to find my victim, however, and a confirmation was unobtainable.'

Mesch was credited with Taplin. Trescowthick saw Lockley shoot down a Fokker out of control as he was diving away. On return from prison camp, Taplin left this graphic account of his fate:

'The formation went over the line in V-formation, Trescowthick leading, Eddie and Carter above and behind him, and Lockley and myself above and behind them again. When a few miles over we turned north. We were flying at about 14,000 feet and our escort could not be seen; I did not like the situation and climbed another 1,000 feet above the patrol. Soon after this, when in the region of Douai, we were attacked. There were three formations in the attacking enemy, all Fokker biplanes. Two formations of about 12 to 15 machines attacked almost simultaneously, one from high up in the west and one from the north. Later a very much larger formation came in from the east, which I first thought was our escort coming to our rescue.

'Trescowthick dived away under the formation coming from the direction of our own lines, but the others were cut off. No German attempted to follow Trescowthick, so evidently he was unobserved. Meanwhile, I was gaining all the height I could and as the formation from the north closed in, I dived into the middle of them. The leader, a red and white tailed Fokker, pulled up and we went at it head-on. I got a good burst into his radiator and he went down on a glide—not out of control, just engine out of action. Next moment I was right in the middle of them and before I could do anything, a German below me pulled his nose up and put a burst right through the bottom of my machine. One bullet went through my right hand, smashing it up and breaking the wrist. My Camel immediately stalled and half rolled itself and to conform with poetic justice, came out of the stall right on the tail of my attacker, who was recovering from his own stall. I was now under control with my left hand and easily shot this German down. Just then I saw Lockley dropping past me completely out of control. I also saw during the fight two machines in flames, which I suppose were Eddie and Carter.

'I was getting shot about and firing at anything I saw, when a Fokker from somewhere (the sky seemed full of them) again got a burst into me. One bullet, an explosive, smashed the breach and crank-handle of one of my guns and sent a splinter through my nose. This dazed me and I fell out of control in an engine-spin. I spun down to about 1,000 feet and then recovered, to find two Fokkers had followed me down. I again had to fight, and luckily shot one down easily; the other then left me alone. After this fight I was down to about 100 feet and started off towards home. My engine was just about done, from being shot about and from running full throttle through everything. I had only one hand and could not properly control the engine to gain height, so just staggered along. After running the gauntlet of ground fire for several miles I was shot down from the ground when within a few hundred yards of the German front line, and taken prisoner. I found out from the Germans that Lockley was buried in Henin Lietard cemetery but could get no news of the others.'

Jasta 39 continued balloon busting, Unteroffizier Ruppert burning the Dury balloon at 1810, the British losing a 5th Company gas-bag—SR134—from which Lieutenant Birchal and Corporal Kneller parachuted down.

Soon afterwards, to the north of Cambrai, 60 Squadron, out on patrol 11-strong escorting DH4s, ran into another large formation of 25 Fokkers near Avesnes-le-Sec and claimed six between them. Captain John Doyle claimed one in flames and one out of control before he was wounded, shot down and captured. A feature of the battle was that it was fought in a heavy rain storm! One Fokker pilot was seen to bale out. Jasta 4 were the main opponents, and they lost Leutnant Joachim von Winterfeld, in flames, and Unteroffizier Josef Doerflinger who survived. Doyle was claimed by the acting commander of the Staffel—and future Luftwaffe General—Leutnant Egon Koepsch, south of Paillencourt at 1815, his 8th victory. Ernst Udet, the Jasta CO, was on leave.

During the final skirmishes, 29 Squadron made claims for a two-seater south-east of Armentières and 88 Squadron's Bristols claimed five Fokkers between here and Douai. 80 Squadron lost a Camel to flak north of Mericourt, while Leutnant Paul Baümer of Jasta 2 Boelcke shot down a DH4 of the long suffering 57 Squadron for his 23rd victory. Finally 79 Squadron's Dolphins claimed two Fokkers by the two Americans, Gillet and Lord, with 74 Squadron ending the fighting with two out of control Fokkers near Lille at 1910. During the day, Gefreiter Katzner from Jasta 43 was killed when separated from his patrol—time unknown.

An interesting item by another Jasta 43 pilot, Josef Raesch, who had just returned to the front after being shot down on 25 July, confirms the German Air Service's problems. Back on active duty in mid-August, he found there was no aeroplane for him until 3 September and that on the 5th, the Jasta's fuel allocation was cut to 2,000 litres per month. He noted: 'The British are superior to us, not only in numbers but in their tactics and organisation.' Fine words, considering the Germans were knocking down more Allied planes than the Allies were of them, but as can be seen, they were losing the war. Raesch put his finger on the main points as to why.

French Front

Action here was rather light, although the weather was good as it had been the day before. An American serving with the French, Lieutenant F C McCormick in Spa.164, was wounded and forced down at Mons. Two aircraft were claimed as probables by this unit and Spa.124 another.

Two Spads were claimed by the Germans, one to Leutnant Karl Ritscherle of Jasta 60, his 6th, north of Soissons and one to Vizefeldwebel Donhauser of Jasta 17 at 1210—the latter probably Lieutenant Mantcewitch of Spa.76, forced down near Champfleury. Leutnant Werner Preuss of Jasta 66 claimed a Bréguet for his 15th victory, over Villeneuve inside French lines, supposedly Caporal Gaillard and Aspirant Marielle.

Sous Lieutenant Claude Haegelen, Brigadier Guerin and Sergent Peuch of Spa.100 shared a balloon at Soult-sur-Suippe for the French (Haegelen's 14th victory), while on the German side, Vizefeldwebel Karl Schlegel claimed a balloon at Fismes at 1720 for his 20th victory. Sous Lieutenant Fournier parachuted down without injury. There was no recorded action on the American sector.

	A/C	KB			DES	OOC	KB
British losses	18			British claims	32	32	3
French losses	—	1		French claims	—		1

American losses	—	—
IAF losses	—	
German claims	25†	5

American claims	—	—
IAF claims	—	—
German losses	6	?

† Including at least one to flak and one FTL inside German lines.

British Casualties

Aircraft type	No.	Squadron	Crew		
DH4	F6168	57 Sqdn	Lt A Platt	KIA	
			Lt C E Kirton	KIA	
DH9	C1124	218 Sqdn	Lt J G Munro	Interned	
			2/Lt T W Brodie	Interned	
BF2b	E2495	48 Sqdn	2/Lt R Beesley	POW	
			2/Lt A M Miller	POW	
Camel	B778	4 AFC	2/Lt M H Eddie	KIA	
Camel	E1407	4 AFC	Lt L E Taplin DFC	POW	
Camel	E7174	4 AFC	Lt D C Carter	KIA	
Camel	D8136	4 AFC	Lt A H Lockley	KIA	
Camel	F5945	73 Sqdn	Lt T K G Oliver	POW	
Camel	F2133	80 Sqdn	2/Lt A R Thatcher	POW	
Camel	F2143	80 Sqdn	Lt G B Wootton	Safe	*
Camel	B7280	210 Sqdn	Capt H A Patey	POW	
Camel	E4390	210 Sqdn	2/Lt L Yerex	POW	
Camel	D1824	213 Sqdn	2/Lt C E Francis	POW	
SE5a	E1397	60 Sqdn	Capt J E Doyle DFC	POW/WIA	
SE5a	C1876	60 Sqdn	2/Lt S A Thomson	MIA	
SE5a	C1909	64 Sqdn	Lt W A F Cowgill	POW	
SE5a	B8428	92 Sqdn	Capt G A Wells	POW	
SE5a	D6889	92 Sqdn	Lt E V Holland	POW	
SE5a	D372	92 Sqdn	Lt H B Good	KIA	
DH4	F5828	57 Sqdn	Sgt D E Edgley	Safe	*
			Sgt J H Bowler (O)	WIA	
DH4		57 Sqdn	Lt G A Riley (O)	WIA	*
SE5a		60 Sqdn	Lt R C Blessley USAS	WIA	*

French Casualties

Aircraft type	No.	Squadron	Crew		
Bréguet XIV		?	Cpl Gaillard	Safe	*
			Asp Marielle	Safe	
Spad XIII		Spa.164	Lt F C McCormack	WIA	*
Spad XIII		Spa.76	Lt Mancewitch	Safe	*

Friday, 6 September 1918

British Front

Despite the weather being described as fair, there was not much activity this Friday. The ground offensive was winding down, although still continuing, with the front approaching Cambrai in the south.

Not deterred by their setback of the previous evening, 4 AFC were out early once again, with the 6′ 3″ tall Lieutenant Roy King claiming a DFW C as his 16th victory east of Wavrin (between Lens and Lille) at 0630. Also out early was Lieutenant Jesse Creech of the 148th Aero, claiming a Fokker DVII destroyed 1,000 yards north of Bourlon at 0705. He reported that the patrol was attacked by five enemy fighters. A climbing turn brought him back on the tail of the Fokker and he fired 150 rounds from 50 yards.

The first major fight of the day was between the Bristols of 20 Squadron and Fokkers near St Quentin, with no less than seven being claimed by the 'Brisfits'. Despite two in flames and another two seen to crash, there is no corresponding information as to which Fokker unit this was.

At 0915, the Dolphins of 23 Squadron were escorting 205 Squadron on a raid which was intercepted by more Fokkers. Each unit claimed one, but 23 lost Captain N Howarth who was killed. Leutnant Wolfram von Richthofen of Jasta 11 (cousin of the famous Richthofen brothers) claimed a Dolphin east of St Quentin at 0945 (G), whilst Oberleutnant Paul

Blumenbach, the Staffelführer of Jasta 31, claimed one at 0950 (G) north of the town, but only the one was lost.

Another German victory was that claimed by Jasta 4's Leutnant Heinrich Maushacke, who shot down a Camel of 80 Squadron flown by Lieutenant J A McGill at 0953 over Le Catelet. Honours were even at 1025 and once again an RE8 crew proved they could survive in combat. Lieutenants G N Dennis and H D Hewett were taking photographs over Bourlon Wood but were suddenly attacked by seven Fokkers. Hewett grabbed his gun and sent one down in flames.

Five minutes later another large fight erupted over an area west of Cambrai. No. 11 Squadron on a 12-machine patrol were engaged by several formations of Fokkers. Four were claimed but two Bristols were lost in the process. Jasta 2 claimed two BF2bs, the 8th victory of Leutnant Otto Löffler north of Bourlon Wood, and the recently returned Paul Baümer, who had been injured in May, got his second kill in two days—his 23rd overall. He was on the way to 16 kills this September. Another German ace, Leutnant Martin Demisch of Jasta 58, shot down a 52 Squadron RE8 near Monchy on the Arras front 40 minutes later, to bring his own score to seven. Victory no. 8 for him came at 1245, downing the 8-1-1 balloon at Monchy-le-Preux. Just over an hour later the British lost another balloon, this time the 14th Company, to Vizefeldwebel Oskar Hennrich of Jasta 46, his 11th victory.

From midday to late afternoon there were few actions, although 103 Squadron fought Fokkers during a bomb raid near Lille and 32 and 29 Squadrons were in action; around Ostende 213 Squadron were in combat too.

At 1830, 208 Squadron claimed four Fokkers over the Canal du Nord on the Arras-Cambrai road but they lost Lieutenant A H Hiscoe. Two Camel claims were made, by Leutnants Alfred Lindberger and Ernst Bormann of Jasta 2 Boelcke. During this late period, 210, 88, 29, 201 and 2 AFC all had combats and made claims. At 1900 4 AFC and 22 Squadron had the last fights of the day, the latter with a Pfalz DXII over Cambrai.

French Front

Action was quite heavy, as the weather was mostly clear with good visibility. In the VIII Armée sector at 1215 hours, a patrol of Spa.90, consisting of Lieutenants Marc Ambrogi, Jean Lemarie and Sergent Gerard Florentin, engaged a two-seater over Azelot. Florentin forced the machine to land at Romain, east of Bayon for his first victory, but he was himself hit and mortally wounded, dying later. The occupants, Unteroffiziers Weiser and Scharg of Schlacht-staffel 20, were on an orientation flight that in reality became a disorientation flight, and were taken prisoner.

In the X Armée sector, a flight of four aircraft from Sal.18 on a photo mission became engaged in two combats, the first against eight, the second against 20 enemy fighters. During these, Caporal Nal and Soldat Jeandemange were shot down in flames, although their comrades claimed one kill and one probable. The Salmson most probably fell to Hans Rolfes of Jasta 45 who claimed one at 1535 near Magneux. The Jasta, on their way to attack balloons, suffered no losses.

On this Aisne front, five balloons were attacked and two destroyed. Balloons of the 68 and 83 Ciés were flamed along the X Armée sector, with the observers, Lieutenant Charotte and Sergent Gaitz-Hocki making safe jumps. At 1645 (G), Jasta 45, continuing on after the Salmson fight, went for these balloons near Magneux, Rolfes, Leutnants Berling and Krayer claiming one each but only the two were lost.

Over the V Armée sector, a Bréguet XIV of Br.260, flown by Sergent Blovac and Lieutenant Millot, was attacked by two Fokkers, two kilometres inside the French lines above Puisieux (SE Reims) and shot down in flames. The victor was Leutnant Max Näther of Jasta 62, his 12th victory, recorded as shot down at 1742 (G) at Sillery, in the above area.

Other combats this day involved Spa.163 at 0830, and later at 1930; then at 1720, north of Soissons, Vizefeldwebel Knaak of Jasta 9 claimed a Spad fighter. Another went to Unteroffizier Dost of Jasta 21 east of Braisne at 1905. Two Spad pilots were wounded during the day, one each from Spa.75 and Spa.86. Leutnant Martin Haenichen, Technical Officer with Jasta 53, claimed two Spad two-seaters near Coucy-le-Château for his 2nd and 3rd kills. Another Spad two-seater went down to Leutnant Buddeberg of Jasta 50, south of Soissons, at 1120. One of these was crewed by Lieutenant Salvetat and Sous Lieutenant Descousis of Spa.269, who failed to return.

No activity of note was reported in the American sector.

	A/C	KB			DES	OOC	KB
British losses	6	2	British claims		21	23	—
French losses	5	2	French claims		5		—
American losses	—	—	American claims		—		—
IAF losses	—		IAF claims		—		—
German claims	17†	4	German losses		2‡		—

† Two to flak. ‡ Two 2-seaters, with two other airmen killed, one belonging to FA(A)219 falling near Bray.

British Casualties

Aircraft type	No.	Squadron	Crew		
RE8	C2479	52 Sqdn	Lt J Talbot	WIA	*
			Sgt H J Sampson	WIA	
DH9	D3249	206 Sqdn	2/Lt S M Desmond	KIA	
			3AM A Halliwell	DOI	
BF2b	D7906	11 Sqdn	2/Lt E N Underwood	KIA	
			2/Lt C M Coleman	KIA	
BF2b	C4745	11 Sqdn	2/Lt C B Seymour	KIA	
			2/Lt E G Bugg	KIA	
BF2b	F5820	22 Sqdn	Lt L C Rowney	Safe	*
			Sgt J Goodman	WIA	
Dolphin	C8166	23 Sqdn	Capt N Howarth	KIA	
Camel	D9483	80 Sqdn	Lt J A McGill	KIA	
Camel	D9484	208 Sqdn	2/Lt A H Hiscox	WIA	*
DH4		57 Sqdn	Lt G Anderson	WIA	*
Camel		201 Sqdn	2/Lt L G Teale	WIA	*
SE5a		2 AFC	Lt J S Ross	WIA	*

French Casualties

Spad XIII		Spa.75	S/Lt S Tourbe	WIA	*
Spad XIII		Spa.83	MdL A Perrot	WIA	*
Bréguet XIV		Br.260	Sgt Blovac	KIA	
			Lt Millot	KIA	
Salmson 2A2		Sal.18	Cpl Nal	KIA	
			Sol Jeandemange	KIA	
Salmson 2A2		Sal.17	MdL Baillodz	Safe	
			Lt Le Floch	KIA	
Bréguet XIV		Br.269	Lt Salvetat	MIA	
			S/Lt Descousis	MIA	
Spad XIII		Spa.90	Sgt G Florentin	DOW	

Saturday, 7 September 1918

British Front

A 19-year-old from Warrington, Lancashire, who would not survive the war, opened the aerial combat on this day of low clouds and afternoon rainstorms. At 0655, Lieutenant Guy Wareing of 29 Squadron destroyed a balloon at Gheluvelt for his 5th victory. A brave, but not entirely sensible German, rushed out of a nearby building and fired at Wareing with a rifle. He was promptly gunned down by Wareing, whose flight commander, Captain Camille 'Large-arse' Lagesse, strafed the defences during the attack. Five minutes later, 4 AFC shot down a two-seater at Henin Lietard, the claimant being Lieutenant Thomas H Barkell.

At 0700, the whole of 203 Squadron took off from Izel-le-Hameau aerodrome, led by Captain Leonard Henry Rochford—known universally as 'Tich' due to his small stature. At 0815 they attacked five Fokkers and Rochford shot down one north of Bourlon Wood for his 27th victory.

Major F I Tanner, serving with 80 Squadron following an extensive stay with 4 AFC, claimed a two-seater in flames south of Cartigny at 0930, while Captain George Gates of 201

Squadron gained his 10th victory with another two-seater at Noyelles. Gates noted that the observer baled out successfully, although actually, both crewmen had jumped from their FA(A) 263 machine, but only the pilot—Vizefeldwebel Hansen—survived. The observer's parachute failed, sending 24-year-old Leutnant Rudolf Brammer to his death. This two-seater was also claimed by Captain M E Ashton and Lieutenant T D Fitzsimon, in a 12 Squadron RE8.

Leutnant Fritz Rumey of Jasta 5 made the first German kill of the day, by downing a lone recce DH4 from 205 Squadron, for his 33rd victory. The pilot, Lieutenant Meller, died but the observer, Lieutenant J C Walker, survived a prisoner. Jasta 5's CO, Oberleutnant Otto Schmidt, gained his 13th victory by claiming a balloon at Bertincourt.

DH9s of 211 Squadron were bombing a road north-east of Gravelines mid-morning, losing one machine possibly through a collision, which dived into the sea. Although the French rescued the men, the observer died.

At around 1130, 84 Squadron went on a balloon strafe and burnt four balloons between St Quentin and Bellenglise. One was the 44th victory of the Squadron's star turn, Captain A W Beauchamp-Proctor who would later be awarded the Victoria Cross. Another SE5a pilot, Second Lieutenant J B Bowen, an American serving with 32 Squadron, was not so lucky as he was caught and shot down by Leutnant Julius Schulte-Frohlinde of Jasta 11.

Bad weather now curtailed flying until the late afternoon. No. 20 Squadron's Bristols and 98 Squadron's DH9s both had combats in the early evening, and then the Dolphins of 23 Squadron claimed a Fokker. Another Jasta 11 pilot, Wolfram von Richthofen, gained his 6th victory by downing an SE5a west of Le Catelet at 1840. This was probably Lieutenant R F Bush of 92 Squadron who failed to return but, due to imprecise records, may only have force-landed. Five minutes later von Richthofen and Jasta 11 ran into a patrol of 84 Squadron, he and Oberleutnant Erich von Wedel each shooting down one. Very unusually, the RAF made no claims at all in this fight.

The last RAF claim for the day was a two-seater at 1910, north-east of Marquion, to a patrol of 54 Squadron. During the day the Germans lost two more two-seater crews in British lines, presumed to ground fire. They were Gefreiter Rudolf Knust, who was killed, and Leutnant von Neufville, prisoner, of FA(A) 259 at St Leger. The other was an LVG crew, Vizefeldwebel Hermann and Leutnant Schneider of FA(A) 219, both taken prisoner.

French Front

The weather on the French front was described as cloudy and windy, but despite this the level of combats was high. Second Lieutenant David W Lewis, an American serving with Spa.79, was engaged by four enemy aircraft near La Fere. He reported shooting one down but the others pursued him, riddling his Spad and wounding him. He crash-landed in the front lines, evidently the victim of Leutnant Hofmann of Jasta 79, who was credited with a Spad at 0710 by Villequier-Aumont, about ten kilometres west-south-west from La Fere, for his second victory.

It was a rough day for the French two-seater crews. On the Aisne front the Spad XI of Sergent Malot and Sous Lieutenant Monin was shot down in flames but they managed to survive—probably downed by Leutnant Bornträger of Jasta 49, near Auberive at 1030. On the IV Armée sector, Sergent Thomas and Sous Lieutenant Miles of Spa.140, on a photo mission, were attacked by two Fokkers and failed to return. They fell victim to Leutnant Hermann Habich, also of Jasta 49, at St Hilaire at 1035.

Another was lost in the II Armée sector, Adjutant Videcoq and Lieutenant Broca of Spa.47 failing to get back from a sortie; they were seen going down near Pannes. They were probably the 'Salmson' shot down by Lieutenant Oliver Freiherr von Beaulieu-Marconnay at 1225, north-east of Montsec, where Pannes is located. 'Beauli' had been the Staffelführer of Jasta 19 for just five days, and this was his 14th victory; one week precisely before his 20th birthday and ten months after he had become operational. Jasta 19 was part of JGII—the BMW Fokker-equipped Circus which was just moving into the St Mihiel salient area.

On the VII Armée sector, Maréchal-des-Logis Clerc and Sous Lieutenant Thirion of Sal.5 were shot down—probably to ground fire—and crashed north of Einville at 1645, the pilot killed and the observer wounded. Adjutant Chenard and Sous Lieutenant Plebert of Br.221 were killed in combat near Chavannes-les-Grandes, apparent victims of Leutnant Hermann Stutz, Staffel-führer of Jasta 71, who claimed a Bréguet XIV west of St Ulrich for his 4th victory. This was the only claim and loss in the VII Armée sector, opposite the German Armee-Abteilung 'B' sector.

To offset these losses, a balloon was burnt by Sous Lieutenant Austin of Spa.92 north of Beaurieux in the X Armée sector, while another was claimed in the V Armée sector by Sous Lieutenants Michel Coiffard, Henri Condemine and a newcomer of three weeks, Sergent Charles Peillard. Coiffard, who was 26 years old, and had now scored 25 victories, had been wounded six times in the infantry before becoming unfit for military service. He promptly joined the aviation service, eventually being assigned to Spa.154 on 28 June 1917. His medal citations, written with Gallic flair, for once, did not overstate their case. He was lauded as being a man of 'exceptional fighting qualities', 'rash bravery' and 'exceptional bravery'. Condemine was 23 and came from the infantry via a severe wound while with the cavalry. He was also a recent arrival, having joined the Escadrille on 22 August, but would gain nine victories by the Armistice.

On the Champagne front, Sous Lieutenant Louis Douillet and Sergent Max Caton of Spa.124 claimed a Fokker west of Dontrien.

American Sector

A Salmson of the 91st Observation Squadron, crewed by Lieutenants A W Lawson and H W Verwohlt, was attacked at 1130 hours over Conflans by six EA and was forced to land behind German lines. It was later learned that both men had been captured, with Verwohlt wounded. They had fallen to one of the units of JGII, the second organised Circus, which was beginning to operate against the US forces. They were to inflict massive losses on the Americans, for the same reason JGIII was doing it to the RAF: the best aircraft and pilots available, added to the general level of inexperience of the Americans. Vizefeldwebel Albert Haussmann of Jasta 13 shot them down—his 13th victory—at 1130, near Jeandelize. Haussmann had been operating since 1916, a fighter pilot since Bloody April, and knew his stuff.

First Lieutenant Warren T Kent, 49th Pursuit Squadron, departed on patrol at 1205 with three other pilots. The patrol was attacked by eight Fokkers over Thiaucourt, and Kent was last seen going down in this vicinity. Later in the month the American infantry found a grave marker being made in a house at Pannes, which is between Thiaucourt and Essey. The marker was for an American First Lieutenant who was killed this day. Vizefeldwebel Josef Hohly of Jasta 65 claimed his 5th victory, a Spad, at 1315, near Essey, about three kilometres south of Pannes.

At 1600, three men of the 213th Aero claimed a two-seater south of Essey, near Flirey, while the 22nd and 94th Squadrons each damaged a two-seater.

IAF

For the first time during this month, the IAF was intercepted in the process of dropping two and three-quarter tons of bombs on various targets. Six planes of 55 Squadron bombed the railway at Ehange, while 11 DH9s of 99 Squadron, led by Major Lawrence A Pattinson and Captain W G Stevenson, with ten more DHs from 104 Squadron, led by Captains R J Gammon and E J Garland, attacked Mannheim with two tons of bombs. Take-off was around 1100, with height and position assumed over base 40 minutes later. Soon after reaching German lines, the force was attacked by six-plus enemy fighters. 104 Squadron's gunners claimed three Germans destroyed, two by Gammon and gunner Second Lieutenant P E Appelby (one a flamer) timed at 1230 and 1400—while at the latter time, Lieutenant J W Richards and Sergeant W E Reast destroyed another. Richards and Reast had a slightly defective engine and staggered to and from the target, 2,000 feet below the rest of the formation. For their courage, they were badly shot up and Reast mortally wounded. Observer gunners, protected only by a piece of fabric, often suffered high casualties, for there was no armour plate in WW1. Given the proximity of the pilot to the observer in a DH9 (they were farther apart in the DH4), the rear man tended, on occasion, to act as 'armour' for the pilot's back!

The fight lasted 70 miles to the target and another 70 back, lasting four hours in all. Three crews of 104 and one from 99 failed to return. Two were shot down by Leutnant Georg Weiner, the commander—since 1 September—of Jasta 3, falling at Burscheid and Dassberg. Weiner, who had turned 23 on 22 August, and who would end up a Major General in the Luftwaffe, had served previously with Kest 3 since August 1917 after being wounded with Jasta 20. He died on 24 January 1957; these DHs brought his score to six. The other two fell to Kest 1a, led by a Jasta 5 veteran of Bloody April, Oberleutnant Rudolf Nebel, for his 2nd kill, and Unteroffizier Heinrich Forstmann for his 1st. One of Kest 1a's victims fell at Frankenthal, the other at Zabern (99 Squadron's machine) where it was contested by Kest 3. Nebel's combat report reads as follows:

'Just before 2 pm on 7 September 1918, as leader of the formation of ten aircraft of Kest 1a, I attacked a British bomber formation of 19 DH9s. I was immediately hit three times in the propeller, and once by an explosive bullet in the hand pump, which was shattered. One part struck me in the face causing me to momentarily lose my senses. In order to assess damage, I descended beneath the enemy formation and then immediately unsuccessfully attacked from there.

'Thereupon I dropped behind the enemy formation and despite most extreme enemy opposition, attacked the last DH9 about ten times. Because of the volume of fire which was met by each attack, I was forced to turn away. I could follow my fire well because I used 'Leucht-spur-Munition' (tracer bullets). Because of my accurate fire, the enemy aeroplane descended lower and lower below his formation. I last attacked in the region of Neidersbrund. During this attack, I received hits which damaged the engine mounting. This, and the damaged propeller, caused excessive vibration which made flying impossible. Whilst the fall of the Englishman was clearly a matter of time, I was denied the pleasure of seeing the crash of the machine I had hit. The enemy aircraft fell about 800 metres beyond the place of my last attack and shortly after my emergency landing. I enquired of its fate and was told that it had fallen at Buchsweiler. I fired 650 rounds at very close range during my attacks, received 29 hits in my propeller, engine, pressure pump and one glancing bullet which hit my shoe.'

Nebel's machine, Fokker DVII (Alb) 666/18, was equipped with wireless telegraphy which had enabled Kest 1a to be directed on to the DH9 formation south-west of Mannheim, where they attacked the bombers at 3,400 metres height. The IAF's bombing missed hitting any significant targets. Whilst Nebel was attacking, Feldwebel Schiller was hit in the lower jaw and spun down unconscious, recovering just in time to pull out of the spin and land. Unteroffizier Forstmann reported:

'On 7 September 1918 near 2.15 pm, in my Albatros DVa, in the company of my Kettenführer, Leutnant Korner and Unteroffizier Sonnabend, I attacked an enemy bombing formation SW of Mannheim. After I had fired about 100 rounds I saw the Englishman suddenly go down. In the meantime, I had come so close to the enemy formation that my radiator was shot up and I had to land immediately. I saw the Englishman, who was gliding down, chased first by a Fokker and then a Roland aeroplane. I could see no more because of hot water splashing in my face.'

Leutnant Kurt Seit of Jasta 80b, also claimed a DH9 as his third victory, which he saw stagger into Allied lines and force-land—Richards and Reast! Major Pattinson, Captain Gammon and Lieutenant Appelby all received the DFC five days later.

As this raid was ending, a lone recce DH4 of 55 Squadron, flown by one of the unit's Americans, Lieutenant Don J Waterous, with Second Lieutenant C L Rayment as observer, was intercepted and shot up by seven EA. The DH4 crew staggered back over the lines, claiming one German possibly out of control over Saarburg at about 1400.

The bloody battles which had been going on all summer between the Germans and the IAF were continuing into September. Most of the damage was inflicted by the German front line Jastas over whose territory the IAF had to fly to reach their mainly German targets. In turn, the IAF, as can be seen, could and did take a lot of their opponents with them. The performance and armament differentials were so small between bomber and fighter that no one had a clear advantage, unless the Fokker DVII-equipped units broke up the IAF formations.

	A/C	KB			DES	OOC	KB
British losses	6		British claims		11	4	5
French losses	4		French claims		1		2
American losses	2	—	American claims		—		—
IAF losses	4		IAF claims		3	1	—
German claims	18†		German losses		4		4‡

† Three to flak. ‡ Plus one that broke loose.

British Casualties

Aircraft type	No.	Squadron	Crew		
DH4	D9271	25 Sqdn	2/Lt C H Saffery	Safe	*
			2/Lt J Harrington	WIA	
DH4	A7587	205 Sqdn	Lt D J Mellor	KIA	
			2/Lt J C Walker	POW	
DH9	D2918	211 Sqdn	Lt E S Morgan DFC	Safe	
			2/Lt R Simpson	KIA	
SE5a	C1123	32 Sqdn	2/Lt J B Bowen	KIA	
SE5a	C8895	84 Sqdn	2/Lt W B Aldred	WIA	
SE5a	D6917	84 Sqdn	Lt E C Bateman	KIA	
SE5a	C9064	92 Sqdn	Lt R F Bush	MIA	
Camel	D1887	65 Sqdn	Capt A W Jones-Williams MC	Safe	*
Dolphin		79 Sqdn	Capt H P Rushforth	WIA	*
DH9	D3268	104 Sqdn	Sgt E Mellor	MIA	
			Sgt I Bryden	POW	
DH9	D7653	104 Sqdn	2/Lt J E Kemp	POW	
			2/Lt E B Smailes	DOW	
DH9	D7210	104 Sqdn	2/Lt W E L Courtney	POW	
			2/Lt A R Sabey	DOW	
DH9	D2916	99 Sqdn	Lt G Broadbent	POW	
			Lt M A Dunn	POW	
DH9		104 Sqdn	Lt W J Richards	Safe	*
			Sgt W E Reast	DOW	
DH4	A7942	55 Sqdn	2/Lt D J Waterous	Safe	*
			2/Lt C L Rayment	Safe	

French Casualties

Aircraft type		Squadron	Crew		
Spad XIII		Spa.79	2/Lt D W Lewis US	WIA	*
Spad XI		Spa.140	Sgt Thomas	MIA	
			S/Lt Moles	MIA	
Bréguet XIV		Br.221	Adj Chenard	KIA	
			S/Lt Plebert	KIA	
Salmson 2A2		Sal.5	MdL Clerc	KIA	
			S/Lt Thirion	KIA	
Spad XI		Spa.47	Adj Videcocq	MIA	
			Lt Broca	MIA	
Spad XI		Spa. ?	Sgt Malot	Safe	*
			S/Lt Morin	Safe	
?		?	S/Lt Le Floch	DOW	*

American Casualties

Aircraft type		Squadron	Crew	
Spad XIII		49th Aero	1/Lt W T Kent	KIA
Salmson 2A2		91st Aero	1/Lt A W Lawson	POW
			1/Lt H W Verwohlt	POW

Sunday, 8 September 1918

British Front

The weather was overcast with some rain. Combats were the fewest for the month so far. At 0635, Captain D H M Carberry and Lieutenant J B V Clements of 59 Squadron, in RE8 C2327, encountered and shot down a Halberstadt two-seater, sent another down out of control ten minutes later and then forced a third to land. The first two constituted Carberry's 3rd and 4th successes in air fighting. One victim was from FA(A)239, crewed by Leutnants von Schwere (wounded) and von Rudzins, who crashed near Flesquières. Lieutenant Roy McConnel of 46 Squadron got another two-seater, this time a Rumpler, in flames south of Peronne at 0700.

The first fighter versus fighter clash came at 0815, 24 Squadron claiming three Fokkers between Le Catelet and St Quentin. The known loss was Gefreiter Kurt Blumener of Jasta 6 who baled out over Beaurevoir but his parachute failed to open. Captain G B Gates of 210 Squadron burnt yet another two-seater over Cantaing at 1020. The Albatros's observer baled out too but the 'chute caught fire. This was probably Leutnant Albert Klingsporn, just eight days short of his 22nd birthday, observer with FA(A)252.

The Germans made no claims against the RAF, who none the less lost two RE8s to ground fire—3 AFC and 15 Squadrons.

French Front

As on the British front, aerial activity was light, due to the weather turning to cloud and rain in the afternoon. One aircraft was shot down by ground fire on the X Armée front, coming down between the lines west of Prosnes. Both men scrambled to the safety of their front line trenches despite intense rifle and machine-gun fire directed at them. Another airman was killed by ground fire in this area.

American Sector

Some action took place here, although most units were held back because of the preparations for the St Mihiel offensive. A five-strong Spad patrol from the 95th Aero departed at 0830 to patrol between Watronville and St Mihiel, but lost Lieutenant Norman Archibald to flak about 0900, being forced to land near Etain to become a prisoner. He later wrote the book *Heaven High, Hell Deep* covering his experiences.

In the afternoon, First Lieutenant Jacques Swaab of the 22nd Aero became separated from his patrol and encountered Fokkers over Morhange. He claimed one in flames at 1235 at 150 metres, having come out of low cloud near a German airfield. He then had to fight his way back, claiming two more Fokkers at 1305 before becoming lost and landing well away from his base aerodrome.

	A/C	KB		DES	OOC	KB
British losses	—	—	British claims	5	2	—
French losses	1	—	French claims	—		—
American losses	1	—	American claims	3		—
IAF losses	—		IAF claims	—		—
German claims	1		German losses	3		—

British Casualties

Aircraft type	No.	Squadron	Crew		
RE8	D4814	3 AFC	Lt T J Pengilly	Safe	*
			Lt O G Whitcombe	Safe	
RE8	D4847	15 Sqdn	Capt A R Cross	Safe	*
			Lt H A Coysh	Safe	
DH9		206 Sqdn	2/Lt J D Russell (P)	WIA	*

French Casualties

			Crew		
Two-seater			Lt Verdieret	Safe	
			Lt Moulloud	Safe	
Caudron R11		C.46	S/Lt P Artur (O)	KIA	*

American Casualties

Spad XIII	4662	28th Aero	2/Lt L Moriarty	WIA	*

Spad XIII	95th Aero	1/Lt N S Archibald	POW	
Salmson 2A2	88th Aero	1/Lt E A Wagner (O)	WIA	*

Monday, 9 September 1918

Strong winds, low clouds and heavy rain storms set in on this day and would remain for the next few days. Very little aerial activity occurred, with almost all flying stopped. This gave the aviators a welcome respite, especially in view of the major offensives coming up.

The RAF made no claims and only reported one combat casualty, a 35 Squadron AWFK8, which force-landed near Epehy at 1600, and had to be struck off, having survived a near disastrous encounter with a shell.

The French and Americans had no combat losses either. The Germans made one claim, by Hauptmann Eduard von Schleich, the commander of Jagdgruppe 8, who claimed a Camel over Queant.

		British Casualties		
Aircraft type	**No.**	**Squadron**	**Crew**	
AWFK8	B4179	35 Sqdn	Lt P E Mercer	WIA
			2/Lt A E Harris	Safe

Tuesday, 10 September 1918

The weather was as foul as the previous day, with the French and Americans having no combats nor losing any machines. The RAF lost three aircraft, one pilot and had an airman wounded. Firstly a RE8 which had to force-land following damage from gunfire at 1020, then an AWFK8 was hit by AA fire, which came down behind the front lines and smashed near Hulloch at 1400 hours. Finally a Camel responded to a wireless call near Lens. This meant that a ground station had reported a two-seater sending signals to the ground, and a fighter of 208 Squadron was sent off to intercept it, but the pilot failed to return. The Germans reported a Camel down south of Merignies at 1545 with engine trouble.

		British Casualties		
Aircraft type	**No.**	**Squadron**	**Crew**	
RE8	D4852	4 Sqdn	2/Lt J Sharp	Safe
			Lt S Leslie	Safe
AWFK8	D5149	10 Sqdn	Lt Stacey	Safe
			Lt Mann	Safe
Camel	F1399	208 Sqdn	Lt J P Lloyde	POW
RE8		59 Sqdn	2/Lt S E Rowley	WIA	*

Wednesday, 11 September 1918

Although on this day the Germans claimed one Allied aircraft by flak, none were lost. This was probably an Australian RE8 hit by machine-gun fire during a contact patrol, but it got back, although its crew had been wounded. However, Allied artillery fire did destroy a German balloon. The weather was again appalling, and bad weather or not, the big offensive was planned for the morrow.

		British Casualties			
Aircraft type	No.	Squadron	Crew		
RE8		3 AFC	Lt T L Baillieu	WIA	*
			2/Lt F A Sewell	WIA	

Thursday, 12 September 1918

British Front

Wind and heavy rain reduced operations. No night bombing was undertaken and only one ton of bombs was dropped by day. Only one RAF machine was lost too—a 48 Squadron Bristol that left at 1715 on an OP to Menin. Jasta 35 claimed two aircraft: an AWFK8 by Leutnant Rudolf Stark, near Hermies, and a RE8 to Gefreiter Caspar Schmidt over Queant. Stark and Schmidt overhauled the RE8 near Cagnicourt, Schmidt following the RE down in a series of steep spirals and seeing it hit the ground between Riencourt and Queant, on the British side. Stark then found another two aircraft at low level, being fired on by AA and he attacked a 'Big Ack' over Havrincourt. His bullets appeared to go into the pilot's cockpit whereupon the two-seater heeled over and spun down to crash on the railway line near Hermies. Despite this, there is no information in RAF records to identify the British crews; either they must both have survived injury and their aircraft could not have been seriously damaged, or Stark's Jasta was guilty of severe optimism and overclaiming. The BF2b had to be too far north to be considered a victim of either Jasta 35 pilot.

French Front

On this first day of the St Mihiel offensive (in an area located between the Moselle and the Meuse Rivers) the weather was shocking. The Heights of the Meuse on the western face of the salient was a hilly, wooded area which extended into the area for quite a distance. The nearby Woevre plain was flat and covered with woods and lakes.

Low clouds and heavy rain, combined with strong winds made flying dangerous enough, without enemy opposition. All the French casualties were from the Division Aérienne, assigned to the operational area of the 1st American Army. Forty-five planes of the 1st Brigade d'Aviation (Groupement De Goys) dropped 9,000 kilos of bombs and fired 3,500 rounds at ground targets for the loss of two aircraft from GB 5.

Forty-five Bréguets of GB5 had bombed and strafed the St Beniot, Beney and Fresnes-en-Woevre areas, as well as attacking barracks near Vigneulles. The two aircraft from Br.29 were lost because, according to the French, they were so low; they were hit by blast from their own bombs. However, both Bréguets were claimed by German fighter pilots.

The Second Brigade (Groupement Duseigneur) sent out 37 aircraft which dropped 4,920 kilos of bombs and fired 1,750 rounds at ground targets. Three aircraft failed to return, including the CO of Br.13, Commandant Rocard, plus one aircraft from each of Br.128 and Br.132.

Two of the Bréguets were lost to fighters near Conflans, well to the rear of the lines—one accounted for by Leutnant Georg von Hantelmann of Jasta 15, an ex-cavalry man who was yet to turn 20, for his 7th victory, west of Conflans at 1035. The other was shot down by Jasta 64w's Unteroffizier Bader at Friauville. The others (the two GB5s and the third 2nd Brigade a/c) were lost near the lines claimed by Jasta 13—Leutnant Kurt Hetze (the second not confirmed) and Leutnant Grimm, all over Thiaucourt. Two bombers returned with wounded gunners. Three of JGII's four Jastas were to make kills this day.

A balloon was shot down by Br.131, showing that the British were not the only bomber crews to attack balloons, although the claimants were both American, Lieutenants Carlyle L Nelson and James M Newell, serving with the French.

American Sector

One of the first sorties by the Americans, into the terrible weather, was by the 22nd Aero, whose unit insignia was a shooting star. Second Lieutenant Vaughn McCormack, one of the veterans with two victories, led off their patrol at dawn. He crashed on landing having apparently been hit by ground fire, and was killed.

The 135th Observation Squadron lost three DH4s during the day. The first was lost heading out into low cloud—in places down to 100 feet—and heavy rain at about 0500, never to return. It was hit by an Allied artillery shell and crashed in flames just north-east of Flirey, whilst supporting the 89th American Division. The crew that left at 0620 did not return either. This crew became lost in bad weather and fierce winds, finally landing in Switzerland where they were interned.

Shortly after 0600, Captain Ray Bridgeman led out another patrol from his 22nd Aero and in appalling weather near the Bois le Pretre encountered a Hannover CLIII, shooting it down at 0655. The Hannover was last seen going straight down, out of control, through low clouds. Bridgeman's engine was then hit by ground fire and he had to force-land beyond the former German front lines near Remanauville. Forty-five minutes later Lieutenant Joseph Fritz Wehner of the 27th Aero attacked and damaged a balloon near Montsec.

The German balloon from Ballonzug 55, north-east of Pont-à-Mousson on the east bank of the Moselle river, was flamed at 0905. The Germans noted the attack was pressed to within 50 metres and that their observer, Leutnant Klemm, was shot through the chest and severely wounded. The American pilot was Lieutenant Frank Luke Jr, in aircraft No.21, also of the 27th Aero:

'Saw 3 EA near Lavigneulle and gave chase following them directly east towards Pont-à-Mousson where they disappeared towards Metz. Saw enemy balloon at Marieville. Destroyed it after three passes at it, each within a few yards of the balloon. The third pass was made when the balloon was very near the ground. Both guns stopped so pulled off to one side. Fixed left gun and turned to make one final effort to burn it, but saw it started, the next instant it burst into great flames and dropped on the winch, destroying it.'

Frank Luke landed near an American balloon to get confirmation of this his first victory. He took off to return home but was forced down again by engine trouble, returning the next morning. Luke, an unknown man from Arizona, had no victories to his credit, like most of his colleagues. He was not over popular in the Squadron, being a bit of a loner, but things were to change for this youngster, who had reached the age of 21 on 19 May, and who had been with the 27th since 26 July. After an unconfirmed claim on 16 August—which is why he made sure of confirmation on this occasion—Luke was to claim 18 times in September, in a meteoric career of unbelievable aggression and courage, combined with an apparent disdain for whether he survived or not. Fellow ace Ken Porter—late in a long life—remembered Luke as being 'mad'. Whatever others thought of him, and of one of his favourite retorts to fellow pilots of '...what's it matter, scared?', he was by far the best USAS fighter pilot of the war.

Major Lewis H Brereton, destined to be a general in the next war, but recently appointed the commander of the 1st US Observation Wing, and Capitaine Vallois (a senior French liaison officer), in a Salmson of the 12th Aero, were attacked at 1000. The pilot most likely to have been responsible for shooting them down was Leutnant Max Klieforth of Jasta 13, who claimed a Salmson at Thiaucourt for his first victory. Brereton's machine crashed near this town—in Allied lines—with Vallois wounded.

Mid-morning, the American fighters, who were doing a vast amount of ground strafing and bombing, encountered more opposition. First Lieutenant Charles D'Olive of the 93rd Aero claimed a Fokker between Jaulny and Vieville-en-Haye:

'Lieut. D'Olive states that at about 1020 Sept. 12th, between Jaulny and Vieville-en-Haye (which is slightly east of Thiaucourt) and at about 500 metres, he in company with Lieut. Cox saw EA, possibly a Fokker monoplane. Thinking Lieut. Cox had not seen the Hun, he dived and began shooting at about 350 or 400 metres. He saw tracers litter the cockpit. He had only fired 25 or 30 rounds when he turned into a cloud. He turned away to come home and just glanced backwards towards the cloud and under it saw the machine going down in a steep spin or spiral at about 250 or 300 metres. One magneto quit then and he lost sight of the Hun.'

The USAS credited D'Olive with a victory, on evidence which even the RAF would not accept at this stage of the war; the French never did. When considering American claims, the reader should be aware that the American confirmation rules were much less rigorous than the other Allies, presumably to encourage their relatively inexperienced pilots who, as they gained experience, tended to dispense with what may best be termed 'faith kills'. This is not a criticism of D'Olive, or other American pilots who would prove over the rest of the war to be as good as anyone at this dangerous profession having learnt far more rapidly than these other nations, but rather of their commanders, who encouraged this form of self-delusion that proved so costly to the RAF.

The American Day Bombardment Group lost three planes during the day. The first was the result of a brave but suicidal action by an extraordinarily brave crew. First Lieutenant Andre Gunderlach, the pilot, was a veteran of French bomber and fighter squadrons and was the flight leader of the first 10 Bréguets of the 96th Squadron standing by on their airfield. Due to bad weather, Gunderlach and his observer, Lieutenant H Pennington 'Pinky' Way, chose to go alone to bomb Bruxières, three miles over the lines near Montsec. They argued the weather was too bad for a formation.

Loaded down with bombs they left at 1045—and almost made it. They were shot down in flames and killed near Commercy, well into Allied lines, by eight Fokkers. Feldwebel Beschow of Jasta 64w, claimed his second and final victory, near Broussey, the only Bréguet claim well inside Allied lines, although the time of the kill, in some accounts, was at 1000, but more likely 1200.

The next loss was that of Lieutenants George M Crawford and James O'Toole, who departed at 1100 for a recce over Dampvitoux in a 96th Aero DH4, although Crawford was on detachment from the 20th Aero. The mission was carried out at 50 metres, with the result that they lost their engine to ground fire, according to Crawford upon release from prison camp, and force-landed east of Pont-à-Mousson, O'Toole dying from a severe leg wound. They were also claimed by Oberleutnant Erwin Wenig, the CO of Jasta 80b, who downed a US DH4, whose crew was captured, at Phlyn, which is east of Pont-à-Mousson.

Before the third loss, a DH4 of the 50th Observation Squadron, crewed by Lieutenants Henry Stevens and Edward Gardner, departed at 1030 on a recce mission over the US 82nd Division, who held the line on both sides of the Moselle river. They fell to Leutnant Franz Büchner, who had turned 20 in January 1918, but who had been on active service since 1914. He had flown through Bloody April with Jasta 9, staying with that unit until August 1917, scoring just one victory. By June 1918 his score was two, then the Fokker DVII arrived. He became leader of Jasta 13 on 15 June with four victories and by the morning of this day, had brought his score to 20. He would score more victories in Black September—17—than any other German pilot.

The 135th's third loss also came after midday, during Jasta 13's foray. Six Fokkers flew down the Moselle to the south of Metz, reportedly burnt a Spad (two-seater)—the 50th Aero DH4—then found and shot down this 135th machine in flames near Vilcey-sur-Trey. The DH4 broke up and the observer was flung—or jumped—from the flaming wreck. The pilot was found dead in the wreckage, mercifully from a bullet in the head. This kill was also made by Büchner. The 135th received six DSCs for this day's work—to Messrs Benell, Blezer, Coleman, Hart, Morse and Suiter.

More losses came. The 12th lost a machine near Fey-en-Haye at 1210, possibly by Jasta 64w, Offizierstellvertreter Trautmann, who put in a claim for a Salmson near Flirey. The crew were unhurt and later claimed a Fokker Triplane during their fight.

Franz Büchner made it three for the day by downing an 8th Observation Squadron DH4 in his green-nosed, blue-fuselaged DVII. Lieutenants Horace W Mitchell and John W Artz had taken off from Ourches aerodrome at 1330 on a counter battery mission. At 1430, having completed their task, they turned for home but were attacked by two Fokkers and a Rumpler. During the fight, their motor was hit, Artz being wounded, and forced down to be taken prisoner. After his eventual return, Artz reported:

'During the engagement, our engine was disabled, forcing us to land about 12 km inside the German lines, near a village. The enemy continued firing until our plane had stopped moving on the ground and we were out of it. I received a flesh wound during the attack.'

(Mitchell was later questioned about the Liberty engine which powered his DH4.)

During a rainstorm, the 1st Observation Squadron lost a Salmson 2A2 which had departed at 1400 on a recce sortie. They were attacked near the lines and came down on the right side, although the machine burst into flames on impact, the observer being killed; Harry Aldrich, the pilot, was seriously burned. They probably fell to Oberleutnant Oskar von Boenigk, commander of JGII, whose 22nd victory was a Salmson at Thiaucourt.

Several American Spad pilots were hit or staggered back with motor troubles during the day. One was Lieutenant Lansing 'Denny' Holden of the 95th, who noted in his diary:

'I was flying low, perhaps 800 metres, 3-4 kilometres behind the lines, when my motor dropped from 1900 revs to 1500, barely enough to keep me in the air. I turned for our lines, the motor turning slower and slower. I was gliding down; there was nothing but shell-torn fields and woods below. I started to land when a shell hit in a trench just below me; was it Allied or German? I kept on, just skimmed over a wood and dropped to the ground on probably the one spot it was possible to alight without smashing. The field was covered with barbed wire and shell holes. I heard the rattle of a machine-gun and saw something with blue move in the woods—French or German? I had expected to see American khaki. Most heavenly sight: a French poilu waved to me—I had landed 600 yards behind the front line.'

Later that day, Holden's machine was repaired and he flew it home.

A Salmson of the 104th Observation Squadron, transferring to a new base, strayed over the lines in bad weather and was shot down by ground fire on the west side of the salient. The crew remained missing until the observer, Corporal A C Johnson—wounded—was discovered in a hospital abandoned by retreating Germans some time later.

The leading ace in the USAS was lost late in the day. First Lieutenant David Endicott Putnam, a Harvard graduate, was still only 19 years old despite a wealth of experience of air fighting. Born 10 December 1898, he had sailed to join the French Air Service in April 1917 while still under age to join the American Aviation Service. He had joined Spa.94 in December on the Chalons front before being moved to a Morane Saulnier monoplane-equipped Escadrille MS.156. Up to 1 June, Putnam had claimed four confirmed and eight probable victories. He then transferred to the famous Spa.38, home of Felix Madon. On 2 June—his first day with the unit—Putnam made two confirmed kills, followed three days later by one confirmed and four probables in one fight. With a score of nine confirmed and 15 probables by mid-June he joined the 139th Aero, having been commissioned into the USAS on the 10th. The aggressive Putnam had operated so far over the German lines he was often unable to get the required ground witnesses needed for a confirmed victory while with the French.

By the morning of the 12th, Putnam had run his score to 12, being the leading light of the newer, younger 2nd Pursuit Group. Near Limey at 1830, a patrol of the 139th ran into Fokkers. He was on patrol with Lieutenant Wendell A Robertson at the time, and shot a Fokker off Robertson's tail before falling in American lines, south-east of Limey, to Leutnant Georg von Hantelmann of Jasta 15, at 1835 (A). He was the 8th of von Hantelmann's eventual 25 victories. The German was also 19 and this, his second claim of the day, robbed the USAS of one of its finest officers.

At the end of the day, despite dreadful weather and fierce opposition, the French and American air crews were in complete command of the battlefield. On the ground the attack had been successful, although the Americans would suffer greatly from inexperience here as well. The cost had been low in terms of the number of sorties flown, but the American army co-operation units and their fighters had shown they could operate as a cohesive force.

During the day, the 'ordinary' Jasta 64w had made three claims and the other 'ordinary' Jastas, 77b and 80b, one each. The three component Jastas of JGII that had scored with their BMW-powered Fokkers, had made the other eight claims. This started JGII on an incredible run of 89 victories in a week for some seven losses!

As will be seen, this slaughter was costly to the French, American and British (in the IAF), but it did not in any way hinder or stop the Allied Air Services from accomplishing their tasks. As with the RAF to the north, all the crack Jagdegeschwaderen could do was to make it a Black September for their victims.

The 28th Aero lost Lieutenant George Woods to the Germans, brought down by flak (FZ69) although his loss has been variously quoted as being on the 12th, 13th, and 14th.

	A/C	KB			DES	OOC	KB
British losses	1	—	British claims		—	—	—
French losses	5	—	French claims		—		1
American losses	15	—	American claims		7		1
IAF losses	—		IAF claims		—	—	
German claims	16	—	German losses		?†		1

† Certainly no apparent personnel lost.

British Casualties

Aircraft type	No.	Squadron	Crew	
BF2b	E2527	48 Sqdn	Lt H A Cole	POW
			2/Lt C R Gage	POW

French Casualties

Bréguet XIV		Br.29	Lt Mariage	KIA
			S/Lt Lavidalie	KIA
Bréguet XIV		Br.29	Lt Quatrebarbe	KIA
			Sgt Delhommeau	WIA
Bréguet XIV		Br.13	Cmdt Rocard	MIA
			Lt de Loisy	MIA
Bréguet XIV		Br.132	Sgt Godin	MIA
			Sgt Laigros	MIA
Bréguet XIV		Br.128	Sgt Cardenne	MIA
			Cpl Mallet	MIA
Bréguet XIV		Br.13	Lt Renon	WIA	*
Bréguet XIV		Br.13	Lt Jicquel	WIA	*

American Casualties

Salmson 2A2		1st Aero	1/Lt H D Aldrich	WIA
			1/Lt D Ker	KIA
DH4		8th Aero	1/Lt H W Mitchell	POW
			2/Lt J W Artz	POW
Salmson 2A2		12th Aero	Maj L H Brereton	Safe
			Capt Vallois (Fr)	WIA
Salmson 2A2		12th Aero	1/Lt D Arthur	Safe
			1/Lt H T Fleeson	Safe
DH4		50th Aero	1/Lt H L Stevens	KIA
			2/Lt F H Gardner	KIA
Bréguet XIV		96th Aero	1/Lt A H Gundelach	KIA
			2/Lt H P Way	KIA
Bréguet XIV		96th Aero	1/Lt G M Crawford	POW
			2/Lt J A O'Toole	POW
Bréguet XIV		96th Aero	1/Lt E M Cronin	Killed
			2/Lt L C Blacker	Inj
Salmson 2A2		104th Aero	1/Lt D Johnson	KIA
			Cpl A D Johnson	Evaded
DH4		135th Aero	2/Lt J W Bowyer	KIA
			1/Lt A T Johnson	KIA
DH4		135th Aero	1/Lt W C Suiter	KIA
			2/Lt G E Morse	KIA
DH4		135th Aero	1/Lt T J D Fuller	Interned
			1/Lt V Brookhart	Interned

Spad XIII	139th Aero	1/Lt D E Putnam	KIA	
Spad XIII	139th Aero	2/Lt V R McCormack	KIA	
Spad XIII	13th Aero	Capt R Bridgeman	Safe	*
Spad XIII	28th Aero	1/Lt G B Woods	POW	

Friday, 13 September 1918

British Front

As in April 1917, the flyers in September 1918 had to contend with a Friday the 13th. On this second day of the St Mihiel offensive there were low clouds and high winds with rain that only began to clear in the afternoon.

There was extremely limited action on the RAF front due to the weather. In fact the first action did not occur until 1050, Jasta 35b engaging DH4 bombers, claiming one—Leutnant Rudolf Stark with Vizefeldwebel Hofmann at Recourt. However, there were no RAF losses this day, except an observer in 48 Squadron being wounded. Perhaps once more, identification was poor and the DH4s were in fact Bristols. At 1500 in the afternoon, Leutnant Josef Jacobs, the highly successful air fighter and CO of Jasta 7 recently back from leave following his award of the Pour le Mérite, claimed an RE8 in the Kemmel-Bailleul area, but inside Allied lines.

At 1759, Lieutenant A E Reed of 29 Squadron claimed a black-fuselaged Halberstadt two-seater south-east of Doulemont, but again there are no known two-seater losses. The final claim of the day was a Fokker biplane to the 17th Aero, one of two that had been attacking a 13 Squadron RE8 at 1850. This may have been Leutnant Karl Plauth of Jasta 20, who was shot down but not wounded on this date. The only real success was a balloon of the British 8th Company which Leutnant Martin Demisch of Jasta 58 burnt near Monchy-le-Preux at 1840 for his 9th victory.

During the evening, however, the most successful fighter unit of the RAF in WWI, at least in terms of a victory to loss ratio, made their first claim of the month. They were 151 Squadron, specialised night fighters, flying Sopwith Camels. Flying at night they hunted German night bombers, mostly caught by searchlights. Manned by highly experienced night flyers from extensive service countering night bombing against England, 151 would score a total of 26 victories for no loss to enemy action by the war's end.

At 15 minutes past nine o'clock, Captain W H Haynes in E5142 shot down a Gotha GV near Bapaume, in flames. Haynes also had another success as his combat report notes:

'At 9.15, I observed EA at 7,000 ft travelling west, held in the Peronne and Somme searchlights. I closed to about 25 yards and below the EA's tail and fired two bursts of 30 rounds each. The EA immediately burst into flames and fell near Manancourt.

'I then proceeded to my patrol at Bapaume. At 9.45 pm I saw an EA travelling NW at 8,500 ft over Bapaume, being held in a concentration of searchlights. I was some distance away and EA turned ENE and passed out of range of the searchlights, when he turned west again. I observed EA's exhaust and followed, eventually overtaking him.

'I closed to within 50 yards and took up a position behind and below the EA's tail. I fired two bursts of 50 rounds each; the EA immediately turned to the right and went down. I could follow his course downwards by the exhaust, the sparks from which increased in number. I last saw him going down in a slow spiral about five miles NE of Bapaume. I did not see it crash.'

Haynes' first kill was witnessed by the CO of 151, Major C J Quintin-Brand DSO MC. At 2150, a Friedrichshaven GIII of Kampstaffel 1 of Bogohl 1 was shot down by Lieutenant E P Mackay in F1979 of 151, near Moislains; the crew of Leutnants Kole, Schwaderer and Gefreiter Vowinkel were all captured. Mackay's Camel was equipped with two 'speeded up' Vickers guns.

French Front

Again action was limited. On the French II Armée front, three aircraft of Br.225 were on artillery spotting duties between Conflans and Jarny. Suddenly they were attacked by a dozen Fokkers. The two Bréguets acting as protection had their controls shot away and were forced to land in the front lines, with one gunner wounded. The spotting Bréguet was reported missing, but strangely there are no matching German claims!

All other French activity were by units now attached to the Americans.

American Sector

The operational orders to the Pursuit Groups from the 1st Pursuit Wing required 'barrier patrols', layered in altitude and in multiples of four, giving a minimum strength of eight Spads. Serviceability and weather would intervene. The other hindering factor was that the 2nd Pursuit Group ordered patrols of five with the top cover from another Squadron. The 3rd Pursuit Group allowed all four squadrons—the 28th, 93rd, 103rd and 213th—to strafe roads; a significant move, as will be seen.

All morning, patrols were hampered by low cloud—down to 100 metres at times—and storms. That they were flown at all is one of the advances from 1917. At 1006, the 22nd Pursuit sent out a patrol, with a DH4 of the 20th Aero bringing up the rear, to the area north of Thiaucourt. However, the 'Four' was hit by flak, or suffered engine trouble, and had to land. This experiment of a DH4 flying at the rear of a Spad formation was soon abandoned as useless, the bomber simply being unable to keep station. The 95th's patrol, 1045-1145, came back without Lieutenant Butz, who force-landed near Rampont and smashed his machine. He was unhurt although there is nothing noted as to the cause, but it was possibly ground fire. Another patrol by this unit around midday was out ground strafing, three Spads being forced down, but with no losses.

A special mission by nine Spads of the 93rd departed at 1145, returning without Lieutenant C P Nash, a member of the US Marine Corps. He was probably shot down by Jasta 13, the unit which claimed three Spads over Allamont during the late morning. One went to Franz Büchner, his 24th, another to his brother Felix, his 1st, and one to Vizefeldwebel Albert Haussmann, his 14th. The Büchner brothers also had unconfirmed claims each but obviously insufficient evidence to produce a confirmed victory. Although these are not timed, they were all in the morning.

Gustav Klaudet of Jasta 15 was also credited with a Spad at 1355 over Vionville, the first of two kills for him for the day. This was a machine from the 213th Aero, Lieutenant Frank Sidler.

If Klaudet's is included with Jasta 13's total, they total six. No other JGII claim time is before 1620 hours Allied time. Furthermore, we know what Jasta 13 and 15's pilots were doing later in the day as they nearly had a total disaster!

What occurred was this: as Leutnant Werner Neithammer wrote in *Kamp and Sieg Eines Jagdgeschwader*, both Büchner brothers, Georg von Hantelmann and Neithammer, set off by car with Leutnant Kurt Hetze to visit the front, looking for confirmation of the six claims. Near Woël, the car was strafed by a lone Spad. Evacuating the car with alacrity, the combat veterans were not silly enough to hide under the vehicle but nearby. However, on the second attack Hetze was wounded in the back, bringing his war to an end. He had five victories. The unknown Spad pilot had not only wounded one ace, but had so nearly taken out two more major aces, as well as a future ace! That would have been one of the most effective strafing attacks of the war. Unfortunately for the French and Americans, Büchner and Hantelmann in particular, would soon exact extreme revenge. It also shows the lengths German pilots went to get confirmation of aircraft shot down, and on this occasion, failed to get any and nearly lost their lives in the attempt!

At 1430, a Salmson flight of the 8th Aero headed out, one falling victim to the star turn of Jasta 18, Leutnant Hans Müller, west of Thiaucourt for his 7th victory. A second crew, Lieutenants C H Johnson and E West, returned to make a safe landing, despite being wounded. Another DH4 crew, this time from the 50th Observation Squadron, were forced to fly low because of cloud and came under intense ground fire. They continued their mission as far as six miles into German territory but the observer, Lieutenant F D Bellows, was hit and killed. Lieutenant D C Beebe brought his riddled 'Four' back and both men received DSCs— Bellows' posthumously.

It was not until 1535 that the next air action was recorded. Four Bréguets of the 96th Squadron raided Chambley, although one dropped out with engine trouble. The others ran into Jasta 19, and although the Germans claimed three—Beaulieu-Marconnay and Leutnant Gewart at Cherey at 1720 (G), and Leutnant Scheller at Rembercourt—only two Bréguets failed to get back.

A flight of 13 Spads from the 28th Aero left on a low bombing and strafing attack at 1610 and 35 minutes later, over Jouy, were engaged by three Fokkers. Lieutenant W S Stephenson, the leader, was last seen in combat with a Fokker, a victim of either von Hantelmann (obviously after his car trip) south-west of Thiaucourt at 1707, or Vizefeldwebel Christian Donhauser of Jasta 17, who claimed a Spad at about the same time.

Meantime, 10 Spads from the most experienced Pursuit Squadron—the 103rd—were attacked by Fokkers at 1700, losing Lieutenant Eugene B Jones in flames at Buvières, north of Chambley. Lieutenants Frank O'D Hunter, a 23-year-old from Georgia, and Gorman deFreest Larner, a 22-year-old from New York, who was also a veteran of seven months and two victories with the French Spa.86, avenged the loss, claiming a Fokker as out of control, apparently on fire. Larner had seen the Spad fall in flames and was then attacked by six Fokkers and an Albatros C-type. When the Fokker began to spin down, Hunter followed up the attack as the Fokker pulled up and it spun away again. Both men recieved DSCs for this action. Other US pilots claimed an Albatros DV and a Fokker, plus a Pfalz in flames. In WW2, Hunter, as a Major-General, commanded the Fighter Command element of the US 8th Air Force in Europe.

Also involved in this fight was a patrol of the 93rd Aero. Seven of their Spads were in the area between 1705 and 1720, Lieutenant Charles D'Olive, from Alabama, aged 21, claimed three Fokkers; the first two were shared with Lieutenant George Furlow of the 103rd.

One of the French escadrilles aiding the Americans in the action was Spa.94, who shared a Fokker between three pilots. One was Sous Lieutenant Andre Martinot de Cordou, a 25-year-old veteran of three years of combat flying, and typical of the long serving, successful pilots that formed the backbone of the typical French escadrilles.

Caporal Boulard of Spa.155 was shot down in flames, north of Pont-à-Mousson from 3,500 metres, his demise witnessed by the Americans of the 147th Aero. Oberleutnant Oskar von Boenigk, commander of JGII, claimed a Spad at 1715 over this location for his 23rd victory. Spa.155 claimed a Fokker over Chambley at 1750, credited as the 5th and final victory of 26-year-old Sergent Paul Montange. Vizefeldwebel Klaudet made his second kill of the day at 1720, south-east of Metz. The German losses in this action were Leutnants Siebert of Jasta 15, crash-landed, and Leutnant Eugen Kelber, of Jasta 12, on only his third combat flight, crashed in flames over Mars-le-Tour, probably the victim of Lieutenants L S Harding and L S Carruthers of the 93rd.

Leutnant Adolf Rienau of Jasta 19 was shot down north of Charey at 1900, during a fight with six Spads. He was following one Spad but was then hit from above and behind by another and his controls were shot away. He tried to keep control but finally had to bale out, but due to his delayed jump (from 550 metres), he was only claimed as 'out of control'. The victors were five Spads of the 13th Pursuit that had flown out at 1745, but did not see him jump. One US pilot would fail to return, however, Lieutenant Rob Roy Converse being shot down and captured by what he described as a black-tailed Fokker. He was the second victory of Leutnant Max Klieforth of Jasta 19. Leutnant Oliver Beaulieu-Marconnay claimed another in Allied lines but there were no other Spad losses. Lieutenant J D Este was nearly shot down and had his engine cut out but it caught again and he survived.

IAF

The IAF bombers dropped over five tons of bombs on Ars, Metz, Mars-le-Tour and Arnaville during the day. In the morning these were flown by formations, but also by solo raiders, helped by the weather. After midday, a 104 Squadron crew claimed a Pfalz DIII out of control, south of Metz at 1300 while bombing Metz-Sablon aerodrome.

The DH9s of 99 Squadron had a scrap east of the Moselle river at 1725, Leutnant Hugo Schäfer of Jasta 15 downing one near Pont-à-Mousson at 1740, one of two that failed to return. The other bomber had been tasked to bomb a bridge north-east of Ars. Its pilot was an American, Lieutenant F A Wood, with Lieutenant C Bridgett in the back.

Other crews, two of 99 and one of 104 Squadrons, had wounded on board, one observer mortally, with one machine also having to force-land in Allied lines. Vizefeldwebel Klose of Jasta 54s was credited with one kill at Pont-à-Mousson at 1650, Vizefeldwebel Kurt Delang of the same unit given the other at St Geneviève at the same time.

The night bombers lost one Handley Page (216 Squadron), with another returning from an attempted raid on Buhl airfield with a burning engine, having been hit by flak as it went over the lines. The pilot got it down with its full bomb load at base.

	A/C	KB			DES	OOC	KB
British losses	—	—		British claims	4	—	—
French losses	2	—		French claims			
American losses	8	?		American claims	15		—
IAF losses	3	—		IAF claims	1	2	—
German claims	21	1		German losses	5		—

British Casualties

Aircraft type	No.	Squadron	Crew		
BF2b		48 Sqdn	2/Lt G C Schofield (O)	WIA	*
DH9	D1670	99 Sqdn	2/Lt E E Crosby	KIA	
			2/Lt C Wyatt-Browne	KIA	
DH9	D3218	99 Sqdn	Lt F Wood USAS	POW	
			2/Lt C Bridgett	POW	
DH9	D1668	99 Sqdn	Lt M S Notley	WIA	*
DH9	B9347	99 Sqdn	2/Lt J L Hunter (O)	WIA	
DH9	D1050	104 Sqdn	2/Lt R H Rose	Safe	*
			2/Lt T J Bond	DOW	
DH9	D3263	104 Sqdn	Lt Malcolm	Safe	*
			Lt Alexander	Safe	
HP O/400	3131	216 Sqdn	Lt R W Heine	POW	
			Lt F F Jewett USAS	POW	
			Lt E A Marchant	POW	
HP O/400	D4590	100 Sqdn	Lt J H L Gower	Safe	*
			Lt W B Warneford	Safe	
			Lt R Shillinglaw	Safe	

French Casualties

Spad XIII		Spa.155	Cpl Boulard	MIA	
Bréguet XIV		Br.225	Sgt de Kermal	MIA	
			S/Lt Girard	MIA	
Bréguet XIV		Br.225	Sgt Metairie (M)	WIA	*

American Casualties

DH4		8th Aero	1/Lt H B Rex	KIA	
			2/Lt W F Gallager	KIA	
DH4		8th Aero	2/Lt C H Johnson	WIA	*
			1/Lt E West	WIA	
Spad XIII		13th Aero	1/Lt R R S Converse	POW	
Spad XIII		28th Aero	Lt W S Stephenson	KIA	
DH4		50th Aero	2/Lt D C Beebe	Safe	*
			2/Lt F B Bellows	KIA	
Spad XIII		93rd Aero	1/Lt C F Nash	POW	
Bréguet XIV		96th Aero	1/Lt T W Farnsworth	KIA	
			2/Lt R E Thompson	KIA	
Bréguet XIV		96th Aero	2/Lt S T Hopkins	MIA	
			1/Lt B Williams	KIA	
Spad XIII		103rd Aero	1/Lt E B Jones	KIA	
Spad XIII		139th Aero	1/Lt R O Lindsay	WIA	*
Spad XIII		213th Aero	1/Lt F Sidler	KIA	

Saturday, 14 September 1918

British Front

Low clouds prevailed on this front but the weather was better than the previous few days, with little rain. In consequence, aerial activity increased.

The first combat was at o800, north-east of Vermand, between a patrol of 46 Squadron and a grey coloured C-type. Captain Charles W Odell, who had started his second tour on 20 August, made his third victory claim and his first on a Camel. Odell was still only 19, and shared the victory with Lieutenant Nigel Bruce, an Englishman who would die in an accident on 19 September. Bruce had been with the Squadron since 23 April 1918. Lieutenant Peter F Paton, a 19-year-old Scotsman, also shared in this kill. He had been with the Squadron for five weeks, and 15 minutes later these three would burn a balloon in the same area.

The next claim was also a balloon, this time west of Quesnoy, between Armentières and Lille, to the SE5a pilot Captain Lagesse of 29 Squadron. This was at 1010, with the next combat following at 1020, by an RE8 crew of 12 Squadron. A Fokker had just burnt a balloon and was attacked and shot down by Lieutenants P F Bovington and H P Elliott at Graincourt. The Fokker fell burning, confirmed by 62nd Division troops.

Five minutes later another RE8 crew—59 Squadron—shot down another Fokker in flames during a photo mission, described as being green, red and black:

> 'When SE of Ribecourt, a Fokker attacked us and we made a running fight at about 65 mph, continually keeping machine in turns. S of Havrincourt the Fokker did an Immelmann turn to the left at the right of our tailplane. We did a gradual turn to the right and observer opened fire into him at 20 yards' range and set his cockpit on fire. He went down in a steep dive with flames and smoke coming from the cockpit and flattened out at 1,000 ft. We saw him crash south of Marcoing with smoke coming from the wreck. Another RE8 fired from a range of about 800 yards; our machine was badly shot about.'

This was the approved RE8 defensive technique: turn and lose height at as slow a speed as possible, to force the attacker to overshoot, or pull out where the observer could shoot at it. Despite these definite claims, there are no corresponding Fokker losses this day. The cockpit fire sounds like the signal flares being hit and ignited which would certainly encourage the Fokker pilot to land quickly.

Two claims were made for RE8s during the day, one at either end of the front. To the north Leutnant Friedrich Kresse of Jasta 7 got one south-east of Ypres in Allied lines, while to the south, Leutnant Paul Baümer of Jasta 2 shot down one near Vermand. Kresse's victim was a 4 Squadron machine. It is possible that Baümer fought the 59 Squadron machine and if so, then neither side inflicted permanent damage.

To finish off the morning's activities, 84 Squadron burnt three balloons at 1030, credited to Captain Southey at Gonnelieu, Lieutenant Highwood at Bantouzelle and Second Lieutenant D C Rees, a 23-year-old South African with three years service with the Royal Engineers, but less than a month with 84, one at Bantouzelle too. Earlier in the patrol, Leutnant Fritz Rumey of Jasta 5 had picked off Lieutenant John E Reid, an 18-year-old Scotsman from Inverness, who had been out four months. He went down over Le Catelet, the German's 34th victory.

The only claim in the afternoon was once again to veteran Captain George Gates of 201 Squadron. He brought his score to 12 by downing a two-seater of FA17 crewed by Unteroffizier Erich Reinecke and Leutnant Dietgen von Salis-Marschlins, who were both killed at Gonnelieu at 1325 (A).

The Germans were active as Unteroffizier Lohrmann of Jasta 42 downed a DH9 which fell in Allied lines at 1432, followed at 1640 by Leutnant Friedrich Noltenius of Jasta 27, flaming the 5th KBS balloon (SR135) at Vis-en-Artois. This balloon had in fact been packed with explosives, and was detonated from the ground with the intention of taking the attacker with it. Noltenius had a narrow escape as his diary records:

> 'I planned to take off at noon for a balloon attack but the engine ran too badly. At 1730, after new magnetos had been installed, I finally took off. There were clouds at 4,000 metres and a

thin layer at 2,000 metres. At an altitude of 3,000 I flew towards the front. And then, with the engine throttled back, flew deeper and deeper into enemy territory, until I was in position behind the balloons. At the Arras-Cambrai road, near Vis-en-Artois, I clearly saw the yellow balloon.

'Enemy single-seaters were nowhere in sight. As thin veils of cloud passed below me, I started my dive. I dived in the direction of and in front of the balloon, until I was a bit lower and then pulled up to lose speed (if the prop revved too fast, there was danger of the bullets hitting the blades). As soon as I was on the same level as the balloon, I applied full throttle and flew directly towards it. At a distance of 300 metres I began to fire and closed in, firing continuously. I only wanted to press the attack home when suddenly, while I was a mere 50 metres away, a gigantic flame arose, which completely engulfed me! The shock hurled me away. I at once took course for the lines after I had discovered that the machine was still in flying condition. But what a shambles she was!

'The cloth covering had become completely slack all over the machine and billowed. Large shreds of balloon cloth hung in the struts and in the empennage. The controls acted perfectly differently. To movements of the rudder, the plane did not react at all. In addition, the plane was excessively tail heavy. In this condition I would have been unable to survive in a dogfight. Fortunately the strong western wind carried me home to our lines very quickly and I was able to land safely on our field.'

Ground fire found targets this day. A two-seater of FA26 was brought down near Langemark, Unteroffizier Bohm being wounded, Leutnant Walter Stangen killed. Second Lieutenant W A Johnston of 201 was brought down too and taken prisoner, while Major Tanner of 80 Squadron was badly shot about but got home. Also during the day, Captain E J K McCloughry of 4 AFC attacked Ennetières aerodrome from 200 feet, claiming to have destroyed two LVGs on the ground and bombing a hangar.

French Front

The weather was a lot better to the south, along the French front, with cloud banks interrupted by the first periods of sun for some days. Once again most of the French activity was in support of the Americans' offensive at St Mihiel, which was drawing to a successful conclusion with the elimination of the salient. The German airmen were also more organised; as a consequence the activity was intense.

During the morning, 42 aircraft from Groupement Duseigneur of the Division Aérienne dropped 6,440 kilos of bombs on Conflans and Jonville. As they were soon to discover, bombing a railway station adjacent to JGII's airfield was a dangerous pursuit.

During the course of this expedition at 0940, a strong enemy patrol of over 20 planes attacked the formation en masse. The resulting combat lasted 35 minutes and eight German aircraft were claimed shot down. However, eight French machines were lost, four Bréguet 14 B2s from Br.132, one from Br.131 and one from Br.243. Two escorting Caudron R.XI gunships were also shot down with another badly damaged, and of its three-man crew, one was dead and a second wounded.

The attacking Germans were from JGII, which had received 17 new Fokkers the previous day. They were supported by Jasta 65, which had been directly subordinated to von Boenigk's Circus. Leutnant Wilhelm Frickert and Vizefeldwebel Josef Hohly of Jasta 65 both accounted for Caudrons, while Felix Büchner claimed another for Jasta 13 at Conflans. The eight Bréguets went to Leutnant Hermann Becker, CO of Jasta 12, Franz Büchner, and Leutnants Grimm and Neithammer of Jasta 13, each with one, while Jasta 19 chipped in with three: von Beaulieu-Marconnay, Leutnants Rudolf Rineau and Max Klieforth also one each. The eighth kill went to Vizefeldwebel Hasenpusch of Jasta 67. It was the single biggest loss of Bréguets during the war.

At 1000, an aircraft of Sal.280 departed on a surveillance patrol over the V Armée sector and failed to return. During the afternoon, the bodies of Adjutant Giafferi and Lieutenant Arquis were found near Veil-Arcy, completely burnt. Jasta 45's Offizierstellvertreter Gustav Dörr had his 26th victory, although he claimed it as a Spad XI.

Leutnant Werner Preuss of Jasta 66 also engaged an unidentified aircraft for his 16th victory, probably Sergent Georges Fuoc of Spa.160. Lieutenant Jacques Senart, the commander of Spa.160 and a 27-year-old Parisian, claimed the newly established GC23's first kill, a Fokker, during the day in the I Armée sector, possibly in this combat.

At 1020 (G), Jasta 50 claimed two Spads at Revillon, by Leutnants Buddeberg and Maletski. Revillon is south of the Aisne river, west of Pont Arcy. In this area Spa.152 lost Maréchal-des-Logis Alain de Freslon, and in return Sergent Couderc claimed a probable Fokker. At 1200 (G), Leutnant Walter Blume of Jasta 9 shot down a Spad at Braye, north-east of Pont Arcy, Spa.92 losing Sergent Bernon at about this time.

In the afternoon, the Gernicourt balloon was burnt at 1345 (A) followed by the Cormicy balloon five minutes later. These went down under the combined fire of Michel Coiffard, Sous Lieutenant Condemine and Caporal Lisle of Spa.154.

Things were now warming up considerably. A machine from Br.287 took off at 1400 hours on a recce flight and ran into Jasta 45's Leutnant Koennemann, who claimed a Salmson at Fismes at 1520. Then the Germans launched a series of attacks on balloons along the French and American sectors. At Mailly, south of Reims, the youngest Jasta commander ever, the 19-year-old Max Näther (he had been a Jasta commander at 18!), burnt the 76 Cié balloon at 1535, his 13th of an eventual 26 victories. He would survive the war only to be killed in January 1919 in a border war with Poland.

Before and after this time, but further south-west, near Verdun, the balloons of 25, 30 and 31 Cié were burnt between 1530 and 1538, by Unteroffizier Hans Heinrich Marwede of Jasta 67, which brought his score to four. His next claim on 3 October was filmed by an American film unit, as he burnt the 6th USBC balloon, followed immediately by him being filmed shot down and captured by the balloon's defences—a unique bit of footage. Two further balloons were shot down during the day, those of 29 and 57 Cié, one being credited to Leutnant Christiansen of Jasta 67.

Adjutant Georges Halberger and Maréchal-des-Logis Emmanuel Aubailly of Spa.153 claimed a balloon near St Mihiel, but the unit lost Maréchal-des-Logis Pierre de Villeneuve, in flames, at 1650 near Erbeviller. Oberleutnant Gottlieb Rassberger of Jasta 80b shot down a Spad in flames by Champenoux, which is about two kilometres south-east of Erbeviller.

A GC17 patrol, consisting of Sous Lieutenant Maurice Boyau, Caporal Edward J Corsi (an American) of Spa.77 and Sous Lieutenant Claude Marcel Haegelen of Spa.100, attacked and flamed a balloon near Etraye at 1745, for their 32nd, 1st and 15th victories respectively. Boyau had been flying fighters for two years with Spa.77 and was its leading pilot. This was his 18th balloon. Aged 30, he was a former captain of the French rugby team. Haegelen was one of the big French aces of 1918, with 20 victories in that year to add to his two in 1917 flying with Spa.3, before being wounded. He had turned 22 the previous day and this was his 8th balloon. The claim was valid, for the Austrian balloon of the k.u.k. Balloonkompanie 13 was lost at 1745.

American Sector

Thirty aircraft from the 1st Day Bombardment Group departed at 0645 to bomb the Conflans rail centre, an hour or so before the French attack already mentioned. On their way back they too were intercepted. The American Liberty-engined DH4s of the 11th Squadron bombed from 3,000 metres, which was the first bomb raid by such aircraft. The Squadron was engaged by pilots of Jasta 15 of JGII, the Geschwader being on its way to 80 sorties and 19 victories for this day. Two 'Fours' were shot down and in return the DH's gunners claimed two Fokkers.

Leutnant von Hantelmann got one, Vizefeldwebel Weischer the other. One of those brought down was Lieutenants F T Shoemaker and R M Groner's machine. Shoemaker got his aircraft down despite nine wounds and did not regain consciousness for five days. Groner was wounded in the leg and did not realise his pilot was wounded until the DH spiralled into a forest.

The 3rd Pursuit Group, the least experienced (with the exception of the 103rd Aero), was out early too and the 28th Aero made its first claim of the war during the 0630 patrol—a Fokker in a spin credited to the unit. Twenty minutes later two more Fokkers were claimed shot down.

The big fight of the day involved Charles Biddle's 13th Pursuit, who were out at 0715, 16-strong. Near Preny the patrol had just driven off some Fokkers from the returning 1st Bombardment Group as more Fokkers came at them, sporting the red and white fuselages of Jasta 18. Four of the Americans went down, three into captivity, one dead. In return the Americans claimed two Fokkers, one being Leutnant Günther von Büren, who had claimed one Spad before being wounded. The other three Spads were all shot down by 22-year-old Leutnant Hans Müller, bringing his score to ten.

At 0840, Leutnant Max Gossner, the 24-year-old commander of Jasta 77, burnt the 5th US Company balloon at Pont-a-Mousson, the first of three kills he would score this day. On the other side, the 27th Acro claimed a balloon destroyed at 1000 at Boinville, although it did not burn.

Twenty minutes later more Spads were in trouble north-west of Lachaussée with JGII. The Germans ran into a patrol of the 95th Aero near Hannonville, Oskar von Boenigk claiming two, and indeed, two 95th pilots were forced down. Lieutenant Sumner Sewell—a future ace—got his burning machine down, while Lieutenant John L Mitchell force-landed near Troyon-sur-Meuse.

At 1145, Vizefeldwebel Bernard Ultsch, a 20-year-old Bavarian, claimed his 11th victory—a Spad—while Gossner got his second kill of the day by claiming another. At 1340 Leutnant Müller of Jasta 18 claimed his fourth Spad of the day, down in Allied lines west of Pont-à-Mousson.

While all this was going on, US Salmsons were having trouble too. The 91st Observation Squadron lost a machine on an early patrol, and at 1100 hours three Salmsons of the 99th, on a photo mission, were attacked by nine Fokkers. The two protection machines were shot down into American lines, while the photo machine was heavily damaged, its observer, Lieutenant Raymond C Hill, badly wounded. Clarence C Kahle, his pilot, managed to get back to base but the aircraft was a write-off. Leutnant Eugen Siempelkamp, CO of Jasta 64w, claimed a Salmson at Bonzee at 1100 but was severely wounded this day, perhaps in this fight. Earlier, Oberleutnant Kohze of Jagdgruppe Nr.9 had claimed a DH4 at Pont -à-Mousson.

The 99th tried again after midday, but Gossner of Jasta 77b struck again, over the Fôret de Petre. He shot up Captain Kenneth P Littauer and Lieutenant Theodore E Boyd of the 88th Aero, one of four protection machines for the 99th photo aircraft. Littauer, his observer severely wounded in the legs and arms, force-landed in the American lines. Littauer, the CO of the 88th, had been a member of the Lafayette Flying Corps since 1916 and had seen action with the French two-seater unit C.74. He was about to be promoted to command the 3rd US Corps Observation Group.

The 27th Aero left on another patrol at 1430, and returned two hours later, having burnt the Etain balloon at 1545. Frank Luke and his partner, Lieutenant Joseph Wehner, had separated from the patrol and attacked. Luke set the 'drachen' ablaze and was planning to attack another but aborted such an idea because of eight Fokker biplanes. Wehner had been heading for another balloon but also broke off due to heavy AA fire, joining up with Luke and the Fokkers. Wehner shot down two Fokkers, one of which he saw spin into the ground near Warcq, and then fired at an Albatros. However, none were confirmed despite far better evidence than a number of other claims that were allowed. The balloon was BZ14, with Vizefeldwebel Munchoff and Gefreiter Gasser taking to their parachutes.

At 1510, nine Spads of the 22nd Aero led by Captain Ray Bridgeman engaged 12 light-blue-fuselaged Fokkers near Mars-la-Tour. Lieutenant Ray Brooks claimed two and shared another with Lieutenant Phil E Hassinger, who was then shot down in flames. Brooks too was shot up and force-landed at Menil-la-Tour. His letter on the fight is most graphic:

'We were ten miles behind the lines of the infantry and my chances of escape were so slight I figured I had come to an end. I was frankly scared, but in spite of much high tension and futile yelling at the top of my voice, I calculated by nature of my training, I suppose, to get as many of the Fokkers as possible before the inevitable.

'The only thing that saved me was that being entirely surrounded, the Germans could not shoot at me without being in their own way. A stream of white ribbons from incendiary bullets and the tracers would cut through my wings so that if I reached out my hand they were close enough to cut it off.

'Twice I tried to ram the Fokkers that had me in a direct line with their guns. One red nose "nightmare" came in from my right and endeavoured to draw me under by playing as a foil with a swoop to my level and then perceptibly below.

'I had just time to dip enough to see his features before I let him have a few incendiary bullets. I wasn't even sorry for him after that. Another I turned upon and after a short, close burst, was satisfied that a second had quit, although he did not, like the first, apparently catch fire.

'Two more of the Boche, in their tactical work, happened to get in the way of my line of fire and I finally had the better feeling, finding myself with a good 2,000 metres, directly over the huge, boomerang [shaped] lake with only four of the enemy paying me too much attention to suit me, This was rather more dangerous than with a swarm, because the individuals could far better get a good shot at me where they had less chance of getting in their own way.

'A 220 hp Spad can out-dive a Fokker DVII and for 1,500 metres, with almost full motor, I spun, nose-dived, and slithered, flattening out just over the rolling country, with a fair chance over those four.'

Brooks got away and force-landed just short of his aerodrome. Hassinger was downed by von Hantelmann, claiming the Spad near Lachaussée at 1515. Brooks was claimed by Leutnant Johannes Klein at the same time and place. One of Brooks' victims was reportedly Leutnant Paul Wolff, of Jasta 13, who was captured in an intact Fokker at 1510 near the Lake. Vizefeld-webel Schmuckle of Jasta 15 made his 5th claim five minutes later at St Beniot, probably Lieutenant Arthur C Kimber who was comprehensively shot up. He survived but would not out-live the month. On this day he staggered back to base, with his Spad—named 'Nick' and numbered No.12 of the Shooting Stars—having over 70 bullet holes in it.

These Spads had been engaged in opening up a safe zone for observation aircraft, and they partly succeeded, but a 24th Observation Squadron Salmson was caught at 1515, shot down into the American lines by Leutnant Gewart of Jasta 19, near Beney at 1820 (G).

Lieutenant Wilber W White, a 29-year-old married man with two children—somewhat unusual for a combat pilot—of the 147th Aero, burnt the balloon of Ballonzug 152, east of Chambley at 1645 for his 3rd victory. Five minutes later he claimed a Fokker, for which actions he received the DSC. White would also fail to survive the war, but in a letter to his wife he wrote:

'Had a rather exciting day yesterday. I was out doing some protection work by myself and ran into three fast two-seater Boche between me and the lines. I fired and then turned tail and beat it, they after me, for a part of the lines I could get through. Went down through a little cloud and shook the three of them and saw an enemy balloon below me so dove on that. They immediately started pulling it down and firing at me from the ground. Just then two scout planes dove on me from the front. I pulled up and fired point blank at the first and he went into a nose-dive. The second one, I fired on and then dove under, crossing the lines and coming home. I put in for confirmation on both the balloon and the plane. Hope I get them both, but I won't want another day like that one, I can tell you that much!'

A Spad numbered '19' of Spa.94 was seen to land south of Thiaucourt by an American balloon crew, after a fight with a German fighter, the enemy pilot being Leutnant Bacher of Jasta 3. The Frenchman was unhurt.

During the day, Spa.95 claimed a probable two-seater at Vittonville on the Moselle river, north of Pont-à-Mousson. Just to the north of here, the crew of Feldwebel Deinlein and Leutnant Georg Baumann of FA(A)199, were shot down by four Spads, 27-year-old Baumann being killed. Among the Fokker pilots lost this afternoon, later reported a prisoner, was Flieger Anton Kempa of Jasta 3.

That low flying was dangerous was shown by a 12th Aero Salmson. Lieutenants S Orr and Goodale ran into a balloon cable, crashed and were killed.

IAF

The IAF's bombers continued to support the Americans, bombing Metz-Sablon railway station twice, and Buhl aerodrome once, with 55 Squadron bombing Enrange railway junction. On one raid 99 Squadron was intercepted by 20 fighters and a running fight carried on back to the lines. No. 110 Squadron's brand new DH9As bombed Boulay aerodrome. Oberleutnant Gottlieb Rassberger of Jasta 80b shot down Second Lieutenants W F Ogilvie and G A Shipton of 99 near Pelter, who were taken prisoner at 0900, the first of two claims for him this date.

Also during this fight, Second Lieutenant J G Dennis was severely wounded in the stomach and signalled his observer to take over the controls, but his observer had also been badly hit and was unable to do so. Dennis then managed to fly the 35 miles back to the aerodrome, keeping in formation and making a good landing. He received the DFC for his courage, while he lay in hospital, hovering between life and death, presented in person by General Hugh Trenchard, the IAF's commander. Leutnant Kandt of Jasta 18 also claimed a DH9 near Pelter which may not have been confirmed. The bombers claimed two enemy fighters shot down.

Night bombers lost two Handley Page O/400s, one from 207, the other from 215, the latter raiding Courcelles.

	A/C	KB			DES	OOC	KB
British losses	2	—		British claims	6	—	5
French losses	15	5		French claims	9		5
American losses	12	?		American claims	12		3
IAF losses	3			IAF claims	2	—	—
German claims	48	6		German losses	6		3†

† On the Fr/US front; British front not known; two fighter pilots also wounded, fate of their aircraft not known.

British Casualties

Aircraft type	No.	Squadron	Crew		
Camel	E4391	201 Sqdn	2/Lt W A Johnston	POW	
SE5a	D6131	84 Sqdn	Lt J E Reid	POW	
Camel	B7434	80 Sqdn	Maj F I Tanner	Inj	*
RE8		4 Sqdn	Lt T O Henderson	WIA	*
			2/Lt F Butterworth	KIA	
SE5a		92 Sqdn	2/Lt L S Davis	WIA	*
DH9a	D3064	99 Sqdn	2/Lt W F Ogilvie	POW	
			2/Lt G A Shipton	POW	
DH9a		99 Sqdn	2/Lt J G Dennis	WIA	*
			Lt H G Ramsey	WIA	
HP O/400	C9683	207 Sqdn	Lt A Tapping	POW	
			2/Lt W J N Chalkin	POW	
			2/Lt J B Richardson	POW	
HP O/400	C9673	215 Sqdn	2/Lt G A Harrison	KIA	
			2/Lt H Davies	MIA	
			2/Lt C Guild	MIA	

French Casualties

Spad XIII		Spa.83	S/Lt Gendreau	WIA	*
Spad XIII		Spa.160	Sgt G Fuoc	MIA	
Spad XIII		Spa.152	MdL A de Freslon	MIA	
Bréguet XIV		Br.231	MdL Bernard	Safe	*
			Lt Toucane	WIA	
Bréguet XIV		Br.226	MdL Jus (O)	WIA	*
Salmson 2A2		Sal.280	Adj Giafferi	KIA	
			Lt Arquis	KIA	
Bréguet XIV		Br.287	Sgt Bonnet	Safe	*
			S/Lt Jounin	KIA	

Spad XIII	Spa.153	MdL P de Villeneuve	KIA
Spad XIII	GC 20	Capt R Bailly	MIA
Spad XIII	Spa.65?	Sgt Descamps	WIA
Spad XIII	Spa.92	Sgt Bernon	MIA
Spad XIII	Spa.78	S/Lt Leroy de Boismarie	POW
Spad XIII	Spa.150	Lt P Mary	MIA
Bréguet XIV	Br.132	Lt Calbet	MIA
		Sgt Destieux	MIA
Bréguet XIV	Br.132	Lt de Villele	MIA
		Cpl Valiat	MIA
Bréguet XIV	Br.132	Cpl Fontaine	MIA
		Cpl Pillot	MIA
Bréguet XIV	Br.132	Cpl Mestre	MIA
		Asp Grant	MIA
Bréguet XIV	Br.131	S/Lt Teilhac	MIA
		Cpl Jacquet	MIA
Bréguet XIV	Br.131	1/Lt C L Nelson US	Safe *
		1/Lt J M Newel US	WIA
Bréguet XIV	Br.243	Sgt Landreux	MIA
		Lt Sabirini	MIA
Caudron R11	C.46	Sgt Boeglin	MIA
		Sol Monfils	MIA
		Sol Rust	MIA
Caudron R11	C.46	Cpl Dubuisson	MIA
		Sol Mantel	MIA
		Sol Vincent	MIA
Caudron R11	C.46	Lt Resel	WIA *
		Sgt Maj Lacassagne	WIA
		Sol Poupougnac	Safe

American Casualties

DH4	11th Aero	2/Lt H Shindler	POW
		2/Lt H Sayre	KIA
DH4	11th Aero	2/Lt F T Shoemaker	POW
		2/Lt R M Groner Jr	POW
Salmson 2A2	12th Aero	1/Lt S Orr	KIA
		1/Lt K C Goodale	KIA
Spad XIII	13th Aero	1/Lt C W Drew	POW
Spad XIII	13th Aero	1/Lt H B Freeman	POW
Spad XIII	13th Aero	Lt G P V Kull	KIA
Spad XIII	13th Aero	Lt A A Brody	POW
Spad XIII	22nd Aero	1/Lt P E Hassinger	KIA
Salmson 2A2	24th Aero	1/Lt J J Goodfellow	KIA
		1/Lt E Durrand	KIA
Salmson 2A2	88th Aero	Capt K P Littauer	Safe *
		2/Lt T E Boyd	WIA
Salmson 2A2	91st Aero	1/Lt P H Hughey	MIA
		Capt K Roper	MIA
Salmson 2A2	99th Aero	1/Lt C C Kahle	Safe *
		1/Lt R C Hill	DOW
Salmson 2A2	99th Aero	1/Lt M W Wickersham	Safe *
		1/Lt C F Spencer	Safe
Salmson 2A2	99th Aero	1/Lt J R Edwards	Safe *
		1/Lt J Hayes-Davis	Safe
Spad XIII	95th Aero	1/Lt S Sewell	Safe
Spad XIII	95th Aero	1/Lt J L Mitchell	Safe *

Sunday, 15 September 1918

British Front

The weather was fine for the first time in some days. As a consequence, aerial combats increased considerably. The Germans were out early, Jasta 39 launching a balloon raid in which they burnt the Queant balloon at 0823, followed by the two at Villers, and one at Drury just minutes later. Among those lost were balloons of the 5th KBS (AR56) and 37th (SR136).

All four victories equalled the best run by a German pilot, Unteroffizier Hans Nülle gaining his 6th to 9th kills.

Captain W R Irwin of 56 Squadron was wounded by Fokkers at 0745, over Bourlon Wood, before the hostile machines left him to attack and burn a balloon. This was of the 43rd KBS, from which Lieutenants H V Williams and R H W Davidson baled out. It would appear Jasta 39 was being escorted by Jasta 34b, as at 0830 Oberleutnant Robert Greim of this unit claimed an SE5 over Hermies, just south-west of Bourlon Wood. The four balloons were just north of this position.

Fifteen minutes later, an 11-man strong patrol of 201 Squadron met Fokkers and Pfalz DXIIs over Fontaine-Notre-Dame, Captain Reg Brading shooting down one of the latter in flames for his 12th victory. Then 84 Squadron shot down a balloon at Bellicourt at 0850. The Camels of the 148th Aero also had a fight with some Halberstadt Cs over Epinoy.

A big fight developed between 20 Squadron and Jastas 6 and 24 between 1100 and 1120, north-east of St Quentin, one Bristol being lost. Oberleutnant von Wedel, CO of Jasta 24, claimed a Bristol at 1115, and Leutnant Ulrich Neckel another at 1125, both over Estrées. However, the second BF2b, with its observer wounded, force-landed inside British lines. The Bristols claimed eight Fokker DVIIs—four destroyed and four out of control, but none were recorded lost!

Four more Fokkers were claimed by 73 Squadron's Camels to the north, between Cambrai and La Folie at the same time. They lost one machine, Second Lieutenant J A Mathews being taken prisoner. Unteroffizier de Ray of Jasta 58 claimed a Camel during the day for his first and only victory.

Leutnant Hermann Leptien of Jasta 63 shot down a 42 Squadron RE8 at 1130, which force-landed west of Armentières. Then, just before midday, Leutnant Wilhelm Kohlbach, a 22-year-old west Prussian, who had begun flying in May 1916 as an observer, claimed a Camel at Cantaing—Sergeant R R Lightbody of 203 Squadron, while the unit was out balloon hunting. Kohlbach had been with Jasta 50 since February 1918 and on 11 August he was transferred to replace the great ace Erich Löwenhardt, head of Jasta 10, who had been killed the previous day. Kohlbach became a bomber pilot in WW2, ending that war as a Major-General. He died in a British PoW camp in 1947.

Jasta 58 attacked and claimed two balloons at 1305 (G), one west of Vitry credited to Unteroffizier Kurt Pietzsch, the other to Leutnant Jeep at Wancourt. The 5th KBS balloon was reported lost at 1205 (A). The next action came at 1300 (A); Lieutenant Oren Rose of 92 Squadron shot down a Hannover CLII west of Lille. It is possible that this was an unknown pilot (who survived) and Leutnant Wilhelm Holtfort of FA(A) 236 who was killed near Armentières. Twenty minutes later, Captain H A Whistler of 80 Squadron burnt the balloon at Etricourt.

As if in reprisal, Vizefeldwebel Oskar Hennrich of Jasta 46 shot down a balloon at Bertincourt at 1440, Lieutenants G H Adams and R G A Holbrook taking to their parachutes as they left the 44th KBS balloon's basket.

Meanwhile, up on the coast, 204 Squadron's Camels got into a scrap with some of the Marine Jasta pilots around Zeebrugge, claiming two with another out of control. They lost Lieutenant R C Pattullo, who had just shared one Fokker, falling in flames after being attacked by Leutnant zur see Reinhold Poss of MFJ 4.

Just to be different from dawn aerodrome raids, at 1530 in the afternoon, during a raid lasting 15 minutes, ten SE5s of 56 Squadron attacked Estourmel aerodrome from low level. Thirty-four 25lb Cooper bombs were dropped and around 1,820 rounds of ammunition fired. The results were claimed as one aeroplane shed destroyed, one hangar on fire, one lorry on fire and two Hannover two-seaters shot up. 56 lost two pilots, Captain Owen Cobb Holleran, an American, and Lieutenant L G Bowen, the former being captured. Laurence Grant Bowen was a 20-year-old Canadian, with just under a month with 56. Holleran had joined 56 on 12 April 1918, and was a 26-year-old from Atlanta. They may have been lost to fighters, as Leutnant Georg Meyer, the 25-year-old CO of Jasta 37, claimed an unidentified fighter at 1700 (G), north of Marcoing. Also claiming an SE5 was Vizefeldwebel Christian Mesch of Jasta 26, near Remy, at an unrecorded time. But most likely they were lost to ground fire.

The next action was again on the coast. Nos. 108 and 218 Squadrons were bombing Bruges when they were intercepted by pilots of MFJ 1 and 5 shortly after 1600 hours. The bombers came under heavy AA fire too, and it was thought three, having been hit, were heading for neutral

Holland. However, the German Marine fighter pilots claimed three. One to Leutnant Freymadl of MFJ 1 over the Schelde estuary, the other two to MFJ 5's Flugmaat Karl Engelfried off Walcheren and Flugmeister Kutsche. 218 Squadron lost one bomber too, coming down in the water off the Schelde estuary after being hit by fighters. An escorting 204 Squadron Camel was also shot up and forced to land—understood to be by flak fire.

There was a big fight between 1700 and 1720, involving 1 Squadron's SE5s and 62 Squadron's Bristols. Several German aircraft were thought to be shot down, but only Leutnant Paul Vogel of Jasta 23b was a definite loss, coming down in Allied lines mortally wounded. Vizefeldwebel Ernst de Ridder of Jasta 27 was wounded by an SE5 pilot. Also in action at this time were the Camels of 209 Squadron, mainly against Jasta 28. Leutnant Hilmer Quittenbaum was killed, while Leutnant Emil Thuy, the CO, claimed a Camel for his 29th victory.

A number of other actions became very confused over the late afternoon. The Germans claimed victories but it is difficult to find who they might have been fighting; some claims were for types of Allied machines not even operating. Identification of types was not as easy as one might imagine. Bristols, AWFK8s, DH4s and DH9s could be and were easily misidentified. For instance, Leutnant Wilhelm Neuenhofen of Jasta 27 claimed a DH4 late in the afternoon which was probably a 20 Squadron BF2b. However, a Big Ack (AWFK8) was shot down by Leutnant Josef Jacobs at 1810 over Passchendaele, which was a machine of 82 Squadron. It was part of a formation bombing Passchendaele railway station, being attacked by two Triplanes and six DVIIs, painted black and white. A patrol of 74 Squadron were out looking for them but failed to make rendezvous. It was Jacobs' 26th victory. Another certain victory was scored by Rudolf Stark of Jasta 35b, downing the 19 Squadron Dolphin flown by Second Lieutenant G F Anderson at Cagnicourt at 1805.

Balloons were easier to identify. Jasta 5's Unteroffizier Karl Treiber burned the 14th KBS bag west of Fins at 1800 hours, thereby gaining his first victory, but he was to become the last ace of the Jasta. Vizefeldwebel Christian Mesch of Jasta 26 shot down the 8th KBS balloon near Boiry-Notre-Dame at 1830, kill number two for the day for him, bringing his score to 11. Another sure kill was that of Leutnant Georg Meyer, Jasta 37's star, who downed Second Lieutenant H S Smith of 60 Squadron near Bourlon at 1945 (G); that brought his score to 18.

The fighting now intensified over the last hour before sunset. Nos. 24, 29, 54, 74 and 148th were all in action and claiming kills. Even the RE8s got in on the act, a 15 Squadron crew downing a Fokker that had just attacked a balloon, while a 5 Squadron machine was forced down in Allied lines by a Fokker.

As darkness finally fell, 151 Squadron's night flyers were in action, Lieutenant F C Broome shooting down one of the few Zeppelin Staaken Giants (Nr.31/16), flown by Leutnant Wogelmuth of Rfa 500, near Bapaume at 2220. The German pilot survived a prisoner, but the rest of his crew perished in the crash and fire. Broome's commanding officer, Major Quintin-Brand, had less luck, attacking a German bomber in searchlights, hitting one engine which covered his Camel with oil. Despite this, Brand continued to engage but finally lost sight of the bomber over Vitry when down to 200 feet. The bomber fired a Red Light, and the Camel was surrounded by ground fire, so Brand broke off and headed home, still smothered in thick oil.

Also this night, the RAF lost two FE2b night bombers, raiding German rear areas. All four crew men were captured, one each from 101 and 102 Squadrons.

French Front

In the VIII Armée sector, which was situated on the Vosges mountains, Lieutenant Marc Ambrogi and Adjutant Charles Mace of Spa.90 shot down a balloon at Bourdonnay at 0700. It was Ambrogi's 10th and Mace's 4th victory. Later in the day, two other Spa.90 pilots, Lieutenants Lemarie and de Ginestete, shot down the two-seater of Leutnants Friedrich Gerke and Willy Beck of FA(A) 281 over Raon l'Etape; both were killed. Then at 1130, Adjutant Jean Pezon burnt the Avricourt balloon, making it three kills for Spa.90 and five for Pezon. The Germans lost BZ26 and BZ43 on this sector this day.

At 1230, the indefatigable iron-man, Sous Lieutenant Michel Coiffard of Spa.154, in company with Sous Lieutenant Theophile Condemine and Adjutant Jacques Ehrlich, burnt three balloons, the first at Brimont, a second at Cormicy one minute later, and the third at Gernicourt at 1232. Despite the rapidity of the attack, Coiffard's Spad was badly shot up and he was forced to land near Trepail. But he had gained his 29th-31st victories, Condemine his 5th-7th and Ehrlich his 16th-18th. In all the Germans were to lose 18 balloons during this day's air fighting on the entire Western Front, although the Allies would claim 25.

At 1400, in the Aisne sector, the balloon of 54 Cié was flamed, its observer parachuting down. Three more were burnt in the X Armée sector, from the 28, 83 and 87 Companies, but the observers, Sergent Bosc, Adjutant Dunard and Sous Lieutenant Lemaire, all made safe descents. The balloon of 33 Cié was attacked too, but not flamed and Sous Lieutenant Aasche landed unhurt. Leutnant Hans von Freden of Jasta 50 got the 28 and 87 balloons at 1505 and 1507(A) near Juvigny. Three other claims for balloons, by Leutnants Meixner of Jasta 45, Fritz Höhn and Vizefeldwebel Arthur Korff of Jasta 60, only netted two kills, but it is not known whose is invalid. Another balloon victory this day was claimed by Leutnant Julius Fichter, a 26-year-old former artillery man, now commander of Jasta 67. He downed a balloon at Douaumont, one of the focal points of the Verdun battlefield. It was his 6th victory.

French casualties included Maréchal-des-Logis Raymond Merklen of Spa.154, killed, his Spad receiving a direct by flak at 1630. Five minutes later, the ace Sous Lieutenant Louis Gros of the same unit was wounded in combat with an unknown Fokker and forced to land near Lhéry, putting him out of the war.

Another confirmed balloon to the Germans was scored by Unteroffizier Bernard Bartels of Jasta 44, burning the St Simon balloon at 1800(G), the first of his five victories. The French reported this balloon lost. From the French side, another of the aces, the 23-year-old Marcel Nogues of Spa.57, veteran of almost two years as a fighter pilot, admittedly interrupted by his capture on 13 April 1917 (see Part One) and subsequent escape, flamed two balloons. These were at Bois de Buttes at 1850 and Craonne five minutes later, but his Spad was soundly shot up by the defences and he was forced to land near Goussancourt. Another pilot was not so fortunate. Caporal Rouanet of Spa.98, attacking a balloon at Caurel, opposite the IV Armée sector, was hit and forced down east of Cernay.

American Sector

First Lieutenant Edward V Rickenbacker of the 94th Pursuit claimed a Fokker out of control near Bois de Waville at 0810, and was credited with his 8th victory.

Meantime, French units attached to the Americans went for balloons in order to blind the enemy. BZ152 was burned near Goin at 0928, Maréchal-des-Logis Sainz of Spa.94 thereby gaining his first victory. Leutnant Krawlewski baled out safely. Later in the day, near Chambley, Spa.93 burnt a balloon, shared by Adjutant Gustave Daladier and Sergents Meyniel and Prarond. However, they lost Caporal Goujat, missing in action north-east of Pont-à-Mousson.

Also at an unknown time, Lieutenant Julien Guertiau, who had turned 33 two days earlier, claimed his 8th victory, shared with two other pilots of Spa.97. Three more victories went down to Spa.97 during the day, but the unit lost Sous Lieutenant L Martin.

The 13th Aero had a stiff fight at mid-morning, with several enemy fighters claimed shot down. One of the victorious pilots was Major Carl Spaatz, who was attached to the unit. He would later become a distinguished USAF General who would head Fighter Command of the US 8th Air Force in WW2, then command the US 12th Air Force and later command the Strategic Air Force in the Far East in 1945.

The next fight also involved another man later to command an American Air Force in WW2 (5th AF), First Lieutenant George C Kenney and his observer, Second Lieutenant William T Badham, flying with the 91st Aero. They claimed a Pfalz DIII shot down, two kilometres south-east of Gorze at 1140. Badham was one of the relatively few American observer aces, and would reach his 23rd birthday this month. From Alabama, he lived to reach 95 years.

In the afternoon at 1230, the 1st Aero, who were very aggressive users of their Salmsons, claimed an aircraft near Mamey, claimed by two crews, the pilot of one being Lieutenant William P Erwin. He was by far the most successful USAS two-seater pilot in terms of aircraft shot down, eventually gaining eight kills with his various observers, but this was his 1st. This was in fact a late confirmation, as the initial American summaries say it was not claimed. The Fokker had just burnt two balloons and as will be seen, the German pilot was not lost.

The pilot was the very active Leutnant Max Gossner, of Jasta 77, and he had destroyed the two balloons at 1325(G) near Lironville—from the 1st and 2nd US Balloon Companies, who lost theirs at 1225 Allied time. The observers, Lieutenants F R Burton and H E Dugan had both got out safely. Their ground defences claimed Gossner shot down, as well as the Salmsons having a go, but Gossner just managed to get his badly damaged machine back and down safely.

At 1250, to continue a big day for the major French aces, Maurice Boyau shared in two balloons, to bring his score to 34. These were at Foulgrey and later at La Haie-des-Allieanos at 1330, shared with three other Spa.77 pilots. Then Sous Lieutenant Claude Haegelen of Spa.100 and his wingman shared the Chapelet-Chery balloon—BZ55—at 1520. A second balloon attack by Haegelen and another wingman, this time at Hannonville at 1615, brought success but in fact BZ152 was not destroyed.

Late afternoon saw the team of Frank Luke and Joe Wehner strike again. Luke burnt the balloon south of Bionville (witnessed by pilots of the 213th Aero) and a second near Bois d'Hingry, while Wehner burnt the one to the south-east of the latter location. One of these was BZ35, reported lost at 1743, another being BZ152, which again was not destroyed, although Leutnant Hoffinghoff baled out. Luke reported:

'I left formation and attacked an enemy balloon near Bionville in accordance with instructions and destroyed it. I fired 125 rounds. I then attacked another balloon near Bois d'Hingry and fired 50 rounds into it. Two confirmations requested.'

Very late in the evening, Luke was out again, and flamed the balloon near Chaumont at 1950. This was BZ52. Luke's score was now six in three days, a long way clear of the next American in the St Mihiel battle.

During the day, JGII put up 69 sorties and claimed eight victories. Leutnant Oliver von Beaulieu-Marconnay, on his 20th birthday, claimed a Spad XIII at Petry but it was uncon-firmed. Leutnant Franz Büchner of Jasta 13 claimed two Spads at Thiaucourt and Lachaussée to make his score 28, and Jasta 19's Leutnants Rienau and Scheller claimed two Spads south of Pagny. The only other Spad claim was by Vizefeldwebel Hohly of Jasta 65 at St Remy. Aside from the American Spad lost, the French lost four Spads in the US sector; the others, apart from the two already mentioned, were Adjutant Edouard Stahl of Spa.150 who fell in flames, and Sergent L Fabel of Spa.95.

Three other claims by JGII were for aircraft of the IAF.

IAF

The IAF sent nine 55 Squadron DH4s to Stuttgart, where Captain Ben Silly MC DFC led the bombing of the Daimler Works. South-east of Strasbourg, EA attacked and 55 claimed two destroyed—one in flames.

Thirteen aircraft of 99 Squadron and 12 of 104 bombed the railways near Metz Sablon. The latter unit claimed one EA but lost three of their DH9s. The Fokkers broke open the 104 formation and then picked on each DH9, attacking right back to the lines. Apart from the three who failed to get back, another just scraped over the lines after being hit in the radiator—Captain R T Gammon and Second Lieutenant P E Appelby in C6264, after claiming a Pfalz DIII destroyed. Two machines got back with wounded observers, one of whom later died.

Jasta 15 had caused all the mayhem, Leutnants Hugo Schäfer, von Hantelmann and Vizefeldwebel Theodor Weischer being the scorers. Leutnant Johannes Klein was slightly wounded.

Once again, a front line Jasta simply burst open a bomber formation and although the targets were well within range of escorts, none were provided. By the end of September, even the RAF saw the need and 45 Squadron Camels were recalled from Italy to act as escort for IAF bombers and promised re-equipment with the keenly awaited Sopwith Snipes.

The DH9s of 110 Squadron bombed Hagenau aerodrome without loss. During their raids, the IAF's day and night bombers had delivered 21½ tons of bombs.

	A/C	KB			DES	OOC	KB
British losses	21	?	British claims		36	20	5
French losses	6	8?	French claims		13		16
American losses	1	?	American claims		13		4
IAF losses	3		IAF claims		1	—	—
German claims	42†	18	German losses		3‡		18

† Including two to flak and two that landed with engine failure. ‡ Plus two fighter pilots wounded, one two-seater crewman wounded and one killed, plus seven other airmen reported killed, six on the British front and all NCOs; units unknown.

British Casualties

Aircraft type	No.	Squadron	Crew		
FE2b (night)	A5610	102 Sqdn	Lt C B Naylor	POW	
			2/Lt H Mercer	POW	
SE5a	F6420	84 Sqdn	Lt C R Thompson	WIA	*
Camel	F6107	73 Sqdn	2/Lt J A Matthews	POW	
RE8	C2341	52 Sqdn	2/Lt J B Smith	Safe	*
			2/Lt B Shaw	WIA	
BF2b	E2512	20 Sqdn	2/Lt F E Finch	POW/W	
			2/Lt C G Russell	POW	
BF2b	F5816	20 Sqdn	Lt A R D Campbell	Safe	*
			Sgt A J Winch	WIA	
Camel	E4404	203 Sqdn	Sgt R R Lightbody	KIA	
RE8	C2649	42 Sqdn	2/Lt R M Marshall	WIA	*
			2/Lt A Mulholland	Safe	
Camel	E4391	201 Sqdn	2/Lt W A Johnston	POW	
DH9	D3107	108 Sqdn	Lt J J Lister	Interned	
			2/Lt F B Cox	Interned	
DH9	D1733	108 Sqdn	Capt W R E Harrison	Interned	
			2/Lt C Thomas	Interned	
DH9	D7336	108 Sqdn	Lt J J Macdonald	Interned	
			2/Lt G E McManus	Interned	
DH9	C2158	218 Sqdn	Lt W S Mars	Interned	
			2/Lt M E Power	Interned	
Dolphin	D5314	19 Sqdn	Lt G F Anderson	POW	
SE5a	C8866	56 Sqdn	Lt L G Bowen	KIA	
SE5a	E1291	56 Sqdn	Capt O C Holleran	POW	
BF2b	E2525	62 Sqdn	Lt T H Bradley	KIA	
			2/Lt R H Dilloway	KIA	
SE5a	C1875	1 Sqdn	Lt Newby	Safe	*
BF2b	D7939	20 Sqdn	2/Lt A R D Campbell	POW	
			Sgt T A Stack	KIA	
AWFK8	C8571	82 Sqdn	2/Lt H T Hempsall	POW	
			Lt J H M Yeomans MC	POW	
SE5a	E4079	29 Sqdn	Lt E F Wright	POW	
Camel	F2144	54 Sqdn	Capt G H Hackwill MC	Safe	*
RE8	C2789	5 Sqdn	Capt C F Galbraith	DOW	
			2/Lt E G W Coward	Safe	
SE5a	D6981	60 Sqdn	2/Lt H S Smith	KIA	
RE8	F5894	5 Sqdn	Lt J M Bright	WIA	
			2/Lt E P Eveleigh	WIA	
Camel	E4418	204 Sqdn	2/Lt R C Pattullo	KIA	
DH9	D7205	104 Sqdn	2/Lt R H Rose	POW	
			2/Lt E L Baddeley	POW	
DH9	D3263	104 Sqdn	2/Lt A D Mackenzie	KIA	
			2/Lt C E Bellord	KIA	
DH9	D3245	104 Sqdn	2/Lt G L Hall USAS	POW	
			2/Lt W D Evans	POW	
DH9	D532	104 Sqdn	2/Lt A A Baker	Safe	*
			Sgt N E Tonge	WIA	
DH9	D3211	104 Sqdn	Lt Wrightman	Safe	*
			2/Lt W E Jackson	DOW	
FE2b (night)	D3783	101 Sqdn	Lt E T Stockman	POW	
			2/Lt T Payne	POW	

DH9	D3210	211 Sqdn	Lt C T Linford (O)	WIA	*
SE5a		56 Sqdn	Capt W R Irwin	WIA	*
FE2b (night)		102 Sqdn	Capt R T Jones	WIA	*

French Casualties

Spad XIII		Spa.154	S/Lt L Gros	WIA	*
Spad XIII		Spa.154	MdL R Merklen	KIA	
Spad XIII		Spa.92	Sgt Mernon	MIA	
Spad XIII		Spa.98	Cpl Rouanet	MIA	
Spad XIII		Spa.150	Adj E Stahl	KIA	
Spad XIII		Spa.95	Sgt L Fabel	MIA	
Spad XIII		Spa.97	S/Lt L Martin	MIA	
Spad XIII		Spa.93	Cpl Goujat	MIA	

American Casualties

Spad XIII		147th Aero	1t E A Love	KIA	
Salmson 2A2		1st Aero	2/Lt J W Corley (O)	WIA	*
Salmson 2A2		91st Aero	2/Lt P D Coles	WIA	*
			Capt A Tabchnich	WIA	
Salmson 2A2		99th Aero	Lt H M Sandford	WIA	*
			Lt W T O'Dell	Safe	

Monday, 16 September 1918

British Front

From this date, the clocks changed, and for the rest of September (and on to 6 October), Allied and German times were the same.

The weather was fine this day, which led to one of the highest claiming days of the war by the RAF—totalling no fewer than 105! With the best will in the world, this was over-claiming of at least ten times German losses!

Right on dawn, at 0515, a 13 Squadron RE8 took off to patrol the XVII Corps front and was shot down by ground fire, both men being killed. The Camels of 4 AFC started their day off at 0625 by getting into a fight with three black Fokkers, claiming two west of Lille. An hour later, in the same area, the other Australian unit, 2 AFC, covered 4 AFC who were out raiding, and encountered 15 more Fokkers—including Triplanes. It is believed the German pilots were Jasta 43, the Aussies claiming one destroyed and four out of control. Leutnant Raesch, one of the leading members of the Jasta, noted in his diary:

'... we took off with nine machines. This is the first time Jasta 43 has been up to strength. We should have formed two echelons because we ran into nine SE5s who were higher up and who dove on us. Before long, there was a tremendous amount of shooting. The moment I saw one coming at me from behind, I zoomed up, turned and attacked him on a collision course. He spun downward away from me. Burberg was in great difficulty with an Englishman sitting on his rudder, so I began firing at the scout. With my first burst, the Englishman zoomed up, then fell, but I could not follow him as we were in thick air, so I struggled along with the other seven. Victories were not forthcoming for either side.'

Later in the patrol, at 0800, 2 AFC attacked two more Fokkers, one going down out of control, another crashing into Allied lines half a mile south of Droglandt, credited to Captain Roby Manuel (who had also made a claim in the first fight). Manuel landed nearby, discovered the NCO pilot dead in the wreck and buried him. Later, Manuel reported that the pilot had been wearing a parachute, and was made to go back and dig up the German so the parachute could be inspected! This pilot is strongly suspected to be Gefreiter Kurt Brandt of Jasta 51.

Further south, 20 and 23 Squadrons got into a fight near St Quentin at 0815, the Bristol boys claiming four destroyed and three out of control, the Dolphins claiming four more, one of which was also strafed on the ground after it had crashed. Back on the northern sectors, 4

AFC were engaged yet again, destroying three Fokkers over Frelinghein. The only known loss in this sector at this time was Leutnant Friedrich Kresse of Jasta 7, who fell at Houplines. But he may have been lost during a fight with 29 Squadron that followed this action—see later.

Then down by Cambrai at 0830 11 Squadron, on a recce show, ran into 25-30 Fokkers of JGIII in company with Jasta 5. Three Bristols were shot down, one by Leutnant Helmut Lange of Jasta 26, north-east of Quievy at 0850; Fritz Rumey claimed his 35th victory west of Villers Guislain, while Bruno Loerzer got his 39th at Doignies on the Bapaume-Cambrai road.

One of those downed was the American, Lieutenant Eugene Coler. His petrol tank was pierced and the aileron controls shot away, following which Coler dived for the ground with full power on—a testimony to the strength of the BF2b—pulling out at 1,000 feet over Cambrai, where two chasing Fokkers overshot, and the Brisfit crew claimed them shot down. Coler then struggled over the lines at 150 feet, and side-slipped into the ground near Beugny. The coolness under severe strain of this experienced pilot and gunner got them out of a tricky situation.

They were probably brought down by Loerzer and Leutnant Fritz Hoffmann of Jasta 2 (his first and only victory; he would not survive the month), the latter also claiming a two-seater south-west of Cambrai. The other claims were well behind the German lines and Coler landed 500 metres west of Doignies. Both were claimed as DH9s although none were involved in this fight. Other Bristols, of 22 Squadron, were also shot up at this time, and Leutnant Fruhner of Jasta 26 also put in a claim for a Bristol. However, two damaged 22 Squadron aircraft managed to get back over the lines.

Just after 0835, south of Linselles, 29 Squadron were in combat with Jasta 7, the SE5 pilots claiming five, while the Germans claimed three—one each to Jacobs, Unteroffizier Peisker and Vizefeldwebel Leiber. No. 29 lost Second Lieutenant Peter John Alexander Fleming, a Liverpool-born 19-year-old who was captured. Jacobs described the fight as follows:

> 'Dawn patrol, 0735 to 0855 with eight DVIIs and one Triplane. As we crossed the lines near Armentières, we saw the white puffs of flak converging on three Sopwith Camels who were pushing our way. I signalled my flight and we jumped into what turned out to be a free-for-all; whereupon, four more Camels joined the fracas and we battled them right down to the ground, when they retreated towards their home base.
>
> 'As we recrossed the lines, we were met by seven SE5s coming in from Ypres, and since our own flight was not in attack formation, the SEs picked on our stragglers. One particular fighter waltzed me down to the ground, clear back to Menin, whereupon I was joined by a couple of DVIIs who assisted me by getting on top of the Englishmen, at which point they decided to break off combat and fly home. One of my guns appeared to be hopelessly jammed during combat with an SE5 flight leader who flew brilliantly. Regaining some altitude, I was able to clear the stoppage in my port gun and soon came across an SE5 and shot off his tail causing him to drop vertically beyond the lines.'

As mentioned above, Leutnant Kresse did not return, and in fact ground observers reported a DVII falling out of formation after a fight with Camels.

It was proving a busy morning. No. 205 Squadron's DH4s were out north of St Quentin at 0845 and had fights, firstly with a Hannover CLIII which was shot down in flames and then with Fokker biplanes. 205 lost a crew with two others being forced to land with dead or wounded airmen aboard. Three Jastas were involved: Leutnant Böhning of Jasta 79b claimed a DH9 north-west of Bellenglise, nine kilometres south of St Quentin, which was the DH4 of Second Lieutenant Anslow who was taken prisoner, coming down with a dead gunner. Another DH4 came down in Allied lines at Germaine, which matches the claim by Leutnant Breidenbach of Jasta 44 at 0850 (although he claimed a BF2b).

Five minutes past the hour saw 201 Squadron's indefatigable George Gates destroy another two-seater, an LVG, near Hayencourt, in company with Lieutenant J M Mackay, from which both crewmen baled out safely. It must have been very galling for Allied airmen to see German airmen saving themselves in parachutes when they were not allowed to have them themselves.

DH9s of 103 Squadron, bombing targets near Lille at 0900, were attacked by Jasta 20 when over Lomme. Leutnant Karl Plauth, a 22-year-old from Munich, shot down one for his 7th victory since arriving at the unit on 14 June. 103 lost another aircraft on this raid. Fifteen minutes later, Leutnant Holle of Jasta 31 claimed another DH9 north-east of Douchy, which in fact was a DH4 crew of 25 Squadron, returning from a photography mission to Maubeuge, west of Valenciennes. No. 62 Squadron also got into a fight with Fokkers while escorting DH9s of 49 Squadron north-east of Douai. They claimed three of the German fighters but lost one machine, possibly to Leutnant Paul Baümer of Jasta 2 Boelcke, north-east of Henin-Lietard— his 26th victory.

Pilots of 29, 19, 87 and 79 Squadrons had scraps mid-morning, then at 1030 1 Squadron were in a fight while escorting 98 Squadron on a bomb raid. Lieutenant Howard Kullberg shot down one in flames but was chased back to the lines by five others, having been wounded in the leg in three places, although he landed safely. Kullberg's combat career was thus ended, with a score of 19, a DFC and bar, but the worst was yet to come, as by a stupefying piece of bureaucracy, he was arrested for possessing a camera while on active service!

No.98 Squadron claimed three fighters shot down but lost one bomber and had another shot up. Leutnant Otto Löffler of Jasta 2 claimed both, one north of Aveluy and one north-east of Arras, bringing his score to 11. Leutnant Emil Thuy of Jasta 28w claimed an SE5a at an unknown time and location which may well have been Kullberg, as his unit was operating in this area.

Up on the Channel coast, 210 Squadron lost Second Lieutenant Edward Burleigh Markquick, an 18-year-old, born in Calcutta, India, after just ten days with the Squadron. He went down north-west of Bruges at 0915, in a fight with MFJ 3, the victim of Vizeflugmeister Hans Goerth.

At 1110, near Zeebrugge, 210 Squadron flew another patrol, claiming two Fokkers but losing Second Lieutenant Jack Arthur Lewis, a 25-year-old from Bristol. He too was a novice, having been with the unit for just a month. Leutnant Theo Osterkamp, the acting CO of the Marine Feld Geschwader, claimed two Camels at Coxyde, while Leutnant Wilhelm of MFJ 4 got another off Zeebrugge. At 1135, Captain T W Nash of 204 Squadron blasted a balloon south of Ostende, bringing his score to five. This 26-year-old Londoner would raise this to eight before being killed in action on 23 October.

British two-seaters did not fare well, 35 losing a Big Ack to AA fire just before noon, then two DH9s of 57 Squadron were shot down, one falling in German lines, the other crash-landing in the front lines with a dead pilot. Jasta 23b got them; Unteroffizier Kleinschrodt over Denain, near Valenciennes, and Leutnant Heinrich Seywald, a 23-year-old from Regensburg, the Staffel-führer, west of Cantin; his 6th and final kill. No. 57 Squadron claimed four!

At about this time Leutnant Noltenius of Jasta 27 had a long fight with an RE8 and had to withdraw after the British crew put ten bullets into his radiator. During the day he was apparently credited with a two-seater for his 8th victory. It is possible that this was the second 103 Squadron machine, but more likely it was a late confirmation of this RE8, although no other RE8s were lost other than the one at dawn.

Fritz Rumey of Jasta 5 added two kills to his score at 1230 and 1235, recording a Camel and an SE5 down. Lieutenant J R Montgomery of 3 Squadron was the Camel pilot, killed two miles west of Cambrai at this time.

It was over an hour before more clashes came, 41 and 84 Squadrons seeing combat, while 70 Squadron lost a pilot on a balloon strafe at 1430, presumably to ground fire. Then 22 Squadron's Bristols met Jasta 37 over Quesnoy Wood. The BF2b crews claimed two enemy fighters but lost one with another being forced down inside British lines. The latter machine, flown by Lieutenant T W Martin and Sergeant M Jones, had their aileron controls shot away, and the Brisfit side-slipped down to 2,000 feet. In order to steady it, Jones climbed out onto the wing to use his weight to help level it out. It worked and they were able to get down without injury. Jones was later awarded a merited DFM. Leutnant Georg Meyer and Unteroffizier Gengelin were the victors, although their claims were for a 'scout'.

More fighting involved 79, 201, 87 and 88 Squadrons, in the latter's case two Fokkers colliding during an attack by Lieutenant Ken Conn, north-east of Habourdin aerodrome, near Lille. Then 56 and 3 Squadrons fought Jasta 26 south of Havrincourt Wood; two Fokkers were shot down, one falling in flames minus its wings. Two Allied machines were claimed by the

Germans, a Camel by Vizefeldwebel Mesch at 1755 and an SE5 to Leutnant Marcard at 1800. The latter was Second Lieutenant Noel Frederick Bishop, an 18-year-old from Worthing, who fell to his death east of the Wood. 32 Squadron dived into this fight later and claimed more Fokkers. The SE5 of Lieutenant M A Tancock lost its air pressure in the middle of this fight but he got back over the lines and crash-landed. He may well have been claimed by the Germans.

At unknown times during the day, Bruno Loerzer and Leutnant Klimke of Jasta 27 claimed an SE5 and a Camel respectively, while Leutnant Rudolf Stark, CO of Jasta 35b, was shot up and wounded in the leg, but not seriously enough to put him in hospital.

Camels of 46 Squadron and then 85 Squadron's SEs were in fights during the afternoon, the latter in company with 203's Camels. All scored victories. One went to Captain Cyril Crowe MC of 85, recently demoted from Squadron Commander by Court Martial, following a car crash. He was driving back from a party at another base when he hit a tree and two senior fellow pilots were killed. It seems rather stupid to demote such a vastly experienced air fighter as Crowe, despite the serious consequences of the crash, but it happened, and now he was just a flight commander. Crowe had come out with and been a founder member of 56 Squadron in April 1917. His recent command had been 60 Squadron but after a month he was again promoted to Major, and took over 85.

Flieger Siegfried Braun of Jasta 23b, was shot down in flames in a Pfalz DXII, over Cantin at 1850. This location is too far north for 46, 203 or 85 Squadrons, as Cantin lies on the Douai-Cambrai road, some ten kilometres north of their locations. The only other claims at this time were for two Fokkers by another ten-strong recce patrol of 11 Squadron, flying over Cambrai at 1850. One was claimed north and the other south of the town. Given the rather imprecise RAF combat reports that tended to mention where fights started but not always where they finished, it would appear Braun was one of the flamers credited.

Back on the Channel coast, just on 1900, 204 rounded off the day for the RAF by claiming no fewer than 11 victories in 15 minutes, during a fight that started at Blankenberghe. Three were LVGs and eight Fokkers. All three two-seaters were destroyed, one falling in the sea, while all the Fokkers, bar three, were out of control.

An interesting fact is that of the nine RAF pilots claiming victories in this fight, only one would survive the war, that man being John Raymond Chisam, a 19-year-old who joined 204 on 25 August. From September to the end of the war, this Squadron suffered the highest losses of any RAF fighter squadron. Their opponents were the Marine Feld Jastas and probably the Marine two-seater units. In this fight, MFJ 1 lost Vizeflugmeister Horst Sawatski and Flugmaat Nacke—both wounded—and the ace, Leutnant zur see Heinrich Wessels, shot down and mortally wounded.

Josef Jacobs of Jasta 7 made the final kill of the day:

'During the 1830-1935 evening mission, we observed a few fighter squadrons in the far distance. In the haze I could make out a few observation balloons, so I first flew north into enemy territory and then dived south on to a balloon. When I was within 200-300 metres range, the observer parachuted to earth, and I fired 40-50 rounds from my guns, then immediately turned back towards my lines. As I looked over my shoulder, I could observe six to eight spots in the balloon, glimmering from tracers, and suddenly it exploded in flames. Being well satisfied, I curved back to the front under very little enemy anti-aircraft fire. This was my 28th victory.'

Jacobs' victim was the 5th Company balloon, situated at Poperinghe, which was burned at 1935 that evening.

French Front

The weather on this part of the front was windy but clear, giving good visibility. Half the French casualties were on the American part of the front, despite the winding down of the St Mihiel offensive. The French lost three missing, plus two airmen wounded, while on the rest of their front they lost two killed, two missing and one taken prisoner.

A patrol of Spa.90, in the VIII Armée sector, that comprised Marc Ambrogi, Adjutant

Jean Pezon and Caporal Rivière, flamed a balloon near Cirey. This was evidently BZ141 which was destroyed at 1010 by three Spads between Juvigny and Cirey. The observer baled out but on the return flight Rivière was hit by fire from Flakzug Abteilung 10, south-west of St Ludwig, force-landed and was taken prisoner. Also in the sector, the French claimed a probable victory over an aircraft. This must have been the two-seater of FA10, which was attacked by two Spads, and crash-landed.

Further balloon attacks were mounted from both sides. Shortly after 1100, a patrol of Spa.77 went for one near Harville, flamed by Maurice Boyau and Aspirant Cessieux. They were then engaged by seven German aircraft which cost the French Air Service one of its greats. Boyau evaded the initial pass, then went to assist Caporal Walk of his patrol, but was then reportedly hit by ground fire, falling in flames. Cessieux was badly wounded but made it back to force-land in friendly territory, and Walk too was forced down. Their attackers were Jasta 15, von Hantelmann and Vizefeldwebel Klaudet both claiming Spads, south-west of Conflans and at St Hilaire, the latter between the lines. Both locations are near Harville, and it would appear Hantelmann claimed Boyau the Frenchman having just achieved his 35th victory.

In the IV Armée sector, the balloon of 50 Cié of the French balloon service was set on fire by two aircraft at 1130. For once the observer did not survive, despite taking to his parachute, for he was hit in the head by a bullet and killed. The balloon was apparently attacked by Jasta 47 but the name of the claimant is unknown.

At 1650, in the V Armée sector, Adjutant Lemetayer of Spa.12 was seen to fall into enemy lines following a fight, and later in the day, at 1815, a patrol from GC22 engaged three German aircraft, which were quickly joined by 15 more. There are three known claims in this area, one by Offizierstellvertreter Gustav Dörr of Jasta 45, who claimed a Spad near Fismes for his 27th kill, and two to Jasta 72, Leutnants Gustav Frädrich and Herbert Mahn.

Near Soissons, a French two-seater was forced to land by four Fokkers, crewed by Lieutenants Seillere and Guillet. Locations for Jasta 72's victories are not known, nor if they were single- or two-seater Spads. Dörr's claim was for a Spad VII, but probably a XIII.

Other air fights during the day netted victories for Spa.57 and Spa.87, Spa.38 and the veteran Sous Lieutenant René Pelissier, a 32-year-old from Versailles, commander of Spa.175 since the start of September after two years' active service. He gained his 6th and final victory in the St Mihiel region. Two pilots of Spa.93 shot down an LVG north-east of Juvilize at 1025, Lieutenant Gustave Daladier gaining his 9th victory and Adjutant Pierre Delage his first. Delage would have a meteoric career as a fighter pilot. He would achieve seven victories by 4 October, on which date this 31-year-old from the Dordogne region would be killed in action.

On the Aisne front a Bréguet XIV was shot down in flames, possibly by ground fire.

American Sector

As the ground fighting lessened in the salient area, so did the American activity, the Americans only losing one fighter and four bombers. The fighter pilot lost was Lieutenant Robert M Stiles of the 13th Pursuit, who had three victories. He departed with the 0545 patrol and was last seen south of Metz at 0720, shot down by Feldwebel Hoffmann of Kest 3. Lieutenant Murray Guthrie—a future ace—lost his engine in this action and was lucky to get back over the lines, force-landing near Dieulouard.

At 1115, Lieutenant George F Fisher of the 49th Aero claimed a Rumpler for his second victory. This may have been Vizefeldwebel Padberg and Leutnant Springorum of FA(A) 279, shot down but not harmed. Otherwise, Spa.100 (Haegelen and Sergeant Peuch) and Spa.93 have valid claims for a two-seater, if they misidentified their LVG. Also making a claim for a two-seater, was Lieutenant Louis Charles Simon Jr of the 147th Pursuit, in the vicinity of Hadonville at 1245. He had left his patrol with engine trouble, but was then attacked by three Hannovers. This was at 4,000 metres and by the time he had despatched one and got back over the lines, he was down to 400.

The 96th Bombardment Squadron sent out a flight of seven aircraft at 1650 to bomb Conflans. Two planes dropped out before the lines were reached, then another, not being able to keep up, fell out and bombed Hadonville. The four others which reached the target were engaged in combat on the return trip, three going down in flames, while the fourth crash-landed behind German lines. They had been attacked by Jasta 19 whose pilots claimed four Bréguet bombers just before 1800 in the Conflans-Briey area, two falling to Beaulieu-Marconnay to bring his score to 19, the other two credited to Leutnant Rudolf Rineau and Gefreiter Felder.

The American day bombers had suffered another 'bloody nose', and for the same reasons all the day bombers were suffering: the formations were too small, they went out unescorted, and whenever quality German pilots got in amongst them, heavy casualties ensued. Remarkably the US 8th Air Force in WW2 were to suffer similar problems at the beginning of their war over France and Germany in 1943. Does no one study history or does each generation have to learn the hard way?

Unfortunately for the Squadrons of the US 'First Team' of the American Day Bombardment Group in 1918, things were only going to get worse—far worse!

Late in the evening, the pair of Frank Luke and Joe Wehner struck again. This 27th Aero deadly duo shared the balloon near Reville at 1903, the flames of which consumed the observer's parachute and he was killed. Then Luke burnt the Romagne balloon at 1915, and the pair finished off their activities by Wehner burning the Mangiennes balloon at 1935. Both men landed in the dark at their aerodrome, with the aid of flares. It brought Wehner's score to three and Luke's to eight.

IAF

The Handley Page bombers had been out during the night of 15/16 September, 97 Squadron having one of its machines damaged, and it crashed on its way back from a raid on Mainz railway centre pre-dawn.

The IAF day bombers had another busy day, dropping a total of thirteen-and-a-half tons of bombs and firing 4,120 rounds of ammunition. No. 55 Squadron sent five planes to raid Mannheim, leaving at 1220. On the way, one DH4 flown by Second Lieutenants W E Johns and A E Amey, became separated from the flight after a flak splinter punctured their main fuel tank, and they had to run for home, pursued by Fokkers. They were shot down, Amey being killed in the air, by Vizefeldwebel Ludwig Prime of Jasta 78 and Leutnant Georg Weiner of Jasta 3 at Alt-Eckendorf, north-east of Zabern at 1330. Prime lost the disputed kill to Weiner, the latter thereby gaining his 7th victory. The other 'Fours' had a running fight with 15 enemy fighters after bombing but all got home.

Following 55 in were 11 DH9s of 110 Squadron, who bombed soon afterwards. The leader of the formation had aborted after take-off with engine trouble, and the lead flight descended to 13,000 feet from 17,400, at which height they had bombed. Flak hit two of them, causing the pilots to leave the formation; one crew was killed, the other came down into captivity. A third DH was shot up, its observer killed, but the pilot got back. Kest 1a, the victors of the week before, failed on this occasion to get sufficient height to engage, the laurels going to Jasta 70, who claimed both DH9s that had been separated: Leutnant Anton Stephen and Feldwebel Metzger were the claimants. Jasta 70's CO, Oberleutnant Hans Schlieter, was slightly wounded in the encounter, 110 claiming one Fokker driven down damaged.

During the night of 16/17 September, 24 aircraft, representing all the IAF's night bombing squadrons, set out to bomb Metz, Frescaty, Boulay, Trier, Merzig, Frankfurt and Cologne. The night was a disaster for 215 Squadron, which lost four Handley Pages. Two crews were interned in Holland and Luxemburg, 100 Squadron lost one; the newly arrived 115 Squadron lost one too, the crew landing in Switzerland. Another 216 aircraft was damaged as it landed back at base, while two of 115 Squadron had already been damaged in crashes near their bases, but without casualties. According to the Germans, they used 173 searchlights to illuminate the raiders, while anti-aircraft guns fired 16,063 shells.

	A/C	KB			DES	OOC	KB
British losses	20	1		British claims	60	42	2
French losses	9	1		French claims	3		3
American losses	5	—		American claims	3		3
IAF losses	11			IAF claims	—	1	—
German claims	49	2		German losses	4†		?

† Three fighter pilots killed and eight wounded.

British Casualties

Aircraft type	No.	Squadron	Crew		
HP O/400 (night)	C9758	97 Sqdn	Lt H Cooper	WIA	
			2/Lt A Hinder	KIA	
			2/Lt O F Bendall	Safe	
RE8	F5977	13 Sqdn	2/Lt J J Elder	KIA	
			Lt A Ostler MC	KIA	
BF2b	C946	11 Sqdn	2/Lt J C Stanley	MIA	
			2/Lt E J Norris	MIA	
BF2b	C878	11 Sqdn	2/Lt L Arnott	KIA	
			2/Lt G L Bryers	KIA	
BF2b	E2215	11 Sqdn	Capt E S Coler MC	WIA	
			2/Lt E J Corbett	WIA	
DH4	D9250	205 Sqdn	2/Lt F F Anslow	POW/W	
			Sgt L Murphy	KIA	
DH4	D8429	205 Sqdn	Lt E D Danger	WIA	*
			2/Lt A G Robertson	KIA	
DH4	B7764	205 Sqdn	2/Lt G C Matthews	WIA	*
			2/Lt H S Mullen	WIA	
BF2b	E2244	62 Sqdn	2/Lt R H Stone	POW	
			2/Lt N F Adams	POW	
BF2b		62 Sqdn	2/Lt C H Moss (P)	WIA	*
DH9	C2221	98 Sqdn	Lt Thomas	Safe	*
			Sgt Allwork	Safe	
DH9	D3267	98 Sqdn	2/Lt F J Keble	POW	
			2/Lt C H Senecal	POW	
DH9	D3254	103 Sqdn	Capt F A Ayrton	POW	
			2/Lt B P Jenkins	POW	
DH9	D489	103 Sqdn	2/Lt W H Cole	KIA	
			Sgt S Hookaway	MIA	
SE5a	E6002	29 Sqdn	2/Lt P J A Fleming	POW	
BF2b	F5824	22 Sqdn	Lt T D Smith	Safe	*
			2/Lt S C Barrow	Safe	
BF2b	C978	22 Sqdn	Lt L N Caple	Safe	*
			Lt G S Routhier	Safe	
DH4	A7788	25 Sqdn	Capt R L Whalley	KIA	
			2/Lt E B Andrews	KIA	
DH4	D8378	25 Sqdn	Lt E W Griffin (O)	WIA	*
Camel	F1962	54 Sqdn	Lt J C MacLennan	Safe	*
Camel	B7271	210 Sqdn	2/Lt E B Markquick	KIA	
AWFK8	D5146	35 Sqdn	Capt J E Phillips	KIA	
			2/Lt C V Hepburn	KIA	
Camel	E5173	54 Sqdn	2/Lt B Dixon	WIA	*
DH4	A7987	57 Sqdn	2/Lt J P Ferreira	MIA	
			2/Lt L B Simmonds	MIA	
Camel	D1946	54 Sqdn	2/Lt B H Matthews	Safe	*
Camel	D3357	210 Sqdn	2/Lt J A Lewis	KIA	
Camel	F5958	3 Sqdn	Lt J R Montgomery	KIA	
Camel	E1597	70 Sqdn	Lt J Glen	KIA	
BF2b	E2519	22 Sqdn	2/Lt W Kellow	MIA	
			2/Lt H A Felton	MIA	
BF2b	D8089	22 Sqdn	Lt T W Martin	Safe	*
			Sgt M Jones	WIA	
SE5a	B8499	56 Sqdn	2/Lt N F Bishop	KIA	
AWFK8		2 Sqdn	2/Lt R P Powell (P)	WIA	*
DH4	F2634	57 Sqdn	Lt G Anderson	KIA	
			Sgt J S Macdonald	WIA	
DH4	F7597	57 Sqdn	Lt P W J Timson	WIA	*
			2/Lt I S Woodhouse	Safe	
SE5a	B8427	1 Sqdn	Lt H A Kullberg	WIA	*
DH9		211 Sqdn	2/Lt H M Moodie (O)	KIA	*
Camel	E1479	148th Aero	Lt G C Dorsey USAS	WIA	*
DH4	F5712	55 Sqdn	2/Lt W E Johns	POW	
			2/Lt A E Amey	KIA	
DH9a	E8410	110 Sqdn	Sgt A Haight	KIA	
			Sgt J West	KIA	

DH9a	F997	110 Sqdn	Lt H V Brisbin	POW	
			Lt R Lipsett	POW	
DH9a		110 Sqdn	Lt K B H Wilkinson	Safe	*
			2/Lt H M Kettener	WIA	
HP O/400 (night)	C9658	215 Sqdn	Lt H R Dodd	KIA	
			2/Lt E C Jeffkins	POW	
			2/Lt A Fairhurst	POW	
HP O/400 „	D4566	215 Sqdn	Lt B Monaghan	POW	
			Lt H E Hyde	POW	
			2/Lt G W Mitchell	POW	
HP O/400 „	C9727	215 Sqdn	2/Lt C C Fisher	Interned	
			2/Lt R S Oakley	Interned	
			2/Lt C J Locke	Interned	
HP O/400 „	D9684	215 Sqdn	2/Lt J B Lacy	POW	
			2/Lt R Down	POW	
			Lt C N Yelverton	POW	
HP O/400 „	D4588	115 Sqdn	Lt R L Cobham	Interned	
			Lt E G Gallagher	Interned	
			2/Lt E E Taylor	Interned	
HP O/400 „	D8302	100 Sqdn	Lt F R Johnson	POW	
			Lt R C Pitman	POW	
			2/Lt F H Chainey	POW	
HP O/400 „	C9662	216 Sqdn	Lt B Norcross	POW	
			2/Lt R H Cole	DOW	
			Sgt G Hall	POW	

French Casualties

Bréguet XIV		Br.?	Sgt Gros	MIA	
			Lt Carre	MIA	
Spad XIII		Spa.12	Adj Lemeteyer	KIA	
?		?	Sgt Garin	Safe	
			Lt Fargeaud	Safe	
?		?	Lt Seillere	Safe	*
			S/Lt Guillet	Safe	
Spad XIII		Spa.?	Sgt Rouanet	MIA	
Spad XIII		Spa.77	Asp Cessieux	WIA	*
Spad XIII		Spa.77	S/Lt M Boyau	KIA	
Spad XIII		Spa.77	Cpl Walk	MIA	
Bréguet XIV		Br.229	Sgt Foiny	MIA	
			Cpl K Becker	MIA	
Spad XIII		Spa.90	Cpl Rivière	POW	
Bomber—GB Pouderoux		?	?	MIA	

American Casualties

Spad XIII		13th Aero	1/Lt R M Stiles	KIA	
Spad XIII		13th Aero	1/Lt M K Guthrie	Safe	*
Bréguet XIV	#14	96th Aero	1/Lt C P Anderson	KIA	
			1/Lt H S Thompson	KIA	
Bréguet XIV	#1	96th Aero	1/Lt N C Rogers	KIA	
			2/Lt K A Strawn	KIA	
Bréguet XIV	#4	96th Aero	1/Lt R C Taylor	KIA	
			1/Lt N A Stuart	KIA	
Bréguet XIV		96th Aero	1/Lt C R Codman	POW	
			2/Lt S A McDowell	POW	

Tuesday, 17 September 1918

British Front

Today was another fine one, with the activity on the front being described by the RAF communiqué as 'normal'. Early on, the recce DH4 of 25 Squadron was intercepted on the way to Maubeuge. Lieutenant C Brown did return at 0830, but his observer, Lieutenant E W Griffin, was dead in his cockpit.

In trying to keep the German Air Service down, two RAF squadrons continued the increasing practice of bombing enemy airfields with an attack on Emerchicourt, beginning soon after dawn. Ninety-one bombs were dropped and the aerodrome and area well strafed by 64 and 209 Squadrons, although they lost one aircraft each to ground fire. No. 22 Squadron provided top cover for the raid. The attack awoke Leutnant Noltenius of Jasta 27, who noted that it achieved practically nothing. However, Jasta 36 had a tent burnt down, lost a Triplane, a DVII and a Fokker E.V monoplane on the ground—not bad for practically nothing!

Two SE5s of 84 Squadron failed to return from an early sentry duty patrol. Both were NCO pilots, sent out alone, Sergeants A Jex and F S Thompson. Jasta 5 got at least one of them, Leutnant Fritz Rumey gaining his 38th victory at 0905 near Romilly, but it is not recorded who claimed the other. Shortly before 1000, 40 Squadron's Lieutenant Arthur T Drinkwater, an Australian from Melbourne, opened his score on his second tour with a Fokker south-east of Cambrai. Drinkwater had earlier flown DH4 bombers with 57 Squadron in 1917. However, 40 lost Second Lieutenant F W King south of this location, being brought down wounded inside German lines to Leutnant Hans Boes of Jasta 34b.

Captain Fred Lord of 79 Squadron downed a Fokker over the River Lys at 1010, seeing it go down with its prop stopped, crashing near the bridge on the south-west edge of Comines. The pilot, however, must have survived as no German fatalities are known.

Bristols of 11 and 88 Squadrons had fights mid-morning, as did 2 AFC's SE5s, while a 59 Squadron crew returned badly shot up by Fokkers. No. 25 Squadron were also in a fight, one DH4 having to force-land on its return to base. Another DH4 from this Squadron failed to return from another show, and was probably the victim of Leutnant Frommherz of Jasta 27, after it had been crippled by a pilot from Jasta 2 Boelcke.

At midday 46 Squadron were in a fight with German fighters, making claims, while 57 Squadron, on another raid, lost a machine to flak near Wahignies at 1310. Another aircraft lost to ground fire was a 24 Squadron SE5, ground strafing near Vermand. Meantime, Fritz Rumey of Jasta 5 added a second kill for the day by downing Lieutenant J E Smith of 60 Squadron. As the afternoon wore on, Leutnant Noltenius set off for another of his balloon attacks. He reported:

'The sky was perfectly cloudless. At 4,000 metres I crossed the lines and flew deep into enemy territory, with the engine throttled back. I had a bad time fighting the violent wind. Finally I was on a level with the balloon, dived vertically, and then raced for the balloon. I did not close in very hard as immediately my guns jammed. On turning away I saw two observers jump. Then I went much closer for a second attempt, but still the balloon did not burn. I followed through with a third attack but departed quickly as the flak became uncomfortably heavy. Fortunately the balloon eventually ignited, a fact I only learned on landing.'

This was his 9th victory, scored at 1530 over the 20th KBS balloon, SR151, which exploded in flames at 2,000 ft.

There was more activity late in the day, beginning on the Channel coast. Off Zeebrugge a German seaplane was shot down by a 217 bomber crew at 1825. A few minutes later, south of Ostende, 210 Squadron had a scrap, losing Second Lieutenant John Edward Harrison, 22, who had been on the Squadron just 17 days. He fell to Flugmaatrose Gerhard Hubrich of MFJ 4, his 4th victory.

Further south, 74 Squadron and 22 Squadron both had fights and claimed victories, while the 17th USAS unit also downed a Fokker but had one Camel forced to land with its controls shot away. A Camel was claimed by ground fire near Neuve Chapelle at 1805.

Jasta 5 were back in action at 1915, meeting 46 Squadron near Bourlon Wood. Lieutenant Harold Toulmin MC, aged 21, another new arrival with just 17 days on the Squadron, was killed, while Second Lieutenant Cronan Edmund Usher-Summers was made a prisoner. They were brought down by Rumey and Josef Mai. This made Rumey's score a round 40, three on this day, and six in two days. Mai's kill was his 26th.

It is interesting to reflect on the German's reluctance to recruit NCOs into their officer corps, despite awards, experience and victories. The famed trio of Jasta 5—Rumey, Mai and Otto Könnecke—had all been senior non-comms. Rumey was commissioned in July 1918 when his score was 25; Mai in September 1918 after 23 victories; and Könnecke in June 1918 after 21 kills. Between them they would bring down 110 Allied aircraft in the war and Rumey and Könnecke received the 'Blue Max', and Mai was recommended for it, but not before any of them had been commissioned.

That night, 151 Squadron struck again, claiming three night raiders. At 2052, Lieutenant E P Mackay shot down an AEG GV of Kampfstaffel 4, five miles south-east of Estrées-en-Chaussée, killing Gefreiter Otto Kurth, with Leutnants Gerlach and Tillmans taken prisoner.

Then at 2240, Major Brand attacked a machine later identified as a Friedrichshafen GIII, which blew up in mid-air, while Captain D V Armstrong shot down another Friedrichshafen in flames east of Bapaume. This was a bomber of Kampfstaffel 5, who lost Leutnants Max Scharf, Josef Freck, and Unteroffiziers Paul Nöller and Paul Kagelmacher—all killed at Pronville. Both had originally been claimed as Gothas.

The Germans lost another aircraft this night, reported as a DFW, crewed by Leutnant Nolte and Flieger Geyger, who were taken prisoner. They were of Kampfstaffel 8 and whether this loss had anything to do with Brand's or Armstrong's claims is not clear.

The night bombers were out, 101 Squadron's FEs running into trouble. One machine was hit by ground fire and had to come down 15 miles behind the German lines. The crew destroyed the machine and then managed to reach the lines on foot and get back. A second FE was also hit and force-landed in the front lines, both men scrambling to safety, but only the engine of their pusher was later salvaged.

French Front

The weather on this front was reported as cloudy in the morning, fine in the afternoon. The fighting let up considerably, but still cost the French flyers three men killed, two wounded and three balloons burned.

Sous Lieutenant William Herisson of Spa.75, a 24-year-old veteran from Nimes, claimed a two-seater over Vailly at 1800 hours, shared with Sergent Le Tilly, and also a Fokker during the day, shared with Sergent Baralis. These brought Herisson's score to 11. Leutnant Hans Siemann of FA(A) 227 was killed at Braisne on this day, possibly one of the two-seater crew.

In the X Armée Sector, the balloon of 33 Cié was flamed, apparently by Vizefeldwebel Artur Korff of Jasta 60, his 7th victory. Adjutant L Flament parachuted safely. The other two balloon losses were on the Aisne front, but with no recorded claimants, perhaps they were hit by artillery fire.

The French lost two-seaters, one being Caporal Dubourg and Adjutant Huart, killed over Nesle. The other was a Bréguet flown by Maréchal-des-Logis Kienne, killed, and Sergent Sauton, wounded, of Br.269, brought down in the front lines by flak fire. The other French combats occurred on the American sector.

American Sector

Balloons were attacked by Spa.100, Caporal Maufras failing to return from going for the balloon at Hattonville, but he came down in French lines and returned the next day. Sous Lieutenant Haegelen and Lieutenant Poulin shared the balloon at 1615.

In the 19 Armee sector, Leutnant Georg Weiner of Jasta 3 claimed a Bréguet XIV for his 8th kill, over Falkenberg during the morning. This aircraft, from Br.111, Groupe de Bombardement VI, crewed by Sous Lieutenant E de Carnell and Sergent A Puel, came down north east of Commercy.

The first American loss occurred at first light. The 24th Aero sent out a Salmson at 0515, and it probably fell to Leutnant Franz Büchner of Jasta 13, for he scored his 29th victory near Dampvitoux on this day.

The other high scoring German pilot on this front, von Hantelmann, of Jasta 15, gained his 15th victory at 1510, north of Gorz. The American pilot was Lieutenant Waldo Heinrichs of the 95th Pursuit. This unit had flown out seven-strong at 1430 to hunt for balloons and got into a fight with Fokkers over the Lac-de-Lachaussée, Heinrichs later giving this graphic account:

> 'An explosive bullet hit me in the left cheek and knocked out 16 teeth, breaking both my jaws and then tearing through the windshield, breaking it also. I remember spitting out teeth and blood and turned for our lines. Pulled a "reversement" and came out underneath the chap who was firing at me from behind. Two more explosive bullets hit me in the left arm, tearing through and breaking the left elbow. Two broke in the right hand and nearly took off the right small finger. Another hit me in the left thigh, one in the left ankle and one in the right heel. Two more hit me in the leg. Saw my left arm hanging broken by my side.'

Despite these terrible injuries (he'd been wounded in ten places) Heinrichs managed to crash-land—and survived a prisoner. The 95th had just been re-equipped with Marlin guns, most of which jammed in this fight, the 95th being lucky to lose just one man. These .30 guns were gas-operated, a modification of the Colt-Browning gun, intended to replace the British Vickers guns. In France their cloth feed belts gave a good deal of trouble in wet weather, which led to a number of jams.

At 1645, between Eply and Waville, Feldwebel Hans Popp, a 24-year-old from Hof and a member of Jasta 77b, was killed, shot down by seven Spads. These were probably the 103rd Aero pilots, who claimed four Fokkers in a long fight in the Bayonville area.

	A/C	KB		DES	OOC	KB
British losses	14	—	British claims	16	13	—
French losses	4	3	French claims	3		1
American losses	3	—	American claims	4		—
IAF losses	—		IAF claims	—		—
German claims	13†	2	German losses	6		?
† 3 to flak.						

British Casualties

Aircraft type	No.	Squadron	Crew		
DH4	D8378	25 Sqdn	Lt C Brown	Safe	*
			Lt E W Griffin	KIA	
SE5a	D6030	64 Sqdn	2/Lt W W Chreiman	POW	
Camel	E4382	209 Sqdn	2/Lt J E Walker	KIA	
BF2b	D8062	88 Sqdn	Lt F Jeffreys	Safe	*
			Lt F W Addison	Safe	
SE5a	C6480	84 Sqdn	Sgt A Jex	POW	
SE5a	C9069	84 Sqdn	Sgt F S Thomson	POW	
DH4	A7820	25 Sqdn	Lt R Dobson	Safe	*
			2/Lt A G Grant	WIA	
SE5a	E4053	40 Sqdn	2/Lt F W King	POW/WIA	
BF2b	D8083	11 Sqdn	Capt A Morrison	Safe	*
			Sgt R Allan	Safe	
RE8	F5971	59 Sqdn	Lt A Ibbotson	Safe	*
			2/Lt W J Carruthers	Safe	
DH4	A8031	25 Sqdn	Lt J H Latchford	MIA	
			2/Lt J Pullar	MIA	
SE5a	B8412	24 Sqdn	2/Lt W J Miller	KIA	
DH4	F6133	57 Sqdn	2/Lt W A Wilson	POW	
			2/Lt H H Senior	POW	
SE5a	C9297	60 Sqdn	2/Lt J E Smith	KIA	
Camel	D9513	17th US	2/Lt J A Ellison	Safe	*
BF2b	E2218	62 Sqdn	2/Lt R A Boxhall	Safe	*
			2/Lt L Miller	Safe	
Camel	F2130	46 Sqdn	Lt H Toulmin MC	KIA	
Camel	F6226	46 Sqdn	2/Lt C E Usher-Summers	POW	
Camel	F3931	210 Sqdn	2/Lt J E Harrison	KIA	
FE2b (night)	C9834	101 Sqdn	Capt H W Stockdale	Evaded	
			2/Lt N C Shergold	Evaded	
FE2b (night)	F5863	101 Sqdn	Lt A W Allen	Safe	
			Lt E H Clarke	Safe	

French Casualties

Bréguet XIV	3.314	Br.269	MdL Kienne	KIA	
			Sgt Sauton	WIA	
?		?	Cpl Dubourg	KIA	
			Adj Huart	KIA	
?		Esc.255	Asp Mokel (O)	WIA	*
Bréguet XIV		Br.111	S/Lt E de Carnell	MIA	
			Sgt A Puel	MIA	
Spad XIII		Spa.100	Cpl Maufras	Safe	

American Casualties

Salmson 2A2	1st Aero	Lt W B Cowart	KIA
		2/Lt H W Dahringer	KIA
Salmson 2A2	24th Aero	1/Lt W L Bradfield	POW
		1/Lt A L Clark	POW
Spad XIII	95th Aero	Lt W H Heinrichs	POW/WIA

Wednesday, 18 September 1918

British Front

Cloudy weather returned on this day and the RAF noted decreased activity by the Germans. On the ground, however, activity increased greatly. The British Army attacked from where their line joined the French line, just north of St Quentin, to Epehy, about 11 miles to the north. Three Corps, comprising eight divisions, attacked. The centre Corps, the Australians, gained the most success, going 'over the top' at 0520. They took positions overlooking the Hindenburg Line's main defences, opposite Bellicourt. Intense fighting occurred along this section of the front, which also reflected where most of the aerial activity took place.

A balloon was shot down at La Barrière, in the Belgian coastal area, by 213 Squadron's Camels. It was shared between First Lieutenant D S Ingalls, an American Navy pilot, and Lieutenants H C Smith and G S Hodson. It fell burning onto a balloon hangar and burnt it and neighbouring hangars as well. This was George Hodson's first claim of his second tour, bringing his score to five. This 19-year-old Englishman from Surrey would end his career as an Air Marshal.

Single-seaters were out looking for ground targets, but one SE5a of 92 Squadron was brought down by ground fire at Wingles at 1030, its pilot taken prisoner. At 1140, bombers of 103 Squadron lost a DH9 north-west of Lille to flak fire. Unteroffizier Sowa of Jasta 52 claimed his 4th victory here, which was contested by flak gunners.

At exactly the same time, Leutnant Garsztka of Jasta 31 scored his 2nd victory, an SE5a in flames at Lempire. This in fact was a Camel of 46 Squadron, Lieutenant H C Saunders being shot down in flames east of Hesbecourt at 1150, which is just south of Lempire. Yet another novice pilot had been lost. Like Toulmin, killed the day before, Herbert Saunders had joined 46 on the last day of August. An ex-infantry man, this Canadian was an old man, in pilot terms, being 33 when he died. A few minutes later Garsztka claimed a DH9 over Saulcourt. His aircraft identification was off again, as his victim was a 35 Squadron 'Big Ack' which went down in flames. The observer either fell or jumped from the burning two-seater at 2,000 feet, and although the pilot was alive when he came down, he died of burns.

At 1215, the Dolphins of 23 Squadron encountered Fokkers over Lihaucourt. Captain James Pearson, an American from New Jersey, claimed one in flames and another out of control, bringing his score to 8. Pearson survived the war and passed away in January 1993, the last known US ace to die.

The next combats were after 1400, 40 and 80 Squadrons having fights with DVIIs. Leutnant Hans Böhning, the commander of Jasta 79b, shot down a balloon north of Vaux for his 17th victory, this being the 22nd KBS balloon, from which Lieutenant Lindsay and Corporal Burgess baled out. At 1510, Leutnant Noltenius burnt another, his 10th victory. He wove his way through clouds, burnt the balloon and returned, damaged in the propeller by ground fire.

This was the 8th KBS balloon—AR37—lost at 1512 according to the balloon casualty report.

The Germans, fully aware of the ground activity, were responding by taking out these observation balloons. Eight minutes after AR37 went down, Leutnant Carl Degelow, commander of Jasta 40s, burnt the 36th Company balloon at Poperinghe, his 14th victory. Another went down at 1540 at Tincourt, near St Quentin, by Unteroffizier Treiber of Jasta 5, which was the 14th KBS balloon.

The final fight of the day was at 1730. Captain Dudley Lloyd-Evans MC of 64 Squadron claimed two Fokkers east of Havrincourt Wood, one destroyed, one out of control. These brought his score to eight and he received the DFC this month, and became tour expired. He was to win a bar to his DFC flying in Mesopotamia in 1920.

All claims this day had been for Fokkers apart from one LVG C, by Howard Burdick, of the 17th US Aero at Rumilly—in flames. This happened at 1100, one of two LVGs located and pursued. Burdick's fire knocked out the gunner of one, shortly before the machine caught fire and crashed. The second LVG was hit and the observer dropped into his cockpit following attacks by Lieutenants George Vaughn and Glenn Wicks.

Rumilly is just south of Cambrai, opposite the German 2 Armee area. This Armee reported one two-seater casualty, Unteroffizier Hoppe and Leutnant Buchwald of FA 17 both wounded, although noted as hit by ground fire! A two-seater of FA 207 may also have been hit this day; the observer, Leutnant Hans Stanger, is recorded as the observer. In two different sets of records, he is noted as being killed on both the 18th and 25th of September—with different pilots! It is possible, of course, that his pilot on the 18th, Flieger Fackart, survived being shot down with Stanger on the 18th, Stanger then being killed a week later.

French Front

The French only suffered two air casualties this day, but both were important men. For the second time in three days, a balloon attack went wrong. In the V Armée sector a patrol from Spa.154, consisting of Adjutants Jacques Ehrlich and Paul Petit with Sergent Charles Peillard, attacked a balloon near Brimont at 1805. They had a difficult time and had to make three passes before they flamed it. It was Ehrlich's 19th, Petit's 6th and Peillard's 2nd victory.

By this time they were very low, and instead of trying to regain altitude, they raced for the lines. They were met by 11 Fokkers and as a result of the combat, Ehrlich and Petit were both shot down and taken prisoner. Petit was badly wounded and died in captivity.

Surprisingly, it is not known which German unit was involved, and it is open to question whether they were credited to ground fire, for balloon defences on this day were credited with two victories, with other flak units accounting for seven more. However, German fighter pilots were credited with 21 kills, including balloons, the authors only having found a corresponding 18.

The only other French claims of the day were a balloon by Aspirant Bonneau of Spa.48, and a two-seater shared on the American sector, near Jonville, by pilots of Spa.89 and Spa.23, at Belrupt. Leutnants Wilhelm Babatz and Willi Thormann of FA(A) 247 were lost at Froidmont, which may relate to this action.

American Sector

Action was more intense—especially in terms of casualties—on the American part of the front, primarily due to another comprehensive slaughter of American day bombers. All the action took place well into the afternoon, no doubt due to weather, as occurred on the French front.

At 1405, Lieutenants Lansing C Holden and W H Taylor of the 95th Aero, departed on a voluntary patrol and ran into a formation of five Fokker biplanes. During the combat, Bill Taylor, who was eager to avenge the loss of his friend Heinrichs on the previous day, was shot down in flames over Dampvitoux, victim of Franz Büchner—his tenth victory in six days and his 30th overall. It would prove a good day for Büchner.

At 1610, the 139th Aero encountered some Pfalz Scouts over Pagny-sur-Meuse, claiming two shot down, shared by seven pilots. However, it would prove a sad day for the 27th Aero. The team of Luke and Wehner departed on a balloon strafe at 1600 hours and located two at Labeuville, west of Mars-la-Tour, both bursting into flames at 1645. The second of these Luke hit at an altitude of just 30 metres. However, the pair were immediately attacked by Fokkers and Wehner, in trying to cover his friend during his second balloon attack, was shot down in flames. Luke then claimed two of the Fokkers at St Hilaire, and later joined in on an attack on a Halberstadt C over Jonville. This latter machine was also attacked by Spa.89 and 23, and it crashed into the American lines, possibly a machine lost by FA 36, brought down in combat with six Spads at Maas-Ost (Leutnants Karl Höhne and Ernst Schulz). Landing back, Luke credited Wehner with a share in the two balloons, which brought his dead friend's score to six.

Luke's five claims in about ten minutes took his total to 13, but he was distraught over the loss of Joe Wehner. He fell at Vionville at 1645, brought down by Georg von Hantelmann— his 18th victory. One of the balloons destroyed was from BZ112. Details of Fokkers lost only show one Jasta 13 pilot, Leutnant Erich Kämpfe, being shot down this day and he took to his parachute. He was wounded by ground fire on his way down, and died of his wounds on the 20th in a hospital in Metz.

The American 11th Bombardment Squadron sent ten DH4s on a mission to bomb Mars-la-Tour, following twenty minutes behind the 20th Bombardment Squadron's similar force. This had meant in the past that the earlier raid stirred up the opposition and the second unit across was invariably the one hit. Why this somewhat bizarre tactic persisted is unclear, but on this occasion, the 11th suffered the almost inevitable consequences.

Three of the DH4s had fallen out before the lines were crossed but the other seven pressed on in cloud. One became separated, leaving just six to bomb Conflans, as they were unable to locate Mars-la-Tour. At 1720, near Conflans, 11 Fokkers of Jasta 12 found them and attacked. These were joined soon afterwards by elements of Jasta 6, part of JGI. As if the presence on the front of JGII was not enough, JGI was beginning to move down opposite the Americans, and Ulrich Neckel's Jasta 6 had just arrived. By coincidence, Neckel had been a long time member of Jasta 12, so may have joined in their patrol.

Two DH4s went down in flames straight away, followed shortly afterwards by another. Eventually, just Lieutenants Vincent P Oatis and Ramon H Guthrie returned to base, two more bombers having fallen during the running fight home. The Germans overclaimed by one, pilots being credited with six in all: Leutnant Hermann Becker got two (victories 15 and 16), both west of Conflans, Leutnant Besser one at Conflans, which blew up when it hit the ground, killing an Austrian soldier. Leutnant Alfred Greven got one south-west of Conflans, as did Flieger Wilke. Neckel downed his—which was his 26th victory—also at Conflans. The sole returning US crew claimed one Fokker shot down between Olley and Moulette.

Late in the evening, patrols were sent out by the 2nd Pursuit Group to strafe near Mars-la-Tour, and several combats took place. Lieutenant David McClure, 213th Aero, who had three victories, failed to return. Jasta 13's Franz Büchner shot down two Spads, one being flown by what he described as a skilled pilot, but who finally went down near Chambley at 1725. Five minutes later, Lieutenant Fred Philbrick of the 28th fell in flames over the same locality.

	A/C	KB			DES	OOC	KB
British losses	4	—	British claims		5	4	1
French losses	2	—	French claims		2		2
American losses	9	—	American claims		11		2
IAF losses	—		IAF claims		—	—	—
German claims	30†	4	German losses		4		?

† Nine to ground fire (possibly including two Breguéts and a Salmson in the C Abteilung area, listed as cause unknown). Only 18 fighter pilot claims found.

British Casualties

Aircraft type	No.	Squadron	Crew		
SE5a	D6971	92 Sqdn	Lt C M Holbrook	POW	
DH9	5572	103 Sqdn	2/Lt T M Phillips	KIA	
			2/Lt R E Owen	KIA	
RE8	C2490	3 AFC Sqdn	Lt D F Dimsey	Safe	*
			2/Lt R F C Machin	KIA	
Camel	D9405	46 Sqdn	Lt H C Saunders	KIA	
AWFK8	F7395	35 Sqdn	Lt M C Sonnenberg	DOW	
			2/Lt J Clarke	KIA	

SE5a		40 Sqdn	2/Lt L C Band	WIA

French Casualties

Spad XIII	7921	Spa.154	Adj J L Ehrlich	POW
Spad XIII	15060	Spa.154	Adj P A Petit	POW/DOW

American Casualties

DH4		11th Aero	1/Lt E T Comegys	KIA
			2/Lt A R Carter	KIA
DH4		11th Aero	1/Lt L S Harter	KIA
			1/Lt M Stephenson	KIA
DH4		11th Aero	1/Lt J C Tyler	KIA
			1/Lt H H Strauch	KIA
DH4		11th Aero	1/Lt R F Chapin	POW
			2/Lt C B Laird	POW
DH4		11th Aero	1/Lt T D Hooper	POW/WIA
			1/Lt R R Root	POW/WIA
Spad XIII		27th Aero	1/Lt J F Wehner	KIA
Spad XIII		28th Aero	1/Lt F Philbrick	KIA
Spad XIII		95th Aero	Lt W H Taylor	KIA
Spad XIII		213rd Aero	Lt D M McClure	POW

Thursday, 19 September 1918

British Front

On the ground, the British Army continued to attack the Hindenburg Line. The weather was overcast with a high wind. Consequently the level of air fighting reduced drastically. Indeed, the RAF only made two claims prior to noon.

The first of these was by the New Zealander, Captain R B Bannerman, who raised his personal score to ten by shooting down a Fokker DVII east of Houthulst Forest at 0735, being seen to break up in the air. Far to the south, 73 Squadron shot down another at 1040.

Late in the morning, 5 Squadron lost an RE8 on the Arras front, its pilot being killed, the observer wounded but lucky to fall into Allied lines, although the RE was wrecked. Unteroffizier Paul Hüttenrauch of Jasta 7 claimed an AWFK8 during the day, which is probably this incident. Identification, as noted before, was often poor among both sides, evidenced by another RAF loss in the afternoon. However, a 10 Squadron Big Ack was attacked by three DVIIs over Voormezeele at 0905, while directing fire for five 9.2 guns. The observer fired at them and they withdrew.

At 1600, a significant event occurred. Jasta 11 claimed a Bristol Fighter near Bellenglise, right in the middle of the battle area. This was the last claim against the RAF made by its nemesis of Bloody April and many battles since. Leutnant Julius Schulte-Frohlinde's 3rd claim was in fact not a Bristol but an RE8 of 3 AFC, supporting the Australian infantry. Its crew were killed, having taken off at 1515.

Late afternoon saw bombers of 57 Squadron intercepted after a raid on Havrincourt. The five DH4s had just turned north off the target as eight Fokkers came down on them. Two of the German machines were thought to have been shot down, with one DH4 being shot up too, having to make a forced landing at Selis on the way home.

At 1810, the veteran commander of 54 Squadron, Major R S Maxwell MC, made his 8th claim, a C-type out of control east of Havrincourt Wood. Maxwell was out on a solo patrol/special mission. He spotted a lone DFW at 13,500 feet north of St Quentin and drove it down at 1730. Continuing on, he then saw another DFW over Bourlon Wood, attacked and reported it had fallen out of control. Twenty-eight-year-old Gefreiter Paul Milkowski and his observer, Leutnant Robert Müller, 25, of FA(A) 224, were killed in action, crashing near Gonnelieu, which is due east of Havrincourt Wood. This is one of the very few 'out of control' claims made in September for which any victim can be identified.

Josef Jacobs of Jasta 7 claimed his 29th victim at 1900, a Camel at an unknown location—

neither is the victim known, although 70 Squadron were attacked by a fighter while low-bombing, but suffered no losses. The only RAF Camel lost was that of Second Lieutenant N Bruce of 46 Squadron, killed in collision with one of his colleagues—who survived. However, the Germans only recorded two claims for the day, and neither of the two Jasta 7 pilots really scored. In his diary, Jacobs recorded Hüttenrauch downing a Big Ack for his 4th victory, which clearly didn't crash if it was the already mentioned 10 Squadron machine. Jacobs' own victory is noted as having crashed, the pilot 'soon abandoned the aircraft'—which seems to indicate the pilot clambered from the wreck(?) and had come down on the British side of the lines.

French Front
The weather was equally as bad on both the French and American fronts, with low cloud and rain. The French lost one aircraft during the day, Caporal J Fonteile in a Spad of Spa.89 being reported missing. He was lost to balloon defence units, who claimed two aircraft shot down.

The French made one claim, at about 0900. It was for a new type of two-seater that had a white fuselage with red wings and tail, brought down by a patrol of Spa.150, which crashed near Rezonville. (German losses this day recorded Leutnant Lorenz, a pilot with FA241, as wounded.)

Some movements took place on the 19th, as GC12 (Spa.3, 26, 67 and 103)—the famed Cigognes (Storks) Group—moved from Lisle-en-Barrois in the II Armée Sector to La Noblette in the IV Armée, in preparation for the offensive being planned in the Meuse-Argonne Sector.

American Sector
The only action of note this day was the loss of First Lieutenant John W Ogden of the 213th Aero. He got himself lost in bad weather and landed by mistake on a German aerodrome, being taken prisoner.

	A/C	KB			DES	OOC	KB
British losses	5	—	British claims		2	3	—
French losses	1	—	French claims		1		—
American losses	1	—	American claims		—		—
IAF losses	—		IAF claims		—		—
German claims	3		German losses		4		—

British Casualties

Aircraft type	No.	Squadron	Crew		
RE8	F6045	5 Sqdn	Lt H W Driver	KIA	
			2/Lt R Greenyer	WIA	
RE8		9 Sqdn	2/Lt J Turnbull (O)	WIA	*
Camel	F2172	46 Sqdn	2/Lt N Bruce	KIFA	
Camel	C8342	46 Sqdn	2/Lt A A Partridge	Inj	
RE8	E120	3 AFC Sqdn	2/Lt J C Peel	KIA	
			Lt J P Jeffers	KIA	

French Casualties

Spad XIII	4720	Spa.89	Cpl J Fonteile	MIA

American Casualties

Spad XIII		213th Aero	1/Lt J W Ogden	POW

Friday, 20 September 1918
British Front
The weather remained wet, with low clouds and continuing high winds. Unlike the previous two days, the Germans were out in force, consequently combats were far more frequent, with the RAF alone totalling over 40 claims.

Two two-seaters were attacked early, one by 24 Squadron, the other by a Dolphin of 79, the latter north of Habourdin, an aerodrome on the outskirts of Lille. An hour after these actions, at 0750, 88 Squadron's Bristol crews fought a number of Fokkers, claiming three, but this appears to have been an action with Jasta 56, who only lost Leutnant Helmut Gantz, severely wounded, and he died the next day in hospital.

At around the same time, near Marcoing, Jasta 27 got into a bitter fight with a number of British single-seaters; 60 and 201 Squadrons were the main units involved. Hermann Frommherz got a Camel for his 23rd kill, while Noltenius and Neuenhofen also shot down fighters, the former over Marcoing for his 11th victory, the latter at Proville, for his 8th. No. 60 Squadron lost Lieutenant G F Caswell to Fokkers north of Marcoing at this time and 201 lost Lieutenant J P Mill at Serenvillers. The third was possibly Lieutenant E B Larrabee of 24 Squadron, who failed to return from a patrol that left at 0600. Noltenius called this the hardest fight of his life, whilst a young flight commander from 201 was also impressed. Noltenius recorded:

'We took off at 0700 when we saw flak bursts appear in the sky. At first we did not see any planes. We flew at an altitude of 4,000 metres and it was atrociously cold. We then proceeded more towards enemy territory and gave the flak a chance to bang away at us. This alerted the Englishmen and before long a Sopwith formation of seven machines arrived overhead. We turned home in order to lure them a bit farther over our territory, but Neuenhofen attacked immediately.

'The Englishman spun instantly with Neuenhofen in pursuit. I closed in too, pulled up and fired. The Englishman I had attacked also spun down with me behind him. When I got rather close, I fired and now the dog-fighting really started, which was not made any easier by the fact that another Englishman sat on my neck. The Englishman carried a pennant as squadron marking, a ribbon of black and white stripes about the fuselage, just in front of the vertical tailplane. He also had a white 'C' on the top wing.

'He flew brilliantly. Spinning had no doubt been only a trick meant to lure me into following him and be killed then. He fired at me from all angles. However, often enough I sat behind him and forced him lower and lower. Finally, with barely 100 metres altitude left, he tried to escape over the lines as the wind had carried us deep into our territory.

'This proved to be his undoing. I now had a good chance and his aircraft rammed into the ground. This was in my memory, the most exciting fight of my life as a fighter pilot. If the wind had not been unfavourable to the Englishman, things might have turned out the other way. My peculiar technique of side-slipping permitted me to escape over and over again, though he tried loops and everything in the bag and even though his plane was the more manoeuvrable one. But the Fokker was faster and he was unable to escape when he tried to fly home. He was wounded and taken prisoner of war.'

Later, Captain Ronald Sykes DFC wrote of this fight:

'Our flight of five Camels met 12 Fokkers at 5,000 feet, south-east of Cambrai and chased them well east, well into enemy territory. They then turned and must have opened their throttles of new, more powerful engines; to our surprise they easily climbed above us and we had to turn west into the misty air under a cloud. They came through the cloud and started a dog-fight. In the streams of mist, identification was difficult but I fired into several "black crosses" as they crossed close ahead.

'A Camel levelled up and looked round again; a misty shape just astern was just starting to go down in flames; I dived below the mist to identify it but all I could see was the top column of black smoke, so I zoomed up and joined a formation of three dim shapes but had the shock of my young life when I got up close and saw their black crosses. They had not seen me so I fired into the nearest one and then pulled up and changed direction in the cloud and dived down into clear air.

'I could see three Camels a long way off going west and no Fokkers but I felt there could be a lot of them above me in the streamers of mist. Did a lot of violent evasive action to avoid being a sitting target. Then "archie" started and I knew the Fokkers had gone and it was safe for me to fly for the other three Camels which were in clear air towards the lines.

'It was Lieutenant Mill who had been shot down, and much later when the infantry advanced through the area, we found his shallow grave beside the remains of his Camel near Seranvillers.

'The Fokkers were in strange green and buff colours, and our Intelligence reported that they belonged to a Circus and had the 185 BMW engine which normally used full throttle only at high altitude; we did not meet them again.'

There are some interesting points to this fight. Firstly, although Noltenius had correctly described the tail markings of 201 Squadron—the black and white stripes—Mills was lost in Camel 'H' and was killed. Noltenius would appear to have picked up one of the SE5s as both these pilots were captured. Also, Sykes reported green and buff Fokkers—almost certainly a misreporting of the SE5s. Possibly involved was Leutnant Georg Meyer of Jasta 37, who took his tally to 20, north of Hermies at 0800. This may have been Larrabee.

Caswell was lost to a blue Fokker at Cantaing at 0740. Also wounded in this fight was a new member of 60 Squadron, who described the fight in his autobiography, published shortly after his death on 4 October 1981. Second Lieutenant Henry Frederick Vulliamy Battle was at the tail of the 60 Squadron formation as they dove away from the eight attacking Fokkers. Battle was hit in the left posterior, but got away into the clouds and managed to land at the friendly aerodrome of 59 Squadron at 0825. His month of active service was over but he would retire an Air Commodore OBE DFC.

There followed a period of fights and overclaiming by the RAF. No. 218 Squadron claimed three out of control victories during a bombing raid up north, near Bruges at 0920, then between 1000 and 1030 a patrol of 20 Squadron, reinforced by a Flight of 84, was engaged in a fight with up to 20 Fokkers near St Quentin. The RAF communiqué noted that this fight handicapped the RAF due to the strong westerly wind blowing the combatants deeper into German territory. However, the two units claimed no fewer than nine destroyed with a further three out of control. Two of these went to 84, the rest to the Brisfit crews.

In fact this fight was with Jasta 5, who in turn claimed two of the two-seater Bristols. Oberleutnant Otto Schmidt, Staffelführer, got one in flames at Fresnoy-le-Grand at 1037 (his 14th), Unteroffizier Leicht the other over Croix Fonsomme at 1040, also in flames. In the event, 20 Squadron only lost one—in flames. Jasta 5 did not lose a single pilot on this date—nor, it seems, any Fokkers.

The whole problem of fighting over German territory, often at high speed and in a twisting, turning dog-fight, in which the Fokkers often dominated, was of reporting what had actually happened. It has to be remembered that the fighter pilot's raison d'être, apart from defending the Corps and bombing aircraft, was to shoot down German machines. Equally, the fighter squadrons existed to score victories.

The RAF treated each combat within a fight as a separate entity. Each pilot in the main wrote his own report of the combat, or certainly dictated it to the Recording Officer who then had it typed up. No one seemed to look at the fight as a whole. By 1918 some squadron commanders and some Wing Staff were cutting down on claims by finally looking at the fight as a whole. Colonel Louis Strange was one. However, as the combat reports were passed along, any report with 'disallowed' written on it was still counted back on the squadrons. No change was made to the squadron copy of the report, nor was any revised total noted in the records changed.

Thus, when awards for medals went forward, a pilot with (say) four destroyed and two out of control claims would be put up for a DFC. (At this stage, some Brigades had set out six claims as a minimum for a medal.) One of the 'ooc' claims may have been made three months previously—and subsequently disallowed at Wing. From reading all the extant combat reports and War Diaries and other records available, it is obvious to the authors that no one checked this! So a pilot (or a gunner/observer) could get a claim credited towards his medal which had long since been disallowed.

However, the two major reasons for overclaiming were as follows: firstly, no ground witnesses were necessary, and no signed air witnesses were required, although quite often another pilot might add his confirmation to a report of a brother officer if he had seen something; secondly, the extremely scant debriefing that followed combat meant little assessment. If two squadrons were in a fight, then double claiming was absolutely certain. It is also evident that often a pilot would see a burning machine hit the ground, but far from being a German, it was one of their own machines, one blazing mass several hundred feet below looking much like any other.

The pilots themselves, with some exceptions, were not liars. They believed what they were accurately claiming. With the insular arrogance of the British Military, which continued into WW2, the British were sure that the Germans were lying about their losses. They were also amazed at the French system not 'trusting' their pilots and crews, by requiring ground witnesses. Their pilots were trusted, and that was that!

The RAF operated 90 per cent of its time over the German lines. It did not have the benefit of counting wrecks. When 151 Squadron claimed, it was nearly totally accurate because it was the only RAF unit that operated under 'German' conditions.

Also, the RAF was completely lacking in any sensible form of overall assessment of results. A failed infantry attack failed. The bodies were there, the ground was not taken. Better efforts would be made next time. In the air there was no system of deciding whether a fight was a failure or not. The evidence was not there—unless they took a massive loss eg: six out of eight machines failing to return. It took camera guns and a stricter assessment system before RAF claims became very accurate later in WW2. As for the Germans, they overclaimed as well, as evidenced by the usual two claims for one loss in big fights. When the front lines were more or less static, things improved, but fighting over a fluid battle-front, confirmations became less strict.

The 'victorious' RAF pilots, if they knew what they were doing, did not follow their 'victims' down, as even watching them overlong was dangerous. They would have been twisting and turning, checking for danger from behind, above, underneath and each side, and only then might they make a quick check to see if their recent spinning target was still going down. What their eyes may have picked out then could have been almost any machine, their's or someone else's, and if near the ground, in low mist or haze, any number of pilots would return home and put in a combat report for an enemy aircraft shot down. It happened with the bombers too, and the two-seater Bristols.

With half a dozen gunners in a formation of, say, DH4s, being engaged by a gaggle of Fokkers, each firing back desperately before they themselves might be hit, and seeing one Fokker spin away—often just getting out of the way when perhaps the odd bullet or two started hitting their machine—any number of the six gunners might claim a victory. And in the confines of their own little world, wholly concentrating on staying alive and getting that Fokker away from them, they might not be totally aware of all that was going on around them in that instant.

It would be very similar in WW2, during the huge daylight battles fought above Germany by the American 8th Air Force bombers. Attacked by scores of Me109s or FW190s, a box of four-engined B17s or B24s might have up to thirty gunners blazing away. If two German fighters went down, more than a dozen gunners would return reporting a kill.

Should anyone suspect that the Germans in WW1 had any reason to hide losses, let it be said that apart from being totally against strict policy there was no reason, and certainly it was very difficult to fabricate even if some unit commander thought it desirable. Each Kofl (Kommandeur der Flieger)—the officer in charge of all flying units assigned to a particular Armee—had to receive accurate reports from each unit each day and there is no defensible reason for any Kofl to try and hide casualties. Those casualties, especially aircraft losses, would have to be made good by the AFP (Armee Flug Park)—aircraft supply depot. The AFPs would have to order replacement machines and crews from FEAs (Flieger Ersatz Abteilung)—aviation replacement units—in order to maintain front line operational strength. Therefore, how would it be possible for a Kofl, or all Kofls, to turn in false reports to Kogenluft (Kommandierenden General der Luftstreitkräfte)—Generals in command of the German Army Air Service—and/or Idflieg (Inspektion der Fliegertruppen)—inspectorate of military aviation? The answer, of course, was that it was not possible. Therefore, although the Germans did keep as meticulous records as the British—certainly in aircraft—their methods of accounting for personnel casualties were little different from the Allies. Most surviving Jasta records appear to be extracts, so one cannot write up one side's losses with the same enthusiasm as 'victories'. A lot of Jastas do not appear to have any non-fatal casualties listed, especially late in the war!

Everyone says from time to time how thorough and meticulous Germans were, how rigid in military matters and so on, so why should anyone doubt their losses. The only reason has to be is that with so many aircraft claimed by Allied units and so few apparent recorded losses, there has to be a discrepancy in those records. But the plain truth is, there isn't. The Allied air forces were simply claiming too many victories, ie: they were not shooting down the number of hostile machines they thought, or would like to think. They had to believe this or the losses sustained were not worth it. And again, this was the first air war in history; who would think that anyone would have the slightest interest in statistics after the war? The winners would win and the losers would lose and that would be sufficient.

To balance the argument, it has to be said that some German claims do not check out, despite the equally meticulous German method of assessing confirmations. Each claim had to have two independent witnesses and be agreed by Kogenluft; yet even so, occasionally the system failed—even with someone as well known as Manfred von Richthofen—but not as much as on the Allied side.

At 1050, a DH9 was claimed in flames south-east of Montigny by Leutnant Karl Odebrett of Jasta 42—an experienced pilot, whose 14th kill this was—yet there is no known loss to match it. Leutnant Hans Böhning, CO of Jasta 79b, was also wounded further north-east, over Soriel, reportedly in a fight with another DH9. It ended his war, with a record of 17 victories; he was to die in a sailplane gliding accident in 1934. The only DH9 casualty this day was a 205 Squadron machine on a bomb raid, whose pilot was mortally wounded. He got his machine back but died of his wounds. 205, who had just started to receive DH9As, were operating from Proyart, midway between Amiens and St Quentin.

Whilst this fight was on, the day's activities were hotting up on the Channel coast. Two Fokkers were claimed at 1015 by 65 Squadron south-west of Bruges. Five minutes later 204 Squadron also became involved, claiming six Fokkers, between Dixmude and Ostende, but losing two Camels with another pilot forced to land. The Marine pilots of MFJ 1 and 2 shot them down, one going to Leutnant P Becht at Beerst, while Leutnant Max Stinsky got his south-east of Pervyse—in Allied lines. Leutnant Theo Osterkamp claimed another at Praet Bosch and Vizeflugmeister Karl Scharon got a fourth at Pervyse. One too many—a double claim.

Just before 1100, Carl Degelow of Jasta 40 brought his score to 15 by shooting down a 48 Squadron BF2b at Annappes, but this was the last fight of the morning.

At 1455, the 148th American Squadron, still fighting on the British front, were in action, First Lieutenant Elliott White Springs shooting down a Fokker north of Cambrai, but the unit lost Harry Jenkinson. They had been out on an intended balloon strafe. Leutnant Noltenius claimed a Camel at Aubigny-au-Bac at 1445 and left us this graphic account:

'We now played a nice game with them. We kept approaching them rather closely while over there, but moved away smartly when they came too close. Then one of them came too close and Klimke rushed into the attack, pursuing him downwards. The fight ended when the Camels disappeared in the clouds. I had to remain upstairs and kept a careful watch. Now I saw another Sopwith turn in our direction, planning to catch Klimke from the rear. I attacked him head-on and shot well from this position. Thereupon, he turned away, but not tightly enough. I positioned myself behind him and after aiming carefully, fired. Though the distance between us was nearly 400 metres, the plane broke into flames after a short burst. It carried two pennants.'

The next fight was a huge affair between JGIII and three squadrons of the RAF. This occurred from the south to the north of Cambrai and slightly to the west. No. 87 Squadron Dolphins made three claims, all destroyed over Noyelles. Lieutenant Leslie Hollinghurst was attacked by a Fokker while accompanied by Captain A W Vigers MC and was comprehensively shot up, but got away and then shot one down off the tail of Lieutenant D C Mangan. In return, Mangan claimed the one that had shot up Hollinghurst, while Captain H A R Biziou claimed a third.

The SE5s of 85 Squadron were also involved, Lieutenant J W Warner claiming a Fokker in flames east of Bourlon Wood at 1530. The main involvement, however, was from 203 Squadron, who had all three of its Flights out on this patrol. They claimed five Fokkers, all near Hayencourt, one destroyed and another breaking up, from which the pilot baled out. They lost two Camels.

The fight had been with Jasta 26, who indeed claimed two Sopwith Camels—credited to Leutnant F Brandt at Ecourt for his 9th, at 1540, the second to Leutnant Otto Fruhner, east of Cagnicourt at 1545, for his 27th. However, his Fokker was then hit and he baled out, landing safely but injured sufficiently to keep him out of the war. Second Lieutenant W H Coghill had claimed the machine from which the pilot parachuted, so this was yet another case of a youngster getting his first kill, by downing a high-scoring and highly experienced fighter pilot; although there is a suggestion that Fruhner may have collided with a Camel first, for he reported that he had been rammed by a crashing Camel which caused his wings to break off This was not the case, for he was hit by Coghill. Leutnant Schneider was also shot down in this fight and survived, but it is not certain if he went down to 87, 85 or 203 Squadron.

Leutnant Paul Baümer of Jasta 2 Boelcke claimed a Camel east of Rumaucourt, reportedly at 1550. None were lost at this time but an hour later, at 1650, Lieutenant D C Ware of 209 Squadron was shot down in flames near here—over Ecourt, by a Fokker. In return, 209 claimed a Fokker out of control.

That night 151 Squadron struck again. At 2135, Captain F C Broome shot down an AEG bomber seen in the moonlight; it fell in flames at Tincourt, in Allied lines, north west of St Quentin. Leutnant Karl Schneider, Vizefeldwebel Johannes Schnabel and Flieger Walther Fischer were all killed at Jeancourt, which is a couple of kilometres from Tincourt. Both Schnabel and Fischer were just short of their 18th birthdays, no doubt a sign of how manpower in Germany was in short supply.

French Front
During the day there was little fighting on this front and only two claims were made. A Bréguet bomber crew claimed one, and a fighter patrol of GC14 another. The Germans recorded losses on this front, Flieger Wilhelm Sudmeyer killed in action at Bouriers, Flieger Karl Porzelt at St Avold and Luftsch Johann Semken killed in action at Montigny—the latter a balloon man.

That evening, Unteroffizier Eddelbuttel and Leutnant Huss of FA276 took off at 2210 and were hit by ground fire and forced to come down in French territory. However, they managed to regain the German lines on the 22nd.

That night the French lost three bombing aircraft. Jasta 73 claimed three night-flying Voisins, credited to Franz Kirchfeld, Offizierstellvertreter Werner Schluckebier and Leutnant Fritz Anders, the Staffelführer. Jasta 73 specialised in night sorties, Fritz Gerhard Anders becoming the first WWI German night ace. Groupement Pouderoux reported three bombers lost, one coming from GB1.

The 1st Brigade d'Aviation was ordered to change its sphere of operations to the area between Montfaucon and the Moselle River, covering part of the French II Armée and all of the American 1st Army front. The 2nd Brigade was to cover the area between Prunay and Montfaucon, covering the rest of the II Armée and IV Armée fronts.

American Sector
Nothing to report.

IAF
All five HP Squadrons made raids this night, to Boulay, Frescaty, Morhange and Buhl airfields, Thourout railway station, Mannheim and the gas works at Karlsruhe. At least one

night fighter was encountered, but this was shot down in flames by Lieutenant E J Whyte, gunner to Lieutenant Firby, which won him the DFC. German AA fire claimed one bomber shot down in flames over Metz, and another crashed on landing but without crew casualties.

	A/C	KB			DES	OOC	KB
British losses	13	—		British claims	30	13	—
French losses	3	—		French claims	3		—
American losses	—	—		American claims	—		—
IAF losses	—			IAF claims	—		—
German claims	21			German losses	4†		—

† Possibly two or three more.

British Casualties

Aircraft type	No.	Squadron	Crew		
SE5a	E4072	24 Sqdn	Lt E P Larrabee	POW	
BF2b	E2183	88 Sqdn	Lt A Williamson	Safe	*
			2/Lt K C Craig	Safe	
Camel	C125	201 Sqdn	2/Lt J P Mill	KIA	
SE5a	D6945	60 Sqdn	2/Lt H F V Battle	WIA	*
SE5a	F5472	60 Sqdn	Lt G F C Caswell	POW	
SE5a	E4000	29 Sqdn	Lt C G Ross DFC	Safe	
BF2b	E2260	48 Sqdn	Lt M R Mahony	POW	
			2/Lt J N Keir	POW	
BF2b	E2158	20 Sqdn	2/Lt A R Strachan	KIA	
			2/Lt D M Calderwood	KIA	
RE8	F6007	9 Sqdn	Lt C Dotzert	Safe	*
			2/Lt K S Hill	WIA	
Camel	B6319	204 Sqdn	2/Lt D F Tysoe	WIA	*
Camel	D8205	204 Sqdn	2/Lt C L Kelly	KIA	
Camel	D3387	204 Sqdn	2/Lt E G Rolph	POW	
Camel	F6192	148th Aero	1/Lt H Jenkinson	KIA	
Camel	E4409	203 Sqdn	2/Lt M G Cruise	KIA	
Camel	E4377	203 Sqdn	2/Lt G C Milne	POW	
Camel	F5986	209 Sqdn	Lt D C Weare	KIA	
RE8		59 Sqdn	2/Lt W G Brown (O)	WIA	*
RE8		21 Sqdn	2/Lt F L W Dowling	WIA	*
DH9	F6119	205 Sqdn	Lt W V Theron	DOW	*
			2/Lt J J Rowe	Safe	
HP O/400 (night)	C9732	215 Sqdn	2/Lt A C G Fowler	KIA	
			2/Lt C C Eaves	KIA	
			2/Lt J S Ferguson	KIA	
HP O/400 „	D4589	115 Sqdn	Lt Firby	Safe	*
			Lt C A Bonar	Safe	
			Lt E J Whyte	Safe	
HP O/400 „	D5424	115 Sqdn	3 crew	Safe	*

French Casualties

Voisin XB2 (Groupement Pounderoux)	GB1		Two crew	MIA
Voisin XB2 „	?		Two crew	MIA
Voisin XB2 „	?		Two crew	MIA

Saturday, 21 September 1918

British Front

The weather continued bad, with a good deal of cloud and a very strong wind. Considering the losses sustained during this month, how much more severe they might have been if fine weather had kept both sides active in the air!

In the early hours of the morning, one of the RAF's night bomber crews put up a good show. Lieutenant H R Hern of 148 Squadron, whilst gliding down to bomb Seclin aerodrome, was caught in a heavy barrage of 'flaming onions' and tracer, being wounded in the shoulder at 1,000 feet. In spite of this wound he dropped his bombs with what was described as good effect. On the way back, against heavy head winds, he was again subjected to much ground fire. His observer, Lieutenant A A Tutte, seeing his pilot was in a fainting condition, climbed onto the top of the FE's gondola and held the 'joystick'. Being in front of the pilot, he would, of course, be facing backwards. At the same time, he forced some brandy down his pilot's throat. In this situation, and in spite of fainting three times, Hern and Tutte returned safely and Hern landed without further damage. Both men received the DFC.

On this night of the 20th/21st, eight FEs of 83 Squadron bombed Bazuel aerodrome, the bombers meeting sporadic gunfire from around Cambrai. Meantime, two other aircraft of the Squadron flew night recce sorties but Major D A MacRae, acting CO of C Flight, and his observer were hit by ground fire, which punctured the fuel tank. He was forced to land near Montigny Farm. It was only his second sortie in France but this 33-year-old Canadian survived and continued with 83 until the war's end. He had previously been with Home Defence units.

The Dolphins of 79 Squadron shot down two two-seaters early on, Captain R B Bannerman sending his down to crash south-west of Hollebeke at 1015, Lieutenant H M S Parsons sending another down east of Oostaverne twenty minutes later. On the debit side, Carl Degelow of Jasta 40s knocked down an RE8 of 7 Squadron at St Julien, north of Ypres at 1045, which went down in flames. The Germans also noted the arrival of an SE5a of 2 AFC, Lieutenant George Cox having to force-land near Armentières after his engine was knocked off its mountings by an unknown object.

Shortly before noon, Jasta 7 found and attacked DH9s of 108 Squadron over Zarren, on the Dunkirk front. Josef Jacobs claimed two, but only one was confirmed, Leutnant Karl Plauth of Jasta 20 getting the second at Staden. The 'Nines' claimed one Fokker out of control.

Other than some scraps by Dolphins of 79 and 19 Squadrons, there was little activity until the evening. At 1745, 84 Squadron claimed two Fokkers north-east of St Quentin, and at 1810, Captain W E Shields of 41 Squadron forced two Fokkers to collide, one being seen to crash, the other spinning down out of control.

Then Captain W R 'Wop' May of 209 Squadron got into a fight, and although he claimed a Fokker, his own machine was damaged sufficiently for it to be written off upon his return to base. Lieutenant G Knight also added a victory to his score of the previous day. This fight took place at 1835 over Ecoust St Quentin, both claims being out of control. However, Vizewfeldwebel Ernst de Ritter of Jasta 27 was shot down unhurt during this encounter. For once the Germans overclaimed, for they reported two Camels shot down, one by Frommherz, the other by Leutnant Klimke, but only May was shot up.

Five minutes later, to the north, near Lille, the RAF lost one of its legends—fortunately as a prisoner. Captain Sidney 'Timbertoes' Carlin was lost in a fight with Jasta 29. Unteroffizier Westphal got him east of La Bassée for his 2nd victory. In return 74 claimed four, two being out of control, but Jasta 29 had no losses.

To the south, JGIII encountered bombers. North of Fontaine Notre Dame, which 57 Squadron had just bombed, the formation was attacked by up to a dozen Fokkers. In a fierce fight, one DH4 was brought down, although three were claimed. Surprisingly, these three were credited to the usually reliable Paul Baümer of Jasta 2 Boelcke, his victories 28 to 30, east of Bourlon Wood, east of Lagnicourt and east of Morchies. However, there was a 205 Squadron DH9 shot up some time during the afternoon, its observer wounded, but the time and location are uncertain. The DH gunners reported shooting down one Fokker out of control, while the whole formation got a share of a red Fokker with a yellow tail—in flames. The only recorded casualty was the 17-victory ace Leutnant Rudolf Klimke of Jasta 27 who was wounded three times in the shoulder at this time, in combat with two-seaters, so it seems pretty certain one of the Fokker pilots was him. (There is a suggestion, however, that he was wounded in a fight with BF2bs.)

Another two-seater DH4 of 205 Squadron however, was lost at 1735, falling to Josef Mai of Jasta 5—his 27th victory—at Le Catelet, although the German records note this to be an hour later; but this, along with other noted records, may be due to historians forgetting that German time was no longer one hour ahead of Allied time at this period.

A German two-seater crew of Schlasta 2, Vizefeldwebel Niemeyer and Unteroffizier Kappel, claimed an RE8 north-west of Epehy at an unrecorded time, but no RE8s feature on the loss reports. However, two AWFK8s on contact patrol work returned with wounded observers, and although one was supposedly hit by ground fire, it would not be the first time AWs would be mistaken for RE8s, despite the size difference!

During the day, the Germans had extensively overclaimed, something they were prone to do when operating near a battle front in bad weather. Obviously the confirmation system broke down when aircraft fell into a battle area or inside Allied lines. However, they never overclaimed as much as the RAF!

That night the real professional operators of the RAF struck another three times (and, it must be said, the only RAF unit that had one-on-one fights over their own lines with thousands of witnesses!). No. 151's commander, Major Brand, shot down a Friedrichshafen GIII at 2126 near Gouzeaucourt. Nine minutes later, to the south of this location, he shared an AEG with Lieutenant J H Summers, a post-war member of the Royal Australian Air Force. Then Lieutenant A A Mitchell struck again, with a Gotha north of Peronne, also at 2135. One of the crews brought down came from Bombenstaffel 23, Bogohl 7—the AEG—crewed by Vizefeldwebel Wilhelm Gudemann and Leutnant Werner Schmidt, who fell at Proyart. Bogohl 7 also lost Unteroffizier Wilhelm Lansberg killed and Gefreiter Bosche wounded, coming down near Sailly. A third crew, Leutnant Delte and Flieger Stocker, also of Bogohl 7, were wounded. In fact, all three aircraft were probably AEGs.

French Front

A patrol from GC16 was engaged in combat with 14 Fokkers at 0800 over Cerney, losing Spa.151's Sergent Frederic Claudet, in flames. The only claims for Spads were by Jasta 18, but all were at 1900 or later in the evening. One assumes someone got the time wrong. Nine machines of Jasta 18 attacked Spads over the Facq Woods and Vizefeldwebel Richard Schleichardt, formally of Jasta 15, gained his 3rd and final kill, in Allied lines at this time. This was followed five minutes later by two more Spads, one to Leutnant Hans Müller, his 12th, and one to Leutnant Erich Spindler, his second and last victory, both falling over the Combres Heights. Sergent Miliot of Spa.65 was reported wounded.

A recce sortie by three aircraft of Br.221 in the VIII Armée sector was attacked at 1000 hours by five hostile machines. During the combat, the Bréguet of Sous Lieutenant Bernard and Sergent Darbonnens was hit and the rear man wounded, but they got back.

Groupe de Combat 11 commenced operations in the IV Armée sector, located at Frencheville, about 15 km south-east of Chalons.

American Sector

At 1750, First Lieutenant Herbert R Hall of the 95th Aero claimed a Fokker at 2,000 metres over Doncourt. This was evidently another misidentification or the aircraft type was recorded wrongly, as a two-seater of FA2 was lost at St Hilaire, in the Armee Abteilung 'C' sector, and Doncourt is about three kilometres to the south-east. This was the only US claim of the day.

This FA2 machine was flown by Unteroffizier Gerhard Schlueter and Leutnant Erwin Sklarek, who were both killed. Another two-seater was lost on this same front, Flieger John and Leutnant Eduard Reichenwaller of FA 46 being killed over Bray. This may relate to a French claim for an aircraft shot down by Sous Lieutenant Cousin of Spa.163, in a combat over Tahure, or a claim made by a patrol from an unknown escadrille.

IAF

IAF bombers dropped a total of fifteen-and-a-half tons of bombs and fired off 7,810 rounds of ammunition at hangars, searchlights, AA batteries, trains and other targets. No. 216 Squadron bombed factories at Rombach, 207 Squadron bombed the airfields at Metz and Frescaty. 115 Squadron attacked Morhange and Leiningen railway stations, while 215 raided the blast furnaces at Hagondange, which were heavily defended by flak. One HP of 216 lost an engine and crashed on landing, injuring the pilot, whose 29th and final operation this turned out to be.

	A/C	KB			DES	OOC	KB
British losses	8	—		British claims	14	6	—
French losses	2	—		French claims	2		—

				American claims	I	—
American losses	—	—				
IAF losses	—			IAF claims	—	—	—
German claims	14	—		German losses	6	—

British Casualties

Aircraft type	No.	Squadron	Crew		
FE2b (night)	5711	83 Sqdn	Maj D A MacRae	Safe	*
RE8	F5976	7 Sqdn	Lt W G Allanson	KIA	
			2/Lt W Anderson	KIA	
SE5a	E5965	2 AFC Sqdn	2/Lt G Cox	POW	
DH9	D5759	108 Sqdn	2/Lt H L McLellan	MIA	
			2/Lt F X Jackson	KIA	
DH9	D3092	108 Sqdn	2/Lt D A Shanks	KIA	
			Sgt R Sear	KIA	
Camel	D9599	209 Sqdn	Capt W R May	Safe	
DH4	F5827	57 Sqdn	2/Lt O McI Turnbull	KIA	
			Lt D F V Page	KIA	
DH9	A8089	205 Sqdn	2/Lt A N Hyde	KIA	
			2/Lt W W Harrison	KIA	
DH9		205 Sqdn	2/Lt W Tunstall (O)	WIA	*
SE5a	D6958	74 Sqdn	Capt S Carlin MC	POW	
AWFK8		8 Sqdn	2/Lt A B McDonald (O)	WIA	*
AWFK8		35 Sqdn	2/Lt A E Harris (O)	WIA	*

French Casualties

Spad XIII		Spa.151	Sgt F Claudet	KIA	
Spad XIII		Spa.65	Sgt Miliot	WIA	
Bréguet XIV		Br.221	S/Lt Bernard	Safe	*
			Sgt Darbonnens	WIA	

Sunday, 22 September 1918

British Front

Low clouds and rain storms returned to the British end of the front, whilst the weather was good in the morning on the French front, later turning to rain.

The Camel pilots of 4 AFC were on patrol early, and three, flown by Lieutenants P J Sims, T C Cox and T H Barkell, were at 6,000 feet preparing to dive-bomb Armentières railway station. Suddenly above them appeared 13 Fokker DVIIs of Jasta 30, who immediately dived. For the second time in the month the Australians had been caught, and once again their patrol was nearly wiped out. Sims got away safely but Cox was forced to land near Sailly. Barkell was nearly lost, as he was attacked by four Fokkers. The first he avoided by a half roll and turn, which took him on to the Fokker's tail, claiming this shot down out of control. He then claimed another in the same fashion but was hit by the others, one of which followed him down to 100 feet, where he crash-landed in British lines near Neuve Eglise. The Aussies timed the fight at 0820, while Jasta 30's CO, Leutnant Hans-Georg von der Marwitz, reported his 12th victory south of Neuve Eglise at 0815, and Leutnant Friedrich Bieling reported his first victory at Ploegsteert Wood at 0820.

Prior to this, Vizefeldwebel Karl Bohnenkamp of Jasta 22s claimed two Camels shot down at 0750 north of Epehy—inside Allied lines. It is not known to which unit these Camels belonged (Epehy is way down south from 4 AFC's area), there being no corresponding British losses.

The next fight took place at 0840. Pilots of the 17th US Aero, escorted by Dolphins of 87 Squadron, ran into Jasta 34 and elements of JGIII. Once again Leutnant Noltenius was involved. His diary records:

'At 0700 hours the whole Geschwader took off. We climbed to great altitude—no activity at all. Finally, six machines—two-seaters—made an appearance. Staffel 26 went after them. It did not take long and soon enemy single-seaters appeared, coming towards Albert. We flew over enemy territory; from our side a squadron of Sopwiths approached. We dived on them at once but I remained higher up because I saw another Sopwith formation approaching. I flew in front of their leader in order to make him attack me. He promptly dived vertically for me and I turned towards him firing at once. Then another Fokker wedged himself between the Sopwith and me and the dog-fight continued.

'Alternately, Mesch, Neuenhofen and I were behind him. Finally Neuenhofen got close enough, kept behind him and forced him down for good. I kept a bit higher up because the cloth covering of the top wing had torn off and several ribs were broken in the hectic dog-fight. The kill was credited to Neuenhofen. Frommherz too shot down one.'

First Lieutenant George Vaughn of the 17th, reported:

'Whilst on OP at 0845, I dived vertically on EA which was circling over a machine of our formation at 7-8,000 feet and fired at him from a range of 80 yards. He dived steeply past others of our machines below, and I could not observe results, since I turned to engage another EA, which I shot down and which was observed to crash by Lieut. Dixon.'

Vaughn was then shot up himself but got back using his emergency fuel tank. Dixon saw Vaughn's Fokker burst into flames and crash; Vaughn was awarded the American DSC for this action. The Americans lost two pilots: Lieutenant Theose E Tillinghast became a prisoner (but later escaped), while Lieutenant Gerald P Thomas was killed. Howard Knotts also claimed a Fokker, which he last saw suspended upside down in a tree! Lieutenant Glen Wicks also claimed a Fokker destroyed west of Rumilly. Sixty years after the war, the noted aviation historian Jon Guttmann showed Vaughn Noltenius's account of the fight, and he immediately recognised himself as the German's opponent.

In all the Germans claimed four kills, the other two by Leutnant Franz Brandt of Jasta 26 and Bruno Loerzer, JGIII's leader, the latter's 41st victory. During the fight, Captain H A R Biziou of 87 Squadron claimed two aircraft destroyed over Bourlon Wood at 0840. Jasta 34b lost Leutnant Karl Bauernfeind, killed south-west of Cambrai—in flames—presumably the victim of George Vaughn.

More fights took place around 0900, Vizefeldwebel Belz of Jasta 1 claiming an RE8 at 0855; none were lost although a 53 Squadron machine returned shot up by ground fire, while 87 Squadron's Captain A W Vigers and Lieutenant Ross MacDonald shared a Rumpler destroyed at 0910. Nos. 64 and 24 Squadrons also made claims for Fokkers during the morning. However, the latter unit lost an SE5, its pilot having both petrol tanks shot through, forcing him to land between the trenches. Lieutenant W C Sterling regained the Allied lines but his fighter had to be abandoned.

Second Lieutenant J G Gunn of 56 Squadron was lost near Hamel at midday to Fokkers, Leutnant Thuy of Jasta 28w claiming his 31st victory near Vitry, not far from Hamel. Also Bruno Loerzer claimed another single-seater during the day, possibly Lieutenant D A Nevill of 41 Squadron, missing over Comines soon after 1300.

At 1325 a 12 Squadron RE8 crew beat off the attentions of some Fokkers. Lieutenants H J Evans and C A Stubbings put up a stout show against a succession of attacks, Stubbings firing at each as it came in. The last Fokker to dive zoomed up, looped, then fell upside down and was seen to crash.

Other than the Jasta 34b loss, the only other recorded German casualty was Leutnant Krayer of Jasta 45, who was wounded on this day, the unit operating on the French front.

French Front

Adjutant Charles Mace made the only claim for the day, shooting down two balloons for his 2nd and 3rd victories. The first was at 1004 near Geline, the other three minutes later at Juvelize. These balloons were BZ62 and BZ36, both lost in this area by a lone Spad.

The Germans claimed a Bréguet south of Flavy le Martel at 0956, Leutnant Karl Odebrett of Jasta 42 seeing it come down inside French lines. This was possibly the Bréguet of Br.123, in which the US observer was wounded (1/Lt E M Powell). Vizefeldwebel Hünninghaus claimed a Spad near Pont Arcy while Oberleutnant Oskar von Boenigk, leader of JGII, claimed an American Salmson near Conflans. None were reported lost.

American Sector

The only American activity was the moving from the Toul area to Vivincourt, 50 km south-south-east of Verdun, of the 1st Army Observation Group. They were preparing for the Meuse-Argonne offensive, due to start on the 26th.

	A/C	KB			DES	OOC	KB
British losses	5	—		British claims	8	6	—
French losses	—	—		French claims	—	2	
American losses	—	—		American claims	—		—
IAF losses	—			IAF claims	—	—	—
German claims	13	—		German losses	2		2

British Casualties

Aircraft type	No.	Squadron	Crew			
Camel		4 AFC	Lt T C Cox	Safe	*	
Camel	E7191	4 AFC	Lt T H Barkell	Safe	*	
Camel	F2157	17th Aero	1/Lt T E Tillinghast	POW		
Camel	F5969	17th Aero	2/Lt G P Thomas	KIA		
Camel	F6034	17th Aero	1/Lt G A Vaughn	Safe	*	
RE8	C2506	53 Sqdn	2/Lt J P Sharpe	Safe	*	
			2/Lt S A Bird	Safe		
SE5a	E6012	24 Sqdn	Lt W C Sterling	Safe		
SE5a	C8864	56 Sqdn	2/Lt J G Gunn	POW		
SE5a	F5453	74 Sqdn	Lt F J Hunt	Safe	*	
SE5a	C9133	41 Sqdn	Lt D A Neville	MIA		

Monday, 23 September 1918

British Front

This Monday was a day of more strong winds, overcast sky and some rain. The RAF communiqué described enemy aircraft activity as slight, and most of that occurred late in the evening.

The Camel-equipped 3 Squadron lost a pilot to Fokker DVIIs at 0800, Second Lieutenant Stuart H Richardson, a Londoner, who would have turned 19 on the 28th, and who had been on the Squadron for just one month. A comrade of his, Lieutenant Albert McManus, an American, left this sad account of how a novice's mistake was usually fatal:

'Just came in from a dawn show which I was leading. There were 18 machines in three layers of six machines each, about 2,000 feet above each other. My flight was the lowest, at about 7,000 feet. The two hours were almost up when I saw nine Fokkers about ten miles north-west of us, and also a two-seater about a mile east. I had a go at the two-seater, to drive him east, and then I turned to run out from the Fokkers. One of my pilots, a new chap, cut right through the formation and in under the Fokkers, who immediately attacked. They were firing explosive bullets at him, and he didn't even try to get away but just flew straight until one of the explosive bullets hit his petrol tank which burst into flames. The flames immediately went out, but burst out at three distinct times during his fall. He must have lost his head, for he was on our side of the lines and could have spun down to the ground and got away. It just made me sick, for it is the first time that I've lost a man, and he just made himself a gift to those Huns. If he had stayed with me he'd have been all right, for the rest of us were not even fired upon.'

Also shot down, but force-landing safely, was Lieutenant Martin Giesecke of the 17th Aero, who was unhurt. Both were possible victims of JGIII, or another Jasta. Leutnant Noltenius of Jasta 27 claimed a two-seater in flames inside German lines and another was claimed by

Leutnant Frommherz, but neither were confirmed and perhaps they were given to another unit. No other German claims appear to have been made during the day that fit the time or location, as total claims for the day were nine, plus a balloon. There is also the possibility that one of the German claims listed on the 22nd was actually for the 23rd.

An RE8 of 13 Squadron then attacked a DFW two-seater, which was circling over a downed Camel. Lieutenant G S Bourner dived on it, fired, then turned to let his observer, Lieutenant F A D Vaughn, fire as well. The enemy machine fell to the ground and burst into flames at 0835, near Sains-les-Marquion.

The next action was over the Belgian coastal plain. A patrol of 213 Squadron drove down a Fokker out of control six miles east of Dixmude, but was disallowed by Wing HQ. In fact, they had accounted for Flugmaatrose Karl Schiffmann, of MFJ 2, who was killed by Camels at Ichtegem, which is due east of Dixmude. In the afternoon, a DH9 of 211 Squadron went down to flak over Bruges, and landed in Holland.

Oberleutnant Hasso von Wedel, of Jasta 24s, reported shooting down an SE5a at 1620 near Villers Outreaux, but there was no such loss. An hour later, at 14,000 feet north of Bourlon, an LVG crew from FA(A) 228 were shot down, crashing near Sailly, under a kilometre north-east of Bourlon. Vizefeldwebel Paul Farber and Sergeant Leopold Bach were both killed—victims of the deadly Captain George Gates of 201 Squadron, whose 14th victim spun straight in after a burst from his guns.

During the day, the 42 Squadron crew of Second Lieutenants G C Upson and A N Thomson, whilst on a photography sortie, were attacked by eight Fokker biplanes, one of which hit their fuel tank, dousing Upson with petrol. The observer fired 30 rounds at this Fokker when his Lewis gun was hit and put out of action. However, another crew saw the Fokker go down and crash. At 1715, another 42 Squadron RE, crewed by Second Lieutenants D A Newson and G E M Browne, was brought down in flames by a Fokker. This was probably Leutnant Hermann Leptien, CO of Jasta 63, who made his 7th and final claim of the war, south of Fleurbaix at 1710.

The bulk of the actions came in two intense fights in the evening. The first was between six Dolphins of 87 Squadron and 14 red and black Fokkers at 1745, although one was described as having black and white checks. In the first encounter they claimed one Fokker destroyed and two out of control, and 25 minutes later in another scrap the Dolphin pilots claimed three more, two out of control, while Lieutenant Leslie Hollinghurst reported the pilot of his Fokker either baled or jumped out. Lieutenant F W Goodman was shot up, wounded, and forced to land near Sailly. Leutnant Fritz Rumey of Jasta 45 claimed a Dolphin south of Barelle at 1815—his 42nd kill.

The Bristols of 20 Squadron encountered a formation of DVIIs north-east of St Quentin at 1815 and over the next 15 minutes claimed six of them, four destroyed and two out of control, whilst losing one, with another observer wounded. This fight was with Jasta 24s, whose Vizefeldwebel Kurt Ungewitter claimed his 4th victory at Levergies at 1825. Jasta 24s recorded no losses.

That evening, 102 Squadron sent out its FE2 bombers at 1940 hours. One machine was hit by AA fire, its crew being forced down at Epehy, between the front line and the support trenches. Both men scrambled into the British trenches, but their machine was shelled and destroyed.

French Front

There was not much activity on this front either. Leutnants von Beaulieu-Marconnay of Jasta 19 and von Hantelmann of Jasta 15 are reported to have claimed on the 23rd or 25th. It is believed the 25th was the correct date. A Spad (two-seater!?) claimed by Vizefeldwebel Hans Donhauser of Jasta 17 near Vrizy at 1255 is believed to have been a Salmson 2A2 of Sal.28—the only French loss this day. However, Caporal Stanley of Spa.23, whilst attacking a German two-seater, was hit by return fire. Making a forced landing in the front lines he smashed his aircraft but it is not certain if it was a total loss.

A balloon was reported shot down by Leutnant Oldenburg of Jasta 22s at Atilly at 1620, while the only French claim was an EA downed by Lieutenants Denis and Beucler of Sal.40, near Mont-sans-Nom.

	A/C	KB			DES	OOC	KB
British losses	4	—		British claims	10	6	—
French losses	1	1?		French claims	1		—
American losses	—	—		American claims	—		—
IAF losses	—	—		IAF claims	—	—	—
German claims	5	1		German losses	2†		—

† Apart from those already mentioned, German casualties also included one Feldwebel, one Gefreiter and two Fliegers as being killed this date, units unknown.

British Casualties

Aircraft type	No.	Squadron	Crew		
Camel	F6029	3 Sqdn	2/Lt S H Richardson	KIA	
Camel	H7275	17th Aero	Lt M Giesecke	Safe	*
RE8	C2300	42 Sqdn	2/Lt D A Newson	KIA	
			2/Lt G E M Browne	KIA	
Dolphin	D3741	87 Sqdn	Lt F W Ferguson	WIA	*
BF2b	E2562	20 Sqdn	Lt J Nicholson	KIA	
			2/Lt B W Wilson	KIA	
BF2b	E2467	20 Sqdn	Lt E A Britton	Safe	*
			Sgt R S Dodds	WIA	
FE2b (night)	A6521	102 Sqdn	Capt P M McSwiney	Safe	
			Lt E R Canning	Safe	
BF2b	E2363	11 Sqdn	2/Lt C Johnson	Safe	*
			Sgt G H Hampson	WIA	

French Casualties

Salmson 2A2		Sal.28	Cpl Latil	MIA
			Sgt Saloman	MIA
Spad XIII		Spa.23	Cpl Stanley	Safe ?
Spad XIII		Spa.95	S/Lt Schroeder	WIA	*

Tuesday, 24 September 1918

British Front

As the weather improved to being fair with some cloud according to the RAF, it was described as being magnificent by Friedrich Noltenius. In consequence there was a marked increase in aerial activity. During the day the RAF were to claim 96 aircraft and balloons; the Germans admit to losing six aircraft, whilst claiming 26 Allied aircraft and seven balloons in return.

Still aggressive despite their near disaster of the 22nd, 4 AFC Squadron were about early again, in pairs. Captain E J K McCloughry claimed a DFW C east of Lille at 0625, followed by a Fokker ten minutes later, both destroyed, taking his victories to 21. The Fokker's colleagues, however, wounded the Australian but he just managed to regain the Allied lines before force-landing. Soon afterwards, George Jones added another Halberstadt two-seater to the Squadron's bag, this time near Lens. Jones and his fighting partner, Lieutenant V H Thornton, attacked it at 3,000 feet, with Jones getting east of the Germans, thereby cutting off their retreat to safety. Jones then attacked from underneath after which the observer was last seen hanging out of the Halberstadt. Going in for the kill, Jones finished it off. Offizierstellvertreter Ernst Hänisch and Leutnant Richard Biermann, of FA19, crashed at Henin Lietard and were killed.

At 0700, 40 Squadron got into a fight with Jasta 58. Captain G J 'Ben' Strange, the younger brother of the 80 Wing Commander Lieutenant Colonel Louis Strange MC DFC, was seen to shoot down one Fokker in flames, the patrol being awarded another in flames (to Second Lieutenant G S Smith) with two more out of control. Leutnant Martin Demisch was seen to shoot down an SE5a at Abancourt at 0725, his 10th victory—which was Ben Strange—but was then shot down himself and killed, most likely by Smith.

The Americans of the 148th Aero were involved in the first large scale fight of the day, running into seven Fokkers near Bourlon Wood, reinforced by up to 40 more. They claimed seven shot down, but had three of their Camels lost, coming down inside Allied lines but without injury to the pilots. This fight had started at 0728, the two bottom sections of Henry Clay's 'C' Flight being engaged by blue-tailed Fokkers; the two other sections then joined in. Lieutenant E H Zistell was wounded after shooting down two Germans and crash-landed, unconscious, near Bapaume. Lieutenant Larry Callahan also force-landed.

The scrap would appear to have been with Jasta 36, whose machines sported blue tails, and then Jasta Boelcke, for whom Leutnant Paul Baümer claimed a Camel at Sailly for his 31st victory. No. 148, after their reverses earlier in the month, were deliberately beginning to fight in teams. Whilst the Americans could still be said to be relatively inexperienced, the capacity to learn and use their brains to develop advanced tactics was perhaps only equalled by the Australians. Colonel Strange had the two Australian Flying Corps fighter squadrons in his 80 Wing (2 and 4 AFC), and bemoaned the lack of any organised tactics before or during the fight by 40 Squadron, which had resulted in the death of his brother.

Around this time, further to the east of Cambrai, 57 Squadron's DH4s were returning from an attack on Beauvois aerodrome, escorted by 62's Bristols. They ran into 30 more Fokkers, with 62 claiming four but losing Lieutenants N N Coope and H S Mantle—both PoW—and had another Brisfit shot up, with yet another being forced down before it reached base. Another pilot, Captain W E 'Bull' Staton MC DFC, having just gained his 25th victory, the unit's most successful air fighter, was wounded, putting an end to his WWI career. No. 57's gunners, meantime, claimed another three shot down. The Germans claimed three Bristols: Vizefeldwebel Robert Wirth of Jasta 37, south of Beauvois at 0830; Leutnant Lehmann of Jasta 59 reported one down in Allied lines at Boursies; while Leutnant Hans Jebens of the same staffel scored one at Bantouzelle.

There was a good deal of SE5 action at this time. 56 Squadron claimed victories over Sailly, although they had one pilot wounded and forced down. No. 32 Squadron also had a pilot forced down about 0930. The Germans claimed several: Leutnant Rumey, his 42nd victory, and Otto Schmidt his 15th, both from Jasta 5. Oberleutnant Krafft of Jasta 59 scored his 1st at Inchy—time unknown—probably Lieutenant D S Atkinson of 32.

A balloon strafe mounted by 84 Squadron netted three balloons at 0915, while covering aircraft downed a Fokker between Estrées and Gouy. This signalled an intense period of combats. No. 88 Squadron engaged Fokkers near Habourdin aerodrome, the experienced crews of Captain Alan Hepburn/Second Lieutenant H G Eldon and Captain Charles Findlay/Second Lieutenant A B Radford each claiming one at 1010. Vizefeldwebel Peter Stenzel of Jasta 14 was shot down at Fort d'Englos, which is exactly in this location.

Twenty minutes later 2 AFC claimed an Albatros C-type out of control then further to the north; 74 Squadron claimed two Siemens-Schukert DIV rotary-engined scouts out of control. This was one of the few specific instances of Siemens-Schukerts being claimed and identified by British pilots. As this patrol continued, they scored a destroyed by downing a Rumpler two-seater near Lille at 1045.

Just before this, at 1040, the last fight of the morning had started, north-west of Havrincourt. It was the second big fight of the day for the Americans, this time the 17th Aero who claimed seven Fokkers; one in flames, four crashed, and two out of control. This fight was with JGIII at least, as Jasta 27's diarist, Noltenius, reported a fight at this time, during which Vizefeldwebel Schmidt was severely wounded in the knee.

The only other claims of the morning were three DH9s by Jasta 20 and another by Jasta 22s. The former three were in a fight in the La Bassée area, with Leutnant Karl Plauth getting the first at 1040—his 9th victory—and Leutnant Hans Gildemeister the second at Lorgies. The third went to Leutnant Joachim von Busse also at Lorgies, for his 8th victory. No. 103 Squadron lost two 'Nines' but the survivors made no claims, although Leutnant Bruno Hobein was wounded during the day, possibly in this action. Vizefeldwebel Karl Bohnenkamp got the Jasta 22s DH9 far to the south at Vermans, just west of St Quentin, in Allied lines, but at the exact same time. The only two-seater lost near here in the morning was an 8 Squadron 'Big Ack' which left its base at Foucaucourt at 0620 for a contact patrol and never returned.

More balloon attacks occurred late morning/early afternoon. Vizefeldwebel Oskar Hennrich of Jasta 46, the unit's chief balloon-buster, claimed one for his 14th victory at 1120, between Etricourt and Manancourt. Then 84 Squadron made their second balloon-busting run at 1350, claiming a further four—all at Cambrai.

The two ex-RNAS Camel units operating on the Belgian coast had a heavy engagement at 1440. 210 Squadron claimed seven Fokkers and 213 four more, for one casualty. This was Captain S C Joseph DFC of 210, who was wounded and forced to land. He was claimed by Leutnant zur see Wilhelm of MFJ 4, at Pervyse—in Allied lines—at 1415. In all, the Camel pilots claimed eight destroyed and three out of control. Despite these claims, the German Marines reported no losses at all! The idea that it was the inexperienced newcomers that were optimistically over-claiming can be discounted here, as all these claiming pilots were experienced—indeed, all were aces!

Four o'clock saw the next combat, Bristols of 20 Squadron claiming two Fokkers destroyed and two out of control south-east of St Quentin. Ten minutes later Jasta 46 struck at the Allied balloon lines near Fins, Hennrich burning his second gas bag of the day at 1612, another falling to Leutnant auf den Haar, also near Fins. The RAF reported Lieutenant J L King and 2AM B C Holmes baling out of their 1 KBS balloon at 1615. This was closely followed by the loss of the 32nd KBS balloon at 1616, from which Second Lieutenant A E Hopkins and Corporal R B Stewart also baled out safely.

About this time, 49 Squadron lost three DH9s to intense fighter attack while they were trying to bomb Aulnoye railway junction, far to the east of Cambrai. They had left at 1450 and during the day, in this vicinity, the Germans claimed three DH9s and a DH4. The only timed claim was at 1730, by Leutnant Josef Mai of Jasta 5, his 28th victory falling at Beauvais. The others went to Jasta Boelcke's Paul Baümer, south-west of Clary, and Otto Löffler, west of Cambrai, while the 'Four' went to Oberleutnant Hans Helmut von Boddien. This veteran of Jasta 11 was now commander of Jasta 59, and it was his second victory of the day, bringing his score to five. In addition, 49's returning machines carried one wounded pilot and two wounded gunners.

Another 'Nine' was shot down up north, Leutnant zur see Paul Achilles downing a 108 Squadron machine at Werckem at 1620. Another DH bomber, from 211 Squadron, force-landed in Holland, brought down by AA fire.

From 1700 onwards, as evening set in, there were three actions in the Cambrai area at one time involving DH9s of 18 Squadron and their escorting Bristols of 22 Squadron. Also in the action was 32 Squadron, who reported that while on patrol between Cambrai, Le Cateau and Bohain they observed the running fight nearing Cambrai from the east.

Captain Andrew Callender led 32 north to Le Cateau and swung in behind seven Fokkers which were following the bombers and attacked from the east with his lower formation. The Fokkers were taken by surprise and scattered. Callender attacked the leading machine which had a streamer on its rudder, claiming it shot down, believed crashed, on the northern edge of Bourlon Wood. Finding himself under a fight between Fokkers and 'Nines' he attacked three of the Germans over Marquion, one of which went down in a steep spiral, apparently out of control and last seen at 5,000 feet over Havrincourt.

Other pilots claimed three Fokkers as out of control north of Cambrai—all timed between 1705 and 1710—while an 18 Squadron crew claimed two Fokkers in flames, over Marquion at 1715. Prior to this the escorting Bristol crews had been in action: Captain S F H Thompson and Sergeant Ronald M Fletcher, the top crew active in 22 Squadron, claimed a Fokker over Cambrai at 1700. Fletcher was the second highest scoring Bristol observer—this was his 26th victory—and the most successful NCO gunner in WW1. It was also Thompson's 29th victory. The Bristols also reported a further three Fokkers shot down.

This fight was with JGIII, who reported no losses. Also involved was Jasta 44, Vizefeldwebel Becker claiming a British two-seater at Metz-en-Couture, south of Cambrai, which went down on the Allied side at 1725.

Two two-seaters were downed by Captain Roy King of 4 AFC east of Ploegsteert at 1720, while on the coast ten minutes later, Lieutenant David Ingalls, the American Navy pilot flying with 213 Squadron, claimed a Rumpler flying east over Nieuport at 13,000 feet. His report continued:

'Camels pursued and engaged EA over St Pierre Capelle. Lt Ingalls USNRF, fired 200 rounds at 100 yards range. Lt Hodson 100 rounds at 200 yards range. Both pilots followed the EA down to 6,000 feet when machine was observed to fall in flames.'

One of Ingalls' letters home added some detail, which shows just how curt combat reports could be:

'This was the closest shave I had, therefore it is interesting to me. We flew along the lines at 15,000 feet for some time, got disgusted and started for home, as it was getting dark. As we left the lines, I saw "Archie" over La Panne and there picked up a machine heading towards Ostende on our side of the lines. I fired my guns to attract Hodson's attention and set out in pursuit, for Archie on our side of the lines meant a Hun... The Hun was an old Rumpler, the slowest I ever saw, and he kept on, so I dove under him and came up from below. But he was so slow that I overshot and could not train my guns on him. So I dove again and tried once more. He would turn one way to give his observer a shot and I would try to keep under him, making a bigger circle, so his observer could not shoot. A few seconds and I tried to come up beneath him again. His machine was too slow again and I almost overshot, but succeeded in firing a few rounds from just beneath.

'Nothing happened, so I dropped and continued working for a good position, completely fed up at not being able to get one. On a turn he very nearly got me, for before I could make the outside circle, his observer fired about ten shots, the tracers all going by between the struts on my left side. We were only ten yards off at the time and I could see the two Huns perfectly in their black helmets, and it was rather fascinating to be so close. All the time we were getting further over the lines and I was getting madder. So I gave up the careful, cautious tactics, got straight behind him and kept firing for probably 100 rounds.

'At last a big puff of smoke came up like an explosion and I felt fine. I turned and dove down to the ground to chase myself home. When way over the lines and not high enough to be safe from Archie, the stunt is to race along just over the ground at about 200 to 300 feet. I had not seen Hodson anywhere.'

Ingalls Camel was none the less damaged by ground fire and he only just got back to base. The 1st Marine Feld Flieger Abteilung lost Leutnant Emil Melcher in this action.

Twenty minutes later, the SE5s of 41 Squadron claimed a Fokker destroyed west of Comines with another out of control. Captain C Crawford was shot down and taken prisoner at 1800, downed by Leutnant Carl Degelow, north of Zillebeke Lake, the 17th victory for this CO and leading ace of Jasta 40s. Another SE5a was claimed south of Ypres at the same time by Vizefeldwebel Maack of Jasta 63—in Allied lines—but none are reported forced down.

Ten minutes after 6 o'clock, 59 Squadron's Captain D H M Carberry took his total to at least five, the second highest for an artillery observation pilot. He and Lieutenant J B V Clements were doing a recce to Gonnelieu at 1,200 feet when they saw two Halberstadts behind the enemy lines three hundred feet higher. One hundred rounds from Carberry's front gun into one of them resulted in some return fire but the two-seater spun down and crashed near Lateau Wood.

The German lost a two-seater crew on the Somme this day, noted as a ground fire casualty. Vizefeldwebels Hermann Hoos and Richard Wagner of Schlasta 15 were both captured.

At 1820, 2 AFC entered their second combat of the day. Fifteen SEs, in three flights of five, were west of Lille at 17,000 feet; then over Habourdin, 11 Fokkers were encountered in two layers. Captain Eric Simonson led a flight on to the top five, with the other ten going for the lower six. Later some Pfalz Scouts attempted to intervene. Total claims by the Australians came to eight. (It is possible the Jasta 14 loss occurred in the fight rather than with 88 Squadron earlier.)

The last fight of the day occurred as darkness approached, at 1845. 204 Squadron attacked a formation of Fokker Biplanes and Triplanes in the Pervyse to Dixmude area. One Triplane and five DVIIs were claimed for the loss of Second Lieutenant T Warburton, brought down and captured by Josef Jacobs of Jasta 7, who generally led his unit in a black Triplane, even at this late stage of the war. Jacobs noted in his diary:

> 'As we flew towards Ypres, three Camels started gliding after us and I pulled my flight up slowly in the direction of Dixmude, and, sure enough, they opened their engines to cut us off. I stood my Triplane on its nose and the highest flying Camel dropped down erratically as my guns stuttered. I kicked rudder and went after him while a couple of my chaps fired bursts across his nose to prevent him from getting away. I finally caught him again, just above the ground, and the Englishman defended himself to the last and did not want to capitulate, but he suddenly banked around and started to land near Moorslede, but turned over when his wheels hit some shell-holes. The pilot, Lieutenant Warburton, was unhurt and taken prisoner. I had a look at his machine that evening which was completely wrecked. The chap must have had incredibly good luck not to have been injured.'

Jasta 7 had set out seven-strong and all returned, so what was considered a six-to-one victory for 204 was actually a one-to-nil loss! Jacobs was probably the only ace still in a Triplane. He liked the Tripe better than a DVII, and he had a good reason for inspecting the downed Camel. His main problem was the supply of suitable rotary engines for his Driedekker and he had a standing arrangement with front line troops to send back any rotary engines they should find undamaged in crashed British aircraft. A case of champagne would be their reward and suffice it to say Jacobs generally obtained a replacement engine for his black machine, with its Nordic 'God of the North Wind' insignia painted on the fuselage.

That night, the CO of 65 Squadron, Major Hugh Champion de Crespigny, together with one of his pilots, Lieutenant Maurice Newnham, attacked Gontrude aerodrome between 2200 and 0030 hours, despite strong winds and a rain storm, one of the earliest examples of night intruder sorties by single-seaters.

This night too, FE2 bombers were out; one 101 machine taking off at 2125 failed to return, its crew being brought down, wounded and taken prisoner. A 102 Squadron FE headed off at 2330 but its engine was hit by ground fire and the pilot had to force-land at Sailleaumont; the observer was injured but the FE was salvaged.

French Front

Sous Lieutenant d'Estainville of Spa.87 burnt the Bourgogne balloon at 0745.

Two French aces added to their scores, Sous Lieutenant Charles Marie Joseph Leon Nuville, a 29-year-old with 22 months on Spa.57, claimed his 12th at 1215, a two-seater down at Cernay-en-Dormies, in company with Maréchal-des-Logis Imhoff. Four hours later, Captain Henri Hay de Slade, CO of Spa.159, gained his 15th by downing an EA north of Suippes. French pilots also scored five probables during the day.

Jasta 44s claimed a French two-seater in the morning, probably Sous Lieutenant Bouillane and Sergent Junot. They were wounded when their Bréguet, along with two others, was in action with 10 EA on the Picardie sector. (Unit not recorded.) The Bréguet was claimed by Offizierstellvertreter Bansmer at 1050, in French lines, south-west of Attigny. Another two-seater victory went to Vizefeldwebel Friedrich Poeschke of Jasta 53. At 1100 he shot down a Salmson 2A2 of Sal.263 at Besine, which crashed south of Somme-Py, although he in fact claimed a Spad XI.

Pilots of Spa.78 claimed a two-seater in the area of Xammes at 1133. The action began at 4,700 metres, the German spinning down to 400, when another 100 rounds were fired into it. The crew were Vizefeldwebel Fittgen and Leutnant Konnigs of FA37.

Balloons were again the target of the German pilots during the day. Unteroffizier Heinrich Haase of Jasta 21s shot down the balloon of 75 Cié south of Braisne at 1350, but Leutnant Wilhelm Meyer of Jasta 47 was lost to ground fire while attacking a balloon at 1630, being taken prisoner. The French balloon of 45 Cié was damaged by French defensive fire during this attack. Either Meyer or Leutnant Wember of Jasta 61 were, however, credited with this balloon, or another that was lost in this area. At 1810, Adjutant Couillard of 43 Cié jumped successfully for the fourth time, after the attentions of Vizefeldwebel Max Kuhn, also Jasta 21s, south of Fismes, at 1815.

American Sector

The front was still fairly quiet as the build-up for the 26th continued. At 1530, a patrol from the 22nd Aero claimed a two-seater near Woël. A C-type of FA29, crewed by Vizefeldwebel Wilkens and Leutnant Rudolf Kaehne, fell near Briey in the Armee Abteilung 'C' Sector, Kaehne certainly being killed.

Jasta 15's acting commander, Leutnant Johannes Klein, shot down a Spad at 1615, and Offizierstellvertreter Gustav Dörr also claimed a Spad near Soissons at 1900, but no corresponding losses have been found. However, Lieutenant E L Moore of the 49th Aero seems to have been slightly wounded on this date.

	A/C	KB			DES	OOC	KB
British losses	14	—		British claims	52	37	7
French losses	2	4		French claims	4	—	1
American losses	—	—		American claims	1		
German claims	26	7		German losses	6†		?

† Possibly at least two more, 17 Armee reporting four men killed, units unknown.

British Casualties

Aircraft type	No.	Squadron	Crew		
SE5a	E4054	40 Sqdn	Capt G J Strange	KIA	
AWFK8	B8837	8 Sqdn	Lt W F R Robinson	MIA	
			Lt J H Roberts	KIA	
Camel	E7160	4 AFC	Capt E J K McCloughry	WIA	*
BF2b	E2515	62 Sqdn	Lt N N Coope	POW	
			2/Lt H S Mantle	POW	
BF2b	D7899?	62 Sqdn	Capt W E Staton MC DFC	WIA	*
			Lt L E Mitchell	Safe	
SE5a	F5488	56 Sqdn	Lt F A Sedore	WIA	*
SE5a	D6983	32 Sqdn	Lt D S Atkinson	Safe	
DH9	5842	103 Sqdn	Lt H C Noel	KIA	
			Sgt L C Owens	POW	
DH9	D2877	103 Sqdn	Lt C Hebner	KIA	
			2/Lt D Davenport	KIA	
DH4	F6165	18 Sqdn	Lt R C Bennett	Safe	*
			Lt A Lilley	Safe	
DH9	D3251	211 Sqdn	2/Lt J Olorenshaw	Interned	
			2/Lt R L Kingham	Interned	
DH9	D7208	108 Sqdn	2/Lt J M Dandy	POW	
			Sgt C P Crites	POW	
DH9	E8869	49 Sqdn	Capt E D Asbury	KIA	
			2/Lt E J Gillman	KIA	
DH9	F6098	49 Sqdn	Lt C C Conover	POW	
			2/Lt H J Pretty	POW	
DH9	E658	49 Sqdn	Lt H J Bennett	POW	
			2/Lt R H Armstrong	POW	
DH9		49 Sqdn	2/Lt L Eteson (O)	WIA	*
DH9		49 Sqdn	2/Lt L C Belcher (O)	WIA	*
DH9		49 Sqdn	2/Lt E C Moore (P)	WIA	*
BF2b	E2363	11 Sqdn	2/Lt C Johnson	WIA	*
			Sgt G H Hampson	WIA	
SE5a	E4074	41 Sqdn	Capt K Crawford	POW	
Camel	C6620	4 Sqdn	Lt D T Warburton	POW	
Camel	B7232	204 Sqdn	Lt O J Orr	Safe	*
Camel	D8147	210 Sqdn	Capt S C Joseph	WIA	*
DH9		207 Sqdn	2/Lt J M Mackinnon	WIA	*
BF2b		22 Sqdn	Capt G McCormack (O)	WIA	*
FE2b (night)	D9922	102 Sqdn	2/Lt W Lloyd-Williams	Safe	*
			Lt O Reilly-Patey DFC	Inj	
FE2b „	D9921	101 Sqdn	Lt B H Kelly	POW	
			2/Lt J W Brown	POW	

French Casualties

Bréguet XIV		Br.?	S/Lt Bouillanne	Safe	?
			Sgt Junot	KIA	

| Salmson 2A2 | Sal.263 | Sgt Delporte | KIA |
| | | S/Lt Burfin | KIA |

American Casualties

| Spad XIII | 49th Aero | 1/Lt E L Moore | WIA ? |

Wednesday, 25 September 1918

British Front

An overcast sky with rain in the morning reduced aerial activity. A patrol of 64 Squadron made the first encounter at 1740, a C-type out of control near Bourlon Wood—possibly Vizefeldwebel Adolf Mertens and Leutnant Hans Stanger of FA(A)207, who were reported lost near La Ferrières, although further south than Bourlon. (See also comment on 18 September re. Stanger.)

There were no other reported actions until 1745, 213 Squadron losing three Camels in a fight with Marine units. No. 213 did claim one Fokker in return but Vizeflugmeister Alexandre Zenses of MFJ 2 got his 8th victory, Paul Achilles of MFJ 5 his 4th and 5th.

A couple more Fokkers were claimed by 208 and then 85 Squadron around 1800, while over Fresnoy, 27 Squadron's bombers ran into Jastas 34b and 31, losing two aircraft. Robert Greim scored his 24th victory by downing one south of Escaufort at 1815, Unteroffizier Brungel the other at Busigny, at 1825. No. 27 did claim one Fokker destroyed and three out of control. The one destroyed was seen to spin into the ground between Bohain and Ponchaux; of the 'OOCs', one disappeared in low cloud after falling like a leaf, another—a most persistent German pilot firing from under the DH9's tail—also went down, confirmed by 148 Squadron as out of control, while the last out of control was finally observed to pull out and land in a field.

In fights between 1800 and 1830, 20 Squadron claimed no fewer than eight Fokkers between Cambrai and St Quentin, 22 claiming two more between Cambrai and Bourlon Wood. Amidst this, 25 Squadron's bombers were in action against Fokkers, claiming one over Bohain and two more over Ponchaux. Gefreiter Franz Wagner of Jasta 79b was killed in action at Preselles Ferme, by either 25 or 22 Squadron, while Leutnant Fritz von Braun claimed a Bristol down at Villers Guislain.

There were no DH4 losses reported, although earlier in the day 25 Squadron's Captain S Jones had to force-land at Haute Avesnes at 1130 with a wounded observer. Jones left the machine ticking over while he arranged for the wounded man to be taken to hospital. He then instructed two orderlies to load the rear cockpit with ballast but the throttle accidentally opened, the aircraft moved forward, ran 50 yards and turned over. The damage needed to be repaired at No.2 ASD.

On the half-hour, Major Geoffrey Bowman MC and bar burnt a Rumpler north-east of Ypres for his 30th victory, possibly a crew lost from Schusta 24. Bowman had first spotted some Fokkers over the Roulers-Menin road but was then attracted to the two-seater by white AA bursts. He wrote:

'I fired 40 rounds from both guns at close range and EA burst into flames. I turned back to the lines and after about half a minute, saw the flames die down. I turned back towards the EA, who was then flying nose-down, due north, and not burning very well. I fired again at long range without effect. At 2,000 feet over Houthulst Forest, owing to bad visibility, I could not see if he crashed. EA burnt slowly the whole way down.'

The former Naval units were in action during the next half hour, with 204 Squadron reporting two Fokkers colliding while attacking Lieutenant C J Sims south-west of Ostende. No. 213 then lost its fourth pilot of the day, Second Lieutenant G Iliff giving Leutnant Franz Piechulek of Jasta 56 his 11th victory at Kortemarck at 1850.

The only other loss this day was an RE8, shot down by ground fire at 1620. The crew force-landed in the front lines, and although the crew were safe, the machine had to be abandoned.

The final action of the day came an hour before midnight over Arras. Lieutenant T R Bloomfield of 151 Squadron shot down an AEG of Bogohl 6, although he reported his kill as a Gotha. As he attacked he could see pamphlets being thrown out of a bottom trap door. Opening fire, the machine almost immediately caught fire and fell burning between Montenescourt and Agny, exploding when it hit the ground. Leutnant Reinhold Lampe, Feldwebel August Platte, Unteroffizier Karl Ruehlicke and Gefreiter Adolf Morch were all killed.

French Front

Two Spad fighters were shot down early in the day. At 0805, Leutnant Rudolf Fuchs of Jasta 77b claimed his first victory over Arnaville; Caporal Abeles of Spa.88 was reported missing in the area. In the same area, Sergent Millot of Spa.65 was attacked by three Fokker Triplanes. he spun vertically and force-landed, his Spad riddled with bullets but he appears not to have been claimed.

To the north of the French line, Vizefeldwebel Karl Treiber of Jasta 5 claimed a Spad two-seater south of St Quentin at 1800, which was probably the Bréguet lost this day. In the II Armée area, a Salmson of Sal.47 broke up in the air during a fight with six Fokkers, falling in German lines at Hageville, shot down by Leutnant Friedrich Hengst of Jasta 64w. Only one German aircraft was claimed by the French, Adjutant Priollaud of Spa.150 shooting down one over Ornes during the day.

The Germans also got a night victory. This was scored by Leutnant Fritz Anders of the night-fighting Jasta 73, over Moronvillers, the location where a Farman of F.114 was lost. Anders had been a pilot since 1912, and this was his second kill of the month, and his 5th night kill. It was also his 7th overall—and last.

American Sector

First Lieutenant Eddie Rickenbacker of the 94th Aero claimed a Fokker and a Halberstadt two-seater near Billy, and north-east of Verdun in the morning. Then at 1002, the 139th destroyed a Rumpler near Damloup.

Jagdgeschwader Nr.1 began offensive operations on the Front this day, Jasta 10's Leutnant Justas Grassmann burning a balloon at 0950 near Pont-à-Mousson. The US 10th Balloon Company lost its gas bag near Jezainville, five kilometres from Pont-à-Mousson, the observer, Lieutenant J W Lavers, taking to his parachute.

IAF

After some days of inactivity, the IAF set out on long range bombing raids today. Twelve aircraft of 55 Squadron took off at 0815 to bomb the munitions factories south of Kaiserslautern, attacking at 1010 with nine 230 lb and six 112 lb bombs. On the return trip they were engaged by 12 enemy fighters, later reinforced as the danger period near the lines was entered. No. 55 claimed two destroyed and two out of control, but lost four. Three fell to Jasta 70, including one in Allied lines; Leutnant Anton Stephen crashed one at Albertsweiler, Vizefeldwebel Lemke one at Bergzabern, and Vizefeldwebel Krist one at Brumath. The other went down near the target area at 1010, under the guns of Leutnant von Beaulieu-Marconnay, the Jasta 19 pilot's 20th victory.

Then 11 aircraft, the modern DH9a machines of 110 Squadron, set out to bomb railway works at Frankfurt, flying in two formations. The first was led by Captain A Lindlay, the other by Captain A C M Groom. The Squadron dropped one-and-a-half tons of bombs at midday, but during the five-hour-40-minute sortie, four bombers were shot down, despite the gunners claiming to have sent down five fighters out of control. Among those lost was the first formation leader. The survivors landed at base with one dead and two wounded gunners.

The first two losses were at 1115 and 1120, on the outward journey, Gefreiter Meyer of Jasta 3 sending his victim down south-east of Sarralben, swiftly followed by Jasta 15's Leutnant Georg Hantelmann's kill south of Metz. The last two, well on the return journey, went to Jasta 78b, Leutnant Richard Schmidt, at Zabern at 1430, and Vizefeldwebel Prime near Buhl airfield at 1500.

In fact, Buhl airfield was also the target assigned to five aircraft of 99 Squadron. They too were engaged, one DH being badly shot up, the crew eventually crash-landing in Allied lines, two miles short of their base at Azelet, south of Nancy.

IAF bombers really needed escorts, but most of their German targets were simply out of range of any fighter types. They would have been happy to meet short-range escorts as they returned to the lines, but of course there was no way of knowing when or where the bombers would re appear. Even if a spot and approximate time were arranged, a running fight with German fighters would invariably split up the bombers and alter their courses and ETA home.

	A/C	KB		DES	OOC	KB
British losses	7	—	British claims	15	7	—
French losses	5	—	French claims	1		—
American losses	—	1	American claims	4		—
IAF losses	8	—	IAF claims	2	7	—
German claims	22	1	German losses	4?†		?

† Personnel casualties suggest at least two or three more may have been lost.

British Casualties

Aircraft type	No.	Squadron	Crew		
DH4	A8051	25 Sqdn	Capt S Jones	Safe	*
			2/Lt J Pullar	WIA	
DH4	D3163	27 Sqdn	2/Lt C B Sanderson	POW	
			Sgt J Wilding	POW	
DH4	E8857	27 Sqdn	2/Lt A V Cosgrove	POW	
			2/Lt S C Read	POW	
RE8	F5892	59 Sqdn	Lt J Stanley	Safe	
			2/Lt J W Elias	Safe	
Camel	B7252	213 Sqdn	Lt C P Sparkes	POW	
Camel	D8216	213 Sqdn	Lt L C Scroggie	POW	
Camel	D3360	213 Sqdn	2/Lt J C Sorley	MIA	
Camel	E4385	213 Sqdn	2/Lt G Iliff	KIA	
DH4	D8413	55 Sqdn	2/Lt A J Robinson	KIA	
			2/Lt M R Burnett	KIA	
DH4	D8356	55 Sqdn	2/Lt J B Dunn	KIA	
			2/Lt H S Orange	KIA	
DH4	D8388	55 Sqdn	2/Lt P G Pretty	KIA	
			2/Lt G R Bartlett	KIA	
DH4	F5714	55 Sqdn	Lt G B Dunlop	POW	
			2/Lt A C Hayes	POW	
DH4		55 Sqdn	2/Lt H Wood	WIA	*
DH4		55 Sqdn	2/Lt C Turner	Safe	*
			2/Lt J T L Atwood	KIA	
DH9a	F992	110 Sqdn	Lt L S Brooke	KIA	
			2/Lt F Proven	KIA	
DH9a	E9660	110 Sqdn	Lt C B E Lloyd	POW	
			2/Lt H J C Elwig	POW	
DH9a	F1030	110 Sqdn	Capt A Lindley	POW	
			Lt C R Cross	POW	
DH9a	E8422	110 Sqdn	Sgt H W Tozier	KIA	
			Sgt W Platt	KIA	
DH9a	F1000	110 Sqdn	2/Lt C M B Stevenson	Safe	*
			Lt H J Cockman	WIA	
DH9a		110 Sqdn	Lt F R Casey (O)	WIA	*
DH9	D3270	99 Sqdn	2/Lt King	Safe	*
			2/Lt J M Oliphant	Safe	

French Casualties

Bréguet XIV	Br.?		Adj Fabiani	MIA
			S/Lt Lormail	MIA
Farman	F.114		Lt Bizard	MIA
			Capt Garnier	MIA
			Asp Rives	MIA
Spad XIII	Spa.88		Cpl Abeles	MIA
Spad XIII	Spa.65		Sgt Millot	Safe
Salmson 2A2	Sal.47		Sgt Chauffeur	KIA
			MdL Alby	KIA

Thursday, 26 September 1918

British Front

The weather which was fine during the previous night, continued fine during this day. There was good activity on the British Front, but the main feature of the day was the opening of the Meuse-Argonne offensive on the French and American sectors. It was not, however, until mid-morning that the air actions began for the RAF.

The first big fight was timed between 1030 and 1100 hours, on the coast north-east of Ostende to Blankenberghe. Camels of 65 and 204 Squadrons were in combat, giving direct or indirect escort to DH4s of 202 Squadron. No. 204 claimed two destroyed and four out of control for the loss of two, to MFJ 5 pilots Flugmaats Karl Engelfried and Christian Kairies, one at Wenduyne, the other at Neumunster. The latter pilot's victory was over the very aggressive Canadian ace Lieutenant W B Craig, from Smith Falls, Ontario, who was killed. Since mid-August he had scored 8 victories and was about to receive the DFC. One DH4 also went down, this last being seen at 16,500 feet over Ostende, being chased by five enemy fighters, the kill going to Leutnant zur see Freymadel. No. 65 also lost a Camel, credited to Vizeflugmeister Sawatski of MFJ 1, also over Ostende, and flown by Lieutenant W R Thornton who was taken prisoner.

During the latter half of the morning, 87 and 65 Squadron both claimed two-seaters, while 74 Squadron shot down a Fokker Biplane. 48 Squadron also got one of eight Fokkers that engaged them over Menin, although the Bristol crew then had their engine shot out and they had to force-land. On the German side, Vizefeldwebel Karl Bohnenkamp of Jasta 22s claimed a Camel down in Allied lines north-west of Ronnsoy as his 12th victory, but there is no obvious corresponding loss.

A big airfield strafe took place soon after lunch, Camels, SE5s and BF2bs of 203, 40 and 22 Squadrons going for Lieu St Amand, 12 km north-east of Cambrai. The SE5s went in first, dropping their 25 lb bombs on hangars and huts, one of the former catching fire, while several huts were destroyed. No. 203 followed them down, setting fire to three more hangars and bombing a fourth. Living quarters were also strafed. A DFW two-seater was also set on fire. Major Ray Collishaw, the Canadian ace and CO of 203, attacked a fighter he saw taking off and shot it down in flames. Later he brought down another enemy machine. Lieutenant D Woodhouse also spotted some mounted troops on a nearby road and shot them up, inflicting several apparent casualties. In all 88 bombs fell on the target, and five aircraft were destroyed by 203, two more by the escorting Bristols.

The Camels did not have it all their own way: Second Lieutenant W H Coghill, having successfully engaged one Fokker, was hit and wounded by another. Two more Camels were shot up, one pilot force-landing in the front line. Lieutenant N C Dixie got into the front trenches but his Camel was shelled. These were probably among the claims of JGIII, Bruno Loerzer getting his last two kills of the war at this time, bringing his score to 44. Ernst Bormann of Jasta 2 also claimed a Camel around this time, north of Cambrai, and if it was not one of 203's machines it may have been a Dolphin of 23 Squadron that was last seen over Bellicourt at 1145. 203 lost another Camel during the day, Lieutenant F J S Britnell DSC being brought down by ground fire while on contact patrol. His engine seized and he too plunged into the front line trenches, surviving, but his fighter was lost. 'Duke' Britnell was an ace, having accounted for his 8th victory this very day.

During the afternoon, the 148th Aero had a big fight east of Bourlon Wood, and Fritz Rumey of Jasta 5 scored his 43rd victory over a Bristol Fighter of 'L' Flight at Gouzeaucourt. At 1433, Vizefeldwebel Christian Mesch of Jasta 26 claimed a Dolphin west of St Quentin, but this was more probably a Bristol Fighter of 20 Squadron, time and location fitting. He was not the first German pilot to confuse the double-bays of the Dolphin (overlooking the wing-stagger) with the BF2b.

More combats abound. No. 80 Squadron fought Jasta 31 at 1740, each claiming one, but it was a Camel that came down in flames north-west of St Quentin, accounted for by Leutnant Sylvester Garsztka for his 5th victory (although he claimed an SE5). At 1805, Jasta 5 attacked DH4s of 57 Squadron, two falling, one to Rumey—his 44th victory—while Karl Treiber gained his 4th kill, all scored this month, with two more to come. Another of the bombers, flown by

Top left: Leutnant Gunther von Buren, Jasta 18, wounded in a fight with the Spads of the 13th Aero, 14 September.

Top right: Three pilots with Jasta 2 were Gerhard Bassenge, Friedrich Kempf and Hermann Vallendor. Bassenge and Vallendor both scored kills in September, while Kempf scored his first victory on the last day of April 1917.

Middle: Fokker DVIIs of Jasta 18. Note the raven on the fuselage, a reference to the unit CO, Leutnant August Raben (raven). The machine in the middle is that of Ltn Heinz Kustner.

Bottom left: Otto Schmidt, leader of Jasta 5, shot down four aircraft and one balloon in September, achieving 20 kills by the war's end.

Bottom centre: Leutnant Rudolf Stark, commander of Jasta 35b, three confirmed kills during September.

Bottom right: Captain Kenneth P Littauer, commander of the 88th Aero, won the DSC for his actions on 14 September, being shot down by Jasta 77b into the Allied lines, his observer wounded.

Top left: Lieutenants C F Galbraith DFC and A T Sprangle, 5 Squadron. Galbraith, from Winnipeg, was mortally wounded on 15 September in air combat but returned to his aerodrome. The name 'Kildonan' refers to his home town.

Top right: Lieutenant A R D 'Archie' Campbell, 20 Squadron, PoW 15 September, by AA fire, the second time he was shot down that day.

Above left: Men of the 90th Aero Observation Squadron: Lts Allan Lockwood, Percy Schuss, Captain William Schauffler (CO), John Sherrick, Fred A Tillman DSC and Van Haydon.

Above right: Lieutenant H A Kullberg DFC, 1 Squadron, wounded 16 September.

Right: Captain J W Pearson, an American flying with 23 Squadron RAF, claimed two Fokkers on 18 September. He was one of the last US WW1 aces to die (1993).

Top left: First Lieutenant Thornton D Hooper, commander of the 11th Aero, taken prisoner on 18 September, during a raid on Mars-le-Tour. Four others of his Squadron failed to return.

Top right: Leutnant Ulrich Neckel was amongst the claimants against the 11th Aero on 18 September, but it was only his second kill of the month.

Above left: Three pilots of Jasta 26: Erich Buder, Otto Fruhner and Otto Esswein. Fruhner scored his last nine kills during September, to bring his score to 27.

Above right: 1/Lieutenant Chester Wright, 93rd Aero, gained the first two of his eventual nine victories in mid-September.

Left: 1/Lieutenant Frank A Llewellyn DSC, C Flight Commander of the 99th Aero, from 19 September. Note pilot's front gun on the Salmson's cowling.

Top left: Lieutenant Arthur Reed DFC, a South African serving with 29 Squadron, brought his score to 19 in September with five victories, and received a Bar to his medal.

Top right: Captain Ron Sykes of 201 Sqn, recorded a memorable fight with Jasta 27 on 20 Sept.

Above left: Lieutenant C G Ross DFC, 29 Squadron, forced down 20 September.

Bottom: Bristol Fighter of 48 Squadron, brought down 20 September, the crew being captured.

Top left: Canadian Major D A MacRae, 83 Squadron, with his observer, hit and forced down by ground fire while in a night recce sortie, 20/21 September.

Top right: Captain Sydney Carlin MC DFC, 74 Squadron, PoW 21 September after a fight with Jasta 29.

Bottom left: Carl Degelow, Jasta 40s, scored six of his 30 kills in September.

Bottom right: Lieutenant W G Allanson, 7 Squadron, killed in action 21 September, shot down by Carl Degelow, Jasta 40s.

Top left: Leutnant Josef Jacobs, CO of Jasta 7, shot down his 30th victory on 21 September - a DH9.

Top right: Two of the main RAF day bombers were the DH9 and DH9a.

Middle left: Major C J Quintin-Brand MC. CO 151 night-fighter Squadron, he shot down three German bombers in September, two on the 21st.

Bottom: An RE8 crew prepare for a sortie.

Top: Another confirmed victory - this time a downed Gotha GV.

Middle left: While Gothas and Friedrichshafens raided into Allied territory, the IAF's Handley Page O/400s attacked targets in occupied territory and Germany. This one is being refuelled - note petrol cans.

Middle right: RAF airmen work on the

wreckage of a Friedrichshafen GIII bomber, two of which were brought down by 151 Squadron on the night of 17/18 September.

Bottom left: The IAF's main day bombers were the DH4 (note cowling on ground)......

Bottom right: ....and the Airco DH9. Note how the gunner's cockpit has been placed nearer the pilot in the later machine.

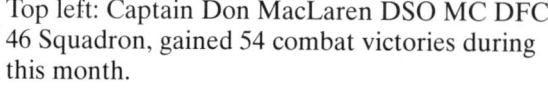

Top left: Captain Don MacLaren DSO MC DFC, 46 Squadron, gained 54 combat victories during this month.

Top right: Leutnant Friedrich Noltenius, Jasta 27, left vivid descriptions of the September fighting in his diary entries. He scored nine victories during this month.

Above left: Hermann Becker of Jasta 19, scored eight of his 25 victories during September 1918.

Above right: Paul Bäumer of Jasta Boelcke, claimed an impressive 16 kills in September, including three triples in a day.

Top left: Hermann Frommherz, Jasta 27; ten September kills.

Top right: Salmson 2A2 flown by Lieutenants William P Erwin and Arthur E Easterbrook, 1st Aero Squadron.

Above left: Easterbrook and 1/Lieutenant Arthur J Coyle, 1st Aero.

Above right: Lieutenants Byrne V Baucom DSC, William P Erwin DSC and Arthur E Easterbrook DSC – 1st Aero Squadron.

Left: Oskar von Boenigk, commanded JGII in September, a unit which caused havoc amongst the Allied aircrews. Boenigk himself shot down five aircraft to bring his score to a final 26.

Top left: Bruno Loerzer, commander of JGIII, scored his final ten victories in September, bringing his score to 44.

Top centre: Amongst the high scores on the German side was Franz Büchner, leader of Jasta 13. He downed 17 aircraft, including four on the 26th. He ended the war with 40 kills.

Top right: Gustav Dörr, Jasta 45, was another high scorer with seven of his 35 kills scored during September - all Spad types.

Above left: Max Näther of Jasta 62, also scored seven victories in September, including two Spads and a balloon on the 26th.

Above right: Oskar Hennrich, Jasta 46, added nine victories to his score in September, including six balloons.

Top left: Oliver von Beaulieu-Marconnay, commander of Jasta 19, netted eight kills during this month, including three Bréguet bombers on the 16th, although only two were confirmed. In all he scored 25.

Top right: Spad XIII, 28th Aero Squadron.

Middle right: Captain Albert W Stevens, operating a camera, 24th Aero.

Bottom: Four stalwarts of the 95th Aero: Ted Curtis, Harold Buckley, Alex McLanahan and John Mitchell.

Top left: Salmson 2A2 of the 91st Observation Squadron.

Top right: René Fonck, of Spa. 103, and the Allied WW1 Ace of aces, scored seven victories in September, six of them on the 26th.

Middle left: French Caudron R. XI 'escort gunship'.

Bottom: French Spad XI, two-seat recce machine.

Top left: Second Lieutenant W R Thornton, 65 Squadron, PoW, brought down by Marine Jasta 1.

Top right: Reinhold Poss and Christian Kairies, MFJ V.

Middle left: Second Lieutenant W B 'Scottie' Craig, 204 Squadron, shot down by Christian Kairies, of MFJ V.

Above right: Fritz Rumey and Paul Bäumer, Jastas 5 and 2, both scored 16 kills in September, but Rumey was killed in action on the 27th.

Left: Ernst Udet of Jasta 4, brought his score to 62 on 26 September by downing two DH9 bombers, although he was wounded on this day.

Top left: Leutnant Georg Meyer, Jasta 37, scored five of his 24 victories during September.

Top right: Lieutenant W H Maxted, 3 Squadron, downed a Balloon and an LVG on 27 September.

Middle: Captain Frank L Hale, an American with 32 Squadron RAF, claimed six of his seven victories during September, including three on the 27th. He received the DFC shortly afterwards.

Left: Josef Mai, Jasta 5, brought his WW1 score to 30 in September with seven victories.

Top left: Lieutenant William W Spriggs flew with Squadron, and was awarded the DFC in October.

Top right: Captain William H Hubbard DFC won a bar to his DFC during September, flying with 73 Squadron. From Toronto he flew low attack sorties against anti-tank guns, in front of the Canadian Corps attacks.

Above left: Another air fighter involved in

September's ground work was 73 Squadron's Lieutenant E J Lussier DFC. Photo taken on the aerodrome at Foucaucourt in September 1918 (Camel E1551).

Above right: Captain Eddie Rickenbacker, 94th Aero. Although he was not to receive his Medal of Honor until 1930, the citation makes mention of his actions near Billy, on 25 September, shooting down a Fokker and a Halberstadt two-seater.

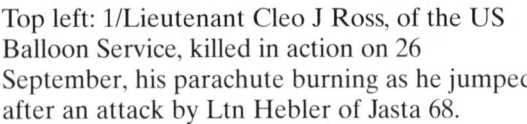

Top left: 1/Lieutenant Cleo J Ross, of the US Balloon Service, killed in action on 26 September, his parachute burning as he jumped after an attack by Ltn Hebler of Jasta 68.

Top right: Airco DH4 (A7845), 202 Squadron. Note under-wing fuel tank.

Above left: Pilots of 92 Squadron, summer 1918. Rear: Lt E T Crabb, Lt E Shapard, Millar; front: Haddon-Smith, Capt O J Rose DFC (an American) and Lt T S Horry. Oren Rose scored four victories during September, Shapard one. Rose, Crabb, Shapard and Horry all ended the was as aces.

Above right: Bristol Fighter with Lieutenant C W M Thompson of 22 Squadron standing by it. He was brought down and taken prisoner on 29 September, by Jasta Boelcke.

Right: Lieutenant Francis R Pemberton was an American who flew with 65 Squadron in September and was wounded in action on 4 November.

Captain A Newman and Lieutenant E G Pernet, claimed a Fokker in flames south-east of Cambrai but Pernet was wounded. The DH force-landed in Allied lines, and so did another DH, also badly shot about. 46 and 208 Squadrons also had scraps with Fokkers in the early evening.

Balloons were attacked and destroyed by Jasta 46, one falling to Vizefeldwebel Oskar Hennrich at 1645—his 16th victory—and one to Unteroffizier Fröhlich at 1745, his first of two kills. Both balloons were at Lieramont, the first belonging to 6-15-5, the second to 14-14-5.

During the day, two Jasta 37 pilots were wounded, Vizefeldwebel Robert Wirth and Leutnant Mappes. It is difficult to know by whom but the fights with 22 and 203 might provide the most probable source.

French Front

Dawn saw the beginnings of a clear and beautiful day, the day the French/American offensive began. A feature of the Allied plan was to capture and disrupt the German rail system, making it difficult for them to bring up supplies and reinforcements, and to hinder any sort of retreat. The main cross-railway line ran from Metz through Montmedy-Mezières-Hirson to Valenciènnes, although the vital section was the Metz-Mezières line. If this could be cut or disrupted between these two points before the Germans could withdraw from France and Belgium, then the ruin of the German Army would be accomplished. Thus the mission of the French/American forces was to cut this vital rail line, while the Germans knew they must hold it to stop a catastrophe. The task was given to the French IV Armée and General Pershing's 1st US Army.

The chosen ground was difficult for the attackers; it was, after all, a forest, and a hilly one at that. At 0200 hours, 3,800 guns opened fire on the German trenches and positions to their rear for the ritual, but not always effective, softening-up process. The French and Americans went 'over the top' at 0530.

Attacks were to continue along this front for the 47 remaining days of the war. The number of aircraft Colonel Mitchell had at his disposal had dropped recently to about 800, 600 of which were American.

The air war was very much more sophisticated by this stage of the war. As an example, the French bombers deliberately bombed German airfields commencing at 0130, to try and keep the German fighters on the ground. The specialist night-bombers of GB7 acted as path-finders with volunteer crews from the three Groupes de Bombardements of Escadre 12. GB's 5, 6 and 9 bombed various airfields. Three crews of GB5 hit St Loup, three more from GB6 went for Attigny while three others of GB9 bombed Leffincourt.

The French Air Service was active all along the front. The Division Aérienne was assigned to cover the attack, with Escadre de Combat No.1 covering the IV Armée, while No.2 covered the right flank and attacked observation balloons between Samogneux and Manheulles.

To the east of Reims, Groupement Menard pilots (Champagne sector) claimed three balloons north of Somme-Py, Saint Hilaire and north of Cerny, one each for Spa.93, 97 and 37. One was shared with Adjutant Georges Lienhard, at 32 years of age a veteran of air operations in Italy, but who had only come to Spa.37 at the end of May 1918. He would score three victories this day to make him an ace.

In the afternoon, another ace, Adjutant Armand Berthelot of Spa.15, shot down a DFW two-seater north of Montfaucon. However, a Spad was lost in the IV Armée sector. Sergent Roger Caillet of Spa.89 was killed in combat, falling near Souain. Vizefeldwebel Alfons Nägler of Jasta 81 claimed a Spad near Suippes, about six kilometres south of Souain, while Unteroffizier Karl Hoffmann of Jasta 60 claimed another at 0900 near Massiges.

Three balloons were also shot down by the Germans on the IV Armée front. The 21 Cié lost a balloon from which Sous Lieutenants Vallier and Defleury baled out. The 19 and 30 Cié balloons were also lost. Leutnant Fritz Höhn of Jasta 60 got one at 1215 by Minaucourt; Leutnant Hermann Habich of Jasta 49 another at 1540 in the same area, while Leutnant Hans von Freden of Jasta 50 claimed his at Perthes at 1755.

Escadre 12's bombers of GB5, escorted by protection units R.239 and R.240, attacked Medeah during the day and were attacked by Fokkers. The Caudron RXI crews of the latter unit shot down two for the cost of a wounded R.239 pilot, Sergent Meynadier, whose aircraft was also damaged. Also active was GB13, whose force of 54 Bréguets, protected by eight Caudron RXIs from C.46, dropped 9,520 kilos of bombs in the area from Manre to Challeronge, mainly on railway targets. The formation engaged in eleven combats during which Br.132 and C.46 each claimed a Fokker.

In the II Armée sector, Lieutenant Hayer and Caporal Chausden of the two-seater Spa.215 were shot down in combat with eight enemy fighters but neither was hurt. Leutnant Blume of Jasta 9 claimed a Spad two-seater at Tahure around 1215, which was probably this crew. However, Gustav Dörr of Jasta 45 also claimed a Spad at Fismes at 1300—his 29th kill—so he too may have been responsible. An earlier Spad two-seater went to Jasta 60's Leutnant Höhn at 0830, at Somme-Py. Without knowing the exact time the Spad came down, any one of these three may have been the victor. A single-seat Spad of Spa.315 crash-landed after a combat near Belfort. Caporal Boutin was injured, and may have been the victim of Leutnant Wilhelm Frickart of Jasta 65, his 9th victory.

On the main IV Armée front, the French claimed four balloons and ten aircraft, six of the latter going to one man, the highly successful, albeit controversial, Lieutenant René Fonck of Spa.103. This action was basically concentrated along the west, or left edge of the offensive, where it overlapped the combats of Menard's units.

Spa.12 started the day by burning two balloons, the aristocrat Capitaine Armand Jean Galliot Joseph de Turenne, its 27-year-old commander, sharing them with two of his pilots. De Turenne had opened his score back in November 1916 and by now was one of the foremost leaders of the French fighter arm. The balloon, shot down over St Genevieve at 0800, took his score to 14. The next balloon went down 20 minutes later, to Sergent Saxon (an American) and Caporal Haller north of Somme-Py.

Late in the morning, an aircraft from Spa.103, flown by Fonck, who had been on leave since mid-August, his score standing at 60, climbed away from his airfield. Fonck spotted five Fokkers at 1145 and attacked. He bounced the outside rear machine, whose pilot saw him coming and tried to warn the others, but was shot down, along with the rear Fokker. The Frenchman reported these two crashed at St Marie-à-Py and St Souplet, following which, never one to lose an advantage, Fonck broke off the action. Soon afterwards, he saw a Halberstadt two-seater being shelled by French AA. He dived on it, firing at the observer who was killed straight away. The pilot dived so violently to get away—he failed—that the body of his observer was flung out before it crashed at Perthes-les-Hurles, at 1210. FA(A)233 lost Unteroffizier Richard Scholl and Leutnant Eugen Anderer, both killed, over Perthes.

Mid-afternoon, Lieutenant George W Eypper, an American serving with Spa.98, shot down a two-seater north-east of Bouconville. Sous Lieutenant Marcel Nogues of Spa.57—who it may be recalled was captured in April 1917 but escaped—gained his 13th and final victory by sharing a balloon north-east of Somme-Py at 1645. Five minutes later, the Sechault balloon, more to the east than the claims so far, was flamed by Sergent Kaminsky of Spa.124.

Later in the evening, a four-man patrol of Spa.103 set out, led by Fonck. In the same area were the pilots of Spa.26, led by Capitaine Joseph de Sevin and aircraft of Spa.165. De Sevin, was 24, and had been a fighter pilot since 11 November 1915, rising from Caporal to Capitaine, while gaining 11 victories and 13 probables. Fonck flew above his three companions, acting as cover. Eight Fokkers attacked the three, and as Fonck was diving to the rescue, de Sevin joined in, as did three more Fokkers. Soon he and Adjutant Brugère of Spa.103 were below the Fokkers and in deep trouble. Fonck claimed two of the Fokkers east of Souain as he tried to extricate them. Unfortunately, de Sevin was last seen spinning down out of control. Fonck then claimed another Fokker north-east of Somme-Py. This is interesting in itself, as these combats are usually described as being with a Fokker, then with two two-seaters! Spa.165 also claimed a Fokker over Souain at 1755, credited to Sergent Gaudry—his first.

Upon his return, Fonck was credited with all three, bringing up his second six-in-a-day claim. He was bemoaning the fact that his guns had jammed, otherwise he would have got more, and also regretting the demise of de Sevin, when the missing man walked in from a crash-landing. The Fokker he claimed himself was also one of those claimed by Fonck, so de Sevin did not receive credit for his victory. This was somewhat embarrassing for the French, as de Sevin was highly respected, and a Capitaine, and not likely to be a liar! As the news of the six for Fonck had already been released, the other side of the story was kept quiet!

This fight had been with Jasta 50, for whom Leutnant Maletzky claimed a Spad at 1800 at Perthes, followed by another at 1810 at Le Mesnil. The latter was de Sevin. The Jasta lost Vizefeldwebel Weinmann, who was captured, and was the victim of either one of the French aces.

Meanwhile, at 1800 Spa.37 and Spa.3 combined to down another Fokker south of Tahure, although the former unit lost Lieutenant Boby de la Chapelle, who died, possibly as a result of this fight. In this general area during the day, Sous Lieutenant Marcel Coadou, the acting commander of Spa.88, crashed a two-seater into Allied lines for his 4th victory, while Sous Lieutenant Pierre Gaudermen, shared an EA west of Ville sur Toube with two other members of Spa.68. Paris-born Gaudermen, at the advanced age of 35, was on his way to becoming an ace, now having gained his 4th kill. Jasta 50 was once more in action, Leutnant Hans von Freden claiming a Salmson near this same locality at an unknown time, bringing his score to 11.

The last French claim of the day also involved two aces, the first being de Turenne, whose second claim of the day was a C-type, also at Ville-sur-Toube, at 1845, shared with pilots of Spa.91 and 89. It was also the 5th victory of Adjutant Emile Regnier, whose Médaille Militaire citation specified that this victim was a two-seater in French lines, and that Regnier was severely wounded in the fight. De Turenne was wounded as well, and there are sufficient reports to indicate that their opposition may well have been a Fokker rather than a two-seater. Also, it is possible that Spa.68 and 88 were involved in this victory.

Despite the dubious nature of some of Fonck's claims on this day, his overall performance far outstrips other top-scorers, British Empire's Bishop and the American, Rickenbacker. Many of the latter's claims were out of controls, probably out of control and forced to land, often while he was out alone—just like Fonck and especially Bishop! Fonck's, because of the stricter French confirmation system, were at least visible (supposedly) from the ground. Upon reflection, it seems all three were overcome by ambition, especially as the number two men for all three countries—Mannock (not forgetting McCudden), Georges Guynemer and Frank Luke—were very accurate claimers.

American Sector

The ground offensive began as the troops came out of their trenches at 0530. The east end of the attack was against the heights on the Meuse River; to the west, the Argonne Forest. In the middle was a ridge with the three German strongpoints of Montfaucon, Cunel and Berricourt. The offensive ground to a halt on the 29th, after three days of bitter fighting. However, more attacks continued into late October, at which time the German Army cracked.

After some days of quiet, resting up for the coming offensive, and changing bases, the Americans went full out on the opening day of the assault. The majority of fighter opposition came from JGII, who had another good day—in the sense of shooting down the opposition— although they barely interrupted the American and French Air Services' work. Major Harold Hartney's 1st Pursuit Group was assigned to burn German balloons and keep the front clear of German two-seater recce aircraft. Top cover for these operations was to be provided by the 2nd and 3rd Pursuit Groups.

Thus the day began with an organised balloon strafe, netting two destroyed and two damaged, one by the 94th Aero (near Nantillois at 0552) the other to the 27th Aero (near Lisson at 0553). Less than an hour later, the 27th destroyed the Romagne balloon, at 0634. In this half hour, three more balloons were damaged and forced down.

The 94th and 95th Aeros had had early skirmishes with Fokkers, with two claimed shot down; one by Rickenbacker, who had damaged his propeller when the interrupter gear failed. Then, shortly after 0700, another wave of combats began, the 28th and 22nd Aeros each claiming victories over Fokkers. At 0710, Leutnant Max Näther of Jasta 62 claimed a Spad at Bezonvaux (his 14th victory), while exactly an hour later Jasta 8's Vizefeldwebel Wilhelm Seitz, an original staffel member, claimed a Spad for his 11th victory in the same vicinity. Both Spads were from the 13th Aero. Flying with them was the future General, Major Carl Spaatz, still gaining combat experience while attached to this outfit.

He reported shooting down a Fokker out of control and damaging another between Flabs and Damvillers, and was chasing a third when he was attacked by two others. Spaatz was saved from this predicament by Captain Charles Biddle and two other pilots who forced the Fokker down out of control. However, the 13th lost two pilots, Lieutenants T P Evans and Van H Burgin, both brought down and captured.

Lieutenant John Sperry of the 22nd Aero, who had already claimed one Fokker in an earlier fight, scored a second—in flames—near Etain at 0820, described as having a green nose and white tail. Vizefeldwebel Robert Mosbacher of Jasta 77b was shot down in flames over Allied lines this day, but despite being wounded, managed to get back over the German side to crash-land. He may have been Sperry's victim.

Between 1015 and 1100, the American day bombers set out on a series of support raids. For the 20th Bombardment Squadron it was to be a tragic day, as they lost five bombers, although they claimed three fighters shot down. The chief killers were Jasta 12, who for the second time in a week obliterated an American bomber formation.

The 96th Aero was the first off, sending eight planes to Dun-sur-Meuse, two of which aborted. The other six, led by First Lieutenant David Young, dropped their bombs on the town but were attacked on the return journey. Two fighters were claimed shot down—one awarded to all six crews—the second, a Pfalz, to Lieutenant Paul J O'Donnell, gunner to Lieutenant Harold J Forshay. O'Donnell was then hit and killed.

The second formation off was from the 11th Aero, but it was soon apparent they had not recovered from the mauling of the 18th, as their formation broke up and the leader aborted. One crew, Lieutenants W W Waring and S A Norris, then joined up with the next formation along—that of the 20th Aero.

This absurd tactic of the American Bomb Group, of sending out very small formations in close succession to the same target, went wrong yet again, although the plan had been to meet up over Vitry. They didn't. The 20th's flight of seven was hit soon after crossing the lines and two planes went down right away, with another crippled and starting to lag behind. The 11th Aero crew dropped back to protect it and both crews made it back, with Waring and Norris claiming a Fokker near Damvillers. Three more bombers went down, while the observer in another was killed. The consolation of a Fokker shot down, credited to the 20th as a whole, was little reward.

The pilots of Jasta 12 claimed five DH4s. Leutnant Hermann Becker claimed two (17th and 18th), Vizefeldwebel Otto Klaiber got his first, Leutnant Besser his second and Leutnant Alfred Greven his second too. This last was Lieutenants Guy B Wiser and Glenn C Richardson, who were captured, with Richardson leaving this account:

'Left Moulin at 9 o'clock in the morning in a heavy ground fog. The flight consisted of eight DH4s with orders to bomb Dun-sur-Meuse. We were to meet three other flights from our Group at Vitry and proceed over the lines. We failed to meet the other three flights and continued on over, reaching the lines at about 1030 at an altitude of 13,000 feet... We were attacked by five Fokkers who kept well to the rear and down. We all opened fire and one Fokker went down and the other four withdrew. At this time we were running parallel to the lines for some reason or other, which we have never ascertained, probably due to a lost sense of direction.

'Almost immediately, 12 more Fokkers attacked from the front and above. The leader dived through our formation attacking our flight leader. I fired one drum of ammunition and then had a jam in both guns. I had jams with each magazine and did not succeed in getting two shots in succession from that time on. I noticed three of our machines go down in flames and then turned to see our engine smoking and steaming as though on fire. I received a shot in the leg which was a flesh wound only but caused my leg to grow numb.

'Turning toward the front, I noticed the reserve tank was shot and a spray of gasoline hit me in the face. At this time we were running engine full on and trying to make the lines but at an altitude of 8,000 feet our propeller stopped dead, necessitating a slow glide. Three Fokkers hung to our tail firing all the way down until we reached 500 feet. We had been side-slipping to present as difficult a target as possible and we pulled out of the last slip at about 200 feet and glided to the ground, landing without smashing on the field which turned out to be the aerodrome of the 12th German Aero Squadron.'

The base was Giraumont. The two Americans were entertained by JGII pilots, led by Greven, and in 1961, Wiser and Richardson were shown a series of photos taken on that occasion. For the other Americans, fate was not so kind. Six were killed and two others also captured. At least one was seen to jump from 13,000 feet, to avoid the dreadful fate of being burnt alive. First Lieutenant Merian C Cooper also reported on his experiences on his return from prison camp:

'My observer ... was shot through the neck. The shot came out through his shoulder and knocked him into his cockpit. I received a graze across the head, which stunned me. Although severely wounded and bleeding heavily, my observer endeavoured to carry on the fight, but collapsed. As my engine was hit and I was unable to keep up with the formation, I was surrounded by enemy airplanes. Just at the instant of kicking into a spin in order to make myself as poor a target as possible, my engine caught fire. I believe that was due to the gas line or carburettor being hit and petrol spurting out onto the hot exhaust pipe. My plane on fire, I fell one or two turns into a spin, during which time my hands and face were burned. By putting the plane into a nose dive and opening the throttle wide, I was able to burn out the gas in the engine and extinguished the fire.'

Cooper force-landed, the victorious German pilot landing alongside, and looking after them.

Late in the morning, at 1140, a patrol of the 139th Aero claimed the first two-seater of the day—a DFW over the Bois de Consenvoye—shared between six pilots. However, this patrol then lost three pilots killed during an engagement with Jastas 13 and 15. Vizefeldwebel Albert Haussmann of Jasta 13 got his at Bertincourt, Leutnants von Hantelmann and Hugo Schäfer of Jasta 15 sending theirs down at Bethincourt and Etain, at 1215. Leutnant Johannes Klein of Jasta 15 also claimed one south of Metz but this was not confirmed.

From midday there was some intense air action. At 1210, the 22nd's Lieutenant William Stovell claimed a blue and red nosed Fokker, with a checkerboard wing, over Havrincourt. During this patrol, Lieutenant A C Kimber ran out of luck. A direct hit from an artillery shell obliterated his Spad as it dived down to strafe. An hour later, a German two-seater investigating the centre of the ground attack was shot down by two pilots of the 49th Aero, and at 1350 two other pilots of the 49th claimed a Fokker near Etain but lost Lieutenant Irving J Roth, who was probably shot down by Jasta 8's Vizefeldwebel Rudolf Francke, who gained his 15th kill at this time and vicinity.

Also during the day, Lieutenants David C Beebe and Milton K 'Micky' Lockwood of the 50th Observation Squadron were forced to land their DH4 near Daucourt aerodrome after a fight with six Fokkers. They were probably claimed by Leutnant Näther, whose 26th victory, and second of the day, was reported as a Salmson at Abancourt, which is due north of where they crashed. A Salmson of the 1st Observation Squadron took off at 1330 but was shot down near Varennes, evidently going down under the guns of the unrivalled killer of American aviators, Franz Büchner. He claimed a Salmson for his 33rd victory five kilometres north of Varennes; he would end this day with four kills.

It was now the Germans who attacked French and US observation balloons. At 1415, Leutnant Haebler of Jasta 68 burnt two at Aubreville and Recicourt. The first was the French 39 Cié, the second the US 8th Company gas bag, from which First Lieutenant C J Ross and Second Lieutenant H D Hudnut parachuted. Unfortunately, Ross waited too long to jump, and pieces of the burning balloon fell onto his parachute, setting it on fire, plunging Ross to his death. His companion landed unharmed.

An hour later, Max Näther with Leutnant Breidenbach burnt two more balloons at Thierville, just north of Verdun. These were the 9th and 3rd US Balloon Company balloons, from which Lieutenants S V Clarke, S E White, H P Neibling and G C Carroll all baled out safely. Soon afterwards, at 1630, the 95th Aero burnt the Reville balloon, shared between

Lieutenants Harold R Buckley and Alex McLanahan. Frank Luke of the 27th Aero was also out after balloons, with a new partner, Lieutenant Ivan A Roberts, but they ran into Fokkers. Luke sent one down out of control but he did not see it crash and then he had gun problems. The last he saw of Roberts was of him fighting over Consenvoye; he did not return, a victim of Franz Büchner, who claimed his 34th kill over this location.

Büchner was in action again at 1756, the 94th getting into a fight with Jasta 13. Although the 94th were credited with a Fokker, Lieutenant Alan Nutt was shot down, followed by Lieutenant Alan B Sherry. His shot up Spad crash-landed in 'no-man's-land', where he remained until the following day. This brought Büchner's score to 36. In the fortnight since the 12th, he had claimed 14 victories—mostly Americans. The day ended with Lieutenant Harvey W Cook of the 94th burning a balloon near Grandham at 1848. At unknown times and locations, Jasta 72s claimed a total of five victories during the day, two to Leutnant Herbert Mahn, and one each to Leutnants Gerold Tschentschel, Gustav Frädrich and Ernst Schultz. The victory types are also unrecorded. The Americans lost a Salmson of the 91st Observation Squadron, but this was to AA fire.

Overall, the Americans would be well pleased with this day's efforts. The most experienced 1st Pursuit Group suffered only three losses while doing its job. The 2nd Group did suffer some heavy casualties, but these lesser experienced units soon learnt. The 3rd Group made some claims for no losses. Unlike St Mihiel, only a couple of Observation aircraft were attacked by the Fokkers, which barely interrupted their important work. The bombers, as usual, bled. For the Germans, some of the lesser Jastas performed well, but none equalled the performance of the three JGII units that engaged the Americans. At least 13 victories for no loss, but also for no result!

IAF

Seven aircraft of 99 Squadron left at 1505 on a bombing mission to Metz. They were intercepted by 40 enemy fighters from Jastas 3, 4, 77b and 15 at least. Fighting their way to the target, six were able to drop their loads, causing fires in the railway junction. There was persistent fighting all the way back, with gunners claiming two fighters destroyed and another out of control. Five DH9s were brought down in the general area south of Metz, west of the Moselle river. Two more crews were forced to come down in crash landings inside Allied lines, both with dead gunners aboard. Leutnant Ernst Udet of Jasta 4, the highest scoring pilot alive in France, who started the day with a score of 60, was wounded in the thigh during this action.

Claims by the opposition are so numerous it is difficult to paint a picture of what actually occurred. A complicating factor is the loss of a DH9 from 104 Squadron, ten of which left on a mission, five aborting, the one being lost to Fokkers while bombing the same general target. German claims were as follows:

1615	Leutnant Heinz Graf von Gluczewski-Kwilicki	Jasta 4	SE of Kemnat
1710	Leutnant Ernst Udet	Jasta 4	Montengingen
1715	Vizefeldwebel Seidel	Jasta 3	SE Frescaty—u/c
1715	Leutnant Richard Kraut	Jasta 4	Buch
1720	Leutnant Ernst Udet	Jasta 4	S of Metz
1725	Leutnant Max Gossner	Jasta 77b	Manningen
1727	OfStv Bernard Ultsch	Jasta 77b	Kubern
1730	Vizefeldwebel Agne	Jasta 77b	Grosspunach
1730	Vizefeldwebel Schaflein	Jasta 77b	Pullingen
?	Leutnant Joachim von Ziegesar	Jasta 15	Pont-à-Mousson—u/c
?	Leutnant Johannes Klein	Jasta 15	Verny, S of Metz

Given the times, it would appear Jasta 15 accounted for the 104 Squadron aircraft, with Leutnant von Ziegesar losing the claim, while the rest were the 99 Squadron losses. To some extent it depends if the two bombers that came down in Allied lines were observed from the German side and allowed, for this would make seven DH9 losses for seven claims, the Jasta 3 victory being in some doubt. However, in some records, Jasta 4 do not receive credit for any of their four claims. Perhaps this was because the famous element of the Circus had just arrived and the Kommander der Flieger of the 19th Armee boosted the morale of Jasta 77b, who had seen some action during September but little beforehand since June 1918.

All four of Jasta 77b's victories are recorded as coming down inside German lines, generally near the sites for Jasta 4. The Germans called such disputes 'strittig' or 'contested'— and had a procedure for settling them. The result of this dispute is not known. If there was any suggestion of Jasta 4's claims being over-ruled in favour of Jasta 77b, perhaps thoughts were revised when it was realised that the now wounded Udet would have increased his score to 62 if his victories were confirmed. Being universally recognised as having scored 62 kills in the war must indicate that they, at least, were upheld. In any event, one of the 99 Squadron gunners had put Udet out of the war, for he saw no further action before the Armistice.

	A/C	KB		DES	OOC	KB
British losses	16	—	British claims	18	10	—
French losses	5	1	French claims	12		7
American losses	17	3	American claims	22		5
IAF losses	5	—	IAF claims	2	1	—
German claims	58	9	German losses	?†		?

† No figure has been found; personnel casualties indicate 15 airmen of all ranks killed, one taken prisoner, at least one wounded and at least one Jasta 68 pilot down in flames but unhurt.

British Casualties

Aircraft type	No.	Squadron	Crew		
Camel	E1552	65 Sqdn	2/Lt W R Thornton	POW	
Camel	D3374	204 Sqdn	Lt W B Craig	KIA	
Camel	C75	204 Sqdn	Lt G E C Howard	KIA	
DH4	A7632	202 Sqdn	Lt F A B Gasson	KIA	
			2/Lt S King	KIA	
Dolphin	H7243	23 Sqdn	Lt E Fulford	POW	
Camel	D9632	203 Sqdn	Lt N C Dixie	Safe	
Camel	D9611	203 Sqdn	Lt F J S Britnell	Safe	
Camel	D9640	203 Sqdn	2/Lt W H Coghill	POW	
BF2b	E2163	'L' Flt	2/Lt C A Harrison	POW	
			Lt J A Parkinson	POW	
BF2b	E2155	20 Sqdn	2/Lt L G Smith	POW	
			2/Lt E S Harvey	KIA	
Camel	B8168	208 Sqdn	Capt A Storey	Safe	*
Camel	F1975	80 Sqdn	2/Lt H Walker	KIA	
DH4	F6187	57 Sqdn	Lt F G Pym	POW	
			Sgt W C E Mason	POW	
DH4	E2155	57 Sqdn	Lt P W J Timson	KIA	
			Lt A N Eyre	KIA	
DH4	D8424	57 Sqdn	Capt A Newman	Safe	
			2/Lt E G Pernet	WIA	*
DH9	D4742	218 Sqdn	2/Lt J T Aitken	MIA	
			2/Lt G F Hibbert	MIA	
DH9	D3271	218 Sqdn	Capt J F Chisholm DSC DFC	Interned	
			Sgt H J Williams	Interned	
RE8	C2800	3 AFC	Lt G M Deans	Safe	*
			Lt T H Prince	WIA	
DH4		25 Sqdn	2/Lt C W Blasdale (O)	WIA	*
RE8		5 Sqdn	Capt G N Moore (P)	WIA	*
RE8		52 Sqdn	Lt W E C Coombs	WIA	*
DH4	D7232	104 Sqdn	Lt O L Malcolm	KIA	
			2/Lt G V Harper	KIA	
DH9	D5573	99 Sqdn	2/Lt L E Stern	KIA	
			2/Lt F O Cook	KIA	
DH9	D3213	99 Sqdn	2/Lt W H C Gillet	POW	
			2/Lt H Crossley	POW	
DH9	E632	99 Sqdn	Lt S C Gilbert	KIA	
			2/Lt R Buckley	KIA	
DH9	D6272	99 Sqdn	2/Lt C R G Abrahams	KIA	
			2/Lt C N Sharp	KIA	
DH9	B9347	99 Sqdn	Capt P C Welchman	POW	
			2/Lt T H Swann	POW	

DH9	B9366	99 Sqdn	2/Lt P Boniface	Safe	*
			2/Lt S McKeever	KIA	
DH9	D544	99 Sqdn	Lt M D West	Safe	*
			2/Lt J W Howard	KIA	

French Casualties

Salmson 2A2	Sal.16	Sgt Lemarie	WIA	*
		Lt Champagnet	Safe	
Salmson 2A2	Sal.16	MdL Neveux	WIA	*
		S/Lt Guinard	Safe	
Spad XIII	Spa.37	Lt B de la Chapelle	DOW	
Spad XIII	Spa.89	Sgt R Caillet	KIA	
Caudron RXI	R.239	Sgt Meynadier (P)	WIA	*
Bréguet XIV	Br.234	Asp Patouret (O)	WIA	*
Bréguet XIV	Br.234	S/Lt Richaud	KIA	
		Lt Sacquin	WIA	
Spad XI	Spa.215	Lt Hayer	Safe	
		Cpl Chausden	Safe	
Spad XIII	Spa.315	Cpl Boutin	Inj	
Bréguet XIV	Br.9	Capt Schlumberger	WIA	*
		Asp Pacquet	WIA	
Spad XIII	Spa.26	Capt J M X De Sevin	Safe	*

American Casualties

Salmson 2A2		1st Aero	1/Lt J F Richards II	KIA	
			2/Lt A F Hanscom	KIA	
Spad XIII		13th Aero	1/Lt T P Evans	POW	
Spad XIII		13th Aero	2/Lt V H Burgin	POW	
DH4	32792	20th Aero	2/Lt D B Harris	KIA	
			2/Lt E Forbes	KIA	
DH4	32819	20th Aero	1/Lt R P Matthews	KIA	
			2/Lt E A Taylor	KIA	
DH4	32915	20th Aero	1/Lt P N Rhinelander	KIA	
			1/Lt H C Preston	KIA	
DH4	32492	20th Aero	1/Lt M C Cooper	POW	
			1/Lt E C Leonard	POW	
DH4	32286	20th Aero	2/Lt G B Wiser	POW	
			1/Lt G C Richardson	POW	
DH4		20th Aero	1/Lt S C Howard	Safe	*
			1/Lt E A Parrott	WIA	
Spad XIII		22nd Aero	1/Lt A C Kimber	KIA	
Spad XIII		27th Aero	2/Lt I A Roberts	KIA	
Spad XIII		49th Aero	1/Lt I J Roth	KIA	
Salmson 2A2		91st Aero	1/Lt A E Kelly	KIA	
			1/Lt F B Lowry	KIA	
Spad XIII		94th Aero	1/Lt A Nutt	KIA	
Spad XIII		94th Aero	1/Lt A B Sherry	Safe	
Bréguet XIV		96th Aero	2/Lt H J Forshay	Safe	*
			2/Lt P J O'Donnell	KIA	
Spad XIII		139th Aero	1/Lt H A Garvie	KIA	
Spad XIII		139th Aero	1/Lt H P Sumner	KIA	
Spad XIII		139th Aero	1/Lt H A Petree	KIA	
DH4		50th Aero	2/Lt D C Beebe	Safe	*
			2/Lt M K Lockwood	Safe	

Friday, 27 September 1918

British Front

The weather was fine, but cloudy. While the French and American attack had gone forward on a 20-mile front the previous day, the very low level of experience of the American troops had led to severe fighting and no immediate breakthrough. Significantly, no German reserves were being moved to that part of the front.

On this morning, General Sir Henry Horne's 1st Army and General Sir Julian Byng's 3rd Army both launched attacks following a day-long bombardment by the overwhelmingly superior artillery of the British Army against the Woton and Hindenburg Lines. The 1st Army attacked between Epehy and St Quentin, while the 3rd Army launched itself across the Canal du Nord, due east of Cambrai. The German Army began to fall back on the whole front, from Lens to Armentières to the north again, to avoid being cut off. Four-to-five mile penetrations were made on this first day, with the front getting to within three miles of Cambrai. Meantime, further north, the British 2nd Army, in co-operation with the Belgians, were preparing to attack on a front from St Eloi to Dixmude.

As would be expected, the RAF was highly active over the battle fronts, and the German Air Service responded making another day of heavy air combat. There would be plenty of targets for the Germans, for the four RAF Brigades in action—I, III, V and IX—mustered over 1,000 aircraft. The more southern battle opened along a 13-mile front between Sauchy Lestrée and Gouzeaucourt, with the Canadian Corps assigned to spearhead the attack, with 8 Squadron's Big Acks used once more as tank support, as well as contact and artillery work.

There was much ground attack and support by both fighters and Corps aircraft, resulting in a number of casualties. On the 1st Army front there were five squadrons allocated exclusively to ground attack work—40, 54, 64, 203 and 209. The 3rd Army had one squadron assigned—201—but others were given roving commissions to fly both air and ground patrols. The first three RAF losses were caused by ground fire between 0645 and 0700, Camels of 70, 73 and 201 were brought down. The latter, flown by Lieutenant W A W Carter, actually came down in German territory with his fuel line cut; with the fighting going on about him, he managed to get back to the British side. In fact he took back a wounded soldier, and when coming across two unescorted German prisoners, got them to help him!

The Dolphins of 19 Squadron had a series of fights between 0715 and 0735, claiming several Pfalz and DVIIs. North-west of Cambrai, Lieutenant Lewis Ray attacked three Triplanes, and claimed all three shot down—one destroyed and two out of control! Then 22 Squadron's Bristols fought a two-seater and some Fokkers, claiming the former and three of the latter. At 0800, the DH4s of 18 Squadron ran into Jasta 57, losing one machine, with another crashing on landing back at base. Leutnant Johannes Jensen claimed a DH9 at Fechain, north-west of Sancourt, but the Staffelführer, Paul Strähle, was hit a glancing blow to the head, from either 18 or 22 Squadron, being forced to land at Aniche aerodrome.

Balloons were yet another obvious target at the start of an attack, 3 Squadron destroying three, the last one having been hauled right down to the ground. Two LVGs were also shot down. However, engaged by Fokkers, they lost Lieutenant Theodore R Hostetter, a 20-year-old American from a well known New York brewery family, who had been just nine days at the front. Lieutenant Jeff Wood, a 22-year-old lad from York, with six weeks on the Squadron, became a prisoner. German pilots scoring victories over Camels at this time were Jasta 2's Leutnant Hermann Vallendor, two, north of Bourlon Wood and at Marquion at 0825, Ernst Bormann and Unteroffizier Karl Fervers, also of Jasta 2, north of Cambrai, while Oberleutnant Robert Greim, CO of Jasta 34b, got a Camel south of Masnières at 0815, seven kilometres south of Cambrai. This fight probably overlapped with the 19 Squadron fight. However, 73 Squadron lost a Camel in flames to ground fire over Bourlon Wood, possibly claimed in the above fight.

At 0800, 56 Squadron's SE5s dived on eight Fokkers over Cambrai and claimed five. Lieutenant George Osborne Mackenzie, a 25-year-old Canadian from Ontario, with four weeks on the Squadron, was last seen with three fighters on his tail near Bourlon Wood at 0820. He was probably the victim of Paul Baümer of Jasta 2, who claimed two SE5s in this area at an unknown time. Jasta Boelcke's Leutnant Fritz Heinz was killed in action over Awoingt, probably in this fight.

On the half hour, 98 Squadron had two DH9s shot up, one coming down to crash-land in a shell-hole at Grevillers, the other staggering back for repair. Vizefeldwebel Fritz Senf of Jasta 59 shot down a DH9 at Goeulzin for his first victory. For the following half hour, 29 and 84 Squadrons downed balloons, a 4 Squadron RE8 force-landed after hits from ground fire, 79 Squadron claimed a two-seater over Armentières and Paul Baümer shot down a DH4, most likely one lost by 25 Squadron during a recce of the Mons area.

At 0915 the first actions of a new British type at the front began—43 Squadron's Sopwith Snipes. No. 107 Squadron were bombing Bohain railway station, escorted by 1 and 43 Squadrons, and near Bertry and Brevillers, Fokkers were engaged. No. 1 Squadron claimed one destroyed and one out of control, while Captain R King and Lieutenant C C Banks, the leading aces of 43, shared another out of control, the first Snipe 'victory', following which Lieutenant R S Johnston claimed a second.

The SEs of 40 Squadron joined combat with Jastas 1 and 27 at 0930, over Oisy-le-Verger. Three SEs went down, and another pilot crash-landed near Cambrai wounded. Jasta 1 claimed two—Leutnant Raven von Barnekow, Unteroffizier Gustav Borm, one each, while Leutnant Hermann Frommherz, Jasta 27, got two.

Bombers of 27 Squadron, escorted by SEs of 32, attacked Emerchicourt at 0945. Lieutenants C M Allan and C E Robinson were attacked by a Fokker which dived and zoomed under them but Robinson got in a burst, hitting the Fokker's petrol tank. The fighter burst into flames, turned over, spinning down on fire. Although the Fokker had shot their controls away they got down without injury. 32 Squadron, in turn, claimed five Fokkers, three destroyed (one in flames!) and two out of control. Oberleutnant Hans-Helmut von Boddien, CO of Jasta 59, was wounded by DH9s in this fight, and Leutnant Hans Jebens jumped over Bouchain from a flaming Fokker, but his parachute failed to deploy.

The Bristol Fighters of 20 Squadron were in action at 1030, claiming four Fokkers shot down for the loss of Lieutenants F E Turner and C E Clarke over Fontaine Notre Dame. This was the victory of Offizierstellvertreter Friedrich Altemeier of Jasta 24s, the 17th kill of this high-scoring NCO, who would end the war with 21 victories.

An RE8 crew had a lucky escape mid-morning. Lieutenants R E Britton and B Hickman of 13 Squadron were attacked by eight Fokkers, Hickman being wounded early in the fight although he believed he shot down one Fokker. Britton was then wounded too, and in trying to avoid further damage went into a spin, landing in German territory. With the Fokkers withdrawing, Britton managed to take off again and got back to base, although he fainted and crashed trying to land. There are no German claims for an RE8 this day, and one can imagine some frustrated pilot and intelligence officer trying in vain to locate the 'downed' two-seater. More successful was Leutnant Richard Ruckle of Jasta 33, who claimed a Bristol at Busigny at 1130, 62 losing a machine east of St Quentin; happily the crew were captured.

Just before midday, up on the coast, 65 Squadron were in a fight over Ghistelles, claiming four Fokkers but losing Second Lieutenant R O Campbell. Leutnant Franz Piechulek of Jasta 56 gained victory No.12—a Camel—north-west of Thorout, which is the only claim all day north of Ypres, although it was timed an hour later (in error?).

Between midday and 1300 the Camels of 54 Squadron lost a pilot—at 1210—and had another pilot shot up. Two Camels were claimed by Jasta 5's two stars Rumey and Mai at this time. Mai probably got Lieutenant P McCraig (victory 29), who was killed, Rumey the other (his 45th), but as he was killed this day, he was probably credited with the kill rather than any detailed investigation being gone into.

Just before 1300, 19 Squadron were in action again, claiming two Pfalz DIIIs, during an escort mission to DH4s near Aubigny-au-Bac. However, 19 lost one of its aces, Captain Cecil Gardner, shot down into Allied lines near Bapaume, severely wounded, dying on the 30th. Unteroffizier Gustav Borm of Jasta 1 claimed a Dolphin at Bourlon Wood at 1300 (his second kill of the day), which fits very well.

In the following half hour, 18 Squadron crews on recce sorties were engaged by fighters. Second Lieutenants J K S Smith and A Lilley being shot up and wounded. Lieutenants R Johnson and A Toes failed to return, no doubt the victims of Leutnant von Barnekow, who claimed a DH4 at Sailly at 1300. Another two-seater—this time a BF2b of 88 Squadron—also failed to return from a scrap around 1400. One DVII was sent down out of control, but Vizefeldwebel Fritz Classen of Jasta 26 secured his 8th victory north-west of Abancourt (south of Brunemont on the Sensee Canal).

The RAF had a casualty break until around 1600, but then lost three more BF2bs of 22 Squadron, one being crewed by Captain S F H Thompson MC DFC and Second Lieutenant C J Tolman; Thompson was the highest scoring ace Brisfit pilot of the war to be killed, falling near Cambrai. The other two crews were taken prisoner, although one pilot died. Claimants were Vizefeldwebel Oskar Hennrich of Jasta 46, at Neuvilly at 1600; Oberleutnant Otto Schmidt of Jasta 5, at Cattenières at 1550 (his 16th victory); and one to Carl Degelow of Jasta 40s, west of Valenciennes. In the past, Degelow is noted as having downed an 88 Squadron crew (see Classen above), but they were killed, and Degelow reported his victims were captured, one of three BF2bs he attacked. It would seem the other two Bristols evaded south of Valenciennes, and ran into Jastas 5 and 46, who were part of the same Jagdgruppe. Degelow got Lieutenants G J Smith and G B Shum, while either Hennrich or Schmidt got Thompson. Only this morning, Thompson had brought his score to 30. The third crew were noted as being interned, but where they could have got to if correct, is unknown.

As already mentioned, the great German ace Fritz Rumey was killed on this day, apparently baling out of his crippled DVII but having his parachute fail. At 1720, four Fokkers were claimed over Cambrai, three to Lieutenant Frank Lucien Hale, one destroyed and two out of control. It has often been thought that Rumey was killed in a collision with Lieutenant G E B Lawson of 32 Squadron, who was credited with two Fokker DVIIs this day, but both were claimed at 0930, and Rumey, as already noted, claimed a Camel at 1208. Did Hale, a 23-year-old American from Syracuse, New York, shoot down Rumey? He noted in his combat report:

'On the second OP of the day, ten Fokkers at 9,000 feet over Cambrai seen attacking DH9s of 27 Squadron. SE5s went to assist, Hale firing 25 rounds into one from point blank range. It fell over, out of control, into clouds 4,000 feet below. He was then attacked himself by one who shot him up from the tail. With a climbing turn and a half roll, Hale came out on the enemy's tail, firing one burst of 150 rounds at point blank range. This machine turned over on its back and was observed to be still falling 2,000 feet below, on its back and completely out of control, side-slipping and spiralling. Another DVII attacked, and Hale put himself into a spin, going into clouds at 5,000 feet, came out underneath and flew west. He then saw a Fokker DVII below. He fired from 500 feet overhead directly into the enemy aircraft, which held its course and was firing into the SE5s. At 50 yards Hale then fired both guns, 75 rounds, and saw tracer going in. The enemy dived, zoomed to stalling point, fell on its back and went down on one wing, then the other, helplessly out of control; at 2,000 feet it was still falling.'

By 1745, 32 had lost Second Lieutenant C A Cawley, taken prisoner after possibly shooting down a Fokker. Jasta 2's Leutnant Gerhard Bassenge claimed an SE5 at Noyelles, just south-west of Cambrai, while Vizefeldwebel Fritz Classen of Jasta 26 claimed one south of Sailly, just west of the city. Jasta 37 had two fighter pilots wounded on the 2 Armee front this day, Leutnant Mappes and Vizefeldwebel Robert Wirth.

As the late afternoon progressed, the 17th Aero, 210 and 11 Squadrons all saw combat, then at 1800 hours 57 Squadron bombed a HQ north of Cambrai and got into a scrap with Fokkers, the gunners claiming two DVIIs out of control—one splendidly coloured black underneath, yellow with red spots on top wings and a grey fuselage. Three DHs were shot up, three men wounded, one bomber force-landing near 13 Squadron's base, another force-landing at 62 Squadron's aerodrome.

At this same time, Second Lieutenant E G Robertson of 85 Squadron was last seen east of St Quentin in combat with two Fokkers, probably being shot down by Ernst Bormann of Jasta Boelcke, who claimed a fighter at St Quentin, although he recorded it as a Camel, not an SE5a.

German flak gunners claimed three aircraft shot down during the day, and in the north the Belgian Willy Coppens flamed yet another balloon over Leffinghe—his 31st victory.

It becomes increasingly difficult to tie up German losses as 1918 progressed due to gaps in the records, especially concerning times and locations. The Germans certainly seemed to lose a number of men and machines this day, other than those already mentioned, and some would have been on the French front. Jasta 31 had Leutnant Holle wounded, while another 17 Armee front casualty appears to have been a Marine two-seater crew, Flugmaat Richard Arfendt and

Leutnant Wilhelm Kreitz who were killed at La Lovie, the nearest British victory being that of Ken Unger of 210 Squadron downing a Halberstadt 'south-east of Nieuport'. Other losses are listed as: Fliegers Gustav Dunkel and Fritz Schuster at La Briquette; Vizefeldwebel Gerhard Meyer and Vizefeldwebel Christian Volquartzen killed at Hachy; Leutnant Eugen Wild killed at Rethal; Leutnant Josef Heckenberger, killed; Gefreiter Heinrich Brinker, killed at Tournai.

French Front

Escadre de Combat No.2 was assigned to cover the American attack between Dun-sur-Meuse and Abaucourt. Despite the assumed activity, there was little real action until the evening due to early rain and low cloud. At 1655, Leutnant Hans von Freden of Jasta 50 shot down a balloon by Minaucourt for his 12th victory, the IV Armée's 31 Cié balloon being burnt at exactly this time.

In turn, Spa. 77 burnt a German 'drachen' south-east of Etain, shared between Sergent Edward J Corsi, an American, and Maréchal-des-Logis Thevenot. This pair were then attacked by three Fokkers that had been guarding the balloon, Thevenot being brought down and killed. Leutnant Max Näther of Jasta 62 claimed a Spad at Montezville, 12 km north-west of Verdun, between Etain and the lines, to bring his personal score to 17.

A number of enemy machines were claimed downed by various units—Spa.163, Spa.124, Spa.95, Spa.89 and Spa.100—then during a bomb raid, Escadre de Bombardement 12 sent out a huge force of 86 Bréguet XIVs, escorted by 14 Caudron RXI 'gun-ships', escorted by aircraft of GC19. They bombed troops at Aaure and Bemont, and convoys between Attigny and Somme-Py. Fokkers tried to intervene, the French gunners claiming two, but two Bréguet crews were wounded but got back. One of the Bréguets may have been claimed by Vizefeldwebel Alfons Nägler of Jasta 81, who reported a Bréguet shot down north of Tahure. The same Jasta claimed a Spad near Ville, by Vizefeldwebel Averes.

Other claims by the Germans were by Leutnant Korff, also north of Tahure, followed by a Spad two-seater near Marfaux by Leutnant Fritz Höln at 1820 (the other Bréguet that was hit?). Two Spad pilots returned wounded during the day, one at least having been hit by ground fire.

American Sector

The battle front was covered in clouds in the morning, with rain continuing until 0900, but it cleared in the afternoon, although low clouds persisted until 1700. Again little action took place until the late afternoon.

Observation aircraft were out, one observer being wounded by a Fokker as the 91st Squadron were engaged, although they claimed a Fokker in flames near Crepion. Then the 99th Aero lost a Salmson, brought down by AA fire with a wounded observer.

Once again the Germans appeared to be over-enthusiastic in claiming Spads. Two were reported shot down by Leutnant Hans Korner of Jasta 19, near Pagny, with Vizefeldwebel Prime of Jasta 78b sending down another near Herbeviller five minutes later. In turn, the 147th Aero claimed a Fokker near Montfaucon; another, with a red nose and blue tail, was shared by two more pilots.

The 95th Aero was involved in the final fight of the day, claiming two Rumplers. The first was at 1814 near Brieulles, the second at 1825 near Fleville, although First Lieutenant Thomas F Butz had to make a forced landing after this fight.

	A/C	KB		DES	OOC	KB
British losses	28	—	British claims	28	30	6
French losses	1	1	French claims	6		1
American losses	1	—	American claims	5		—
IAF losses	—		IAF claims	—		
German claims	43†	1	German losses	6/10‡		?

† Three to flak. ‡ Total personnel casualties were at least 17 killed, and six wounded.

British Casualties

Aircraft type	No.	Squadron	Crew		
Camel	D9460	70 Sqdn	2/Lt P M Wallace	POW	
Camel	F1917	73 Sqdn	Capt W H Hubbard DFC	Safe	
DH4	A7899	18 Sqdn	Lt R C Bennett DFC	POW	
			Lt N W Helwig DFC	KIA	
DH4		18 Sqdn	2/Lt Daniel	Safe	*
			2/Lt H F Lee	WIA	
Camel	E4375	201 Sqdn	Lt W A W Carter	Safe	
SE5a	F5495	56 Sqdn	Lt G O Mackenzie	MIA	
SE5a	F5482	56 Sqdn	Lt J A Pouchet DSM	Safe	*
Dolphin	E4501	19 Sqdn	Capt C V Gardiner	DOW	
Camel	F6117	3 Sqdn	2/Lt J A Wood	POW	
Camel	F2158	3 Sqdn	Lt T R Hostetter	KIA	
DH9	D7334	98 Sqdn	Lt E A R Lee	Inj	*
			2/Lt E G Banham	WIA	
DH9	D1106	98 Sqdn	Lt Richmond	Safe	*
			Lt Fish	Safe	
DH4	A8031	25 Sqdn	Lt H D Hazell	KIA	
			2/Lt D B Robertson	KIA	
SE5a	E1350	40 Sqdn	2/Lt C M G Morton	KIA	
SE5a	B8442	40 Sqdn	Lt N D Willis	POW	
SE5a	C9135	40 Sqdn	2/Lt P B Myers	KIA	
SE5a	E1345	40 Sqdn	Lt R Mooney USAS	WIA	
BF2b	C944	62 Sqdn	2/Lt P S Manley	POW	
			Sgt G F Hines	POW	
Camel	D9472	73 Sqdn	2/Lt W A Brett	KIA	
RE8	F6011	59 Sqdn	Capt L M Woodhouse MC DFC	MIA	
			Lt W S Peel MC	MIA	
RE8	D4939	13 Sqdn	Lt R E Britton	WIA	*
			2/Lt B Hickman	WIA	
BF2b	E2566	20 Sqdn	2/Lt F E Turner	MIA	
			2/Lt C E Clarke	MIA	
DH4	A7887	18 Sqdn	2/Lt J K S Smith	Safe	*
			2/Lt A Lilley	Safe	
DH4	A7851	18 Sqdn	Lt R Johnson	MIA	
			2/Lt A Toes	MIA	
Camel	E1549	65 Sqdn	2/Lt R O Campbell	KIA	
DH9	E669	108 Sqdn	2/Lt A S Jones	MIA	
			Sgt N Richardson	MIA	
Camel	B6421	54 Sqdn	Lt P McCaig	KIA	
Camel	F2135	54 Sqdn	2/Lt J M Stevenson	Safe	*
BF2b	E2153	88 Sqdn	Lt C Foster	KIA	
			Sgt T Proctor	KIA	
BF2b	D8089	22 Sqdn	Lt G J Smith	POW	
			2/Lt G B Shum	POW	
BF2b	E2243	22 Sqdn	Lt J R Drummond	KIA	
			2/Lt C H Wilcox	POW	
BF2b	E2477	22 Sqdn	Capt S F H Thompson MC	KIA	
			2/Lt C J Tolman	KIA	
SE5a	B8355	32 Sqdn	2/Lt C F Crawley	POW	
DH4	A8085	57 Sqdn	2/Lt G J Dickins	WIA	*
			2/Lt A H Aitken	Safe	
DH4	A8086	57 Sqdn	2/Lt F deM Hyde	Safe	*
			Lt E H Eyres	WIA	
DH4	F6114	57 Sqdn	Lt E M Coles	Safe	*
			2/Lt C Wilkinson	WIA	
SE5a	H7249	85 Sqdn	2/Lt E G Robertson	MIA	
Camel	E4407	210 Sqdn	2/Lt H E Light	Inj	
RE8		12 Sqdn	Lt C R Pithey DFC	WIA	*
			Lt H Rhodes DFC	WIA	
RE8		52 Sqdn	Lt J W H Scales (P)	WIA	*
AWFK8		8 Sqdn	2/Lt S F Blackwell (O)	WIA	*
BF2b		62 Sqdn	2/Lt R F Hunter (O)	WIA	*

French Casualties

Spad XIII		Spa.100	Sgt Gantois	WIA	*
Spad XIII		Spa.77	MdL Thevenot	MIA	
Spad XIII		Spa.60	Lt Cuvelier	WIA	*
Bréguet XIV		Br.108	Lt Metayer	WIA	*
			Asp Mullet	WIA	
Bréguet XIV		Br.111	Sgt/Maj Leteneur	WIA	*
			Asp Etchberry	WIA	
Bréguet XIV		GB4	Lt Delephine	KIA	*

American Casualties

Salmson 2A2		91st Aero	1/Lt W F Baker	Safe	*
			2/Lt R S Jannopulo	WIA	
Salmson 2A2	1156	99th Aero	1/Lt J E Eaton	Safe	
			1/Lt E R Case	WIA	
Spad XIII		95th Aero	1/Lt T F Butz	Safe	*

Saturday, 28 September 1918

British Front

Low clouds and rain predominated in the morning, clearing in the afternoon. In fact the weather was foul and was responsible for some heavy casualties. The Fourth—and last—Battle for Ypres opened on this day. General Sir Herbert Plumer's 2nd Army and the Belgian Army's attacks were great successes. By nightfall the Germans had been cleared out of Houthulst Forest and at the end of the next day, all the territory lost in April 1918 had been regained. This also meant all the territory gained at such a frightful cost the previous autumn was regained too. Crews of 7, 10 and 53 Squadrons did much valuable work in this sector.

One of the reasons for this success was that the German Army had run out of men, and increasing sections of them were not prepared to fight any more. Another reason was the dominant RAF which enabled all attacks in this month to be surprises. While the air forces' efforts in WW1, of all sides, need to be taken in context, there is no doubt that by 1918 Allied air to ground attack especially was making its impact on German troops. These were mainly carried out by the RAF, but it became increasingly obvious to the German soldier that he was constantly being buzzed, bombed, shot up and generally harassed by enemy fighters, while the Allied two-seaters, now protected far better than hitherto, were able to range artillery on them almost with impunity.

This same strafing, and the day bombing, often met good and accurate ground fire as witnessed this morning, for soon after dawn, 202 Squadron lost three crews during an attack on a dump at Engel, and no Jasta pilots claimed DH4s this day. Also a 204 Camel pilot failed to return while strafing near Thorout. No. 29 Squadron had three of its SE pilots fail to return, all ending up as prisoners.

Air fighting began around 0700, the RE8 team of Carberry and Clements knocked down a Halberstadt over La Vacquerie valley, but Lieutenant J A Fenton of 209 Squadron was lost south of the Scarpe River at 0745, possibly by Unteroffizier Fervers of Jasta Boelcke. An RE8 was also shot down by Unteroffizier Jeckert of Jasta 56, over Moorslede, which was a 7 Squadron loss.

Fighters and ground fire caused other losses, plus at least one to weather during this early morning period. No. 203 Squadron tangled with Jasta 2 at 0830 losing Sergeant W N Mayger MM, down in flames to Leutnant Gerhard Bassenge, although he claimed an SE5a. There were also more multiple losses. 41 Squadron lost five SE5s at this time, mostly to ground fire and the weather, although Josef Jacobs was credited with two SE kills at this time, his 33rd and 34th victories. No. 65 Squadron lost no fewer than six Camels with another force-landing, to ground fire and weather. Three pilots were taken prisoner, two more being interned in Holland. At 0900, 213 Squadron lost three Camels, with another force-landing at Moeres aerodrome after an encounter with fighters and ground fire.

Towards midday, Leutnant Piechulek of Jasta 56 claimed a DH bomber, which was either a 211 Squadron machine, lost while raiding Staden, or a 217 Squadron machine that failed to return; 217 also had a DH4 shot up but it got back. As the afternoon progressed and the weather improved, there were constant combats going on all along the front, with claims and losses difficult to tie up. One fight at 1230 was between 204 Squadron and MFJ 2, the Camel pilots claiming three Fokkers but having one machine force-land, Lieutenant E R Brown being injured. Two German pilots claimed him—Alexandre Zenses for his 9th victory, and Theo Osterkamp for his 27th, both at 1230, both at Woumen.

At 1430, Engel was again raided, 202 losing another machine to this target, but this time to fighters, Flugmaat Nake of MFJ1 making his first victory claim. German fighter pilots had more success during the afternoon. Leutnant Ernst Baumgärtel of Jasta 56 shot down an SE5a near Ypres at 1740, into Allied lines, while a few minutes later, Leutnant Josef Raesch of Jasta 43 shot down another SE5, which fell east of Ypres in German lines. Colours seen on the Fokkers seem to indicate Jasta 56, but Captain E C Hoy DFC of 29 Squadron was brought down at this time to become a prisoner. Hoy had brought his own score to 13 the previous day, and Raesch now had a score of four which would rise to seven by the end of the war.

Combats now came thick and fast and it is difficult to match opposing units. Those that can be included a scrap between 210 Squadron and MFJ 4 south-east of Nieuport at 1745. However, in the general area were Camels of 70 Squadron, Dolphins of 79 and some two-seaters, said to be Bristols by the Germans but probably the DH4s of 218 Squadron. There might also have been some French Spads about, from Spa.62 (see later). No. 70 Squadron lost a Camel north of Gheluwe, but while both sides claimed a number of victories, few aircraft were actually lost.

Shortly afterwards, Marine pilots engaged two-seaters, Theo Osterkamp claiming a Bréguet XIV near Pierkenshoeck at 1810, possibly a Belgian machine lost this day. The two Belgian losses were Warrant Officer Robert J M M Cajot and Lieutenant Alfred T M Bricoult, of 2 Escadrille, who came down at Cortemarck in a Bréguet XIV A-2 to be taken prisoner, and Sous Lieutenant Jean M A G de Roest d'Alkemede and Lieutenant Charles G N F Coomans of 7 Escadrille, flying a Spad XI, who came down near Clercken (Houthulst), although they were apparently hit by flak. Robert Cajot, in WW2, was the CO of the Belgian detachment at the Franco/Belgian school at RAF Odiham, England, having escaped from his native country in July 1940.

Leutnant Bargmann of MFJ 2 shot down a DH9 at Beerst at 1815, perhaps the other Belgian aircraft that failed to get home? With the heavy fighting on this northern part of the front, it is not surprising that further German claims were made, Carl Degelow of Jasta 40s shooting down a Camel here, his 19th victory, Flugmaat Pfeiffer of MFJ 3 another Camel at Woumen at 1815, and this appears to have been Lieutenant R M Bennett of 204 Squadron. From Beckenham, Kent, Bennett at 18 years of age was probably the youngest British ace to die in action. Another claim was for a Spad, to Vizefeldwebel Krebs of Jasta 56 at Kastelhoek— again possibly the Belgian Spad XI. However, the French lost two Spads in the VI Armée Sector, Caporaux Gerard and Gaulhaic of Spa.62. The other claim was an SE5a by Unteroffizier Eduard Binge of Jasta 16, his 4th and final victory of the war.

French Front

The weather here was bad all day, with low clouds and strong winds. Once again, the first job was to try and blind German observations of the battle area by balloon observers, and during the day the French burnt four German 'drachens'. At 0845, at Orfeuil, Sous Lieutenant Jean Charles Romatet, the 25-year-old Corsican CO of Spa.165, got his 5th victory, sharing the balloon with two of his pilots. Then at 0900, the incomparable Michel Coiffard burnt his 23rd balloon (victory 31) south of Semide. Half an hour later, Spa.163's Sergent Onillon flamed the Challerange balloon. Finally, at 1115, the American, Sergent James Connelly, also of Spa.163, claimed the fourth, bringing his own total to six. This too was floating above Challerange, on the west end of the assault area.

In the IV Armée sector, Sal.252 lost a crew to Fokkers, Sergent Bal and Sous Lieutenant Nouvellon being killed as they crashed into French lines. Then a Bréguet of Br.9 failed to return, crewed by Caporal Moser and Sous Lieutenant le Comte des Floris.

Three French two-seaters were claimed by the Germans. Vizefeldwebel Friedrich Poeschke, Jasta 53, shot down his 4th victory at Somme-Py, at 1145, while Leutnant Gustav Frädrich and Vizefeldwebel Karl Arnold each claimed AR2s near Manre. Two observers were wounded by ground fire on this sector, but whether either were involved with enemy fighters is not known. However, Adjutant Montel and Sergent Pautrat of Br.123 were reported missing this day, which may have been the third.

Groupe de Combat 13 engaged in five combats between 1330 and 1530 in the Somme-Py to Manre area, claiming one destroyed and two probables. Adjutant Marcel Laurent Henriot, a

22-year-old from Saulnat in the Haute-Saone region of France, and who had been with Spa.65 since March, claimed his 6th and final victory north of Somme-Py. Sergent Dambet, also of Spa.65, claimed a second. The Escadrille lost Sergent Milhau.

The Germans brought down two Spads: Leutnants Ernst Schulz and Herbert Mahn of Jasta 72s both reported Spads down at Ardeuil, two kilometres north of Manre. Sergent Bourgeois was injured during the day, possibly as the result of combat. Also operating on this front was Spa.124, their Russian GC21 staff commander, Capitaine Paul d'Argueff, bringing down two two-seaters, one at 1010 over Manre, the other at 1520 at Sechault, to bring his score to 13. In between, Lieutenant Henri Berge, the CO of this unit, claimed a probable north of Forges Woods at midday. At 1645, Lieutenant Henri de Sevin, commander of Spa.151, got his second victory over Somme-Py.

Lieutenant René Fonck of Spa.103 claimed a two-seater north-east of Somme-Py at 1030 to bring his score to 67. A patrol of Spa.31 also reported a Fokker biplane down north of Bois de Buoc at 1145, while on the German side Unteroffizier Boness of Jasta 53 claimed a Spad at Somme-Py at 1050.

American Sector

On the front of the Meuse-Argonne offensive, the French and Americans kept up the pressure. The Germans reacted in the air, starting at 0815, with Leutnant Fritz Höhn of Jasta 60 returning the compliment by flaming a balloon near Tahure. Lieutenant Weiss jumped from the burning 67 Cié gas bag. Then at 0850, Höhn returned to burn the American 6th BC's balloon at Bethelainville, from which First Lieutenants H F Gossett and G R Nixon baled out safely.

However, the Americans claimed three balloons at this time too. The first at 0600 went to First Lieutenant Eddie Rickenbacker, near Sivry-sur-Meuse. Six minutes later another 94th Aero pilot, Harvey Cook, flamed a balloon near Clery le Petit. Frank Luke got the third— near Bantheville at 0609—the pilot's 14th victory.

The 22nd Aero were busy in combat shortly between 0840 and 0900, claiming five Fokkers and a Rumpler two-seater. One of the Fokkers was that probably flown by Unteroffizier Karl Hofmann of Jasta 60, who was killed in combat over the Argonne Forest during the day. At 0915, the 139th Aero claimed three Pfalz DIIIs over Clery le Petit, then a Rumpler over Forges at 1030 by a flight commander of the 27th Aero, Jerry Vasconcells.

During the day, the specialist night observation 9th Aero was caught in daylight. Two of their aircraft had been joined by a Salmson of 88 Aero, then proceeded to patrol. Over the front they were attacked by five Fokkers north-east of Montfaucon. The DVII pilot that came in on Second Lieutenants Harry A Dolan and Basil D Woom scored with his first burst, shooting away the aileron contols and sending the DH4 down in a spin to crash-land; the crew were shaken but unharmed.

Second Lieutenant Lee D Warrender and First Lieutenant Harry C Crumb were wounded, Warrender through the neck, Crumb through the abdomen—they crashed in no-man's-land. Crumb was severely wounded and told his pilot to leave him and save himself; he later died of his wound. The accompanying Salmson was shot down in flames, but surprisingly, the crew of Second Lieutenant H E Loud and Captain C T Trickey survived, though wounded, and Loud later succumbed.

Franz Büchner shot down the Salmson, his 37th kill, while Leutnant Werner Niethammer, also Jasta 13, reported downing a Salmson near Pagny, and Leutnant Oliver von Beaulieu-Marconnay of Jasta 19 reported downing a Spad two-seater for his 23rd kill, both most probably misidentification of the DH4s.

At 0950, the balloon of the 1st US Company was attacked by seven Fokkers south of Dannevoux. One Fokker was brought down by the protective fire of the nearby 2nd Balloon Company gunners, Vizefeldwebel Heinrich Brobowski of Jasta 53 being captured. The balloon was damaged but not destroyed, although First Lieutenant S I Howell sensibly baled out.

A lull followed until the afternoon. Several combats and claims occurred, involving the 147th, 213th, 93rd and 103rd Aeros. Another DH4, this time from the 50th Observation Squadron, was shot down by ground fire late in the day, having taken off at 1552. The crew were rescued safely from in front of the lines.

The last victory of the day went to Frank Luke at 1550, a Hannover CLIII near the Bois d'Apremont, bringing the American's score to 15. Bad weather then closed in, ending combat for the day.

	A/C	KB		DES	OOC	KB
British losses	33	—	British claims	24	7	—
French losses	7	1	French claims	8		4
American losses	4	—	American claims	20		3
Belgian losses	2	—	Belgian claims	—		—
IAF losses	—	—	IAF claims	—	—	—
German claims	33†	2	German losses	5‡		?

† At least two to flak. ‡ At least five, with an additional five airmen reported killed, which may or may not have resulted in lost aeroplanes; one of the airmen being from FA205.

British Casualties

Aircraft type	No.	Squadron	Crew		
SE5a	F5456	29 Sqdn	Lt B R Rolfe	POW	
SE5a	F5480	29 Sqdn	Lt D A O'Leary	POW	
SE5a	D6947	29 Sqdn	2/Lt W L Dougan	POW	
DH4	N5962	202 Sqdn	Lt R Ringrose	KIA	
			2/Lt H Hollings	KIA	
DH4	A8025	202 Sqdn	Capt A V Bowater	POW	
			Lt D L Melvin	POW	
DH4	A8066	202 Sqdn	Lt C R Moore	MIA	
			2/Lt E Darby	MIA	
DH4	A7924	217 Sqdn	1/Lt J E Gregory USAS	KIA	
			2/Lt E Martin-Bell	KIA	
Camel	H7288	65 Sqdn	2/Lt W J Brooks	KIA	
Camel	F1542	65 Sqdn	2/Lt D M John	Interned	
Camel	B7864	65 Sqdn	Lt F Edsted	Interned	
Camel	D8145	65 Sqdn	Lt J C Malcolmson DFC	POW	
Camel	E1487	65 Sqdn	Lt J McM Maclennon DFC	POW	
Camel	D8158	65 Sqdn	2/Lt R C Mitten	POW	
Camel	F5937	209 Sqdn	Lt J A Fenton	KIA	
Camel	D8187	204 Sqdn	Lt R M Bennett	KIA	
RE8	C2530	7 Sqdn	2/Lt H M Matthews	DOW	
			2/Lt C Fletcher	KIA	
Camel	F3220	203 Sqdn	Sgt W N Mayger MM	MIA	
Camel	E7199	70 Sqdn	Sgt A C Hall	POW	
SE5a	B7900	64 Sqdn	2/Lt A T Sheldrake	MIA	
SE5a	E4048	41 Sqdn	Lt A F Smith	POW	
SE5a	F5484	41 Sqdn	2/Lt H C Telfer	POW	
SE5a	F5506	41 Sqdn	2/Lt W Mitchell	POW	
SE5a	E4061	41 Sqdn	Lt P B Cooke	POW	
SE5a	C8887	41 Sqdn	2/Lt H B Hewat	POW	
Camel	D3326	213 Sqdn	2/Lt A Fletcher	POW	
Camel	D3372	213 Sqdn	Lt P C Jenner	MIA	
Camel	F3948	213 Sqdn	Lt W A Rankin	POW	
DH9	B8936	211 Sqdn	2/Lt W J Johnson	POW	
			Sgt W E Jones MM	POW	
Dolphin	F6020	79 Sqdn	Lt R J Morgan	POW	
AWFK8	D5152	10 Sqdn	Lt C F J Lisle	WIA	*
			2/Lt M de Verteuil	Safe	
RE8	D6741	7 Sqdn	2/Lt W K Rose	Safe	*
			2/Lt A E Jenkins	KIA	
RE8	E273	7 Sqdn	2/Lt G A J Henry	DOW	
			2/Lt A Westall	WIA	
SE5a	C9294	56 Sqdn	Lt D W Grinnell-Milne	Safe	*
Camel	D8175	70 Sqdn	2/Lt J S Wilson	KIA	
DH9	D5622	108 Sqdn	2/Lt P L Phillips	Safe	*
			2/Lt P S McCrea	Safe	
DH4	A7849	202 Sqdn	Lt A M Stevens	MIA	
			2/Lt W H L Halford	MIA	
Camel	D8218	204 Sqdn	2/Lt E R Brown	WIA	*
Dolphin	C8115	87 Sqdn	2/Lt D A Thomson	POW	
SE5a	C1914	29 Sqdn	Capt E C Hoy DFC	POW	

DH9	C1206	218 Sqdn	2/Lt F Nelson USMCR	WIA	*
			2/Lt L L Barr	DOW	
BF2b	C1036	4 Sqdn	Lt R H Schroeder	Safe	*
			2/Lt B R Jones	WIA	
RE8		7 Sqdn	2/Lt S Kennono (O)	WIA	*
AWFK8	C8643	82 Sqdn	Lt J Sangster	WIA	*
			2/Lt L J Skinner	WIA	
Camel		3 Sqdn	2/Lt R L McLeod	WIA	*
RE8		13 Sqdn	2/Lt J Nicole (P)	WIA	*
SE5a		56 Sqdn	Lt J C Speaks	WIA	*
DH4		27 Sqdn	2/Lt C M Allan (P)	WIA	*
Camel		70 Sqdn	Lt C L Frank	WIA	*

French Casualties

Spad XIII	Spa.62		Cpl Gerard	MIA	
Spad XIII	Spa.62		Cpl Gaulhiac	MIA	
Bréguet XIV	Br.282		Sgt Roux	Safe	*
			Asp Bertrand	WIA	
Spad XIII	Spa.65		Sgt Milhau	MIA	
Spad XIII	Spa.65		Sgt Bourgeois	Inj	
Bréguet XIV	Br.123		Adj Montez	MIA	
			Sgt Pautrat	MIA	
Salmson 2A2	Sal.252		Sgt Bal	KIA	
			S/Lt Nouvellon	KIA	
Bréguet XIV	Br.9		Cpl Moser	MIA	
			S/Lt Le Comte des Floris	MIA	
Bréguet XIV	Br.269		Lt Gilles (O)	KIA	*
Bréguet XIV	Br.55		Lt Mailloux (O)	WIA	*

Belgian Casualties

Bréguet XIV A-2	2me Esc		WO R J M M Cajot	POW
			Lt A T M Bricoult	POW
Spad XI	7me Esc		S/Lt J de R d'Alkemade	?
			Lt C G N F Coomans	?

American Casualties

Spad XIII	27th Aero		1/Lt P V Stout	WIA	*
Salmson 2A2	88th Aero		2/Lt H E Laud	DOW
			Capt C T Trickey	WIA
DH4	50th Aero		1/Lt F McCook	Safe
			2/Lt M K Lochwood	Safe
DH4	9th Aero		2/Lt H A Dolan	Safe
			2/Lt B D Woom	Safe
DH4	9th Aero		2/Lt L D Warrender	WIA
			1/Lt H C Crumb	DOW

Sunday, 29 September 1918

British Front

The weather began fine in the morning, with overcast, cloudy conditions settling in during the afternoon. This day saw yet another sector of the German front being attacked; the fourth day in a row this had occurred. This time, General Sir Henry Rawlinson's 4th Army smashed straight through the main Hindenburg Line positions near Bellicourt, called the Battle of the St Quentin Canal. The main thrust went in between Bellenglise and Venduille. This resulted in pushing the Germans into a retreat which would not stop until the end of the war. On other sections of the front, Passchendaele was retaken by Allied troops, while the Belgians recaptured Dixmude.

As luck would have it, on this front, captured German documents enabled the British commanders to know the exact location of every German machine-gun position, trench mortar and battery, as well as ammunition and supply dumps, telephone and signals centres.

The day's first action took place near Estourmel at 0730, seven of 87 Squadron's Dolphins encountering 11 Fokkers. Lieutenant Hollinghurst claimed one down out of control for his 10th victory, but the unit lost the veteran Canadian Ross Macdonald, although by whom is difficult to discover as no Dolphins were noted as claimed this day. At this same time, Captain J D Breakey of 203 Squadron, engaged on a low bombing patrol, saw a lone LVG two-seater and attacked. Firing 150 rounds into it, the LVG climbed steeply, stalled and crashed near the Sensee Canel. This is believed to be a machine from FA33, who lost two aircraft this day.

On the hour Camels and Fokkers clashed near Wijnendaele Wood. 210 Squadron claimed eight, one German pilot being seen to jump. The Camel boys lost one pilot, Second Lieutenant John F Stafford, a 22-year-old American from Fall River, Massachusetts. He was probably on his first sortie, as he had only arrived four days earlier! MFJ 1 pilots claimed victories—Vizeflugmaat Hackebusch, Leutnant Freydmadl and Flugmaat Reiss, all timed at 0820. Vizefeldwebel Krebs of Jasta 56 claimed an SE5a at Westroosbeke at 0815 although none were lost. (It is just possible the MFJ claims fit losses the day before!)

At 0830 an RE8 was shot down by Unteroffizier Ludwig Jeckert of Jasta 56 near Zonnebeke. The only RE8 crew downed had left their base at 0730, a 6 Squadron machine, but as they were operating from Moslains, well south of Cambrai, it could not have been them. They were most probably brought down by ground fire when operating north of St Quentin.

Bombers of 211 Squadron were in action at 0810 over Roulers and 1 Squadron's SE5s had a fight at 0845. At this latter time too, 11 Squadron's Bristols were in action against DVIIs south-east of Cambrai, one falling to Josef Mai of Jasta 5, on fire, east of Caudry at 0850—the German's 30th victory.

Over Busigny at this same moment, 27 Squadron were fighting Fokkers after bombing the place. One DVII came up under the tail of two of them and was promptly shot down, bursting into flames and breaking up. However, one DH9 was shot down in turn by Unteroffizier Treiber, also of Jasta 5, north of Caudry.

More bombers were out an hour later, escorted by 1 Squadron's SE5s. The fighters claimed two DVIIs but one SE also went down, victim of Leutnant Karl Odebrett of Jasta 42, who notched up his 16th kill at Bohain. A 3 Squadron Camel force-landed just behind the front at 0945 after a low patrol and a fight with Fokkers. Paul Baümer of Jasta 2 claimed two Camels this day at unknown times, and this may have been one of them.

Just prior to 10 am, 84 Squadron went on one of their famous balloon strafes, reporting no less than five 'drachens' burnt, north of Villers-Outreaux (two), Beaurevoir, L'Espagne and north of Montbrehain. One SE5 failed to return, the South African Second Lieutenant D C Rees—probably the SE brought down by Vizefeldwebel Oskar Hennrich of Jasta 46 at Villers-Outreaux at 1020. Three more balloons fell to 29 Squadron at around the same moment, further north, near Comines and Armentières. However, Lieutenant R G Robertson had to force-land near Ypres after being hit by ground fire.

Towards 1030, 20 Squadron were in a fight with Fokkers, putting in claims of six victories north of St Quentin, but they too lost a machine and an ace pilot—Lieutenant N S Boulton and Second Lieutenant C H Case. It has been noted elsewhere that they were brought down by Mai of Jasta 5, but the times do not agree. Jasta 2 claimed two Bristols at undisclosed times—possibly three as Baümer is noted as having downed an RE8 which may have been another type. However, 22 Squadron lost two Bristols mid-morning. The main possibility is that the 20 Squadron BF2b was the 20th victory of Offizierstellvertreter Friedrich Altemeier of Jasta 24s, at Montbrehain, north of St Quentin.

This really is the problem with these last September days: there is so much confused fighting over several overlapping sectors of the front, that it is difficult to have any understanding of who was fighting who. This even applies to aircraft brought down on the Allied side—a rare occurrence. Captain C W Cudemore of 64 Squadron is a case in point. He saw a formation of four Fokkers apparently flying protection to balloons and attacked, shooting down one out of control. The second Fokker he went for fell away and crashed north-west of Sailly, inside British lines, where it burst into flames. This may have been Leutnant Fritz Hoffmann of Jasta Boelcke, killed west of Cambrai.

The fight which cost 22 Squadron two machines occurred between 1130 and midday, and they probably went down to Baümer and Unteroffizier Karl Fervers. A difficulty now is that the surviving German records are not so good as in earlier months and years of the war. For instance, 211 Squadron lost two DH9s with another two shot up at this same time, but there are no apparent claims. Jasta 7 were in the area, and may have been the unknown Jasta, for it is understood that some pilot scores are missing for this unit. Combats abound in this late morning period, with 41, 70, 92, 213 and the 148th Aero all seeing action.

At 1220, 218 Squadron lost two bombers to fighters; Leutnant Willi Rosenstein of Jasta 40s claimed a two-seater at 1240, and Leutnant Kohlpoth of Jasta 56 another at Beythem at 1230. As the morning had been, so too was the afternoon: massed combats and air fights. And it was not always the inexperienced pilots who were caught out. At 1315, Captain E B Drake of 209 Squadron was lost over Cambrai, probably to ground fire. Drake was 20 and came from Weymouth, and had been in the RNAS since October 1916. The Camels of 43, 203 and 209 had been ground strafing the crossings over the Sensee Canal, west of Hem Lenglet, to the north of Cambrai. This dangerous yet exhilarating task would claim many more lives before the war's end. Another pilot gaining experience but lost this day was Lieutenant Francis R Christiani, an American with 84 Squadron. He had gained four victories during this month, but was last seen over Montbrehain.

Another experienced pilot was Captain R C L Holme MC of 29 Squadron. His SE was also hit by ground fire, and although he staggered back to the lines, he had to crash-land in some shell holes and was lucky to get into front line trenches. Age and experience did not necessarily go hand-in-hand. However, experience was necessary when in action against the aces. Two pilots of 46 Squadron, Second Lieutenants A M Allan and N F Moxon, were 21 and 28 respectively, the former from Toronto, the latter from London. The common factor was that they had both been on the Squadron three weeks. This day they were both shot down and taken prisoner—possibly to the vastly experienced Paul Baümer of Jasta Boelcke, who downed his two Camel victories this day over Sailly and Bourlon Wood.

It happened on both sides too. During the day, the Staffelführer of Jasta 51 was brought down and taken prisoner after an attempted attack on a balloon. Hans Gandert, who had eight victories, had commanded his unit since the previous December. Yet experience was obviously necessary, and one who had it was Willi Coppens; this day he shot down a balloon, again at Leffinghe—victory No.32. However, during this day he flew near to a British RE8 and was continually fired on by the observer, despite Coppens trying to show the British crew his Belgian roundels and the fact that they were well inside British lines. The RE8 eventually landed at Proven airfield, so it was probably a 7 Squadron machine. Coppens, more than a little upset, landed too and protested. The observer inspected Coppens machine, finding one bullet hole in the left wing, a second through the tailplane!

French Front

The weather was still atrocious, with more high winds and low clouds. The French lost four aircraft. Capitaine Paul Reverchon, the commander of Spa.31, failed to return from a patrol near Orfeuil, on the IV Armée front, just after 0945. Sous Lieutenant Robert Waddington was also shot up and force-landed, but after claiming a Fokker for his 12th and final victory. Reverchon was shot down by Leutnant Hans von Freden, of Jasta 50, at Somme-Py at 1000, the German's 13th victory.

Unteroffizier Otto Bieleit of Jasta 66 shot down what he thought was a Bréguet north of Jouy, which was in fact a Spad XI of Spa.42 flown by Sergent Kalley and Lieutenant Kervadoe. However, a Bréguet of Br.282 was forced to land in French front lines after a combat.

Up on the northern Flanders front, a Spad two-seater of Spa.34 was engaged by Theo Osterkamp, commander of MFJ 2, west of Zarren, although he reported the machine as a Bréguet (Germans often failed to distinguish between Bréguets, Spad XIs, Salmsons and DH4s). Both crew members were wounded but got their aircraft down inside Allied lines; however, Osterkamp had his 29th victory. On the Reims front French fighter pilots also claimed eight probable victories.

American Sector

The previous evening JGII had moved west to get fully in front of the main direction of the Allied offensive. Jastas 12 and 13 went to Charmois, while 15 and 19 moved into Stenay, just north of Charmois.

A Salmson of the 12th Observation Squadron was brought down by ground fire between Fleville and Cornay, north of Varennes. The pilot, First Lieutenant Wistar Morris, was killed, the observer, Cassius H Styles, captured. His later account stated:

'... we had gone to the front again for a reconnaissance, and having sufficient gasoline, had gone well over the lines to look at Fleville. While there we saw a German battery of field artillery, crossing an open field west of the Aire River. We attacked them with our machine-guns and put two of the four guns and their horses out of commission. One gun tumbled into the river. As a machine-gun was set up to fire at us, we silenced it with a couple of bursts from our guns. When there were no more soldiers in sight, we again returned to HQ and made another report.

'Then we left to go home, but as we had more gas than we needed, we decided to take another look at Fleville. When we reached there, we saw a good number of soldiers around the second cannon we had shot up and started firing on them. After a few bursts we were hit by a machine-gun hidden in some bushes. We crashed and a few minutes afterwards, Lt Morris died, although first aid was given him by some German soldiers.'

The 93rd Pursuit claimed the first USAS victory of the day, at 1625. Three Spads teamed up to down an Albatros two-seater near Chaumont; Leutnant Karl Metzler of FA(A)287 was killed near this location. Ten minutes later, Fokkers were encountered, the Americans claiming four shot down for the loss of one. First Lieutenant Roswell H Fuller crashed near Damvillers about 1635, brought down by Unteroffizier Bader of Jasta 64w, whose victim, he reported, fell south-west of Chaumont, although the time was noted as 1720.

Two-seater fought two-seater at 1655. Lieutenants William P Erwin and Byrne V Baucom in their Salmson 2A2 of the 1st Aero Squadron did battle with a Rumpler two-seater at 150 metres, sending it down north of Fleville. This aggressive observation pilot would achieve eight victories in WW1, while Baucom scored three.

The half hour around sunset of this day saw the end of the remarkable career of the determined, intense, relentlessly aggressive—and abnormally brave—Frank Luke Jr. Luke had set out at 1722 to go for three balloons along the Meuse River, near Dun-sur-Meuse. Ground observers saw him burn all three—the BZ95, 64 and 35 balloons—but then saw him no more.

Apparently he had started at the Meuse and headed east, burning the balloon at Dun, then at Brière Ferme, and the last at Milly. Here he was hit by the defences of Leutnant Mangel's BZ35, suffering a chest wound. He then headed for the small village at Murvaux, passing over it, heading east, circled, and turned back west, landing in near darkness on a slope west of the village, just 50 yards from a creek.

He got out of his Spad and started to crawl towards the stream in order, it must be assumed, to drink, as his type of wound induces a raging thirst. Knowing that the Germans would be looking for him, he fired one round from his revolver, in order to attract attention, before slumping over dead. The later stories about shoot-outs on the ground are simply not true; Luke's career does not need such embellishments. After his last three victories, bringing his score to 18, the end had come to an American warrior of the highest order. And his country awarded him their highest award for bravery and courage, the Medal of Honour, Luke having already been the recipient of the Distinguished Service Cross with Oak Leaf Cluster. More Spads were lost this evening. First Lieutenant T A Gabel of the 49th Pursuit failed to return, last seen in the vicinity of Souilly at 1730. Just before 1800, a flight of three Spads of the 95th departed to patrol the Dun-sur-Meuse area. One dropped out, leaving First Lieutenants Lansing Holden and Granville O Woodard to continue. At about 1855, they attacked and burned two balloons but were then bounced by four Fokkers. Leutnant Rudolf Rienau of Jasta 19 shot down Woodard, who was taken prisoner. Holden left a letter in his own, somewhat disjointed, style describing these events:

'Woody and I went over just above the clouds. We hunted for perhaps half an hour before I spotted two balloons, almost on the ground. Somehow I had a hunch that everything wasn't all right—they weren't shooting at us. We circled for some time—luckily. Four German planes appeared between us and the lines; it was another trap. I climbed into the scattered clouds; that was the last time I saw Woody. Then they opened with the hottest "archie" fire I ever went through. I waited for developments—it was almost dark—and I was at about 2,500 metres, too dark to see the balloons till one burst into flames—Woody must have gotten it. I don't know if he had seen the German planes coming; he never came home. I won't forget him in a hurry, he was one of the most modest, all around good fellows I have met over here.

'It was so dark by this time that the Huns must have gone. The gunners, I don't think, saw me till I started shooting—the balloon was only 100 metres up. I waited as patiently as I could till I was very close, then fired [but] my guns jammed! They were shooting machine-guns and "flaming onions". I was so mad it didn't faze me. I just got the hammer and started fixing the guns. I got the guns fixed and was turning to fire again when up she went. Can you picture that great sausage wrapped in flames in the dead of night?'

The other American loss this day was a Salmson of the 99th Aero, brought down by flak fire near Romagne. Lieutenants John W McElroy and Howard T Kinne were killed.

	A/C	KB			DES	OOC	KB
British losses	22		British claims		37	20	9
French losses	2		French claims		6		1
American losses	6		American claims		7		5
IAF losses	—		IAF claims		—		
German claims	29	1	German losses		4†		3?

† At least four, but probably more, as a further 10/12 airmen of mostly unknown units were reported killed in action, including one from FA287. Leutnant Gerold Tschentschel, an ace of Jasta 72, was also severely wounded this day on the French Front.

British Casualties

Aircraft type	No.	Squadron	Crew		
Dolphin	C4155	87 Sqdn	Lt R M Macdonald	POW	
DH9	D3172	27 Sqdn	2/Lt H S Thomas	MIA	
			2/Lt T Brown	MIA	
DH9	D482	211 Sqdn	2/Lt J L McAdam	Safe	
			2/Lt T W Kelly	WIA	
BF2b	E2509	62 Sqdn	Lt R H O'Reilly	KIA	
			2/Lt L E Mitchell	KIA	
RE8	D4734	6 Sqdn	2/Lt H H Scott	KIA	
			2/Lt A C J Payne	POW	
BF2b	F5814	11 Sqdn	2/Lt T T Smith	KIA	
			Lt J L Bromley	KIA	
Camel	F6175	3 Sqdn	2/Lt A W Tinham	Safe	*
Camel	D9664	210 Sqdn	2/Lt J F Stafford	KIA	
SE5a	C8841	1 Sqdn	Lt L N Elworthy	POW	
BF2b	E2266	22 Sqdn	Lt E Adams USAS	POW	
			Sgt G H Bissell	POW?	
BF2b	E2517	22 Sqdn	Lt C W M Thompson	POW	
			Lt L R James	POW	
Camel	H7274	80 Sqdn	2/Lt R Bramwell	KIA	
BF2b	E2561	20 Sqdn	2/Lt N S Boulton	KIA	
			2/Lt C H Case	KIA	
SE5a	C9293	84 Sqdn	2/Lt D C Rees	MIA	
DH9	D3093	211 Sqdn	2/Lt A G White	KIA	
			2/Lt J B Blundell	KIA	
DH9	D565	211 Sqdn	Lt W H Mooney USAS	POW	
			2/Lt V A Fair MC	MIA	
Camel	F6188	80 Sqdn	Capt H J Welch	KIA	
Camel	E4376	209 Sqdn	Capt E B Drake	KIA	
RE8	C2693	5 Sqdn	2/Lt E A Harrison	Safe	*
			2/Lt E M Patterson	Safe	
Camel	F5960	46 Sqdn	2/Lt A M Allan	POW	

Camel	D6572	46 Sqdn	2/Lt N F Moxon	KIA	
SE5a	D6982	84 Sqdn	2/Lt F R Christiani	KIA	
SE5a	D6942	29 Sqdn	Capt R C L Holme MC	Safe	
AWFK8	C8643	82 Sqdn	Lt J Sangster	WIA	
			2/Lt L J Skinner	WIA	
RE8		6 Sqdn	2/Lt W M Anderson (O)	WIA	*
AWFK8		8 Sqdn	2/Lt J B Ballantyne (O)	WIA	*
DH9		205 Sqdn	2/Lt C O'N Daunt (O)	KIA	*
DH9		205 Sqdn	Lt H G Kirkland (O)	WIA	*
RE8		3 AFC	2/Lt S H Deamer (P)	WIA	*
DH9		27 Sqdn	2/Lt C E Robinson (O)	WIA	*
DH9		103 Sqdn	Capt J Austin-Sparkes	WIA	*
			2/Lt B Russell	WIA	
DH9		206 Sqdn	2/Lt A G Squire (O)	WIA	*

French Casualties

Spad XI		Spa.?	MdL de Bellencourt	WIA	*
			Lt de Bussy	WIA	
Spad XIII		Spa.31	Capt P Reverchon	MIA	
Spad XIII		Spa.31	S/Lt R Waddington	Safe	*
Spad XIII		Spa.?	Adj Naudin	WIA	*
Spad XI		Spa.42	Sgt Kalley	MIA	
			Lt Kervadoe	MIA	
?		Esc.8	Adj Coudreau (P)	WIA	*

American Casualties

Salmson 2A2		12th Aero	1/Lt W Morris	DOW	
			1/Lt C H Styles	POW	
Spad XIII		93rd Aero	1/Lt R H Fuller	KIA	
Spad XIII		13th Aero	1/Lt E R Richards	WIA	*
Spad XIII		49th Aero	1/Lt T A Gabel	MIA	
Spad XIII		27th Aero	1/Lt F Luke Jr	DOW	
Spad XIII		95th Aero	1/Lt G O Woodard	POW	
Salmson 2A2		99th Aero	1/Lt J W McElroy	KIA	
			1/Lt H T Kinne	KIA	

Monday, 30 September 1918

British Front

Unlike the last day of Bloody April, the last day of Black September ended in a whimper compared to some other days. This was due in part to the continued bad weather, which was even worse than it had been of late; it was all low cloud and heavy rainstorms.

The RAF made no claims at all during the day, but lost three planes—all late in the day. As always the poor two-seater crews had to be out trying to locate the front line troops or to range artillery. They had not been slaughtered as much as in April 1917, but Leutnant Heinrich Henkel of Jasta 37 caught an RE8 of 12 Squadron flying a patrol for VI Corps over Crevecoeur at 1700 hours and shot it down. Lieutenants T H Jacques and F N Billington became victory No.5 for Henkel, who would gain three more in October. An hour later, Second Lieutenant L S Davis on an OP with 92 Squadron became the 6th and final victory of Leutnant Sylvester Garsztka of Jasta 31 over Lehaucourt.

The final casualty inflicted on the RAF was to a Bristol crew of 48 Squadron, wounded by ground machine-gun fire this date.

On the German side, FA(A)207 lost a crew at Aubencheul-au-Bac, probably to ground fire, killing Unteroffizier Hermann Geithner and Leutnant Johann Schwartz.

For the ground troops, the war would go on, but for the Royal Air Force, at least Black September was finally over.

French Front

In the IV Armée sector, Caporal Heine and Caporal Gerain of Spa.164 attacked an enemy aircraft at 1823 over Challeronge, the German falling in what was described as a damaged condition. Then Heine was shot down and killed near the Bois de Cernay, the victim of Vizefeldwebel Alfons Nägler of Jasta 81, who claimed a Spad at Ville, which is just south of here. Leutnant Hans Rolfes of Jasta 45 crash-landed on this day, possibly a victim of this air fight. Rolfes had downed his 17th victory just the day before. He had just been placed in command of Jagdgruppe Ost (Jastas 9, 21, 45 and 66), although he retained command of Jasta 45, which he had formed and led since December 1917.

Leutnant Herman Habrich and Leutnant Franz Ray, both of Jasta 49, the latter being the Staffelführer, each claimed a Spad at Somme-Py and Manre at 1820 for their 5th and 17th victories respectively. The problem sometimes is that the Germans tended to note a Spad victory without mentioning if it was a single- or two-seater. The problem too was that their identification of a Spad XI could be for a Salmson, DH4 or a Bréguet, as mentioned before. As no single-seaters appear to have been lost, it is possible they were two-seaters. One known loss was a Salmson of Sal.106, flown by Adjutant Couderc and Sous Lieutenant Zuber, who crashed and had their machine written off near Mont Murat, neither man being injured. Another casualty was a Bréguet of Br.123, which failed to return.

The only confirmed claim of the day was by Spa.163, a two-seater shot down near Cerny at 1823 shared by three pilots, one being an American member of the Lafayette Flying Corps, David S Paden.

American Sector

The Americans ended the month with just one loss, a Salmson 2A2 of the 104th Aero, which was forced down in German lines where the crew were taken prisoner. With no German making a claim, they either fell victim to ground fire or mechanical failure. One Spad pilot, First Lieutenant Irwin W Fish, of the 213th Aero, was wounded during the day, probably by ground fire.

	A/C	KB		DES	OOC	KB
British losses	2	—	British claims	—	—	—
French losses	3	—	French claims	1		—
American losses	1	—	American claims	—		—
German claims	7	—	German losses	?†		—

† Total unknown but other than those mentioned above, an observer in FA241 was wounded by ground fire, Leutnant Georg Schlenker, leader of Jasta 41 with 14 victories, was severely wounded, while 11 other airmen were reported killed, although not all may have been due to combat.

British Casualties

Aircraft type	No.	Squadron	Crew		
RE8	C2442	12 Sqdn	2/Lt T H Jacques	KIA	
			Lt F N Billington	KIA	
SE5a	C9298	92 Sqdn	2/Lt L S Davis	KIA	
BF2b		48 Sqdn	2/Lt W S Rycroft	WIA	*
			2/Lt H C Wood	WIA	

French Casualties

Spad XIII		Spa.164	Cpl Heine	KIA	
Salmson 2A2		Sal.106	Adj Couderc	Safe	
			S/Lt Zuber	Safe	
Bréguet XIV		Br.123	Adj A Montel	MIA	
			Sgt M Pollet	MIA	

American Casualties

Salmson 2A2		104th Aero	2/Lt M F Saunders	POW	
			1/Lt R E Davis	POW	
Spad XIII		213th Aero	1/Lt I W Fish	WIA	*

Summary and Conclusions

What does the intense aerial combat of September 1918 tell us of the changes in aerial warfare since the previous April 1917? Firstly it was a much larger affair, with the sizes of the main protagonists being at least twice that of before. It was also a good deal more specialised.

April 1917 had seen the RFC introduce specialised night bombing squadrons to add to the standard artillery observation, reconnaissance, bombing and scout squadrons. This had expanded into strategic bombing by day and night, tactical bombing day and night, long range recce flights, specialised long range recce squadrons, night fighter squadrons, fighter squadrons and fighter squadrons doubling as ground attack and close support units. These last units—particularly the Sopwith Camel squadrons—signalled the rise of the fighter-bomber, which ended up dominating close support work in WW2 and into more modern times. The Independent Air Force was about to introduce the dedicated long range single-seater fighter escort to bombers. This was No.45 Squadron, back from Italy, which saw out the war waiting for long range Snipes in order to begin this duty. Most of the tactical bomber raids were escorted. The IAF were not, and suffered accordingly.

The French had long range multi-crewed and multi-gunned escort fighters (Caudron RXIs) for their bombers. They had also, perhaps, advanced the furthest of the Allies in using concentrations of fighters, kept in large multi-squadron combinations, to be used to support offensives. In the Groupe de Combats of the Division Aerienne were the best of the Spad units.

The RAF did not copy this. Except for transfers of units between more active and less active fronts, the only Wing that approached the French in terms of mobility was the Head-quarters Wing. Most RAF fighter squadrons stayed on the same army front. When they fought in wings they combined fighter recce and fighter squadrons and, except for No.61 Wing—the mainly ex-RNAS Wing based at Dunkirk—which was all Camel-equipped, always mixed up the different types of fighters with the concept of each type being the best for low level, medium escort and high cover work. Squadrons on a front were reinforced for major offensives by having units added to the Wing, but the RAF never developed tactical groupings at Wing level that fought and trained together. The Wing was mainly administrative and not operational. Louis Strange's 80 Wing was different and would have become the more common style, as it had begun in August 1918 deliberately to use large formations to match the German Circuses. This did not happen all the time, as 4 AFC's loss of four or five Camels showed.

Where the RAF totally excelled, especially in April 1917, was in the performance of the Corps (or Army Co-operation) organisations where the observation squadrons of RE8s and AWFK8s operated fairly freely over the German lines, providing aerial photographic coverage, total mapping requirements and complete capacity for artillery co-operation for the Army. They had also begun ammunition drops to forward troops, smoke-screen laying and dedicated tank support while maintaining their low level contact patrol work.

April 1917 had seen the slaughter of the fighter and recce squadrons of Nieuports and Sopwith 1½ Strutters on the Arras sector, during which the fighter squadrons had not been able to stop the depredations of the Jastas on the BE2s. September 1918 saw perhaps one day when JGII had some impact on a small section of the front, in interfering with the RE8s. Mostly they did not. Few RE8 units lost more than three or four machines for the month, and some of them were to ground fire, and all operated more or less how they chose. The RAF's September 1918 casualties had shifted to the fighter-bombers and the day bombers of both the tactical and strategic kind. In the main, the Bristol F2b fighter-recce units carried out their tasks with low casualties, although both 11 and 48 Squadrons did lose a number of machines, but it was nothing near the level of the Strutter units of Bloody April.

The Americans were able to contribute fully to the Allied cause for the first time during September 1918. Given their late arrival in the war, and some of the obvious difficulties of operating in a service that was a part of the Signal Corps, it is perhaps surprising that they did so well. The reason their fighter pilots did was that their tactical leadership was drawn from the Americans (and Harold Hartney, a Canadian), who had current modern operational experience with the French, embracing the Lafayette Flying Corps, and the British.

They also introduced a high level of teamwork to their efforts like the French, matched the British aggression, but only when needed, and introduced far more commonly than the RAF the operation in patrols of large numbers and multi-squadrons. Their Pursuit Groups were the equivalent of Groupes de Combat, rather than RAF wings, ie: operational units of single types of fighters that were coordinated to achieve specific tasks. They also operated as fighter-bombers.

In day bombing, the Americans took a lot longer to learn, primarily handicapped by a level of incompetence at the Bombardment Group level, matched only by the bravery of the crews. No escorts were provided until massacres forced them to do so (a lesson re-learnt in WW2!). Sending flights of under twelve across the lines in separate formations, to bomb the same target, separated by small time differences resulted in three disasters during the month. If the Jastas did not get the first small group, they would effectively eliminate one of the following formations.

The American observation and recce squadrons, given the low level of experience, were very good at their work and extremely aggressive. Overall, despite significant casualties, by the end of September the Americans could operate effectively against the best that Germany could offer. Their equipment was very good, but their aircrew were far better than any other air service. This was because the best and brightest—mainly highly educated young men of high physical standards—had gravitated to the USAS. This was no different from the other services, except the Americans had not had theirs killed off over the previous three years of mass casualties on the Western Front. Physical standards were, perhaps, too strict, as many a good pilot in the other services would have failed the medicals, but overall the Americans had an extremely motivated group of men who were bursting to fight, confident they would beat the Germans, in order to get the war ended. It was also the first and only chance many would have of seeing Europe and being part of what was still, for many, the great adventure. There were also no inborn class hang-ups as with the British and French; all aviators were officers. Such enthusiasm was tempered somewhat in the French Air Service and the RAF by their more realistic and experienced view on the hazards of operations against a dangerous foe.

The numbers of the 'colonials' in the RAF also aided its capabilities. Large numbers of Canadians, Australians, Americans, South Africans and New Zealanders served in the RAF, in roughly the listed order in terms of numbers. The Americans were also present in the French Air Service.

The German Air Service had also been reorganised since Bloody April. They had concentrated on night bombing, particularly of tactical targets by 1918. Indeed, on one raid on No.1 Aeroplane Supply Depot on 23 September, a total of 41 airmen were killed, with four more missing and 114 wounded. The two-seater Schlachtstaffeln had been expanded to carry out ground attack and other support tasks. Their effectiveness appears to have been very low. It is hard to find in Allied army unit records any major inconveniences caused by their activities. The Australians, for example, took more notice of the night bombing and would lose more men in any one of their major assaults than by aerial attacks for the whole war. Aside from doubling the manpower needed, a two-seater's performance was always less than the fighter opposition. Another fifty Jastas equipped with Fokker DVIIs, that had a prime ground attack role, and dual fighter role—such as was undertaken by the Camels, SE5s and Spads—would have been far more effective.

The German reconnaissance crews were doing their best, and were operating on their lone high altitude sorties all the time, but did not manage to detect the major Allied attack build-ups of the month. They did suffer casualties, particularly when climbing and descending, as their aerodromes were within range of RAF fighter patrols. The German artillery co-operation flyers also suffered during the month and were beginning to suffer from severe shortages, particularly petrol, as indeed the other sections of the service were. They carried on with their tasks as they had all through the war, but were now under constant harassment.

The German fighter force had doubled in early 1918 to 80 Jastas and nine Kests. They were the only arm of the German Air Service that could really impact on the Allied air services. The quality of their equipment had improved over the summer of 1918 with the arrival of the Fokker DVII, and most of the Jastas were at least partially equipped with this type, or the slightly less efficient Pfalz DXII. There were still numbers of Albatros DV and Pfalz DIII fighters in service, mainly with the newest Jastas, or those on very quiet parts of the front, and small numbers of Fokker Triplanes were still operating. In addition there were also five Marine Feld Jastas available, operating in the north, which were well equipped, well trained and successful.

The Germans grouped twelve of their leading Jastas into three Jagdgeschwader—more commonly known to the Allies as Flying Circuses. The impact these units had, being a mere 15 per cent of the whole fighter force, was tremendous and they inflicted casualties out of all proportion to their numbers. By September, JGI 'Richthofen' was a shadow of its former self having absorbed most of the pressure from the Amiens battle of August 1918. Oskar von Boenigk, an alumnus of JGI in the summer of 1917, led JGII, and in September 1918, the 40-odd Fokkers of this group claimed over 100 Allied planes, mainly American, for minimal losses. Despite this impressive performance, the star turns of September were the four (three after 4 September) Jastas of JGIII, claiming 129 RAF aircraft during the month: the staff scored 11, Jasta 2 got 46, Jasta 26 got 33, Jasta 27 got 32 and Jasta 36 nine (the latter disappearing from the scene after the 4th, having been reduced to three serviceable aircraft). The three other BMW-powered Fokker-equipped units inflicted heavy casualties on the RAF. Jasta scores for September were:

Jasta			Jasta			Jasta			Jasta		
Jasta	1	6	Jasta	23	8	Jasta	47	—	Jasta	70	5
Jasta	2	46	Jasta	24	5	Jasta	48	—	Jasta	71	—
Jasta	3	6	Jasta	26	33	Jasta	49	9	Jasta	72	12
Jasta	4	2	Jasta	27	32	Jasta	50	14	Jasta	73	5
Jasta	5	37	Jasta	28	6	Jasta	51	—	Jasta	74	—
Jasta	6	5	Jasta	29	5	Jasta	52	2	Jasta	75	—
Jasta	7	14	Jasta	30	2	Jasta	53	6	Jasta	76	—
Jasta	8	3	Jasta	31	10	Jasta	54	4	Jasta	77	12
Jasta	9	9	Jasta	32	—	Jasta	56	12	Jasta	78	3
Jasta	10	2	Jasta	33	3	Jasta	57	2	Jasta	79	4
Jasta	11	8	Jasta	34	5	Jasta	58	12	Jasta	80	7
Jasta	12	11	Jasta	35	6	Jasta	59	6	Jasta	81	9
Jasta	13	27	Jasta	36	9	Jasta	60	18	Jasta	82	—
Jasta	14	—	Jasta	37	11	Jasta	61	2	Jasta	83	2
Jasta	15	24	Jasta	39	17	Jasta	62	7	MFJ	1	9
Jasta	16	3	Jasta	40	7	Jasta	63	4	MFJ	2	11
Jasta	17	4	Jasta	41	—	Jasta	64	9	MFJ	3	5
Jasta	18	10	Jasta	42	5	Jasta	65	5	MFJ	4	6
Jasta	19	22	Jasta	43	1	Jasta	66	8	MFJ	5	9
Jasta	20	9	Jasta	44	4	Jasta	67	9	Stab JGI		—
Jasta	21	6	Jasta	45	26	Jasta	68	5	Stab JGII	5	
Jasta	22	8	Jasta	46	15	Jasta	69	—	Stab JGIII	11	

(Note: Jastas 35, 38 and 55 were not operating on the Western Front; some Jastas would have scored more than shown here, while some which have no victories noted may well have scored some but records are incomplete for this late period; while Jastas 2 and 5 did well as they had done in April 1917, Jasta 11 was a shadow of its former self in terms of kills.)

This list shows a total of 721 Allied aircraft and balloons brought down for the month of September. To these scores must be added the claims of Flak units, infantry ground fire and successes by two-seater crews of the Flieger Abteilungen and Schutzstaffeln. This latter figure could be shown in the region of 715 aircraft and 87 balloons (total victories claimed—802).

As mentioned at the end of Part One, numbers are difficult to agree or reconcile, and the September figures are just as difficult. However, although they cannot be totally accurate, the following figures of what we know will give an indication of the combat losses. These indicate:

RAF aircraft lost	= 373 (incl. 37 IAF)
French aircraft lost	= 100
USAS aircraft lost	= 87
Total	560

Thus with some 715 German claims, there is something like 155 more claims than losses, but obviously some aircraft seen to fall inside Allied lines were counted but not actually lost to the Allied cause.

Again we can break down the Allied aircraft types lost:

British

Camel	109		RE8	24
SE5s	74		AWFK8	13
DH9/9a	54		HP O/400	12
BF2b	38		Dolphin	9
DH4	32		FE2b	8

French

Spad XIII	42		Voisin	4
Bréguet XIV	32		Caudron R11	2
Salmson 2A2	9		Farman	1
Spad XI	4		Others	6

American

Spad XIII	37		DH4	21
Salmson 2A2	20		Bréguet XIV	9

Personnel Casualties

	Killed	Missing	POW	Wounded	Inj	Interned	Evaded
British	209	67	301	163	7	22	2
French†	49	87	3	62	3	—	—
American‡	76	4	37	25	1	2	1
Totals	334	158	341	250	11	24	3

† Obviously a number of the missing were in fact captured. ‡ But not including USAS men serving with either the British or French.

The RAF, in turn, claimed prodigious quantities of Fokkers shot down, which did not match even slightly the actual German losses. Even though it is difficult to know exactly their losses, fighter pilots dead, wounded, and prisoners are known, and even if one trebled this figure to cover lost machines from which pilots parachuted or survived crashes, it still falls very short of the claims. This has led to the idea among students of WWI aviation that the German fighters were inflicting a severe defeat on the RAF, which only the over optimistic claims of the RAF refuted. This is total rubbish. While JGIII and other units inflicted large casualties, their impact on the RAF's activities was minimal. No RAF squadron was stopped from operating. The most that was achieved was in modifying the way in which these activities were carried out.

According to 'our' figures, the Allies claimed:

RAF	= 521 aircraft destroyed plus 353 'out of control' (total 874)
IAF	= 11 aircraft destroyed plus 12 'out of control' (total 23)
French	= 98 aircraft destroyed (there were also some 50 probables)
USAS	= 135 aircraft destroyed (but including probables)
Total	= 765 plus 365 'ooc' by the RAF/IAF = 1,130 (plus KBs): (—1,180 if one adds French probables)

German losses, as we have said already, are hard to determine. Those that seem fairly certain, total in the region of 107-plus for September 1918, but even if we are 100 per cent wrong/underestimating, that would still only make it 214! (A possible 11 claims for every German loss.)

The question might be asked, did the RAF commanders at HQ have any idea that their fighter pilots were overclaiming, to the extent that they appeared to destroy each month the total number of enemy fighters their intelligence gatherers, however primitive their sources might or might not have been, reported the Germans had available? Yet still they had sufficient men and machines to came up and inflict enormous losses on the Allies. (Shades of '... the last 50 Spitfires ...' in the latter half of the Battle of Britain in 1940!) Did these same WWI commanders and intelligence people believe that the Germans 'had' over 1,000 aircraft on the

Western Front to shoot down, which must mean that, in total, the Germans had to have somewhere in the region of at least 6,000 aircraft opposing them in the first place?

As for the German Jastas, the quality varied greatly. Jasta 5 was certainly the next most successful unit, and most of the other Jastas achieved something. But their impact was minimal and would become more so as their lack of fuel supplies restricted operations. They were also running out of pilots—few of the Jasta ever being at full strength—and their successes often depended on one or two quality pilots in each Jasta. Some Jastas operating on both the RAF and French/American fronts achieved little. Even if they were vastly outnumbered, the defensive posture, lack of aggression and an avoidance of losses meant that a considerable proportion of the German fighter units were basically wasting petrol!

The lack of accurate German casualty records (aircraft), especially of unwounded pilots, make assessment of claims by the RAF difficult, as has already been said. However, one point of note is that the Jastas, throughout their entire period of service, never destroyed an RAF aircraft on its aerodromes, whereas considerable numbers of German aircraft were lost in attacks on theirs. Jasta 40, for example, did not operate until mid-September because their machines had been destroyed on the ground by 80 Wing on 17 August. Power projection, as it is now called, belonged entirely to the Allies.

The Germans, despite a number of historians defending them vigorously, also over-claimed, although not in the same proportions; but that is, in the perspective of the aerial war, irrelevant. The RAF, in its basic roles of army support and co-operation, was basically doing precisely what it wanted to do or was asked to do. Every now and then, three or four times a month on average, a large fight would ensue when they were engaged by the Germans, and more often than not the RAF were severely dealt with. We think the point has been made that despite its lack of numbers in comparison, the German Jastas were by no means defeated, either in September or in the final six weeks the war had to run. Fuel and numbers were on the decline, but their morale was still as high as in the spring of 1917.

The Aces

The current fashion amongst a school of the 'serious' historians is to decry the role of the aces, and state that they received undue publicity and recognition for achieving very little.[1] This idea too is rubbish. To use the RAF as an example: their main striking arm in the battle for aerial supremacy, i.e. the capacity to carry out their roles and prevent the Germans from doing theirs, was the fighter force. In April 1917, the RAF fighter force was simply unable to achieve this due to a number of factors. One of these factors was that the average fighter unit had one or two experienced pilots per flight and a number of these were very much less experienced than the German Jasta leaders.

By September 1918 this had changed. It is important to remember that the tactical leadership of the RAF was vested in the captains—the flight commanders, who led the three Flights in each squadron. Some squadron commanders flew, others did not, but the major day-to-day tactical decisions rested with the flight commanders.

In April 1917, the RFC and RNAS had 23 fighter units in the field (counting single-seater and the FE2 units), and of these 23 squadron commanders only one was an ace—Mulock of 3 Naval. Of the 78 flight commanders at the start of the month, 21 were or would become aces during April—roughly 25 per cent. By September 1918, the RAF had 32 fighter squadrons (single-seater and BF2b units). Of the 43 squadron commanders, 19 were aces; this is over 40 per cent. Of the 126 flight commanders (on 1 September three were vacant positions), 104 were aces—over 80 per cent. In addition, the average flight would have at least one more pilot who would become the next flight commander in it, or would be ready for a posting to a vacancy elsewhere and they too would almost without exclusion be aces. While it is acknowledged that by 1918 surviving pilots had had the opportunity of raising their status to aces due to the

---

[1] History terms an ace as a pilot with a score of five victories or more, despite acknowledging that, with over-claiming, a number of recognised aces would not fall into such a category; but we would not even contemplate a change to the long established historical precedent.

passage of time, the fact remains that on average about 25 per cent of pilots on strength at any one time in 1918 were aces. Therefore, aces are represented in command positions over three times more than the percentage of pilots they made up.

In April 1917 too, the fighter arm of the British was being led by a large percentage of inexperienced men, undoubtedly brave but often not tactically astute and not provided with sufficient support of trained men to raise the experience level of their units. There is also the factor that promotion was in many instances on length of service rather than proven ability, which was about to change. Following the subsequent story of these units during 1917 is to follow the story of the slow building up of experience in the squadrons, and leadership provided by those pilots with the gift of being able to become an ace.

By September 1918, the conclusion can be drawn that the tactical fighter leaders of the RAF were aces. This small percentage of pilots, perhaps 10 per cent at any one time, not only did the vast majority of the scoring, they were doing the vast majority of leading as well. Therefore, the significant role played by aces in the RAF's operational capacity should not be minimised. The idea that teamwork and the good solid average pilot were the backbone of the RAF rather than the aces is simply a misunderstanding of what was involved. Aces were the prime motivators of teamwork and leadership. The lone wolf aces, of whom in reality there were very few, had been replaced by leaders of tactical teams called Flights. The RAF's tactical commanders were confident, experienced men, well aware of the risks and managing to project the confidence that they were totally capable of dealing with the German fighters.

Of course, this was not always true; aces would die during the month as would the novice pilots, but their loss would not lower the leadership and experience level of the squadron. It must be acknowledged too that there were a number of valuable and experienced pilots who proved good leaders, but who did not have the ability to shoot straight—or get the deflection right. This happened in both world wars, just as some with the ability to shoot well and bring down enemy aircraft simply had no head for tactical leadership (but these were usually the exception). There were too the pilots who would survive months of active service and score no victories, but survive, so they had to be good, solid pilots, accumulating vast experience from what was happening. There are no records, diaries or other memoirs the authors have seen that indicate anything other than that the RAF was confident it could handle the Germans in aerial combat. What terrified most of them was ground fire when strafing—and burning in the air!

The Corps and bomber crews were doing valuable work, but they were able to do this work to the extent they did only by the presence of the fighter pilots. The Fokkers were generally 'blotted-up' in attacking the fighters. It was when the fighters were not present (the IAF and long range raids by the RAF day bombers) that they suffered. Remember that almost all RAF fighter squadrons were involved in extensive ground attack duties as well; the significance of the fighter pilots increases again.

One of the biggest errors the British RFC/RAF command made in WWI was in failing to establish any real process of authenticating the claims made by their pilots. This led them to vastly overrate their success against the German Air Service and their victory to loss ratio. (But as mentioned earlier, it seems logical to assume someone must have realised the estimated German strength was not being destroyed with such regularity.) This led to no attempt being made to improve this situation or to eradicate a complacency about their methods that would have dire consequences in the Second World War. The RAF's failure officially to recognise the identities of their leading pilots, unlike the French and the Germans, contributed to this malaise. By 1918 decorations to fighter pilots were awarded, in the main, on the basis of victories but no system was in place to check what resulted. *The Times* of London newspaper in 1918 published the communiqués each side put out at the end of each month, listing the claims and losses of each air force. The paper, its readers and the RAF simply assumed the Germans were liars to admit to so few losses. Combined with the abysmal decision not to supply their airmen with parachutes, all the RAF managed to do was to live, as one of the songs their cynical pilots often sang put it, '...in a world of illusion'.

The French were much more realistic and in general made by far the most accurate claims. However, in the English-speaking world, the achievements of the French Air Service have always been underrated. One reason was undoubtedly the far lower casualties sustained, and lower total claims than the British!

As for the Americans, they also failed to set up a realistic claims system, although many of the early claims mirrored the French system, but at least they made their pilots famous. They too were to forget some of the lessons of the war over the peace, but the one lesson that should not have been lost on the rest of the world but by the Germans and the Japanese in WW2, and by others since was never, ever, to underestimate the quality of the men the Americans could put into their fighting aeroplanes. Frank Luke, Joe Wehner, Wilbur Wright, Ray Brooks, and the men of the Day Bombardment Group were as good as any, despite a lot less experience. The other way in which the American contribution to the air war has also been underestimated is the number of them that were in the RFC, RNAS and RAF.

The RAF Fighter Squadron in September 1918

The following section attempts to provide a view of the background of the fighter pilots that made up the RAF on 1 September 1918. It is by way of a sample, not scientifically selected, but rather selected on the basis of what units have reasonable officers' records still available to the historian, mainly retained in the Public Record Office, London. This analysis covers the records of Nos. 1, 4 AFC, 29, 46, 56, 84, 204 and 210 Squadrons. They are split evenly between SE5a and Camel units, the former being 1, 29, 56 and 84. On 1 September, the strength of these units varied between 21 pilots (210 Squadron) and 30 pilots (204).

Nationality

The following table indicates what country the pilots came from, based on where their next of kin or bank was located.

	1	4AFC	29	46	56	84	204	210	Total
English	11	—	7	13	6	4	8	11	60
Scottish	—	—	—	1	4	3	3	—	11
Welsh	1	—	—	—	2	1	—	—	4
Irish	2	—	—	1	—	—	1	—	4
Canadian	5	—	5	8	9	4	12	4	47
Australian	—	28	—	1	—	—	—	1	30
American	3	—	5	1	5	4	1	5	24
South African	3	—	6	1	—	8	1	—	19
New Zealanders	—	1	—	—	—	—	—	—	1
West Indian	—	—	1	—	—	—	—	—	1
Unknown	—	—	—	—	—	—	2	—	2
Totals:	25	29	24	26	26	24	28	21	203

From this, the English contributed about a third of the RAF; and with the rest of the British Isles added in, about 40 per cent. Allowing for the distortion caused by the presence of an Australian unit, the Canadians and Americans were the next biggest component. In particular the Canadians predominated in the two former RNAS squadrons. The South Africans tended to be concentrated in one or two units, the largest two groups in the RAF being 29 and 84.

Age of the Pilots on 1 September 1918

Age	1	4 AFC	29	46	56	84	204	210	Total
18	1	—	—	3	1	1	2	1	9
19	4	—	6	12	3	5	7	5	42
20	5	2	4	2	3	1	3	2	22
21	2	3	3	3	2	5	5	1	24
22	1	2	1	1	2	—	3	3	13
23	5	7	2	—	2	4	6	3	29
24	2	2	4	—	4	4	—	—	16
25	2	3	1	1	7	1	1	5	21
26+	3	6	3	3	2	3	1	1	22
unknown	—	4	—	1	—	—	—	—	5
Totals:	25	29	24	26	26	24	28	21	203

From this can be drawn the inference that 19-year-olds predominated in 1918. These would be men that had enlisted as soon as they were old enough, and took about ten months to train. The Australians were older, which is explained by the large majority of the AFC's pilots being ex-Army men who had been overseas since 1915-16. But the spread of men in their early twenties indicates the idea that the majority of pilots being under 20 is incorrect. However, as a word of warning, the RNAS units tended to be a good deal younger, and this sample may not be typical.

Length of Service
The following table illustrates the length of service of pilots in these units, in months.

Months	1	4 AFC	29	46	56	84	204	210	Total
0-1	8†	7	4	11‡	13	15†	14	2	74
1-2	2	9	5	5	3	—	1	1	26
2-3	7	2	4	—	2	—	3	10	28
3-4	4	3	4	3	3	3	2	3	25
4-5	4	1	—	3	2	1	3	—	14
5-6	—	2	3	2	1	2	2	2	14
6-7	—	3	2	—	1	2	—	1	9
7-8	—	—	1	1	1	—	—	1	4
8-9	—	—	—	—	—	—	1	—	1
9-10	—	2	1	1	—	—	—	—	4
10-11	—	—	—	—	—	—	—	—	—
11-12	—	—	—	—	—	—	—	—	—
12-plus	—	—	—	—	—	1§	2	1§	4
Totals:	25	29	24	26	26	24	28	21	203

† Includes one pilot on second tour as a flight commander. ‡ Includes two pilots on second tour as flight commanders. § Both men were the squadron commander.

The largest number of pilots had less than one month's experience. There are two reasons for this: firstly, the large number of casualties during August, and secondly, those pilots who had arrived over the quiet winter months of early 1918 had completed their tours in July and August. The pilots that counted were the ones with two to six months' experience. All units had at least eight of these. The longest serving pilots (as distinct from the commanders) of all these men were Captains C R R Hickey and A J B Tonks of 204 Squadron.[1]

The average tour lasted between six and eight months. Another reason for the high number of pilots that had arrived on some units in July 1918, was the spreading influenza epidemic beginning to decimate Europe, which would continue well into 1919. Also, the Australians had received a number of RAF pilots to maintain strength during June and July and many of these had left in August.

The Claims
This table analyses what scores pilots who were on these units on 1 September had on that date.

	1	4 AFC	29	46	56	84	204	210	Total
0	16	14	5	11	18	14	14	6	98
1	—	6	3	6	3	1	2	2	23
2	2	2	3	3	1	2	4	3	20
3	1	—	5	3	1	2	2	2	16
4	1	1	1	—	—	—	2	2	7
5-9	1	2	3	2	2	2	2	3	17
10-19	3	3	4	—	1	2	2	3	18
20-29	1	1	—	—	—	—	—	—	2
30-39	—	—	—	—	—	—	—	—	—
40-49	—	—	—	—	—	1	—	—	1
50-plus	—	—	—	1	—	—	—	—	1

[1] Hickey (aged 21), a Canadian, had operated with 4 Naval/204 RAF from August 1917 and was still in action on 3 October, the date he collided with another pilot and was killed. He had 21 victories. Tonks (aged 20), from London, England, also joined 4 Naval/204 RAF in August 1917, and was rested from operations on 13 October 1918. He had 12 victories but died in a crash in July 1919.

This table shows that at any one time, over 45 per cent of pilots had not scored. Another 30 per cent had scored between one and five times, while just about 25 per cent were aces!

The really big scorers are few and far between. Only four of the 203 Squadron pilots had over 20 claims. Of these, Captain R T C Hoidge of 1 Squadron had just started his second tour; Captain A H Cobby of 4 AFC ended his tour on 4 September; Captain A W Beauchamp Proctor of 84 Squadron had also just started a second tour; while Captain D R MacLaren of 46 Squadron was just rolling along towards the end of his first year of combat.

Although not analysed here, it is apparent that the average fighter pilot who survived operations took two to three months to score. Under a month was exceptional—these men were either very aggressive, burned a balloon, shared in a kill, or were just plain lucky. It was not uncommon for a pilot to fly a whole tour without scoring. The import of this is that the fighter pilot's job was to shoot down the opposition. Nevertheless, those pilots who generally survived a tour would show themselves as sound pilots, perhaps good patrol members, or did not have the overall ability to shoot well. Even in WW2, there were any number of successful fighter pilot leaders with small scores, but whose experience and ability were unquestioned.

The Casualties

This table shows what happened to our sample of the 203 pilots on strength on 1 September 1918. Casualties are defined as either killed or missing in action, prisoners of war, and accidents that were either fatal or resulted in the pilot leaving the unit. Posted means the pilot was posted out of combat, tour expired or ill, or promoted to another unit. In the case of some Americans, they transferred to the USAS.

	1	4 AFC	29	46	56	84	204	210	Total
September	1	5	6	7	10	6	9	5	49
October	2	1	3	4	5	1	10	4	30
November	—	3	1	—	—	—	—	—	4
Posted	2	6	8	6	6	7	4	4	43
End of War	20	14	6	9	5	10	5	8	77
Totals:	25	29	24	26	26	24	28	21	203

Approximately a quarter of these pilots became casualties in September, not including those that arrived during the month and were lost that same month. Another third survived to the end of the war, while just over 20 per cent were posted. Roughly 30 per cent of the pilots on strength were turned over during the month. No.1 Squadron would only suffer three losses in combat of the 35 pilots on strength. This was mainly because they had by far the fewest combats of the units in this sample. Nos. 56 and 204 Squadrons had by far the most casualties. No. 56 lost many pilots ground strafing and also lost one or two in fights for the rest of the war. No. 204 lost some in September, but had two really bad days in October, losing more than four Camels at a time. Most of 4 AFC's casualties came in two fights, on 5 September and 4 November, both at the hands of JGIII.

Given the 50 per cent or so of pilots that were either posted or lasted to the end of the war, the RAF fighter pilots were surviving quite well, relative to earlier periods such as Bloody April. However, it indicated that one in two RAF pilots at this late stage of the war was going to be lost in action or accidents. The air war was not easy, flying unarmoured, slow aeroplanes strafing troops, or in combat with Fokkers, especially when not equipped with parachutes.

Training

By 1918 the RAF had established a reasonably sophisticated training system. A trainee pilot would be taught to fly, then taught aerobatics and other advanced flying before specialising in single-seaters. Then the neophyte fighter pilot went to Fighting Schools, to be taught combat tactics and air gunnery. On arrival in France, he would spend about a week at a Depot— perhaps less in times of high battle casualties—awaiting a vacancy at the front. Most squadrons then tried to initiate the novice slowly, showing them around the front and allowing them to settle in.

Allowing for this advance on earlier times, the dangers for the novice were still immense. Squadron commanders, especially Major W E Young of No.1 Squadron for example, were pushing for training units on quiet sectors of the front to break in these tyros, instead of sending them into combat in the intense areas. This was how the RNAS had done it in 1917 and early 1918, using Nos 11 and 12 Naval Squadrons in the Dunkirk area as early examples of operational training units.

The Lessons Learnt—Only to be Forgotten

The major lesson learnt from this study is that history repeats itself. At the outbreak of WW2, the RAF had seemingly forgotten most of what its fighter pilots had learnt through bitter experience. This new generation of fighter pilots would die under-trained, never having been taught to shoot properly, nor had they the right combat tactics. It was well into the war before the same basic processes were introduced. And it was well into 1941 before fighter-bombers were rediscovered. Army co-operation, as it had been used in WW1, had totally disappeared, because no aeroplane built for the task could survive the flak and fighters.

Despite the emergence of large formations of aircraft in 1917-18—a wing for the Allies, Jagdgeschwader for the Germans—WW2's early conflicts were fought by the RAF, in Flight or Squadron strengths, inevitably overwhelmed by the continued employment of large numbers of fighters by the Germans. Between the wars, the RAF, at least partially to justify their independent service status, promoted the role of the strategic bomber. Despite the losses sustained by unescorted day bombers of the IAF in 1918, the policy followed in the early WW2 days was for unescorted day bombers, deemed to be able to fight their way to a target. Even more amazing was that while Bomber Command thought this policy would work, Fighter Command was just as sure they would be able to stop German bombers reaching British targets.

The lessons that unescorted day bombers would be extremely vulnerable were ignored, and even in 1942 the Americans experienced losses when unescorted. Tactical day bombing was only able to operate successfully when escorted.

The big loss, however, was of almost all capacity to support the army at a tactical level, something the Germans developed with their Stuka dive-bombers. It was not until well into 1942 that the Desert Air Force re-learned the value of ground attack, and remembered how well the RAF had done in 1918 by ground strafing and bombing with fighters.

However, the Germans too lost their way a little between the wars. While they improved their army support capacity it was at the cost of strategic bombing, producing only medium range bombers. Whilst they developed long range escort fighters (as the British and French tried to do) such as the Me110 for these medium bombers, they could not survive against single-seat fighters, and their own single-seaters lacked the range to escort with any hope of success.

However, the main reasons why they lost the air war in WW1 were repeated in WW2. They had insufficient numbers of day fighters; quality and quantity will defeat quality any time. The Germans also underestimated the Americans. Germany's training system and operations broke down under the strain of a lack of resources and increasing fuel shortages. The extraordinary resilience and quality of their veteran pilots was just not enough. Another generation later, the equivalent of Paul Baümer, Fritz Rumey, Franz Büchner, Georg von Hantelmann, etc. had to try and beat off overwhelming numbers in defence of the Fatherland. That both generations did not succeed was not because of lack of courage and dedication of the Jasta pilots in WW1 nor the Geschwader pilots of WW2.

This brings the authors to the final conclusion they hope readers will draw from this book. We have tried to show how and why the Allied Air Forces suffered so many casualties in the hardest two months of the war; April 1917 in percentage terms, and September 1918 in total numbers terms. The Germans lost the air war, but it took many lives of brave yet frightened young French, American and British aviators to achieve this, just as it took many youngsters on the ground to overcome the Germans in the land battles.

Any denigration of their German opponents in the air only devalues this sacrifice. German fighter pilots were as good as any, and perhaps more so. Their strategic and tactical circumstances—outnumbered and with much longer tours of duty—resulted in them having many opportunities for combat. That resulted in a good deal of aces scoring victories, and the differential in aces' scores would be vastly greater in the second war.

The German Air Service fought to the last. It took the best of the Allied world to triumph in both wars. The cost of victory in the Second World War would have been a great deal less if the RAF had remembered some of the basic lessons learnt at such a high price in the First.

APPENDIX I
RAF Victory Claims September 1918

1 September 1918

Time	Pilot/Crew	Sqdn	Vic No	E/A	Location	
0740	Lt L E Taplin	4AFC	9	Balloon	Fromelles	DF
0745	Lt R King	4AFC	13	Balloon	Le Grand Riez	DF
0750	Lt W E G Mann	208	8	DFW C	S Scarpe River	DF
0815	Capt G C Dixon	40	6	2-seater	SE Henin-Lietard	OOC
0830	Lt F E Luff	74	3	Balloon	Menin	DF
0925	Lt J W Wright	4AFC	1	Fokker DVII	SE Bailleul	OOC
1025	Capt E C Hoy	29	6	Balloon	NE Armentières	DF
1125	Lt R F McCrae	46	4	Fokker DVII	E Brie Bridge	OOC
1320	Lt F W Gillet	79	4	LVG C	NE Armentières	D
1330	Lt G K Runciman &	62	3⎫	Fokker DVII	NE Cambrai	OOC
	Sgt H H Inglis	62	1⎭			
1330	Lt A W Blowes &	62	3⎫	Fokker DVII	E Cambrai	OOC
	2/Lt H S Hind	62	3⎭			
1345	Sgt D E Edgley &	57	3⎫	Fokker DVII	Cambrai	DF
	Sgt N Sandison	57	2⎭			
1345	Sgt D E Edgley &	57	4⎫	Fokker DVII	Cambrai	OOC
	Sgt N Sandison	57	3⎭			
1345	Lt F O Thornton &	57	2⎫	Fokker DVII	Cambrai	DF
	2/Lt F C Craig	57	3⎭			
1350	2/Lt F J Hunt	74	1	Balloon	NE Armentières	DF
1400	Lt E M Coles &	57	3⎫	Fokker DVII	Cambrai	OOC
	Sgt J Grant	57	5⎭			
1430	Lt M A Tancock	32	1	Albatros DV	Doignies	D
1810	Capt E C Hoy	29	7	Fokker DVII	NE Armentières	OOC
1815	Lt A E Reed	29	15	Fokker DVII	W Armentières	OOC
1830	Lt E Swale	210	10	Fokker DVII	E Ypres	OOC
1850	Capt G K Cooper	208	6	Fokker DVII	Ecourt-St Quentin	OOC
1900	Lt H A S Molyneaux	56	2	Fokker DVII	S Reincourt	OOC
1910	Capt A Hepburn &	88	8⎫	Fokker DVII	E Becelaere	DF
	Sgt E Antcliffe	88	6⎭			

2 September 1918

Time	Pilot/Crew	Sqdn	Vic No	E/A	Location	
0630	Capt R C B Brading	201	9	Fokker DVII	Heudicourt	OOC
0715	Capt R C B Brading	201	10	Fokker DVII	Lagnicourt	D
0715	Lt R Sykes	201	5	Fokker DVII	Lagnicourt	D
0915	Lt H H Beddow &	22	9⎫	Fokker DVII	Arras-Cambrai Road	D
	2/Lt T Birmingham	22	7⎭			
0915	Lt I O Stead &	22	5⎫	Fokker DVII	Arras-Cambria Road	OOC
	2/Lt W A Cowle	22	4⎭			
1005	2/Lt M D Sinclair	60	2	LVG C	Bruhemont	D
1015	Major F I Tanner	80	4	2-seater	Le Mesnil	D
1015	Lt J Collier	80	1	2-seater	Le Mesnil	D
1115	Lt F G Gibbons &	22	9⎫	Fokker DVII	Haynecourt	D
	Sgt G Shannon	22	2⎭			
1115	Capt S F Thompson &	22	26⎫	Fokker DVII	Haynecourt	D
	Sgt R M Fletcher	22	23⎭			
1115	Lt F G Gibbons &	22	10⎫	Fokker DVII	Haynecourt	D
	Sgt G Shannon	22	3⎭			
1130	Sgt A S Cowlishaw	64	2	Fokker DVII	Marquion	D
1150	1/Lt F E Kindley	148US	5	Fokker DVII	S Rumaucourt	D
1150	1/Lt C T McLean	148US	2	Fokker DVII	Buissy	D
1150	Lt W B Knox	148US	1	Fokker DVII	S Rumaucourt	OOC
1200	Capt W H Farrow	64	10	Fokker DVII	Aubencheul	OOC
1435	Capt G C Dixon	40	7	Fokker DVII	Ecourt St Quentin	OOC
1900	Lt L E Taplin	4AFC	10	Halb C	E Aubers	OOC
1910	1/Lt O P Johnson	60	1	Albatros DV	Marquion	D
1930	2/Lt W S Rycroft &	48	1⎫	Fokker DVII	N Menin	OOC
	2/Lt H L Ward	48	1⎭			

1930	Lt H A Cole &	48	2⎫		Fokker VIID	Menin	OOC
	2/Lt J W London	48	1⎭				
1930	Lt J B Cowan &	48	1⎫		Fokker DVII	W Lille	DF
	Lt T L Jones	48	1⎭				
1945	Lt J B Cowan &	48	2⎫		Fokker DVII	W Lille	OOC
	Lt T L Jones	48	2⎭				

3 September 1918

0615	Capt W A Southey,	84	11⎫				
	Lt Wilson,	84	1 ⎪		Rumpler C	S Manancourt-Nurlu Rd	D
	Lt Miller &	84	1 ⎬				
	Lt F R Christiani	84	1 ⎭				
0630	Lt S E Searson &	5	1⎫		DFW C	Baralle	DF
	Lt T K Green	5	1⎭				
0645	Capt W A Southey	84	12		Balloon	Fins	DF
0700	Lt M G Burger	54	2		Hannover C	Moeuvres	D
0700	Lt C W M Thompson &	22	4⎫		Pfalz DXII	Sailly-Sailisal	D
	2/Lt G McCormack	22	1⎭				
0705	Lt L E Taplin	4AFC	9		Balloon	Le Plouich	DF
0710	Capt W R Irwin	56	10		Fokker DVII	Etaing	D
0710	Capt W R Irwin	56	11		Fokker DVII	Haynecourt	D
0710	Lt H P Chubb	56	1		Fokker DVII	Etaing	D
0710	Lt H A S Molyneaux	56	3		Fokker DVII	Etaing	OOC
0730	Capt D Lloyd-Evans	64	5		Fokker DVII	Brebieres	OOC
0910	Capt J I Morgan	70	5		Fokker DVII	S Roulers	OOC
0910	Lt S T Liversedge	70	10		Fokker DVII	S Roulers	D
0910	Lt McPhee	70	1		Fokker DVII	S Roulers	OOC
0910	Lt J A Spilhaus	70	1		Fokker DVII	S Roulers	OOC
0930	2/Lt C R Thompson	84	4		Balloon	S Poeuilly	DF
0935	Lt J A Glen	70	1		Balloon	Warneton-Deulemont	DF
1010	Capt J E Doyle	60	7		Fokker DVII	Inchy	D
1055	Capt J L M White	65	13		Fokker DVII	Engel	OOC
1100	Capt J L M White	65	14		Fokker DVII	Engel	OOC
1110	Lt H E Browne	65	4		Fokker DVII	Engel	OOC
1110	2/Lt R O Campbell	65	1		Fokker DVII	Engel	OOC
1150	Lt R C Pattullo	204	1		Fokker DVII	Dixmuide-Ypres	OOC
1150	Lt B E Barnum	204	2		Fokker DVII	Gheluvelt	OOC
1150	Lt R M Gordon	204	7		Fokker DVII	Gheluvelt	OOC
1150	Capt F I Lord	79	6		Fokker DVII	Armentières	DF
1215	Lt E J Jacques &	27	1⎫		Fokker DVII	SW Valenciennes	D
	2/Lt N P Wood	27	1⎭				
1310	Capt G B Gates	201	9		Hannover C	Moeuvres	DF
1315	Lt A S Compton	54	2		Hannover C	E Moeuvres	DF
1325	Lt F W Gillet	79	5		Balloon	Armentières	DF
1425	Capt W E G Mann	208	9		Fokker DVII	Marquion	OOC
1520	Lt L G Bowen	56	1		Fokker DVII	Roisel	OOC
1530	Capt W A Southey	84	13		Balloon	N Fins	DF
1600	Capt G B Bailey &	13	1⎫		Fokker DVII	Inchy-Moeuvres	D
	Lt A Ostler	13	1⎭				
1600	Capt G B Bailey &	13	2⎫		Fokker DVII	Inchy-Moeuvres	D
	Lt A Ostler	13	2⎭				
1645	Lt H R Carson	32	1		Fokker DVII	Douai	OOC
1715	Lt C R Pithey &	12	10⎫		LVG C	Lagnicourt	D
	Lt H Rhodes	12	11⎭				
1720	Lt C O Stone	2AFC	1		Fokker DVII	NW Cambrai	OOC
1720	Lt F R Smith	2AFC	5		Fokker DVII	NW Cambrai	OOC
1745	Capt H P Lale &	20	13⎫		Fokker DVII	S Havrincourt Wood	OOC
	2/Lt R J Ralph	20	13⎭				
1745	Lt P T Iaccaci &	20	15⎫		Fokker DVII	Havrincourt Wood	D
	Lt A Mills	20	10⎭				
1745	Lt G E Randall &	20	4⎫		Fokker DVII	S Havrincourt Wood	OOC
	Lt G V Learmond	20	3⎭				
1750	Lt C R Oberst &	20	1⎫		Pfalz DIII	Havrincourt Wood	D
	Lt R Gordon-Bennett	20	2⎭				
1750	Lt C R Oberst &	20	2⎫		Pfalz DIII	Havrincourt Wood	OOC
	Lt R Gordon-Bennett	20	3⎭				
1810	Lt W S Jenkins	210	6		Fokker DVII	Lille	OOC

Time	Name	Sqn	No.	Aircraft	Location	Result
1820	Lt H A Kullberg	1	18	Fokker DVII	Avesnes-le-Sec	D
1830	Capt H A Patey	210	11	Fokker DVII	NE Roulers	DF
1830	Lt E Swale	210	11	Fokker DVII	Courtrai	D
1830	Capt S C Joseph,	210	12			
	Lt C W Payton,	210	5			
	Lt Hughes,	210	2	Fokker DVII	Menin-Courtrai	D
	Lt Lewis &	210	1			
	Lt I C Sanderson	210	6			
1830	Capt H J Larkin	87	9	Fokker DVII	Epinoy	OOC
1830	Capt A W Vigors	87	9	Fokker DVII	Epinoy	D
1830	Capt H J Larkin	87	10	Fokker DVII	Epinoy	OOC
1830	Capt A W Vigors	87	10	Fokker DVII	Epinoy	OOC
1830	Capt W F Staton &	62	23	Fokker DVII	SE Marquion	D
	Lt L F Mitchell	62	5			
1845	Capt G E Gibbons &	62	13	Fokker DVII	N Cambrai	OOC
	Lt T Elliott	62	7			
1845	Capt G E Gibbons &	62	14	Fokker DVII	N Cambrai	OOC
	Lt T Elliott	62	8			
1845	Lt L N Hollinghurst	87	6	Hannover C	Masnières	D
1845	Lt E J Stephens	41	6	Fokker DVII	S Vitry	D
1900	Lt L E Taplin	4AFC	10	Balloon	Herlies	D
1925	Capt G B Gates	201	9	Albatros C	E Metz-en-Couture	DF
1930	Capt E C Hoy	29	10	Fokker DVII	N Comines	D

4 September 1918

Time	Name	Sqn	No.	Aircraft	Location	Result
0555	Capt E J McCloughry	4AFC	18	Balloon	Erquinghem	DF
0605	Lt O B Ramsey	4AFC	1	Balloon	La Bassée	DF
0630	2/Lt M D Sinclair	60	3	Fokker DVII	Rallincourt	D
0630	Lt O P Johnson	60	2	Fokker DVII	Epinoy	DF
0630	Lt G M Duncan	60	7	Fokker DVII	Cambrai	D
0645	Lt G C Whitney	148 US	1	Fokker DVII	Marquion	OOC
0700	Capt R Atkinson &	206	4	Balloon	Frelinghein	DF
	2/Lt W T Ganter	206	2			
0710	Lt R King	4AFC	15	LVG C	Erquinghem-le-Sec	D
0710	1/Lt H R Clay	148US	5	Fokker DVII	Sains-les-Marquion	D
0710	1/Lt C Bissell	148US	2	Fokker DVII	SW Marquion	D
0714	1/Lt H R Clay	148US	6	Fokker DVII	Marquion	D
0715	1/Lt C Bissell	148US	3	Fokker DVII	W Marquion	OOC
0715	Capt A H Cobby	4AFC	29	Fokker DVII	Wattignies	OOC
0745	Capt S Carlin	74	9	Balloon	NE Armentières	DF
0750	Capt G W F Darvill &	18	8	Fokker DVII	Cantin	DF
	Lt W Miller	18	5			
0750	Capt G W F Darvill &	18	9	Fokker DVII	Aubigny-au-Bac	D
	Lt W Miller	18	6			
0805	Lt F S Gordon	74	6	Balloon	S Roulers	DF
0815	Lt D H S Gilbertson &	70	5	Fokker DVII	Escaillon	D
	Lt J S Wilson	70	3			
0815	Lt K B Watson	70	3	Fokker DVII	Escaillon	DF
0900	Capt E C Johnston &	88	11	Fokker DVII	Seclin	DF
	Lt W I N Grant	88	2			
0900	Lt C Foster &	88	3	Fokker DVII	Seclin	OOC
	Lt B R Smyth	88	6			
0915	Capt E C Johnston &	88	12	Fokker DVII	Phalempin	OOC
	Lt W I N Grant	88	3			
0930	Lt C Findlay &	88	9	Fokker DVII	S Don	D
	2/Lt C T Gauntlett	88	1			
0930	Capt E C Johnston &	88	13	Fokker DVII	Provin	OOC
	Lt W I N Grant	88	4			
0930	Lt K B Conn &	88	9	Fokker DVII	Provin	OOC
	Sgt C M Maxwell	88	1			
0930	Lt C Foster &	88	4	Fokker DVII	Provin	OOC
	Lt B R Smyth	88	7			
0930	Lt R Schallaire &	62	2	Fokker DVII	Marcq	D
	2/Lt R Lowe	62	2			
0930	Capt G F Gibbons &	62	15	Fokker DVII	Abancourt	D
	2/Lt T Elliott	62	10			

Time	Crew	Sqn	No.	Aircraft	Location	Result
0930	Capt G F Gibbons &	62	16⎫	Fokker DVII	Cambrai	OOC
	2/Lt T Elliott	62	11⎭			
0930	Capt W E Staton &	62	23⎫	Fokker DVII	Marquette	OOC
	Lt L E Mitchell	62	6⎭			
0940	Lt G F Manning &	48	1⎫	Fokker DVII	W Armentières	D
	2/Lt P A Clayton	48	2⎭			
0940	Lt V E Knight	2AFC	1	Fokker DVII	SE Douai	OOC
0945	Lt F L Hale	32	2	Fokker DVII	N Cambrai	DF
0950	Lt F L Hale	32	3	Fokker DVII	SE Arras	OOC
0950	2/Lt F T Stott &	107	2⎫	Fokker DVII	La Sentinelle	DF
	Sgt W J Palmer	107	2⎭			
1000	Lt A B Agnew &	12	1⎫	Fokker DVII	Moeuvres-Inchy	D
	2/Lt A E Chadwick	12	1⎭			
1000	Capt A MacGregor &	57	4⎫	Fokker DVII	Bourlon Wood	OOC
	Sgt J Grant	57	6⎭			
1010	Lt W Hubbard	3	10	Fokker DVII		D
1010	Lt A W Franklyn	3	6	Fokker DrI		D
1010	Lt S D Lavalle	3	1	Fokker DVII		D
1010	Lt D J Hughes	3	4	Fokker DVII	POW	
1015	Lt F M Tudhope	46	4	Fokker DVII	Pronville	OOC
1040	Capt T F Hazell,	24	37⎫			
	Lt W A Southey &	24	22⎬	Balloon	Bernes	D
	2/Lt A L Bloom	24	1⎭			
1045	Capt T F Hazell	24	38	Fokker DVII	Gouzeaucourt	D
1045	Lt A D Shannon &	11	2⎫	Fokker DVII	E Cambrai	OOC
	2/Lt C E Spinks	11	1⎭			
1045	Lt E N Underwood &	11	1⎫	Fokker DVII	E Cambrai	OOC
	2/Lt G S Turner	11	1⎭			
1045	Lt C R Smythe &	11	3⎫	Fokker DVII	S St Hilaire	DF
	2/Lt W T Barnes	11	3⎭			
1110	Lt O J Rose	92	7	Halb C	Quiery-Douai	D
1235	Lt A E James	4AFC	1	Balloon	SE La Bassée	DF
	Lt F E Hyatt &	5	1⎫	Fokker DVII	NW Epinoy	OOC
	Lt R Greenyer	5	1⎭			
1255	Lt A H Lockley	4AFC	1	Balloon	S Armentières	DF
1330	Lt C B Seymour &	11	1⎫	Fokker DVII	Douai-Cambrai	OOC
	Sgt W J Gillespie	11	1⎭			
1330	2/Lt S W Highwood &	84	4⎫	Balloon	Douvieux	DF
	2/Lt C R Thompson	84	5⎭			
1345	Lt R C Bennett &	18	4⎫	Fokker DVII	Bailleul	OOC
	2/Lt A Lilley	18	1⎭			
1615	Capt A T Whealy	203	29	Fokker DVII	Trescault	D
1715	Lt D J T Mellor &	205	2⎫	Fokker DVII	Roisel	OOC
	Sgt W J Middleton	205	6⎭			
1815	Capt A Morrison &	11	3⎫	Fokker DVII	Douai	D
	Sgt R Allen	11	3⎭			
1825	2/Lt L Arnott &	11	1⎫	Fokker DVII	Auberchicourt	OOC
	Sgt C W Cooke	11	1⎭			
1930	Major K L Caldwell	74	20	Fokker DVII	S Lille	D
1930	2/Lt F J Hunt	74	2	Fokker DVII	S Lille	OOC

5 September 1918

Time	Crew	Sqn	No.	Aircraft	Location	Result
0625	Lt A H Lockley	4AFC	2	Balloon	Perenchies	DF
0655	Lt C L Childs	70	1	Fokker DVII	E Ploegsteert Wood	DF
0950	2/Lt S W Highwood	84	5	Balloon	S Poeuilly	DF
0950	2/Lt C R Thompson	84	6	Balloon	S Poeuilly	DF
1015	Sgt A S Cowlishaw	64	3	Fokker DVII	NE Cambrai	D
1015	Sgt A S Cowlishaw	64	4	Fokker DVII	NE Cambrai	OOC
1015	Capt W H Farrow	64	11	Fokker DVII	NE Cambrai	D
1015	Capt D Lloyd-Evans	64	6	Fokker DVII	NE Cambrai	D
1030	Lt H J Welch	80	1	Fokker DVII	Havrincourt Wood	OOC
1045	Lt G R Hicks	74	4	Fokker DVII	S Cambrai	D
1045	Lt F E Luff	74	4	Fokker DVII	S Cambrai	D
1045	Lt A C Kiddie	74	8	Fokker DVII	S Cambrai	D
1100	Maj A Coningham	92	13	Fokker DVII	W Cambrai	D
1110	Capt W E Reed	92	4	Fokker DVII	SW Cambrai	D
1115	Lt E Shapard	92	2	Fokker DVII	Cambrai	D

Time	Crew	Unit	Score	Aircraft	Location	Result
1120	2/Lt D V Thomas &	57	1	Fokker DVII	Marcoing	OOC
	2/Lt I S Woodhouse	57	1			
1125	Lt F O Thornton &	57	3	Fokker DVII	W Marcoing	OOC
	2/Lt F C Craig	57	4			
1125	Capt A MacGregor &	57	4	Fokker DVII	SW Marcoing	DF
	Sgt J Grant	57	7			
1125	Sgt D E Edgley &	57	5	Fokker DVII	Marcoing	OOC
	Sgt J H Bowler	57	2			
1145	Lt A W Franklyn	3	7	Fokker DVII		DF
1205	Lt W Hubbard	3	11	Albatros C	Peronne	D
1215	Capt E L Zink	32	5	2-seater	N Equabcourt	D
1240	Capt H A Oaks &	48	10	Fokker DVII	Courtrai-Roulers	DF
	Lt T Beck	48	1			
1240	Capt H A Oaks &	48	11	Fokker DVII	Courtrai-Roulers	OOC
	Lt T Beck	48	2			
1345	2/Lt F Suckling	65	1	Fokker DVII	Ostende	D
1345	2/Lt W Thornton	65	2	Fokker DVII	E Ostende	OOC
1345	2/Lt B Lockey	65	1	Fokker DVII	E Ostende	DF
1345	2/Lt W H Bland	65	1	Fokker DVII	E Ostende	OOC
1345	Capt Jones-Williams	65	13	Fokker DVII	E Ostende	OOC
1440	Capt J E Greene	213	11	Fokker DVII	S Varsenaere	D
1440	Lt G C Mackay	213	13	Fokker DVII	S Varsenaere	D
1520	Capt H P Lale &	20	14	Fokker DVII	SE Cambrai	D
	2/Lt H L Edwards	20	3			
1520	2/Lt R B D Campbell &	20	1	Fokker DVII	SE Cambrai	OOC
	2/Lt G C Russell	20	1			
1520	Lt G E Randall &	20	5	Fokker DVII	SE Cambrai	OOC
	Lt G V Learmond	20	4			
1605	Capt A MacGregor &	57	5	Fokker DVII	W Avesnes-le-Sec	DF
	Sgt J Grant	57	8			
1615	'B' Flight	57		Fokker DVII	W Avesnes-le-Sec	OOC
1650	Lt G Howarth &	218	1	Pfalz DIII	Bruges	OOC
	2/Lt F Gallant	218	1			
1500	Major R Collishaw	203	56	Fokker DVII	Inchy-en-Artois	D
1700	Capt S Thompson &	22	27	Fokker DVII	Douai	DF
	Sgt R M Fletcher	22	24			
1700	Capt S Thompson &	22	28	Fokker DVII	Douai	OOC
	Sgt R M Fletcher	22	25			
1700	Lt H H Beddow &	22	10	Fokker DVII	Douai	OOC
	Lt W U Tyrrell	22	1			
1700	Lt C W Thompson &	22	5	Fokker DVII	Douai	OOC
	2/Lt G McCormack	22	2			
1700	Lt F G Gibbons &	22	11	Fokker DVII	Douai	OOC
	2/Lt J McDonald	22	8			
1720	1/Lt F E Kindley	148US	6	Fokker DVII	St Quentin Lake	OOC
1720	1/Lt E W Springs	148US	11	Fokker DVII	Canal du Nord	OOC
1730	Lt L Yerex	210	4	Fokker DVII	NE Roulers	OOC
1730	Lt I C Sanderson	210	11	Fokker DVII	SE Roulers	D
1805	Lt A H Lockley	4AFC	3	Fokker DVII	S Brebières	OOC
1805	Lt L E Taplin	4AFC	12	Fokker DVII	S Brebières	OOC
1810	Capt J E Doyle	60	8	Fokker DVII	Avesnes-le-Sec	DF
1810	Capt J E Doyle	60	9	Fokker DVII	Avesnes-le-Sec	OOC
1820	Lt J W Rayner	60	1	Fokker DVII	Avesnes-le-Sec	DF
1820	Lt G M Duncan	60	9	Fokker DVII	Avesnes-le-Sec	OOC
1825	Lt J W Rayner	60	2	Fokker DVII	Avesnes-le-Sec	OOC
1825	Lt G M Duncan	60	9	Fokker DVII	Avesnes-le-Sec	OOC
1830	Lt A E Reed	29	16	LVG C	SE Armentières	D
1845	Lt K B Conn &	88	10	Fokker DVII	NE Armentières	OOC
	2/Lt B Digby-Worsley	88	12			
1845	Lt V Voss &	88	3	Fokker DVII	Armentières	D
	Sgt C Hill	88	3			
1845	Capt J R Swanston	204	2	Fokker DVII	Ouckene	DF
1850	Lt C Findlay &	88	10	Fokker DVII	E Perenchies	D
	2/Lt G T Gauntlett	88	2			
1855	Lt F W Gillet	79	6	Fokker DVII	E Armentières	D
1900	Capt F I Lord	79	7	Fokker DVII	E Ploegsteert	OOC
1900	Capt H P Rushworth	79	1	Fokker DVII	NE Armentières	OOC

1900	Capt A Hepburn &	88	9⎱	Fokker DVII	N Douai	OOC
	2/Lt H G Eldon	88	1⎰			
1900	Capt A Hepburn &	88	10⎱	Fokker DVII	Armentières	DF
	2/Lt H G Eldon	88	2⎰			
1910	Lt A C Kiddie	74	9	Fokker DVII	W Lille	OOC
1910	Lt G R Hicks	74	5	Fokker DVII	W Lille	OOC

6 September 1918

0630	Lt R King	4AFC	16	DFW C	E Wavrin	OOC
0705	1/Lt J O Creech	148US	3	Fokker DVII	NE Bourlon	D
0830	Lt A T Iaccaci &	20	12⎱	Fokker DVII	Cambrai-St Quentin	OOC
	Sgt A Newland	20	15⎰			
0830	Lt P T Iaccaci &	20	16⎱	Fokker DVII	Cambrai-Peronne Road	D
	Lt A Mills	20	11⎰			
0845	Capt H P Lale &	20	15⎱	Fokker DVII	St Quentin	DF
	2/Lt H L Edwards	20	4⎰			
0845	Capt H P Lale &	20	16⎱	Fokker DVII	St Quentin	DF
	2/Lt H L Edwards	20	5⎰			
0850	Lt P T Iaccaci &	20	17⎱	Fokker DVII	St Quenton	OOC
	Lt A Mills	20	12⎰			
0850	Lt R B D Campbell &	20	2⎱	Fokker DVII	St Quentin	OOC
	2/Lt D M Calderwood	20	1⎰			
0850	Lt A T Iaccaci &	20	13⎱	Fokker DVII	NE St Quentin	OOC
	Sgt A Newland	20	16⎰			
0915	Lt H N Compton	23	3	Fokker DVII	St Quentin	DF
0915	Lt E H Johnston &	205	4⎱	Fokker DVII	St Quentin	D
	2/Lt A Crosthwaite	205	4⎰			
1025	Lt G N Dennis &	13	1⎱	Fokker DVII	Bourlon Wood	DF
	Lt H G Hewett	13	1⎰			
1030	Lt E S Coler &	11	11⎱	Fokker DVII	W Cambrai	D
	2/Lt D P Conyngham	11	1⎰			
1030	Capt H A Hay &	11	4⎱	Fokker DVII	W Cambrai	D
	Lt A H Craig	11	1⎰			
1030	Lt E S Coler &	11	12⎱	Fokker DVII	W Cambrai	OOC
	2/Lt D P Conyngham	11	2⎰			
1030	Capt H A Hay &	11	5⎱	Fokker DVII	W Cambrai	OOC
	Lt A H Craig	11	2⎰			
1100	1/Lt B Rogers	32	2	Rumpler C	E Roisel	OOC
1130	Capt J S Stubbs &	103	7⎱	Fokker DVII	W St Andre-Lille	D
	2/Lt C C Dance	103	5⎰			
1145	Lt J Whitham &	103	1⎱	Fokker DVII	Lille	OOC
	Sgt E G Stevens	103	2⎰			
1700	Lt G E B Lawson	32	2	Fokker DVII	Holnon	D
1700	1/Lt B Rogers	32	3	Fokker DVII	Holnon	DF
1800	Lt G W Wareing	29	4	DFW C	SE Perenchies	D
1815	Lt F C Jenner	213	2	Fokker DVII	N Ostende	OOC
1830	Capt J B White	208	8	Fokker DVII	Arras-Cambrai Road	DF
1830	Lt J S McDonald	208	6	Fokker DVII	Arras-Cambrai Road	DF
1830	Capt W E G Mann	208	10	Fokker DVII	Canal du Nord	DF
1830	Capt W E G Mann	208	11	Fokker DVII	Canal du Nord	OOC
1835	Lt E Swale	210	12	Fokker DVII	W Ostende	D
1835	Lt C F Pineau	210	2	Fokker DVII	W Ostende	OOC
1840	Lt T S Harrison	29	13	Fokker DVII	SE Armentières	OOC
1845	Capt E J McCloughry	4AFC	19	LVG C	N Don	OOC
1845	Lt J P Findlay &	88	4⎱	Fokker DVII	N Douai	OOC
	2/Lt W Tinsley	88	7⎰			
1845	Capt A Hepburn &	88	11⎱	Fokker DVII	N Douai	OOC
	2/Lt H G Eldon	88	3⎰			
1845	2/Lt A Fowles	201	1	Fokker DVII	Cambrai	OOC
1845	Capt R C B Brading	201	11	Fokker DVII	Cambrai	OOC
1845	2/Lt H J Ewan	201	1	Fokker DVII	Cambrai	OOC
1855	Lt V G M Sheppard	4AFC	1	Fokker DVII	Douai	OOC
1855	Lt J W Wright	4AFC	2	Fokker DVII	Douai	OOC
1855	Lt G Jones	4AFC	2	Fokker DVII	Douai	OOC
1900	Lt J J Wellworth	2AFC	4	Fokker DVII	NW Douai	OOC
1900	Lt F R Smith	2AFC	6	Fokker DVII	NNE Douai	D
1900	Lt D A O'Leary	29	2	Fokker DVII	N Menin	D

Time	Name	Sqn	No.	Aircraft	Location	Result
1910	Lt A E Reed	29	17	Fokker DVII	S Lille	OOC
1915	Lt L N Caple &	22	2⎫	Pfalz DXII	Cambrai	OO
	2/Lt S G Barrow	22	2⎭			

7 September 1918

Time	Name	Sqn	No.	Aircraft	Location	Result
0655	Lt G W Wareing	29	5	Balloon	Gheluvelt	DF
0700	2/Lt T H Barkell	4AFC	1	2-seater	Henin-Lietard	D
0815	Capt L H Rochford	203	26	Fokker DVII	N Bourlon Wood	D
0930	Major F I Tanner	80	4	Fokker DVII	S Cartigny	D
1020	Capt G B Gates	201	10	Albatros C	Noyelles	D
1100	Lt R B Bannerman	79	7	DFW C	NE Ploegsteert	D
1120	2/Lt R Russell &	108	1⎫			
	2/Lt G B Pike	108	1⎟			
	2/Lt C R Knott &	108	1⎬	Fokker DVII	Ostende	D
	2/Lt E D McClinton	108	1⎟			
	2/Lt H L McLellan	108	1⎟			
	2/Lt F X Jackson	108	1⎭			
1130	1/Lt I P Corse	84	3	Balloon	N St Quentin	DF
1130	2/Lt S W Highwood	84	6	Balloon	Bellenglise	DF
1135	Capt A F W B Proctor	84	44	Balloon	Cambrai-St Quentin	DF
1140	2/Lt F R Christiani	84	2	Balloon	Cambrai-St Quentin	DF
1205	Lt A E Reed	29	18	Halb C	Warneton	OOC
1800	2/Lt E A R Lee &	98	1⎫			
	2/Lt E G Banham	98	1⎭	Pfalz DXII	Demicourt	D
1810	Capt H P Lale &	20	17⎫	Fokker DVII	NE St Quentin	D
	2/Lt H L Edwards	20	6⎭			
1815	2/Lt T W Sleigh &	98	1⎫	Pfalz DXII	SW Cambrai	D
	2/Lt A H Fuller	98	1⎭			
1815	2/Lt C B Gowing &	98	1⎫	Fokker DVII	SW Cambrai	OOC
	2/Lt J G W Holliday	98	1⎭			
1840	2/Lt H F Taylor &	205	1⎫	Fokker DVII	W St Quentin	OOC
	2/Lt J Golding	205	1⎭			
1845	2/Lt E J Taylor &	23	1⎫	Fokker DVII	Ronssoy	OOC
	Lt H A White	23	4⎭			
1900	2/Lt C G Vandyk,	54	1⎫			
	2/Lt Berrington,	54	1⎟			
	2/Lt Fuller,	54	1⎬	2-seater	NE Marquion	D
	Capt G Hackwill,	54	8⎟			
	Lt M G Burger &	54	3⎟			
	Lt J C MacLennan	54	2⎭			
	Capt M E Ashton &	12	1⎫	LVG C	Noyelles	D
	Lt T D Fitzsimon	12	1⎭			

8 September 1918

Time	Name	Sqn	No.	Aircraft	Location	Result
0635	Capt D H M Carberry &	59	4⎫	Halb C		D
	Lt J V B Clements	59	2⎭			
0645	Capt D H M Carberry &	59	5⎫	Halb C		OOC
	Lt J V B Clements	59	3⎭			
0650	Cape G B Gates	201	11	Albatros C	Cantaing	D
0700	Lt R K McConnell	46	7	Rumpler C	S Peronne	DF
0815	Capt T F Hazell	24	38	Fokker DVII	Le Catelet	D
0815	Capt H D Barton	24	14	Fokker DVII	Le Catelet	OOC
0820	2/Lt H L Bair	24	5	Fokker DVII	N St Quentin	D

13 September 1918

Time	Name	Sqn	No.	Aircraft	Location	Result
1750	Lt A E Reed	29	19	Halb C	SE Deulemont	D
1850	1/Lt H C Knotts	17US	2	Fokker DVII		D

14 September 1918

Time	Name	Sqn	No.	Aircraft	Location	Result
0035	Lt W Atiken	151	1	Gotha GV	Beauquesnes	DF
0115	Capt A B Yuille	151	3	Fried G	Doullens-Arras	POW
0800	Capt C W Odell,	46	3⎫			
	Lt N Bruce &	46	2⎬	2-seater	NE Vermand	D
	Lt P F Paton	46	3⎭			
0805	Capt C W Odell &	46	4⎫	Balloon	NE Vermand	DF
	Lt P F Paton	46	4⎭			

1010	Capt C H R Lagesse	29	9	Balloon	W Quesnoy	DF
1020	2/Lt P F Bovington &	12	1⎱	Fokker DVII	Graincourt	DF
	Lt H P Elliott	12	1⎰			
1025	Lt A Ibotson &	59	1⎱	Fokker DVII	S Marcoing	DF
	2/Lt W J Carruthers	59	1⎰			
1030	Capt W A Southey	84	14	Balloon	Gonnelieu	DF
1030	2/Lt S W Highwood	84	7	Balloon	Bantouzelle	DF
1030	2/Lt D C Rees	84	1	Balloon	Bantouzelle	DF
1325	Capt G B Gates	201	12	LVG C	E Villers-Plouich	DF

15 September 1918

0845	Capt R C B Brading	201	12	Pfalz DXII	W Cambrai	D
0850	Capt A W B Proctor &	84	45⎱	Balloon	Bellicourt	DF
	Capt D Carruthers	84	3⎰			
0955	Lt C R J Thompson	84	7	Balloon	E St Quentin	DF
1040	2/Lt P E Cunnius,	148US	1⎱			
	1/Lt O A Ralston,	148US	3	Halb C	Epinoy	OOC
	1/Lt E W Springs &	148US	13			
	1/Lt H Starkey, Jr	148US	1⎰			
1050	1/Lt F E Kindley	148US	7	Fokker DVII	Epinoy	OOC
1100	Lt R B D Campbell &	20	3⎱	Fokker DVII	NE St Quentin	OOC
	Sgt A J Winch	20	1⎰			
1105	Capt O M Baldwin	73	10	Fokker DVII	Cambrai	D
1105	Lt N Cooper	73	5	Fokker DVII	Cambrai	OOC
1110	Lt N S Boulton &	20	1⎱	Fokker DVII	NE St Quentin	OOC
	2/Lt G W Pearce	20	1⎰			
1110	Capt O M Baldwin	73	11	Fokker DVII	Cambrai	OOC
1115	Lt A T Iaccaci &	20	14⎱	Fokker DVII	S Lesdain	D
	Sgt A Newland	20	17⎰			
1120	Lt A T Iaccaci &	20	15⎱	Fokker DVII	S Morcourt	D
	Sgt A Newland	20	18⎰			
1120	Capt O M Baldwin	73	12	2-seater	La Folie	D
1120	Lt A R Strachan &	20	2⎱	Fokker DVII	Omissy	D
	Lt D M Calderwood	20	2⎰			
1120	Lt A R Strachan &	20	3⎱	Fokker DVII	Omissy	OOC
	Lt D M Calderwood	20	3⎰			
1120	Lt W M Thomson &	20	22⎱	Fokker DVII	St Quentin	D
	2/Lt H L Edwards	20	7⎰			
1120	Lt W M Thomson &	20	23⎱	Fokker DVII	St Quentin	OOC
	2/Lt H L Edwards	20	8⎰			
1200	Capt E S Coler &	11	13⎱	Fokker DVII	W Esnes	D
	2/Lt E J Corbett	11	1⎰			
1200	Capt E S Coler &	11	14⎱	Fokker DVII	SW Lesdain	D
	2/Lt E J Corbett	11	2⎰			
1300	Lt O J Rose	92	7	Hannover C	W Lille	D
1320	Capt H A Whistler	80	18	Balloon	Etricourt	DF
1400	Lt B E Barnum &	204	3⎱	Fokker DVII	Zeebrugge	D
	Lt R C Pattullo	204	1⎰			
1400	Capt C R R Hickey	204	16	Fokker DVII	Zeebrugge	OOC
1400	Lt D S Ingalls &	213	3⎱	Rumpler C	Ostende	DF
	Lt H C Smith	213	3⎰			
1415	Capt D R MacLaren	46	46	Fokker DVII	N Gouzeaucourt	OOC
1520	Lt C J H Haywood &	205	6⎱	Fokker DVII	Busigny	OOC
	Sgt S F Longstone	205	5⎰			
1645	Capt W E Shields	41	14	Fokker DVII	Houthem	OOC
1700	Capt F O Soden	41	20	Balloon	Beaucamps	DF
1700	Capt R M Foster	209	14	Fokker DVII	Ecoust-St Quentin	D
1700	2/Lt F O McDonald &	205	2⎱	2-seater	W Roisel	DF
	2/Lt J B Leach	205	4⎰			
1705	Capt G W D Allen,	62	11⎱			
	Capt C S T Lavers,	62	8			
	Lt D E Cameron,	62	1	Pfalz DXII	Recourt	POW
	Lt B H Moody,	62	5			
	Capt W E Staton &	62	24			
	Lt L E Mitchell	62	6⎰			
1705	Capt W Pallister	1	1	Fokker DVII	N W Cambrai	D

1705	Lt R Schallaire &	62	3 ⎫	Fokker DVII	Marquion	D
	2/Lt R Lowe	62	3 ⎭			
1705	2/Lt P S Manley &	62	1 ⎫	Fokker DVII	Marquion	OOC
	Sgt G F Hines	62	1 ⎭			
1715	Lt C W Arning	1	1	Fokker DVII	Haynecourt	OOC
1715	Lt C G Pegg	1	3	Fokker DVII	E Raillencourt	D
1715	Capt W R May	209	11	Fokker DVII	E Epinoy	D
1720	Capt E E Cummings &	2AFC	5 ⎫	Albatros C	Wez Marquart	D
	Lt E E Davies	2AFC	2 ⎭			
1720	Capt R M Foster	209	15	Fokker DVII	Ecoust-St Quentin	D
1745	Lt E Lussier	73	9	Fokker DVII	Aubigny-au-Bac	D
1750	Capt T P Middleton &	20	26 ⎫	Hannover C	SE St Quentin	D
	Lt A Mills	20	13 ⎭			
1750	2/Lt H F Taylor &	205	2 ⎫	Fokker DVII	St Quentin	OOC
	2/Lt H S Mullen	205	1 ⎭			
1805	Lt J W Warner	85	5	Fokker DVII	Bourlon Wood	D
1810	Capt W H Hubbard	73	11	Fokker DVII	Gouy-sous-Bellone	D
1815	Lt S T Liversedge	70	11	Fokker DVII	Houthulst	OOC
1815	Lt N Cooper	73	6	Fokker DVII	NE Bourlon Wood	D
1815	Capt O M Baldwin	73	13	Fokker DVII	Gouy-sous-Bellone	D
1815	Capt O M Baldwin	73	14	Fokker DVII	Gouy-sous-Bellone	OOC
1830	Capt H D Barton	24	15	Albatros C	Cambrai	OOC
1830	2/Lt M J Ward	70	1	Balloon	E Armentières	DF
1840	Capt G H Hackwill	54	9	Fokker DVII	Fernin	OOC
1840	1/Lt J O Creech	148US	4	Fokker DVII	Epinoy	D
1845	1/Lt T L Moore	148US	1	Fokker DVII	NE Hamel	D
1845	Lt C W Wareing	29	6	Fokker DVII	Roulers-Rumbeke	DF
1845	1/Lt W W Lauer	29	1	Fokker DVII	Moorslede-Roulers	D
1850	Capt S Carlin	74	10	Fokker DVII	NE Lille	DF
1850	Lt F E Luff	74	5	Fokker DVII	NE Armentières	D
1855	Capt H D Barton &	24	16 ⎫	Hannover C	Hannescourt Wood	D
	2/Lt H L Bair	24	6 ⎭			
2220	Capt F C Broome	151	2	Staaken	Bapaume	POW
	Lt G F Anderson &	88	3 ⎫	Fokker DVII	E Seclin	OOC
	Lt T F Chiltern	88	4 ⎭			
	Lt V W Kilroe &	15	1 ⎫	Fokker DVII		D
	Lt G E Izzard	15	1 ⎭			

16 September 1918

0625	Lt R King	4AFC	17	Fokker DVII	Le Quesnoy	D
0625	Capt H G Watson	4AFC	13	Fokker DVII	Le Quesnoy	OOC
0630	Lt S W Highwood &	84	8 ⎫	Rumpler C	Selenoy	D
	Lt C F C Wilson	84	4 ⎭			
0730	Lt F R Smith	2AFC	7	Fokker DVII	Lille	OOC
0730	Lt F R Smith	2AFC	8	Fokker DVII	Lille	OOC
0730	Lt F Alberry	2AFC	1	Fokker DVII	NW Lille	DF
0730	Capt R L Manuel	2AFC	10	Fokker DVII	Habourdin	OOC
0735	Lt G E Holroyde	2AFC	1	Fokker DVII	Habourdin	OOC
0800	Lt C H Copp	2AFC	1	Fokker DVII	Steenvoorde	OOC
0800	Capt R L Manuel	2AFC	11	Fokker DVII	S Droglandt	POW
0815	Lt W M Thomson &	20	24 ⎫	Fokker DVII	NE St Quentin	D
	2/Lt H L Edwards	20	9 ⎭			
0815	Lt A R Strachan &	20	4 ⎫			
	2/Lt D M Calderwood	20	4 ⎰	Fokker DVII	NW St Quentin	D
	Lt W M Thomson &	20	25 ⎱			
	2/Lt H L Edwards	20	10 ⎭			
0820	Lt W M Thomson &	20	26 ⎫	Fokker DVII	St Quentin	D
	2/Lt H L Edwards	20	11 ⎭			
0820	2/Lt T H Barkell	4AFC	2	Fokker DVII	Frelinghien	D
0820	Lt A J Pallister	4AFC	1	Fokker DVII	Frelinghien	D
0820	Lt G Jones	4AFC	3	Fokker DVII	Frelinghien	D
0825	Lt A T Iaccaci &	20	16 ⎫	Fokker DVII	W Lesdain	D
	Sgt A Newland	20	19 ⎭			
0825	Lt H E Johnson &	20	1 ⎫	Fokker DVII	W Lesdain	OOC
	2/Lt E S Harvey	20	1 ⎭			
0825	Lt N S Boulton &	20	2 ⎫	Fokker DVII	W Lesdain	OOC
	Sgt R S Dodds	20	1 ⎭			

Time	Pilot	Sqn	Score	Aircraft	Location	Result
0825	Lt J Nicholson &	20	1⎱	Fokker DVII	W Lesdain	OOC
	2/Lt B W Wilson	20	1⎰			
0825	Lt J Adam	23	3	Fokker DVII	W St Quentin	D
0830	2/Lt E J Taylor &	23	3⎱	Fokker DVII	W Itancourt	D
	Lt R L M Robb	23	1⎰			
0830	Lt H A White &	23	5⎱	Fokker DVII	St Quentin	OOC
	Lt A P Pherson	23	3⎰			
0830	Lt H A White	23	6	Fokker DVII	St Quentin	DF
0830	Capt E S Coler &	11	14⎱	Fokker DVII	Cambrai	DF
	2/Lt E J Corbett	11	3⎰			
0830	Capt E S Coler &	11	15⎱	Fokker DVII	E Cambrai	D
	2/Lt E J Corbett	11	4⎰			
0835	1/Lt W L Dougan	29	4	Fokker DVII	S Wervicq	D
0835	Capt C H R Lagesse	29	10	Fokker DVII	S Linselles	D
0835	Lt E O Amm	29	4	Fokker DVII	Bois Warneton	D
0840	Capt E C Hoy	29	11	Fokker DVII	N Quesnoy	D
0845	Capt E C Hoy	29	12	Fokker DVII	E Becelaere	D
0845	Lt W E Macpherson &	205	1⎱	Hannover C	N St Quentin	DF
	2/Lt S F Ambler	205	1⎰			
0845	Lt W E Macpherson &	205	2⎱	Fokker DVII	St Quentin	D
	2/Lt S F Ambler	205	2⎰			
0900	Capt G B Gates &	201	13⎱	LVG C	Haynecourt	DF
	Lt J M Mackay	201	1⎰			
0917	Lt C M Wilson	29	8	Fokker DrI	N Loos	D
0920	Lt E G Davies	29	1	Fokker DrI	E Lille	D
0920	Lt A F Diamond	29	2	Balloon	W Perenchies	D
0930	2/Lt K G Nairn &	205	1⎱	Fokker DVII	W Bray	OOC
	2/Lt N R McKinley	205	1⎰			
0940	Capt R A Del Haye	19	6	Pfalz DIII	Fort Carnot	D
0940	Lt D P Laird	19	1	Pfalz DIII	Lille	OOC
0940	Capt C V Gardner &	19	9⎱	Fokker DVII	Lille	OOC
	Lt J D Hardman	19	6⎰			
0940	Lt L H Ray	19	3	Pfalz DIII	Lille	OOC
0945	Capt F I Lord	79	8	Fokker DVII	Messines	OOC
1030	Capt A W Vigers	87	11	Rumpler C	N Cambrai	D
1030	2/Lt T W Sleigh &	98	2⎱	Fokker DVII	Valenciennes	OOC
	2/Lt A H Fuller	98	2⎰			
1030	Lt H A Kullberg	1	20	Fokker DVII	Valenciennes	DF
1035	2/Lt J H Nicholas &	98	1⎱	Pfalz DIII	W Valenciennes	D
	2/Lt A P C Bruce	98	1⎰			
1045	Capt O W C Johnsen &	98	5⎱	Fokker DVII	Oisy	OOC
	2/Lt C H Thompson	98	1⎰			
1105	Lt L H Pearson &	202	4⎱	Pfalz DIII	Lisseweghe	OOC
	2/Lt E Darby	202	4⎰			
1105	Capt N Keeble &	202	5⎱	Pfalz DIII	Lisseweghe	D
	Capt E B C Betts	202	5⎰			
1105	Lt H N Witter &	202	1⎱	Fokker DVII	Lisseweghe	OOC
	2/Lt A E Lee	202	1⎰			
1110	Lt C F Pineau	210	3	Fokker DVII	NW Zeebrugge	D
1115	Lt A Buchanan	210	5	Fokker DVII	N Zeebrugge	D
1125	Lt L H Pearson &	202	5⎱	Fokker DVII	Dudzeele	DF
	2/Lt E Darby	202	5⎰			
1125	Capt N Keeble &	202	6⎱	Pfalz DIII	Dudzeele	DF
	Capt E B C Betts	202	6⎰			
1135	Capt T W Nash	204	5	Balloon	SE Ostende	DF
1145	Capt R B Bannerman	79	8	2-seater	N Hollebeke	D
1200	Capt R B Bannerman	79	9	2-seater	Hooge	OOC
1215	Capt C H Stokes &	57	3⎱	Fokker DVII	Havrincourt Wood	D
	Lt R D Bovill	57	1⎰			
1215	Lt P W J Timson &	57	1⎱	Fokker DVII	Havrincourt Wood	DF
	2/Lt I S Woodhouse	57	1⎰			
1230	Capt C H Stokes &	57	4⎱	Fokker DVII	Havrincourt Wood	OOC
	Lt R D Bovill	57	2⎰			
1230	Sgt D E Edgeley &	57	6⎱	Fokker DVII	Havrincourt Wood	OOC
	Sgt A Lovesay	57	2⎰			
1340	Lt C V A Bucknell &	41	1⎱	DFW C	W Roubaix	OOC
	Lt W Mitchell	41	1⎰			
1350	Major G H Bowman	41	29	2-seater	Hooglede	DF

1400	Capt C F Falkenberg	84	12	Fokker DVII	Montigny	OOC
1410	Major G H Bowman	41	30	Fokker DVII	Houthulst	OOC
1530	Lt T W Martin &	22	6⎫	Fokker DVII	Quesnoy Wood	D
	Sgt M Jones	22	1⎭			
1530	Lt F G Gibbons &	22	12⎫	Fokker DVII	Quesnoy Wood	OOC
	Sgt G Shannon	22	4⎭			
1615	Lt J H McNeaney	79	1	Fokker DVII	NW Tourcoing	OOC
1730	Capt H J Larkin	87	11	Fokker DVII	W Abancourt	D
1735	Capt H A R Biziou	87	4	Fokker DVII	N Cambrai	D
1735	Capt H A R Biziou	87	5	Fokker DVII	N Cambrai	OOC
1735	Capt R C B Brading	201	13	Fokker DVII	SE Cambrai	D
1735	Capt R McLaughlin	201	4	Fokker DVII	SE Cambrai	OOC
1750	Lt K B Conn &	88	11⎫	Fokker DVII	NE Havrincourt	D
	2/Lt B Digby-Worsley	88	13⎭			
1750	Lt K B Conn &	88	12⎫	Fokker DVII	NE Haubourdin	D
	2/Lt B Digby-Worsley	88	14⎭			
1755	Lt H A S Molyneaux	56	4	Fokker DVII	Havrincourt Wood	D
1755	2/Lt V H Hervey	56	1	Fokker DVII	Havrincourt Wood	OOC
1800	Lt G E B Lawson	32	3	Fokker DVII	E Marquion	OOC
1810	Lt F L Hale	32	4	Fokker DVII	Brunemont	DF
1810	1/Lt B Rogers	32	4	Fokker DVII	Sancourt	OOC
1810	Lt A A Callander	32	6	Fokker DVII	Sancourt	OOC
1810	2/Lt W H Maxted	3	5	Fokker DVII	Bourlon Wood	OOC
1810	2/Lt A H Betteridge	3	1	Fokker DVII	Bourlon Wood	OOC
1815	Capt D R MacLaren,	46	47⎫	Fokker DVII	Cambrai	DF
	Lt R Viall &	46	1⎬			
	Lt C H Swayer	46	2⎭			
1815	Capt D R MacLaren	46	48	Fokker DVII	Cambrai	OOC
1840	Lt F J S Britnell	203	6	Fokker DVII	Haynecourt	DF
1845	Major C W Crowe	85	14	Fokker DVII	Souchy-Couchy	D
1845	2/Lt R A H Lloyd	85	1	Fokker DVII	Biache	DF
1850	Lt B S B Thomas &	11	2⎫	Fokker DVII	N Cambrai	D
	Lt W T Barnes	11	5⎭			
1855	Capt C R R Hickey,	204	15⎫			
	2/Lt N Smith,	204	1⎪			
	Lt R M Bennett,	204	4⎬	Fokker DVII	Blankenberghe	DF
	Lt F G Bayley &	204	2⎪			
	2/Lt C R Chisman	204	11⎭			
1900	2/Lt N Smith	204	2	Fokker DVII	Blankenberghe	OOC
1900	2/Lt C L Kelly	204	1	Fokker DVII	Blankenberghe	OOC
1900	Lt R M Bennett	204	5	LVG C	Blankenberghe	D
1900	Lt P F Cormack	204	1	2-seater	Blankenberghe	D
1900	Lt B S B Thomas &	11	3⎫	Fokker DVII	S Cambrai	D
	Lt W T Barnes	11	6⎭			
1905	Lt W B Craig	204	3	Fokker DVII	Blankenberghe	D
1905	Lt W B Craig	204	4	Fokker DVII	Blankenberghe	OOC
1905	Lt W B Craig	204	5	Fokker DVII	Blankenberghe	OOC
1910	Capt C R R Hickey,	204	16⎫			
	2/Lt N Smith,	204	3⎪			
	Lt R M Bennett,	204	5⎬	Fokker DVII	Blankenberghe	DF
	Lt F G Bayley &	204	3⎪			
	2/Lt C R Chisman	204	2⎭			
1910	Lt G E C Howard	204	1	LVG C	Blankenberghe	D
	Lt C H Moss &	62	1⎫	Fokker DVII		D
	2/Lt R Lowe	62	4⎭			
	Lt L Campbell &	62	7⎫	Fokker DVII		OOC
	2/Lt L Egan	62	2⎭			
	2/Lt P S Manley &	62	2⎫	Fokker DVII		OOC
	Sgt G F Hines	62	2⎭			

17 September 1918

0955	Lt A T Drinkwater	40	7	Fokker DVII	SE Cambrai	OOC
1010	Capt F I Lord	79	9	Fokker DVII	Comines	OOC
1020	Lt F Alberry	2AFC	2	Fokker DVII	Lille	OOC
1020	Lt F Alberry	2AFC	3	Fokker DVII	Lille	OOC
1055	Lt B S B Thomas &	11	4⎫	Fokker DVII	Cambrai-Wasnes	D
	Lt W T Barnes	11	6⎭			

1100	Lt L L K Straw &	25	2⎫	Fokker DVII	E Bourlon Wood	OOC
	Lt G M Lawson	25	1⎭			
1115	Lt R G Dobson &	25	1⎫	Fokker DVII	Le Catelet	OOC
	2/Lt A G Grant	25	1⎭			
1115	Capt W S Philcox	92	1	Albatros C	Le Catelet	OOC
1200	Capt D R MacLaren,	46	49⎫			
	2/Lt R Gilpin-Brown,	46	1			
	Lt P M Tudhope,	46	5	Fokker DVII	Cambrai	OOC
	Lt C H Sawyer,	46	3			
	Capt C W Odell &	46	5			
	2/Lt L Skerrington	46	2⎭			
1200	Capt D R MacLaren,	46	50⎫			
	2/Lt R Gilpin-Brown,	46	2			
	Lt P M Tudhope,	46	6	Fokker DVII	Cambrai	OOC
	Lt C H Sawyer	46	4			
	Capt C W Odell &	46	6			
	2/Lt Skerrington	46	3⎭			
1230	Capt O M Baldwin	73	15	Rumpler C	E Cambrai	D
1300	1/Lt F E Kindley &	148US	8⎫	Fokker DVII	Epinoy	D
	1/Lt J O Creech	148US	5⎭			
1305	1/Lt L T Wyly	148US	4	Fokker DVII	NW Cambrai	OOC
1410	Capt S B Horn	85	13	2-seater	SE Graincourt	D
1825	Major K L Caldwell	74	21	Fokker DVII	N Courtrai	D
1825	Lt F J Hunt	74	3	Fokker DVII	N Courtrai	DF
1825	Lt A M Phillips &	217	3⎫	Seaplane	Zeebrugge	D
	Lt N S Dougall	217	2⎭			
1830	Lt C W M Thompson &	22	6⎫	Fokker DVII	SW Douai	D
	Lt G McCormack	22	3⎭			
1830	Lt C W M Thompson &	22	7⎫	Fokker DVII	Brebières	OOC
	Lt G McCormack	22	4⎭			
1830	Lt W S Jenkins	210	7	Fokker DVII	S Ostende	DF
1830	Lt W S Jenkins	210	8	Fokker DVII	S Ostende	DF
1840	Major K L Caldwell	74	22	Fokker DVII	NW Courtrai	OOC
1845	1/Lt W T Clements &	17US	1⎫	Fokker DVII	Arleux	D
	2/Lt H C Knotts	17US	3⎭			
2050	Lt E P Mackay	151	2	AEG G	Estrées	D
2240	Capt D V Armstrong	151	5	Fried G	Fletre	DF
2241	Major C J Q Brand	151	10	Fried G	E Bapaume	D
	2/Lt P S Manley &	62	3⎫	Fokker DVII		OOC
	Sgt G F Hines	62	3⎭			
	Lt F Jeffreys &	88	1⎫	Fokker DVII	Lille	DF
	Lt F W Addison	88	1⎭			
	Lt F Jeffreys &	88	2⎫	Fokker DVII	Lommelet	D
	Lt F W Addison	88	2⎭			
	Lt R Britton &	13	1⎫	2-seater		D
	2/Lt B Hickman	13	1⎭			

18 September 1918

1050	Lt D S Ingalls,	213	4⎫			
	Lt H C Smith &	213	3⎬	Balloon	La Barrière	DF
	Lt G S Hodson	213	5⎭			
1100	2/Lt H C Burdick	17US	1	LVG C	Rumilly	DF
1215	Capt J W Pearson	23	7	Fokker DVII	Lihaucourt	DF
1215	Capt J W Pearson	23	8	Fokker DVII	Lihaucourt	OOC
1420	Lt N D Willis	40	2	Fokker DVII	Cambrai	OOC
1445	Capt H A Whistler	80	19	Fokker DVII	E Pontruet	D
1445	Lt E O C Parsons	80	1	Fokker D VII	E Pontruet	D
1445	Lt H J Welch	80	2	Fokker DVII	E Pontruet	D
1730	Capt D Lloyd-Evans	64	7	Fokker DVII	E Havrincourt	D
1730	Capt D Lloyd-Evans	64	8	Fokker DVII	E Havrincourt	OOC

19 September 1918

0735	Capt R B Bannerman	79	10	Fokker DVII	E Houthulst Wood	D
1040	Lt G Carr-Harris	73	2	Fokker DVII	Magny-la-Fosse	D
1725	Lt F G Pym &	57	1⎫	Fokker DVII	Havrincourt Wood	OOC
	Sgt W G E Mason	57	1⎭			

1725	Capt W E Green &	57	9⎫	Fokker DVII	Havrincourt Wood	OOC
	Lt A M Barron	57	2⎭			
1810	Major R S Maxwell	54	8	2-seater	E Havrincourt Wood	OOC

20 September 1918

0630	Capt H D Barton	24	17	LVG C	Wassigny	D
0655	Capt F I Lord	79	10	Hannover C	N Haubourdin	D
0750	Lt K B Conn &	88	13⎫	Fokker DVII	Quesnoy	OOC
	2/Lt B Digby-Worsley	88	15⎭			
0750	Lt G R Poole &	88	5⎫	Fokker DVII	SE Capinghem	D
	Sgt C Hill	88	5⎭			
0755	Capt E C Johnston,	88	15⎫			
	2/Lt W J N Grant,	88	5			
	Lt K B Conn,	88	14⎪	Fokker DVII	SE Quesnoy	D
	2/Lt D Digby-Worsley	88	6⎧			
	Lt G R Poole &	88	6			
	Sgt C Hill	88	6⎭			
0920	Capt J F Chisholm &	218	2⎫	Fokker DVII	Bruges	OOC
	Sgt R J Williams	218	2⎭			
0930	Lt E H Attwood &	218	1⎫	Fokker DVII	W Bruges	OOC
	2/Lt A E Smith	218	1⎭			
0943	Lt A M Anderson &	218	1⎫	Fokker DVII	Stahlhille	OOC
	Sgt J Harris	218	3⎭			
1000	Lt F G Harlock &	20	3⎫	Fokker DVII	Mesnil	D
	2/Lt A S Draisey	20	3⎭			
1000	Lt W J B Nel	84	6	Fokker DVII	E Mont d'Origny	D
1015	Capt N E Chandler	65	1	Fokker DVII	SW Bruge	D
1015	Lt M A Newnham	65	8	Fokker DVII	Jabberke	D
1015	Lt F G Harlock &	20	4⎫	Fokker DVII	Mesnil	DF
	2/Lt A S Draisey	20	4⎭			
1015	Lt N S Boulton &	20	3⎫	Fokker DVII	NE St Quentin	D
	Sgt E G Mitchell	20	1⎭			
1015	Capt C F Falkenberg	84	13	Fokker DVII	Mont d'Origny	OOC
1020	2/Lt D F Tysoe	204	1	Fokker DVII	Beerst	D
1020	Lt M McCall &	20	2⎫	Fokker DVII	E Longchamps	D
	2/Lt C G Boothroyd	20	4⎭			
1020	Lt S Walters &	20	2⎫	Fokker DVII	St Quentin	OOC
	Lt T Kirkpatrick	20	1⎭			
1025	Lt G E C Howard	204	2	Fokker DVII	NE Dixmuide	OOC
1025	Lt W B Craig	204	6	Fokker DVII	NE Dixmuide	OOC
1025	2/Lt H G Clappison	204	1	Fokker DVII	NE Dixmuide	DF
1025	Lt F R Brown	204	1	Fokker DVII	NE Dixmuide	D
1025	Lt M McCall &	20	3⎫	Fokker DVII	N Longchamps	OOC
	2/Lt C G Boothroyd	20	5⎭			
1025	Lt S Walters &	20	3⎫	Fokker DVII	St Quentin	D
	Lt T Kirkpatrick	20	2⎭			
1030	Capt T P Middleton &	20	27⎫	Fokker DVII	Rouvroy	D
	Lt A Mills	20	14⎭			
1030	Capt T P Middleton &	20	28⎫	Fokker DVII	Rouvroy	D
	Lt A Mills	20	15⎭			
1030	Capt C F Falkenberg	84	14	Fokker DVII	Mont d'Origny	D
1030	Lt W B Craig	204	7	Fokker DVII	SW Ostende	OOC
1045	Lt D S Ingalls	213	5	Fokker DVII	Vlisseghem	D
1245	Lt H A White &	23	7⎫	Fokker DVII	N St Quentin	DF
	Lt C Thomas	23	1⎭			
1455	1/Lt E W Springs	148US	13	Fokker DVII	Canal-du-Nord-Aubigny	D
1530	Lt J W Warner	85	6	Fokker DVII	E Bourlon Wood	D
1530	Lt D C Mangan	87	3	Fokker DVII	Noyelles	D
1530	Lt L N Hollinghurst	87	7	Fokker DVII	Noyelles	D
1530	Capt H A Biziou	87	6	Fokker DVII	Noyelles	D
1530	1/Lt H C Starkey	148US	2	Hannover C	N Cambrai-Arras Road	OOC
1530	Lt F J S Britnell	203	7	Fokker DVII	Haynecourt	OOC
1530	Capt J D Breakey	203	6	Fokker DVII	Haynecourt	OOC
1530	2/Lt W H Coghill	203	1	Fokker DVII	Haynecourt	D
1530	2/Lt M G Cruise	203	1	Fokker DVII	Haynecourt	DF
1530	Lt H W Skinner	203	2	Fokker DVII	Haynecourt	D

1645	Capt W R May &	209	12⎫	Fokker DVII	Sauchy-Lestrées	D
	Lt C Knight	209	1⎭			
2135	Capt F C Broome	151	3	AEG C	Tincourt	D

21 September 1918

1015	Capt R B Bannerman	79	11	2-seater	SW Hollebeke	D
1035	Lt H M S Parsons	79	1	2-seater	E Oostaverne	D
1145	Patrol	108	—	Fokker DVII	Zarren	OOC
1150	Lt F W Gillet	79	7	Fokker DVII	Habourdin-Wavrin	D
1155	Capt F McQuistan	19	6	Fokker DVII	E Thorout	D
1745	Lt D C Rees	84	2	Fokker DVII	NNE St Quentin	D
1745	2/Lt J A Jackson	84	1	Fokker DVII	NE St Quentin	D
1810	Capt W E Shields	41	15	Fokker DVII	Don	D
1810	Capt W E Shields	41	16	Fokker DVII	Don	OOC
1835	Capt C H Stokes &	57	5⎫	Fokker DVII	Fontaine-Notre Dame	OOC
	Lt R D Bovill	57	3⎭			
1835	Capt W R May	209	13	Fokker DVII	Ecoust-St Quentin	D
1835	Lt G Knight	209	2	Fokker DVII	Ecoust-St Quentin	OOC
1840	Patrol	57	—	Fokker DVII	Bourlon Wood	DF
1840	Lt F J Hunt	74	4	Fokker DVII	Lille	D
1845	Capt C B Glynn	74	5	Fokker DVII	Lille	D
1845	Major K L Caldwell	74	23	Fokker DVII	Lille	OOC
1845	Capt B Roxburgh-Smith	74	15	Fokker DVII	Lille	OOC
2126	Major C J Q Brand	151	12	Fried G	Gouzeaucourt	POW
2135	Major C J Q Brand &	151	13⎫	AEG G	S Gouzeaucourt	D
	Lt J H Summers	151	2⎭			
2135	Lt A A Mitchell	151	2	Gotha G	N Peronne	D

22 September 1918

0820	2/Lt T H Barkell	4AFC	3	Fokker DVII	E Armentières	OOC
0820	2/Lt T H Barkell	4AFC	4	Fokker DVII	Armentières	OOC
0840	Capt H A R Biziou	87	7	Fokker DVII	Bourlon Wood	D
0840	Capt H A R Biziou	87	8	Fokker DVII	Bourlon Wood	D
0845	1/Lt G A Vaughn	17US	8	Fokker DVII	Fontaine-Notre Dame	D
0845	1/Lt G D Wicks	17US	2	Fokker DVII	W Rumilly	D
0845	1/Lt G A Vaughn	17US	9	Fokker DVII	W Cambrai	DF
0910	2/Lt H C Knotts	17US	4	Fokker DVII	SW Cambrai	D
0910	Capt A W Vigers &	87	12⎫	Rumpler C	NE Bapaume	OOC
	Lt R M MacDonald	87	2⎭			
0910	Lt E C Worthington	87	5	Rumpler C	NE Bapaume	OOC
1030	Capt C W Cudemore	64	9	Fokker DVII	S Cambrai	OOC
1040	Capt H D Barton	24	18	Fokker DVII	E Bourlon Wood	D
	Capt E C Johnston &	88	16⎫	LVG C		OOC
	Lt W J N Grant	88	5⎭			
	2/Lt H J Evans &	12	1⎫	Fokker DVII		D
	Lt C A Stubbings	12	1⎭			

23 September 1918

0835	Lt G S Bourner &	13	1⎫	2-seater	Sains-les-Marquion	DF
	Lt F A D Vaughn	13	1⎭			
1425	Lt W E Grey,	213	6⎫	Fokker DVII	E Dixmuide	OOC
	Lt M N Hancocks,	213	3⎪			
	Lt A R Talbert &	213	2⎥			
	Lt C P Sparkes	213	3⎭			
1725	Capt G B Gates	201	14	LVG C	N Bourlon Wood	D
1745	Capt A W Vigers	87	13	Fokker DVII	NE Cambrai	OOC
1745	Lt C K Oliver	87	4	Fokker DVII	NE Cambrai	OOC
1748	Lt R M McDonald	87	3	Fokker DVII	NE Cambrai	D
1810	Lt L N Hollinghurst	87	8	Fokker DVII	Bourlon Wood	D
1810	Lt R M McDonald	87	4	Fokker DVII	Bourlon Wood	OOC
1810	Capt A W Vigers	87	14	Fokker DVII	Bourlon Wood	OOC
1815	Lt N S Boulton &	20	4⎫	Fokker DVII	NE St Quentin	D
	2/Lt H L Edwards	20	12⎭			
1818	Lt N S Boulton &	20	5⎫	Fokker DVII	NE St Quentin	DF
	2/Lt H L Edwards	20	13⎭			
1820	Lt N S Boulton &	20	6⎫	Fokker DVII	NE St Quentin	D
	2/Lt H L Edwards	20	14⎭			

1820	Lt A E Kiernander &	20	1⎱	Fokker DVII	NE St Quentin	D
	Lt C G Boothroyd	20	5⎰			
1820	Lt E A Britton &	20	1⎱	Fokker DVII	W Rouvroy	D
	Sgt R S Dodds	20	2⎰			
1820	Lt E A Britton &	20	2⎱	Fokker DVII	W Rouvroy	OOC
	Sgt R S Dodds	20	3⎰			
1715	2/Lt G C Upson &	42	1⎱	Fokker DVII	Fleurbaix	D
	2/Lt A N Thomson	42	1⎰			

24 September 1918

0625	Capt E J McCloughry	4AFC	20	DFW C E	Lille	D
0635	Capt E J McCloughry	4AFC	21	Fokker DVII	Lille	D
0645	Lt G Jones	4AFC	4	2-seater	Lens	D
0700	Capt G J Strange	40	7	Fokker DVII	Cambrai	D
0700	Patrol	40	—	Fokker DVII	Cambrai	OOC
0700	Patrol	40	—	Fokker DVII	Cambrai	OOC
0705	Major R Collishaw	203	57	Fokker DVII	Epinoy	D
0710	2/Lt G S Smith	40	1	Fokker DVII	Cambrai	DF
0728	1/Lt F E Kindley	148US	9	Fokker DVII	W Cambrai	D
0735	1/Lt H R Clay	148US	8	Fokker DVII	Bourlon-Epinoy	DF
0738	1/Lt E H Zistell	148US	3	Fokker DVII	Bourlon Wood	D
0740	1/Lt L T Wyly	148US	4	Fokker DVII	Bourlon Wood	D
0740	1/Lt E W Springs	148US	14	Fokker DVII	NE Bourlon	D
0740	1/Lt W B Knox	148US	2	Fokker DVII	W Cambrai	D
0745	1/Lt E H Zistell	148US	4	Fokker DVII	N Bourlon Wood	OOC
0810	Lt A Newman &	57	3⎱	Fokker DVII		D
	2/Lt C Wilkinson	57	1⎰			
0810	Lt F G Pym	57	2⎱	Fokker DVII		DF
	Sgt W G E Mason	57	2⎰			
0810	2/Lt F de N Hyde &	57	1⎱	Fokker DVII		OOC
	2/Lt L H Eyres	57	1⎰			
0815	Capt H P Chubb	56	2	Fokker DVII	Sailly	D
0830	Lt H A S Molyneaux	56	5	Fokker DVII	Haynecourt	D
0900	Lt W Sidebottom &	203	7⎱	Hannover C	SE Lens	D
	2/Lt W H Coghill	203	2⎰			
0900	Sgt E Campbell &	11	1⎱	Fokker DVII	SE Havrincourt	D
	Sgt H C Taylor	11	1⎰			
0910	Lt W J B Nel	84	7	Fokker DVII	Estrées-Gouy	D
0915	Capt A W F B Proctor	84	46	Balloon	Gouy	DF
0915	2/Lt S W Highwood	84	9	Balloon	Gouy	DF
0915	2/Lt D C Ress	84	3	Balloon	Gouy	DF
1010	Capt A Hepburn &	88	12⎱	Fokker DVII	Habourdin	D
	2/Lt H G Eldon	88	4⎰			
1010	Capt C F Findley &	88	11⎱	Fokker DVII	Habourdin	DF
	2/Lt A B Radford	88	1⎰			
1030	Capt C W Cudemore	64	9	Fokker DVII	S Cambrai	OOC
1030	Capt R L Manuel &	2AFC	12⎱	Albatros C	La Bassée-Bethune	OOC
	Lt F R Smith	2AFC	9⎰			
1030	Lt G R Hicks	74	6	SS DIV	E Armentières	OOC
1030	Major K L Caldwell	74	24	SS DIV	E Armentières	OOC
1040	2/Lt H C Knotts	17US	5	Fokker DVII	Loupez Mill	D
1040	2/Lt H Burdick	17US	2	Fokker DVII	NW Havrincourt	D
1040	2/Lt H C Knotts	17US	6	Fokker DVII	NW Havrincourt	D
1040	1/Lt W T Clements	17US	2	Fokker DVII	NW Loupez Mill	D
1040	1/Lt J F Campbell	17US	3	Fokker DVII	NW Havrincourt	OOC
1045	2/Lt H C Knotts	17US	7	Fokker DVII	NW Havrincourt	DF
1045	Lt G R Hicks &	74	7⎱	Rumpler C	Capingham	D
	Capt B Roxburgh-Smith	74	16⎰			
1050	2/Lt A J Schneider	17US	1	Fokker DVII	Havrincourt	OOC
1350	2/Lt S W Highwood	84	10	Balloon	Cambrai	DF
1350	2/Lt S W Highwood	84	11	Balloon	Cambrai	DF
1350	2/Lt F R Christiani	84	3	Balloon	Cambrai	DF
1350	Capt C F Falkenberg	84	15	Balloon	Cambrai	DF
1440	Capt E Swale	210	13	Fokker DVII	St Pierre Capelle	D
1440	Lt W S Jenkins	210	9	Fokker DVII	Schooze-Keyem	D
1440	Lt G A Welsh	210	2	Fokker DVII	NE Nieuport	OOC
1440	Lt K R Unger	210	7	Fokker DVII	S St Pierre Capelle	OOC

Time	Name	Sqn	Score	Aircraft	Location	Result
1440	Lt P Boulton	210	3	Fokker DVII	S St Pierre Capelle	OOC
1440	Lt C F Pineau	210	4	Fokker DVII	N St Pierre Capelle	D
1445	Lt C F Pineau	210	5	Fokker DVII	SE Nieuport	OOC
1445	Capt C P Brown	213	9	Fokker DVII	Couckelaere	D
1445	Lt G S Hodson	213	6	Fokker DVII	SW Thorout	OOC
1450	Capt C P Brown	213	10	Fokker DVII	SW Thorout	D
1455	Lt G S Hodson	213	7	Fokker DVII	W Mitswaere	D
1600	Lt T C Traill & Lt R Gordon-Bennett	20, 20	5, 4	Fokker DVII	W Busigny	OOC
1600	Capt G H Hooper & Lt H L Edwards	20, 20	4, 15	Fokker DVII	E St Quentin	D
1610	Lt G E Randall & Lt J Hackett	20, 20	6, 1	Fokker DVII	S Clery	D
1610	Lt G E Randall & Lt J Hackett	20, 20	7, 2	Fokker DVII	S Clery	OOC
1700	Lt L C Rowney & Lt W U Tyrrell	22, 22	1, 4	Fokker DVII	Masnières-Crevecoeur	D
1700	Lt L C Rowney & Lt W U Tyrrell	22, 22	2, 5	Fokker DVII	Masnières-Crevecoeur	OOC
1700	Capt S F H Thompson & Sgt R M Fletcher	22, 22	29, 26	Fokker DVII	Cambrai	OOC
1700	Lt C W M Thompson & Lt G McCormack	22, 22	8, 8	Fokker DVII	Cambrai	OOC
1705	Capt A A Callander	32	7	Fokker DVII	Cambrai	D
1705	Capt A A Callander	32	8	Fokker DVII	Cambrai	OOC
1705	Lt C Wilderspin	32	1	Fokker DVII	Cambrai	OOC
1705	Lt R W Farquhar	32	1	Fokker DVII	N Cambrai	OOC
1710	Lt H R Carson	32	2	Fokker DVII	N Cambrai	OOC
1710	Lt G E B Lawson	32	4	Fokker DVII	N Cambrai	OOC
1715	2/Lt R Champion & Sgt R H Favell	18, 18	2, 1	Fokker DVII	Marquion	DF
1715	2/Lt R Champion & Sgt R H Favell	18, 18	3, 2	Fokker DVII	Marquion	DF
1720	Capt R King	4AFC	18	2-seater	E Ploegsteert	D
1730	Lt D S Ingalls & Lt G S Hodson	213, 213	6, 8	Rumpler C	St Pierre Capelle	DF
1750	Capt W E Shields	41	17	Fokker DVII	W Comines	D
1800	2/Lt H C Telfer	41	1	Fokker DVII	NW Comines	OOC
1800	Capt H P Chubb	56	3	Fokker DVII	E Noyelles	OOC
1810	Capt D H M Carberry & Lt J B V Clements	59	5	Halb C	Lateau Wood	D
1815	Lt L Franks	2AFC	1	Fokker DVII	E Sequedin	D
1815	Lt F C M Mills	2AFC	4	Fokker DVII	Habourdin	OOC
1820	Lt F R Smith	2AFC	10	Fokker DVII	S Capinghem	D
1820	Lt F L Roberts	2AFC	1	Fokker DVII	Habourdin	OOC
1820	Capt E L Simonsen	2AFC	1	Fokker DVII	Habourdin	OOC
1820	Capt E L Simonsen	2AFC	2	Pfalz DXII	S Habourdin	D
1820	Lt J J Wellwood	2AFC	5	Pfalz DXII	NW Habourdin	DF
1830	Lt H J Welch	80	3	Fokker DVII	St Quentin	OOC
1835	Capt A T Cole	2AFC	9	Pfalz DIII	Habourdin-Perenchies	D
1845	Lt W B Craig	204	8	Fokker DVII	Dixmuide	DF
1850	Lt C P Allen	204	4	Fokker DVII	Pervyse	OOC
1850	Lt P F Cormack	204	2	Fokker DVII	NE Dixmuide	OOC
1850	Capt T W Nash	204	6	Fokker DVII	Pervyse	D
1850	Capt T W Nash	204	7	Fokker DVII	Pervyse	OOC
	2/Lt P S Manley & Sgt G F Hines	62, 62	4, 4	Fokker DVII	E Cambrai	DF
	2/Lt F S Manley & Sgt G F Hines	62, 62	5, 5	Fokker DVII	E Cambrai	DF
	Lt L W Hudson & 2/Lt A W Palmer	62, 62	2, 1	Fokker DVII	E Cambrai	OOC
	Capt W E Staton & 2/Lt L E Mitchell	62, 62	25, 7	Fokker DVII	E Cambrai	OOC

25 September 1918

Time	Name	Unit	Score	Aircraft	Location	Result
1740	Capt C W Cudemore,	64	10			
	2/Lt T Bullough,	64	1			
	Lt A H S Youll,	64	1	Hannover C	Bourlon	OOC
	Lt A G Donald,	64	4			
	Lt G W Graham &	64	1			
	2/Lt R B Francis	64	1			
1745	Lt W E Gray	213	5	Fokker DVII	W Thorout	OOC
1750	Capt W E G Mann	208	12	Halb C	Gouy	DF
1750	Lt Bayly	208	1	Halb C	Gouy	OOC
1755	LT J W Warner	85	7	Fokker DVII	Urvillers	D
1810	Lt F G Gibbons &	22	13	Fokker DVII	Bourlon Wood-Cambrai	D
	2/Lt J A Oliver	22	2			
1810	Lt C W M Thompson &	22	9	Fokker DVII	Bourlon Wood-Cambrai	OOC
	Lt L R James	22	1			
1815	Capt J R Webb &	25	1	Fokker DVII	Bohain	OOC
	2/Lt W A Hall	25	1			
1815	Capt G H Hooper &	20	5	Fokker DVII	NE St Quentin	D
	Lt H L Edwards	20	16			
1015	Capt G H Hooper &	20	6	Fokker DVII	NE St Quentin	DF
	Lt H L Edwards	20	17			
1820	Lt T C Traill &	20	6	Fokker DVII	NE St Quentin	DF
	Lt R Gordon-Bennett	20	5			
1820	Lt F G Harlock &	20	5	Fokker DVII	Magny	D
	Lt A S Draisey	20	5			
1820	Capt G H Hooper &	20	7	Fokker DVII	E Bellenglise	D
	Lt H L Edwards	20	18			
1821	Lt F G Harlock &	20	6	Fokker DVII	Lehaucourt	D
	Lt A S Draisey	20	6			
1825	2/Lt J Locksedge &	25	1	Fokker DVII	Ponchaux	OOC
	Sgt H W J Roach	25	1			
1825	2/Lt C M Allen &	25	1	Fokker DVII	Ponchaux	D
	Sgt W E Smith	25	2			
1830	Lt M McCall &	20	4	Fokker DVII	Estrées	DF
	Lt C G Boothroyd	20	6			
1830	S/Lt S L Walters	20	3	Fokker DVII	St Quentin	OOC
	Lt T Kirkpatrick	20	3			
1830	Major G H Bowman	41	30	Rumpler C	NE Ypres	DF
1835	Lt C J Sims	213	4	Fokker DVII	SW Ostende	D
1835	Lt C J Sims	213	5	Fokker DVII	SW Ostende	D
2300	Lt T R Bloomfield	151	1	AEG G	Montenescourt	D

26 September 1918

Time	Name	Unit	Score	Aircraft	Location	Result
1045	2/Lt G H Clappison	204	2	Fokker DVII	Blankenbergh	OOC
1045	2/Lt F R Brown	204	2	Fokker DVII	Blankenbergh	OOC
1045	Lt N Smith	204	4	Fokker DVII	NE Ostende	D
1050	Lt B E Barnum	204	4	Fokker DVII	Blankenbergh	OOC
1050	Capt C R R Hickey	204	20	Fokker DVII	Blankenbergh	D
1050	2/Lt S E Mathey	204	1	Fokker DVII	Blankenbergh	OOC
1120	Major C J W Darwin	87	5	LVG C	Latteau Wood	D
1125	2/Lt R C Mitten	65	1	Rumpler C	Clemkerke	OOC
1130	2/Lt W S Rycroft &	48	1	Fokker DVII	Menin	D
	2/Lt H L Ward	48	1			
1130	Capt B Roxburgh-Smith	74	17	Fokker DVII	SE Warneton	DF
1300	Lt C W H Thompson &	22	10	Fokker DVII	Arras-Cambrai Road	D
	Lt W U Tyrrell	22	4			
1300	Lt C W H Thompson &	22	11	Fokker DVII	Arras-Cambrai Road	D
	Lt W U Tyrrell	22	5			
1300	Capt J D Breakey	203	7	Fokker DVII	SW Lieu St Amand	DF
1305	Major R Collishaw	203	58	Fokker DVII	Lieu St Amand	D
1315	2/Lt W H Coghill	203	3	Fokker DVII	E Combles	D
1315	Lt F S J Britnell	203	8	Fokker DVII	E Combles	DF
1325	1/Lt F E Kindley	148US	10	Fokker DVII	E Bourlon Wood	D
1325	1/Lt J O Creech	148US	6	Fokker DVII	E Bourlon Wood	D
1325	1/Lt O A Ralston	148US	4	Fokker DVII	E Bourlon Wood	D
1330	1/Lt L T Wyly	148US	4	Fokker DVII	Epinoy	OOC
1335	Major R Collishaw	203	59	Fokker DVII	E Lieu St Amand	D

1510	Lt G R Hicks &	74	7⎫	DFW C	SE Armentières	D
	Capt B Roxburgh-Smith	74	18⎭			
1745	Lt G W Hales	80	1	Fokker DVII	Lehaucourt	OOC
1745	Lt R E Thompson	80	1	Fokker DVII	Lehaucourt	OOC
1815	Capt D R MacLaren	46	51	Fokker DVII	Havrincourt	D
1818	Capt A Newman &	57	4⎫	Fokker DVII	SE Cambrai	DF
	Lt E G Pernet	57	1⎭			
1825	Lt M C Howell	208	4	Fokker DVII	N St Quentin	OOC
1840	Capt W E G Mann	208	13	Fokker DVII	SE St Quentin	OOC

27 September 1918

0715	Lt L H Ray	19	4	Fokker DrI	Haynecourt	D
0715	Lt L H Ray	19	5	Fokker DrI	Haynecourt	OOC
0720	Lt L H Ray	19	6	Fokker DrI	Haynecourt	OOC
0720	Lt L H Ray	19	7	Balloon	Haynecourt	DF
0720	Capt S F H Thompson &	22	30⎫	Halb C	N Noyelles	D
	2/Lt C J Tolman	22	10⎭			
0725	Capt R A Del Haye &	19	7⎫	Pfalz DIII	Haynecourt	D
	Lt C M Moore	19	1⎭			
0725	Lt G R Riley	3	10	Balloon		DF
0725	Lt G R Riley	3	11	Balloon		DF
0730	Lt F G Gibbons &	22	14⎫	Fokker DVII	Sensee Canal-Cambrai	OOC
	Sgt G Shannon	22	5⎭			
0730	Lt C W M Thompson &	22	12⎫			
	Lt L R James	22	2⎪	Fokker DVII	Oisy-le-Verger	D
	Lt Lt L C Rowney &	22	3⎪			
	Lt W U Tyrrell	22	6⎭			
0730	Lt J R Drummond &	22	1⎫	Fokker DVII	Oisy-le-Verger	OOC
	2/Lt C H Wilcox	22	1⎭			
0735	Lt J A Aldridge	19	6	Fokker DVII	NW Cambrai	OOC
0755	Lt G F Anderson &	88	4⎫	Fokker DVII	Lambersart	OOC
	2/Lt T S Chiltern	88	5⎭			
0800	Capt H P Chubb	56	4	Fokker DVII	Cambrai	D
0800	Lt C B Stenning	56	3	Fokker DVII	Cambrai	D
0800	Lt J A Pouchot	56	1	Fokker DVII	Cambrai	D
0800	Lt W E Clarkson	56	1	Fokker DVII	Cambrai	OOC
0800	Lt I W Awde	56	1	Fokker DVII	Cambrai	OOC
0805	2/Lt W H Maxted	3	2	LVG C		DF
0810	2/Lt W H Maxted	3	3	LVG C		D
0820	Lt G R Riley &	3	12⎫	Balloon		DF
	2/Lt W H Maxted	3	4⎭			
0845	Lt C W Wareing	29	7	Balloon	Moorslede	D
0850	Capt A W B Proctor	84	47	Balloon	Crevecoeur	DF
0855	Lt F Woolley	79	1	Albatros C	Armentières	D
0915	Lt B H Mooney	1	3	Fokker DVII	Bertry	DF
0915	Lt C W Anning	1	2	Fokker DVII	Bevillers	OOC
0920	1/Lt F E Kindley	148US	11	Halb C	Marcoing	D
0925	Capt C F King,	43	20⎫	Fokker DVII	Cambrai	OOC
	Lt C C Banks	43	10⎭			
0930	Lt R S Johnston	43	1	Fokker DVII	SE Cambrai	OOC
0930	2/Lt G S Smith	40	2	Fokker DVII	Oisy-le-Verger	OOC
0940	Capt G E B Lawson	32	5	Fokker DVII	Emerchicourt	DF
0940	Capt G E B Lawson	32	6	Fokker DVII	Emerchicourt	D
0940	Lt B Rogers	32	5	Fokker DVII	Emerchicourt	D
0940	Lt R E L McBean	32	3	Fokker DVII	Emerchicourt	OOC
0940	Lt M A Tancock	32	2	Fokker DVII	Emerchicourt	OOC
0940	Lt C F Cawley	32	1	Fokker DVII	Emerchicourt	OOC
0945	Lt C M Allen &	27	2⎫	Fokker DVII	Emerchicourt	DF
	2/Lt C E Robinson	27	1⎭			
0955	1/Lt E W Springs &	148US	16⎫	Halb C	Fontaine-Notre Dame	D
	1/Lt H R Clay	148US	8⎭			
1030	Lt F G Harlock &	20	7⎫	Fokker DVII	NE Marcy	D
	Lt A S Draisey	20	7⎭			
1030	Lt A T Iaccaci &	20	16⎫	Fokker DVII	Fontaine-Notre Dame	D
	Sgt A Newland	20	20⎭			
1030	Lt A T Iaccaci &	20	17⎫	Fokker DVII	N Bernart	OOC
	Sgt A Newland	20	21⎭			

Time	Pilot	Sqn	Score	Aircraft	Location	Result
1030	Lt M McCall &	20	5⎱	Fokker DVII	W Bernot	D
	Lt C G Boothroyd	20	7⎰			
1120	Lt L N Hollinghurst	87	9	Fokker DVII	Rumilly	OOC
1130	Capt G B Gates	201	15	Balloon		DF
1150	Capt M A Newnham	65	9	Fokker DVII	Ghistelles	D
1150	Lt G Richardson	65	1	Fokker DVII	Ghistelles	
1150	Lt F Edsted	65	3	Fokker DVII	Ghistelles	OOC
1150	Lt J Reid	65	1	Fokker DVII	Ghistelles	OOC
1240	Capt F McQuistan	19	7	Pfalz DIII	E Aubigny	OOC
1250	Capt R A Del Haye	19	8	Pfalz DIII	Aubigny	OOC
1410	Capt O M Baldwin	73	16	LVG C	N Graincourt	DF
1410	Capt E C Johnston &	88	17⎱	Fokker DVII	Abancourt	OOC
	2/Lt H R Goss	88	3⎰			
1720	Lt F L Hale	32	5	Fokker DVII	Cambrai	D
1720	Lt F L Hale	32	6	Fokker DVII	Cambrai	OOC
1720	Lt F L Hale	32	7	Fokker DVII	Cambrai	OOC
1735	1/Lt J F Campbell	17US	4	Fokker DVII		OOC
1745	Lt K R Unger	210	8	Halb C	SE Nieuport	D
1800	Patrol	11	—	Fokker DVII	SE Cambrai	D
1800	Capt V S Bennett	54	2	Fokker DVII	SE Bourlon Wood	D
1800	2/Lt F de N Hyde &	18	2⎱	Fokker DVII	Cambrai	OOC
	2/Lt L H Eyres	18	2⎰			
1800	Lt F L Harding &	57	1⎱			
	2/Lt I Woodhouse	57	1⎟	Fokker DVII	Cambrai	OOC
	Lt F O Thornton &	57	4⎟			
	2/Lt F C Craig	57	5⎰			
1815	Capt E C Hoy	29	13	Fokker DVII	Passchendaele	D
1940	Lt C F Lane &	18	1⎱	Fokker DVII	Wasnes-au-Bac	OOC
	2/Lt C Thompson	18	1⎰			
	Lt R E Britton &	13	2⎱	Fokker DVII		OOC
	2/Lt B Hickman	13	2⎰			

28 September 1918

Time	Pilot	Sqn	Score	Aircraft	Location	Result
0700	Capt D H M Carberry &	59	5⎱	Halb C	La Vacquerie valley	D
	Lt Clements	59	3⎰			
0825	Capt A Beck	60	5	LVG C	Cambrai	D
0830	Lt W Sidebottom	203	8	Fokker DVII	Hem-Lenglet	OOC
1145	Lt O A P Heron	70	4	Fokker DVII	NE Passchendaele	D
1150	Capt W M Carlaw	70	7	LVG C	NE Gheluwe	D
1230	Capt A J B Tonks	204	13	Fokker DVII	Werckem	D
1230	Capt A J B Tonks	204	14	Fokker DVII	Werckem	OOC
1230	Capt C R R Hickey	204	22	Fokker DVII	NW Werckem	D
1235	Capt R B Bannerman	79	12	Fokker DVII	SW Comines	D
1255	Lt F W Gillett	79	9	Albatros C	Bousbecque	D
1315	Lt M G Burger	54	4	Fokker DVII	NW Raillencourt	D
1315	Capt F I Lord	79	11	Pfalz DIII	Werckem	D
1445	Capt F Cunninghame &	48	2⎱	Fokker DVII	SE Roulers	D
	Lt R A Brunton	48	2⎰			
1610	Lt G R Riley	3	12	Fokker DVII		OOC
1625	2/Lt S M Brown	29	3	Fokker DVII	Menin	D
1710	Lt C G Ross	29	13	Fokker DVII	S Menin	DF
1725	Lt F Boulton	210	4	Fokker DVII	E Staden	D
1730	Lt C G Ross	29	14	Fokker DVII	Menin-Ghelguvelt Road	D
1745	1/Lt G A Vaughn	17US	10	LVG C		D
1745	2/Lt H Burdick	17US	3	LVG C		DF
1745	Lt K R Unger	210	9	Fokker DVII	NE Dixmuide	D
1745	Lt G A Welsh	210	3	Fokker DVII	SE Nieuport	OOC
1750	Lt J H McNeaney	79	2	Fokker DVII	Passchendaele	D
1750	Lt F W Gillett	79	9	Fokker DVII	SE Nieuport	D
1750	Lt G A Welsh	210	4	Fokker DVII	SE Nieuport	D
1750	Lt H D MacLaren &	218	1⎱	Fokker DrI	Cortemarck	D
	Sgt G Barlow	218	1⎰			
1750	Lt H D MacLaren &	218	2⎱	Fokker DrI	Cortemarck	OOC
	Sgt G Barlow	218	2⎰			
1750	Lt E R Brewer USMC &	218	1⎱	Fokker DrI	Cortemarck	OOC
	Sgt Wershimer USMC	218	1⎰			
1755	Lt J H McNeaney	79	3	Fokker DVII	Passchendaele	OOC

1755	Lt T H Newsome &	22	4⎱			
	Lt R S E Walshe	22	1⎰	Pfalz DXII	E Bugnicourt	D
1810	2/Lt H Burdick	17US	4	Fokker DVII	Cambrai	D

29 September 1918

0730	Capt J D Breakey	203	6	LVG C	Hem	D
0730	Lt L N Hollinghurst	87	10	Fokker DVII	Estourmel	OOC
0755	Lt W S Jenkins	210	10	Fokker DVII	W Lichtervelde	D
0757	Lt G W Hopkins	210	1	Fokker DVII	N Wijnendaele Wood	DF
0800	Lt G A Welsh	210	5	Fokker DVII	N Wijnendaele Wood	D
0800	Lt C W Payton	210	9	Fokker DVII	Wijnendaele Wood	D
0800	Capt E Swale	210	14	Fokker DVII	Cortemarck	D
0800	Lt A Buchanan	210	6	Fokker DVII	Wijnendaele Wood	D
0800	Lt P Boulton	210	5	Fokker DVII	Wijnendaele Wood	OOC
0805	Lt A Buchanan	210	7	Fokker DVII	Wijnendaele Wood	OOC
0810	2/Lt H H Palmer &	211	1⎱	Fokker DVII	Roulers	D
	2/Lt W C Snowden	211	1⎰			
0845	Lt D E Cameron	1	2	Fokker DVII	Bohain	OOC
0845	Lt D M Bisset	1	1	Fokker DVII	Bohain	OOC
0845	2/Lt T Peacock &	11	1⎱	Fokker DVII	SE Cambrai	OOC
	2/Lt G W A Kelly	11	1⎰			
0845	2/Lt T Peacock &	11	2⎱	Fokker DVII	SE Cambrai	D
	2/Lt G W A Kelly	11	2⎰			
0845	Capt J R Webb &	27	2⎱			
	2/Lt W A Hall	57	2⎰	Fokker DVII	Busigny	D
	2/Lt T A Dickinson &	57	1⎱			
	2/Lt W J Dimest	57	1⎰			
0845	Patrol	27	—	Fokker DVII	Busigny	OOC
0935	Lt J H Sprott &	218	1⎱	Fokker DVII	Lichtervelde	OOC
	2/Lt J S Lewis	218	1⎰			
0940	Lt F P Mulcahy USMC	218	1⎱	Fokker DVII	Cortemarck	OOC
	Cpl T McCullough USMC	218	1⎰			
0940	Capt C S Iron &	218	1⎱	Fokker DrI	Thorout	OOC
	2/Lt C Ford	218	1⎰			
0950	Lt J G Coots	84	1	Balloon	N Villers-Outreaux	DF
0955	Lt E G Davies	29	2	Balloon	SE Comines	DF
1000	Lt C W Wareing	29	8	Balloon	SE Armentières	DF
1000	Lt E O Amm	29	5	Balloon	E Armentières	DF
1010	Lt F W Gillett	79	10	Fokker DVII	W Roulers	DF
1010	2/Lt D C Rees &	84	4⎱	Balloon	Beaurevoir	DF
	2/Lt S W Highwood	84	12⎰			
1010	Lt F R Christiani	84	4	Balloon	Villers-Outreaux	DF
1011	Lt E R W Miller	84	2	Balloon	N Montbrehain	DF
1015	Capt H A Whistler	80	20	Fokker DVII	N Fontain	D
1015	Capt A H Orlebar	43	9	Fokker DVII	Remaucourt	OOC
1020	Capt G H Hooper &	20	8⎱	Fokker DVII	N St Quentin	OOC
	Lt H L Edwards	20	19⎰			
1025	Capt G H Hooper &	20	9⎱	Fokker DVII	N St Quentin	D
	Lt H L Edwards	20	20⎰			
1025	Capt G H Hooper &	20	10⎱	Fokker DVII	N St Quentin	D
	Lt H L Edwards	20	21⎰			
1025	Lt T C Traill &	20	7⎱	Fokker DVII	N St Quentin	D
	Capt L W Burbridge	20	6⎰			
1030	2/Lt S L Walters &	20	4⎱	Fokker DVII	Levergies	D
	Lt T Kirkpatrick	20	4⎰			
1030	Lt M McCall &	20	6⎱	Fokker DVII	Lihaucourt	D
	2/Lt C G Boothroyd	20	6⎰			
1030	Capt C F Falkenberg	84	16	Fokker DVII	Beaurevoir	D
1030	Capt H A Whistler	80	21	Fokker DVII	Joncourt	D
1115	Capt C W Cudemore	64	11	Fokker DVII	NW Cambrai	D
1115	Capt C W Cudemore	64	12	Fokker DVII	NW Cambrai	OOC
1115	2/Lt L W Rabe	148US	1	Fokker DVII	W Ramillies	DF
1130	Lt C T MacLean	148US	3	Fokker DVII	N Cambrai-Ramillies	D
1130	Lt R M Attwater	70	1	Fokker DVII	E Roulers	D
1130	Lt O S Clefsted	70	1	Fokker DVII	SE Roulers	OOC
1130	Lt J H Latchford &	25	2⎱	Fokker DVII	N Cambrai	DF
	Sgt A H Mabey	25	2⎰			

1140	Lt K B Watson	70	4	Fokker DVII	Oostnieuwkerke	D
1145	Lt E J Stephens	41	7	Fokker DVII	NE Roulers	D
1145	Lt O J Rose	92	8	Fokker DVII	E Beaurevoir	DF
1150	Lt O J Rose	92	9	Halb C	Bellicourt	D
1200	Capt C P Brown	213	11	Fokker DVII	E Roulers	OOC
1220	2/Lt C H Dickens &	211	1 ⎫	Fokker DVII	Dadizeele	D
	2/Lt A M Adam	211	1 ⎭			
1230	Capt J B White	208	10	Fokker DVII	N Lesdins	D
1230	Lt R C D'A Gifford	208	5	Fokker DVII	Lesdins	OOC
1230	2/Lt H J Botterill	208	1	Fokker DVII	Lesdins	OOC
1230	2/Lt H J Philip	208	1	Fokker DVII	Lesdins	OOC
1240	Capt W E Shields	41	18	Balloon	SE Comines	D
1340	2/Lt G S Smith,	40	3 ⎫			
	Lt Field &	40	1 ⎬	Balloon	NE Cambrai	DF
	Cpt R Chidlaw-Roberts	40	10 ⎭			
1340	Lt R L M Barbour &	205	4 ⎫	Fokker DVII	Montbrehain	D
	Capt M F M Wright	205	1 ⎭			
1410	Lt C W Wareing	29	9	Balloon	E Comines	DF
1640	Capt D R MacLaren &	46	52 ⎫	Fokker DVII	Le Cateau	OOC
	Lt C H Sawyer	46	5 ⎭			
1640	Capt C W Odell	46	7	Fokker DVII	Le Cateau	OOC
1700	Capt G B Gates	201	16	Balloon	Bantouzelle	DF
1740	Capt R B Bannerman	79	13	Hannover C	Estaires	D
	Capt G T Richardson &	62	1 ⎫	Fokker DVII		D
	2/Lt I P Aitken	62	1 ⎭			
	Capt G T Richardson &	62	2 ⎫	Fokker DVII		D
	2/Lt I P Aitken	62	2 ⎭			
	2/Lt N J Nock &	10	1 ⎫	Fokker DVII		DF
	2/Lt W E Grainger	10	1 ⎭			

APPENDIX II

French Air Service Victory Claims September 1918

1 September 1918

Time	Pilot/Crew	Unit	Vic No	E/A	Location
1840	S/Lt L Bourjade &	152	17 ⎫	Balloon	St Arcy
	S/Lt E Maunoury	152	6 ⎭		
	Sgt C Veil	150	2	EA	Flavy-le-Meldeux
	Lt H Stickney &	150	1 ⎫	EA	Flavy-le-Meldeux
	Sgt L Bagarry	150	1 ⎭		

2 September 1918

0900	Lt H Dencausse	90	2	Balloon	Geline
0930	Lt M Ambrogi,	90	9 ⎫		
	Adj M Bizot &	90	6 ⎬	Balloon	Juvelize
	Adj J Pezon	90	3 ⎭		
1030	Adj Dutrey &	20	1 ⎫	Fokker DVII	La Neuvillette
	Sgt Latapie	20	2 ⎭		
1045	Lt H Hay de Slade	159	14	EA	W Terny-Sorny
1500	Adj-Chef Thevenin &	111	1 ⎫		
	Adj Thomas	111	1 ⎪		
	Adj Loustalot &	111	1 ⎬	EA	Baslieux-les-Fismes
	Lt Oise	111	1 ⎪		
	2/Lt de Carheil &	111	1 ⎪		
	Lt Hegon	111	1 ⎭		
1535	MdL Galland &	2	1 ⎫	Fokker DVII	Baslieux-les-Fismes
	Lt Heuzeel	2	1 ⎭		

Time	Name	Unit	No.	Type	Location
1800	Sgt P Rozes	99	1	EA	Sorny
	Adj J Lucas	97	1	Balloon	
	Lt F Bonneton	69	4	Balloon	Beaurieux-Pontavert
	Lt Clavel &	20	1 ⎫	Fokker DVII	N La Neuvillette
	Lt Puisieux	20	1 ⎭		
	Patrol	GC14	—	DFW C	
	MdL Verges &	34	1 ⎫	EA	Coucy-la-Ville
	Lt Barat	34	1 ⎭		
	Adj P Bentejac &	124	2 ⎫	Balloon	Manre
	Sgt E Grillot	124	2 ⎭		
	Lt H Berge &	124	2 ⎫	Balloon	Bois de la Taille
	Sgt M Caton	124	1 ⎭		
	Adj E Pillon	98	4	Scout	Servon
	S/Lt H Pretre,	91	2 ⎫		
	MdL de Caso &	91	1 ⎬	EA	Crécy-au-Mont
	Cpl Leblanc	91	1 ⎭		
	Sgt P Montange	155	3	2-seater	Vauxillon
	Sgt P Montange	155	4	Balloon	Bauris
	72 Balloon Cié AA fire		POW	Fokker DVII	Prosnes
	Flak		POW	Fokker DVII	Dommartin-la-Planchette
1830	Patrol	38	P	EA	Reservoir
	Lt F Bonneton	69	P	Fokker DVII	Beaurieux-Pontavert
	Adj A Cousin	163	P	2-seater	Tahure
	Patrol	163	P	Balloon	Bouconville
	Patrol	124	P	Balloon	Bouconville

3 September 1918

Time	Name	Unit	No.	Type	Location
0830	MdL A de Freslon	152	2	Balloon	Concevreux
0930	Lt P Schneider	15	1	Balloon	N Fismes
1625	Lt G Madon	38	41	Scout	N Fismes
1730	Adj J Pezon	90	4	Balloon	Goin
	MdL A Courtieu	96	2	2-seater	
	Sgt Maillon &	96	1 ⎫	EA	
	Sgt H Hutreau	96	1 ⎭		
	Lt H Pretre	91	3	EA	Noyon
	Adj F Guerrier,	77	4 ⎫		
	Mdl J Thevenod,	77	1 ⎪	Balloon	
	Cpl Maria &	77	1 ⎬		
	Brig Coquelin	77	1 ⎭		
	Adj F Guerrier	77	5	Balloon	
1630	Lt G Madon	38	P	Scout	N Fismes
1705	Patrol	31	P	Fokker DVII	Muizon
	Patrol	GC14	P	EA	
	Patrol	203	P	2-seater	

4 September 1918

Time	Name	Unit	No.	Type	Location
0645	S/Lt L Bourjade,	152	17 ⎫		
	S/Lt E Maunoury &	152	6 ⎬	Balloon	Pont Arcy
	Cpl E Manson	152	1 ⎭		
1135	Adj A Berthelot,	15	8 ⎫		
	Sgt Fourcade &	15	1 ⎬	EA	
	Sgt Barat	15	1 ⎭		
1145	Adj J Jacquot	100	1	EA	Breuil-sur-Vesles
1200	Lt R Volmeraude	38	2	2-seater	W Lavannes
1815	S/Lt A Coadou,	88	3 ⎫		
	Adj F Delzenne &	88	4 ⎬	EA	Juvigny
	Adj E Pinot	84	1 ⎭		
	Capt J de Luppe	83	2 ⎫	Balloon	Filain
	S/Lt M Devilder	83	2 ⎭		
0730	Sgt C Couderc	152	P	Balloon	Concevreux
1200	Sgt J Fabre	38	P	EA	Grandelain

5 September 1918

Time	Name	Unit	No.	Type	Location
1545	S/Lt Haegelen,	100	14 ⎫		
	Brig Guerin &	100	2 ⎬	Balloon	Boult-sur-Suippe
	Sgt P Peuch	100	1 ⎭		

	Patrol	GC14	P	EA	
	Sgt E Grillot	124	P	EA	Monts
	Patrol	GC21	P	EA	Monts
	Patrol	GC21	P	EA	Monts

6 September 1918

0830	Sgt J Connelly &	163	5 ⎫	Fokker DVII	Navarin
	MdL J Morvan	163	1 ⎭		
1215	Sgt G Florentin	90	1	EA	Bayon
1930	Adj E Corso &	124	1 ⎫	EA	
	Adj P Bentejac	124	3 ⎭		W Dontrien
	Sgt Rouzand &	18	1 ⎫		
	Sol Martin	18	1 ⎭	Scout	
	FTL/POW			2-seater	Coucy-le-Château

7 September 1918

0730	S/Lt L Austin	92	1	Balloon	N Beaurieux
	S/Lt M Coiffard,	154	25 ⎫		
	S/Lt T Condemine &	154	2 ⎬	Balloon	
	Sgt C Peillard	154	1 ⎭		
	S/Lt L Douillet &	124	4 ⎫	Fokker DVII	W Dontrien
	Sgt M Caton	124	2 ⎭		

10 September 1918

	Adj A Petit-Delchet	57	P	EA	

12 September 1918

	1/Lt Nelson &	131	1 ⎫	Balloon	
	1/Lt Newell	131	1 ⎭		

13 September 1918

1720	S/Lt A Martenot,	94	6 ⎫		
	Lt A Laganne &	94	2 ⎬	Fokker DVII	Vieville-en-Haye
	Lt A Carbonel	94	1 ⎭		
1750	Sgt J Pustienne &	155	1 ⎫	EA	Haumont
	Cpl Charties	155	1 ⎭		
1750	S/Lt P Montange	155	5	EA	Chambley
	Adj J Fleury	95	P	Fokker DVII	Ancy

14 September 1918

0910	Sgt P Bourgeois	68	1	EA	Jonville
0920	Lt C Couderc	152	P	EA	Pont Arcy
1300	Patrol	154	P	Fokker DVII	Bouvancourt
1345	S/Lt M Coiffard,	154	26 ⎫		
	S/Lt T Condemine &	154	3 ⎬	Balloon	Gernicourt
	Cpl M Lisle	154	1 ⎭		
1350	S/Lt M Coiffard,	154	27 ⎫		
	S/Lt T Condemine &	154	4 ⎬	Balloon	Cormicy
	Cpl M Lisle	154	2 ⎭		
1745	S/Lt M Boyau,	77	32 ⎫		
	Cpl E Corsi &	77	1 ⎬	Balloon	Etraye
	S/Lt M Haegelen	100	15 ⎭		
	Lt J Senart	160	3	Fokker DVII	
	MdL G Halberger &	153	4 ⎫	Balloon	Goin
	MdL E Aubailly	153	1 ⎭		
	Capt A Mezergues &	131	5 ⎫		
	Asp Collin	131	1 ⎪		
	MdL Jacquot &	131	1 ⎬	EA	
	MdL Gautier	131	1 ⎭		
	1/Lt Nelson &	131	2 ⎫		
	1/Lt Newel	131	2 ⎪		
	MdL Pradel de Lamze &	131	1 ⎬	EA	
	Sgt Rayez	131	1 ⎭		

S/Lt Truchement &	131	1		
Asp Hogenville	131	1	EA	
Sgt Depuy &	131	1		
Cpl Magnenot	131	1		
Capt J Jannekeyn &	132	2	Fokker DVII	
Lt E Weissmann	132	3		
Brig Vollet &	132	1	Fokker DVII	
Sol Malacrida	132	1		
Sgt Brideland &	132	1	Fokker DVII	
Lt Pechine	132	1		
Lt A Paillard &	132	2	Fokker DVII	
Sgt Hincelin	132	1		
S/Lt Resel,	46	1		
Sol Poupougnac &	46	1	EA	
Sgt-Maj Lacassange	46	1		
Sgt Duval &	23	1	Balloon	Etraye
Sgt Bacque	23	2		
MdL G Uteau	315	4	2-seater	
S/Lt Schroeder &	95	P	2-seater	Vittonville
Sgt L Lacouture	95	P		

15 September 1918

0700	Lt M Ambrogi &	90	10	Balloon	Bourdonnay
	Adj C Mace	90	1		
0930	MdL M Sainz	94	1	Balloon	Goin
1050	Adj H Garaud	38	P	2-seater	Hermonville
1100	Lt J Lemarie &	90	3	EA	Raon l'Etape
	Lt H de Ginestet	90	1		
1130	Adj J Pezon	90	5	Balloon	Avricourt
1230	S/Lt M Boyau,	77	33		
	Lt H Decoin,	77	3	Balloon	Château-Vhehery
	S/Lt Y Barbaza &	77	3		
	Adj-Chef E Strohl	77	1		
1230	S/Lt M Coiffard,	154	28		
	S/Lt T Condemine &	154	5	Balloon	Brimont
	Adj J Ehrlich	154	16		
1233	S/Lt M Coiffard,	154	29		
	S/Lt T Condemine &	154	6	Balloon	Cormicy
	Adj J Ehrlich	154	17		
1235	S/Lt M Coiffard,	154	30		
	S/Lt T Condemine &	154	7	Balloon	Gernicourt
	Adj J Ehrlich	154	18		
1300	Cpl D Chollet	92	1	2-seater	N Vieil Arcy
1520	S/Lt M Haegelen &	100	16	Balloon	Chatelet-Chehery
	Sgt Douzant	100	1		
1630	Sgt G Courcelle	97	2	Fokker DVII	Lorry
1630	Sgt W York	97	1	Fokker DVII	Preny
1640	Sgt S Jacob	163	2	EA	N Servon
1730	S/Lt L Bourjade &	152	18	Balloon	Ailles
	S/Lt E Maunoury	152	7		
1735	S/Lt M Boyau,	154	34		
	Lt Decoin	77	4	Balloon	Brieulles
	S/Lt Y Barbaza &	77	4		
	Adj-Chef Strohl	77	2		
1735	S/Lt L Bourjade &	152	19	Balloon	Hurtebise
	S/Lt E Maunoury	152	8		
1735	S/Lt M Haegelen &	100	17	Balloon	Brieulles
	Sgt P Peuch	100	2		
1850	Lt M Nogues	57	11	Balloon	Bois de Buttes
1855	Lt M Nogues	57	12	Balloon	Craonne
	Lt Jallois &	19	1		
	Lt Delagoutte	19	1		
	Lt Canivet &	19	1	Fokker DVII	Saint Thierry
	Lt Desmaroux	19	2		
	Sgt Hall &	19	1		
	S/Lt Serre	19	1		

	Name	Unit	Score	Aircraft	Location
	Lt Jallois &	19	2		
	Lt Delagoutte	19	2		
	Lt Canivet &	19	2	Fokker DVII	Saint Thierry
	Lt Desmaroux	19	3		
	Sgt Hall &	19	2		
	S/Lt Serre	19	2		
	Patrol	GC14	P	EA	
	Patrol	98	P	EA	
	S/Lt G Daladier,	93	6		
	Sgt H Meyniel &	93	1	Balloon	Chambley
	Sgt E Prarond	93	1		
	S/Lt J Guertiau,	97	8		
	Adj J Lucas &	97	2	EA	Gorze
	Sgt G Courcelle	97	1		
	Escadre de Combat 2			Balloon	
	MdL J de Gaillard	95	P	EA	St Die
	Adj J Fleury	95	P	2-seater	Forêt de Mondon

16 September 1918

	Name	Unit	Score	Aircraft	Location
1030	Lt M Ambrogi,	90	11		
	Adj J Pezon &	90	6	Balloon	Cirey
	Cpl Rivière	90	1		
1117	S/Lt M Boyau,	77	35	Balloon	Marville
	Asp H Cessieux	77	1		
1200	S/Lt M Haegelen &	100	18	Balloon	Bois de Sept-Sarges
	Sgt P Peuch	100	1		
1215	S/Lt C Nuville &	57	11	2-seater	Breuil
	Adj R Vanier	57	4		
	S/Lt R Pelissier	155	6	2-seater	
	S/Lt G Daladier &	93	9	LVG C	Juvelize
	Adj P Delage	93	2		
0700	S/Lt J Casale	38	P	2-seater	Concevreux
0800	Lt J Lanez	87	P	Fokker DVII	Allemont
1615	S/Lt C Philibert	12	P	Fokker DVII	Revillon

17 September 1918

	Name	Unit	Score	Aircraft	Location
1615	S/Lt M Haegelen &	100	19	Balloon	Hannonville
	Lt C Poulin	100	1		
1619	Patrol	GC14	P	Fokker DVII	
1619	Patrol	GC14	P	Fokker DVII	
	S/Lt W Herisson &	75	10	2-seater	Soissons
	Sgt R Le Tilly	75	1		
	S/Lt W Herrisson &	75	11	Fokker DVII	Soissons
	Sgt Baralis	75	1		
	Patrol	GC23	P	EA	
	Flak			EA	
	Adj L Marot &	37	3	EA	
	Adj G Lienhard	37	2		

18 September 1918

	Name	Unit	Score	Aircraft	Location
1805	Adj J Ehrlich,	154	19		
	Adj P Petit &	154	5	Balloon	Brimont
	Sgt C Peillard	154	2		
	Asp G Bonneau	48	1	Balloon	Onville
	Adj E Regnier,	89	4		
	S/Lt V Federoff,	89	4		
	Sgt G Lasne,	89	2		
	Cpl J Havard,	89	1	Halb C	Belrupt
	Sgt A Stanley &	23	1		
	2/Lt F Luke, Jr USAS	27th	13		
	S/Lt P Gaudermen &	68	4	Halb C	Jonville
	Adj R Sinclaire	68	2		

19 September 1918

	Name	Unit	Score	Aircraft	Location
	Lt L Delrieu,	150	3		
	Sgt C Veil &	150	3	2-seater	Rezonville
	MdL P Lebigre	150	1		

20 September 1918

	Patrol	GC14	P	EA	
	Patrol	132	—	EA	

21 September 1918

	S/Lt A Cousin	163	1	EA	Tahure
	Patrol			EA	

22 September 1918

0740	Sgt L Decatoire	92	P	Balloon	Gernicourt
1004	Adj C Mace	90	2	Balloon	Geline
1007	Adj C Mace	90	3	Balloon	Juvelize
	Patrol	69	P	EA	

23 September 1918

	Lt Denis &	40	1}	EA	Mont-sans-Nom
	S/Lt Beucler	40	1}		

24 September 1918

0745	S/Lt R d'Estainville	87	2	Balloon	Bourgogne
0805	Patrol	GC12	P	Scout	Rouvroy
1800	Patrol	26	P	2-seater	Ripont
1810	Lt J Casale &	38	P}	Fokker DVII	Pevy-Prouilly
	Adj H Garaud	38	P}		
	Patrol	GC14	P	EA	
	S/Lt C Nuville &	57	12}	EA	Cernay-en-Dormois
	MdL Imhoff	57	1}		
	Patrol	67	P	EA	St Etienne-au-Temple
	Flak			Fokker DVII	
	Capt H Hay de Slade	159	15	EA	N Suippes
	Capt G Lagache,	78	2}		
	Sgt G Tscheoberle &	78	1}	2-seater	Xammes
	Sgt Le Fustec	78	1}		

25 September 1918

	Adj G Priollaud	150	3	EA	Ornes

26 September 1918

0800	Capt A de Turenne,	12	14}		
	S/Lt Herlemont &	12	2}	Balloon	Sainte Geneviève
	Sgt Maurio	12	2}		
0820	Sgt H Y Saxon &	12	2}	Balloon	N Somme-Py
	Cpl E Haller	12	2}		
0827	Lt H Barancy	164	P	Fokker DVII	Massiges
0827	Lt M Robert	164	P	Fokker DVII	Massiges
1050	Adj E Corso &	124	P}	Scout	E Sechault
	Sgt J Kamisky	124	P}		
1115	Patrol	26	P	2-seater	Grateuil
1145	Lt R Fonck	103	61	Fokker DVII	St Marie-a-Py
to	Lt R Fonck	103	62	Fokker DVII	St Soupley
1210	Lt R Fonck	103	63	Halb C	Perth-les-Hurles
1245	S/Lt M Nogues &	57	13}	Balloon	NE Somme-Py
	Cpl Beaume	57	1}		
1410	Adj A Berthelot	15	9	DFW C	N Montfaucon
1510	MdL Dequeker	163	P	2-seater	Monthois
1545	1/Lt G W Eypper USAS	98	1	2-seater	NE Bouconville
1650	Sgt J Kamisky	124	1	Balloon	Sechault
1705	Cpl F Tailler	124	P	Scout	Manre-Aure
1720	Patrol	167	P	Scout	Navarin
1745	Patrol	3	P	Scout	Auberive
1755	Sgt L Caudry	165	1	Fokker DVII	Souain
1800	Patrol	67	P	Scout	S Tahure
1800	Lt P Pendaires,	67	6}		
	Adj E Parsons &	3	6}	Scout	S Tahure
	MdL Denneulin	3	2}		

1810	Lt R Fonck	103	64	Fokker DVII	St Souplet
1820	Lt R Fonck	103	65	Fokker DVII	Souain
1845	Capt A de Turenne,	12	13⎫		
	Adj E Regnier &	89	5⎬	Scout	Ville-sur-Tourbe
	S/Lt R Schurck	91	2⎭		
	Lt R Fonck	103	66	DFW C	E Souain
	S/Lt G Daladier,	93	10⎫		
	Adj P Delage &	93	2⎬	Balloon	N Somme-Py
	MdL H Meyniel	93	2⎭		
	S/Lt J Lostalot,	97	2⎫		
	Adj Joubert &	97	2⎬	Balloon	Saint Hilaire
	MdL R Gaston	97	1⎭		
	S/Lt F Guyou &	37	8⎫	Balloon	N Cerny
	Adj G Lienhard	37	3⎭		
	S/Lt G Daladier	93	11	EA	
	S/Lt F Guyou &	37	9⎫	2-seater	
	Adj G Lienhard	37	4⎭		
	Adj G Lienhard &	37	5⎫	EA	Butte du Mesnil
	Adj L Marot	37	4⎭		
	Adj Damanez,	46	2⎫		
	Sgt Jourde &	46	1⎬	EA	
	Cpl Galotte	46	1⎭		
	Lt Robert &	14CA	P⎫	Scout	St Souplet
	Lt Dupuy	14CA	P⎭		
	S/Lt A Coadou	88	4	EA	
	S/Lt P Gaudermen,	68	5⎫		
	Adj E Prevost &	68	3⎬	EA	Ville-sur-Tourbe
	Cpl Chirac	68	1⎭		
	Patrol	132	—	EA	

27 September 1918

1720	Patrol	103	P	EA	NE Somme-Py
1735	Sgt M Guillet	163	3	Pfalz	Somme-Py
	Adj J Fleury &	95	4⎫	EA	
	Sgt L Lacouture	95	3⎭		
	Capt G Tourangin,	89	4⎫		
	Adj E Regnier &	89	6⎬	EA	Somme-Py—Manre
	Sgt G Lasne	89	1⎭		
	Capt de Vaubicourt,	100	2⎫		
	Lt C Poulin,	100	2⎬	EA	
	Sgt Coursic &	100	1⎭		
	Sgt R Hummel	100	1		
	Sgt E Corsi &	77	2⎫	Balloon	SE Etain
	MdL J Thevenod	77	2⎭		
	Lt Fouan &	108	2⎫		
	Asp Blanc	108	1⎬	EA	
	Adj Robyn &	108	1⎭		
	Adj Douville	108	1		
	Lt Coubaz &	29	1⎫		
	MdL Fremont	29	1⎬	EA	
	Lt Charmess &	29	1⎭		
	Sgt Lascourrages	29	1		
	Capt P d'Argueeff &	GC21	11⎫	Fokker DVII	N Cerny
	Lt Marolle	124	1⎭		
	Lt Thiberge	EMIV	2	EA	Grateuil

28 September 1918

0845	S/Lt J Romatet,	165	5⎫		
	S/Lt R Decugis &	165	3⎬	Balloon	Orfeuil
	Lt Besse	165	1⎭		
0900	S/Lt M Coiffard	154	31	Balloon	SW Semide
0930	Sgt R Onillon	163	2	Balloon	Challeronge
1010	Capt P d'Argueff	GC21	12	2-seater	Manre
1030	Lt R Fonck	103	67	2-seater	N Somme-Py
1115	Sgt J Connelly	163	6	Balloon	Challeronge

1145	S/Lt F Portron,	31	4⎫		N Bois de Bouc
	S/Lt L Chartoire &	31	3⎬	Fokker DVII	
	MdL Jacquet	31	1⎭		
1520	Capt P d'Argueff	GC21	13	2-seater	Sechault
1645	Lt H de Sevin	151	2	EA	Somme-Py
	Adj P Delage	93	3	EA	
	Adj M Henriot	65	5	EA	N Somme-Py
	Sgt R Damhet	65	1	EA	N Somme-Py
1130	Patrol	3	P	2-seater	Geneviève Ferme
1200	Lt H Berge	124	P	EA	N Bois de Forges
	S/Lt M Coiffard	154	P	Fokker DVII	

29 September 1918

0945	S/Lt P Waddington	31	10	Fokker DVII	Orfeuil
1740	Sgt G Rotureau	57	2	Fokker DVII	N Auberive
1825	Adj F Delzenne	88	5	EA	Monthois
1845	S/Lt Cousin	163	2	2-seater	Sechault
	Adj Droziers &	69	1⎫	Balloon	
	Sgt Fugier	69	1⎭		
	MdL P Ducornet	93	2	Balloon	Machault
	MdL H Meyneil	93	3	EA	
	Sgt Lucci,	240	1⎫		
	Sol Devillers &	240	1⎬	EA	
	Sol O'Farrell	240	1⎭		
	Sgt Bellat &	127	1⎫	EA	
	Asp Steiner	127	1⎭		
1015	Capt A de Turenne	12	P	Scout	NE Somme-Py
1030	Lt Herlemont	12	P	Scout	NE Somme-Py
1135	Patrol	67	P	EA	Somme-Py
1210	Adj G Discours	87	P	Balloon	Parisy
1515	Lt G Madon	38	P	2-seater	Chevrigny
1545	Sgt D Paden	163	P	Fokker DVII	Machault
1550	Sgt S Lederlin	163	P	Fokker DVII	Challeronge
1720	Adj M Paulnier &	98	P⎫	Fokker DVII	Vaux-les-Mouron
	MdL Champaver	98	P⎭		
1800	MdL Julien	156	P	Fokker DVII	Machault
	Sgt Savaurel &	8	P⎫	EA	
	Sgt Petit	8	P⎭		

30 September 1918

1823	Sgt R Onillon,	163	3⎫		
	Sgt D Paden &	163	1⎬	2-seater	Cerny
	Sgt Lefebvre	163	1⎭		
1823	Cpl Heine &	164	P⎫	EA	Challeronge
	Cpl Gerian	164	P⎭		

APPENDIX III

US Air Service Victory Claims September 1918

2 September 1918

Time	Pilot/Crew	Unit	Vic No	E/A	Location
0930	2/Lt A R Brooks	22	2	Rumpler C	Armaucourt
	1/Lt C G Grey,	213	1⎫		
	1/Lt P Phelen &	213	1⎬	2-seater	Filrey
	1/Lt S P Gaillard, Jr	213	1⎭		
	1/Lt G M Comey &	88	1⎫		
	1/Lt R B Bagby	88	1⎬	Hannover CLIII	Filrey
	1/Lt R C Page &	88	1⎪		
	1/Lt P F Carl, Jr	88	1⎭		

3 September 1918

	Capt J A Summersett &	96	1		
	2/Lt R I Coryell	96	1		
	1/Lt A W Gundelach &	96	2		
	2/Lt P W Way	96	1		
	1/Lt D W Young &	96	1		
	1/Lt S M Lunt	96	1	Pfalz DIII	Laubeville
	1/Lt A N Alexander &	96	1		
	1/Lt J C E McLennan	96	1		
	1/Lt R C Taylor &	96	1		
	1/Lt W A Stuart	96	1		
	1/Lt E E Bates &	96	1		
	1/Lt D W Warner	96	1		

4 September 1918

1100	1/Lt V H Strahm &	91	1	Pfalz	Rembercourt
	Capt J A Wallis	91	1		
1100	1/Lt P H Hughey &	91	—	Pfalz	Rembercourt
	Capt K Roper	91	—		
1220	Patrol	96	—	Pfalz	Laubeville
1330	2/Lt A R Brooks,	22	3		
	1/Lt F B Tyndall &	22	1	Fokker DVII	Barnecourt
	2/Lt C Jones	22	2		

8 September 1918

1235	1/Lt J M Swaab	22	1	2-seater	Cirey-Saarburg
to	1/Lt J M Swaab	22	2	Fokker DVII	Cirey-Saarburg
1305	1/Lt J M Swaab	22	3	Fokker DVII	Cirey-Saarburg

10 September 1918

1650	1/Lt W A Robertson	139	1	Pfalz	Bayonville

12 September 1918

0655	Capt R C Bridgman	22	2	Hannover C	Bois de Pretre
0809	2/Lt F Luke, Jr	27	1	Balloon	Marieulles
1020	1/Lt L J Rummell	93	1	Fokker DVII	Thiaucourt
1020	1/Lt C R D'Olive	93	1	Fokker DVII	Vieville-en-Haye
1210	Capt D H Arthur &	12	1	EA	Vieville-en-Haye
	1/Lt H T Fleeson	12	1		
	1/Lt D E Putnam	139	—	Pfalz	Lachaussée
	1/Lt W A Coleman &	135	1	Fokker	Limey
	1/Lt J H Nathan	135	1		
	1/Lt J J Curtin &	135	1	Fokker	Thiaucourt
	1/Lt P G Hart	135	1		
	1/Lt G D Ream &	135	1	Fokker	Thiaucourt
	1/Lt J H Nathan	135	2		

13 September 1918

1530	1/Lt V H Strahm	91	2	Fokker	Orly Ferme
	Capt J A Wallis	91	2		
1700	1/Lt C R D'Olive	93	2	Fokker DVII	Charey
1700	1/Lt C R D'Olive	93	3	Fokker CVII	Chery
1700	1/Lt L Carruthers &	93	1	Pfalz	Woel
	1/Lt L S Harding	93	1		
1700	1/Lt G W Furlow	103	2	Fokker DVII	Charey
1705	1/Lt G W Furlow	103	3	Fokker DVII	Charey
1710	1/Lt H D Kenyon	103	1	Albatros	St Julien
1710	1/Lt F O'D Hunter &	103	2	Fokker DVII	Chambley
	1/Lt G de F Larner	103	3		
1713	1/Lt C R D'Olive	93	4	Fokker DVII	St Benoit
1830	1/Lt D E Putnam	139	13	Fokker DVII	Limey
1830	1/Lt J D Este,	13	1		
	1/Lt J J Seerley,	13	3		
to	1/Lt R R Converse,	13	1	Fokker DVII	Chambley
	1/Lt D W Howe &	13	1		
1955	1/Lt F K Hayes	13	1		

1830	1/Lt J D Este,	13	2		
	1/Lt J J Seerley,	13	4		
to	1/Lt R R Converse,	13	2	Fokker DVII	Chambley
	1/Lt D W Howe &	13	2		
1955	1/Lt F K Hayes	13	2		
1830	1/Lt J D Este,	13	3		
	1/Lt J J Seerley,	13	5		
to	1/Lt R R Converse,	13	3	Fokker DVII	Chambley
	1/Lt D W Howe &	13	3		
1955	1/Lt F K Hayes	13	3		
	1/Lt B J Gaylord &	96	1		
	2/Lt H G Rath	96	1		
	1/Lt T W Farnsworth &	96	1	Fokker DVII	Chambley
	2/Lt S E Thompson	96	1		
	2/Lt S T Hopkins &	96	1		
	1/Lt B Williams	96	1		

14 September 1918

0733	Patrol	28	—	Fokker DVII	Villers-sur-Troy
0755	1/Lt H L Fontaine &	49	1	Fokker DVII	Chambley
	1/Lt H Brewster	49	1		
0755	1/Lt H L Fontaine &	49	2	Fokker DVII	Chambley
	1/Lt H Brewster	49	2		
0805	1/Lt R Biggs &	11	2		
	1/Lt H Greer	11	2		
	1/Lt E Comegys &	11	1		
	2/Lt A R Carter	11	1		
	1/Lt R Chapin &	11	1		
	2/Lt C Laird	11	1	Pfalz	Mars-la-Tour
	1/Lt L Harter &	11	1		
	1/Lt MacC Stephenson	11	1		
	2/Lt H Schindler &	11	1		
	2/Lt H Sayre	11	1		
	2/Lt R Guthrie &	11	1		
	1/Lt V Otis	11	1		
0805	1/Lt E F Richards	13	1	Pfalz	Cernay
0805	1/Lt E F Richards	13	2	Pfalz	Cernay
0805	1/Lt R M Stiles,	13	2		
	1/Lt G D Stivers &	13	1	Fokker DVII	Preny
	1/Lt M K Guthrie	13	1		
0805	1/Lt R M Stiles,	13	3		
	1/Lt G D Stivers &	13	2	Fokker DVII	Preny
	1/Lt M K Guthrie	13	2		
0815	1/Lt E V Rickenbacker	94	7	Fokker DVII	Waville
1000	1/Lt T F Lennon,	27	1		
	1/Lt L H Dawson &	27	2	Balloon	Boinville
	2/Lt F Luke, Jr	27	3		
1310	1/Lt C G Grey,	213	2		
	1/Lt R W Richardson &	213	1	Fokker DVII	Spandville
	1/Lt S P Gaillard, Jr	213	2		
1520	2/Lt A R Brooks &	22	4	Fokker DVII	Mars-la-Tour
	1/Lt P E Hassinger	22	1		
1525	2/Lt A R Brooks &	22	5	Fokker DVII	Mars-la-Tour
	1/Lt P E Hassinger	22	2		
1635	1/Lt W W White, Jr	147	3	Balloon	Chambley
1640	1/Lt W W White, Jr	147	4	Fokker DVII	Chambley
	2/Lt F Luke, Jr	27	2	Balloon	Buzy

15 September 1918

0810	1/Lt E V Rickenbacker	94	8	Fokker DVII	Bois de Waville
0945	1/Lt L W Powell &	91	1	Pfalz	Conflans
	1/Lt J H Stricker	91	1		
1000	2/Lt R E Wells &	24	1	Fokker	Conflans
	2/Lt A W Swineboard	24	1		
1015	Major C Spaatz	13	1	Fokker DVII	Vaux

1030	1/Lt W H Stovall	13	3	Fokker DVII	Cernay
1030	1/Lt L Brewer	13	1	Fokker DVII	Cernay
1030	1/Lt M K Guthrie &	13	3⎫	Fokker DVII	Vaux
	1/Lt F K Hayes	13	4⎭		
1140	1/Lt G C Kenney &	91	1⎫	Pfalz DIII	N Gorze
	2/Lt W T Badham	91	1⎭		
1230	1/Lt W P Erwin &	1	1⎫		
	1/Lt H W Dahringer	1	1⎬	EA	Mammey
	2/Lt J M Richardson &	1	1⎫		
	1/Lt A W Duckstein	1	1⎭		
1705	2/Lt F Luke, Jr	27	4	Balloon	Boinville
1710	1/Lt J Wehner	27	2	Balloon	Bois d'Hingry
1725	2/Lt F Luke, Jr	27	5	Balloon	Bois d'Hingry
1815	1/Lt C E Wright &	93	1⎫	Fokker DVII	Charey
	1/Lt H D Lindsay	93	1⎭		
1950	2/Lt F Luke, Jr	27	6	Balloon	Chaumont
	1/Lt J Wehner	27	1	Fokker DVII	Rouvres

16 September 1918

1115	1/Lt G F Fisher	49	2	Rumpler C	Benville
1245	1/Lt L C Simon	147	1	Halb C	Hadonville
1220	1/Lt C E Wright &	93	2⎫	Fokker DVII	Chambley
	1/Lt H D Lindsay	93	2⎭		
1940	2/Lt F Luke, Jr &	27	7⎫	Balloon	Romagne
	1/Lt J Wehner	27	3⎭		
1945	1/Lt J Wehner	27	4	Balloon	Mangiennes
	2/Lt F Luke, Jr	27	8	Balloon	Reville

17 September 1918

1125	1/Lt G S Robertson	147	1	Halb C	Etain
1545	1/Lt F O'D Hunter	103	3	Fokker DVII	Verneville
1545	1/Lt F O'D Hunter	103	4	Fokker DVII	Bayonville
1620	1/Lt G W Furlow	103	4	Fokker DVII	Verneville
1620	1/Lt J Frost	103	1	Fokker DVII	Bayonville

18 September 1918

1610	2/Lt J S Owens,	139	1⎫		
	1/Lt R O Lindsay	139	1⎪		
	1/Lt G V Moy	139	1⎪		
	1/Lt W A Robertson,	139	2⎬	Pfalz DIII	Bayonville
	1/Lt K J Schoen	139	1⎪		
	1/Lt R D Shelby &	139	1⎪		
	1/Lt H A Garvie	139	1⎭		
1610	2/Lt J S Owens,	139	2⎫		
	1/Lt R O Lindsay,	139	2⎪		
	1/Lt G V Moy,	139	2⎪		
	1/Lt W A Robertson,	139	3⎬	Pfalz DIII	Bayonville
	1/Lt K J Schoen	139	2⎪		
	1/Lt R D Shelby &	139	2⎪		
	1/Lt H A Garvie	139	2⎭		
1635	1/Lt S Sewell	95	5	Fokker DVII	Landres
1640	2/Lt F Luke, Jr &	27	9⎫	Balloon	Mars-la-Tour
	1/Lt J Wehner	27	5⎭		
1640	2/Lt F Luke, Jr &	27	10⎫	Balloon	Mars-la-Tour
	1/Lt J Wehner	27	6⎭		
1645	2/Lt F Luke, Jr	27	11	Fokker DVII	St Hilaire
1645	2/Lt F Luke, Jr	27	12	Fokker DVII	St Hilaire
1645	2/Lt F Luke, Jr	27	13	Halb C	Jonville
1650	1/Lt H A Garvey	139	3	Pfalz	
1720	1/Lt D m McClure	213	1	Fokker DVII	Mars-la-Tour
1720	1/Lt D M McClure	213	2	Fokker DVII	Mars-la-Tour
1720	1/Lt D M McClure	213	3	Fokker DVII	Mars-la-Tour
1730	2/Lt R Guthrie &	11	2⎫	Fokker DVII	Oiley
	1/Lt V Otis	11	2⎭		

20 September 1918

| 1745 | 2/Lt F H Hart & | 90 | 1 | Fokker DVII | Dampvitoux |
| | 2/Lt A T Grier | 90 | 1 | | |

21 September 1918

| 1750 | 1/Lt H R Hall | 95 | 1 | Fokker DVII | Dancourt |

24 September 1918

1530	Capt R C Bridgman,	22	3		
	2/Lt R J Little &	22	1	DFW C	Woel
	1/Lt H B Hudson	22	1		

25 September 1918

0840	1/Lt E V Rickenbacker	94	9	Fokker DVII	Billy
0850	1/Lt E v Rickenbacker	94	10	Halb C	Spincourt
1002	1/Lt G V Moy,	139	3		
	2/Lt R O Seevers &	139	2		
	2/Lt J S Owens	139	3	Fokker DVII	Arnacourt
	2/Lt P W Chase &	8	1		
	1/Lt R Smith	8	1		

26 September 1918

0552	1/Lt R M Chambers	94	1	Balloon	Nantillois
0600	1/Lt E V Rickenbacker	94	11	Fokker DVII	Damvillers
0605	1/Lt H R Buckley &	95	3	Balloon	Nantillois
	1/Lt A H McLanahan	95	2		
0625	1/Lt I A Roberts	27	3	Balloon	Romagne
0715	1/Lt J A Sperry	22	1	Fokker DVII	Bois de Merles
0715	1/Lt H B Hudson &	22	2	Fokker DVII	Etain
	2/Lt B M Doolin	22	1		
0723	1/Lt T G Cassady	28	7	Fokker DVII	St Marie-à-Py
0730	1/Lt J D Beane	22	1	Fokker DVII	Charpentrie
0735	Capt C J Biddle,	13	6		
to	1/Lt L Brewer &	13	2	Fokker DVII	Flabas
0750	1/Lt S M Avery	13	1		
1735	Major C Spaatz	13	2	Fokker DVII	Flabas
0820	1/Lt J A Sperry	22	2	Fokker DVII	Etain
1000	2/Lt S V Peters &	24	1	Fokker DVII	Doumprix
	1/Lt L A Weitishek	24	1		
1015	1/Lt B F Beverly &	96	1		
	1/Lt F J Newbury	96	1		
	1/Lt D M Young &	96	2		
	2/Lt R I Coryell	96	2		
	1/Lt B C Hopper &	96	1		
	2/Lt A N Kelly	96	1		
	1/Lt L S Turnbull &	96	1	Fokker DVII	Clery-le-Grand
	2/Lt L C Bleecker	96	1		
	1/Lt R P Elliott &	96	1		
	1/Lt A O Ellis	96	1		
	2/Lt H J Forshay &	96	1		
	2/Lt P J O'Donnell	96	1		
1015	2/Lt H J Forshay &	96	2	Fokker DVII	Clery-le-Grand
	2/Lt P J O'Donnell	96	2		
1050	1/Lt W W Waring &	11	1	Fokker DVII	Dun-sur-Meuse
	2/Lt S A G Morris	11	1		
1055	1/Lt P N Rhinelander &	20	1		
	1/Lt H C Preston	20	1		
	1/Lt M C Cooper &	20	1		
	1/Lt E C Leonard	20	1		
	1/Lt R P Mathews &	20	1		
	2/Lt E A Taylor	20	1		
	1/Lt W C Potter &	20	1		
	2/Lt G W Schultz	20	1	Fokker DVII	Damvillers
	2/Lt G B Wiser &	20	1		
	1/Lt G C Richardson	20	1		
	2/Lt D B Harris &	20	1		
	2/Lt E Forbes	20	1		
	1/Lt S C Howard &	20	1		
	1/Lt E A Parrott	20	1		

1140	2/Lt S J Owens,	139	4		
	1/Lt S J De France	139	1		
	1/Lt H S Garvie,	139	4	DFW C	Consenvoye
	1/Lt L H Germer	139	1		
	1/Lt K J Schoen &	139	3		
	1/Lt H R Sumner	139	1		
1310	1/Lt W H Stovall	13	4	Fokker DVII	Etain
1315	1/Lt J F Manning &	49	1	Rumpler C	Hagecourt
	1/Lt J Wentworth	49	1		
1350	1/Lt D H Backus &	49	1	Fokker DVII	Etain
	1/Lt H W Heiber	49	1		
1620	1/Lt M Stenseth	28	1	Fokker DVII	Grimmcourt
1748	1/Lt C M Gravett	95	1	Fokker DVII	Dullancourt
1750	1/Lt J Vasconcells	27	3	Balloon	Lisson
1800	1/Lt A Nutt	94	1	Fokker DVII	Dullancourt
1800	1/Lt L H Dawson	27	3	Fokker DVII	Charey
1805	1/Lt A N McLanahan	95	3	Fokker DVII	Montfaucon
1845	1/Lt H W Cook	94	2	Balloon	Grand Ham

27 September 1918

1600	1/Lt E R Cook &	91	1		
	1/Lt W R Lawson	91	1		
	1/Lt J W Van Heuvel &	91	1	Fokker DVII	Crepion
	1/Lt L C Hammond	91	1		
	1/Lt W F Baker &	91	1		
	1/Lt R S Jannopoulo	91	1		
1745	1/Lt E R Scroggie,	94	1		
	1/Lt J P Herron &	147	1	Fokker DVII	Montfaucon
	1/Lt W W White, Jr	147	5		
1745	1/Lt W W White, Jr	147	6	Fokker DVII	Montfaucon
1814	1/Lt H R Buckley,	95	4		
	1/Lt E P Curtis &	95	3	Rumpler C	Brieulles
	1/Lt H Poperfuss	95	1		
1925	1/Lt H R Buckley,	95	5		
	1/Lt T F Butz &	95	1	Rumpler C	Fleville
	1/Lt G O Woodard	95	1		

28 September 1918

0500	1/Lt E V Rickenbacker	94	12	Balloon	Sivry-sur-Meuse
0600	2/Lt F Luke, Jr	27	14	Balloon	Bethenville
0606	1/Lt H W Cook	94	3	Balloon	Clery-le-Petit
0650	1/Lt K L Porter &	147	2	Rumpler C	Langres
	1/Lt E S Ennis	147	1		
0840	1/Lt J D Beane &	22	2	Fokker DVII	Ivoiry
	1/Lt J M Swaab	22	4		
0840	1/Lt H B Hudson	22	3	Fokker DVII	Ivoiry
0845	Capt R C Bridgman &	22	4	Fokker DVII	Montfaucon
	2/Lt W W La Force	22	1		
0850	1/Lt F B Tyndall	22	2	Fokker DVII	Montfaucon
0900	2/Lt C Jones	22	2	Fokker DVII	Ivoiry
0900	2/Lt C Jones	22	3	Fokker DVII	Montfaucon
0915	2/Lt S J De France	139	2	Pfalz DIII	Clery-le-Petit
0915	1/Lt R D Seevers	139	2	Pfalz DIII	Clery-le-Petit
0915	1/Lt W A Robertson,	139	4		
	1/Lt E M Haight &	139	1	Pfalz DIII	Clery-le-Petit
	1/Lt R O Lindsay	139	3		
1030	1/Lt J Vasconcells	27	4	Rumpler C	Forges
1240	1/Lt K L Porter,	147	2		
	1/Lt O B Myers &	147	1	Rumpler C	Cierges
	1/Lt L C Simon	147	2		
1310	1/Lt M Stenseth	28	2	Fokker DVII	Grand Pre
1310	1/Lt M Stenseth	28	3	Fokker DVII	Grand Pre
1325	1/Lt W J Hoover	27	3	Halb C	Forges
1325	1/Lt A H Treadwell	213	2	Fokker DVII	Bantheville
1330	1/Lt E G Tobin	103	6	Fokker DVII	Chatel-Chehery
1335	1/Lt T H Hubbard	103	1	Fokker DVII	Chatel-Chehery
1340	1/Lt R N Weatherbee	93	1	Fokker DVII	Grandham

1550	2/Lt F Luke, Jr	27	15	Hannover C	Monthainville

29 September 1918

0455	1/Lt W P Erwin &	1	2⎫	Rumpler C	Fleville
	2/Lt B V Baucom	1	1⎭		
1635	1/Lt A B Patterson, Jr	93	1	Fokker DVII	Damvillers
1635	1/Lt R H Fuller	93	1	Fokker DVII	Damvillers
1635	1/Lt L J Rummell	93	2	Fokker DVII	Damvillers
1635	1/Lt L J Rummell	93	3	Fokker DVII	Damvillers
1635	1/Lt L J Rummell,	93	4⎫		
	1/Lt A B Patterson Jr &	93	2⎬	Albatros C	Chaumont
	1/Lt R H Fuller	93	2⎭		
1705	2/Lt F Luke, Jr	27	16	Balloon	Avocourt
1710	2/Lt F Luke, Jr	27	17	Balloon	Avocourt
1712	2/Lt F Luke, Jr	27	18	Balloon	Avocourt
1720	1/Lt R M Chambers &	94	2⎫		
	1/Lt S Kaye, Jr	94	1⎭	Fokker DVII	Cunel
1850	1/Lt G O Woodard	95	3	Balloon	Dun-sur-Meuse
1850	1/Lt L C Holden	95	1	Balloon	Cunel

APPENDIX IV

German Victory Claims September 1918

1 September 1918

Time	Pilot/Crew	Unit	Vic No	Type	Place
1005	Vfw K Schlegel	45	19	Balloon	Oueilly
1100	Oblt R Greim	34b	22	Camel	St Pierre Waast
1555	Lt T Quandt	36	11	SE5	S Pronville
1750	Flg H Nülle	39	3	Camel	Bailleul
1830	Flak			Dolphin	Armentières
2100	Lt W Sommer	39	3	Balloon	Tilloy
	Lt E Bormann	B	5	BF2b	S Lecluse
	Oblt B Loerzer	JGIII	34	BF2b	
	Uffz Schaak	28w	2	DH4	Tilloy
	Vfw W Skworz	36	2	DH4	Brunemont
	Sgt F Poeschke	53	2	Spad	Bretigny
	Vfw H Gockel	33	3	Camel	Queant
	Lt W Blume	9	—		

2 September 1918

Time	Pilot/Crew	Unit	Vic No	Type	Place
0820	Lt T Quandt	36	12	Camel	Ecourt-St Quentin
0820	Uffz O Bieliet	45	1	Spad	Baslieux
0955	Oblt R v Wedel	11	11	EA	
1010	Lt A Brandenstein	49	5	Spad	Suippes
1015	Lt H Lange	26	6	SE5	Villers
1025	Lt O Frühner	26	18	SE5	Baralle
1030	Lt H Frommherz	27	17	BF2b	Hamel
1100	Lt F Noltenius	27	6	Sopwith	Etaing
1100	Lt Buddeberg	50	1	Spad 2	Braisne
1100	Gefr Jacob	17	1	Spad 2	Savigny
1110	Vfw O Frühner	26	19	SE5	Villers
1125	OStv G Dörr	45	23	Spad 2	Ormes
1130	Lt F Noltenius	27	5	Sopwith	Rumaucourt
1130	OStv G Dörr	45	24	Spad 2	Reims
1130	Lt Meixner	45	1	Spad	Reims
1150	Lt K Brendle	45	8	Balloon	Reims
1210	Lt Christians	21s	1	Spad	NW Reims
1220	Lt W Sommer	39	4	RE8	Fampoux
1230	Lt W Nebgen	7	3	AWFK8	Lomme

1230	Vfw Mack	63	1	AWFK8	Lomme
1240	Vfw C Mesch	26	7	Camel	Haucourt
1240	Oblt H Dahlmann	JGIII	4	Camel	Haucourt
1242	Vfw C Mesch	26	8	Camel	Raucourt
1245	Lt H Lange	26	4	Camel	NE Baralle
1245	Lt Ehlers	26	1	Camel	NE Baralle
1245	Oblt B Loerzer	JGIII	35	Camel	NE Baralle
1320	Lt H Habich	49	2	Bréguet XIV	Chalons
1330	Lt M Demisch	58	5	RE8	Vis-en-Artois
1515	Gefr H Nülle	39	1	Balloon	Tilloy
1555	Lt Krayer	45	3	Balloon	Reims
1600	Lt U Koennemann	45	2	Spad 2	Magneux
1600	Lt F Rolfes	45	12	Spad 2	Magneux
1605	Lt F Rolfes	45	13	Spad 2	Magneux
1720	Lt G Buerck	54	3	Balloon	Champenoux
1740	Lt Christians	21s	2	Spad	E Fismes
1833	Lt H Hentzen	9	2	Spad	Terny-Sorny
1845	Vfw Duennhaupt	58	1	DH9	Hamel
1920	Lt H Brunig	50	7	Spad	Fismes
1930	Flg J Wolff	17	1	Spad	Savigny
2000	Lt B Hobein	20	3	BF2b	Gheluvelt
2000	Lt R v Barnekow	20	5	BF2b	Gheluvelt
2100	Lt W Sommer	39	5	Balloon	N Bapaume
	Lt O Löffler	9		Camel	Palleul
	Lt E Bormann	B	8	Camel	Sauchy-Lestrées
	Lt F Heinz	B	2	Camel	Boiry
	Lt E Bormann	B	6	Camel	SE Dury
	Lt E Bormann	B	7	Camel	W Havrincourt
	Lt O Löffler	B	4	Camel	Beugnatre
	Lt O Löffler	B	7	Camel	S Pelves
	Oblt E v Schleich	23b	31	RE8	NW Bapaume
	Vfw A Lux	27	5	RE8	Hamel
	Vfw A Lux	27	—	BF2b	Vis-en-Artois
	Lt Stoltenhoff	27	2	EA	
	Uffz Kahle	27	1	Sopwith	Beugnatre
	Vfw R Jorke	39	13	RE8	Bailleul
	Lt W Preuss	66	10	Bréguet XIV	Bagneux
	Flg Eyssler	66	1	Spad	N Soissons
	Lt H Quartier	67	2	Balloon	
	Uffz Baumgarten	67	2	Balloon	
	Lt R Otto	68	4	Bréguet XIV	Remy Wald
	Uffz Huar	68	3	Bréguet XIV	Remy Wald
	Lt G Clausnitzer	72s	1	Balloon	
	Oblt G Rasberger	80b	1	Balloon	
	Lt J Filbig	80b	2	Balloon	Laroxne
	Vfw F Classen	26	—	Camel	Bailleul
	Lt K v Schönebeck	33	7	EA	
	Lt F Höhn	81	11	Spad	Coucy-le-Château

3 September 1918

1015	Lt Schramm	56	3	BF2b	Moorseele
1030	Lt W Blume	9	20	Spad	S Fismes
1031	Lt H Rolle	9	3	Spad	S Fismes
1040	Flg E Mix	54	2	Balloon	Tremblecourt
1125	Lt T Quandt	36	13	SE5	Moreuil
1515	Gefr H Nülle	39	2	Balloon	Vis-en-Artois
1517	Gefr H Nülle	39	4	Balloon	Haucourt
1625	Lt O Löffler	B	5	DH9	Epehy
1700	Lt G Wember	61	1	Balloon	
1735	Vfw O Frühner	26	21	Camel	Sin-le-Noble
1740	Oblt B Loerzer	JGIII	36	SE5	Douai
1805	Lt A Lindenberger	B	9	BF2b	Combles
1805	Lt T Quandt	36	14	BF2b	Eterpigny
1840	Lt Vollbracht	5	2	BF2b	W Havrincourt
1847	Lt F Rumey	5	30	BF2b	S Peronne
1850	OStv J Mai	5	23	BF2b	N Bertincourt
2000	Oblt A Auffarht	29	20	SE5	Guemappe

2000	Lt F Weber	29	2	SE5	Pelves
2000	Uffz S Westphal	29	1	SE5	Agny
2000	Uffz P Schönfelder	29	1	SE5	Agny
2010	Lt Hencke	31	2	Camel	Rony-le-Petit
2035	Vfw O Hennrich	46	11	SE5a	SW Moreuil
2050	Lt z Brockhoff	MFJ3	3	Bréguet XIV	E Furnes
	Vfw H Donhauser	17	5	Spad	Sissone
	Rittm H v Brederlow	JGpII	2	Spad	Sissone
	Vfw M Hutterer	23b	4	DH9	Arleux
	Vfw M Hutterer	23b	5	Dolphin	Marcoing
	Lt H Frommherz	27	18	RE8	Beugnatre
	Lt H Frommherz	27	19	RE8	Beugny
	Fw A Hübner	36	3	SE5	Aubenscheul
	Lt F Thiede	38	6	BF2b	
	Uffz Mack	60	1	Spad	
	Vfw W Stör	68	4	Balloon	Remy Wald
	Lt F Höhn	81	12	Spad	Soissons
	Vfw D Averes	81	5	Spad	Soissons
	Vfw D Averes	81	6	Spad	Soissons
	Lt Bleibtreu	45	1	Bréguet XIV	Conde
	Uffz F Engler	62	1	Balloon	
	Vfw W Skworz	36	3	SE5	Sancourt

4 September 1918

0910	Oblt H Dahlmann	JGIII	5	Camel	Palleul
0910	Lt Ehlers	26	2	Camel	Palleul
0912	Oblt H Dahlmann	JGIII	6	Camel	Palleul
9012	Vfw E Buder	26	9	Camel	Cantin
0915	Vfw O Frühner	26	22	Camel	W Cantin
0915	Vfw O Frühner	26	23	Camel	Douai
0918	Vfw F Classen	26	6	Camel	Cantin
0920	Oblt B Loerzer	JGIII	37	Camel	Monchecourt
0925	Vfw E Buder	26	10	Camel	Gouy
0930	Vfw O Frühner	26	24	Camel	W Corbehem
0930	Oblt F Röth	16b	23	DH9	Neuf Berquin
1010	Uffz A Müller	39	2	DH9	Chelmes
1015	Uffz H Nülle	39	5	DH9	St Aubert
1015	Uffz H Haase	21s	3	Balloon	E Sarcy
1040	Lt Spille	58	2	DH9	Helesmes
1045	Vfw Jeep	58	3	DH9	d'Hivergies-Fe
1100	Lt M Demisch	58	6	BF2b	Emerchicourt
1100	Lt R Wenzl	6	2	Camel	Raillencourt
1100	Vfw G Staudacher	1	6	Camel	Sailly-Cambrai
1100	Lt E Bormann	2	9	SE5a	Pelves
1110	Lt G Meyer	37	15	2-seater	W Cambrai
1115	Oblt O Schmidt	5	12	BF2b	Gouzeaucourt
1205	Lt E Siempelkamp	64w	1	Salmson 2A2	E Thiaucourt
1230	Lt Siefert	17	1	Spad	Soilly
1335	Uffz Bader	64w	2	Balloon	Mandres
1400	Lt F Rolfes	45	16	Spad	N Fismes
1400	OStv G Dörr	45	25	Spad	N Fismes
1400	OStv G Dörr	5	26	Spad VII	Fismes
1450	Oblt O Schmidt	5	—	Balloon	Loos
1715	Lt E Just	11	6	Balloon	Barastre
1815	Lt W Peckmann	9	3	Spad	Soissons
1830	Lt F Rumey	5	31	Camel	Queant
1930	Lt Berling	45	3	Balloon	Mont Notre Dame
	Lt A Laumann	10	28		
	Lt H Frommherz	27	20	EA	Recourt
	Vfw A Lux	27	6	Sopwith	Cantin
	Fw A Hübner	36	4	SE5	Mercatel
	Lt T Quandt	36	15	SE5	Queant
	Vfw K Schlegel	45	21	Balloon	Sarcy
	Vfw A Korff	60	4	Spad	
	Lt W Preuss	66	14	2-seater	Crécy-au-Mont
	Uffz Baumgarten	67	3	Balloon	
	Lt F Jacobsen	73	6	RE6/AR2	

5 September 1918

0910	Flak			Camel	N Mericourt
1005	Lt F Rumey	5	32	SE5a	N Bouchain
1010	OStv J Mai	5	25	SE5a	W Bugnicourt
1200	G Meyer	37	16	SE5a	E Havrincourt
1200	Lt Auf den Haar	46	—	SE5a	E Havrincourt
1210	Lt Auf den Haar	46	—	SE5a	NE Ribecourt
1210	Lt T Himmer	37	2	SE5a	NE Ribecourt
1210	Oblt B Loerzer	JGIII	38	SE5	Inchy
1350	Lt B Hobein	20	4	BF2b	Espières
1415	FTL Motor trouble			Scout	Ostricourt
1515	Vfw Krautz	46	2	Balloon	NE Bapaume
1525	Lt R Wenzl	6	8	Balloon	Croiselles
1525	Vzflgmstr Mayer	MFJ3	4	Camel	Stalhille
1530	Lt F Schliewen	6	1	Balloon	Croiselles
1730	Vfw K Schlegel	45	20	Balloon	Fismes
1825	Uffz L Jeckert	56	2	Camel	Lenvelere
1827	Lt L Beckmann	56	8	Camel	Vorsmohlen
1840	Lt P Baümer	B	24	BF2b	S Douai
1845	Uffz A Müller	39	3	2-seater	Douai
1900	Vfw C Mesch	26	9	Camel	Coincy
1900	Lt H Frommherz	27	21	Camel	Marquion
1905	Lt A Lux	27	7	Camel	Baralle
1905	Vfw F Classen	26	7	Camel	Henin-Lietard
1910	Uffz Ruppert	39	1	Balloon	S Dury
1915	Lt E Koepsch	4	8	SE5a	S Paillencourt
2010	Lt W Ott	16b	1	Camel	Langemarck
	Oblt E v Schleich	23b	32	Dolphin	Landres
	Lt K Ritscherle	60	6	Spad	Leury
	Lt W Preuss	66	15	Bréguet XIV	Villeneuve
	Flgmt K Engelfried	MFJ5	2	DH9	W Knocke

6 September 1918

0945	Lt W v Richthofen	11	5	Dolphin	
0950	Oblt P Blumenbach	31	3	Dolphin	N St Quentin
1053	Lt H Maushacke	4	7	Camel	Le Catelet
1220	Lt Buddeberg	50	2	Spad 2	S Soissons
1315	Lt M Demisch	58	8	Balloon	Monchy
1340	Lt M Demisch	58	7	RE8	Monchy le Preux
1455	Vfw O Hennrich	46	12	Balloon	S Le Mesnil
1635	Lt F Rolfes	45	15	Balloon	Magneux
1645	Lt F Rolfes	45	14	Balloon	Magneux
1645	Lt Berling	45	2	Balloon	Magneux
1645	Lt Krayer	45	2	Balloon	Magneux
1820	Vfw H Knaak	9	1	Spad	N Soissons
1842	Lt M Näther	62	12	Bréguet XIV	Sillery
2005	Uffz W Dost	21s	3	Spad	E Braisne
	Lt O Löffler	B	8	BF2b	N Bourlon Wood
	Lt P Baümer	B	23	BF2b	W Cantaing
	Lt E Bormann	B	10	Camel	N Bourlon Wood
	Lt A Lindenberger	B	10	Camel	Lagnicourt
	Vfw O Frühner	26	—		
	Lt F Noltenius	27	—		
	Lt S Garaztka	31	—	DH9	St Quentin
	Vfw Amschl	31	—	DH9	Noyon
	Lt M Haenichen	53	2	Spad 2	
	Lt M Haenichen	53	3	Spad 2	Coucy-le-Château

7 September 1918

0810	Lt Hofmann	79b	2	Spad	Villequier-Aumont
1125	Lt F Rumey	5	33	SE5a	St Quentin
1130	Lt F Bornträger	49	2	Bréguet XIV	Auberive
1135	Lt H Habich	49	3	Spad	St Hilaire
1145	Oblt O Schmidt	5	13	Balloon	SW Bertincourt
1230	Vfw A Haussmann	13	13	Salmson 2A2	Jeandelize
1300	Lt J Schulte-Frohlinde	11	2	SE5	
1325	Lt O v Beaulieu-Marconnay	19	14	Salmson 2A2	NE Montsec

1400	Lt Schulte-Schlutius	3	1	DH9	Buschweiler
1415	Vfw J Hohly	65	5	Spad 2	Essey
1415	Oblt R Nebel	Kest1a	2	DH4	Niederbronn
1430	Uffz Forstmann	Kest1a	1	DH4	Frankenthal-Morsch
1940	Lt W v Richthofen	11	6	SE5a	W Le Catelet
1945	Lt W v Richthofen	11	7	SE5a	
1945	Oblt R v Wedel	11	12	SE5	Le Catelet
	Lt G Weiner	3	5	DH9	Dassberg
	Lt G Weiner	3	6	DH9	Burscheid
	Lt A Laumann	10	—		
	Lt H Stutz	71	4	Bréguet XIV	W St Ulrich
	Lt K Seit	80b	3	DH9	

8 September 1918

	FTL Motor trouble			Spad	E Etain

9 September 1918

	Oblt E v Schleich	23b	33	Camel	W Douai
	Lt H Frommherz	27	—	DH9	

10 September 1918

1400	Flak			AWFK8	Hulluch
1645	Cause unknown			Camel	S Merignies

11 September 1918

	Flak			EA	

12 September 1918

1135	Lt G v Hantelmann	15	7	Bréguet XIV	W Conflans
1235	Vfw R Moosbacher	77b	3	Salmson 2A2	Thimmenheim
1310	Oblt O v Boenigk	JGII	22	Salmson 2A2	Thiaucourt
1935	Lt G v Hantelmann	15	8	Spad	SE Limey
	Lt F Büchner	13	21	2-seater	Vieville-en-Haye
	Lt F Büchner	13	22	Bréguet XIV	E Thiaucourt
	Lt Grimm	13	2	Bréguet XIV	Thiaucourt
	Lt K Hetze	13	5	Bréguet XIV	Thiaucourt
	Lt F Büchner	13	23	DH4	N Hattonville
	Lt Klieforth	19	1	Spad 2	Thiaucourt
	Gefr C Schmidt	35b	1	RE8	NW Queant
	Lt R Stark	35b	7	AWFK8	Hermies
	OStv Trautmann	64w	1	Salmson 2A2	Flirey-Brusay
	Uffz Beschow	64w	2	Salmson 2A2	Broussey
	Uffz Bader	64w	1	Bréguet XIV	
	Oblt E Wenig	80b	4	DH4	Phyln
	MFlakzug 69			Spad	Bouxières

13 September 1918

1005	Lt R Stark	35b	8	DH4	Recourt
1355	Vfw G Klaudat	15	4	Spad	Vionville
1500	Lt J Jacobs	7	25	RE8	N Bailleul
1720	Lt G v Beaulieu-Marconnay	19	15	Bréguet XIV	Charey
1720	Lt Gewert	19	1	Bréguet XIV	Charey
1720	Lt Scheller	19	3	Bréguet XIV	Rembercourt
1750	Vfw H Klose	54s	2	DH4	Recourt
1750	Vfw K Delang	54s	3	DH4	St Geneviève
1805	Lt G v Hantelmann	15	9	Spad	SW Thiaucourt
1820	Vfw G Klaudat	15	5	Spad	SE Metz
1840	Lt H Schäfer	15	7	DH4	Pont-à-Mousson
1930	Lt G v Beaulieu-Marconnay	19	16	Spad	Jaulny
1930	Lt M Klieforth	19	2	Spad	Jaulny
1940	Lt M Demisch	58	9	Balloon	Monchy
	Oblt O v Boenigk	JGII	23	Spad	Thiaucourt
	Lt F Büchner	13	24	Spad	Allamont
	Vfw A Haussmann	13	14	Spad	Allamont

	Lt Büchner	13	1	Spad	Allamont
	Lt H Müller	18	7	DH4	W Thiaucourt
	Lt B Hobein	20	—	EA	
	Lt B Hobein	20	—	EA	
	Lt R v Barnekow	20	—	EA	
	Uffz Buenning	83	1	Spad	
	OStv Kapfhammer	FAA298	1	2-seater	Buillonville

14 September 1918

0900	Lt H Müller	18	8	Spad	Gorze
0900	Vfw T Weischer	15	2	DH4	Bayonville
0900	Lt G v Hantelmann	15	10	DH4	N Gorze
0905	Lt G v Buren	18	2	Spad	Gorze
0910	Lt H Müller	18	9	Spad	SW Sillingen
0915	Lt H Müller	18	10	Spad	SE Gohn
0940	Lt M Gossner	77b	8	Balloon	Pont-à-Mousson
1000	Oblt G Rasberger	80b	2	DH9	Rolters
1005	Lt Kandt	18	1	DH4	Pelter
1020	Lt Buddeberg	50	3	Spad	Revillon
1020	Lt Maletzky	50	1	Spad	Revillon
1110	Lt F Rumey	5	34	SE5a	S Le Catelet
1140	Lt J Klein	15	14	Spad	N Lachaussée
1145	Lt G v Hantelmann	15	11	Spad	St Benoit
1150	Oblt H Kohze	JGp9	2	DH	Pont-à-Mousson
1155	Lt W Blume	9	24	Spad 2	S Laffaux
1200	Lt W Blume	9	25	Spad	Braye
1245	Lt M Gossner	77b	7	Spad XIII	Bois de Rappes
1245	Vfw B Ultsch	77b	10	Spad XIII	Jaulny
1320	Lt M Gossner	77b	9	Salmson 2A2	Villecrey
1440	Lt H Müller	18	11	Spad	Pont-à-Mousson
1445	Vfw Glatz	18	1	Spad	
1532	Uffz Lohrmann	42	2	DH9	W Holnon Wood
1615	Lt G v Hantelmann	15	12	Spad	Lachaussée
1615	Lt J Klein	15	15	Spad	Lachaussée
1620	Vfw K Schmuckle	15	5	Spad	St Benoit
1620	Lt U Koennemann	45	3	Salmson 2A2	Fismes
1630	Lt Christiansen	67	2	Balloon	Clermont-Verdun
1630	Uffz H Marwede	67	2	Balloon	Clermont-Verdun
1634	Uffz H Marwede	67	3	Balloon	Clermont-Verdun
1635	Lt M Näther	62	13	Balloon	Mailly
1638	Uffz H Marwede	67	4	Balloon	Clermont-Verdun
1730	Oblt G Rasberger	80b	3	Spad XIII	Champeneaux
1815	Lt Bacher	3	2	Spad	S Thiaucourt
1920	Lt Gewert	19	2	Salmson 2A2	Beney
	Lt P Baümer	B	25	RE8	Cantaing
	Lt F Kresse	7	1	RE8	SE Ypres
	Oblt O v Boenigk	JGII	24	Spad	Lachaussée
	Oblt O v Boenigk	JGII	25	Spad	Lachaussée
	Lt H Becker	12	14	Bréguet XIV	Luttingen
	Lt F Büchner	13	25	2-seater	Mars-la-Tour
	Lt F Büchner	13	26	Bréguet XIV	Mars-la-Tour
	Lt Grimm	13	3	Bréguet XIV	Conflans
	Lt W Niethammer	13	3	Bréguet XIV	Puxe
	Lt Büchner	13	2	Caudron	Conflans
	Lt O v Beaulieu-Marconnay	19	17	Bréguet XIV	Jouville
	Lt R Rineau	19	3	Bréguet XIV	Conflans
	Lt M Klieforth	19	3	Bréguet XIV	Conflans
	Lt F Noltenius	27	7	Balloon	Vis-en-Artois
	OStv G Dörr	45	26	Spad 2	Blanzy
	Lt K Ritscherle	60	7	Spad	
	Lt G Wember	61	4	Balloon	
	Lt E Siempelkamp	64w	—	Spad XIII	W Auvillers
	Lt E Siempelkamp	64w	5	Salmson 2A2	Bonzée
	Lt W Frickert	65	8	Caudron	Lateur
	Lt J Hohly	65	6	Caudron	St Maurice
	Lt W Preuss	66	16	2-seater	
	Vfw Hasenpusch	67	2	Bréguet XIV	Doncourt

Vfw Wimmer	80b	2	Spad XIII	
Uffz Goetz &	1			
Flg Golz	FA296	1	Spad	

15 September 1918

0923	Uffz H Nülle	39	6	Balloon	Queant
0924	Uffz H Nülle	39	7	Balloon	Villers
0925	Uffz H Nülle	39	8	Balloon	Villers
0926	Uffz H Nülle	39	9	Balloon	Dury
0930	Oblt R Greim	34b	24	SE5a	S Hermies
1210	Lt H Schäfer	15	8	DH9	SW Metz
1215	Vfw T Weischer	15	3	DH9	S Metz
1215	Lt G v Hantelmann	15	13	DH9	SE Metz
1215	Oblt H v Wedel	24s	3	EA	Nauroy-Estrées
1225	Lt U Neckel	6	25	BF2b	Estrées
1230	Lt H Leptien	63	6	RE8	W Armentières
1245	Vfw O Hennrich	46	13	Balloon	Bertincourt
1250	Vfw W Kohlbach	10	4	Camel	Cantaing
1305	Lt Jeep	58	2	Balloon	Vitry
1305	Uffz K Pietzsch	58	2	Balloon	Wancourt
1325	Lt M Gossner	77b	5	Balloon	Lironville
1505	Lt H v Freden	50	8	Balloon	Jumigny
1507	Lt H v Freden	50	9	Balloon	Jumigny
1510	Lt zS R Poss	MFJ4	6	Camel	Zeebrugge
1700	Lt G Meyer	37	17	EA	N Marcoing
1705	Flgmt Hackbusch	MFJ1	2	Dolphin	Coucelaere
1705	Flgmt Kutschke	MFJ5	1	DH9	Walvhern
1710	Flgmt K Engelfried	MFJ5	3	DH9	Walchern
1720	Lt Fraymadl	MFJ5	1	DH9	Middleberg
1745	Vfw R Jörke	39	14	SE5a	
1800	Gefr B Bartels	44s	1	Balloon	St Simonm
1800	Vfw K Treiber	5	1	Balloon	W Fins
1905	Vfw O Frühner	26	25	RE8	Palleul
1905	Lt R Stark	35b	9	Dolphin	Cagnicourt
1906	Uffz C Schmidt	35b	2	Camel	
1908	St H Stor	35b	1	SE5a	N Marquion
1910	Lt J Jacobs	7	33	AWFK8	Passchendaele
1920	Lt F Reimer	26	7	SE5	Pallcul
1930	Vfw C Mesch	26	10	Balloon	Boiry-Notre Dame
1940	Vfw Schneck	9	2	Spad	E Vailly
1940	Lt W Neuenhofen	27	7	SE5a	Bourlon Wood
1945	Lt G Meyer	37	18	SE5a	Bourlon
	Lt F Büchner	13	27	Spad	Thiaucourt
	Lt F Büchner	13	28	Spad	Lachaussée
	Lt Scheller	19	4	Spad	Pagny
	Lt R Rineau	19	4	Spad	S Pagny
	Oblt E v Schleich	23b	34	AWFK8	Marcoing
	Lt H Seywald	23b	5	Camel	Marquette
	Vfw M Hutterer	23b	6	SE5a	St Leger
	Uffz H Kleinschred	23b	1	Camel	Arleux
	Flg S Braun	23b	1	Camel	Ecoust
	Lt F Classen	26	—	Camel	Reincourt
	Vfw C Mesch	26	11	SE5	Remy
	Lt E Thuy	28w	29	Camel	
	Lt Meixner	45	2	Balloon	Braisne
	Uffz De Ray	58	1	Camel	
	Lt F Höhn	60	11	Balloon	
	Lt A Korff	60	5	Balloon	
	Lt Leibfried	64w	1	Salmson 2A2	Blened
	Vfw J Hohly	65	7	Spad 2	St Remy
	Lt J Fichter	67	6	Balloon	Douaumont
	Lt M Gossner	77b	6	Balloon	Lironville
	Flak			2-seater	Marimbois
	Flak			2-seater	Conflans
	FTL, became lost, POW			2-seater	Doncourt
	FTL motor trouble, POW			Scout	Conflans

16 September 1918

Time	Name	Unit	No.	Aircraft	Location
0740	Fw Hoffmann	Kest3	1	Spad	SW Frescaty
0840	Lt J Jacobs	7	26	SE5a	W Menin
0840	Ltn H Boehning	79b	16	DH9	NW Bellenglise
0845	Lt O Frühner	26	26	BF2b	Fontaine
0845	Uffz Brungel	31	1	Scout	Gricourt
0850	Lt H Lange	26	7	BF2b	NW Quiery
0850	Lt Breidenbach	44s	1	BF2b	Roupy
0900	Lt K Plauth	20	7	DH9	Bondues
0900	Oblt B Loerzer	JGIII	39	BF2b	Dourges
0900	Lt F Rumey	5	35	DH9a	Villers-Guislain
0915	Vzflgmstr H Goerth	MFJ3	5	Camel	Zerkeghem
0915	Lt Holle	31	1	DH9	NE Douchy
1120	Lt G v Hantelmann	15	14	Spad	SW Conflans
1125	Vfw G Klaudat	15	6	Spad	St Hilaire
1150	Bz 152 FTL POW			Spad	Kemnat
1230	Lt F Rumey	5	36	SE5a	Marquion
1235	Lt F Rumey	5	37	Camel	Marquion
1330	Lt G Weiner	3	7	DH4	Ettendorf
1530	Lt G Meyer	37	19	Scout	Marquion
1540	Uffz Gengelin	37	2	Scout NW	Cambrai
1755	Lt O v Beaulieu-Marconnay	19	19	Bréguet XIV	SW Briey
1755	Lt R Rineau	19	5	Bréguet XIV	SW Briey
1755	Gefr Felder	19	2	Bréguet XIV	Conflans
1755	Vfw C Mesch	26	13	Camel	Reincourt
1755	Vfw F Classen	26	11	Camel	Recourt
1755	Lt C Reimer	26	—	Camel	Baralle
1800	Lt Macard	26	2	SE5	Sauchy-Couchy
1935	Lt J Jacobs	7	28	Balloon	Poperinghe
	Lt P Baümer	B	26	DH4	Henin-Lietard
	Lt O Löffler	B	10	DH4	Haveluy
	Lt O Löffler	B	11	DH4	NE Arras
	Lt F Hoffmann	B	1	BF2b	SW Cambrai
	Vfw Lieber	7	1	SE5a	
	Uffz Piesker	7	1	SE5a	
	Lt O v Beaulieu-Marconnay	19	18	Bréguet XIV	Fleville
	Lt H Seywald	23b	6	DH4	W Cantin
	Uffz H Kleinschred	23b	2	DH4	Denain
	Oblt B Loerzer	JGIII	40	SE5	
	Lt R Klimke	27	16	Camel	
	Lt F Noltenius	27	8	BF2b	
	Vfw E de Ridder	27	—	SE5a	
	Lt E Thuy	28w	30	SE5a	
	Oblt R Greim	34b	—	EA	
	OStv G Dörr	45	27	Spad	Fismes
	????	47	—	Balloon	
	Lt J Jensen	57	4	RE8	S Sauchy-Cauchy
	Vfw A Korff	60	6	Spad	
	Lt A Stephan	70	1	DH9a	Germersheim
	Sgt Metzger	70	1	DH9a	SE Landau
	Lt G Frädrich	72s	3	Spad	
	Lt H Mahn	72s	2	Spad	
	Lt G Anders	73	—	Voisin	Warnerville
	Lt zS Wilhelm	MFJ4	1	Camel	Zeebrugge
	Oblt E v Schleich	JGp8	34	AWFK8	Marquion
	Lt zS T Osterkamp	MFJ2	24	Camel	Coxyde
	Lt zS T Osterkamp	MFJ2	25	Camel	Coxyde
	Flak FTL POW			Spad	Xammes
	Lt Ahrens &		1		
	Sgt Koppel	FA44	1	Spad	Pierrefitte
	Flakzug 422			Spad	SE St Ludwig

17 September 1918

Time	Name	Unit	No.	Aircraft	Location
0905	Lt F Rumey	5	38	SE5a	Rumilly
1157	Lt F Brandt	26	—	Camel	Hermies
1300	Lt F Rumey	5	39	Camel	NW Cambrai
1310	Flak			DH4	Wahagnies

1510	Lt G v Hantelmann	15	15	Spad	N Gorze
1530	Lt F Noltenius	27	8	Balloon	
1805	Flak			Camel	Neuve Chapelle
1833	Flgmt G Hubrich	MFJ4	4	Camel	Batt Zeppelin
1910	Lt F Rumey	5	40	Camel	SW Cambrai
1910	OStv J Mai	5	27	Camel	S Bus
	Lt G Weiner	3	7	Bréguet XIV	Falkenberg
	Lt F Büchner	15	29	Salmson 2A2	Dampvitoux
	Lt H Frommherz	27	22	DH9	
	Lt H Boes	34b	2	SE5a	
	Vfw A Korff	60	6	Balloon	
	Flak FTL POW			Salmson 2A2	Bruville

18 September 1918

1030	Flak			SE5	Wingles
1135	Vfw Sowa/Flak	52	—	DH9	Lomme
1140	Lt S Garsztka	31	2	SE5a	Lempire
1430	Lt H Boehning	79b	17	Balloon	N Vaux
1510	Lt F Noltenius	27	10	Balloon	
1520	Lt C Degelow	40s	14	Balloon	Oosthoek
1540	Vfw K Trieber	5	2	Balloon	Tincourt
1645	Lt G v Hantelmann	15	16	Spad	Vionville
1725	Lt F Büchner	13	31	Spad	Chambley
1730	Lt F Büchner	13	32	Spad	W Chambley
1730	Lt U Neckel	6	26	DH4	Conflans
1730	Lt H Becker	12	15	Bréguet XIV	W Conflans
1730	Lt H Becker	12	16	Bréguet XIV	W Conflans
1730	Lt H Besser	12	1	Bréguet XIV	W Conflans
1730	Flg Wilke	12	1	Bréguet XIV	SW Conflans
1730	Lt A Greven	12	1	Bréguet XIV	SW Conflans
	Lt F Büchner	13	30	Spad XIII	Dampvitoux
	Lt S Garsztka	31	3	DH9	Saulcourt
	FTL, Cause unknown			Salmson 2A2	Chambley
	FTL, Cause unknown			Bréguet XIV	Conflans
	FTL, Cause unknown			Bréguet XIV	Conflans

19 September 1918

1600	Lt J Schulte-Frohlinde	11	3	BF2b	Bellenglise
1900	Lt J Jacobs	7	29	Camel	
	Uffz P Huttenrauch	7	4	AWFK8	
	Lt Maletzky	50	—	Balloon	Noyon

20 September 1918

0745	Lt W Neuenhofen	27	8	Camel	Proville
0745	Lt H Frommherz	27	23	Camel	Marcoing
0745	Lt F Noltenius	27	11	Camel	Marcoing
0800	Lt G Meyer	37	20	SE5a	N Hermies
1005	Lt zS Stinsky	MFJ2	2	Camel	SE Pervyse
1005	Vzflgmstr K Scharon	MFJ2	1	Camel	Pervyse
1037	Oblt O Schmidt	5	14	BF2b	Fresnoy-le-Grand
1040	Uffz Leicht	5	2	BF2b	Croix Fonsomme
1050	Lt K Odebrett	42	14	DH9	SE Montigny
1055	Lt C Degelow	40s	15	BF2b	Annappes
1445	Lt F Noltenius	27	12	Camel	Aubigny-au-Bac
1540	Lt F Barndt	26	9	Camel	Ecourt
1545	Vfw O Frühner	26	27	Camel	E Cagnicourt
1550	Lt P Bäumer	B	27	Camel	E Rumaucourt
	Lt J Jacobs	7	—	Camel	
	Lt F Kirchfield	73	2	Voisin	
	OStv W Schluckebier	73	2	Voisin	
	Lt G Anders	73	6	Voisin	
	Lt P Becht	MFJ1	2	Camel	Beerst
	Lt zS T Osterkamp	MFJ2	26	Camel	Preat Bosch
	Ground fire			H.P.	AFP C Airfield
	Flak			Camel	N Mericourt

21 September 1918

0945	Vfw Niemeyer &	I			
	Uffz Kappel	SchSt 29	2	Camel	NW Ephey
1045	Lt C Degelow	40s	16	RE8	St Julien
1120	Flak			SE5a	E La Bassée
1210	Lt J Jacobs	7	30	DH9	Dixmuide
1222	Lt J Jacobs	7	—	DH9	NW Roulers
1830	Lt Oldenberg	22s	1	DH9	Cambrai
1840	OStv J Mai	5	26	DH9	Montecouvez-Fe
1845	Uffz Westphal	29	2	SE5	E La Bassée
1900	Vfw R Schleichardt	18	1	Spad	Facqwald
1905	Lt H Müller	18	12	Spad	Combreshohen
1905	Lt Spindler	18	2	Spad	Combreshohen
	Lt P Baümer	B	28	DH4	E Bourlon Wood
	Lt P Baümer	B	29	DH4	E Lagnicourt
	Lt P Baümer	B	30	DH4	E Morchies
	Lt K Plauth	20	8	RE8	Staden
	Lt R Klimke	27	17	Camel	
	Lt H Frommherz	27	33	Sopwith	
	Lt F Noltenius	27	—	EA	
	Lt R Klimke	27	—	EA	

22 September 1918

0750	Vfw K Bohnenkamp	22s	9	Camel	N Ephey
0750	Vfw K Bohnenkamp	22s	10	Camel	N Ephey
0815	Lt H v d Marwitz	30	12	Camel	S Neuve Eglise
0820	Lt F Bieling	30	1	Camel	Ploegsteert Wald
0850	Lt W Neuenhofen	27	9	Sopwith	
0850	Vfw C Reimer	26	8	Camel	W Sauchy-Cauchy
0855	Vfw Belz	1	2	RE8	Cambrai
0858	Lt F Brandt	26	10	Camel	Sains
0956	Lt K Odebrett	42	15	Bréguet XIV	S Flavy-le-Martel
	Oblt B Loerzer	JGIII	41	Camel	
	Oblt B Loerzer	JGIII	42	EA	
	Lt H Frommherz	27	24	Sopwith	
	Lt E Thuy	28w	31	SE5a	Vitry
	Vfw H Hunninghaus	66	3	Spad	Pont Arcy
	Oblt O v Boenigk	JGII	26	Salmson 2A2	Conflans

23 September 1918

1620	Lt Oldenberg	22s	2	Balloon	Attilly
1620	Oblt H v Wedel	24s	4	SE5	Villers-Outreaux
1710	Lt H Leptein	63	7	RE8	S Fleurbaix
1725	Vfw K Ungewitter	24s	4	BF2b	Levergies
1725	OStv F Altemeier	24s	—	BF2b	Levergies
1815	Lt F Rumey	5	41	Dolphin	SW Baralle
	Lt B Hobein	20	—	BF2b	Baralle

24 September 1918

0730	Lt M Demisch	58	10	SE5a	Abancourt
0820	Lt F Rumey	5	42	SE5a	S Buissy
0830	Oblt O Schmidt	5	15	SE5a	Rumaucourt
0830	Uffz Leicht	5	3	SE5a	N Hamel
0830	Vfw R Wirth	37	4	BF2b	S Beauvois
1030	OStv Bansmer	44s	2	Spad 2	SW Attigny
1040	Vfw K Bohnenkamp	22s	10	DH9	Vermand
1040	Lt K Plauth	20	9	DH9	Sainghin
1050	Lt J Gildemeister	20	3	DH9	Lorgies
1050	Lt J v Busse	20	8	DH9	Lorgies
1100	Vfw F Poeschke	53	3	Spad 2	Besine
1120	Vfw O Hennrich	46	14	Balloon	NE Manancourt
1350	Uffz H Haase	21s	4	Balloon	S Braisne
1415	Lt zS Wilhelm	MFJ4	2	Camel	Pervyse
1610	Vfw O Hennrich	46	15	Balloon	Fins
1612	Vfw O Hennrich	46	16	Balloon	Fins
1612	Lt Auf den Haar	46	1	Balloon	Fins

1725	Vfw Becker	44s	3	2-seater	Metz-en-Couture
1730	OStv J Mai	5	28	DH9	S Beauvais
1800	Lt C Degelow	40s	17	SE5a	Zillebekesee
1800	Vfw Mack	63	2	SE5a	S Ypres
1815	Vfw M Kuhn	21s	9	Balloon	SE Fismes
1835	Lt J Jacobs	7	35	Camel	Moorslede
1900	OStv G Dörr	45	28	Spad	Soissons
	Lt P Baümer	B	31	Camel	Sailly
	Lt P Baümer	B	32	DH9	SW Clary
	Lt O Löffler	B	12	DH9	W Cambrai
	Oblt H v Boddein	59	4	SE5a	Anneux
	Oblt F Krafft	59	2	SE5a	Inchy
	Oblt H v Boddein	59	5	DH4	Le Pave
	Lt Lehmann	59	1	BF2b	Boursies
	Lt H Jebens	59	1	BF2b	Bantounelle
	Lt G Wember	61	2	Balloon	
	Lt zS P Achilles	MFJ5	2	DH9	Werckem

25 September 1918

0805	Lt R Fuchs	77b	1	Spad	Arnaville
0950	Lt J Grassmann	10	6	Balloon	Pont-à-Mousson
1010	Lt O v Beaulieu-Marconnay	19	20	Bréguet XIV	Pont-à-Mousson
1115	Gefr Meyer	3	1	DH9a	SE Sarralben
1120	Lt G v Hantelmann	15	17	DH4	S Metz
1430	Lt W Schmidt	78b	1	DH4	Zabern
1430	Lt Keisze	Kest 1b	1	DH4	Zabern
1500	Vfw E Prime	78b	—	DH4	Buhl Airfield
1500	2/Flamga 911			DH9	Buhl Airdrome
1750	Lt zS P Achilles	MFJ5	3	Camel	Hooglede
1800	Vfw K Treiber	5	3	Spad	S St Quentin
1800	Lt S Garsztka	31	4	DH9	Fresnoy
1800	Vzflgmstr A Zenses	MFJ2	8	Camel	Wynendaele
1805	Uffz Brungel	31	2	DH9	Busigny
1805	Lt zS P Achilles	MFJ5	4	Camel	NW Roulers
1815	Oblt R v Greim	34b	23	DH9	S Escaufourt
1825	Lt F v Braun	79b	2	BF2b	Villers-Guislain
1850	Ltn F Piechulek	56	11	Camel	Kortemarck
	Lt F Noltenius	27	13	Camel	
	Lt F Hengst	64w	3	Salmson 2A2	
	Lt A Stephen	70	2	DH4	Alberschweiler
	Vfw Lemke	70	2	DH4	Bergzabern
	Vfw Krist	70	1	DH4	Brumath
	Lt G Anders	73	5	Farman	Moronvillers
	Uffz Neilputs &		1		
	Uffz Rogge	SchSt19	1	SE5	Nurlu

26 September 1918

0710	Lt M Näther	62	14	Spad	Nezonvaux
0810	Vfw W Seitz	8	—	Spad	Etain
0830	Lt F Höhn	60	14	Spad 2	Somme-Py
0831	Gefr Rohr	50	1	Bréguet XIV	SE Perthies
0900	Uffz K Hoffmann	60	1	Spad	Massiges
1025	Vfw K Bohnenkamp	22s	12	Camel	NW Rossoy
1030	Flgmt K Engelfried	MFJ5	4	Camel	Wenduyne
1030	Flgomt C Kairies	MFJ5	6	Camel	Meumunster
1050	Uffz Ernst	49	1	Bréguet XIV	Tahure
1115	Lt Freymadl	MFJ1	2	DH4	Ostende
1115	Vzflgmstr Sawatzki	MFJ1	1	Camel	Ostende
1215	Lt W Blume	9	26	Spad 2	Tahure
1215	Lt F Höhn	60	15	Balloon	Minaucourt
1300	OStv G Dorr	45	29	Spad 2	Fismes
1350	Vfw R Francke	8	—	Spad	
1410	Lt F Rumey	5	43	DH4	Gouzeaucourt
1415	Lt Hebler	68	2	Balloon	Auberive
1415	Lt Hebler	68	3	Balloon	Auberive
1433	Vfw C Mesch	26	12	Dolphin	W St Quentin
1535	Lt M Näther	62	15	Balloon	Thierville

1535	Lt Briedenbach	62	1	Balloon	Thierville
1540	Lt H Häbich	49	4	Balloon	Minaucourt
1545	Lt M Näther	62	16	Salmson 2A2	Abaucourt
1600	Vfw A Juehe	8	4	Spad	
1630	Oblt G Rasberger	8ob	4	Spad XIII	Athienville
1645	Vfw O Hennrich	46	17	Balloon	Lieramont
1710	Oblt E Udet	4	61	DH4	SW Metz
1715	Oblt E Udet	4	62	DH4	SW Metz
1715	Vfw Seidel	3	1	DH9	SE Frescaty
1715	Lt Bacher	3	3	DH	
1715	Vfw Glasemann	3	1	DH	
1715	Lt R Kraut	4	1	DH	
1720	Lt J Klein	15	16	DH4	NE Vern
1727	Vfw B Ultsch	77b	10	DH9	Kubern
1730	Vfw Schaflein	77b	1	DH9	Pullingen
1730	Vfw Agne	77b	1	DH9	Grossprunach
1740	Lt J v Ziegesar	15	3	DH4	Pont-à-Mousson
1740	Lt S Garsztka	31	5	SE5a	Fresnoy-le-Petit
1745	Uffz Fröhlich	46	1	Balloon	Lieramont
1755	Lt H v Freden	50	10	Balloon	Perthes
1800	Lt Matetsky	50	3	Spad	Perthes
1805	Lt F Rumey	5	44	BF2b	Cambrai
1810	Lt Matetsky	50	4	Spad	Le Mesnil
	Lt E Bormann	B	11	Camel	N Cambrai
	Lt v Gluszewski	4	1	DH4	N Leveningen
	Vfw K Treiber	5	4	DH4	E Le Pave
	Lt H Becker	12	17	DH4	SE Longuyon
	Lt H Becker	12	18	DH4	Anoux
	Lt A Greven	12	2	DH4	Giraumont
	Vfw Klaiber	12	1	DH4	NW Longuyon
	Lt H Besser	12	—	DH4	Landres
	Lt F Büchner	13	33	Spad	Consenvoye
	Lt F Büchner	13	34	Salmson 2A2	Charpentrie
	Lt F Büchner	13	35	Spad	Gercourt
	Lt F Büchner	13	36	Spad	Etreillers
	Vfw A Haussmann	13	15	Spad	Bertincourt
	Lt G v Hantelmann	15	18	Spad	Etain
	Lt H Schäfer	15	9	Spad	SW Etain
	Oblt B Loerzer	JGIII	43	EA	
	Oblt B Loerzer	JGIII	44	EA	
	Lt H v Freden	50	11	Salmson 2A2	Ville-sur-Tourbe
	Lt W Frickart	65	9	Spad	S Delut
	????	69	—	Spad	Montreux
	Lt H Mann	72s	3	EA	
	Lt H Mann	72s	4	EA	
	Lt G Tschentschel	72s	5	EA	
	Lt G Frädrich	72s	4	EA	
	Lt Schulz	72s	1	EA	
	Lt M Gossner	77b	8	DH9	Menningen
	Vfw D Averes	81	7	Bréguet XIV	Tahure
	Vfw A Nägler	81	7	Spad	Suippes
	Flak			DH4	Noyelles-le-Sec

27 September 1918

0755	Vfw H Juhnke	52	—	BF2b	W Armentières
0815	Oblt R v Greim	34b	25	Camel	S Masnières
0930	Lt R v Barnekow	1	6	SE5a	Bourlonwald
0940	Uffz G Born	1	3	SE5a	St Olle-Cambrai
1020	OStv F Altemeier	24s	17	BF2b	Marcy-Fontaine
1130	Lt R Ruckle	33	2	BF2b	Busigny
1208	Lt F Rumey	5	45	Camel	E Marquion
1210	OStv J Mai	5	29	Camel	Sauchy-Cauchy
1250	Vfw K Treiber	5	5	SE5a	W Cambrai
1300	Lt R v Barnekow	1	7	DH4	Sailly
1300	Uffz G Born	1	4	Dolphin	Bourlonwald
1403	Vfw F Classen	26	8	BF2b	S Brunemont
1550	Oblt O Schmidt	5	16	BF2b	Cattenières

1600	Vfw O Hennrich	46	18	BF2b	Neuvilly
1655	Lt H Korner	19	4	Spad	Pagny
1655	Lt H v Freden	50	12	Balloon	Minaucourt
1700	Vfw E Prime	78b	—	Spad VII	Herbeville
1730	Gefr Meyer	3	2	Spad	Champenoux
1735	Lt G Bassenge	B	4	SE5a	Noyelles
1735	Vfw F Classen	26	9	SE5	S Sailly
1810	Vfe A Korff	60	8	Spad	N Tahure
1820	Lt F Höhn	60	16	Spad	Marfaux
1820	Vfw Zimmermann	60	1	Spad	Tahure
1820	Uffz H Pfaffenreiter	60	3	Spad	
	Lt P Bäumer	B	33	SE5a	W Cambrai
	Lt P Bäumer	B	34	SE5a	W Cambrai
	Lt H Vallendor	B	4	Camel	Marquion
	Lt P Bäumer	B	35	DH4	Oisy-le-Verger
	Lt E Bormann	B	12	Camel	Ecourt-St Quentin
	Lt E Bormann	B	13	Camel	E Epinoy
	Lt H Vallendor	B	5	Camel	N Bourlonwald
	Uffz K Feveres	B	1	Camel	Aubenscheul
	Lt H Frommherz	27	25	SE5	
	Lt H Frommherz	27	26	SE5	
	Lt E Thuy	28w	32	SE5a	
	Lt C Degelow	40s	18	BF2b	W Valenciennes
	Lt F Piechulek	56	12	Camel	Torhout
	Lt J Jensen	57	5	DH9	Fechain
	Vfw Senf	59	1	DH9	Goeulzin
	Lt M Näther	62	17	Spad	Mantzeville
	Vfw D Averes	81	8	Spad	Ville
	Vfw A Nägler	81	8	Bréguet XIV	N Tahure

28 September 1918

0800	Uffz Jeckert	56	3	AR2	Moorslede
0810	Lt F Höhn	60	17	Balloon	Tahure
0830	Lt F Höhn	60	18	Balloon	Bethelainville
0835	Lt G Bassenge	B	5	SE5a	Hem-Lenglet
1024	Flak			SE5	N Carvin
1035	Lt O v Beaulieu-Marconnay	19	21	Spad	Dannevoux
1130	Flak			Camel	S Drocourt
1145	Vfw F Poeschke	53	4	Spad 2	Somme-Py
1150	Uffz K Boness	53	1	Spad	
1230	Vzflgmstr A Zenses	MFJ2	9	Camel	Woumen
1230	Lt zS T Osterkamp	MFJ2	27	Camel	Woumen
1240	Lt E Baumgartel	56	1	SE5	Ypern
1315	Lt Wolff	60	1	Spad	Vienne-le-Château
1430	FlgMt Nake	MFJ1	1	DH9	Leke
1545	Lt A Brandenstein	49	6	Spad	Cerny
1620	Vfw K Bohnenkamp	22s	15	DH9	Wassigny
1740	Lt K Plauth	20	10	Camel	S Roulers
1740	Lt K Plauth	20	11	Camel	S Roulers
1745	Lt zS R Poss	MFJ4	7	Dolphin	W Roulers
1745	FlgMstr A Buhl	MFJ4	4	Dolphin	Roulers
1750	Lt J J Raesch	43	2	SE5a	E Ypern
1810	Lt zS T Osterkamp	MFJ2	28	Camel	Pierkenshoeck
1815	Lt zS Bargmann	MFJ2	1	DH9	Beerst
1815	Flgmt Pfeiffer	MFJ3	1	Camel	Woumen
	Lt O Löffler	B	13	SE5a	Epinoy
	Uffz K Feveres	B	2	Camel	Epinoy
	Lt J Jacobs	7	30	SE5a	
	Lt F Büchner	13	37	Salmson 2A2	Nantillois
	Lt W Niethammer	13	4	Bréguet XIV	
	Uffz E Binge	16b	4	SE5a	
	Oblt R v Greim	34b	—	Camel	S Masnières
	Lt C Degelow	40s	19	Camel	Armentières
	Lt F Piechulek	56	13	DH4	Wervicq
	Vfw Krebs	56	1	Spad	Kastelhoek
	Vfw R Ruebe	67	—	Balloon	
	Lt G Frädrich	72s	5	AR2	Maure

	Vfw K Arnold	72s	4	AR2	Maure
	Lt E Schulz	72s	2	Spad	VII Ardeuil
	Lt H Mahn	72s	5	Spad	VII Ardeuil

29 September 1918

	Pilot/Crew	Unit	Vic No	E/A	Location
0815	Vfw Krebs	56	2	SE5	Westroosebeke
0820	Vzflgmstr Hackbusch	MFJ1	3	Camel	SW Oostkamp
0820	Lt Freymadl	MFJ1	3	Camel	SW Oostkamp
0820	Flgmt Reiss	MFJ1	1	Camel	SW Oostkamp
0830	Uffz Jeckert	56	4	RE8	Zonnebeke
0845	Vfw K Treiber	5	6	DH9	N Caudry
0850	OStv J Mai	5	30	BF2b	N Caudry
0940	Lt K Odebrett	42	16	SE5a	Bohain
1000	Lt H v Freden	50	13	Spad	Somme-Py
1020	Oblt H v Wedel	24s	5	SE5	Hesdins
1020	Vfw O Hennrich	46	19	SE5a	Villers-Outreaux
1030	Lt Auf den Haar	46	2	Scout	Aubenscheul
1040	OStv F Altemeier	24s	18	Scout	Montbrehain
1050	Lt A Lenz	22s	6	SE5a	Bellenglise
1205	Flgmt E Blaass	MFJ3	3	Camel	Oudekapelle
1230	Lt Kohlpoth	56	1	DH4	Beythem
1240	Lt W Rosenstein	40s	5	BF2b	
1400	Lt H Henkel	37	4	Balloon	Graincourt
1720	Uffz Bader	64w	3	Spad XIII	SW Chambley
1855	Lt R Rineau	19	6	Spad	Brieulles
1900	Lt F Rolfes	45	17	BF2b	Masnières
	Uffz Keusen	B	2	BF2b	E Irony
	Uffz K Fervers	B	2	BF2b	Cagnoucles
	Lt P Baümer	B	36	RE8	Marcoing
	Lt P Baümer	B	37	Camel	Bourlonwald
	Lt P Baümer	B	38	Camel	SE Sailly
	Lt J Jacobs	7	—	EA	
	Lt Zicke	8	2	Spad	
	Lt K Plauth	20	12	DH9	Roulers
	Vfw H Huenninghaus	66	4	Spad	N Jouy
	Uffz O Bieleit	66	1	Bréguet XIV	N Jouy
	Lt zS T Osterkamp	MFJ2	29	Bréguet XIV	W Zarren

30 September 1918

0940	Vfw W Schmelter	42	3	SE5a	Bohain
1025	Vfw F Nuesch	22s	2	Camel	Omissy
1540	Gefr Pissowotsky	54	1	Balloon	Monsard
1700	Lt H Henkel	37	5	BF2b	Crevecoeur
1800	Lt S Garsztka	31	6	SE5a	Lehaucourt
1820	Lt H Habich	49	5	Spad	Maure
1820	Lt F Ray	49	17	Spad	Somme-Py
	Lt A Wunsch	67	—	Salmson 2A2	
	Vfw A Nägler	81	9	Spad	Ville

APPENDIX V

Belgian Victory Claims September 1918

3 September 1918

Time	Pilot/Crew	Unit	Vic No	E/A	Location	How
	Lt W Coppens	Esc.1	29	Balloon	Tenbrielen	DF

4 September 1918

| | Lt W Coppens | Esc.1 | 30 | Balloon | | DF |

27 September 1918

| Ltn W Coppens | Esc.1 | 31 | Balloon | Leffinghe | DF |

29 September 1918

| Ltn W Coppens | Esc.1 | 32 | Balloon | Leffinghe | DF |

APPENDIX VI

Known German Casualties September 1918

1 September

Vfw Pilartz	FA294	WIA, near Roeux	
Uffz Gottfried Eberle	"	KIA	
Ltn Hermann Aschoff		KIA, Hendecourt	
Ltn Friedrich Ohlf	FA208	KIA, Gendecourt	
Uffz Alfred Donnevert		KIA, Le Cateau	

night of 1/2 September

Ltn Paul Berthold	BGIII	Killed, Gontrude	4 Armee
Uffz Kurt Peuckert	"	Killed	
Ltn Hertel	"	Injured	

2 September

Ltn Hartung (O)	FAA279	WIA	Armee-A 'C'
Flg Rau (O)	FA37	WIA	"
Ltn Gottfried Clausnitzer	J72	KIA	1 Armee
Uffz Hennies	J49	WIA	3 Armee
Flg Prillwitz	J81	POW	"
Uffz Herzberg	FA250	WIA	4 Armee
Ltn Hans Quartier	J67	POW	5 Armee
Ltn Konrad Brendle	J45	POW/DOW, Reims	7 Armee
Flg Karl Pabst	J50	KIA	"
Ltn Friedrich Noltenius	J27	Safe	17 Armee
Vfw Heinrich Gockel	J33	Safe, a/c burnt	"
Uffz Josef Kraemer (P)	FA2	KIA, Nesle	19 Armee
Ltn Eugen Weber (O)	"	KIA	
Uffz Otto Reichart		KIA, Coincy	"
Ltn Adolf Thomas (O)	FAA210	KIA, Cambrai	"
Ltn Walter Lucas (O)	FAA232	WIA, DOW 22 September	"

3 September

Vfw Friedrich Engler	J62	WIA	1 Armee
Gefr Wilhelm Becker	SS16	KIA, Jonkershove	4 Armee
Uffz Hugo Holtmaier	"	KIA	
Ltn Wilhelm Asimus (O)	FAA248	KIA, Metz-en-Couture	
Gefr Karl Noelpp (P)	"	KIA	
Uffz Karl Grunwald		KIA, Valenciennes	
Ltn Keimens Hoffstadt		KIA, Reims	
Vfw Wilhelm Skworz	J36	KIA, Abancourt	
Flg Hermann Wirth	J33	KIA, Douai	
Vfw Max Siewert		KIA, Anizy-le-Château	
Vfw Fritz Schloeter		KIA	

4 September

Vfw Kurt Jentsch	J2	WIA	
Vfw Alfred Baeder	J65	WIA	Armee-A 'C'
Vfw Hans Reimers	J6	DOW, 5 September	2 Armee
Ltn Kurt Waldheim	J36	KIA, Abancourt	17 Armee
Uffz Reinhold Neumann	J36	KIA, Abancourt	"
Gefr Tegtmeyer	J57	WIA	"
Vfw Duennhaupt	J58	WIA	"
Flg Otto Wagner	J79b	POW; DVII 4504/18	18 Armee

Gefr Jakob Katzner	J43	WIA, DOW 16 September	6 Armee
Ltn Lauscher	J31	Injured	
Gefr Anton Freyler	BS27	KIA, Etreux	
Uffz Hans Lienhardt	"	KIA	
Uffz Oskar Brachmann		KIA, Charleroi	
Gefr Eugen Reudt		KIA, Wambaix	

5 September

Ltn Jochim v Winterfeld	J4	KIA, Avesnes-le-Sec	2 Armee
Ltn Schenk	J5	WIA	"
Gefr Jakob Katzner	J43	KIA	6 Armee
Vfw Ernst de Ritter	J27	Shot down — safe	17 Armee
Ltn Heinrich Hager	J32b	WIA	"
Uffz Otto Rösler	J37	KIA, Flesquières	"

6 September

Uffz Weiser (P)	SS20	POW	
Uffz Scharg	"	POW	
Flgr Bonifazius Baal		KIA, Bisigny	Armee-A 'C'
Ltn Karl Rommel (O)	FAA219	KIA, SW Bray	"
Flgr Otto Ruden		KIA "	
Uffz Richard Mann		KIA	

7 September

Vfw Rudolf Besel	SS30	KIA	
Ltn Rudolf Brammer (O)	FAA203	KIA, Flesquières	
Flgr Otto Goldtree		KIA, Valenciennes	
Flgr Julius Jansen (P)	FA1	KIA	
Ltn Johann Neumann (O)		KIA	
Gefr Rudolf Knust (P)	FA259	KIA, St Leger	
Oblt Neufulle (O)		POW	
Vfw Hermann (P)		POW (LVG crew)	
Ltn Schneider (O)		POW	

8 September

Gefr Kurt Bluemener	J6	KIA, Beaurevoir	2 Armee
Lftsch Kurt Rehn		KIA, Villers-Outreaux	"

13 September

Ltn Eugen Kelber	J12	KIA, Mars-la-Tour	Armee-A 'C'
Ltn Kohler	FA37	WIA	"
Ltn Rudolf Reinau	J19	Baled out safely, over Charey	
Ltn Kole	KG	POW; Friedrichshafen crew	
Ltn Schwaderer		POW	
Gefr Vowinkel		POW/WIA	

14 September

Ltn Paul Wolff	J13	POW, Lachaussée	Armee-A 'C'
Ltn Eugen Siempelkamp	J64w	WIA	"
Uffz Boehm (P)	FA25	WIA, Langemarck	4 Armee
Ltn Walter Stangen (O)	"	KIA	
Fw Deinlein (P)	FAA199	Safe	
Ltn Georg Baumann (O)	"	KIA, Monhofen	19 Armee
Flgr Anton Kempa	J3	POW "	
Ltn Günther von Büren	J18	WIA	"
Gefr Willi Thom		KIA, Etreux	
Ltn Gustav Proemmel		KIA	
Flgr Wilhelm Arnold		KIA	
Uffz Erich Reinecke (P)	FA17	KIA, Gonnelieu	
Ltn Dietegen v Salis-Marschlins	"	KIA	

15 September

Ltn Friedrich Gerke	FAA281	MIA, Roan l'Etape	Armee-A 'A'
Ltn Willy Beck	"	MIA	
Ltn Johannes Klein	J15	WIA	Armee-A 'C'
Fw Elze (P)	FAA206	WIA	"
Ltn Wilhelm Holtfort (O)	FA236	KIA, Armentières	6 Armee

Ltn Paul Vogel	J23b	POW/DOW, Amiens	17 Armee
Vfw Ernst de Ritter	J27	WIA	„
Ltn Hilmar Quittenbaum	J28w	KIA, nr Douai	„
Uffz Ottowell	J33	WIA	„
Vfw Wilhelm Lubrecht		KIA, St Quentin	
Vfw Hermann Sandtvos		KIA, Cambrai	
Vfw Wilhelm Mitschein		KIA, Cambrai	
Gefr Walter Leingruber		KIA, Cambrai	
Gefr Hermann Gieseler		KIA, Cambrai	
Lftsch Otto Foshac		KIA, Cambrai	

16 September

Oblt Hans Schleiter	J70	WIA	Armee-A 'A'
Two-seater	FA10	crew safe, nr Hochfeld	„
Vfw Padberg (P)	FAA279	Safe Armee-A 'C'	
Ltn Springerum (O)		Safe	
Ltn Friedrich Kresse	J7	KIA, Houplines	4 Armee
Gefr Kurt Brandt	J51	KIA, nr Quesnoy	
Flgr Siegfried Braun	J23b	KIA, Cantin	17 Armee
Ltn Friedrich Noltenius	J27	Safe, nr Mons	„
Ltn Heinrich Wessels	MFJ1	DOW	
Vzflugmstr Lawatski	MFJ1	WIA	
Flgmt Nake	MFJ1	WIA	
Oblt Alfred Braungard (O)	FA40	KIA, Caudry	
Ltn Paul Marten (O)	FAA222	KIA, Laon	
Vfw Walter Sieg	J71	KIA, Habsheim	
Uffz Georg Steinemann		KIA, Rethel	

17 September

Vfw Johannes	FA253	WIA	6 Armee
Fw Hans Popp	J77b	KIA, Warville-Eply	19 Armee
Ltn Max Scharf (O)	KG5	KIA, Pronville, Friedrichshafen	
Uffz Paul Noeller	„	KIA crew	
Uffz Paul Kagelmacher	„	KIA	
Ltn Josef Freck	„	KIA	
Gefr Otto Kurth (P)		KIA, Athies, AEG crew	
Ltn Gerlach		POW	
Ltn Tillmanns		POW	
Flgr Geiger (P)	BS6	POW, DFW crew	
Ltn Nolte		POW	
Ltn Hans Siemann (O)	FA227	KIA, Braisne	

18 September

Ltn Erich Kaempfe	J13	WIA/DOW on 20th	Armee-A 'C'
Uffz Hoppe (P)	FA17	WIA	2 Armee
Ltn Buchwald (O)	„	WIA	
Ltn Karl Höhne (O)	FA36	KIA, Maas-Ost	5 Armee
Ltn Ernst Schulz (P)	„	KIA	
Ltn Wilhelm Thormann (P)	FAA247	KIA, Froidmont	6 Armee
Ltn Wilhelm Babetz (O)	„	KIA	
Vfw Karl Zickgraf		KIA, Nivelle, Belg	„

19 September

Ltn Lorenz (P)	FA241	WIA	2 Armee
Gefr Paul Miltowski (P)	FA224	KIA, Gonnelieu	„
Ltn Robert Müller (O)	„	KIA	

20 September

Uffz Eddelbuttel	FA276b	Evaded, returned 22nd	
Ltn Huss	„	Evaded	Armee-A 'A'
Ltn Helmut Gantz	J56	DOW, Armentières	4 Armee
Vfw Otto Frühner	J26	Baled out safely	17 Armee
Ltn Han Böhning	J79b	WIA, Soreil	18 Armee
Flgr Walter Fischer		KIA, Jeancourt	
Vfw Johannes Schnabel		KIA	
Ltn Karl Schneider		KIA	
Gefr Fritz Mey		KIA, Charleroi	

Ltn Walter Mohnke		KIA, Nivelles	
Fw Christian Rothweiler		KIA, Villers-Outreaux	
Flgr Wilhelm Sudmeyer		KIA, Bouriers	

21 September

Uffz Gerhard Schleuter (P)	FA2	KIA, St Hilaire	Armee-A 'C'
Ltn Erwin Sklarek (O)		KIA	
Flgr John (P)	F46b	KIA, Briey	"
Ltn Eduard Reichenwallner		KIA	
Ltn Rudolf Klimke	J27	WIA	17 Armee
Uffz August Buecker		KIA, Valenciennes	"
Uffz Wilhelm Landsberg (P)		KIA, Sailly	"
Gefr Bosche (O)		WIA	
Ltn Paul Baümer	J2	Baled out safely	
Gefr Wilhelm Pieper		KIA, Pass am Strumitza, Belg	
Vfw Wilhelm Güdemann (P)	BS7	KIA, Proyart	2 Armee
Oblt Werner Schmidt (O)		KIA	
Flgr Konrad Wieclorek		KIA, Lanboucy-la-Ville	

22 September

Ltn Karl Bauernfeind	J34b	KIA, Demicourt	2 Armee
Ltn Krayer	J45	WIA	7 Armee
Flgr Otto Muhr		KIA, Avesnes	19 Armee

23 September

Fw Leopold Bach	FAA	KIA	Sailly
Vfw Paul Färber		KIA	
Gefr August Brenner		KIA, St Armond	
Flgr Paul Joos		KIA, Briey	
Fw Adolf Mörch		KIA, Arras	
Flgr Josef Uklei		KIA, Valenciennes	
FlgObmt Karl Schiffmann	MFJ2	KIA, Ichteghem	

24 September

Vfw Fittgen (P)	FA37	KIA	Armee-A 'C'
Ltn Konnigs		KIA	
Vfw Wilkens (P)	FA29	MIA, Briey	"
Ltn Rudolf Kaehne (O)		MIA	
Ltn Wilhelm Meyer	J47	POW, Suippes	3 Armee
Ltn Melcher	MFJ1	WIA	4 Armee
Ltn Bruno Hobein	J20	WIA	"
Vfw Peter Stenzel	J14	KIA, Fort d'Englos	
Vfw Willi Schmidt	J27	DOW 26th	17 Armee
Ltn Martin Demisch	J58	DOW 25th	"
Ltn Richard Biermann (O)	FA19	KIA, Henin-Lietard	
Gefr Max Hess		KIA, Lille	
Uffz Franz Joscht		KIA, Peuvilly	
Ltn Walter Klemann (O)	FA205	KIA, Crécy	
Ltn Emil Melcher		KIA, Ghistelles	
Uffz Paul Müller		KIA, Neuville-Cambrai	

25 September

Vfw Adolf Martens (P)	FA207	KIA, La Fontaine	2 Armee
Ltn Hans Stanger (O)	"	KIA	
Gefr Franz Wagner	J79b	KIA, Preselles Ferme	18 Armee
Ltn Franz Hausmann	BG4	KIA, Cambrai	
Ltn Fritz Knipp		KIA, Maas-Ost	
Ltn Reinhold Lampe	BG9	KIA, Arras	
Fw August Platte	"	KIA	
Uffz Karl Rühlicke	"	KIA	

26 September

Vfw Huar	J68	WIA	5 Armee
Vfw Robert Mossbacher	J77b	Safe	19 Armee
Vfw Weinmann	J50	POW	3 Armee
Ltn Ernst Udet	J4	WIA	
Vfw Meppes	J37	WIA	

Flgr Ewald Feuchtner	J69	KIA, Etain	
Flgr Michael Reiner		KIA, Mont Brehain	
Flgr Georg Schmidt		KIA, Aubigny-au-Bac	

27 September

Ltn Max Näther	J62	WIA	Armee-A 'C'
Ltn Mappes	J37	WIA	2 Armee
Vfw Robert Wirth	J37	WIA	,,
Ltn Fritz Rumey	J5	KIA, Neuville	,,
Ltn Fritz Heinz	J2	KIA, nr Cambrai	17 Armee
Ltn Paul Strähle	J57	WIA	,,
Ltn Hans Jebens	J59	KIA, Bouchain	,,
Oblt Hans v Boddien	J59	WIA	,,
Ltn Holle	J31	WIA	
FlugMt Richard Arfendt		KIA, La Lovie	
Ltn Wilhelm Kreitz		KIA, La Lovie	
Gefr Heinrich Brinker		KIA, Tournai	
Flgr Gustav Dunkel		KIA, La Briquette	
Flgr Fritz Schtster		KIA	
Ltn Josef Heckenberger	FA290	KIA	
Uffz Karl Kessel		KIA, Valenciennes	
Ltn Eugen Wild (O)	FA261	DOW, Rethel	

28 September

Vfw Heinrich Brobowski	J53	POW	3 Armee
Uffz Karl Hofmann	J60	KIA, Argonne Forest	,,
Ltn Hugo Fleisher (O)	BGIII	KIA, Ypres	
Ltn Willi Meyer (P)	,,	KIA	
Flgr Josef Jansen		KIA, Marquion	
Flgr Johann Kohler		KIA, Valenciennes	
Gefr Theodor Kaufhold		KIA	
Flgr Walter Koulen		KIA, Mouchin	
Fw Otto Stollberg		KIA	
Flgr Andreas Schaetzhauer		KIA, Beauchamps	
Ltn Gustav Spaich (P)	BGIV		KIA, Catillon
Vfw Walter Tischmann		KIA, Harly	

29 September

Ltn Gerold Tschentschel	J72	WIA	Armee-A 'C'
Fw von Kamp (P)	FA33	WIA	2 Armee
Ltn Weise (O)	,,	WIA	
Gefr Kurt Grossmann (P)	FA33	KIA, Gorth	,,
Ltn Richard Brauss (O)	,,	KIA	
Oblt Eberhardt Gandert	J51	POW	4 Armee
Ltn Fritz Hoffmann	J2	KIA, W Cambrai	17 Armee
Flgr Willi Benkert		KIA, Coudron	
Flgr August Bendrin		KIA, End-Auz	
Fw Friedrich Geiger		KIA, Bernot	
OffStv Paul Haack		KIA, Gardy	
Ltn Ernst Köther		KIA, Bonne-Evance	
Vfw Gerhard Köth		KIA, Furstenwald	
Ltn Karl Metzler	FA287	KIA, Breuil	
Gefr Gerhard Müller		KIA, Fontaine	
Uffz Fritz Stein		KIA, Harly	

30 September

Ltn Gaspary (O)	FA241	WIA	2 Armee
Ltn Georg Schenker	J41	WIA	
Gefr Ernst Bruck		KIA, Hauving	
Gefr Karl Faerber		KIA, Osterode	
Gefr Friedrich Heinz		KIA	
Flgr Willi Glaser		KIA, Wahn	
OffStv Ambrosius Haas		KIA	
Vfw Wilhelm Hagendorf		KIA, Rethel	
Ltn Willi Herrmann		KIA, Putzig	
Ltn Martin Miehe		KIA	
ObMt Albert Günner		KIA	
ObflgMstr August Ponater		KIA	

APPENDIX VII

IAF Victory Claims

Date	Pilot/Crew	A/C	Sqn	E/A Type	Claim
7 Sep	Capt R J Gammon	C6274	104	Fokker DVII	DF
	2/Lt P E Appleby			Fokker DVII	D
"	Lt J W Richards		104		
	Sgt W E Reast			Fokker DVII	D
"	1/Lt D J Waterous	A7942	55	Fokker DVII	OOC
	2/Lt C L Rayment				
13 Sep	2/Lt A D Mackenzie	D3263	104		
	2/Lt C E Bellord			Pfalz DIII	OOC
"	Lt Malcolm	D5483	104		
	Lt Alexander			Fokker DVII	OOC
"	2/Lt W T Jones	C6260	99		
	2/Lt E C Black			Fokker DVII	D
14 Sep	Capt W G Stephenson	D3041	99		
	Sgt J Jones			EA	D
"	Capt E J Garland	D6023	104		
	Lt W E Bottrell			Fokker DVII	D
15 Sep	Capt B J Silly	F5701	55		
	Lt J Parke			Albatros DV	DF
"	2/Lt C Turner	A7427	55		
	2/Lt J T L Attwood			Fokker DVII	D
"	Capt R T Gammon	C6264	99		
	2/Lt P E Appleby			Pfalz DIII	D
16 Sep	Lt A Stephen		110		
	Sgt Metzger			EA	OOC
25 Sep	2/Lt H Wood	D8392	55	Fokker DVII	D
	2/Lt J D Evans			Fokker DVII	OOC
"	Lt W G Braid	D8386	55		
	2/Lt G S Barber			Pfalz DIII	D
"	Lt J Cunliffe		55		
	2/Lt G E Little			Fokker DVII	OOC
"	Capt A C M Groom	F1008	110		
	Capt G E Lange			Fokker DVII	OOC
"	Capt A G Inglis	F1010	110		
	2/Lt G W L Bodley			Fokker DVII	OOC
"	Lt R P Brailli	F995	110	EA	OOC
	Lt R F Casey			EA	OOC
"	2/Lt A Brandrich	F980	110		
	Sgt T W Harman			EA	OOC
26 Sep	Lt D M West	D544	99		
	2/Lt J W Howard			Fokker DVII	OOC
"	110 Squadron			Fokker DVII	D
"	110 Squadron			Fokker DVII	D

Index

British Empire

Abbey, Maj J 64
Adams, Lt A T 17
Adams, Lt G H 176
Allan, 2/Lt A M 238
Allan, Sgt R 144
Allen, Lt C M 228
Allum, 2AM T E 18, 23, 77
Amey, 2/Lt A E 186
Anderson, 2/Lt G F 177
Andrews Capt J O 83
Anslow, 2/Lt F F 182
Appleby, 2/Lt P E 155-6, 179
Applin, 2/Lt R 58, 77
Armstrong, 2/Lt B H 74
Armstrong, Capt D V 190
Arnold, FL A R 56
Ashton, Capt M E 154
Aspinall, 2/Lt J V 41
Atkinson, Capt E D 57, 79
Atkinson, Lt D S 210
Atkinson, Capt R N G 141

Baker, 2/Lt H E 10
Baker, Lt J W 46
Balfour, Capt H H 15, 72
Ball, Capt A 49-50, 60, 61, 70, 74
Ball, Lt D H 33
Ball, Lt O G F 18
Banks, Lt C C 228
Banks, Cpl 137
Bannerman, Capt R B 195, 203
Barkell, Lt J H 153
Barkell, Lt T H 205
Barker, 2/Lt W G 68
Baring, Maj M 76-7
Barlow, Lt L M 65
Barney, Lt L W 15
Barnham, Lt B E 137
Barritt, 2/Lt G L 42
Barwell, Capt F L 78
Bate, 2/Lt G B 77
Battle, 2/Lt H F V 198
Beauchamp-Proctor, Capt A W 154, 251
Beck, Lt W 177
Benbow, Lt E L 14, 16
Benjamin, Lt M A 68
Bennett, Lt R M 233
Bennett, FSL S L 36, 60, 76
Berigny, 2/Lt C E 13
Berry, 2/Lt C W 58
Bevington, Lt R J 26
Billinge, Capt 55
Billington, Lt F W 241
Binnie, Capt A 45
Birchel, Lt 150
Bird, Capt 37
Birks, Lt N A 19
Bishop, 2/Lt N F 184
Bishop, Lt W A 26, 30, 55, 58, 72, 76, 84
Bishop, 2/Lt 55
Biziou, Capt H A R 201, 206
Bloomfield, Lt T R 216
Bolton, 2AM J H 12, 18
Bond, 2AM W 61, 64
Bond, Lt W A 76
Bonner, 1AM P 12
Booker, FL C D 65, 70
Boulton, Lt N S 237
Bourner, Lt G S 208
Bousfield, 2/Lt C 68
Bovington, Lt P F 169
Bowen, 2AM E 13
Bowen, Lt E G 137
Bowen, 2/Lt J E 154
Bowen, Lt L G 176
Bowler, Sgt J H 148
Bowman, Maj G H 215
Boyd, Capt W W 33
Brading, Capt R C B 129, 176
Breadner, FC L S 36, 60, 76
Breakey, Capt J D 237
Brettell, 2/Lt W P M 46

Brewis, Lt J A G 65, 76
Bridgett, Lt C 168
Brink, Lt J H 34
Britnell, Lt F J S 218
Britton, Lt R E 228
Brodie, Lt T W 148
Brookes, 2/Lt G E 18
Broome, Capt F C 177, 201
Brown, 2/Lt C 21
Brown, Lt C 188
Brown, Lt E R 232
Brown, Lt F E 46
Browne, 2/Lt G E M 208
Bruce, Lt N 169, 196
Buck, Lt G S 43
Buckton, 2/Lt N C 42, 74
Burbury, Lt A V 65, 69
Burgess, Cpl 192
Bush, Lt R F 154
Byng, Gen Sir J 126, 227

Callender, Capt A A 211
Campbell, 2/Lt R O 228
Cant, 2AM, A W 18, 35
Capper, Lt E W 46
Carberry, Capt D H M 158, 212
Carlin, Capt S 141, 203
Carr, FSL 57
Carson, Lt H R 137
Carter, Lt D C 149
Carter, Lt W A W 227
Case, 2/Lt C H 237
Casey, FSL F D 66
Caswell, Lt G F 197, 198
Catchpole, Capt B 127
Caton, 2/Lt E F 148
Cawley 2/Lt CA 229
Chambers, 2/Lt P W 11
Champagne, Lt E O 144
Chapman, 2/Lt L C 45
Child, Lt J M 61, 70, 83
Childs, Lt C L 147
Chisam, Lt J R 184
Clark, 2/Lt A E 74
Clark, 2/Lt R B 66
Clarke, Capt A J M 22
Clarke, Lt C E 228
Clarke, FL I N C 28
Clayton, Sgt 18
Clement, Capt C M 24, 30, 60
Clements, Lt J B V 158, 212
Coates, Capt L C 46
Cobby, Capt A H 141, 148, 251
Cochrane, 2/Lt 9
Cochrane-Patrick, Capt W J C K 84
Cock, 2/Lt J H 45
Cockerell, Lt S 11
Coghill, Lt W H 201, 218
Cole, Lt E S T 30, 57
Cole, Lt M B 45
Coler, Lt E S 182
Coles, Lt E M 127
Collier, Lt J 130
Collishaw, Maj R 74, 148, 218
Compton, Lt A S 137
Coningham, Maj A 147
Conn, Lt K B 183
Coope, Lt N N 210
Cooper, 2/Lt S 43
Coote, Lt M H 61
Cotton, 2/Lt J C 46
Cowie, 2/Lt W A 130
Cowgill, 2/Lt W A F 147
Cowlishaw, Sgt A S 131
Cox, Capt C R 11
Cox, 2/Lt G 203
Cox, Lt T C 205
Craig, Lt W B 218
Crawford, Capt C 212
Crawford, Lt K 11
Crisp, 2/Lt A E 54
Critchley, 2/Lt G A 77, 82
Crowe, Maj C M 60, 65, 75, 184
Crossen, Lt E P 143

Crundell, FSL E D 70
Cubbon, Capt F R 63
Cuckney, FSL E J 16
Cudemore, Capt C W 237
Cull, Capt A T 17, 35
Cullen, Lt 40
Culling, FSL T G 57, 58, 60
Cunniffe, Sgt J A 15
Curphey, Capt W G S 15
Cuzner, FSL A E 78

Dallas, FC R S 57, 58, 60, 82, 83
D'Arcy, 2/Lt S H 54
Darvill, Capt G W F 141
Davies, 2/Lt L G 24
Davies, 2/Lt R 42
Davidson, Capt D A L 83
Davidson, Lt R H W 176
Davis, 2/Lt L S 241
deCrespigny, Maj H V C 61, 213
Dennis, Lt G N 152
Dennis, 2/Lt J G 174
deSelincourt, Capt A 68
Dinsmore, 2/Lt G H
Dixie, Lt N C 218
Dixon, Capt G C 126
Dixon, Lt J L 18, 68
Douglas, Maj W S 35
Downing, 2/Lt H G 76
Doyle, Capt J E 136, 150
Drake, Capt E B 238
Dreshfield, 2/Lt W G 27
Drinkwater, Lt A T 189
Duncan, Lt G M 140, 141
Dunn, Sgt R 13

Eddy, 2/Lt M H 149
Edgley, Sgt D E 148
Edwards, Lt H 47
Edwards, Cpl 35
Elderton, Capt E F 56, 61
Eldon, 2/Lt H G 210
Elliott, Lt H P 169
Elliott, Lt J M 26
Ellis, Lt H E O 43, 70, 72, 74
Elworthy, Lt L M 13
Emsden, Cpl L 24
Evans, Lt H J 206
Eyre, FC C A 33

Fall, FSL J S T 36
Farley, Maj R L 58
Fenton, Lt J A 232
Ferguson, Lt F W 138
Fernihough, Capt F 34
Findlay, Capt C 210
Firby, Lt 202
Fitzsimon, Lt T O 154
Fleming, 2/Lt P J A 211
Fletcher, FSL A H 78
Fletcher, Sgt R M 211
Foreman, Capt J H 142
Foster, 2/Lt R M 23
Fowler, Capt H 46
Freshney, Lt 127
Friend, 1AM 15
Fry, Lt W M 66

Galbraith, Lt C F 136
Gammon, Capt R J 155-6, 179
Ganter, 2/Lt W T 141
Gardner, Lt C G 228
Garland, Capt E J 155
Gates, Capt G B 137, 138, 153-4, 158, 169, 208
Geddes, Maj A C B 54
George, 2/Lt H D K 17
Gerrard, FL T F N 20
Gilbertson, Lt D H S 141
Gillet, Lt F 127, 137, 150
Glen, Lt J A 136
Good, Lt H B 147
Goodman, Lt F W 208
Goody, Lt H E 62
Gordon, 2/Lt D 10

French

Belgian

German